COMPARATIVE ANIMAL BEHAVIOR

AN EVOLUTIONARY AND ECOLOGICAL APPROACH

RICHARD MAIER

Loyola University of Chicago

ALLYN AND BACON

Boston ◆ London ◆ Toronto ◆ Sydney ◆ Tokyo ◆ Singapore

Vice President, Editor in Chief, Social Sciences: *Sean W. Wakely*
Senior Editor: *Carolyn O. Merrill*
Editorial Assistant: *Amy Goldmacher*
Vice President, Director of Field Marketing: *Joyce Nilsen*
Production Administrator: *Annette Joseph*
Editorial–Production Service: *Susan Freese, Communicáto, Ltd.*
Copyeditor: *Jay Howland*
Photo Researcher: *Laurie Frankenthaler*
Artists: *Asterisk Group and Deborah Schneck (animal drawings)*
Design/Electronic Composition: *Denise Hoffman*
Composition Buyer: *Linda Cox*
Manufacturing Buyer: *Suzanne Lareau*
Cover Administrator: *Linda Knowles*
Cover Designer: *Studio Nine*

Library of Congress Cataloging-in-Publication Data

Maier, Richard A.
     Comparative animal behavior : an evolutionary and ecological
approach / Richard Maier.
          p.   cm.
     Includes bibliographical references and index.
     ISBN 0–205–19985–2 (alk. paper)
     1. Animal behavior.   2. Animal behavior—Evolution.   I. Title.
QL751.M217   1998
591.5—DC21   97–27885
                                                               CIP

Printed in the United States of America

10 9 8 7 6 5 4 3 2   02 01 00 99 98

*The photo and figure credits appear on p. 570, which constitutes a continuation of the
copyright page.*

To my wife, Mary Gene,
with great love and appreciation

CONTENTS

◆ ◆ ◆ PART TWO   LEARNING AND COGNITION

CHAPTER 4 ◆ LEARNING   72

CHAPTER 5 ◆ COGNITION   98

◆ ◆ ◆ PART THREE   FEEDING AND DEFENSE AGAINST PREDATION

CHAPTER 6 ◆ FEEDING   122

◆ ◆ ◆   PART FIVE   SOCIAL BEHAVIOR

CHAPTER 12 ◆ COOPERATION AND COMMUNICATION   270

CHAPTER 15 ◆ SOCIAL RELATIONSHIPS BETWEEN DIFFERENT SPECIES   344

◆ ◆ ◆ PART SIX   BIOLOGICAL MECHANISMS

PREFACE

This book is intended primarily as an undergraduate text for courses in animal behavior, comparative psychology, and behavioral ecology. Like other texts that emphasize both research and theory, *Comparative Animal Behavior* presents a mixture of recent research and conceptualization along with classic studies of animal behavior. However, some organizational aspects are different from those in the standard texts.

Because I have found that students tend to lose interest in the presentation of the history of any discipline in one large dose, I have spread small discussions of history over several chapters. Communication, a topic that is often presented in one chapter, is included in parts of three chapters—courtship communication (in conjunction with attractiveness), social communication (as an adjunct to social systems), and pheromonal communication (as part of chemical control of behavior). I have delayed the presentation of neural and chemical mechanisms until relatively late in the book. My students seem to comprehend these mechanisms most thoroughly after they have been exposed to evolutionary theory, basic behavioral genetics, and a general analysis of functional behavior patterns.

Some changes in the emphasis of this book reflect recent shifts in research and theoretical interests. In the last few years a vast amount of excellent and thorough research has been published on animal learning and cognition; to address this new knowledge, I have included a separate chapter on each of these subjects. Also, much recent work on various forms of parasitism and mutualism is directly relevant to an evolutionary approach to animal behavior; therefore I have included a chapter on social relationships that covers these subjects.

In response to the rapid development of the field of evolutionary psychology, I have included more information related to the evolution of human processes than is found in most other texts. In fact, each chapter closes with a section entitled Human Evolution. These sections may be of particular value to students interested in psychology, because the research cited ties in with several areas of psychology as well as biology. For all students, speculation on human evolution provides a fertile ground for discussion.

A boxed feature entitled Unusual Adaptations appears in most chapters. Because it is often difficult to know if an example given in an animal behavior text occurs commonly or only rarely, this feature emphasizes the uniqueness of some adaptations. It also provides an opportunity to speculate on the evolution of such exceptional behavior. As in the case of the Human Evolution section, the regular occurrence of the Unusual Adaptations feature adds a consistency to the style of presentation.

A table entitled Changing Perspectives is also included near the end of each chapter. Each table presents a very short summary of past perspectives compared with present conceptualizations discussed in the chapter. These summaries help put present-day concepts in historical perspective; they also suggest that some myths from the past are still widely accepted. The "Future" perspectives column in each of these tables raises a few unanswered questions and emphasizes a need for continued research and theoretical development.

As illustrated in the Contents, this book is divided into seven parts. Each part contains two to four chapters on closely related topics and thus should be read as a unit. However, the parts may be studied in an alternative sequence. For example, some teachers may prefer to cover Part Six (Biological Mechanisms) earlier in the course.

Because of the recent explosion of research on animal behavior and related mechanisms, space limitations prevent me from listing the primary references for all research cited. I have tried, however, to include references on classical research and theoretical formulations as well as the most recent studies. In some cases I have indicated review articles (prefaced by the term *see*), which typically include the relevant primary sources.

Several pedagogical devices will help students master the material in the chapters. First, each chapter begins with an outline and an overview of material to be covered; each chapter then concludes with a summary. Second, key terms are defined and printed in boldface in the body of each chapter; these terms are listed at the end of the chapter and also defined in the Glossary at the end of the book. Finally, the Appendix provides an abbreviated discussion of animal classification; this feature may be helpful for students with limited background in biology.

ACKNOWLEDGMENTS

I believe a debt of gratitude is due the many researchers and scholars whose work is cited in the References section of this book. Without them, there would be no scientific study of animal behavior.

I would also like to thank my students, who have given me helpful feedback and inspiration at many stages of this project. In particular, I wish to thank the following graduates and undergraduates, who read large sections of the manuscript and offered their suggestions: Jen Brockway, Cori Hillman, Lisa Hoffman, Ann-Marie Kambanis, Aimee Lesperance, Sharon Massel, Christine Mattson, Zehra Metovic, Erik Moyer, Justin Nauth, Jennie Picciola, Justin Resnik, Holly Richards, Kim Rosa, Patty Spyrakos, and Diane Stephens.

I am especially indebted to my colleague Lois Leidahl, of Loyola University, who spent numerous hours critiquing the manuscript, helping me locate sources, and making valuable suggestions at many stages of development. A number of other Loyola colleagues also helped in various stages of planning, organizing, and advising during this project. Thanks go to Fred Bryant, Al Dewolfe, Dick Fay, Anne Grauer, Linda Heath, Fred Morrison, Robert Russell, and Gene Zechmeister. The office staff also provided great support, particularly Marilyn Domingo, Lillian Hardison, and Stacy Rivas.

Many of the professionals at Allyn and Bacon have labored hard and effectively behind the scenes in producing this book. I have been particularly fortunate to have worked directly with Sue Freese, Annette Joseph, Andrea Iorio, and Carolyn Merrill. My thanks to everyone on the Allyn and Bacon team for their cooperation and dedication.

Finally, I would like those individuals who reviewed the book in its early stages for Allyn and Bacon and offered their valuable insights: Michael Casey, Virginia Polytechnic; Roger Fouts, Central Washington University; James Holland, University of Pittsburgh; Victoria Luine, Hunter College; Thomas McBride, Princeton University; Dennis Mitchell, University of Southern California; Regina Sullivan, University of Oklahoma; and Barbara Turpin, Southwest Missouri State University.

CHAPTER 1

INTRODUCTION AND OVERVIEW

◆ *Why are the male elephant seals larger than the females?*

◆ *Why do females usually live longer than males?*

When I was a young boy, I was fascinated by the behavior of animals. Our household always included various types of pets, and our whole family made frequent visits to the zoo. I was particularly fortunate because my father studied animal behavior. As a special treat, I was sometimes allowed to accompany him to his animal behavior laboratory at the University of Michigan, where he and his graduate students would patiently try to answer my endless questions. My love of animals and my curiosity

1

about their behavior has continued throughout my life and has provided an impetus
for me to share my enthusiasm through teaching and writing.

*We will begin our study of animal behavior by considering some of the reasons
people in general have found animal behavior interesting and worthy of study. Next,
we will look briefly at the history of the scientific study of animal behavior. Then we
will turn to modern approaches to studying animal behavior and the basic tenets of
evolutionary theory. We will then focus on some of the research strategies and techniques that have provided many answers to questions about animal behavior—and, at
the same time, have stimulated provocative new questions. Finally, we will look at the
place of evolutionary theory in our understanding of the human animal.*

REASONS FOR STUDYING ANIMAL BEHAVIOR

Humans have been interested in animal behavior for thousands or perhaps hundreds of
thousands of years. This interest clearly pre-
dates the development of scientific methods of
inquiry. Fossil evidence suggests the earliest
humans were hunter–gatherers, and our ancestors must have carefully observed the behavior of their quarry. In fact, Native Americans in preliterate hunting societies had great
knowledge of the behavior of the animals in
their area, especially those they hunted.

There is also evidence of interest in animals from early written records. The oldest
Sumerian clay tablets still in existence, which
date back more than 5,000 years, contain de-
pictions of more than 100 kinds of birds and 50
types of fish (Kramer, 1963; Mountjoy, 1980).

Most people today do not depend on
hunting animals for their survival, however;
so why does this interest continue? The answer is that there are still practical advantages,
both direct and indirect, to understanding animal behavior. We can benefit from knowing
how domestic animals and pets feed, reproduce, and fight disease as well as how they
react to social conditions such as crowding. It
is also possible to train animals to serve disadvantaged people. For example, dogs can lead
blind persons, and monkeys can bring objects
to individuals confined to wheelchairs.

In addition, there may be future-oriented
reasons for studying animals and protecting
them from destructive forces. For example, recent evidence suggests that skin secretions of

certain frogs found in tropical rain forests could be highly useful to humans. A poison-arrow frog found in Ecuador produces a substance that is 200 times more effective in blocking pain than morphine. Yet many species of frogs may become extinct before we have time to research their potential usefulness (see Stebbins & Cohen, 1995).

Beyond the possibility of direct usefulness, an understanding of animals' behavior may facilitate the survival of endangered species not only in the wild, but also in zoos and animal sanctuaries. Many of us are alarmed at the increasing rate of extinction of animals brought about by the encroachment of human civilization on animals' natural habitats.

A study of animal behavior may also help us gain a better understanding of human behavior and of the mechanisms that influence our behavior. For example, we have learned a great deal about the human nervous system and human physiological reactions to stress through experiments with animals that would be impossible to conduct with human subjects (see Domjan & Purdy, 1995).

Although some experiments cause stress for animal subjects, an attempt has been made in recent years to reduce the negative effects of research on animal subjects as much as possible. Most universities that conduct animal research have developed guidelines that prohibit the misuse of animal subjects (see Association for the Study of Animal Behaviour, 1996). Furthermore, many scientists are making efforts to focus attention on the welfare of farm and laboratory animals, animals in zoos, and animal pets (see Webster, 1995).

Pulitzer Prize–winning naturalist E. O. Wilson suggests still another reason for our interest in animal behavior. Because animals were basic to the survival of our ancient ancestors, who lived as hunter–gatherers for more than a million years, there would be a strong, natural human tendency to pay attention to animals. (Individuals who failed to pay attention to animals—both predators and potential prey—would be less likely to survive and pass on their genes.) In other words, there may be deep-seated evolutionary roots to our interest in animals—and in other parts of our natural environment as well. Wilson calls this interest **biophilia** or, literally, a love of living things (Wilson, 1984) (Figure 1.1).

Whatever the explanation, people of all ages and cultural backgrounds find animals interesting and, in many cases, respect the great diversity found in animals' solutions to the fundamental challenges of surviving and reproducing. There is also a growing appreciation of the complex ways in which different forms of life are intertwined and a feeling of kinship with animals as dynamic related life forms. Finally, since we humans have evolved in the natural world and faced the same types of pressures as other animals, we can learn something basic and meaningful about ourselves by studying the evolution of nonhuman animals.

A BRIEF HISTORY OF THE SCIENTIFIC STUDY OF ANIMAL BEHAVIOR

Early humans had undoubtedly observed and speculated about animals for many thousands of years; but, as in the case of many types of inquiry, the ancient Greeks seem to have been the first to systematically record animal behavior.

FIGURE 1.1 ◆ **An example of biophilia.** According to Wilson's biophilia hypothesis, healthy trees and other naturally occurring objects are perceived as positive or beautiful because they were associated with fitness-enhancing conditions in our early evolutionary history.

Before 1900

In the fourth century B.C., Aristotle wrote two volumes in which he identified and classified animal behavior. Some of the material was based on the observations and interpretations of travelers from distant areas, and understandably there are several inaccuracies. For example, Aristotle included some references to unicorns, which he believed to be real. However, Aristotle also included ideas such as evolutionary development across species, which, 2,000 years later, proved to be basic to our understanding of animal behavior (Denny, 1980).

Unfortunately, much of the enthusiasm for systematically studying animal behavior died with Aristotle. In fact, as late as the seventeenth century, the renowned French philosopher René Descartes argued that animals behave in a strictly mechanical way and therefore are not worthy of study.

It was not until the nineteenth century, with the publication of Charles Darwin's *On the Origin of Species,* that the scientific study of animal behavior began in earnest (Darwin,

1859). Darwin's theory provided an explanation for a large variety of animal behaviors. In addition, the theory generated a number of testable hypotheses and, as we shall see, raised a multitude of interesting questions about animal behavior. The nineteenth century also witnessed the first experimental studies of animal behavior.

1900–1950

In the first half of the twentieth century, the study of animal behavior blossomed into an extremely active field of research. Three European pioneers in the experimental study of animal behavior in natural settings—Karl von Frisch, Konrad Lorenz, and Niko Tinbergen—shared a Nobel Prize in 1973 honoring their contributions to the field. The study of animal behavior in natural or seminatural settings became known as **ethology.** Lorenz and Tinbergen also developed a theory that emphasized what they called instinctive behavior (Tinbergen, 1951).

The ethologists studied behavior in a large variety of animals and emphasized the need to look at behavior in natural settings rather than in the sterile conditions associated with a laboratory. The ethologists also focused on the development of behavior, which they believed took place independent of learning.

Across the Atlantic Ocean, American scientists who called themselves **comparative psychologists** conducted numerous laboratory investigations of animal behavior. For example, Frank Beach studied the effects of hormones on sexual behavior in various classes of vertebrates. Beach (1950) made an especially strong argument for examining comparable behavior patterns in different animals and identifying the mechanisms behind the behaviors.

Other American psychologists, studying mainly pigeons, rats, and monkeys, tried to develop learning theories that could account for behavioral development in general. B. F. Skinner, for example, developed a set of learning principles that attempted to explain the development of a large number of behaviors in nonhuman animals as well as humans (Skinner, 1953).

For several years there was controversy between European ethologists and American psychologists. As just suggested, the Europeans emphasized field studies and behavior that was presumed to be independent of learning, whereas the Americans often focused on learning in laboratory settings. In some cases, arguments between the two groups became heated.

Since 1950

In the second half of the twentieth century, several of these earlier controversies subsided as the differences between ethologists and comparative psychologists began to fade. For example, T. C. Schneirla, an American, began experiments on army ants in seminaturalistic settings, while Niko Tinbergen conducted laboratory research on stickleback fish in an aquarium. In many cases, a synthesis of ideas resulted after North American scientists visited research centers in Europe and ethologists crossed the Atlantic to meet with American scientists (Dewsbury, 1995).

Today, as we shall see, research strategies on both sides of the Atlantic often combine laboratory research and research in natural settings. Furthermore, few if any differences remain in our conceptualization of the role of learning in behavior. Scientists now view behavior as the result of a complex interaction between genetic and experiential factors. Finally, regional differences in research strategies have virtually disappeared; and scientists on all continents, including numerous developing countries, are studying the behavior of animals. Many of the animals studied in developing countries are species indigenous to those areas, so the variety of animals studied has increased markedly in recent years.

Modern Approaches to Studying Animal Behavior

As the arguments between ethologists and American scientists subsided, several important theoretical approaches emerged that have had a significant effect on our conceptualizations of animal behavior, including the behavior of humans.

Behavioral Ecology

John Crook (1964) was an early pioneer in the study of what came to be known as **behavioral ecology,** or the study of the relationship between ecology and behavioral patterns. Behavioral ecologists point to the strong involvement of ecology in the evolution of behavior. As we shall see in Chapter 10, the distribution of food influences not only the evolution of feeding patterns, but, indirectly, the evolution of mating systems as well. Similarly, the presence and mode of operation of predators, also considered part of the ecology, can influence more than the evolution of defensive behav-

ior. As we shall see in Chapters 14 and 19, predators are a driving force in the evolution of social behavior and patterns of migration. In fact, we can often predict more about an animal's behavior by knowing how its food source is distributed and what types of predators the animal faces than by knowing the class to which the animal belongs.

Behavioral ecology also had an influence on traditional comparative psychology. Rather than focusing strictly on the comparison of animals based on their taxonomy, comparative approaches now take into consideration similarities and differences in the ecology of animals. For example, Donald Dewsbury and his colleagues (1992) have focused on the habitats of rodents as a factor in the evolution of their mating systems. Another comparative psychologist, Gordon Gallup (1982), has compared the evolutionary history of cognitive processes of primates, taking into account ecological factors such as the environments in which the animals live and the types of food they eat.

Sociobiology and Evolutionary Psychology

In 1975 E. O. Wilson introduced the term **sociobiology** to designate an evolutionary approach to understanding social behavior. Expanding on the theoretical formulations of several scientists (which will be discussed in some detail shortly), Wilson applied modern evolutionary principles to a wide variety of social behaviors. In the last chapter of his book, Wilson generalized sociobiological principles to humans and, in the process, stirred up a controversy.

Partly because sociobiology took on a negative connotation as the result of this controversy, social scientists interested in the evolution of human behavior often prefer to call themselves **evolutionary psychologists.** David Buss, Leda Cosmides, and John Tooby are representative of evolutionary psychologists. These researchers place heavy emphasis on the complex interaction between genetic and environmental or contextual factors. Furthermore, evolutionary psychologists focus on cognitive factors as basic determinants of behavior, especially in primates.

Although some controversies have subsided, others have lingered on, especially in areas that involve humans. For example, scientists frequently disagree on whether or not concepts traditionally associated with humans, such as emotions and thoughts, can be applied to nonhuman animals. Furthermore, as I've mentioned, there is often controversy surrounding the use of evolutionary principles to explain human behavior. We will revisit these controversies, as well as the arguments on each side of the issue, at several points in later chapters.

FIGURE 1.2 ◆ Charles Darwin (1809–1882).

EVOLUTIONARY THEORY

As suggested earlier, Darwin's theory of evolution by natural selection ushered in vigorous attempts to apply evolutionary principles to an understanding of animal behavior. We will start our discussion of evolution by looking at Darwin's theory and then consider more recent advances in evolutionary theory.

The Theory of Natural Selection

Charles Darwin is the name most closely linked with the concept of evolution—the theory that life processes change over time and that, in many cases, one life form develops into a distinctly different form (Figure 1.2). Nonetheless, evolution was originally postulated by many earlier thinkers, including Aristotle and Erasmus Darwin, Charles Darwin's grandfather. The younger Darwin's great contribution was to propose how evolutionary changes could occur, explain why evolution took the form it did, and collect data from an extensive trip around the world to support his position.

The heart of Darwin's theory of evolution is the **theory of natural selection.** Natural selection means that only animals well equipped to survive and reproduce will pass on their inherited traits. Actually, Alfred Wallace and

Charles Darwin both arrived independently at the theory. However, Darwin developed the theory in detail and gathered vast amounts of supporting evidence. Consequently, Darwin's name is generally associated with evolution by natural selection.

In presenting the theory of natural selection, Darwin emphasized three sets of well-established observations. First, variations exist in traits exhibited by plants and animals, especially by sexually reproducing plants and animals. Darwin had amassed enormous amounts of evidence supporting this observation on his voyage, and other scientists had noted this variation as well.

Second, Darwin proposed that at least some aspects of traits are inherited. The work of Mendel suggesting how inheritance might take place was not known to Darwin (or to most other scientists) at the time. However, there was a good deal of indirect evidence that many traits were indeed affected by inheritance.

Third, many more offspring are produced than will survive. Darwin was reminded of this observation when he read an 1826 work by Thomas Malthus that focused on the population pressure resulting from a plethora of offspring. Darwin saw the tendency to produce an overabundance of offspring as a basis for competition among living things. This perception of the significance of competition provided the foundation of his theory.

The Concept of Fitness

Building logically on these three observations, Darwin argued that individual animals vary in **fitness;** that is, some are more likely to survive and to reproduce successfully than others. Furthermore, animals with traits that promote survival and successful reproduction are presumably going to pass these traits on to succeeding generations. (Organisms with "inferior" traits are not as likely to survive and reproduce, so their traits will not be passed on.) Finally, over time, the average trait in a population of animals should undergo distinct changes, especially when there are changes in conditions that promote survival and reproductive success. For example, a large body provides insulation from the cold. If the climate becomes colder, large deer are more likely to survive than small ones. Consequently, the large deer are most likely to pass on the genes that are associated with greater size.

Darwin's concept of fitness refers primarily to producing offspring that have a high probability of surviving and reproducing. Surviving in itself does not contribute to fitness if the animal does not reproduce. The fittest animals are ones that leave a relatively large number of offspring that not only survive, but are themselves relatively successful in attracting mates and reproducing.

As we shall see in later chapters, fitness means different things for different types of animals. For example, fitness for rabbits may mean ability to outdistance predators and reproduce rapidly. For apes, however, fitness may mean winning encounters with competitors and investing large amounts of energy in parenting a small number of offspring. The end result is the same—producing as many surviving offspring as possible.

The Concept of Adaptation

Darwin defined an **adaptation** as an inherited trait or behavioral disposition that provides fitness advantages in some way. More specifically, he defined adaptive structures or behaviors as providing more total fitness value than competing traits in a given environment. As many theorists following Darwin have argued, an adaptation is not a perfect solution, but one that is better than other alternatives available to the animal.

Darwin hypothesized that adaptations usually result from a series of small steps. Furthermore, the changes must build on structures and/or behaviors already present in the animal. Therefore, different animals exhibit a great variety of adaptations related to the same type of problem, because they are starting from different points.

Later theorists have pointed out that adaptations are more than traits with which animals are born; an openness to certain types of developmental modification is also an adaptation. As I'll explain at several points in the book, the potential for learning certain types of relationships can be a very important adaptation.

At first glance, it might appear that all traits must be adaptive—or they would not have evolved. However, a trait may be advantageous at one point in an animal's evolutionary history but later, after conditions have changed, may no longer be beneficial. Yet if the trait does not have a significant deleterious effect, it will remain in the population. For example, humans do not use their coccyx, or tailbone. But the coccyx does not present a problem, so it is retained as a **vestigial structure** (the remnant of a structure that was useful at an earlier time in the evolutionary history of the species).

A trait that does not promote fitness may also evolve in a population of animals as a by-product of the evolution of another trait that was adaptive. For example, the extreme dependency of a newborn human baby is not adaptive; but it probably evolved, to a certain extent, as a by-product of bipedal locomotion—standing erect and walking on two feet. Bipedal locomotion is most efficient when a woman has a relatively small pelvis. Because a large baby's head cannot pass through a small pelvis, natural selection in humans tended to favor a small head encasing a relatively undeveloped brain at birth. Much of the development of the brain then had to take place after birth; thus, necessarily, the baby is highly dependent during this period.

Experimental Tests of Hypothesized Adaptations

It is not always clear which traits are adaptive and which are vestigial or by-products of other evolutionary trends. Evolutionary theorist Stephen J. Gould (1984) has warned that some theorists tend to go overboard in attributing adaptations, creating highly inventive myths comparable to Kipling's "just-so story" about how the leopard got its spots.

Fortunately, in many cases, scientists are able to test hypotheses related to adaptations. For example, W. E. Cooper and L. J. Vitt (1985) hypothesized that brightly colored blue tails in lizards known as blue-tailed skinks were adaptive because the tails acted as decoys; the bright tail directed the strikes of predators away from the lizard's vulnerable head end. (The tails of lizards can be regenerated, so their loss is relatively insignificant.)

Cooper and Vitt found that lizards whose tails were painted black to match the color of the rest of their bodies were killed by snakes significantly more often than the lizards with normal, blue tails. Consequently, the hypothesis of adaptiveness was confirmed. We will see

◆ UNUSUAL ADAPTATIONS

The Panda's Thumb

In some cases, adaptations appear to be clumsy compared to something a human engineer might design. Stephen J. Gould (1965) gave a classic example of an unusual adaptation as well as a hypothesis concerning how it may have evolved. Gould pointed out that a panda has a structure modified from the wrist bone that operates as a "thumb." This "thumb" functions in opposition to the panda's "fingers" and enables the panda to strip leaves from bamboo shoots.

Why didn't the panda evolve a more serviceable opposable thumb like that of an ape or a human? The panda apparently evolved from predatory ancestors that chased down their prey. Once the digits of the feet of these predators became highly specialized for running, they lost the possibility of evolving in another direction; that is, of developing an opposable thumb.

As we shall see at several points in later chapters, specialization in one evolutionary direction limits an animal's potential to develop in other directions. In some respects this limitation is analogous to what happens when a human worker is trained on a highly specialized job. The flexibility necessary to start out in an entirely different direction is reduced.

In contrast to a human engineer or designer, evolution does not "know where it is going"; consequently, normal rules of design do not apply. The only rule that evolution by natural selection follows is "Go with the best solution immediately available."

many similar tests for the adaptiveness of traits in later chapters as we revisit controversies surrounding the concept of adaptation.

Evolutionary Trends

Typically, when a change takes place that is adaptive, the change will continue in a certain direction for a period of time or for several generations. Then, when the total benefit reaches a certain point, there is no advantage—or perhaps there is a disadvantage—to further developments in that direction. At this point the evolutionary trend comes to an end. For example, in order to escape predators, it might be beneficial for an animal to develop a shell. Once the animal is able to hide from virtually all of its predators, there is no advantage in developing a thicker or larger shell. As a matter of fact, a thicker or larger shell might slow it down. Thus, evolutionary trends such as the development of thicker and larger shells tend to have their natural limits (Simpson, 1958).

When a trend nears its limit, the animal is said to be **specialized** or highly evolved in regard to the mechanism or behavior in question. (At the other extreme, an animal that has not developed significant evolutionary trends is said to be **ancestral.**) As we have seen in the panda example, animals that are highly specialized are not likely to undergo new evolutionary trends.

When a group of animals enters a hospitable area in which there are few if any competing animals, they tend to exhibit **adaptive radiation;** that is, the animals evolve rapidly in several different directions and fill each available **niche** (habitat and role within that habitat). Darwin first identified adaptive radiation among finches in the Galapagos Islands. He reasoned that a few finches had arrived on the islands from the mainland several generations earlier. Since there were no small birds filling several types of possible niches, the finches evolved specializations relatively rapidly and filled a variety of niches (Figure 1.3). After a period of time, the animals in different niches failed to interbreed, and in each niche a new species was formed.

Adaptive radiation tends to promote **divergence:** Animals that start out as similar become more distinct over a period of many generations as they live in very different niches. For example, whales and cattle both evolved from an ancestral mammal but are now extremely different in structure and behavior. The opposite type of evolutionary process can take place when animals that are very different fill niches that are similar—a process known as **convergence,** or starting out dissimilar and becoming more similar. Sharks and dolphins, for example, look similar at a superficial level, although they have very different evolutionary roots and are not closely related. (Sharks evolved from primitive fishes, while dolphins evolved from land mammals.)

Sexual Selection

In conjunction with the natural selection we have just considered, Darwin proposed a special type of selection process called **sexual selection** (Darwin, 1871). He defined sexual selection as a type of natural selection that emphasizes traits associated with reproductive success. To use modern terminology, through sexual selection, traits associated with reproductive success are passed on and increase in frequency in the gene pool.

Geospiza magnirostris
Diet: Large seeds
Beak: Crushing

Geospiza scandens
Diet: Cactus fruits
Beak: Probing

Certhidea olivacea
Diet: Small insects
Beak: Forcepslike

FIGURE 1.3 ◆ **Diversity in the structure of the beaks of Darwin's finches found on the Galapagos Islands.**

For many years following the death of Darwin, the theory of sexual selection was neglected. In recent years, however, the theory has gained a great deal of support; it is now considered a cornerstone of evolutionary theory (Andersson, 1994).

Essentially sexual selection is a process that involves competition between members of one sex or gender for access to members of the other gender. As we shall see when we consider attraction and courtship in Chapter 9, females are generally more discriminating than males, so intragender competition is greatest among males.

There are several types of intragender competition. In one, males compete with each other and the male who wins becomes dominant or claims an attractive territory and gains access to females. In another type, the competition involves less direct interaction between males. The males simply compete with each other to advertise their fitness, and each female chooses a male on the basis of some trait or combination of traits. In still another type of competition, there is a selection process favoring males that develop sensory capacities enabling them to locate females efficiently (Schwagmeyer, 1995).

In many cases, two or more of these types of intragender competition occur at the same time. For example, as Chapter 9 explains, there is experimental evidence that male characteristics enabling a male to win an encounter with another male are also perceived as attractive by females.

The sexual selection process tends to create morphological differences (differences in form or structure) between the sexes, because different factors are adaptive for the male than for the female. This difference in morphology—which is reflected in such things as size, color, or the presence of ornamentation—is called **sexual dimorphism.**

Some species of animals are **polygynous;** that is, a few males mate with many females while other males do not mate at all. Species that are polygynous are most likely to exhibit sexual dimorphism, because intramale competition produces a strong evolutionary trend toward characteristics that provide competitive advantages or high levels of attractiveness to females. In contrast, **monogamous** mating systems (systems that feature one male mating exclusively with one female) produce approximately equal evolutionary pressures on the two sexes. Consequently, there tends to be little or no trend toward sexual dimorphism in monogamous systems.

Support for this hypothesis of the relationship between the type of mating system and the degree of sexual dimorphism comes from observations of seals. The degree of sexual dimorphism is significantly correlated with the degree of polygyny in different seal species. At one extreme, an elephant seal male, which may have a harem of as many as 100 females, is much larger than the female. Male fur seals, which are moderately polygynous and mate with half a dozen or so females during a breeding season, are only slightly larger than the females. At the other extreme, monogamous harbor seal males are approximately the same size as the females.

Refinements and Extensions of Evolutionary Theory

As we have seen, the Darwinian model indicates that animals gain fitness by passing on adaptive inherited traits. Following the development of modern genetics, an updated version of this model suggests that fitness consists of an animal's success in passing on copies of its genes.

Several developments in evolutionary theory have followed this genetically oriented view of fitness. Furthermore, modern breakthroughs in neurophysiology and endocrinology (described in Chapters 17 and 18) have indicated that animals may inherit behavioral tendencies as well as structural adaptations. We will now look at some modern theories that represent refinements and extensions of evolutionary theory and that have made particularly important contributions to our understanding of animal behavior. These theories were basic to the development of the modern evolutionary orientations discussed earlier—behavioral ecology, sociobiology, and evolutionary psychology. The theories apply to a wide range of behaviors, so I will introduce them here and then refer to them in more detail in later chapters.

The Theory of Kin Selection

William Hamilton (1964) carried the concept of fitness one step farther than Darwin had. In his **theory of kin selection,** Hamilton argued that animals can gain fitness by behaving in ways that facilitate the survival and reproduction of their close relatives. This type of fitness results from the fact that close relatives have a large number of genes that are identical.

Hamilton called the fitness Darwin described—passing on copies of one's genes by parenting offspring that survive and reproduce—**direct fitness.** The direct fitness of an individual is determined by the survival and reproduction of the individual's direct descendants.

In addition to direct fitness, Hamilton reasoned that animals must also benefit from the successful reproduction of close relatives who are not direct descendants—a type of fitness he called **indirect fitness.** Since very close relatives such as siblings share a greater percentage of genes than less close relatives such as cousins, the closer the relationship, the greater the indirect fitness an individual may experience.

Hamilton called the sum of direct and indirect fitness **inclusive fitness,** and he reasoned that this inclusive fitness was the driving force of natural selection. Thanks to this extension of the concept of fitness to imply inclusive fitness, scientists can now conceptualize many more structures and behaviors as adaptive than was possible during Darwin's time. Furthermore, sophisticated ways of quantifying inclusive fitness allow scientists to make and test specific predictions related to fitness considerations (Lucas et al., 1996).

Hamilton's theory of kin selection assumes that animals are naturally selected to help relatives because this helping behavior has inclusive fitness value. The degree of fit-

TABLE 1.1 ◆ Degree of Relatedness (r) of Various Relatives

Relationship	r
Parent–offspring	.50
Full siblings	.50
Grandparent–grandchild	.25
Individual–niece or –nephew	.25
Cousins	.125

ness value depends on how many relatives are helped, how closely related the relatives are, and how much help the behavior provides. In essence, Hamilton provides an explanation for a critical link in the evolution of social behavior. Close relatives often stay together and help each other because, ultimately, this association results in high degrees of inclusive fitness.

The Theory of Natural Selection at the Individual Level

For many years following the publication of Darwin's theory, theorists assumed that evolution could take place at the group level. However, in his **individual level of selection hypothesis,** George Williams argued that there must be a selective advantage for individual animals if evolution is to occur. For example, if there were two types of individuals in a population—one that limited its reproduction for the good of the species and another that was selfish and reproduced excessively—the selfish one would have greater fitness. Thus, it would be difficult or impossible for the genes associated with selfishness to be eliminated by natural selection. In fact, the selfish individuals would probably increase because they would be able to survive and reproduce quite successfully. Consequently, it would be impossible for evolution of self-sacrificing behavior to take place at the group level.

If selfishness is likely to remain in a population—or perhaps win out, as in the preceding example—how can self-sacrificing behavior ever evolve? Consistent with Hamilton's theory, there are some instances where self-sacrificing behavior provides more inclusive

fitness than selfish behavior. If an animal can only produce one offspring that survives, it will do better to help its siblings to produce three or four than to reproduce itself. Thus, as Williams suggests, altruistic or self-sacrificing behavior may evolve at the individual level.

Elaborating on the idea that self-sacrificing behavior has fitness value in certain circumstances, Richard Dawkins (1976) argues in *The Selfish Gene* that genes have evolved in such a way that they necessarily "behave" selfishly. However, this does not imply that individuals are necessarily selfish in the broad sense. Rather, it suggests that certain characteristics such as helping behavior may have underpinnings of selfishness in that the behavior may facilitate passing on copies of genes.

Optimality Theory

In an attempt to understand and predict feeding behaviors of animals, R. H. MacArthur and Eric Pianka (1966) hypothesized that animals evolve an ability to forage with high levels of efficiency. More specifically, they suggested that animals evolve ways of maximizing their food intake (benefit) while minimizing time and energy expended (cost). The theory was consistent with the theory of natural selection in that, over time, there should be a selection process favoring efficiency. Clearly, less efficient plans would eventually be defeated by the most successful plan. Phrased somewhat differently, animals should be naturally selected to engage in behaviors that have a favorable cost–benefit ratio. If several comparable behaviors are available, animals should ultimately engage in the one that has the most favorable cost–benefit ratio.

A pattern of behavior that provides optimal solutions to problems presumably reflects a **strategy** or set of rules. The term *strategy* does *not* imply conscious intent or an animal's knowledge of the reasons behind a behavior or set of behaviors. A strategy is, in the simplest sense, a rule of thumb that, in an animal's evolutionary history, has resulted in generally favorable outcomes.

Like Hamilton, MacArthur and Pianka were able to make predictions based on a quantitative analysis of factors involved. To make this analysis, MacArthur and Pianka expressed food taken in and energy spent in terms of calories. Thus, these researchers identified a cost–benefit ratio for many foraging behaviors.

Later theorists extended optimal foraging theory to include many behaviors in addition to feeding. This general approach resulted in the formulation of what is known as **optimality theory.** Optimality theory proposes that there has been a natural selection process for efficiency in regard to virtually all behaviors. The theory assumes that animals balance large numbers of needs for overall efficiency in satisfying fitness requirements. For example, animals should behave so as to balance such factors as the need for food, the need to escape from predators, and the need to reproduce effectively in terms of a generally favorable cost–benefit ratio.

As we shall see, optimality theory applies to virtually all of the behaviors we will discuss in later chapters. The idea of looking at animal behavior strategies in terms of a cost–benefit ratio represents an extremely important breakthrough in evolutionary theory.

Tests of optimality theory indicate that animals are not perfectly adapted in terms of the cost–benefit ratio, but that they come reasonably close given certain imperfections in their sensory and information-processing systems (Bateson & Kacelnik, 1995). As we have seen, evolutionary processes result not in perfect solutions but simply in the best solutions available given various kinds of restraints.

Game Theory

Despite its impressive utility, optimality theory does not predict all types of decisions animals make. In many cases animals must compete with other animals for the same, limited resources; so an animal must often take into account a competing animal's behavior. For example, an animal feeding in a group and competing with **conspecifics** (other members of the same species) must behave differently than a solitary feeder. John Maynard Smith (1974; listed under Maynard Smith) applied **game theory**—borrowed from economic theory—to explain how animals develop a strategy that considers competitors' behaviors.

Perhaps the best way to understand game theory is to imagine the attempts of a coach to devise an offensive strategy for a football game. Let us simplify the situation and assume that there are two general types of plays, passing plays and running plays; and that the team has been slightly more successful using running plays. If the defense were the same on every play, the optimum strategy would be to call a running play every time. However, the defense anticipates and makes adjustments; so game theory predicts that the optimum strategy will be to use both running and passing plays in a somewhat unpredictable sequence. But because running plays gain more on the average, it will be best to use a higher percentage of running plays.

An **evolutionarily stable strategy** is a strategy that is so effective that it is not likely to be replaced by an alternative strategy—unless conditions change drastically. Thus, we are quite certain that a football team will always utilize some running plays; however, if a team is in desperate circumstances—six points behind and a long distance to go with only a few seconds left—the circumstances may eliminate the possibility of a running play.

A **mixed evolutionarily stable strategy** is a tendency to employ more than one strategy; for instance, both running and passing plays. Because the opponent is going to benefit by anticipating particular strategies, the mixed strategy is an evolutionarily stable one in situations involving direct competition. In the example of the football game, the individual strategy (running or passing) is typically chosen in proportion to its relative effectiveness—something like 60 percent running plays and 40 percent passing plays.

As Chapter 13 will show, game theory can be extended to explain more complex types of competition. At this point, it is enough to remember that game theory is basically an elaboration of optimality theory. Strict optimality theory applies to situations where there is little or no interaction between animals, while game theory is used to predict optimal outcomes when there is a significant interaction effect.

The Theory of Parental Investment

Robert Trivers's (1972) **theory of parental investment** is, essentially, an optimality theory applied to the development of reproductive strategies. Trivers argues that investing in off-spring at one point in time uses up time and energy and reduces the probability of successful reproduction in the future. For example, a young female fish that produces and deposits eggs sacrifices growth potential: In the future, she will not be able to produce as many eggs as a female that waits to produce eggs until she is older and larger. For animals that show parental responses to the young, the expenditure of time and energy and the increased risk of predation may be even greater. On the other hand, if an animal waits too long to invest in reproduction, it may die before it leaves any offspring.

The main thrust of Trivers's theory is that animals, in the long run, reach a balance that maximizes the probability of producing a large number of offspring that survive to reproductive age. Over the course of evolution, natural selection results in each species' producing the optimum number of young at the most appropriate time.

As we shall see when we consider reproduction in Chapters 8 through 11, the theory of parental investment helps to explain differences between species with respect to the timing of reproduction, the number of offspring produced, and the amount of parental behavior invested. Furthermore, the theory explains why different types of environments are associated with alternative reproductive patterns in animals of the same species.

RESEARCH STRATEGIES

Now that we have considered the theoretical bases from which hypotheses about animal behavior are derived, we will turn to the types of questions researchers ask and some of the methods scientists use to test hypotheses.

TABLE 1.2 ◆ Theories That Refined and Extended Darwin's Evolutionary Theory

Theory	Primary Contribution
Theory of kin selection	Accounted for the evolution of a tendency to help relatives.
Theory of natural selection at the individual level	Indicated the need for selection to take place at an individual rather than a group level.
Optimality theory	Emphasized the importance of cost–benefit ratios in natural selection.
Game theory	Applied game theory to the evolution of behavioral strategies and introduced the concept of evolutionarily stable strategies.
Theory of parental investment	Applied optimality theory to an analysis of reproductive strategies.

Asking Questions

Do you recall the barrage of questions I raised as a child while visiting my father's animal behavior laboratory? We can separate researchers' questions into two general categories. **Proximate questions** were concerned with the immediate causes of behavior. How do male rats identify a female? How does the rat know where to go to get food? More sophisticated proximate questions asked by scientists include queries into the nervous, hormonal, and sensory mechanisms that regulate behavior. Researchers also ask proximate questions about how behavior develops.

In contrast to proximate questions, the **ultimate questions** I asked as a child were concerned with causes less closely related in time, often beginning with the word *why*. Why does the rat stop and look around when entering a new area? Why do rats have whiskers? Ulti-

mate questions often refer to evolutionary processes that have taken place over many generations. The more sophisticated questions asked by scientists include questions about function and about the probable evolutionary history of a behavior pattern.

In addition to these traditional questions, modern animal behaviorists ask two other types: cognitive questions, such as How does an animal process the information it acquires? and comparative questions, such as How do the abilities of one animal compare to those of another animal?

When scientists are in the process of investigating one type of question, other types of questions frequently arise. For example, as we compare courtship patterns in different mammals, we are likely to develop a curiosity about the evolution of courtship patterns. As we contemplate the evolution of courtship patterns, we find ourselves asking questions about why certain types of cues have become important in courtship. And as we think about the types of cues that are important, we begin to wonder how an animal develops sensitivity to these cues. In fact we frequently end up with more questions than we had at the start of our inquiry. This expansion of our curiosity is part of what makes scientific research so exciting.

Designing Experiments and Testing Hypotheses

We have already seen how an ultimate question about the function of the blue tail of a lizard led to the design of an experiment testing the hypothesis that the tail was a defensive adaptation. Let us now turn to an example of a proximate question: How does a herring gull chick recognize its parent's beak?

The early ethologists developed a laboratory method of systematically presenting a series of models of what seemed to be critical stimuli for an animal and then measuring and comparing the animal's response to each model. In a classic experiment, Tinbergen and Perdeck (1950) presented models of adult gull beaks to baby gulls and counted the number of times the chicks pecked at each model.

Under natural circumstances, baby gulls beg by pecking at the parent's beak; this stimulation evokes a regurgitation of food for the chicks. As Figure 1.4 shows, the experimental model that evoked the most consistent pecking was a rough configuration of a head, bill, and red spot that was moved slowly from side to side. The experimenters concluded that the red spot was especially critical to the gull chick's recognition of its parent's beak. (We will look at the development of pecking in

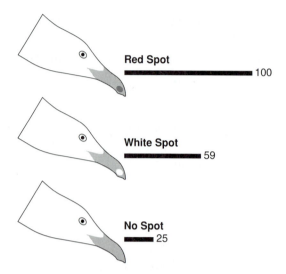

FIGURE 1.4 ◆ **Relative effectiveness of three models of herring gulls' heads in eliciting chicks' begging response.** The response to one model is designated 100, and responses to the others are expressed relative to this standard.

more detail when we discuss behavioral development in Chapter 3.)

With technological advances in the last half of the twentieth century, it has been possible to develop more sophisticated models. For example, many recent experiments involve displaying series of photographic slides to birds. The birds peck or fail to peck at a circle in response to each slide. By observing the birds' responses, experimenters can make inferences about the birds' perceptions. As we will see when we consider animal cognitions in Chapter 5, experimenters may also draw inferences about the length of time it takes a bird to process information by noting the delay between the slide presentation and the bird's response.

◆ HUMAN EVOLUTION

Scientists in increasing numbers have applied evolutionary principles to the study of humans. Because we are primates, we can often gain significant insights by comparing ourselves with other primates. However, we can also benefit from comparing ourselves to other types of animals that have similar feeding or mating habits, or that live in environments similar to those of our ancestors. Throughout this book, I will conclude each chapter with a comparison between humans and other animals and will speculate on the evolution of various aspects of human behavior.

Early **hominids**—species classified within the family of humans—lived as hunter–gatherers during the vast majority of the past two million years or so. It was during this time period that much of our human behavior potential and cognition evolved. In contrast, humans have been living in agricultural communities for less than 20,000 years and in urban environments for an even shorter period. Consequently, we have not had time to evolve adaptations consistent with our modern style of living. Because we evolved as hunter–gatherers over 99 percent of our existence as a species, we are in certain respects Paleolithic humans living in an age for which we are not always well adapted (see Allman, 1994).

I will begin my consideration of human evolution by looking at the adaptations of hunter–gatherers. Here (and in many of the chapters that follow) I will mention instances in which technological societies are sometimes out of step with the evolved behavioral tendencies and preferences of the human species. Then I will focus on sexual selection and sexual dimorphism as they apply to humans. As we shall see, some interesting gender differences can be related to these evolutionary mechanisms.

ADAPTATIONS OF HUNTER–GATHERERS

The million-year-plus time period during which the ancestors of modern humans lived as hunter–gatherers provided ample time for these hominids to evolve behavioral strategies and mental mechanisms consistent with a hunter–gatherer style of life. Although we cannot know directly how our ancestors lived hundreds of thousands of years ago, we can gain some insight by looking at certain preliterate hunter–gatherer societies that exist today.

For example, individuals in hunter–gatherer societies are active physically, often walking long distances during the day. Clearly, we have inherited from our hunter–gatherer ancestors a strong need to be physically active. Unfortunately, however, many people in technologically advanced societies work at jobs and engage in leisure activities that require little physical activity. Technological advances have created a multitude of sedentary jobs that place people behind desks and have encouraged sedentary leisure activities such as watching television or playing video games. The good news is that many and varied kinds of exercise are beneficial to modern humans. For people of all ages, engaging in a moderately strenuous but enjoyable activity three or more times a week has been found to increase feelings of well-being and self-esteem. In addition, regular exercise strengthens the immune system and increases longevity (see Seraganian, 1993).

Another example: Hunter–gatherers live in harmony with their natural environment, thriving where there are abundant plants, fresh water, and wildlife. As indicated earlier, E. O. Wilson's biophilia hypothesis suggests that there is an evolved tendency for modern humans to thrive under conditions where we feel close to nature. Research testing the biophilia hypothesis has demonstrated that humans do in fact have greater feelings of well-being when they work in buildings that have windows looking out on natural scenes or even pictures of pleasant natural scenes than when there are no windows or pictures. Furthermore, the speed of recovery from illnesses and operations is enhanced by access to windows or pictures of pleasant natural scenes (see Kellert & Wilson, 1993).

In the recent past, especially in the nineteenth century and the early part of the twentieth century, fast-growing communities often ignored people's need for access to pleasant natural environments such as parks. However, it is encouraging that many communities are now committing resources to protect the few remaining natural areas and restore blighted districts. These attempts not only increase people's deep-seated appreciation of our natural environment but can provide significant social benefits. For example, people who are happy, have solid self-esteem, and live in harmony with their surroundings make good citizens (see Myers, 1983).

SEXUAL SELECTION AND SEXUAL DIMORPHISM

Like many other animals, humans are sexually dimorphic; and as with other animals, the evolution of human sexual dimorphism was probably driven by sexual selection strongly related to polygyny. Therefore, it is possible to make certain inferences about the behavior of early hominids by analyzing their degree of sexual dimorphism. Fossils of Australopithecines (hominids that lived from approximately 4 million to 2 million years ago) exhibit a large degree of sexual dimorphism—which, as explained in relation to nonhuman animals, is associated with polygynous mating systems.

Humans (*Homo sapiens*), who first appeared in the fossil record about 200,000 years ago, have less sexual dimorphism than Australopithecines. Therefore, we may assume that in our more recent ancestors, the high degree of polygyny associated with Australopithecines more than 2 million years ago was modified and probably included some degree of monogamy (Hrdy, 1988).

As I'll discuss further in Chapter 9, the relatively large size and aggressiveness of male animals in polygynous species promotes the males' potential to attract and mate with females. However, large size represents a compromise in terms of health and longevity. The sexual dimorphism of humans is associated with gender differences in life expectancy—differences that have been observed in many different human cultures. Females live approximately seven years longer on average than males in virtually all societies studied.

It is difficult to know the proximate cause of this gender difference in human longevity. However, a study conducted in the 1960s using a group of mentally retarded men who had been castrated—at a time when castration was an accepted treatment for retarded males—found that castrated males lived significantly longer than a comparison group of intact males (Hamilton & Mestler, 1969). Apparently testosterone was a basic causal factor in limiting male longevity, but the reasons behind this effect were not clear. Fortunately, from a humanitarian standpoint, castration of mentally retarded humans is no longer sanctioned; so we can only guess at the exact reasons why testosterone "costs" males years of longevity.

◆ CHANGING PERSPECTIVES

PAST	PRESENT	FUTURE
A huge gulf exists between human and nonhuman animal behavior (believed throughout history until nineteenth century, pre-Darwin).	Many of the same evolutionary and ecological principles explain human and nonhuman animal behavior.	What are the limits to the explanatory power of evolutionary and ecological principles?

SUMMARY

Interest in animal behavior has deep roots and provided significant benefits for our ancient ancestors, which lived as hunter–gatherers. A systematic study of animal behavior began with Aristotle, lay dormant for hundreds of years, but was reawakened by the advent of Darwin's theory of evolution by natural selection. In the twentieth century, interest continued with the development of such fields of inquiry as ethology, comparative psychology, learning theory, behavioral ecology, sociobiology, and evolutionary psychology.

Darwin's theory of natural selection has been a driving force in the investigation of animal behavior since the latter part of the nineteenth century. The concepts of fitness and adaptation are basic to Darwin's theory and to all succeeding extensions of evolutionary theory.

Over a period of many generations, evolutionary trends develop and, in some cases, result in specialization, divergence, or convergence. Sexual selection appears when there are different evolutionary pressures on males than on females, resulting in the development of sexual dimorphism.

In recent decades, several evolutionary theories related to behavior have had a strong effect on our understanding of animal behavior. Recent extensions of evolutionary theory include Hamilton's theory of kin selection; Williams's theory of natural selection at the individual level; MacArthur and Pianka's theory of feeding that developed into optimality theory; Maynard Smith's game theory applied to animal behavior; and Trivers's theory of parental investment.

Questions about animal behavior can be divided into two general types: proximate and ultimate. The various types of questions asked include questions about mechanisms, development, function, evolutionary history, cognition, and comparisons between species. Often, the pursuit of one question leads to the development of other questions.

Hypotheses about animal behavior are often generated from the theories discussed and then tested in laboratories or natural settings.

Looking at the probable evolutionary history of humans enables us to gain insight into our basic humanness. For example, our need for exercise and our need to live in harmony with the environment make sense in the light of our hunter–gatherer heritage. Our sexual dimorphism helps to explain gender differences in life expectancy.

KEY TERMS

adaptation, p. 8
adaptive radiation, p. 11
ancestral, p. 11
behavioral ecology, p. 6
biophilia, p. 3

comparative psychologists, p. 5
conspecifics, p. 15
convergence, p. 11
direct fitness, p. 13
divergence, p. 11

ethology, p. 5
evolutionarily stable strategy, p. 16
evolutionary psychologists, p. 7
fitness, p. 8
game theory, p. 15
hominids, p. 19
inclusive fitness, p. 13
indirect fitness, p. 13
individual level of selection hypothesis, p. 14
mixed evolutionarily stable strategy, p. 16
monogamous, p. 12
niche, p. 11
optimality theory, p. 15

polygynous, p. 12
proximate questions, p. 17
sexual dimorphism, p. 12
sexual selection, p. 11
sociobiology, p. 6
specialized, p. 11
strategy, p. 15
theory of kin selection, p. 13
theory of natural selection, p. 7
theory of parental investment, p. 16
ultimate questions, p. 17
vestigial structure, p. 9

CHAPTER 2

GENES AND BEHAVIOR

- ◆ *Why is it advantageous for an animal to avoid mating with a close relative?*

- ◆ *Why is too much of a difference between mates nonadaptive?*

2

Genes, the basic blueprints for development, are fundamental to all life processes. Furthermore, genes are necessary for the continuing existence of life forms, because genetic material is intimately involved in reproduction. A powerful finding supporting the theory of natural selection is the fact that basically all of the information we have discovered about genes since Darwin's death is consistent with the theory. Thus, in some respects, this chapter is simply a continuation of our discussion of evolutionary theory.

In this chapter we will focus on the relationship between genes and animal behavior. We'll begin with a consideration of the genetic foundations of heredity. Then we will look at the role of genes in behavior and at the interaction between genes and the environment. Next, we will discuss research techniques related to the role of genes in behavior. Finally, we will examine genetic factors in human evolution.

GENETIC FOUNDATIONS OF REPRODUCTION AND HEREDITY

In 1866 an obscure Czech monk named Gregor Mendel gave a lecture and published a paper on his work on the inheritance of characteristics in pea plants. Ironically, Charles Darwin, who died in 1882, was not aware that Mendel had quietly laid the foundations for understanding heredity, the concept that lay at the core of Darwin's theory of evolution. It was not until the turn of the century that Mendel's work was rediscovered and the science of genetics became established.

In the twentieth century, scientists achieved several remarkable breakthroughs that extended Mendel's findings and elaborated the molecular bases of inheritance. T. H. Morgan, working with fruit flies, identified genes—the basic structures responsible for inheritance. Although Morgan was unable to observe genes directly, he demonstrated that genes were located on specific areas of the chromosomes in the nucleus of every cell.

Genes consist of deoxyribonucleic acid (**DNA**), and in 1944 Oswald Avery and two associates identified DNA as the molecular "blueprint" or record of precise instructions for heredity. These instructions are coded as genes that may be copied and passed on to an organism's descendants.

In 1953 James Watson and Francis Crick achieved one of the greatest scientific feats of the century by uncovering the specific molecular structure of DNA. The molecular structure includes a double-stranded polynucleotide consisting of a sugar, phosphate, and four bases—guanine (G), cytosine (C), adenine (A), and thymine (T). The genetic code consists of the specific sequence of these bases in a DNA strand (see Figure 2.1).

Genetic Coding

We now know that genes affect inheritance by acting as a template for the production of another nucleic acid, ribonucleic acid (**RNA**). A type of RNA known as transfer RNA carries or transfers critical information from the DNA to another part of the cell, where a protein is constructed. And proteins, among other things, function as the building blocks of an organism's body.

Specifically, the sequence of nitrogenous bases that make up the "rungs" on the DNA "ladder" function as the code or the blueprint. Since there are four different bases—and the "ladder" may be extremely long—a large number of bits of information may be coded in a DNA strand. Periodically, the coded information is transferred to the RNA by a process known as transcription. Transcription can be accomplished relatively easily because RNA is biochemically similar to DNA. In fact, the

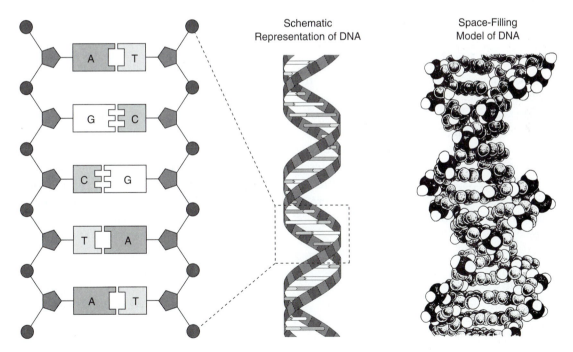

Schematic Representation of DNA

Space-Filling Model of DNA

FIGURE 2.1 ◆ **A schematic representation of DNA.** Note the sequence of nucleic bases—G, C, A, and T.

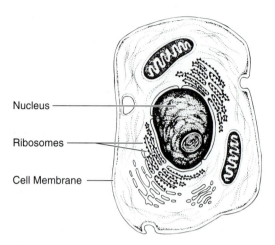

FIGURE 2.2 ◆ **A cell.** The nucleus contains RNA; protein synthesis takes place in the ribosomes. RNA from the nucleus enters the ribosomes and functions as a blueprint for the synthesis.

Nucleus

Ribosomes

Cell Membrane

two substances are identical except for one nitrogenous base: In RNA, uracil occurs in place of thymine.

The transfer RNA then leaves the nucleus of the cell and migrates to the **ribosomes**—specialized structures within the cell that function as the "workshop." Inside the ribosomes, the RNA directs the synthesis of a protein molecule (see Figure 2.2). In other words, proteins are constructed in the ribosome workshop.

The Role of Proteins in Behavior

Proteins have several critical functions related to behavior. For example, some proteins serve as building blocks for the nervous system. As Chapter 16 will explain, the nervous system functions to initiate, coordinate, and control behavior and cognitive processes.

As in the case of the nervous system, proteins are the building blocks for sensory systems. Sensory systems provide information about the external world; they also provide information about the internal world, such as information about the position of the body or the blood sugar level—or, in some cases, about specific deficits such as pathologically low levels of sodium.

Proteins may also act as enzymes, which regulate the production of chemical substances that function as chemical communicators. Among these chemical communicators are **neurotransmitters,** which regulate the transmission of neural impulses and, consequently, are intimately involved with the functioning of the nervous system.

Another class of chemical substances, **hormones,** facilitate the development of several neural structures and of other structures related to reproduction. Hormones also alter the activities of tissues and organs, including the nervous system. Consequently, hormones can have a direct effect on behavior.

Still another class of chemical substances, **pheromones,** act as messengers and influence the behavior of other individuals in the same species. We will discuss these substances in more detail when we consider the neural and chemical control of behavior in Chapters 16 and 17.

Proteins may also affect behavior in subtle, indirect ways. For example, slight differences in protein structure cause noticeable differences in the smell of an animal's urine. Consequently, animals with a good sense of smell, such as mice, can recognize individuals by the smell of their urine and can also assess their degree of relatedness (Agosta, 1992).

TABLE 2.1 ◆ The Functions of Proteins in Behavior

Site of Protein Action	Function
Building blocks in the nervous system	Control behavior and cognition.
Building blocks in the sensory systems	Provide information about the internal and external worlds.
Neurotransmitters	Transmit neural messages.
Hormones	Facilitate development of neural structures; alter activity in the nervous system and in other parts of the body.
Pheromones	Influence behavior of conspecifics.

Genes and Reproduction

How are genetic codes passed from one generation to the next during reproduction? As we shall see, there are two basic types of reproduction—asexual and sexual.

Asexual Reproduction

Asexual reproduction involves simple **mitosis**—the process of cell replication (Figure 2.3). Consequently, two parent organisms are not required. At the beginning of the mitotic process, the genetic material in the nucleus of the cell is duplicated, resulting in twice the normal number of chromosomes. Then the cell divides, and the duplicate half of the chromosomes are included in a separate daughter cell while the other half remain in the original cell. Consequently, each cell has the normal complement of chromosomes and genetic material. In other words, the daughter cell is basically a genetic duplicate or clone of the

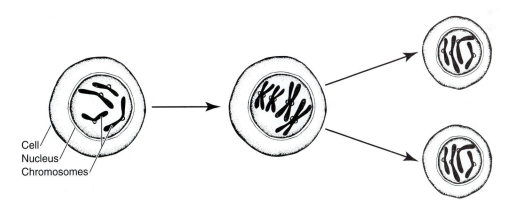

Cell
Nucleus
Chromosomes

A. Nucleus with normal (diploid) number of chromosomes

B. Replication results in twice the number of chromosomes

C. Division results in two identical cells with normal number of chromosomes

FIGURE 2.3 ◆ **A schematic representation of mitosis.**

parent cell as it was before the process of mitosis began.

As we shall see when we discuss reproduction in Chapter 8, there are several types of asexual processes. One of the most common is **binary fission;** after duplicating its chromosomes, the animal simply splits into two more or less equal parts. In the genus *Paramecium* the split takes place longitudinally while the animal is moving freely. Some flatworms, in contrast, attach their posterior ends to a substrate and then move forward until they snap in two. There may be some genetic variation due to random errors in the process of genetic duplication, but the effects of these errors are usually minimal.

Sexual Reproduction

In contrast to asexual reproduction, sexual reproduction involves the mixing of genes from two parents. In most cases the offspring receive a mixture of 50 percent of their genes from one parent and 50 percent from the other. Because the mixture is different for each individual offspring, the mixing of genetic material results in great variability in the offspring. With the exception of identical twins, the possibility that any two offspring will be genetic duplicates—or that any one offspring will be a duplicate of either parent—is microscopically small.

This variability in genetic makeup is brought about by **meiosis**—a process that results in the production of **gametes,** or cells that contain half the organism's original number of chromosomes and enter into the process of fertilization (Figure 2.4). Every animal has a certain number of paired chromosomes; humans, for example, have 23 pairs.

The first stage of meiosis is similar to mitosis: In a reproductive cell, the homologous pairs of chromosomes gather together and each chromosome replicates itself. Thus, the

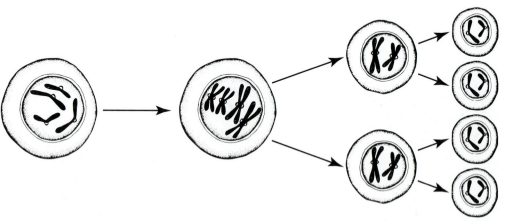

A. Nucleus with normal (diploid) number of chromosomes

B. Replication results in twice the number of chromosomes

C. Two divisions result in four cells, each with half the normal number of chromosomes (haploid number)

FIGURE 2.4 ◆ **A schematic representation of meiosis.**

◆ UNUSUAL ADAPTATIONS

Haplodiploidy

Certain insects have evolved a type of sex determination known as **haplodiploidy:** males develop from unfertilized (haploid) eggs while females develop from fertilized (diploid) eggs. Because the female can lay either fertilized or unfertilized eggs, she can determine the sex of her offspring.

Another important feature of haplodiploidy is the degree of relationship between kin. As we saw in Chapter 1, members of most sexually reproducing species have duplicates of approximately 50 percent of the genes of their siblings. The relationship is commonly referred to as sharing 50 percent of the genes. But in haplodiploidy insects such as ants and bees, sisters share approximately 75 percent of their genes. This unusually high degree of genetic sharing means that it is relatively advantageous, from a fitness standpoint, for sisters to forgo their own reproduction and support the reproduction of a sister (Hamilton, 1972). Chapter 12 will explore further the tendency of many individual females (workers) to become infertile and support the reproduction of the queen, who is their sister; this tendency is basic to the evolution of the highly complex social behavior seen in ants and in certain species of bees and wasps.

cell temporarily has twice the normal number of chromosomes. The cell then divides twice, resulting in four cells, each containing half the original number of chromosomes—the **haploid** number. It is only through fertilization that a fertilized egg cell becomes **diploid;** that is, contains the full complement of chromosomes.

In males, each cell containing the haploid number of chromosomes develops into a male gamete or sperm cell. In females, however, only one out of each four comparable cells develops into a female gamete or egg. (The other three cells do not have a function in reproduction.) Consequently, the physiological cost of producing eggs is greater than the cost of producing sperm.

In addition, females of many species provide each egg with a certain amount of yolk, which provides nutrients for the developing embryo. For this reason too, in most species, eggs are much more "expensive" to produce than sperm. Furthermore, there is a longer period of delay before mature eggs can be replaced by the female than before mature sperm can be replaced by the male. As Chapter 9 will discuss, the relatively long waiting period before females can regain fertility has important ramifications for the differential evolution of sexual strategies in males and females.

POPULATION GENETICS

With this simplified introduction to genetics, we can now turn to an updated version of evolutionary theory. Genes function as the basic blueprints for the development of behavior. Copies of genes are passed on to the succeeding generation, so the genes also function as the agents for inheritance.

The Gene Pool

Because most animals reproduce sexually, the genes of the offspring are not duplicates of those of the parents. A similar statement can be made about the **gene pool**—the aggregate of the types of genes found in a population of interbreeding animals. The gene pool varies from one generation to the next. Let's consider factors that influence shifts in the makeup of the gene pool.

Mutations

Mutations, or random errors in genetic coding and replication, continually introduce new genes and **alleles** (alternative forms of genes) into each animal population. Although most mutations have deleterious effects, some are associated with positive events. For example, if a mutated allele is associated with a light coloration and this trait has an advantage in providing protection from predators, the allele will tend to increase in the population.

However, the advantage of light coloration may occur in only certain populations of animals. Thus, individuals that spend the winter in the far north may benefit from light coloration because they blend in with the snow, while individuals in southern climates may be at a disadvantage. There will tend to be a natural selection against the same allele in the southern population.

Genetic Drift

In some cases there is **genetic drift;** that is, changes in the frequency of alleles in a population occur by chance alone. Genetic drift is most likely to take place in small populations of interbreeding animals. Thus, one light-colored individual may happen to survive just because it happened to be in the right place at the right time. This chance event will have greater significance in a small population of animals than in a large population. By way of analogy, one person becoming suddenly rich in a small community will have a greater impact on the community than the same person becoming rich in a large community.

Gene Flow

Changes in a population may also occur as the result of **gene flow**—the introduction of the genes from potentially interbreeding individuals from different populations. To continue with our example related to coloration, the arrival of a light-colored animal from the north that breeds with individuals from the southern population can result in the introduction of the allele associated with light coloration into the population. Even though the light coloration may be selected against in the long run, there are likely to be some of the newly introduced alleles in the population for a period of time.

Under certain theoretical conditions, the frequency of alleles would remain stable and no evolution would take place. But for the frequency of alleles to remain stable, there must be no mutations, an extremely large population of individuals, and no new members entering the population from another area; and all animals must have an equal chance of reproducing.

In actuality these conditions are rarely if ever met, so evolution continues to take place. And the more the theoretical conditions are violated, the greater the speed of evolutionary change. Furthermore, since the environment is typically in a state of flux, the alleles that provide the greatest fitness may differ from one time to another. Consequently, over a period of several generations, the distribution of alleles or genes in a population changes—and, as later chapters will document, evolution continues and results in some amazing variations and adaptations.

Toxins in the Environment

Toxins in the environment, especially those induced by humans, can have a rapid effect on animal gene pools. For example, when a new type of pesticide is introduced, mosquitoes that possess alleles related to immunity to the toxin survive and pass on the toxin-resistant alleles to their offspring. In just a few generations, the mosquitoes' gene pool is significantly altered and the toxin loses its effectiveness.

Unfortunately, many human-introduced toxins have indirect effects that can be extremely damaging to the environment and can even bring about extinctions. For example, birds that eat insects that have absorbed a pesticide may retain the toxin and suffer reduced

TABLE 2.2 ◆ Factors That Induce Changes in the Gene Pool

Factor	Definition	Significance
Mutation	Random errors in genetic coding within an individual	Mutations bring about changes in the gene pool and alter natural selection.
Genetic drift	Changes in the frequency of alleles in the population related to chance	Changes are more rapid in small populations.
Gene flow	Introduction of genes from different populations	The introduction of new, inter-breeding individuals facilitates changes in the gene pool.
Toxins	Substances, often introduced by humans, that affect the health and survival of animals	Toxins cause changes in the gene pool and alter natural selection. In some cases, extinction results.

ability to reproduce. By the 1970s the use of DDT had seriously reduced the populations of many songbird populations in the United States. The identification of this deleterious effect by researchers led to the outlawing of this particular pesticide in this country. As we shall see at many points throughout this book, however, other toxins continue to have far-reaching effects.

Dominant and Recessive Characteristics

Mendel discovered that the expression of one genetically determined trait can be dominant over another; that is, one trait may mask the expression of another trait. For example, when a pea plant with round seeds was bred to a plant with wrinkled seeds, all of the progeny had round seeds. In other words, the **phenotype** (observable characteristic) in the progeny was identical to that in just one of the parent plants.

This expression of **dominance** can be understood on the basis of the interaction of alleles. Let us use R to stand for the dominant (expressed) allele and r to represent the **recessive** (masked) allele. The pea plants' progeny receive an allele from each of the parents, and all of the progeny possess both the R and the r alleles; so the **genotype** or genetic makeup of the progeny can be represented as Rr.

When the two alleles differ, as in this case, the condition is called **heterozygous;** when the alleles are identical, the condition is described as **homozygous.** Thus, in our example, the parent plants are homozygous while the progeny are heterozygous. Only the dominant characteristic is expressed in the Rr, heterozygous condition. Nonetheless, animals with heterozygous traits (heterozygotes) have the potential to produce progeny that express the recessive trait. If two Rr individuals mate, some of the progeny (approximately 25 percent) will be homozygous (rr), and the recessive trait will be expressed (Figure 2.5).

Recessive traits are difficult to eliminate by natural selection. Even if a recessive trait has deleterious effects, heterozygotes carry and pass on the recessive allele to their offspring. Two closely related individuals are particularly likely to carry alleles for the same recessive traits. Consequently, fitness is reduced when close relatives mate. For example, when closely related animals have been mated in zoos, there has been an unusually high rate of infant mortality (Ralls et al., 1979). This reduced fitness associated with the breeding of close relatives, known as **inbreeding depression,** presents a significant problem for endangered species. When populations are small, the incidence of close relatives breeding is greatest.

The effects of genes are usually more complex than that illustrated by the pea plant example. For example, there may be incomplete dominance resulting in progeny that are

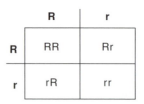

FIGURE 2.5 ◆ The four types of combinations possible with a mating of heterozygous individuals. Note that only one in four of the combinations results in the expression of the recessive trait (rr).

intermediate in regard to a particular trait. This intermediate effect is graphically illustrated by a study of two closely related species of migrating birds that were bred under laboratory conditions. German blackcaps normally fly in a southwesterly direction on their migratory route, while Austrian blackcaps normally migrate in a southeasterly direction. The hybrid offspring of these birds were found to orient due south—a compromise between the normal migratory patterns of the two parents (Helbig, 1991). Incidentally, this study also illustrates one of the dangers of cross-breeding, because the southward flight of these hybrid offspring would be an inappropriate behavior in the wild; it would not promote survival.

Optimal Outbreeding

In a tendency related to the avoidance of inbreeding depression, animals have evolved methods of avoiding mating with close relatives. For example, when given a choice of mates, laboratory white-footed mice tend to avoid mating with siblings (Keane, 1990). And as we shall see in Chapter 20, in many different species of animals there is reduced possibility of inbreeding because either male or female juveniles tend to leave the area where they were born.

At the other extreme, as in the example of the migrating blackcaps, too much genetic dissimilarity in mates may also present a problem. Because each animal tends to be specialized for survival in its own microhabitat, too much outbreeding leads to **outbreeding depression**—the failure of offspring from parents of excessively diverse genetic backgrounds to thrive or even to survive.

As a compromise between avoiding inbreeding and risking outbreeding depression, most animals tend to be **optimal outbreeders;** that is, to mate with partners that are *somewhat* similar to themselves. For example, when given a choice, Japanese quail tend to mate with first cousins rather than with siblings or nonrelatives (Bateson, 1982). We will return to the subject of optimal outbreeding when we consider animal dispersal in Chapter 20.

Polygeny and Pleiotropy

Another example of the complex nature of genetic effects is provided by **polygeny**—the fact that several different genes may influence the expression of a given trait or behavior. Polygeny is the general rule because most traits, especially behavioral traits, require the integrated action of several different types of processes. If each process, in turn, requires a specific enzyme, then several genes are necessary to synthesize the appropriate enzymes.

When there is simple dominance of one allele over another, traits in a population tend to be distributed into discrete categories. In this case, animals are either black or white, for instance. However, polygeny typically results in a continuous distribution of traits; that is, in many shades of gray. Since polygeny is very common in regard to behavioral traits, especially in birds and mammals, most behavioral traits are distributed along a continuous spectrum.

If one gene is found to have a negative effect on a trait, this does not mean that only that one gene is involved in the expression of the trait. But as in the case of any group effort, the failure on the part of one individual may be enough to damage the whole system. For example, a single gene deficit in humans can result in brain dysfunction and a serious form of mental retardation known as phenylketonuria, or PKU. (Fortunately, it is possible to forestall the problem effectively by regulating the newborn's diet.)

Just as several genes are usually involved in one trait or behavior pattern, one gene often influences the development of several different structures and behaviors—an effect known as **pleiotropy.** In mice, for example, a single gene is involved in the development of such phenotypically different traits as fur color, kidney function, and visual sensitivity (Balkema et al., 1983).

The existence of pleiotropy helps to explain why not all of the traits possessed by an animal are adaptive. Traits that are associated with a favorable characteristic sometimes continue to be passed on even if they are not beneficial or mildly deleterious. The reason is that the organism has no way of separating traits that are bound together by pleiotropism; thus, some nonadaptive traits continue to exist in a population because of this "free ride" effect.

TABLE 2.3 ◆ Polygeny and Pleiotropy

Mechanism	Definition	Significance
Polygeny	Several genes influence the expression of a trait.	Since most traits are the result of polygeny, most traits vary along a continuum.
Pleiotropy	A single gene may affect several traits.	Not all traits are adaptive.

THE INTERACTION BETWEEN GENES AND THE ENVIRONMENT

Historically, our failure to understand how genes operate led to a controversy that is now seen as meaningless. Some people argued that certain behaviors were caused by genetic factors, or "nature"; others countered that those behaviors were the result of experience or the environment, referred to as "nurture." Both arguments, however, can now be seen as invalid. Behavioral development necessarily results from an interaction of genetic and environmental factors. Just as we must have a recipe as well as ingredients and an oven to make cake, we need a combination of a blueprint, a body, and some sort of an environment in order to produce behavior.

The interaction between environmental and genetic factors takes place in complex ways; that is, genetic and environmental influences do not simply add together. Furthermore, genes may have their influence at many different points in development. Some genes are active over a long period of time, but others must be activated by cues from the internal or external environment before they can synthesize proteins. In some cases, one gene or set of genes is activated by other genes, but only under certain specific circumstances.

This complex interaction between genetic and environmental factors is called **epigenesis** (Figure 2.6). The epigenetic approach assumes that because the expression of genes is dependent upon environmental factors, the same genes may express themselves differently at different times. Consequently, an animal may behave very differently under various environmental conditions.

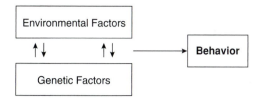

FIGURE 2.6 ◆ **Epigenesis.** Complex interactions among environmental and genetic factors result in behavior development. Neither environmental nor genetic factors alone are responsible for the development of any given behavior.

The term *environment* includes internal factors, such as conditions within the nervous system, as well as stimulation coming from outside the body. As I shall discuss shortly, experiential factors result in changes in the nervous system. Thus, the epigenetic approach also emphasizes that development involves an interaction between genes and experience. In other words, experience is coded within the nervous system and becomes part of the internal environment.

This complex interaction among genes, environment, and experience allows for much greater variability and adjustment to unusual circumstances than if development were entirely dependent on one factor alone. To illustrate this point, let us imagine the interaction between a architect and a carpenter building a house. Working together, the architect and carpenter can overcome many problems that arise; but such adaptations would be impossible if the architect had to spell out rules for every conceivable adjustment that might have to be made at each step during the construction process.

Neural Development

Neural development presents some clear examples of how epigenesis proceeds. Part of the recipe for the development of the brain and the rest of the nervous system is contained within genes. For many years, scientists assumed that the nervous system developed in a straightforward manner according to the gene recipe. However, research in the last 25 years indicates that neural development is also influenced by the environment. Whether or not the neurons survive, how the endings on neural processes grow, and the direction of neural growth are influenced by such factors as other neurons in the environment. This developmental plan provides for the considerable flexibility in neural growth, both prenatally and after birth.

Prenatal Development

Using a sophisticated and complicated procedure, researchers were able to trace the early development of a neuron (nerve cell) within the nervous system of a fetal rat. The nerve's development was highly dependent upon the other cells in the area. In other words, the neuron received some of its developmental "instructions" from components of other cells, not simply from the genes within its own cell nucleus (Walsh & Cepko, 1992).

If there is injury to certain parts of the brain during prenatal development, neurons may grow in a different pattern and form different synapses than if the brain tissue remains healthy. This neural plasticity enables animals to adjust to even severe prenatal brain injuries (Jacobson, 1978). Similar types of adjustment occur in response to certain genetic abnormalities. For example, as the result of a genetic mutation, Siamese cats lack pigment in tissue underlying the retina of the eye. This disturbance causes optic nerve fibers to be routed to the wrong side of the brain. However, the abnormally routed fibers reorganize nerve cells in the brain in such a way that, despite this unorthodox "wiring," the cat develops a normal visual system (Hubel & Wiesel, 1979).

Environmental factors are also related to the survival of neurons. Early in embryonic development, the number of neurons generated greatly exceeds the number that ultimately survive. The neurons then compete with each other for survival. One form of competition is for synaptic sites: Those neurons that do not obtain a site generally die. As a result of this selective survival of neurons, more neurons are found in areas of the brain where they are "needed" than in other areas.

There is recent evidence that the pattern of prenatal nerve death helps to account for important species differences. For example, Spanish wildcats and domestic cats have the same number and types of neurons early in fetal development. Just before birth, however, different types of neurons die in the two species. In the domestic cat, nerve cells that would normally mediate color vision die off in large numbers. In contrast, the wildcat experiences a large loss of cells that are sensitive to motion and objects in dim light. These differences make sense, because the Spanish wildcat hunts in bright sunlight while the domestic cat hunts at night (Williams et al., 1993).

Postnatal Development

The effects of the environment on neural development continue after birth. In many different kinds of animals, experimental lesions that disrupt neurons at their synapses result in the growth of new end processes and synapses. Some of the new synapses occur at a considerable distance from the site of the lesions, suggesting that the neural growth is a reorganizational process as well as a replacement process (Cotman & Nieto-Sampedro, 1982).

TABLE 2.4 ◆ Neural Development

Factor	Effect	Result
Prenatal injury or abnormality of nerve cells	Other nerve cells grow differently.	Adjustment to brain injuries is possible.
Prenatal competition for synaptic sites	The greater the number of possible synaptic sites, the greater the number of surviving neurons.	Production of neurons in areas where they are needed takes place.
Postnatal stimulation of brain cells	The more nerve cells are stimulated, the more dendritic branching, etc.	The more brain cells are used, the more effective they become.

A classic series of experiments with rats indicates that the degree of stimulation from the outside environment affects the brain's development. An "enriched" environment—in which 10 to 12 animals live with various objects, undergo frequent handling by humans, and are given periodic experiences with mazes—produces rats with a thicker cerebral cortex, larger neural cells, and more dendritic branching than are found in rats reared under the usual isolated laboratory condition of one rat to a cage. Furthermore, even a "social" environment—defined as 3 animals living together in a laboratory cage without extra objects or special experiences—results in some increased neuronal development compared to the usual laboratory isolation (Rosenzweig et al., 1962).

The "enriched" condition probably represents an environment comparable, in terms of stimulation, to the natural environment of the rat. In contrast, the "social" and isolated conditions seem to represent varying degrees of deprivation. Thus, it is probably more accurate to say that deprivation has negative effects on neural development than to conclude that enrichment enhances development. At any rate, the differences in neural development clearly represent neural changes associated with learning.

The Development of Gender Differences

As in the case of neural development, there has been a tradition of thinking that differences between males and females were entirely the result of a genetic recipe. However, gender differences also illustrate epigenesis.

The Development of Sex Organs

In embryonic mammals, potential males have one X chromosome and one Y chromosome while potential females have two X chromosomes. For many years people assumed that the presence of a Y chromosome in itself determined that an individual would develop male sex organs. And in fact the presence of the Y chromosome is necessary for the development of testes (rather than ovaries). However, it is the presence of testosterone secreted by the newly formed testes that orchestrates the development of the penis and other male organs. In contrast, the absence of testosterone leads to the development of a clitoris and other female sex organs.

More specifically, a single gene on the Y chromosome leads to the production of an enzyme called testes-determining factor. This enzyme causes the undifferentiated gonads to develop into testes. In contrast, the absence of this enzyme results in the development of ovaries. Thus, if the testes-determining factor is experimentally injected into a "female" embryonic mouse, the individual will develop into a male (Koopman et al., 1991).

Masculinization and Defeminization of Behavior

Masculinization is the effect of testosterone on the development of structures and behaviors related to male mating patterns. As this definition implies, the presence (or absence) of testosterone is important to behavioral development as well as to the development of sex organs.

Fortunately, from a research standpoint, the physical arrangement of rodent fetuses allows researchers to assess the role of testosterone under seminatural conditions. Rodent fetuses are arranged sequentially in the two horns of the uterus. A fetus may be placed between two males (2M), between a male and a female (1M), or between two females (0M). Male fetuses produce large amounts of testosterone just before the time of birth, and this testosterone strongly stimulates adjacent fetuses but has a less significant effect on distant fetuses. Consequently, both male and female fetuses may be evaluated in regard to conditions of strong (2M), medium (1M), and weak (0M) testosterone stimulation.

The testosterone stimulation has a masculinizing effect on males. The 2M males sire significantly more offspring than do 0M males when all the males are given unlimited access to females. At some level, the females seem to be aware of this difference in reproductive potential; when given a choice between 2M and 0M males, females in estrus prefer to associate with the more successful 2M males (Clark & Galef, 1989).

Masculinization is not the only effect that testosterone has on fetuses. In some cases the testosterone inhibits the development of female reproductive traits, an effect known as **defeminization.** In gerbils, for example, 2M females show delayed sexual maturity. Furthermore, these females produce only half as many offspring as 0M females (Clark et al., 1992).

In conclusion, the principles of masculinization and defeminization, related to the presence or absence of testosterone during a critical period of development, apply to the development of several structures and behaviors related to mating. However, the critical periods are different for the development of sex organs and the development of sexual be-

TABLE 2.5 ◆ The Effects of Testosterone on Development in Rodents

Effect	Time of Effect
Development of male genitals	Early fetal development
Masculinization, including male mounting behavior	Late fetal development
Male attractiveness	Late fetal development
Defeminization, including inhibitions of female patterns	Late fetal development

havior potential. Consequently, an abnormal quantity of testosterone at one point in fetal development is not likely to affect both aspects. In such a case, an animal may develop masculinized genitals but not masculinized sexual behavior, or vice versa.

RESEARCH TECHNIQUES

We have looked at how genetic information is coded and passed on from one generation to another. Now let us consider some of the experimental methods scientists use to study the relationship between genes and behavior.

Crossbreeding

Mendel demonstrated the phenomenon of dominance in peas by crossbreeding varieties that produce round and wrinkled seeds. Much later, scientists investigated the relationship between genes and behavior by crossbreeding closely related animals that differed from one another in a significant way. For example, two species of lovebirds carry nesting material in very different ways; one species carries the material in its beak, while the other tucks it between feathers on its back. Hybrid offspring of the two species show elements of both transporting techniques; sometimes they carry the material in their beaks and at other times in the back feathers. Furthermore, the hybrids spend a good deal of time in apparent conflict before they finally transport material to the nest—picking up the material, placing it in the back feathers, then removing it again (Dilger, 1962).

In looking at these crossbreeding studies, we might incorrectly assume that differences between groups of animals are attributable to genetic factors alone. However, the animals have been reared in experimental situations where the internal and external environments for each group are very similar, so the effects of environment are not apparent. We must remember that genes in themselves do not *cause* behaviors. It is ultimately an interaction between genetic factors and environment that produces the effect. What crossbreeding research demonstrates is simply the relatively strong influence that genetic factors have on the traits in question.

Selective Breeding

Researchers also investigate the contribution of genetic factors to behavioral development by selectively breeding for a particular trait. Investigators may mate individual animals that rate highest on a particular trait and, after a few generations, assess changes in regard to

that trait. However, changes that take place over generations may be affected by changes in environmental conditions as well as by genetic factors. To control for this possible environmental effect, experimenters usually have a control condition in which animals mate randomly, or a condition in which individuals with the lowest scores for the trait are bred. Offspring from the highest condition may then be compared to offspring from the control or the lowest condition.

As an example, mice were divided into two groups on the basis of their levels of general activity. Individuals with the highest levels were interbred, as were individuals with the lowest levels. After four generations there was a clear distinction between the active and lethargic mice strains (De Fries et al., 1974).

In a study employing a similar technique, rats were separated into two groups on the basis of their performance on mazes. Rats that learned a maze in relatively few trials, termed maze-bright rats, were mated with other maze-bright rats. Similarly, rats that took a large number of trials to learn a maze (maze-dull rats) were mated together. The average rats in the two groups differed greatly from each other by the seventh generation, and there was little overlap between the groups (Tryon, 1940).

It is also possible to look at selection under natural conditions. For example, garter snakes face different types of predators in different habitats. In response to these differences, the snakes undergo rapid evolutionary change in regard to defensive strategies. In contrast, animals that face the same types of predators no matter what their habitat tend to be resistant to change (Garland, 1988).

Overall, studies of selective breeding and selection under natural conditions indicate that some traits are relatively resistant to change over several generations while other traits, such as the ones just considered, can be molded rather easily. This plasticity is important as a potential facilitator for beneficial change within a few generations. Conversely, resistance to change is a safeguard against change taking place as the result of chance or for relatively unimportant reasons.

It seems that the potential for rapid genetic change in a trait, like other characteristics in animals, is driven by natural selection. Generally, the characteristics that have paid off for many generations and under a large variety of circumstances, such as the stalking behavior of a cat, have evolved a resistance to change. In contrast, high activity levels in mice may pay off in some types of environments but not in others. And indeed, the activity levels of mice turn out to be relatively plastic, changing significantly in a few generations.

Gene Insertion

In recent years researchers have developed sophisticated techniques that enable them to produce **recombinant DNA,** or DNA spliced together from two separate organisms. Consequently, it is sometimes possible to insert a single gene from one animal (the donor) into the cells of the embryo of another animal (the recipient). Then, after the embryo develops into an adult, the recipient's behavior can be observed.

Scientists using this technique have investigated the role of genes associated with biological rhythms in fruit flies. Fortunately for the researchers, one strain of flies exhibits a 24-hour rhythm of activity, whereas a closely related strain is arrhythmic, showing no consistent activity rhythm. The insertion of a gene known as the *per* gene from the rhythmic strain into arrhythmic individuals induces rhythmic behavior, indicating that the *per* gene is responsible for the rhythmic behavior under normal conditions (Jackson et al., 1986).

The gene insertion technique shows great promise as a research strategy, because it can identify precisely where a gene that affects behavior is normally located on a chromosome. Furthermore, this technique enables researchers to identify where in the body the gene products have an effect. For example, researchers have located many areas in the adult fruit fly's body that are influenced by the *per* gene (Liu et al., 1988). Thus, it may be concluded that there are several biological "clock" sites in the fruit fly. (Biological clock mechanisms will be discussed in more detail in Chapter 18.)

DNA Fingerprinting

Sophisticated molecular techniques have now been developed that allow researchers to analyze the DNA of individuals on the basis of blood or tissue samples. Essentially, DNA molecules are labeled radioactively and separated from one another by molecular weight and electric charge. Photographs are then made of the fragments. The photographs produce a record comparable to those of fingerprints. As in the case of human fingerprints, each individual animal's DNA "fingerprint" is unique. Consequently, it is possible to identify the tissue or blood as belonging to a particular individual with an extremely high degree of certainty.

By the use of DNA fingerprinting it is also possible to evaluate the degree of relationship between two animals. For example, DNA fingerprinting identifies paternity with great accuracy, an identification that is difficult to make by means of other techniques. Scientists have learned through DNA identification of the paternity of birds in monogamous species that there is much more extrapair copulation than was previously expected (Burke et al., 1989). As we shall see when we examine postcopulatory competition in Chapter 10, this finding of relatively large amounts of extrapair copulation is significant; it suggests that there have been strong evolutionary pressures promoting sperm competition within the female's reproductive tract.

Karyotyping

Karyotyping is a method of identifying the pattern of the chromosomes in an individual of any species of animal. Typically, karyotypes are prepared from white blood cells. Karyotypes from two species of animals can then be compared and fairly accurate assumptions made about how closely the two species are related. Karyotypes also allow scientists to make fairly good estimates of how many years the two species have been separate.

As we shall see in several later chapters, information from karyotypes helps researchers trace the evolutionary history of animals, especially humans and other primates. Karotypes of primates reveal that our closest living relatives are chimpanzees and that the common ancestor of humans and chimpanzees lived approximately 6 million years ago.

TABLE 2.6 ◆ Research Techniques

Technique	Definition	Information Provided
Crossbreeding	Representatives of different populations or subspecies are interbred.	Relative contribution of genetic factors can be pinpointed.
Selective breeding	Individuals either high or low on a trait are bred.	Relative contributions of genetic factors can be determined.
Gene insertion	Recombinant DNA is produced.	Location of a gene on a chromosome can be identified.
DNA fingerprinting	DNA is analyzed.	Degree of relatedness between two conspecifics can be established.
Karyotyping	An individual's pattern of chromosomes is identified.	Degree of relatedness between two heterospecifics and the evolutionary relationship between species can be established.

◆ HUMAN EVOLUTION

Many of the principles of behavioral genetics apply to humans as well as to nonhuman animals. We will begin by looking at certain myths that have fostered misconceptions about the role of genes in human behavior. Then we will consider some research on the interaction of genes and the environment in human behavior.

MYTHS RELATED TO GENETIC FACTORS IN HUMAN BEHAVIOR

A relatively old myth is that human behavior is entirely the result of experience and is therefore extremely malleable. The leading proponent of this philosphy was the Englishman John Locke, who in 1690 compared the human mind to a blank slate on which experience writes. Locke's philosophy was especially popular with political philosophers in America, because it was consistent with democratic ideals; it influenced the formation of the Declaration of Independence and the Constitution.

Despite the positive influence of Locke's philosophy, the blank slate analogy is faulty: There is strong evidence that human behavior, like that of nonhuman animals, is the result of an interaction between genetic potential and environmental factors—including experience.

Another myth, somewhat related to the first, is that nonhuman animals are driven solely by genetic programming, whereas humans are shaped by experience. As we shall see in the next several chapters, experience plays a large role in the development of many nonhuman animal behaviors.

A third myth is that developmental processes are influenced by genetic factors prior to birth and that it is only after birth that environmental factors have their effect. As we have seen, however, the embryonic development of the mammalian brain is influenced by environmental factors. Furthermore, there is research evidence that even human mothers' speech patterns can affect prenatal development (Busnel et al., 1992).

Still another myth is quite common today, despite increasing publicity concerning genetic research (see Begley, 1996). This myth is that some human behaviors are genetically determined while others develop under the sole influence of environmental factors. In fact, *all* behavior is the result of interaction between genes and environmental factors. It is true that some behaviors reflect more variability as the result of experience than others. This does not mean, however, that genes have no effect on those behaviors. Nor does it mean that we can assign percentages to environmental and genetic influences.

TWIN STUDIES

Three of the general methods used for researching genetic factors in nonhuman animals—crossbreeding, selective breeding, and gene insertion—are obviously unethical for the study of humans. However, research with identical twins can provide insight into genetic factors in human behavior.

Because identical, or monozygotic, twins develop from the same fertilized egg, they have identical genes. Simply looking at the similarities between identical twins presents a biased picture of the role of genes, however, because at least some of the similarities between the individuals may be due to their having been raised in a similar environment.

To partially control for this bias, we can compare the degree of similarity of traits in identical twins with the similarities found in same-sex fraternal, or dizygotic, twins—twins that develop from separate eggs and are no more alike genetically than nontwin siblings. The degree of similarity between identical twins is often expressed in terms of **concordance rate,** an objective measure of similarity. For example, a concordance rate of .60 means that if one twin smokes, the probability that his or her twin sibling smokes is .60. Presumably, fraternal twins also share a similar environment, so higher concordance rates for certain traits in identical twins than in fraternal twins implicate genetic factors in the development of these traits.

Twin studies have been especially important in debunking the myth that some human traits develop entirely as the result of environmental factors. For example, it was long assumed that smoking and drinking patterns were completely determined by a person's environment and experiences. However, concordance rates for smoking are much higher for identical twins than for fraternal twins. The differences between these concordance rates occur for both the initiation of smoking and the persistence of smoking (Heath & Martin, 1993). Similarly, concordance rates for alcoholism are significantly higher for identical twins than for fraternal twins (Kendler et al., 1992).

Nonetheless, since concordance rates are always less than 1.00, there are still a large number of cases in which one identical twin smokes or becomes alcoholic while the other does not. These observations suggest that environmental factors are also important in the development of substance abuse (see Prescott et al., 1994).

A comparison of identical twins and fraternal twins raised in intact families is not completely free of bias; identical twins are more alike physically than fraternal twins and, consequently, may be treated more similarly by other people. However, it is possible in some cases to evaluate similarities in twins raised apart from each other. In these cases, it is less likely that similarities in the environment could account for similarities in behavior.

Thomas Bouchard and his associates (1990) conducted an extensive study of several pairs of twins separated from each other before the age of five. On several behavioral and personality measures, the concordance rates of identical twins were significantly higher than those of fraternal twins. In fact, the concordance rates of identical twins reared apart were even higher than those of fraternal twins reared together.

Unfortunately, these types of studies are not free from bias either. Separated identical twins shared a prenatal environment and, for some period of time, a postnatal environment (see Wahlsten & Gottlieb, in press). In conclusion, twin studies give a general indication of the interaction between genetic and environmental factors. However, it is impossible to establish any precise quantitative measure of the relative contributions of environmental and genetic influences.

GENES, ENVIRONMENT, AND EVOLUTION

Michael Rutter (1997) emphasizes the complexity of interactions between genes and the environment in the development of human behavior. For example, research by Rutter and his colleagues has demonstrated that genetic factors can influence the development of antisocial behavior by influencing personality development, a person's physical appearance, and/or the way in which a person processes information. In other words, genes may influence antisocial behavior in many different ways rather than simply having a direct influence on a person's tendency to commit a crime.

Furthermore, genes can indirectly influence the environment to which a person is exposed. For instance, a person may react differently to others if they have one type of genetically influenced personality trait than if they have a very different type. Finally, the interaction between genetic and environmental influences may change as a person ages (see Azar, 1997).

David Buss (1991) has considered the interaction between genes and environment in the development of human personality from an evolutionary perspective. Humans, like other animals, live in environments that vary a great deal. These environments differ from one another not only in terms of physical characteristics but in social milieus as well. For example, the trait of extroversion may have greater fitness benefits in some types of milieus than in others. Therefore, there has been a natural selection for a certain amount of variability among individuals in regard to extroversion, rather than simply a tendency for one optimum level of this trait. An interaction between environment and genes influences the development of extroversion, enabling the trait to develop great variability, even among individuals in the same family.

But why, from an evolutionary perspective, does a personality trait such as extroversion show relatively little variability throughout a person's lifetime? As we have all observed, outgoing children tend to develop into outgoing adults. Such consistency in salient personality traits may contribute to our ability to interact consistently with other people. If individuals were extremely extroverted at one point in their lives and introverted at another, interpersonal communication would be very difficult.

◆ CHANGING PERSPECTIVES

PAST	PRESENT	FUTURE
Nonhuman animal behavior is mechanistic or instinctive; human behavior is rational and based on experience (seventeenth century).	*All* behavior development is epigenetic; i.e., involves interaction between genetic factors and environmental influences (including the role of experience mediated via neurological changes).	How do genetic and environmental influences interact? What are the relative influences of genetic and environmental factors for various behaviors?

SUMMARY

Genes are basic to all life processes, functioning as part of a code or blueprint. The genes (consisting of DNA) transfer information to RNA, which directs the synthesis of proteins. Proteins, in turn, influence behavior by functioning as building blocks for the nervous and sensory systems. Proteins also act as neurotransmitters, hormones, and pheromones.

Sexual reproduction results in greater genetic variability in the offspring than is seen in asexual reproduction. The variability associated with sexual processes is related to the mixing of genetic material that takes place during meiosis. Although males and females make equal genetic contributions to the offspring, females often invest more energy in gamete production than males.

An updated version of evolutionary theory suggests that evolution is facilitated by mutations, genetic drift, and gene flow. Higher mutation rates, smaller populations, and greater numbers of new alleles introduced into the gene pool all tend to speed the rate of evolution.

Some traits are dominant and recessive in relation to each other. Because recessive traits cannot be successfully eliminated from the gene pool by natural selection, many of these traits are deleterious and lead to problems such as inbreeding depression. At the other extreme, too much outbreeding can also produce negative effects. Polygeny (several genes influencing a single trait) and pleiotropy (a single gene affecting several traits) are the general rule, especially in multicellular animals.

Epigenesis, which is the general rule for all development, involves complex interactions between genes and the environment (both internal and external). Experience is coded as part of the internal environment, so experiential factors also affect development. Some previously unexpected examples of epigenesis are illustrated in the development of the brain and the development of gender differences.

Scientists may investigate the relationship between genes and behavior by crossbreeding closely related strains of animals, by selectively breeding animals over several generations, and by inserting genes from one animal into another. DNA fingerprinting allows researchers to compare the degree of relationship between individual animals and to identify paternity. Karyotyping enables researchers to identify the closeness of the relationship between individuals of different species and to speculate on the evolutionary history of a species.

There are several myths regarding the role of genes in human behavior. Research findings, especially the results of twin studies, have debunked these myths and shed light on the complex interactions between genes and environment in the development of human behavior.

KEY TERMS

alleles, p. 32
binary fission, p. 30
concordance rate, p. 45
defeminization, p. 40
diploid, p. 31
DNA, p. 26
dominance, p. 34
epigenesis, p. 36
gametes, p. 30
gene flow, p. 32
gene pool, p. 32
genes, p. 26
genetic drift, p. 32

genotype, p. 34
haplodiploidy, p. 31
haploid, p. 31
heterozygous, p. 34
homozygous, p. 34
hormones, p. 28
inbreeding depression, p. 34
masculinization, p. 39
meiosis, p. 30
mitosis, p. 29
mutations, p. 32
neurotransmitters, p. 28
optimal outbreeders, p. 35

CHAPTER 3

THE DEVELOPMENT OF BEHAVIOR

- ◆ *Why do birds sing?*
- ◆ *How do birdsongs develop?*
- ◆ *Do different populations of birds have distinct dialects?*

*I*n the previous chapter we considered some aspects of development related to neural processes and gender development. In this chapter we will continue our discussion of development, this time focusing on the early development of representative behavior patterns. We will begin with a discussion of developmental homeostasis, a concept basic to all structural and behavioral development. Then we will look at behavioral development in three classes of vertebrates—amphibians, birds, and mammals. Finally, we will look at human development in relation to some nonhuman counterparts.

3

DEVELOPMENTAL HOMEOSTASIS

Chapter 2 explained that the epigenetic development of the nervous system results in a certain amount of flexibility, allowing the nervous system to make adjustments in structures to compensate for various types of traumas. However, there is also a strong degree of similarity in the structure and behavior of animals. For example, the brains of two normal individual animals in the same species are remarkably similar. Similarly, anyone who has watched two kittens batting at a piece of dangling string cannot help but notice the similarity of their play pattern. Much of this similarity results from **developmental homeostasis**—the tendency for organisms to buffer themselves against adapting to extreme conditions that may occur. Developmental homeostasis protects animals from developing extreme behavior patterns that would be likely to prove nonadapative.

The flexibility resulting from epigenetic development allows animals to adapt to changes in the environment. If development were rigidly programmed by genes, environmental changes such as shifts in the strategies of predators would leave prey animals unable to adjust and extremely vulnerable. Developmental homeostasis, on the other hand, promotes more or less consistent development under normal conditions. The resulting homogeneity is beneficial not only because animals are buffered against extreme adaptations, but because individuals of the same species tend to respond consistently to one another. For example, imagine how chaotic it would be if each duckling responded differently to calls from the mother!

As we shall see in this and the following two chapters, there are many different types of developmental paths. Such diversity enables some types of behavior patterns to show relatively great flexibility, while other patterns become quite inflexible. In essence, natural selection has shaped the types of developmental paths in much the same way that the selection process has shaped the types of behavior an animal exhibits.

Although the amount of variation in behavior that animals develop is effectively limited under natural conditions, certain nonadaptive behaviors may develop under unnatural conditions, as in laboratories or zoos. Such abnormalities are rare or nonexistent in nature. The fact that animals sometimes act abnormally in zoos emphasizes the need to simulate as much as possible the natural habitats of captive animals. For example, polar bears in zoos often walk around in circles in a highly stereotypical pattern. When we consider that under normal circumstances polar bears walk hundreds of miles over ice fields, it is not surprising that these animals are severely stressed by confinement. One of the major contributions of animal behavior research is to identify which conditions are especially important and then to promote better design of zoos and other places where animals are restrained.

Unfortunately, some people tend to pass judgment on the behavior of animals and may even label an animal as "stupid" for failing to behave in an expected way in an artificial setting such as a zoo. Similarly, certain animals are portrayed as vicious or wanton killers because they show extreme aggression under unnatural conditions; white sharks artificially attracted to divers protected by cages represent a familiar example. But animals are necessarily adapted to respond appropriately in their natural surroundings. In nature, strategies that are unsuccessful are not passed on to offspring. We are certainly better able to appreciate and live in harmony with animals of other species if we can observe them in the wild or at least take into account the nature of their natural environment.

BEHAVIORAL DEVELOPMENT IN AMPHIBIANS

We will begin our consideration of the specifics of behavioral development by considering amphibians. Swimming is a behavior that is extremely important to the survival of larval amphibians, such as frog tadpoles; thus, it is not surprising that the development of swimming in amphibians is quite independent of experience. If experience were necessary, many tadpoles would become victims of predators before they had a chance to develop swimming ability.

Even the embryonic movements inside the freshly fertilized egg of a South African clawed frog are not necessary for normal swimming to develop. Lanny Haverkamp and Ronald Oppenheim (1986) immobilized a group of embryos with an injection of a drug that acted on the nervous system to suppress all embryonic movement. The tadpoles that developed from the movement-suppressed embryos swam as well as a control group of tadpoles that had developed normally.

Nonetheless, it would be an oversimplification to assume that all amphibian behavior develops independent of early experience. In fact, research by Pfennig and his associates (1993) suggests that experience can have some unexpected effects on amphibian behavioral development. Spadefoot toad tadpoles that eat a normal diet do not eat members of their own species. However, tadpoles experimentally fed a whole-animal diet (a diet of small whole animals) become cannibalistic, preying on conspecifics when they are encountered.

As I'll discuss further in Chapter 6, a disadvantage of cannibalism is that it reduces indirect fitness when relatives are killed and eaten. Interestingly, however, the tadpoles exhibit another adaptation that tends to reduce the chance that they will cannibalize relatives. Tadpoles fed an early whole-animal diet show a reduced tendency to swim in proximity to their relatives—a tendency common in normally fed tadpoles. Consequently, the cannibalistic tadpoles reduce the possibility of suffering indirect fitness losses associated with eating individuals that are relatives.

BEHAVIORAL DEVELOPMENT IN BIRDS

Generally speaking, the development of avian (bird) behavior is more open to modification as the result of experience than that of amphibian behavior. Several types of avian behaviors develop as the result of **imprinting**—the rapid development of a strong, stable preference for a particular type of stimulus present during a short, sensitive period of development.

At one time, the short period during which a bird was imprinted, or strongly influenced by experiential factors, was called the "critical period." However, "critical" implies a rigidity, and we now understand that the imprinting period is not as rigidly determined as we once believed. Therefore, many animal behaviorists now prefer to use the term *sensitive period.*

Imprinting differs from many types of development in response to experience in that imprinting occurs only during a specific, relatively short period of development. Furthermore, once imprinting occurs, the imprinted response is extremely resistant to alteration.

The Following Response in Precocial Birds

Classic research of the Nobel Prize–winning ethologist Konrad Lorenz (1935) graphically illustrated what has come to be known as **filial imprinting**—the development of a tendency for young birds such as ducks and geese to follow their mother. By rearing young ducks and geese by himself, Lorenz found that they quickly developed the tendency to follow him instead of other geese. He also found that

the birds' response was consistent and highly resistant to modification. Lorenz concluded that he had become the object of imprinting because he was the first moving object the young birds saw.

This type of imprinting occurs only in **precocial species**—species in which the young are well developed at hatching (Figure 3.1). Under natural conditions, filial imprinting enables the young to develop a tendency to follow their mother, who is almost always the only relevant stimulus present during this sensitive period. Consequently, the young stay near their mother and are protected and sheltered, particularly when there is a danger from predators. The tendency for the young to follow the mother also enables the mother to lead the young to water or food resources, or away from areas in which the risk of predation is high.

Laboratory Studies of Filial Imprinting

Controlled research indicates that the sensitive period for the development of filial imprinting is very short and occurs early in the bird's life. In mallard ducks, the most effective period for imprinting is 13 to 16 hours after hatching. Why is the sensitive period so early and so short?

A proximate explanation suggests that the reason is related to the interaction of two factors: the development of locomotion and the onset of a fear of novel objects. Support for this explanation comes from the finding that a bird fails to imprint if it is deprived of the experience of moving independently. When a bird is experimentally pulled in a cart—as opposed to actively following a model of the parent during the sensitive period—the bird fails

FIGURE 3.1 ◆ **One-day-old young of a precocial species (on the left).**
Compare to the *altricial* species' one-day-old nestling on the right; altricial birds
are relatively undeveloped at hatching.

to imprint. Then, at around 16 hours after hatching, a bird develops a fear of novel objects. A bird cannot imprint to feared objects, so there is little chance of a bird becoming inappropriately imprinted under natural conditions (Hess, 1973).

A physiological explanation consistent with this model is related to neural growth. That is, the sensitive period is marked by relatively great neural plasticity. This plasticity promotes the type of neural changes involved in imprinting. The termination of the period of plasticity heralds the end of the sensitive period (Immelmann, 1985).

Whatever the explanation, filial imprinting takes place at a most propitious time. The mother (the appropriate stimulus) is invariably present; and inappropriate moving objects such as other animals are not likely to be present—at least, not in any consistent way. When the sensitive period has passed and the young encounter many more types of stimuli, the young are inhibited from developing an attachment or tendency to imprint.

Researchers investigate filial imprinting in precocial birds through experiments with an apparatus similar to that shown in Figure 3.2. The young birds that serve as subjects are typically hatched in incubators to ensure that they have had no previous exposure to other birds, either visual or auditory. Researchers can then present various types of models to the young, naive birds and can also vary the speed of models' movement and the time of exposure. It is also possible to play recordings of sounds during the presentation of the models.

Results of studies of ducklings done with this type of apparatus indicate that several different types of stimuli will function as effective visual models for filial imprinting, including inanimate objects such as beach balls, as long as experimenters move the objects at a speed that roughly approximates the speed of a mother duck. Models that resemble the mother duck, however, evoke more immediate and consistent imprinting. In other words, the natural stimulus of the mother has a

FIGURE 3.2 ◆ **Apparatus used in the study of imprinting.** The speed of movement, size, and shape of the decoy may be varied, and recordings of rhythmic sounds may be played in the presence of the moving decoy.

greater likelihood of becoming the object of imprinting than other types of stimuli (Hess, 1973).

The Role of Auditory Cues

A mother duck normally vocalizes while she is leading her brood; it is not surprising, then, that in imprinting research rhythmic sounds experimentally presented with the model increase the strength of imprinting. The sounds of mallard calls are more effective in promoting imprinting in baby mallards than the rhythmic calls of other species such as wood ducks or domestic hens, even if the baby ducks are reared in incubators and have no experience with mallard calls (Gottlieb, 1965).

How do the ducklings develop a sensitivity to mallard calls if they never hear the calls of an adult? Experimental research suggests that ducklings become sensitive to the sound of their own calls and then identify mallard calls on the basis of this sensitivity. Thus, if mallard ducklings are reared in isolation and made mute just before they begin to vocalize within their eggs, they will show no preference for the mallard call. Apparently, the ducklings must have the experience of hearing their own voices before they can develop a tendency to show appropriate imprinting (Gottlieb, 1978).

In some cases, sound functions as the exclusive stimulus for imprinting. Wood ducklings become imprinted to the sound of the mother's voice while they are still embryos in the shells. Later, when the mother calls from outside the nest, which may be located several meters above the ground, the young ducklings leap down to join her on the ground (Gottlieb, 1971). The wood ducklings' correct identification of their own mother's call is very important to their survival, because the mother calls at a time when her ducklings are at the appropriate age for leaving the nest. A response to simply any wood duck's call could come at an inappropriate time, with disastrous consequences.

Another example of an auditory influence that occurs while bird embryos are still in the shell is seen in bobwhite quail of eastern and central North America. The embryos make clicking sounds inside their shells. These sounds stimulate an increased speed of development in the less advanced embryos in the clutch and slow down the development of the most advanced embryos. Such communication results in a **synchronization of hatching** (Vince, 1969). This synchronization is adaptive because the young will hatch about the same time and can be reared in a group within a relatively short period. Consequently, the mother's period of parental investment is limited and the young benefit from the protection of the group.

Sexual Imprinting

After Lorenz had induced his geese to follow him in his classic study of imprinting, he observed something even more surprising than filial imprinting. When the geese became sexually mature, they began to court and make sexual advances toward him. This phenomenon later became known as **sexual imprint-**ing: the development of a tendency to show sexual responses to a type of animal or object that is present during a sensitive period.

In the case of the geese that Lorenz studied, the sensitive period for the development of sexual imprinting was the same as that for filial imprinting. In most species of precocial birds, however, the sensitive period occurs later in development. As a result, subsequent studies of duck and chick imprinting early in development failed to identify sexual imprinting.

Sexual imprinting also occurs in a few species of birds other than ducks and geese. One study found that if male zebra finches are experimentally reared with a closely related species of Bengalese finch, the males show a preference for the Bengalese finch females. If no Bengalese finches are available, however, the zebra finches mate with females of their own species (Immelmann, 1972).

A later study with zebra finches helps to explain why the early sexual imprinting to Bengalese finches is not irreversible. There are actually two stages to the sexual imprinting process in zebra finches. The first stage, which occurs shortly after hatching, enables the zebra finches to develop a general social preference for a certain type of bird. A later stage, which begins with approaching sexual maturity, functions to consolidate the earlier preference. If the Bengalese finches to whom the hatchlings became socially imprinted are not available as the young zebra finches approach sexual maturity, the young birds can still imprint to zebra finches in the consolidation stage (Oetting et al., 1995).

Under specific laboratory conditions, male finches may become sexually imprinted to two different species; this phenomenon is known as **double imprinting.** For example, when young zebra finch males are exposed to adults of both zebra and Bengalese finches during the sensitive periods for sexual imprinting, the males vacillate between the two species in their preference (ten Cate, 1987).

The effects of sexual imprinting are greater for male zebra finches than for females. Thus, male zebra finches become imprinted to the color of their mother's bill and then, as adults, are most likely to choose partners with bills the same color as their mother's. In contrast, females do not show a consistent preference for bill color (Vos, 1995). As we shall see when we discuss attraction in Chapter 9, females generally take into account a greater variety of factors in choosing mates than do males.

The Development of Birdsong

The development of filial imprinting is basic to the survival of young precocial birds, such as geese and ducks, that spend considerable time on the ground. However, **altricial species** of birds, such as songbirds—that is, species whose young are relatively undeveloped at hatching—are incapable of locomotion, and their eyes are closed for some time after hatching. Consequently, filial imprinting cannot occur in altricial species of birds.

Also in contrast to ducks and geese, which vocalize in a fairly stereotypical manner and have limited communication functions, songbirds develop complex vocalizations that enable them to communicate in complex ways. Birdsong is related to mate attraction, territorial defense, synchronization of reproductive behavior between mates, and "tutoring" of the young (Albrecht & Oring, 1995).

In the fairy wren, both the male and the female sing to defend their territory (Cooney & Cockburn, 1995); in most species of songbirds, however, while both genders produce sounds, only the male makes the complex vocalizations classified as songs. Consequently, the majority of research has centered on the development of birdsong in males.

Despite the differences between precocial and altricial species, some of the same principles apply to both filial imprinting and the development of singing in songbirds. Specifically, both following responses and singing develop at an early, sensitive period of development, and both are resistant to alteration after they become established.

If birdsongs were completely dependent on species-specific genetic factors, the variability in song patterns and the birds' ability to convey recently acquired information would be limited. On the other hand, if song learning were not somewhat restricted by species-specific genetic factors, birds would be unable to differentiate their own songs from those of another species. Thus, it is not surprising that the development of birdsongs involves complex interactions among genetic and experiential factors.

Early Laboratory Studies of Birdsong Development

Classic experiments with chaffinches by W. H. Thorpe during the 1950s demonstrated the role of early auditory experience. Thorpe reared some birds in isolation from all visual and acoustic stimulation; he reared others in visual isolation but let them hear tapes of birdsongs.

The birds exposed to the tapes developed a **full song;** that is, the normal, complex song of the species. However, the birds reared in acoustic isolation developed only a **subsong**— a simple song that is the precursor of the full song in normally reared birds. Apparently the subsong develops relatively independent of auditory stimulation, but the full song depends on auditory input from a **tutor** or model (Thorpe, 1961).

Bias in Song Learning

Despite the importance of a tutor in birdsong development, white-crowned sparrows who are played recordings of the songs of other species will not develop an adult song. Furthermore, if the sparrows hear the songs of both their own and another species, they will develop their own species' song (Konishi, 1985; Marler, 1970). Birds seem to have a bias for learning their own song as opposed to those of other species. This bias functions to reduce the possibility of inappropriate song learning.

Laboratory studies indicate that in some cases young birds develop songs that represent elements of the songs of two or more tutors (ten Cate & Slater, 1991). Under natural conditions there may be more than one male in the immediate vicinity, so the young bird may integrate various aspects of each tutor's song. Consequently, a particular individual bird is able to develop complex songs that are unique to him in some respects.

The Thorpe chaffinch studies suggest that songbirds have an early sensitive period during which they must hear the species-specific song in order for the song to develop. For song sparrows and zebra finches, this sensitive period occurs during the first few weeks after fledging. At this time the young male is still in the breeding area, where he is most likely to

learn the song from his father (Böhner, 1990). The indigo bunting, however, learns at least part of the song in adulthood (Margoliash et al., 1991). The bunting's greater freedom from the rigidity imposed by a short sensitive period enables the adult birds to develop considerable variability and complexity in their songs. As Chapters 9 and 13 will make clear, song variability and complexity have considerable advantages for both mate attraction and territorial defense.

Among inbred canaries, there are two subspecies that sing somewhat different songs. Recent experiments indicate that each subspecies has a bias to learn the song of its own subspecies. However, hybrid offspring learn songs from both subspecies (Mundinger, 1995).

As we would predict on the basis of epigenetic rules, there is clearly an interaction between genetic and experiential factors in the development of birdsong. Nonetheless, there are significant differences among species in the nature of the interaction.

The Role of Practice

One of the most surprising findings of research on birdsong learning is that birds typically learn the nature of the song at one time and then practice producing the song several months later. At this later time, they apparently match their vocalizations to their memory of the tutor's song. Thus, if young birds are experimentally deafened at five months— well after their sensitive period for learning the song, but before they begin adult vocalizations—they fail to develop the adult song. However, if they are deafened after they have begun adult vocalizations, they sing normally (Konishi, 1965).

Although the effective stimulus for song learning is primarily auditory, some birds are strongly affected by the physical presence of a live tutor. For example, white-crowned sparrows will learn a song twice as fast from a live tutor as from a tape recording of the song (Petrinovich, 1990).

Young zebra finches are even more dependent on the presence of the tutor; if only a tape recording is presented, these birds do not learn the song at all. It is not clear exactly what role the live tutor plays, but at least part of the effectiveness of the live tutor is that he interacts behaviorally with the young bird (ten Cate, 1991). Since the father tends to interact more with his offspring than do other males, it is not surprising that the father is the most influential tutor (Mann & Slater, 1995).

Dialects

Some species of songbirds that have highly complex songs develop **dialects;** that is, songs that vary from one geographic region to another. For example, the songs of white-crowned sparrows differ in each of three California locations. These dialects occur because young birds learn their songs from adults in their area and then remain in that same area to breed.

Sensitivity to dialect is used by some birds in mate selection. For example, female zebra finches may learn the song of their father and then compare a suitor's song with that of their father. A female may then be able to avoid inbreeding by rejecting a male that sings a duplicate of her father's song (Nottebohm, 1991). It is also possible that females effect optimal outbreeding by not choosing a male whose song is too different from that of their father.

The process of dialect development results in genetic isolation and rapid evolutionary divergence and may result in the development of new species in a relatively short period of time (Gibbs et al., 1990). At any rate, the development of dialects represents one of the few examples of what might be called cultural evolution.

Although it has been generally believed that dialects develop entirely as the result of differential learning experiences, recent evidence suggests that genetic variation may also be involved (Nelson et al., 1995). This conclusion adds further support to the epigenetic approach to understanding development.

Species Differences

Although the general principles that I have just discussed apply to the learning of songs in most birds, there are specific adaptations for particular challenges that a species faces. For example, the bird's habitat—whether in a heavily forested area or in an open area—will influence some specific aspects of birdsong development, because the acoustic properties of the two habitats are different. For example, research involving the broadcast and reception of various frequencies of sounds indicate that medium-frequency sounds (between 1,500 and 2,500 Hz) travel most efficiently in forested areas. In contrast, high-frequency sounds travel with relatively great efficiency in grassland habitats. The songbirds in Panamanian forests are apparently sensitive to the effectiveness of medium-frequency sounds, because most of them sing within this range (Morton, 1977).

Another factor that is related to song learning is whether or not the bird is a nest parasite. (Nest parasites are birds hatched from eggs that their mothers have deposited in the nests of birds of other species.) If a nest parasite such as a cowbird learned its song from a tutor when it was young, it would learn an inappropriate song, because the birds in the nest vicinity during the cowbird's sensitive song-learning period are not cowbirds but the host species.

Nonetheless, the cowbird does exhibit a subtle type of learning that influences its song development—as illustrated by an experiment involving the rearing of male cowbirds in isolation from other males. Somewhat surprisingly, males reared in isolation (isolates) sing songs that are more attractive to cowbird females than do males reared under more normal conditions. Apparently the isolates do not learn to inhibit certain aspects of their songs—whereas normal cowbird males do inhibit themselves when they are in the presence of more dominant males, because the same song characteristics that attract females threaten cther males. Consequently, isolates attract females but also end up getting attacked by more dominant males, and many isolates are literally killed in reaction to their "boldness" (King & West, 1990).

Pecking

Songbirds do not need to develop songs rapidly, because the songs do not serve a function until adulthood. In contrast, precocial birds such as domestic fowl must be able to peck with accuracy soon after hatching, or they will die from starvation. Consequently, as in the case of tadpole swimming, there is a need for a rapid and reasonably accurate de-

velopment of the precocial chick's pecking response.

In the 1870s Charles Spalding, who was a tutor of the famous philosopher Bertrand Russell, conducted one of the first experiments in animal behavior and demonstrated that little or no practice is required for accurate pecking to develop. Spalding placed tiny hoods over the eyes of domestic chicks immediately after they hatched, even before their eyes had opened. Several hours later he removed the hoods and found that the chicks pecked with normal accuracy.

Later animal behaviorists observed that older chicks do peck with greater accuracy than young chicks. However, we can explain this observation without assuming that practice is important. Eckert Hess (1956) reared baby chicks with goggles that deflected their vision 7 degrees to the right. He then tested the chicks for several days to see if they would learn to adjust their aim, deflected by the goggles, and strike a seed with accuracy. The chicks did *not* adjust their aim, but the older chicks did show less variability in their pecking; apparently the maturation of the chicks' motor and perceptual systems resulted in increased pecking consistency. Nonetheless, Spalding's earlier conclusion that eye-to-beak coordination develops relatively independent of pecking practice after hatching was supported.

BEHAVIORAL DEVELOPMENT IN MAMMALS

The developmental principles of early sensitive periods and resistance to change apply to mammals as well as to amphibians and birds.

In mammals, however, the sensitive periods are generally longer, and there is more of a tendency for animals to change as the result of experience in adulthood. This is the case especially among primates; these differences between primates and other groups of animals arise at least partly from the relatively large degree of flexibility in primate behavior.

Socialization

The social interaction among social primates such as rhesus monkeys and chimpanzees is highly complex, as we shall see when we discuss cooperation in Chapter 12. Basic to this interaction is a sensitivity to cues emitted by other members of the social group. A classic series of experiments with rhesus monkeys performed by Harry Harlow and his associates in the 1950s through the 1970s identifies some of the developmental factors related to this sensitivity.

Monkeys Reared in Isolation

Individual rhesus monkeys reared in complete isolation from other animals, including humans, become so emotionally disturbed that they typically huddle in the corner of their cage or bite themselves at the approach of a stranger. The effects of the social isolation last indefinitely, even if the disturbed monkeys are exposed to contact with normal monkeys as adults. It seems that there is a need for social experience when the monkeys are at a young, critical age for normal social development—that is, when they are about three to nine months old. Without social experience during this time, the monkeys develop inappropriate

social behavior that is difficult or impossible to alter.

Social deprivation also affects monkeys' reproductive behaviors: Monkeys reared in isolation are unable to mate with one another as adults, even though they show some appropriate sexual responses such as erections and pelvic gyrations. Their lack of appropriate social behavior seems to make it impossible for them to court and engage in the kinds of social responses required for successful sexual interaction.

Because the disturbed monkeys are unable to mate with one another and even have problems mating with normal monkeys, it is difficult to study the parental responses of a female reared in isolation. However, it is possible to impregnate females artificially. Furthermore, a few extremely patient normally reared males have been able to impregnate certain females that have been reared in isolation. When these females give birth, they typically ignore the infant and, in some cases, even show abusive behavior. Normal parental behavior, like sexual behavior, seems to depend on social interaction that occurs long before the animals reach adulthood (Harlow & Zimmerman, 1958; Harlow, 1960).

Even when monkeys have normal interaction with their mothers, isolation from peers has disruptive effects. Peer-deprived monkeys show excessive fear and aggression when they interact with other monkeys as adults. However, if isolated monkeys are exposed to peers for only 15 minutes a day, the isolates are able to relate fairly normally as adults (Harlow & Harlow, 1962). It seems that normally occurring play and other types of social interaction among juveniles is crucial to the development of social behavior. Under extreme circumstances, even a small amount of interaction allows the social behavior to develop.

Later studies suggest that the original conclusion of social deprivation studies—that social damage in isolation-reared monkeys is always irreversible—does not hold true in all circumstances. If 6-month-old isolation-reared monkeys are placed with normally reared monkeys 3 months younger, the younger monkeys reduce the effects of the isolation. The age of these young "therapists" is a critical factor. Three-month-old monkeys are old enough to initiate social contact, but young enough so that they do not react to the isolates' initial rejection with aggression. After a few weeks, the isolate monkeys respond to the clinging of the young monkeys by clinging back and playing with them. As a result of this interaction, the isolates show an almost complete recovery within about 6 months (Suomi, 1973).

Monkeys Reared by Mother Surrogates

Perhaps Harlow's most famous isolation experiment involved rearing two groups of rhesus monkeys with mother surrogates in their cages. One type of surrogate was a wire cylinder; the other was a cloth-covered contraption of comparable size. These surrogates were designed in such a way that they could deliver milk to the baby monkeys. Although the wire surrogate provided reinforcement via the milk for one group, all of the babies preferred to spend their time in the vicinity of the cloth surrogate and clung to this soft object when they were frightened. Apparently warmth and softness is rewarding, independent of any association with food (Harlow & Zimmerman, 1958; Harlow & Harlow, 1962).

Both groups of monkeys that were reared on mother surrogates were socially disturbed as adults, especially those that were nourished by the wire mother surrogate. However, monkeys reared with dogs as mother surrogates exhibited close-to-normal social development (Mason, 1978). Even an animal of another species can apparently facilitate social development in these monkeys.

Play Behavior

Much of the interaction between baby monkeys and their mothers or peers involves **play,** which is defined as activity that imitates elements of goal-directed behavior but does not lead to an immediate goal. The Harlow research raised many questions and stimulated a large amount of subsequent research concerning play behavior, not only in primates but in other mammals as well.

Patterns of play in juveniles are related to the lifestyles of the adults of the species. For example, young predators exhibit play behaviors related to killing, while young ungulates (hoofed animals) such as horses engage in running behavior similar to that used in escape, and young social mammals play at the establishment of dominance and social communication. One reason that play is so common in mammals—as opposed to other groups of animals—is that in mammals there is a large difference between the behavior of juveniles and that of adults.

Although it is sometimes difficult to differentiate play from other activities, play seems to have several distinctive characteristics. First, play combines different functional activities over a short period of time. For example, a juvenile mongoose may exhibit elements of prey catching and sexual behavior in rapid succession. Second, sequences within a behavior pattern may be quickly abandoned. A kitten will leap on another kitten as if in concerted attack and then immediately walk away as if nothing had happened. Third, play behavior will develop suddenly in the absence of any apparent provocation. It is not unusual to see a kitten suddenly attack an inanimate object or roll over on its back and make biting movements as if an object or animal of some kind was present. Finally, play behaviors usually develop in juveniles but tend to diminish as animals become older and reach adulthood. The greater incidence of play in juveniles, of course, is related to the role of play in development.

Gender Differences

A mother mammal may play with her young, especially if she has a single offspring; usually, however, play takes place between siblings or individuals of the same age. In rhesus monkeys, play groups are typically made up of individuals of the same sex. Male juveniles spend more time in play–fighting and fight more vigorously than female juveniles. In contrast, female juveniles spend much more time in play–mothering than male juveniles. The quality of juvenile–infant interactions also differ. While females exhibit caregiving behavior, males often play aggressively with the infants.

Recent research indicates that there are also gender differences in types of play in mice. If most or all of the mouse siblings are female, play is more social than if siblings are mostly or all male (Laviola & Alleva, 1995).

The Functions of Play

Play seems to serve a variety of purposes, but these functions of play are difficult to demonstrate experimentally (see Baldwin, 1986). One of the reasons that many studies have failed to confirm the dependence of adult behavior patterns on juvenile play is that it sometimes takes only a minimal amount of activity to produce a developmental effect. As we saw earlier, only 15 minutes a day of interaction with peers was enough to mitigate the effects of social deprivation in monkeys. Another reason is that studies have not always been sensitive to relatively small benefits of play activities; but, even small benefits can have a significant effect over an animal's life span (Caro et al., 1989).

One of the major functions of play is related to physical training. For example, the high-speed turns of juvenile horses seem to facilitate locomotory flexibility in adult horses (Fagen & George, 1977). Similarly, the play of juveniles in several different species of arboreal (tree-dwelling) monkeys has been found to increase dynamic and static flexibility in the adult monkeys (Fontaine, 1994).

In wolves, playfulness is related to the development of a highly developed social organization. Wolf pups exhibit a great deal of play solicitation, which seems to be the precursor of the complex cooperative behavior seen in an adult wolf hunt (Caro et al., 1989).

A more subtle function of play is to enhance cognitive abilities. For example, playing with a novel object may increase an animal's chances of finding a productive use for the object. The role of early experience in the use of novel objects is illustrated by a classic study with chimpanzees. Chimpanzees reared under conditions where they do not have exposure to sticks are unable to learn to use sticklike tools as adults (Birch, 1945). In contrast, chimpanzees reared under natural conditions or in laboratory conditions where sticks are available develop an ability to use sticks as tools in a variety of ways.

Chimpanzees sometimes engage in play that is both elaborate and inventive. They may initiate social play with one of two particular signals: the "play walk" and the "play face" (see Figure 3.3). Their play activities consist of chasing, mounting, and rough-and-tumble play as well as various games involving tickling and sparring with soft punches and kicks.

Cognitive components of play are particularly noticeable in bonobo chimpanzees. For example, juvenile bonobos in the San Diego Zoo have been observed playing what looks like "blindman's buff"; they cover their eyes with a banana leaf or with their arms and stumble around until they almost lose their balance. These chimpanzees also make unusual facial expressions that do not seem to be directed at anyone in particular. For example, they may poke a finger in their cheek or push out their lower jaws (DeWaal, 1989). This type of play behavior may be related to the control of facial expression that is important in the social communication of apes.

The Costs of Play

Although play has several important benefits, it also has costs. For example, the play of domestic kittens takes up about 9 percent of their waking time and energy (Martin, 1984).

FIGURE 3.3 ◆ The play face of a young chimpanzee.

Moreover, play may interfere with some aspects of the mother's life. The play of cheetah cubs sometimes blocks the mother's hunting success (Caro, 1987).

Play may also reduce the vigilance of young and make them vulnerable to predation. At one extreme, an observational study of fur seal pups indicates that of pups killed by predators, 85 percent were caught while playing, even though play took up only 6 percent of the animals' time (Harcourt, 1991). At the other extreme, various cheetah cubs were observed for 2,600 hours and were never preyed upon or injured during play (Caro, 1995). Clearly, the risks of predation and injury differ greatly from one species to another; and in the long run these risks, balanced against potential benefits, have undoubtedly influenced the evolution of play behavior.

Reproductive Behavior

Imprinting or mechanisms very similar to imprinting take place in certain mammals with regard to reproductive behaviors. Sheep mothers, whose lambs are able to walk shortly after birth, develop a remarkable ability to recognize their lambs. A mother ewe licks her lamb as it emerges from the birth canal. She apparently imprints to the odor and taste of her lamb during and shortly after the birth process. This learning ability enables the mother lamb to discriminate her own lamb from other lambs and to allow only her own to nurse.

Experimental research indicates that if a newborn lamb is experimentally taken away from its mother at birth before she has had a chance to lick it, the ewe will reject the lamb when it is presented to her several hours later (Poindron & LeNeidre, 1980). Apparently there is a short critical period during which the mother ewe must learn the chemical cues associated with her offspring.

Recognition of the ewe by the lamb also develops very quickly. The lamb is able to identify its mother at close range within the first day, and from a distance of several yards by the third day. Experimental tests indicate that the lamb uses a combination of acoustic and visual cues—but not olfactory (smell) cues—in discriminating between its own mother and other ewes (Nowak, 1991). Thus, it seems that the bond that forms between the mother and the lamb involves recognition by both mother and young, though mother and young utilize different cues. This mutual recognition—and the ability of the young to recognize the mother from a distance—seems to be the rule in ungulates (Nowak et al., 1989).

◆ HUMAN EVOLUTION

Some human behavior patterns develop according to the same principles as those observed in nonhuman animals, while other human patterns develop quite differently than anything seen in nonhumans. Let's look at language and social development in humans and compare the developmental patterns with some nonhuman counterparts. Then we will look at the development of two human systems that do not have clear counterparts in nonhuman animals—reading and complex mathematical ability.

THE DEVELOPMENT OF LANGUAGE

Although songbirds and humans are not closely related, several of the basic principles associated with song learning in birds also apply to human language learning. First, as we have seen, there is a sensitive period during which songbirds must be exposed to appropriate songs: If a songbird is raised in auditory isolation during the early sensitive period, later exposure to the song fails to produce song learning. The sensitive period is longer for humans, but it still exists. If for some unfortunate reason children do not hear normal speech during their first 8 years of life, they have great difficulty learning a language (Elliot, 1981).

Second, the production of birdsong comes after the bird hears the song and develops a template of the song. Similarly, human infants show evidence of becoming sensitive to the relevant sounds of their native language long before they produce the specific language-related sounds. For example, 4.5-month-old infants turn their heads toward loudspeakers broadcasting their names more frequently than toward broadcasts of other names, even names that are similar to theirs. Apparently these infants have learned to recognize sound patterns frequently heard, although they will not produce language-related sounds for several more weeks (see Azar, 1996).

Third, songbirds are highly specialized for learning their species-specific songs during the sensitive period of development. They are not good at other types of auditory learning during this period. Human infants and children are also highly specialized for language learning during the sensitive period. Before the age of 7, children are inferior to adults in most types of learning but can learn a second language faster than adults (see Azar, 1996).

Although there are some variations in the expression of birdsong within a species, all individuals in a given species sing songs that have a similar basic structure. Similarly, human languages have variation in the sense that the languages sound quite different. However, all spoken languages have a comparable basic structure. For every language this structure includes an inventory of 30 to 40 basic sounds, or phonemes; a small number of types of words such as nouns, verbs, and adjectives; and a set of rules about word placement within sentences (see Basic Behavioral Science Task Force, 1996). Among both songbirds and humans, then, there is a definite preadaptation for developing vocal communication within a highly predictable framework.

It seems that at least some of the developmental foundations of human language evolved in birds long before humans evolved; birds communicate a great deal of information vocally. Clearly, human language is not as far removed from nonhuman communication systems as we once believed. In Chapter 5 we will see examples of how parrots can be trained to communicate high levels of information using human words, and we will discuss language training with apes.

THE DEVELOPMENT OF SOCIALITY

As in the case of rhesus monkeys, rare and tragic situations in which children are raised in social isolation produce severe abnormalities. The children not only fail to develop normal social responses but experience severe cognitive deficits. With social development as with language development, humans seem to have an early sensitive period for normal development. Severely deprived individuals are relatively unresponsive to attempts at therapy after age 10. However, in some cases a limited recovery occurs (Clarke & Clarke, 1976).

It seems that social mammals in general depend on early social experiences for the development of normal behavior patterns. Mammals such as cats, which are less social than dogs and rhesus monkeys, suffer less severe deficits. In general, the greater the sociality and the more complex the brain, the more important early experience becomes. Thus, it is not surprising that a dearth of social experience—or inappropriate social experiences—can have profoundly negative affects on human development.

THE DEVELOPMENT OF READING AND COMPLEX MATHEMATICAL ABILITY

Human language and sociality have clear counterparts in other animals. However, there is nothing analogous to reading or complex mathematical ability in nonhuman animals. Is it possible to relate human evolution to the development of these two uniquely human abilities?

Recently David Geary (1995) proposed an evolutionary model of development that attempts to account for reading and complex mathematical ability. Geary suggests that there are two classes of cognitive ability: primary and secondary. Biologically primary cognitive abilities include language and a primitive estimate of numerosity—an ability to determine that one array of items includes more individual items than another array. These primary abilities clearly evolved according to the principles of natural selection. The roots of these abilities are found in nonhuman animals; and these abilities perform important fitness functions in our closest primate relatives, and presumably performed comparable functions for our hominid ancestors. These abilities are also deeply rooted and appear in all human cultures.

In contrast, the secondary cognitive abilities, such as reading and the ability to do algebra, develop in specific cultural contexts. These abilities are not found in all human cultures and consequently cannot be considered to serve a general human fitness function.

In keeping with the idea that primary cognitive abilities evolved according to natural selection, acquisition of these abilities is understandably enjoyable for children, as is the aquisition of an ability to fish or hunt. In the absense of a natural selection for an ability to read or learn algebra, however, the effective learning of these abilities generally depends on the ability of teachers and school systems to motivate the students.

Because intelligence tests measure secondary cognitive abilities, Geary (1995) concludes that these tests are sensitive to cultural attitudes about academic achievement and to the effectiveness of schools rather than to some basic attribute of intelligence. Carrying the argument further, it seems unlikely that intelligence tests measure abilities that have been strongly affected by natural selection. Racial differences in intelligence quotient, or IQ, are basically reflections of cultural and educational factors.

The conclusion that racial differences in IQ reflect cultural and educational factors is encouraging, because it suggests that societies can successfully address people's problems in reading and mathematics by changing environmental conditions. In fact, even a very minor change in the environment, such as the addition of a dietary supplement, can make a major improvement in secondary cognitive skills (see Wahlsten, 1995).

TABLE 3.1 ◆ Primary and Secondary Cognitive Abilities

Type of Ability	Examples	Etiology	Consequences
Primary	Spoken language Estimate of numerosity	Strong natural selection	Universal Enjoyable
Secondary	Reading Algebra	Not naturally selected	Not universal Difficult to learn

◆ CHANGING PERSPECTIVES

PAST	PRESENT	FUTURE
Development is rigidly programmed by genetic factors and/or early experience (early part of the twentieth century).	Many early developing behavior patterns can be modified by later experience.	What are the physiological correlates of the early development of behavior? Research on this question will most likely continue. Practical questions related to the facilitation of early development will probably be at the forefront.

SUMMARY

A certain amount of flexibility in behavioral development enables species to adjust to changing conditions. However, there is also a remarkable degree of consistency related to developmental homeostasis. This consistency enables animals of the same species to respond somewhat predictably to one another.

In amphibians the development of behavior occurs relatively independent of experience. In birds and mammals, however, behavioral development is often dependent on specific types of experiences that occur during a short, sensitive period early in development.

The preference for a particular type of stimulus—filial imprinting—results in the tendency of young precocial birds to follow the first moving object to which they are exposed. A similar imprinting response, known as sexual imprinting, influences birds' later choice of a sex partner.

Like imprinting, song learning in birds is constrained by sensitive periods of development. In an early period, the young bird must hear the species-specific song. During a later sensitive period, the bird must practice producing the song.

In a social primate such as the rhesus monkey, socialization is highly dependent on early experience. Experimental studies of social deprivation in monkeys indicate that these animals need a certain amount of social interaction—particularly with peers—for normal development. Studies of monkeys reared by artificial surrogates indicate that physical contact associated with warmth and softness are also basic to normal socialization.

Play behavior in mammals facilitates social behavior and enhances certain sensorimotor and cognitive functions. However, play also has costs, including exposing the young to predation. The most complex play occurs in the social primates, particularly chimpanzees.

Certain aspects of mammalian reproductive behavior are also influenced by experience during a sensitive period of development. For example, an imprintinglike phenomenon occurs between mother sheep and their lambs.

Human language and social development follow developmental principles similar to those seen in certain nonhuman animals. Reading and complex mathematical ability are secondary cognitive abilities, however, and there is no clear analogy to their development in nonhuman animals.

KEY TERMS

altricial species, p. 71
developmental homeostasis, p. 52
dialects, p. 60
double imprinting, p. 58
filial imprinting, p. 54
full song, p. 58
imprinting, p. 54

play, p. 63
precocial species, p. 54
sexual imprinting, p. 57
subsong, p. 59
synchronization of hatching, p. 57
tutor, p. 59

CHAPTER 4

LEARNING

- ◆ *What can animals learn from observing other animals?*

- ◆ *Why does the mother chimpanzee exert more influence on her baby than other chimpanzees do?*

Chapter 3 examined how experiential factors such as imprinting, song learning, and play influence the development of behavior. In this chapter we will look further at the role of experience in the development of behavior—that is, learning.

There have been numerous recent developments in the study of learning, many of which contradict older, well-established conceptions about how and why learning occurs. We will begin by discussing some of the older myths in light of modern theories of the evolution of learning. Then we will focus on several types of learning and the specific functions they serve, and we'll finish with a general examination of aspects of learning in humans.

4

THE EVOLUTION OF LEARNING

As we saw in the last chapter, imprinting and birdsong learning, which take place during sensitive periods of development, contribute to the development of behaviors related to survival and reproduction. The **learning** discussed in this chapter, defined as a relatively persistent change in behavior resulting from experience, also contributes to the development of critical behaviors. However, this type of learning may occur throughout the life span.

Because learning can be more beneficial in some cases than in others, different types of animals have evolved a sensitivity to certain stimuli and are more likely to learn some types of relationships than others. Such **domain-specific learning** is adapted to the learning of specific types of relationships (Buss, 1991). For example, monkeys are especially adapted for learning differences between monkey faces. In contrast, dogs have a highly developed ability to learn differences among the smells of other dogs. It is meaningless to say that monkeys are better or worse at learning than dogs; monkeys and dogs simply tend to learn the kinds of relationships that are important to their particular survival and reproduction needs.

In some cases a dependence on learning can be a disadvantage. For example, if an animal must learn to avoid predators, it may be eaten before it has a chance to learn to make an adaptive response. Similarly, if newly hatched chicks had to learn how to peck, they might starve before the necessary learning could take place (Johnston, 1981).

Learning may also involve physiological costs. Because brain cells involved in some types of learning require a relatively large amount of energy for growth and maintenance (brain cells require more energy than do cells in the rest of the body), an animal pays a certain price for learning ability. This price is especially high for complex learning abilities, because these abilities involve a large number of cells in various parts of the brain (Nottebohm, 1987). The relatively high physiological cost of complex learning abilities may be one reason why complex learning abilities are more rare in the animal world than simple learning abilities. In essence, a cost–benefit ratio affects the evolution of learning ability in the same general way that it influences the evolution of other systems.

Myths

As I have suggested before, several myths have developed that tend to cloud our understanding of the functions and evolution of learning. For example, learning is often considered "advanced" and associated with "higher" or highly evolved animals. But some types of learning take place in ancestral animals such as the sea slug; and conversely, some highly evolved animals are resistant to learning certain types of relationships.

Another myth is that an inability to learn is the primitive condition and that evolution always moves in the direction of increasing learning ability. However, a resistance to learning sometimes evolves after an animal has learned a response. In other words, learning ability may evolve in either direction—toward greater sensitivity to particular stimuli, or toward less sensitivity.

Still another myth is that the evolution of learning follows a path leading to a more and more general learning ability. But in reality, virtually all types of learning tend to be domain specific. In some cases the specialization of a learning ability is extreme. A rat, for example, shows a remarkable ability to associate becoming ill with eating a novel type of food, even if it ate the food hours earlier. However, a rat shows no comparable learning ability for other delayed effects (Garcia & Koelling, 1967).

Ecological Factors

Factors in an animal's environment often have an impact on the evolution of learning. Animals that evolve in extremely stable environments benefit less from learning abilities than do animals that evolve in unstable environments. Consequently, marine animals generally exhibit less complex learning abilities than terrestrial animals. (Remember, whales, dolphins, and seals are mammals that evolved first on land, so they should not be considered typical marine animals.)

Food supply often fluctuates, especially for feeding generalists—that is, species that eat a wide variety of foods. For several reasons, generalists have evolved a greater tendency to learn in relation to feeding than specialists. In the first place, because generalists eat a large variety of food, they are more likely to sample poisonous plants or noxious prey than specialists. Second, because many food items included in the diet of generalists supply only part of their nutritional requirement, generalists must exhibit a certain amount of selectivity in their diet. Nutritional learning facilitates this selection process. Third, generalists tend to live in unstable habitats, so they must be prepared to adjust to frequent shifts in the availability of certain foods. In contrast, a specialist may eat the same kind of food in the same way for many generations and does not benefit very much from a well-developed learning ability.

Another food-related factor that influences the evolution of learning abilities is the mobility of the food that must be obtained. For example, weaver birds that eat insects learn some types of problems more efficiently than do closely related weaver birds that feed on seeds. Apparently the need to identify where and at what time insects are available drives the evolution of spatial and temporal learning to a greater extent than does the need to locate seeds—which tend to stay put.

Ecological factors related to reproduction may also influence the evolution of learning ability. For example, ground-nesting birds such as gulls face the possibility that their young will wander off. Quite understandably, these birds have evolved an ability to recognize their individual offspring—and to differentiate them from the offspring of other parents—within a few days after the young hatch. In contrast, tree-nesting birds, whose young do not wander off, do not benefit from an ability to distinguish their own from other

TABLE 4.1 ◆ Some Ecological Factors
Related to the Evolution of Learning

Condition	Result
Instability of the environment	Complex learning abilities
Mobility of food source	Spatial learning ability
Ground nesting (in birds)	Learning to discriminate offspring

birds' young. And indeed these birds fail to develop an ability to recognize their own young.

Prior Adaptations

Although a need for a particular learning mechanism is an important factor, need in itself does not guarantee that the mechanism will evolve. An animal must have a **prior adaptation** or preadaptation—a foundation upon which to build. In many cases this kind of prior adaptation has evolved in association with other functions and then served as a foundation for a new function.

Structural Preadaptations

The basic aspects of learning take place at the level of the synapse, so a nervous system is a necessary structural requisite for any type of learning. Consistent with this hypothesis, no learning ability has been demonstrated in one-celled organisms. Nonetheless, even animals with a primitive nervous system, such as the sea slug and the flatworm, are capable of simple learning.

Animals tend to become most effective at learning responses in conjunction with sensory systems that are highly developed. For example, rats, which have well-developed chemosensory systems but relatively poor visual systems, are able to learn to avoid food that later makes them sick on the basis of taste cues; but they are not able to learn a comparable avoidance on the basis of visual cues (Garcia & Koelling, 1966). In contrast, chickens, which have well-developed visual systems, are able to learn food avoidance on the basis of visual cues but not by using taste cues (Martin & Bellingham, 1979).

Another type of preadaptation is related to the tendency to associate certain types of sensory cues with particular types of learning. Although rats easily learn to associate a certain taste with nausea, they are unable to learn the association between a sound and the experience of nausea. On the other hand, rats easily learn shock avoidance in response to a sound cue but cannot learn to avoid shock after a taste cue (Garcia et al., 1974). Apparently the rat has a prior adaptation for learning associations between cues that are likely to be predictive of certain consequences; that is, a taste cue is more likely to be indicative of poisoning than a sound cue, and a sound is more likely to predict the approach of a predator than a taste cue.

Behavioral Preadaptations

Well-established behavioral patterns also predispose animals to learn certain types of responses to stimuli. Rats can easily learn to run from a shock, but cannot learn to avoid a shock by standing upright. Similarly, dolphins are unable to learn to press a paddle with a flipper; the flipper is intimately associated with locomotion. But dolphins can easily learn to manipulate a paddle with their snout.

On the other side of the coin, some types of behaviors associated with well-established feeding patterns may function as restraints on learning. At one time animal trainers attempted to teach pigs to pick up large wooden coins and then deposit them in a "piggy bank" as part of an advertising gimmick. The initial learning proceeded quickly and without much of a problem. After a few weeks, however, the pigs would consistently drop the coins, push them with their snouts, drop them again and root, or toss them into the air over and over again. Eventually, the pigs were delaying putting the coins in the bank for so long that they were not getting enough to eat during the training period. One explanation for this outcome is that the basically unlearned behavior of rooting food competed with the learned response, and over time there was a drift back to the more primitive, unlearned response (Breland & Breland, 1961).

The findings that animals are predisposed to learn certain types of relationships indicates that learning is more delicately affected by natural selection than we once believed. Natural selection has not only produced a learning mechanism; it has increased the probability that particular species of animals will learn the types of relationships that will facilitate their fitness, and has decreased the probability that species will learn nonadaptive relationships.

TYPES OF LEARNING

Although researchers agree that there are several types of learning, they are not in complete agreement as to exactly how many distinct types of learning there are—or even how these different types should be named. Rather than dwell on the questions of classification or naming, I will concentrate on the mechanisms and functions of representative types of learning.

Habituation

Habituation is defined as an animal's developing tendency to react *less* vigorously to a stimulus that has been consistently present but that has had little or no effect on the animal. Reacting less vigorously—and eventually failing to react at all—may result in a significant saving of time and energy. If it were not for this primitive type of learning, animals might continue to respond to events that were meaningless.

Habituation occurs in a great variety of animals, ranging from animals with very simple nervous systems to the large-brained primates. An example of habituation in a relatively simple animal is seen in the sea slug, genus *Aplysia*. If the slug is touched on its siphon, it withdraws its gill. But if the siphon is touched several times and no noxious stimulus appears, the gill reflex will cease to occur (Kandel, 1979).

The information processing that accompanies habituation in vertebrates may be quite complex. Some of these animals are able to take several variables into account before they inhibit a reaction (i.e., become habituated). For example, iguanas in a Costa Rican field station show less and less avoidance of humans (which sometimes prey on iguanas) and allow people to approach within a short distance before fleeing. When they do flee, however, they react not simply to the distance that separates them from the potential predator but to the human's direct approach. In addition, iguanas consider a person's line of vision, fleeing most rapidly when a person looks directly at them (Burger et al., 1992).

Many birds and mammals show an avoidance or fear reaction to strange or unfamiliar objects that is known as **neophobia.** The neophobia is functional in that it discourages animals from approaching objects that may prove to be harmful. However, this avoidance may have a disadvantage for feeding generalists, which may benefit from investigating and exploiting new food sources. Thus, it is not surprising that generalists habituate to novel objects more rapidly than specialists (Greenberg, 1990).

Once habituation to novel objects or unfamiliar areas takes place, animals often explore the object or area. The exploration may provide information about a potential food source and may also indicate an escape route in case danger threatens. Scientists have measured rats' tendency to explore in the laboratory by observing the number of times each animal pokes its head into a hole in the wall. Once a rat adjusts to the unfamiliar situation, it pokes its head into the wall frequently; but within a short period of time, it habituates and reduces the response tendency. The habituation takes place more rapidly in older rats than in 15-day-old rats, suggesting that young rats may need more time to process new types of information than do older rats (Spear & Rudy, 1991).

Pavlovian Conditioning

Pavlovian or **classical conditioning**—the passive development of a response to a previously neutral stimulus—is named after the Russian physiologist and Nobel Prize winner who first identified the phenomenon in his laboratory work with dogs (Pavlov, 1927). From a functional standpoint, Pavlovian conditioning results in the development of a sensitivity to a signal indicating that a biologically important event is about to occur. This signaling or warning effect is important because it allows the animal to prepare for various eventualities—and to avoid wasting time and energy preparing for events that are unlikely to occur.

In the simplest sense, Pavlovian conditioning involves the pairing of a neutral stimulus—called the **conditioned stimulus** or **CS**—with a stimulus that normally evokes a response, the **unconditioned stimulus** or **UCS.** After several pairings of the CS and the UCS, the CS alone evokes the response (Pavlov, 1927). To use the example from Pavlov's laboratory, when the sound of a bell (the CS) is consistently followed by the presentation of meat (the UCS), a dog salivates to the sound of the bell, even when meat is not presented (Figure 4.1).

For many years following Pavlov's work, theorists assumed that this type of conditioning was relatively unsophisticated; as suggested in the definition just given, animals seemed to become conditioned as the result of a simple association between stimuli. However, research since the 1970s suggests that, at least in some animals, Pavlovian conditioning results in the perception of relationships between events. This relationship learning enables animals to cognitively (mentally) represent their environment (Rescorla, 1988).

According to this viewpoint, not any stimulus will act as a CS. In order for a given stimulus to become effective as a CS, the animal must have developed the cognition that that stimulus has **predictive value:** that it consis-

FIGURE 4.1 ◆ **Pavlov's apparatus.** The meat functioned as the unconditioned stimulus, the bell as the conditioned stimulus. The amount of saliva (an objective measure of the dog's response) can be measured after each trial.

tently precedes the UCS (Rescorla & Wagner, 1972). The greater the correlation between the presentation of the CS and the UCS, the stronger the conditioned response. Taking predictive value into account functions to protect animals against becoming conditioned to inappropriate stimuli.

Another principle related to a more sophisticated function of Pavlovian conditioning is **blocking;** if a CS is presented in combination with a second stimulus, it is unlikely that an animal will learn to respond to the second stimulus presented alone (Kamin, 1968). For example, if a dog learns to salivate to a bell, and then both a bell and a whistle precede the arrival of meat, the dog will probably not salivate to the sound of a whistle alone. This blocking or overshadowing effect reduces the

probability that an animal will learn redundant information. If we assume that there is a certain cost to learning each piece of information, then protection against redundancy is adaptive.

Finally, conditioning is most likely to take place if the CS is discriminable and intense. Because discriminable and intense stimuli are more likely to be associated with significant events, the greater probability of developing a conditioned response to stimuli with these qualities is generally adaptive. This principle may also help to explain why bright coloration that serves as a warning to potential predators has evolved in certain prey animals; predators will learn faster to avoid animals with intense coloration than to avoid animals with less bright coloration.

Feeding

As you might expect, Pavlovian conditioning is related to feeding in several ways. For example, the conditioning typically decreases the time necessary to begin eating. If an animal salivates before the arrival of food, it has a head start on consuming the food—an advantage that is especially important when the animal is competing with conspecifics for food.

A second function of Pavlovian conditioning is to promote the development of an association between a feeding response and hunger reduction. Contrary to what one might assume, animals have to learn to associate catching and consuming food with satisfying hunger. For example, hungry kittens will often kill mice without feeding on them until they learn the association between the mouse (the CS) and the taste and ingestion of food. In some cases a mother cat will facilitate this learning by bringing back to her kittens rodents that she has captured and killed (Baerends-van Roon & Baerends, 1979).

Third, Pavlovian conditioning may facilitate feeding by stimulating animals to forage in an area that is likely to include food. This search is brought about by a phenomenon known as **sign tracking:** the development of a food-related response such as biting, clawing, or pecking at a CS even though this response does not bring about food reinforcement. For example, pigeons peck at a spot of light that, on previous trials, signaled the arrival of food (Brown & Jenkins, 1968).

For pigeons in a natural setting, a stimulus that precedes the arrival of food, such as the sound of movement in the underbrush, can be a reliable indication of the presence of food. Therefore, pecking in the area would increase the probability of finding food. For rats, however, a sound is not a reliable indicator of food, and, not too surprisingly, rats do not undergo sign tracking to localized sounds (Cleland & Davey, 1983).

Finally, Pavlovian conditioning is involved in **taste aversion learning**—the development of an avoidance of certain foods whose taste has become associated with illness. John Garcia and R. A. Koelling (1966) demonstrated the powerful effects of taste aversion learning in a classic laboratory experiment. The researchers gave rats water with a novel taste and then, 24 hours later, subjected the rats to illness-producing X rays. On subsequent tests the rats showed an aversion to the specific taste cues associated with the water. In a natural setting this learning ability enables the rats to identify and avoid foods whose consumption leads to illness—that is, to identify poisonous foods.

Incidentally, there is a practical use for taste aversion learning. In parts of the western United States, where coyotes sometimes prey on lambs, a carcass of a sheep laced with a poison may be left out in an area visited by coyotes. After a small bite, the coyotes tend to avoid lambs and concentrate on their natural prey (Gustavson et al., 1974).

Defense

Pavlovian conditioning is especially relevant to defense—against both predators and threatening conspecifics. By making autonomic (reflexive) responses that mobilize energy reserves in response to reliable cues signaling the presence of danger, an animal increases the likelihood of a successful defense. Generally, animals become conditioned to stimuli associated with negative effects faster than they become conditioned to stimuli with positive implications. At least part of the reason for this difference in speed of learning is related to what the animals have to lose if they make a mistake. If an animal is a slow learner in regard to predation or feeding in general, the cost may be a meal; but if it is a slow learner in regard to identifying poisons or escaping from predators, the cost is likely to be its life. Therefore, there is even more evolutionary pressure to develop speed and efficiency in learning to avoid a predator or poison than there is to learn to locate food.

Up to this point, we have considered only examples of adaptive learning. However, as I intimated earlier in the chapter, it is also possible for an animal to be taught inappropriate responses. In fact, laboratory experiments indicate that animals can develop a classically conditioned response of fear to a stimulus and that this fear can then interfere with adaptive responses. For example, cats that were punished by a blast of air while feeding—and presumably developed a fear response—developed neurotic-seeming symptoms: trembling, restlessness, and crouching that interrupted their daily living pattern (Masserman, 1943). There is also evidence that the effectiveness of the immune system may be compromised by classical conditioning. After repeated pairings of sweetened water with a drug that causes a lowering of immunity in rats, the sweetened water alone will eventually trigger immune suppression (Ader & Cohen, 1984). Under natural conditions, however, such inappropriate learning appears to be rare.

Reproduction

As in the case of defensive behavior, the reproductive success of animals may be facilitated by classical conditioning. For example, sexual arousal can be classically conditioned. In a laboratory setting, a group of male Japanese quail were presented with a red light just be-

fore the arrival of a female. After a few trials, the red-light males were able to begin copulating with newly arrived females sooner than a control group that had not been conditioned (Domjan & Burkhard, 1986). Since, under natural conditions, the males compete vigorously with each other—and the courtship with the females is very brief—the time advantage gained is significant.

In mammals, classical conditioning may be important in the nursing relationship. Stimulation of the new mother's nipples provided by the suckling of the newborn prompts the letting down of the milk to the area just behind the nipples. Once this milk let-down occurs—after a "latency" period of 2 to 3 minutes—the milk is available to the young. However, the latency of let-down is soon reduced by classical conditioning; the visual and auditory cues that precede nursing soon allow the female to deliver milk the moment the infant begins to suckle (Hollis, 1982).

Classical conditioning may also facilitate reproduction indirectly by increasing the probability that a male animal will win a territorial battle and, consequently, be able to mate. In a laboratory study, blue gourami fish classically conditioned to a light that signaled the arrival of a competitor almost always won the encounter with the competitor. The conditioning apparently helped the males because these fish secrete testosterone in response to an anticipated encounter, which increases their aggressiveness (Hollis, 1990). And the advantage obtained through the conditioning and the winning of the encounter lasted beyond the original encounter. The winning fish almost always won an encounter up to 3 days later. Apparently the experience of winning has a durable effect, and thus there is a strong natural selection for this type of learning (Hollis et al., 1995).

Operant Conditioning

In contrast to classical conditioning, **operant conditioning** is a more active type of learning; the animal actively operates on its environment to produce favorable consequences. Central to operant conditioning is the concept of **reinforcement**—the presentation or removal of a stimulus that functions to increase the probability of a behavior.

Reinforcers have a critical function, encouraging the expression of behaviors at times that are generally adaptive. Scientists investigate the role of reinforcement in the laboratory by operantly conditioning rats and other animals in an apparatus known as a Skinner box, providing food as reinforcement (Figure 4.2).

In addition to seeking reinforcement that meets biological needs, such as food or water, many animals will work for rewards that are unrelated to biological needs. For example, baby monkeys make extreme attempts to obtain contact with a soft, warm object, even if the object has never been associated with feeding or any other biological need reduction (Harlow & Zimmerman, 1958). Similarly, adult monkeys will learn to perform a task when the only reinforcement is an opportunity to visually explore stimuli (Butler, 1954).

According to **Premack's principle,** any activity may be reinforced by a preferred activity (Premack, 1965). Consequently, if an animal engages in a large number of activities that are innately satisfying, many of these activities may be reinforcing. Also, different animals have different innate preferences, so there are large species differences in the types of activities that are reinforcing. For example, birds and mammals are strongly reinforced by food. In contrast, snakes—which often go for long periods without food—are more strongly

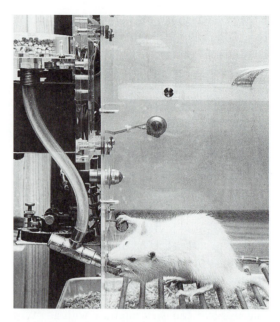

FIGURE 4.2 ◆ The Skinner box, an apparatus used for operantly conditioning a rat. When the rat presses the bar, reinforcement (a pellet of food) is automatically presented.

motivated to work for an opportunity to return to a favorable environment than to seek a food reward.

A comparable reward discrepancy occurs when birds and mammals are compared to ants. Getting food—and, typically, consuming it after it is found—is a strong reinforcer for birds and mammals. In contrast, ants are more reinforced by returning to the nest with food than by getting the food in the first place. In other words, ants learn a maze faster when going back to the nest with food than when going from the nest to the food source (see Maier & Schneirla, 1935). This finding is consistent with the basic ant worker pattern of returning to the nest with food after food is discovered rather than eating it on the spot.

Consistent with Premack's principle, the reinforcing value of a preferred activity varies according to how long it has been since the animal engaged in that activity. For example, a monkey will stop working for the opportunity to explore a novel stimulus after repeated exposure to that stimulus, and a rat will stop pressing a bar for food after having eaten for a period of time.

There are two general types of reinforcement schedules: **continuous reinforcement** (in which the reinforcement follows a behavior 100 percent of the time) and **partial reinforcement** (in which the reinforcement follows the behavior less than 100 percent of the time). Each type of reinforcement schedule has a particular advantage. Continuous reinforcement results in rapid learning, but also in rapid extinction (forgetting of the learned response). In contrast, partial reinforcement produces slower learning, but the response is more durable; that is, more resistant to extinction. This durability of partially reinforced responses is especially beneficial to animals that live in unpredictable environments.

Although there are alternative explanations, the most widely accepted explanation for the differential durability of continuous

TABLE 4.2 ◆ Advantages and Disadvantages of Two Types of Reinforcement

Type of Reinforcement	Advantage	Disadvantage
Continuous	Fast learning	Little resistance to extinction
Partial	Slow learning	Considerable resistance to extinction

and partial reinforcement is couched in cognitive terms: If the animal does not receive a reinforcement after having been reinforced on every previous trial, this change is immediately noticeable, and the animal's "expectancy" is not met. Therefore, the animal begins to abandon its conditioned behavior. However, if the animal has been partially reinforced all along, the shift to no reinforcement is more consistent with the animal's "expectancy" and the animal will continue to respond.

Feeding

In most animals, operant conditioning may take place at almost any time. Honey bees, however, exhibit a type of operant conditioning that is established at a very specific time. When the foraging bees arrive at the feeding site, they develop a preference for the color of the flowers on which they feed. But if bees are artificially prevented from approaching the flowers on their own, they do not develop the preference. Thus, if they are passively placed at the feeding site by an experimenter, they fail to return consistently to the color associated with the nectar from the flower. In contrast, if bees are allowed to approach and feed before they are captured and moved to another location, they will consistently choose the reinforced color. It seems that operant conditioning may take place when the bees approach the flower, but not at other times (J. L. Gould, 1986).

Generally, operant conditioning enables animals to develop appropriate responses toward stimuli that they may have "overlooked" in the past. Operant conditioning also enables animals to become responsive to new types of stimuli that may be introduced into their habitat. For example, pigeon hawks apparently began to follow slow-moving trains that were introduced into northern Mexico during the 1940s because of an association between the trains and the small prey birds the trains stirred up. A similar adjustment to a new foraging opportunity occurred in the British Isles after door-to-door milk delivery began in the 1920s. Much to the disgust of human residents, titmice and certain other birds became conditioned to milk caps; they would peck through the caps and drink the cream off the top of the milk (see Welty & Baptista, 1988).

Defense

Animals can be operantly conditioned not only to seek rewards but to avoid unpleasant stimuli. For example, animals quickly learn to stay away from a location where they have encountered predators; or, if the location is a watering hole they cannot avoid completely, they learn to be wary. They also learn to repeat behaviors that have been associated with escape.

Fortunately, researchers can investigate how animals learn to escape from predators by observing the development of laboratory animals' responses to an electric shock, because shock simulates the appearance of a predator (Bouton & Bolles, 1979). Shock-avoidance learning takes place very rapidly: Rats that have been shocked in a compartment learn to leave the compartment after only one trial.

Animals do not learn all types of avoidance responses equally well, however. For example, we can easily condition a rat to avoid shock by running in a running wheel—but it is virtually impossible to condition a rat to avoid a shock by standing upright. We can understand this difference if we look at an animal's natural responses to a predator. A shock—analogous to the appearance of a predator—is naturally associated with running. In contrast, standing upright is incompatible with escape responses (Bolles, 1973).

The Development of a Skill

An animal makes a slightly different response to a stimulus each time the stimulus appears. Consequently, an experimenter can "shape" a behavior; that is, reinforce a response that is close to the desired one and then, little by little, demand higher and higher levels of performance before giving reinforcement. This process of **shaping** has been used to train animals in a variety of settings. Some colorful results of shaping include raccoons that "dunk" miniature basketballs when a buzzer sounds (Figure 4.3) and chickens that "dance" when a light is turned on. Raccoons naturally manipulate food with their paws and chickens scratch for food with their feet, so these responses are readily available for shaping. In contrast, there are constraints that limit the types of behaviors

FIGURE 4.3 ◆ A raccoon trained through shaping. The animal has learned to dunk a miniature basketball in response to a buzzer.

capable of being operantly conditioned. Because chickens do not manipulate food with their limbs and raccoons do not scratch for food with their feet, a chicken cannot learn to shoot a basket nor a raccoon to "dance."

On the practical side, it is possible to use operant conditioning techniques to train animals to perform services for humans. For example, law enforcement officials have taken advantage of dogs' unusually well developed sense of smell to teach dogs to identify hidden drugs. Similarly, military personnel have trained dolphins and sea lions to identify underwater mines in war zones. More surprisingly, pigeons are able to aid in the search for persons lost at sea. The pigeons are trained to peck at a key when they detect a speck of orange. Then the birds are carried in a chamber beneath a helicopter, and whenever they spot

orange—the international color of life jackets—their pecks set off a buzzer that alerts the pilot. Pigeons are better able to spot distant objects at sea than humans; pigeons can focus over a large area, have excellent distance vision, and do not suffer significant eye fatigue as the result of staring over water.

In natural settings, improvement in an animal's performance of a complex skill is at least partly the result of shaping. For example, chimpanzees in Tanzania learn to insert a probe such as a twig or a blade of grass into termite nests; when a termite seizes the probe in its mandibles, the chimpanzee withdraws the probe and eats the termite (Goodall, 1963; Figure 4.4). The role of operant conditioning in this **termite fishing** is suggested by the observation that adult chimpanzees without previous experience are virtually never successful

FIGURE 4.4 ◆ A chimpanzee "termite fishing" with a twig.

in their first attempts. Furthermore, improvement in termite fishing continues until the animals are 6 or 7 years old. Improvements are apparently related to the chimpanzees' increased skill both in fashioning the tools and in manipulating the tools once they are introduced into the termite nest (Beck, 1980).

Temporal Learning

In some respects, **temporal learning**—the ability to learn time intervals—is similar to operant conditioning. However, temporal learning involves the development of associations between time and reinforcement, whereas operant conditioning involves associations between actions in specific locations and reinforcement. In many cases temporal learning and operant conditioning occur together; an animal learns to go to a specific location or choose a specific object within a predictable time frame. For instance, bees will return to an area the following day at approximately the same time of day that they found food in that area the previous day. Bees are also able to learn to go to different locations at different times of the day. It seems that the bees learn to associate a temporal cue with a cue that indicates location.

Do the bees learn any particular time interval, or are they predisposed to go to the site at a 24-hour interval after their last feeding? There is some support for the latter explanation. Experiments indicate that bees can easily be trained to 24-hour intervals but cannot learn intervals somewhat shorter or longer than 24 hours (see Gallistel, 1990).

A logical explanation for these findings might be that the bees simply learn the time of day the food appears; then they return to the food site the next day at the time when celestial cues indicate the appropriate time of day. A simple experiment suggests that this explanation is incorrect, however. When bees are flown overnight from Paris to New York, they search for food 24 hours after their last feeding in Paris, even though the New York sky gives "inappropriate" cues (Renner, 1960). Apparently bees have an internal biological clock that indicates when 24 hours have elapsed.

Rats also exhibit temporal learning. For example, laboratory rats given a food reward for pressing a bar at a certain time of day soon learn to press only during the appropriate time frame. As in the case of the bee, however, if intervals vary significantly from 24 hours, the rat cannot learn the temporal association (Bolles & Moot, 1973). Because bees and rats usually find food at about the same time each day in a natural state, such a specific learning ability is clearly adaptive.

Under different testing conditions, however, rats are able to learn intervals of time that are much shorter than 24 hours. For example, if rats are reinforced for pressing one bar for a stimulus that lasts for a short duration (1 to 4 seconds), and for pressing another bar for a stimulus that lasts for a longer duration (4 to 16 seconds), they learn to make the appropriate discrimination. The rats appear to have a memory with a biological clock that times the stimuli, some representation of the stimulus, and an ability to make a comparison between the stimuli (Gibbon, 1991).

The American snowshoe hare presents one of the most engaging examples of temporal learning within a short time frame. The doe nurses the young once a day but, unlike most other mammals, does not stay with them the rest of the time. After giving birth, she simultaneously nurses all the young at some time between 10 and 70 minutes after sunset. (With each litter, the mother chooses a different time interval.) Thereafter, on every night until weaning, the doe and her young meet back at the birth place at precisely the same time interval following sunset (Rongstad & Tester, 1971). Since nursing takes only about 5 minutes—and the young all arrive at about the same time—the hares are vulnerable to predation for only a short period. Furthermore, because each litter has a different nursing time, predators have difficulty establishing an optimal time to search for vulnerable snowshoe hares.

Spatial Learning

Spatial learning—the acquisition of information about spatial relationships in the environment—is important in helping animals develop efficient pathways to a burrow or nest, locate safe places in the event of predation or unfavorable weather, and discover areas where food is likely to be found. In some cases, the information an animal gains by spatial learning may be used in situations distinct from any the animal has previously encountered.

To a certain extent, animals learn to go from one location to another by making the same types of movements that resulted in their arrival on the previous occasion. However, this type of learning has important limitations. The animal can easily become lost and may also have difficulty developing efficient paths of movement. Furthermore, predators can learn the animal's pattern of movements and take advantage of this information.

Most animal behaviorists believe that some animals are able to to move about effi-

ciently by developing a **cognitive map**—a mental codification or framework representing the spatial environment. With such a map an animal could presumably use stored information and possibly plan movement strategies that would be difficult or impossible for predators to predict.

Cognitive Maps and Navigation

Edward Tolman and his associates (1946) conducted classic experiments that presented strong evidence for the operation of a cognitive map in rats. The experimenters gave rats the opportunity to explore and become familiar with a maze. Then, in a test situation, the rats took the shortest route between two points, even though they had never had the experience of traversing the path between the two points before. The experimenters concluded that "response learning" (learning to make a series of turns) was an inadequate explanation for the rats' performance; it was reasonable to assume that the rats had developed a cognitive map that enabled them to solve the problem.

In the years following this apparent demonstration of cognitive map formation in rats, additional evidence tended to support the cognitive map hypothesis not only in rats but in many other animals as well. For example, James Gould (1986) demonstrated that honeybees moved from one point to another in a manner consistent with the cognitive map hypothesis (Figure 4.5). Gould trained bees to go from the hive (H) to a feeding station at point A. He then transported them in a closed, dark container to point B. When released, all of the bees flew directly to point A, even though it was impossible for the bees to see their destination from the release site. Gould concluded

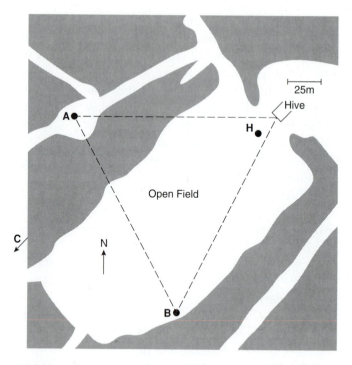

FIGURE 4.5 ◆ **Map of area used in honeybee displacement experiment.**

that the bees had constructed a cognitive map of the area that enabled them to fly a direct route to the food source.

An even more dramatic experiment with bees also tends to support the cognitive map hypothesis. Researchers trained foraging bees to feed from a boat in the middle of a lake. On the bees' return to the hive, their dance failed to recruit any of their fellow worker bees to visit the boat. But when the boat was moved to a spot along the opposite shore (the same distance from the hive), the returning foragers easily recruited bees to this site (Dyer, cited by Gould, 1984). The cognitive explanation for the results is that the bees in the hive had developed a cognitive map of the area and were aware that there was, under normal condi-

tions, no likelihood of a food source in the middle of the lake. A food source along the shore, however, was a real possibility.

Experiments with geese suggest an ability to form a cognitive map based on some type of calculation of distance and direction. For example, tame geese are transported passively in carts along twisting routes and released in areas that are unfamiliar to them. On release, the birds are able to orient in the general direction of their home site and follow a more direct route back than the one along which they were transported. Results obtained from a simple experimental manipulation indicate that the geese gain information about direction and distance from observing the passing terrain. When the geese are covered for part—

but not all—of the journey, they orient in a direction that would be appropriate only for the travel during the times they were uncovered. It is as though the geese are oblivious to what happened to them when they did not have access to visual cues (St. Paul, 1982).

Finally, some young birds apparently construct a cognitive map and then utilize the map much later, as adults, when they navigate during periods of migration. For example, indigo buntings appear to learn the position of the celestial pole in the night sky when they are only a few days old. (The celestial pole is the center of rotation of the night sky: the only point that does not apparently move during the night.) This ability is quite remarkable, because no animal can learn the position of the celestial pole on the basis of one observation. The bird must store the image of the sky it receives at one time and integrate it with other images it receives hours or days later. It takes at least two observations, made at different times of the night, for the bird to extract the necessary information. Once the birds identify the celestial pole, they can learn the position of stars within 35 degrees of the celestial pole and use this information to obtain a sense of direction (Gallistel, 1990). As we shall see when we discuss migration and navigation in more detail in Chapter 19, indigo buntings are able to migrate at night by using the pattern of stars as a compass.

The Nature of Cognitive Maps

Although the evidence is strong that many animals use a cognitive map, the nature of this map is unclear. Certain theorists conceptualize a map in a somewhat literal sense, likening it to an aerial view of an area (Pearce, 1987).

Other theorists define a cognitive map more abstractly—as a record of geometric re-

lationships (Gallistel, 1990). The studies of homing in ants and geese are consistent with this hypothesis.

Still other theorists conceptualize a cognitive map as including both topographical and geometric information—an integration of both a picturelike representation and information about angles and distances (Poucet, 1993). Support for this integrated model comes from studies of certain brain structures—the hippocampus and the posterior parietal cortex—areas of the brain that seem to process information related to cognitive maps.

Whatever the nature of cognitive maps, it seems likely that different animals develop different types of maps, some based on visual information, others on olfactory or auditory information, and still others on information from a combination of sensory cues. In fact, there is experimental evidence that information processed by more than one sense may be integrated into one cognitive map; hamsters are able to remember and use spatial information based on olfactory cues and to combine this information with information derived from visual cues (Tomlinson & Johnston, 1991).

Gender Differences in Spatial Learning

Male and female animals usually face very similar types of tasks, so it is not surprising that the learning abilities of the two genders are similar. In certain polygynous species, however, males move about in search of females while the females are less mobile. Consequently, the males have a greater area in which to navigate. For example, the polygynous meadow vole male has a much larger home range than the female. Related to the challenge of this greater area to navigate, the meadow vole male shows greater maze-learning ability than the meadow vole female. In the monogamous pine voles, by contrast, males and females live in the same home range and face similar challenges to find their way around—and these males and females show similar maze-learning ability in the laboratory (Gaulin & FitzGerald, 1986).

Apparently there has been a differential natural selection for a spatial learning ability related to navigation in the polygynous male vole. This finding is especially interesting because it illustrates how the evolution of mating systems can go hand in hand with the evolution of types of spatial learning ability.

Social Learning

In some cases an animal may learn not by engaging in a relevant activity but by being sensitive to cues from other animals. This type of learning, known as **social learning,** is defined as the transfer of skills developed or information obtained by one animal (the model or tutor) to another animal (the observer). Clearly, the observer benefits from this type of learning, because it can develop skills and obtain information without having to undergo trial-and-error learning. Moreover, the tutor may also benefit—as the result of indirect fitness—if the observer is a relative.

Social learning may take place at several levels. At the simplest level, the learning may simply involve **stimulus enhancement;** that is, the model may emphasize the location or object to which the observer must orient. At a somewhat higher level of social learning, the observer imitates the behavior of the model. Imitation involves paying attention to the location and object and also copying some aspects of the model's behavior (see Whiten et

al., 1996). At what could be considered the highest cognitive level, the observer may gain information from observing the tutor and may then use this information at a later time and in a different context.

Visual Social Learning

Research evidence indicates that an octopus can learn by observing another octopus perform a discrimination task. In a laboratory setting, scientists rewarded an octopus for attacking one of two balls introduced into its aquarium—and punished it for attacking the other ball. (In some cases a white ball served as the positive stimulus, while a red ball was the negative stimulus; in other cases the color contingency was reversed.) In a critical test situation, a second octopus observed the correct responses of the tutor from its aquarium; it was then able to choose the correct ball the vast majority of the time when it was tested (Fiorito & Scotto, 1992).

As far as we know, the relatively large-brained octopus is the only invertebrate capable of visual social learning. In contrast, this ability is well developed in mammals, especially in primates. When one rhesus monkey watches another perform in a series of discrimination problems in the laboratory, the observer monkey learns from watching mistakes as well as from seeing correct responses. In other words, the observer monkey does not simply copy responses but obtains information that it then uses to solve problems (Darby & Riopelle, 1959).

Social learning seems to be involved in a famous example of the development of food washing in Japanese macaque monkeys. Scientists who were studying the social behavior of a troop of monkeys after the scientists had left sweet potatoes as food for the animals noted that one young female monkey in a troop was the only individual to wash dirt from her sweet potato. Then other monkeys—typically playmates of the young female—began to wash their food. Within the next 5 years, food washing spread, typically among the peers, to most of the monkeys under 7 years of age. Finally, the food-washing tradition spread from mother to offspring (Itani, 1958; Kawai, 1965).

It is difficult to know how this social learning took place, because the scientists' report did not specify exactly what happened preceding the development of food washing in each individual monkey. In an attempt to observe more closely the possible development of food washing, other researchers created a laboratory environment that presumably encouraged the development of food washing. The researchers presented two types of monkeys—New World capuchins and Old World crab-eating macaques—with water and toys simultaneously and, later, with water and sandy fruit. Eventually, some of the monkeys consistently washed their sandy food before eating. However, there was no evidence of direct imitation. Rather, it seems that the social learning resulted from individuals washing food on their own in the context of a supportive environment (Visalberghi & Fragaszy, 1990). This study is a good example of how laboratory research can help explain the development of behaviors originally observed in a natural or seminatural setting.

Visual social learning is well developed in apes. In a study in which a chimpanzee named Vicki was raised by humans, the trainers were able to induce Vicki to reproduce a large number of human gestures (Hayes & Hayes, 1952). Observation of orangutans in Indonesian Borneo indicates that these apes reproduce a variety of behaviors, especially behaviors modeled by a caregiver or older sibling. A behavior is most likely to be reproduced if it is relevant and reflects an area of competence (Russon & Galdikas, 1995).

Olfactory Social Learning

Rats, which do not exhibit any apparent visual social learning, show rather complex olfactory social learning. Even though two rats may eat at different times and in separate places, they are able to exchange information about what they have eaten, apparently via odor cues. For example, in a laboratory setting, one rat (the model) was fed a specific type of food and then later was allowed to interact with another rat (the observer). When given a choice of various types of food, the observer rat showed a preference for the type of food the model had eaten (Galef & Wigmore, 1983).

A later experiment provided more direct support for the conclusion that the transfer of information was olfactory. A rat (the model) ate food flavored with a fragrant substance such as cinnamon. This rat was then anesthetized and placed in close proximity to an awake, observer rat. The observer later showed a significant preference for food with the same fragrance as that eaten by the model (Galef, 1990).

Not only does a rat show a preference for a food consumed by a demonstrator, but the observer rat is sensitive to the relative quantities of food eaten. When demonstrator rats eat two flavors of food, but more of one flavor than of the other, the observers eat the flavored food in the same proportion (Galef & Whiskin, 1995).

The transfer of olfactory information can go two ways: A rat may act as both demonstrator and observer during the same interaction (Galef, 1990). This communication is highly sophisticated, in the sense that information about several different foods as well as information about multiflavored foods may be communicated (Galef, 1990; Galef & Whiskin, 1992).

As we shall see when we consider feeding in Chapter 6, a young rat's ability to learn by olfactory observation is important in the development of a balanced diet. Furthermore, because rats are especially vulnerable to poisonous foods (they are unable to regurgitate), these animals benefit greatly from adapting to new food sources.

Auditory Social Learning

The development of songs in songbirds involves auditory social learning: A model presents information that is stored and not used until several weeks later, when the young bird begins apparent attempts to duplicate or at least to approximate the song of the model.

Evidence supporting the role of auditory social learning comes from the study I described in Chapter 3, in which experimental deafening of the bird prevented the normal development of the adult song (Marler, 1970).

Although song learning takes place at an early, sensitive period in a songbird's life, certain birds show another type of auditory social learning—**vocal mimicry,** or the ability to copy sounds in the environment in addition to those produced by their conspecifics. Parrots and mynah birds may learn to imitate hundreds of words and sounds from the environment. Vocal mimicry leads to the development of a large vocal repertoire—which, as we have seen, is related to the attraction of females and territorial defense. This mimicry may also facilitate competition between species. For example, if a parrot is able to mimic the song of a territorial bird of a different species, the parrot may be able to intimidate other birds of that species.

◆ HUMAN EVOLUTION

Earlier in this chapter I mentioned that certain myths have contributed to the mistaken belief that human learning is very different from learning in nonhuman animals. Let's examine these myths as they relate to human learning, then look at several examples of the continuity of learning principles across animal species—including humans. Then we will look at some apparent gender differences in learning ability. Finally, we will look at a type of learning that is especially important in human behavior—social–cognitive learning.

MYTHS ABOUT HUMAN LEARNING

Historically, there has been a general belief that humans are very good general learners and that we can learn relationships between objects or events in a great variety of situations. But actually our learning ability is domain specific rather than general. Like nonhuman animals, in other words, we have evolved a predisposition to learn specific associations that have facilitated our fitness. For example, we find it very difficult to learn to differentiate two rectangles that are similar in shape. However, we are extremely good at learning to perceive small differences in human faces. This ability has great fitness value for us, because social recognition is extremely important in the development of social strategies.

Related to the myth of domain-general learning ability in humans is the myth that humans are superior to nonhuman animals in all types of learning ability. In fact, all animals evolve domain-specific learning abilities, and some nonhuman animals that have become highly specialized for a certain type of learning are superior to humans in that specialized area. For example, few humans can match rats' ability to learn to avoid poison or honeybees' ability to find their way back to several different food sites 24 hours after they first found the food.

Another myth is that learning does not take place in very young infants. However, as we saw in the last chapter, young infants are extremely efficient at learning certain aspects of language, even more efficient than adults. Consistent with the concept of domain specificity, the brains of infants and adults are each specialized for certain types of learning—learning relationships that have a large payoff during a particular developmental stage.

Just as we have failed to give infants their due as far as learning is concerned, we have held a bias against older adults by assuming that "old dogs cannot learn new tricks." Although there is a slowing down in reaction time in older adults, most types of learning do not suffer deficits with aging. In fact, learning of material that is facilitated by previous knowledge is often more efficient and rapid in older, experienced adults than in young, inexperienced ones. What does in fact lead to a decline in learning ability is a failure to challenge oneself with learning tasks. As Chapter 16 will explain, the failure to activate nerve cells via practice results in the premature dysfunction or death of the cells.

THE CONTINUITY OF LEARNING PRINCIPLES ACROSS SPECIES

If we assume that human learning ability evolved out of learning abilities displayed by the ancestors of nonhuman animals, we should be able to identify similarities between nonhuman learning and that of humans. And in fact, the various types of learning discussed earlier in this chapter, widely represented in the animal world, are also well represented in humans.

For example, habituation is basic to the development of attention in humans; without habituation, we would be unable to avoid distractions of various kinds. Pavlovian conditioning is important in our development of food aversions similar to those that develop in rats. Pavlovian conditioning also accounts for many of our learned social preferences, many of which we acquire unconsciously. The operant principle of partial reinforcement helps to explain countless human behaviors—including the way people are drawn to slot machines, even though the payoff is erratic and the total payoff is usually less than the total investment.

Temporal and spatial learning are also well developed in humans. We are able to learn time intervals of varying lengths and can formulate highly sophisticated cognitive maps. Interestingly, humans do not learn 24-hour time intervals as fast or efficiently as honeybees. As we have seen, honeybees return to the location where they found food at virtually the same time the following day. However, humans can learn a much greater variety of time intervals—seconds, days, weeks, or years.

A similar comparison can be made between ants and humans in regard to spatial learning. Although ants can develop a cognitive map of a small area as quickly as humans, humans can build cognitive maps of vary large areas as well as of small areas. Compared to the temporal and spatial learning abilities of insects such as honeybees and ants, the human abilities can be applied to a much greater variety of situations and purposes. Also, humans are able to generalize what they have learned to the extent that they can develop secondary cognitve abilities such as reading and algebra.

HUMAN SOCIAL LEARNING

Like other social primates, humans are very efficient social learners. More than any other animal, humans apply social learning principles to teaching their offspring and also to passing on cultural traditions. Much of this highly developed social learning is related to the high level of cognitive development found in humans; that is, to humans' abilities to think, plan ahead, and develop expectancies.

Certain nonhuman animals, especially chimpanzees, exhibit fairly well-developed cognitive abilities and may plan and develop expectancies to some extent. However, humans utilize these ways of thinking to a much greater extent and, consequently, are much more future oriented.

Albert Bandura's (1986) **social–cognitive theory** combines social learning and cognitive factors to explain large amounts of human behavior. Bandura maintains that humans have "self-maintained" goals; that is, goals that are established by our cognitions, or thoughts. Thus, our behavior is determined by a combination of external factors such as the physical and social environment and internal factors including beliefs and thoughts.

These external and internal factors together affect our behavior. For example, a child who saw two people arguing violently might perceive danger and experience fear. This perception might then lead the child to behave in a distrusting way and influence his or her future interactions with people. The child's future social behavior would reflect the interaction of what actually took place with the child's cognitions about the event.

Human learning, then, is similar to the learning of many other types of animals and reflects several of the same developmental principles. However, our abilities to generalize and to utilize social cognitions, including cognitions about ourselves, greatly enrich human learning. The next chapter will consider how these and other cognitive abilities have contributed to human uniqueness.

GENDER DIFFERENCES IN LEARNING ABILITY

The finding that there are gender differences in a type of spatial learning ability in meadow voles raises the question, Are there differences in the learning abilities of men and women that make sense in terms of differential natural selection pressures?

For many years it has been known that men are superior to women in their ability to mentally rotate figures in space. This spatial ability would have helped with the task that our male ancestors often faced while hunting—finding their orientation after chasing or tracking moving prey. Our female ancestors, in contrast, would have benefited from remembering the specific location and nature of objects—especially the location of objects in relation to each other. Consistent with this hypothesis, laboratory research indicates that women are better than men at learning the position of objects in a room (Silverman & Eals, 1992).

Thus, it seems that men and women have been somewhat differentially naturally selected as a result of the differentiation of roles in our hunter–gatherer ancestors. Although many of the cognitive abilities of men and women are similar, there is some tendency to develop the types of learning abilities that are basic to the primary tasks of women gathering and men hunting. Men typically navigate in terms of the "big picture," using distances and directions, while women tend to utilize landmarks. It is not hard to think of other examples of how men tend to focus on the big picture while women notice details.

◆ CHANGING PERSPECTIVES

PAST	PRESENT	FUTURE
Learning ability in all animals is domain general. The learning ability of humans is superior to that of nonhumans (late nineteenth century).	Most learning ability is domain specific. Humans, like all animals, are predisposed to learn certain types of relationships. Humans are superior in some learning abilities but inferior in others.	What domain-specific learning abilities does each species of animal possess? How did these abilities evolve over time?

SUMMARY

Learning is basic to the development and modification of a large variety of behaviors. Learning is not a general ability but tends to be domain specific; that is, animals are adapted to learning specific types of relationships. This domain specificity reduces the probability of learning meaningless or inappropriate relationships.

The evolution of learning in any animal is strongly influenced by ecological factors such as the type of food available, the mobility of the food source, and the surroundings in which the animal reproduces. However, the mere fact that a certain type of learning ability would prove beneficial is not enough to ensure that that ability will evolve: The animal must have prior adaptations upon which to build. Prior adaptations include a nervous system, appropriately developed motor and sensory systems, and established behavior patterns that predispose an animal to learn certain types of responses to stimuli.

Habituation—the developing tendency to react less vigorously to a stimulus that has little or no effect on an animal—may result in significant savings of time and energy. Although it is a relatively simple type of learning, habituation may be related to some complex types of information processing.

Pavlovian conditioning—the passive development of a response to a previously neutral stimulus—enables an animal to prepare for various significant eventualities. Processes and principles such as the cognition of predictive value, blocking, sign tracking, and taste aversion learning facilitate Pavlovian conditioning in specific situations.

The active process of operant conditioning leads animals to develop appropriate responses toward stimuli they may have "overlooked" in the past; to become responsive to new types of stimuli; and, in some cases, to develop skills. Principles of reinforcement and punishment are basic to operant conditioning.

Temporal learning—the ability to learn intervals of time—enables some animals to feed at the same time each day. Furthermore, certain animals are able to make appropriate comparisons between stimuli based on the duration of a stimulus.

Social learning—the ability to learn by being sensitive to cues from other animals—is important to the communication of information between conspecifics. Social learning may be visual, auditory, or olfactory.

There is a general continuity of learning principles across animal species, including humans. However, humans utilize social cognitive learning to a much greater extent than any other species. As in nonhuman animals, sexual selection has apparently produced certain gender differences in human learning ability.

KEY TERMS

blocking, p. 79
classical conditioning, p. 78
cognitive map, p. 87
conditioned stimulus (CS), p. 78
continuous reinforcement, p. 83
domain-specific learning, p. 74
habituation, p. 77
learning, p. 74
neophobia, p. 78
cperant conditioning, p. 82
partial reinforcement, p. 83
Pavlovian conditioning, p. 78
predictive value, p. 78
Premack's principle, p. 82

prior adaptation, p. 76
reinforcement, p. 82
shaping, p. 84
sign tracking, p. 80
social–cognitive theory, p. 90
social learning, p. 90
spatial learning, p. 87
stimulus enhancement, p. 90
taste aversion learning, p. 80
temporal learning, p. 86
termite fishing, p. 85
unconditioned stimulus (UCS), p. 78
vocal mimicry, p. 92

CHAPTER 5

COGNITION

- ◆ *Can dolphins be trained to develop language?*
- ◆ *What kinds of information can animals communicate?*
- ◆ *Can animals form concepts?*

For much of the twentieth century, as I indicated in Chapter 1 and also in Chapter 4, it was considered inappropriate to apply the term cognition, or thought, to brain processes in nonhuman animals. And as we shall see, controversies still surround the interpretation of studies that appear to demonstrate many types of cognitive abilities in

5

animals. However, these studies have generated a great deal of interest, and cognition is now the subject of a significant area of specialization within the field of animal behavior.

This chapter will examine five major aspects of cognition in animals: concept formation, language learning, quantitative ability, memory and perception, and complex cognitive processes (which, until very recently, were considered only within the domain of humans). Finally, we will examine the evolution of cognitive abilities in humans.

CONCEPT FORMATION

Concept formation—the formation of a category or the extraction of a general principle—involves using information obtained in one context to solve problems in another context. An animal with an ability to form concepts extends its problem-solving ability, because the animal can solve problems that are different in some way from problems it encountered in the past. We will consider three general kinds of concepts: object concepts, abstract concepts, and equivalent class concepts (Wasserman, 1993).

Object Concepts

Object concepts are concepts that apply to groups of objects belonging together or functionally classified together in some way. For example, the categories *human, tree,* and *water*

represent three functionally distinct natural classes of objects. (There are also object concepts, such as the concept of *chair,* that apply to human-made categories.) Are animals able to recognize and classify individual representations of object concepts? We can test for this conceptual ability by presenting an animal with various photographs—some of the photos including examples of an object category, such as humans, and some devoid of humans. We then reward the animal for making the correct response; for example, we can reward a pigeon for pecking at a key when a human is present in the photo. If the pigeon consistently responds only to photos containing humans, we may assume the bird has formed an object concept. In such experiments a pigeon may make a "correct" response but in fact be reacting to some simpler aspect of the photo, such as total brightness or whether or not objects are depicted close up (Edwards & Honig, 1987). But when researchers control for these simpler aspects, pigeons are still able to develop concepts of humans, trees, and water.

A pigeon's ability to conceptualize these three categories has clear functional significance; pigeons interact in significant ways with representatives of these categories under natural conditions. For example, pigeons are able to apply information gathered as the result of an interaction with one human to situations involving human beings in general. Nonetheless, rather surprisingly, pigeons are also able to develop the concept of fish (Hernstein, 1985). Perhaps the ability to correctly categorize fish is simply a by-product of a general conceptual potential.

In some respects, monkeys have a concept formation ability even more advanced than that of pigeons. For example, in only 29 trials, one rhesus monkey learned to differentiate slides showing humans from slides in which humans were not present (Schrier & Brady, 1987). Rhesus monkeys can also learn to distinguish slides depicting their own species from slides of Japanese macaques—which are quite closely related and similar in appearance to rhesus monkeys (Yoshikubo, 1985). This ability to respond to subtle facial characteristics is probably related to a ground-dwelling primate's need to form concepts that facilitate the development of social strategies.

Abstract Concepts

While object concepts require a certain level of abstraction, **abstract concepts** depend on an even greater degree of abstraction; to form an abstract concept, an animal must extract a principle that applies to a large variety of situations. One type of abstract concept problem involves bilateral symmetry. To study pigeons' grasp of bilateral symmetry, researchers trained laboratory pigeons to discriminate among 26 pairs of objects; in each pair, one object was symmetrical and the other asymmetrical. After this training the birds were able to discriminate between novel pairs of objects on the basis of their symmetry (Delius & Nowak, 1982). Animals' tendency to attend to symmetry relates to the fact that many prey animals are symmetrical, so symmetry detection may facilitate the identification and capture of prey (Braitenberg, 1986).

Experimenters have also investigated the formation of the abstract concept of similarity in birds and mammals. In an experimental situation, an animal must choose among three stimuli, two of which are similar and the third, different from the other two (e.g., A, A, and B). The animal is rewarded each time it chooses one of the A's. Then, after the animal has learned this task, it is given another series of tasks in which it must learn a new problem (e.g., C, C, and D). If the animal shows improvement in learning with each new task (i.e., it learns to choose C relatively quickly), it appears to have developed a concept of similarity or sameness.

Comparable problems measure the concept of difference or oddity. The procedure is basically the same as for similarity, except that the animal is rewarded for choosing the odd stimulus (e.g., B and D). Several species of birds and mammals exhibit an ability to develop concepts of both similarity and oddity.

It is in chimpanzees that researchers have found the highest level of performance on abstract concept formation problems. For example, four young chimpanzees applied the matching rule in a similarity task after training on only one pair of objects (Oden et al., 1988). This level of performance was possible only when three-dimensional objects were used and the animals had some familiarity with the objects, however.

For many years animal behaviorists assumed that birds were limited in their cognitive capabilities, because birds have small brains and practically no cerebral cortex. However, some birds are able to solve concept formation problems. Irene Pepperberg (1992) gave an African gray parrot named Alex extensive training and found that he not only comprehended the concepts *same* and *different* but was able to express this comprehension vocally. Alex could discriminate among more than 80 different objects and could answer questions about shape and color. Furthermore, the experimenter could present two novel objects that differed in either shape or color and ask, "What is the same?" Alex would then respond by saying either "same color" or "same shape," whichever was appropriate. Because these objects were novel, his response cannot be considered stimulus specific, so it fits the criterion for concept formation.

More recent studies of Alex indicate that when asked a question about an object defined by *two* categories, Alex was still able to answer with a high degree of accuracy. For example, when presented with a collection of items that differed in shape, color, and material, Alex could respond appropriately to questions like "What color is the round object that is made of wood?" We will return to Alex's apparent use of language when we consider language-learning ability later in the chapter.

LANGUAGE-LEARNING ABILITY

For humans, many concepts are represented by symbols or words. If some nonhuman animals are capable of concept formation, are they also capable of learning the meanings of symbols and the rudiments of language? The possibility of a rudimentary language-learning ability in nonhuman animals is especially interesting because its presence could help to define how great a gap exists between certain nonhuman animals and humans.

As might be expected, research investigating the possibility of teaching language or certain aspects of language to nonhumans has resulted in considerable controversy, particularly because language has traditionally been considered uniquely human. Generally speaking, scientists have had more heated exchanges of opinion over nonhuman animal language learning than over any other area of animal behavior (Wasserman, 1993).

One of the earliest language-related controversies occurred in Germany around the turn of the twentieth century. A horse named Clever Hans and his owner played to packed audiences with an act that seemed to show that the horse could understand the owner's questions and tap out correct answers to complex mathematical problems with his hoof. Later controlled tests indicated, however, that the owner was unconsciously cuing the horse with barely perceptible movements of his head. After the horse had tapped the correct number of times, these subtle movements cued the horse to stop. Ever since Clever Hans, language ability in nonhuman animals has been suspect; and the phenomenon of a human's cuing a nonhuman animal to give a putatively intelligent response has been called the **Clever Hans phenomenon.** It is important for researchers to rule out this phenomenon when studying complex processes such as language comprehension.

Apes

Because apes are our closest living relatives, many researchers have considered apes to be the best candidates for language learning.

Early Studies and Controversies

Hayes and Hayes (1952) attempted to teach a spoken language to a chimpanzee named Vicki. Vicki seemed to exhibit considerable observational learning ability, but the language-teaching attempts met with little success. Nonetheless, the Hayeses noted that Vicki often used gestures to express her needs.

The Hayeses' observation of Vicki's use of gestures stimulated a later pair of researchers (Gardner & Gardner, 1969) to attempt to teach a chimpanzee named Washoe American Sign Language—the language of hand signals utilized by the deaf. After almost 2 years of training, Washoe had acquired about 40 signs; she could use the signs appropriately as well as transfer them to new situations. The Gardners reported that Washoe was even able to combine known signs to designate new objects. For example, she signed "water" and "bird" to indicate a duck.

Skeptics, however, argued that Washoe could have been signing about the water and a bird independently. Furthermore, many of the observations of Washoe were made under informal conditions and were not subject to ex-

perimental control. Finally, it was possible that the trainers could have inadvertently cued Washoe's responses, producing a Clever Hans phenomenon. Thus, it was not at all clear that Washoe really understood the meaning of the signs she was using (see Sebeok, 1979).

Later researchers tried to standardize the use of symbols with chimpanzees by using a computer. For example, they presented a female chimpanzee named Lana with a computer console whose keys showed various symbols, each referring to a specific object or action. When Lana pressed a key, that key's symbol was illuminated on a display panel. The experimenters also communicated with Lana via the computer console. Lana was able to learn names for colors and various items and often initiated "conversations," primarily conversations aimed at getting something she wanted or correcting a deviation from the usual routine (Rumbaugh & Gill, 1976).

A chimpanzee named Sarah was taught a vocabulary and could answer questions by using symbols that consisted of pieces of plastic; the pieces varied in shape and color and had magnets on the back so that they could be attached to a board to make up sentences. Of particular significance is the finding that Sarah could learn the basics of syntax and the importance of sequencing. For example, Sarah could "understand" the difference between the phrases "the apple is in the bucket" and "the bucket is in the apple" (Premack, 1971).

Nonetheless, critics were not convinced. For example, Herbert Terrace, who had worked on a similar computer project with a chimpanzee named Nim, carefully reviewed videotapes of Nim's interactions. He concluded there was no solid evidence that chimpanzees understood the meaning of the computer symbols. Although Nim was able to produce some meaningful word combinations, Terrace believed this represented nothing more than an imitation of the teacher's input (Terrace et al., 1979).

Evidence from a Bonobo Chimpanzee Named Kanzi

Following the damaging critiques of the 1970s, the most convincing demonstration of language-learning ability in apes has been provided by a male bonobo chimpanzee named Kanzi. Significantly, Sue Savage-Rumbaugh and her associates used a very different approach to training Kanzi (see Savage-Rumbaugh & Lewin, 1994).

To begin with, Kanzi happened to learn a great deal about the computer symbols at a young age while in the presence of his mother, who was in the process of traditional ape language training. (Ironically, the mother learned much less than Kanzi.) Kanzi's early learning was probably successful because it was similar to the natural language learning of human children. As we saw in Chapter 3, children have an early, sensitive period for language learning, learn their native language in a language-rich social context where relatively few demands are made of them, and develop language comprehension before language expression.

Much of the further training of Kanzi continued in a relaxed, social setting—a 55-acre forest where Kanzi could reliably find food at 17 locations as he traveled with his human trainer–companions. Kanzi carried a portable version of the keyboard with him and communicated with his trainer–companions via the keyboard—and often "talked" to himself by pointing at symbols in private. Kanzi also spontaneously used gestures and vocalizations. When the trainer–companions communicated with Kanzi, they pointed at symbols and concurrently expressed themselves in spoken language (Figure 5.1).

Kanzi often made spontaneous references to various objects in the environment. He would also communicate his intentions before engaging in any action and would make reference to places that were not visible at the time, showing an apparent ability to plan and form mental images. Finally, in contrast to many of the other apes tested, Kanzi was able to follow directions given to him in spoken English, even when the directions were given by a computer-driven voice synthesizer. This latter test ruled out any possibility of a Clever Hans effect (Savage-Rumbaugh, 1988).

Other apes have also learned to communicate in fairly complex ways, though not on Kanzi's level. Two common chimpanzees, Sherman and Austin, were trained on a computer console similar to the one used by Kanzi. They learned to communicate with each other when in separate rooms by using the consoles. For example, Austin once asked to "borrow" a tool from Sherman; Austin needed the tool in order to obtain a food reward (Savage-Rumbaugh, 1986).

Why was Kanzi so exceptional in his ability? Are bonobos better at learning the rudiments of language than other apes? It appears that it was the trainers' approach rather than some unique character of Kanzi that was of primary importance. Savage-Rumbaugh has had reasonably good success teaching both another bonobo and a common chimpanzee using the "Kanzi approach." Once again, this

FIGURE 5.1 ◆ Kanzi, the bonobo chimpanzee, with his portable keyboard. He was able to understand spoken language and communicated by means of gestures and by pointing to symbols on the keyboard.

approach emphasizes early training, a language-rich social environment, and an understanding that naturally stimulated language comprehension precedes language production (Savage-Rumbaugh & Lewin, 1994).

From a humanitarian standpoint, the Kanzi approach shows promise of helping severely retarded humans. Retarded children who have failed to learn a spoken language have learned to communicate with computer-generated symbols similar to those used by Kanzi. Not only has this technique increased the children's ability to communicate, but the children show definite signs of increased satisfaction and feelings of well-being (see Savage-Rumbaugh & Lewin, 1994).

In conclusion, it appears that, after extensive training, apes are able to learn symbolic communication—substituting symbols for objects and actions. In some cases apes can make non-goal-oriented comments about their environment and can communicate their intentions before their actions occur. Apes do not develop language on their own, however, nor do they seem capable of developing complex rules of syntax. Nonetheless, there is clearly less of a language gulf between humans and apes than we once assumed.

If there is not a large gulf, why haven't apes developed some sort of language on their own? One of the primary factors is related to the anatomy of an ape's vocal apparatus. It is impossible for an ape to produce consonants, and without consonant sounds a spoken language is difficult if not impossible. In other words, language development in apes seems to be hindered more by speech production than by speech comprehension.

Why did humans—but not apes—develop the vocal apparatus capable of producing speech? One hypothesis is that the vocal apparatus evolved into one capable of speech as a result of our becoming bipedal. As early hominids began to walk on their hind feet, they benefited from carrying the head in an erect position above the spine. With the head in this position, the vocal tract bends at a right angle and the tongue is farther back in the throat than it is in apes. In this hominid position speech is possible because, among other things, the tongue can greatly modify sounds and produce consonants (see Crelin, 1987).

Marine Mammals

Following the moderate success in training apes to use language, scientists attempted to train dolphins in an artificial language. Dolphins have large brains and, as we shall see in Chapter 14, engage in complex types of social behavior.

One individual, a female bottle-nosed dolphin named Phoenix, was trained primarily to respond to acoustic signals—computer-generated sounds broadcast into a seawater tank. The signals were whistlelike in character, generally resembling some of the natural sounds made by dolphins. Another female, named Ake, was trained primarily in a gestural language. In this case, the words were indicated by movements of the trainer's arms and hands in the manner of a semaphore.

The trainer wore opaque goggles so that it was impossible to inadvertently cue the dolphin with eye movements and produce a Clever Hans phenomenon. Furthermore, independent observers scored the responses of the dolphins, eliminating the possibility that a bias on the part of the trainer might influence the scoring of responses.

The dolphins could be given instructions (e.g., *fetch, toss,* or *go under*) regarding various objects in the tank, and each dolphin could be given a command that would identify her as either an agent or an object. For example, the statement "Ake Phoenix under" meant that Ake was to swim under Phoenix. Conversely, "Phoenix Ake under" meant that Phoenix was to swim under Ake.

By using an interrogative symbol, the scientists could also ask the dolphins questions such as "Is there a Frisbee in the tank?" The dolphins could then give answers to the questions by pressing one of two paddles, one indicating "yes" and the other indicating "no."

After this training the dolphins' comprehension was found to be very good. Phoenix and Ake had little trouble with any of the examples just given and usually understood immediately even sentences they had never been given before. In addition, questions about objects not immediately present were typically answered correctly by both of the dolphins. Ake was also able to develop the expressive component of her language. For example, she could apply labels to any of five objects shown to her (Herman, 1987).

A language similar to the gestural one used for the dolphins was also developed for two female California sea lions. Sea lions seem to be good candidates for such training because they have relatively large brains and are well motivated to work for food reinforcement. Like the dolphins, the sea lions followed instructions—which included responding to objects on land as well as in the water. Furthermore, the sea lion named Rocky was adept at following commands that involved more than one modifier ("Go over the *large gray ball*") and demonstrated an understanding of simple syntax (Gisiner & Schusterman, 1992).

The dolphin and sea lion studies are significant in that they suggest that rudimentary language-learning potential is present in mammals other than apes. An important message from the language research on nonhuman mammals in general is that if early attempts to identify language-learning ability in an animal fail, this does not mean that the animal and related animals do not have the ability. New insights, new techniques, and a great deal of patience on the part of researchers can produce large advances in our understanding of animal behavior and cognition.

Parrots

Another example of the successful use of new techniques in research on language-related abilities is found in the training of Alex, the gray parrot whose ability to form concepts I discussed earlier. For years people had assumed that parrots were capable of mimicking human speech but incapable of attaching any meaning to the words. The superiority of Alex's performance seems to be related to the method of training.

The experimenters in earlier studies of "talking" in parrots tried to shape the birds' vocal responses by giving extrinsic reinforcement (rewards in the form of food) for correct responses. In contrast, Irene Pepperberg (1992) and her associates presented Alex with the object under "discussion" after he made appropriate responses. Alex could then ask for food reinforcement and would be given the food. If Alex failed to respond appropriately to questions, however, his requests for food were denied. Thus, Alex experienced **intrinsic reinforcement**—reinforcement directly associated with the activity itself. Furthermore, for each set of objects, two humans engaged in a simple dialogue about the objects in question in front of Alex. Consequently, Alex had two types of experiences that are very important in human language learning—intrinsic reinforcement and models of language communication (Figure 5.2). In essence, the training of Alex was similar to that of Kanzi in important ways.

Of particular interest is the finding that Alex's development of the expressive components of language did not occur at the same rate as his receptive capacity. As had been found in the studies of apes and marine mammals, the development of receptive ability preceded the expressive ability. On the basis of this evidence, it seems that the receptive language ability is phylogenetically older—older in terms of the genetic evolution of species—than the expressive ability (Herman, 1987; Savage-Rumbaugh & Lewin, 1994).

One of the most notable findings of the studies of both Alex the parrot and Kanzi the bonobo is that the development of even a rudi-

FIGURE 5.2 ◆ **Irene Pepperberg with Alex the parrot.** Alex is able to use simple words to communicate answers to fairly complex questions.

mentary language greatly increased the animals' cognitive capacities. Language may not be necessary for certain types of cognition; but, as we know from studies of humans, language is a tool that certainly increases cognitive potential.

QUANTITATIVE ABILITY

We often consider verbal ability and quantitative ability to be central to human cognition. Thus, the question arises, Do nonhuman animals have a quantitative ability? Apparently

some animals do. As we shall see in Chapter 6, certain birds behave optimally in regard to the time they spend in patches of food that differ in density. That is, the birds feed as though they had made an estimate of the average level of food supply in the patches sampled (Charnov, 1976).

Laboratory studies also indicate that pigeons are capable of making judgments of "more" and "less." For example, researchers trained pigeons to respond to a sequence of red and blue flashes of light. If more red flashes than blue flashes occurred in the sequence, the correct response was to peck at one key; if more blue flashes occurred, a peck at another key was reinforced. Pigeons' ability to solve this problem suggests that they are capable of judgments of relative quantity beyond single digits (Alsop & Honig, 1991). The ability to make these types of judgments has an important energy conservation function for animals that must make foraging decisions based on the relative numbers of food items in various locations.

Chimpanzees, too, have an ability to make judgments of more and less. In addition, chimpanzees can learn to associate various symbols with numbers up to seven. It is particularly interesting that one chimpanzee named Sheba made indicating acts such as pointing while counting, a behavior similar to that observed in human children who are learning to count (Boysen & Berntson, 1995).

Two rhesus monkeys were taught to associate different symbols with different quantities of food. The experimenters gave the monkeys a choice of two Arabic numerals—for example, 2 and 9. If the monkeys chose 2, they would get two pellets of food; if they chose 9, they would get nine pellets. After several trials in which different numerals were paired in several different combinations, the monkeys showed a definite tendency to choose the larger of the two numerals. One of the monkeys was even able to make an optimal choice when presented with two numerals that were paired together for the first time (Washburn & Rumbaugh, 1991).

To summarize, certain birds seem to be able to make quantitative judgments related to fitness. In the case of rhesus monkeys and chimpanzees, there is some evidence that these primates have the rudiments of abstract quantitative concepts.

MEMORY AND PERCEPTION

Although it seems obvious that nonhuman animals must have systems that organize and store information, memory and perception have been neglected as areas of research until relatively recently (see Wasserman, 1993). On the basis of several different types of research, it now seems clear that memory and perceptual systems have evolved according the same evolutionary principles that influence the evolution of other systems.

Memory

We will begin by discussing a few of the experimental techniques used to measure memory processes. Then we will look at some of the major principles related to memory and at specialized memory formation in rats and birds.

The Measurement of Memory

Many laboratory studies of animal memory involve a technique known as the **delayed matching-to-sample paradigm.** Experimenters present an animal with a stimulus and then, after a period of time, test to determine if the animal can recognize the stimulus. In a popular version of this technique, the experimenter presents a test stimulus, removes it, and then, after a period of delay, presents two other stimuli, one of which matches the first. If the animal responds to the matched stimulus, it receives food reinforcement. After several trials, a consistent choice of the correct, matched stimulus indicates an animal's ability to remember the test stimulus (Blough, 1959).

The experimenter can vary such factors as the duration of presentation of the test stimulus, the length of delay between stimulus presentations, and the qualities of the stimulus the animal is required to match.

Olton and Samuelson (1976) used a radial maze to test for an animal's ability to remember a location associated with feeding. In this technique food is hidden in cups at the ends of the arms of the maze (Figure 5.3). Researchers place a test animal in the center of the maze; after the animal runs to the end of an arm and eats the food, it is returned to the center of the maze. The animal is then retested to see if it consistently goes to arms different from the one just chosen and depleted of food. This technique lets researchers determine if the test animal has a memory for places already visited as opposed to simply a tendency to follow some rule of search.

David Sherry and his associates (1981) developed an apparatus that simulated an area where a seed-storing bird would store or cache its seeds. The apparatus consisted of trays of moss arranged in such a way that after storing a seed, the bird could not see the seed. The experimenters allowed the bird to store seeds and then placed the bird in a separate holding area. During the bird's absence from the apparatus, the experimenters removed the seeds to prevent the possible influence of visual or olfactory cues. The experimenters then returned the bird and observed the bird's recovery attempts. By means of this approach, it was possible to investigate whether the recovery attempts were random, or depended on cues emanating from the seeds, or demonstrated memory in the bird.

General Principles of Memory Formation

Studies using the delayed matching-to-sample technique indicate that pigeons can remember a variety of components of sample stimuli, including color, shape, orientation, and spatial location (see Spear et al., 1990). As the duration of delay between presentation of the sample and presentation of the test stimuli is increased, the accuracy of the birds' memory decreases. This finding is consistent with the **trace theory of memory**—a theory conceptualizing memory as some type of neural trace that fades over time, much the way an electronic charge dissipates from a capacitor (Roberts & Grant, 1976).

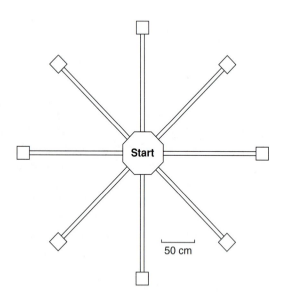

FIGURE 5.3 ◆ **Radial maze.** Food can be hidden in any of the cups at the ends of the maze arms.

Further research suggests, however, that some aspects of animal memory are much more complex than the trace theory would predict. Furthermore, this research suggests that certain cognitive (thinking) processes may be involved. For example, a cue that provides information about the length of delay between stimuli may enhance the animal's memory. When a pigeon is presented with a tone signifying that there will be a short delay of 2 seconds—as opposed to a longer delay of 8 seconds—between stimulus presentations, the bird is highly accurate in its choice. Specifically, the bird is more accurate for 2-second delays with the cue than without the cue (Wasserman et al., 1982). These findings suggest the operation of some type of **expectancy,** or anticipatory behavior that may facilitate memory. Clearly, anticipation—a form of cognition—may facilitate fitness by enhancing the memory of relevant information.

Finally, both pigeons and monkeys show a **serial position effect**—the tendency to remember information at the beginning and at the end of a series more effectively than items in the middle of the series (Wright et al., 1985). This tendency makes an animal especially sensitive to information surrounding the arrival and departure of a predator, competitor, or potential mate.

In conclusion, the cognitive processes just discussed—expectancy and the factors underlying the serial position effect—all seem to facilitate fitness by enhancing the memory of relevant information. What is relevant tends to differ from one species to another, depending upon where the animal lives, what kind of predators it faces, and the type of food it eats. As I have explained, species have been naturally selected to develop an ability to learn one type of problem faster and more accurately than other types. Similarly, animals have been selected to remember certain types of information more than other types. Let's look at examples of specialized memory in the rat and in food-storing birds.

Specialized Memory in Rats

Because rats often deplete a nonrenewable food source (e.g., an overturned garbage can), it is presumably beneficial for them to remember areas where they have recently fed and to avoid these areas when other potential sources are available. Thus, the radial maze test (refer to Figure 5.3) is especially appropriate to test rats' memory for relevant information.

Tests reveal that after a rat has had some experience with the radial maze, the rat typically goes only to arms *not* previously visited. That is, because the rat does not visit the arms in a stereotyped sequence we may conclude that the rat has a memory for places visited and is not showing a simple tendency to follow some rule of search (Olton & Samuelson, 1976).

Rats also have an ability to remember somewhat specific information about food. When tested in a radial maze, rats visit the arms of the maze in a sequence that takes into account the amount of food present in each arm on previous trials; they visit the arm with the largest amount first, the one with the second largest amount next, and so forth (Roberts, 1992).

Do rats have a better memory for information that is organized in some meaningful way than for information presented randomly? Evidence from a radial maze experiment suggests that the answer is yes. Rats remembered places visited with greater accuracy if the experimenters placed preferred food in a predictable sequence than if preferred food was placed randomly in the arms of the maze. Apparently the rats were able to learn the meaningful information faster because it was possible to **chunk** the information: to organize the information into a small number of manageable categories (Macuda & Roberts, 1995).

Specialized Memory in Food-Storing Birds

For many years scientists assumed that birds located hoarding or cache sites by using relatively simple retrieval strategies. It seemed beyond the capacity of birds to process and retain the large amounts of information that would be necessary for them to remember the location of these sites. Since the early 1980s, however, researchers have assembled evidence indicating that several species of birds do indeed remember the location of their cache sites. In the first of a series of laboratory experiments, Sherry and his associates (1981) found that food-storing birds known as marsh tits visited cache sites in the simulated storing site significantly more often than would have occurred by chance. This finding indicates that random searching and the use of cues from the seeds were not viable explanations for the successful cache retrieval (Sherry et al., 1981).

In another experiment, researchers allowed two nutcrackers to cache seeds in the same apparatus. When given a chance to recover the seeds, each bird retrieved its own seeds the great majority of the time. Once again, a random search strategy could not explain these results. Nor does it appear that there is a specific rule for caching that is used by nutcrackers in general (Vander Wall, 1982).

Do birds simply remember that there is food available in a particular location, or do they remember something more specific about the type of food at the cache site? Experimental evidence suggests that the memory is quite specific. Researchers allowed chickadees to cache two types of seeds, one of which the birds preferred over the other. The sites were cleared of seeds between trials. When given a chance to retrieve, the birds went first to the sites that previously contained the preferred food (Sherry, 1982).

There is also experimental evidence for an ability to remember if the food was retrieved. In one study, for example, chickadees were allowed to store seeds and then, a day later, to recover seeds from half of their caches. (The remaining seeds were removed by the experimenter to eliminate any direct cues.) Later, in the critical test, the birds were given a chance to search for seeds; they searched in cache sites from which they had *not* already removed seeds (Sherry, 1984).

Do birds that cache food have a generally superior memory? Or is the superiority in memory restricted to situations related to storing food? Research comparing two closely related species of tits—the marsh tit, which caches food, and the blue tit, which does not—supports the latter hypothesis. Both species of tits were presented with a problem in which they had to return to an area where they had been allowed to eat part of a peanut. There was no difference in the ability of the two species to solve this problem and remember the solution. However, the food-caching marsh tit could learn and remember information related to caches, while the blue tit could not (Healy & Krebs, 1992).

In conclusion, it seems that some animals—especially food-caching birds—have evolved a remarkable ability to remember the location of cache sites. Why did memory for specific cache sites, as opposed to some inflexible instinctive mechanism for establishing rules of search, evolve as a method of retrieving seeds? The most likely explanation is that if there were innate species-wide rules for caching and retrieving, other members of the species would be just as likely to find the cache as the original hoarder. The ability to remember specific information about the type of food stored and whether or not it has already been retrieved further enhances the effective memory of these birds.

Perception

As we shall see at several points in the following chapters, some animals follow sophisticated strategies, especially with regard to foraging. Part of the ability to develop these strategies reflects cognitive factors related to complex learning and memory. We will now consider another part of this strategic ability—perceptual processes based on cognitive principles.

Search Image

Animals that search for food, or for other animals that are difficult to identify, clearly benefit when they have a **search image**—a cognitive representation of the stimulus they are seeking. In other words, it is easier for animals to find something if they know exactly what they are looking for.

How can we determine if animals develop a search image? There is considerable anecdotal evidence supporting the existence of such a cognitive representation. In an early study, for example, a researcher gave monkeys bananas as reinforcement and then secretly substituted lettuce, a less preferred food. The monkeys responded by looking around as if searching for the bananas and by throwing the lettuce on the floor in apparent frustration (Tinklepaugh, 1928).

Some scientists argued against this anecdotal evidence, however, because there were other possible explanations for the behavior of the monkeys. Experimental studies with objective measures such as reaction time present more convincing evidence of a search image. For example, when pigeons are cued to know exactly what kind of stimulus to expect, they respond faster than if they are cued that either of two stimuli will be presented (Blough, 1991).

Not only can the development of a search image facilitate foraging; it can have advantages in the identification of predators. And in highly social animals such as ground-dwelling primates, a search image may also help individuals develop social recognition. Ground-dwelling monkeys and apes show a highly developed ability to identify individuals within their group. These primates even show evidence of perceiving familial relationships. For example, a vervet monkey that has observed a baby monkey being hit by another monkey will typically look toward the mother of the baby, even if the mother is some distance away (Cheney & Seyfarth, 1990).

Object Permanence

Another perceptual phenomenon, the concept of **object permanence**—the ability to perceive the continued existence of an object when it is no longer visible—also facilitates foraging and related activities. If a desired object disappears from sight, it may be present but simply hidden in some way. Thus, it is to an animal's advantage to engage in searching behavior that could result in the recovery of the object.

Do nonhuman animals possess the concept of object permanence? At a relatively simple level, researchers can investigate an animal's grasp of object permanence by hiding an object in front of the animal and determining if the animal searches in the area where the object disappeared. In view of the fact that a solution to this problem involves little more than a memory for recent events, it is not too surprising that a variety of animals exhibit perception of object permanence at this relatively simple level.

In a more complex test of the concept of object permanence, an object is hidden in one of two places—for example, in a cup or behind a screen. The experimenter then demonstrates that the object is not in one of the places, such as the cup. If the animal consistently searches behind the screen (the appropriate place), we may assume some cognitive process more complex than simple memory. Dogs and ground-dwelling primates demonstrate perception of object permanence (see Gagnon & Dore, 1992). Such complex object permanence perception would seem to be particularly beneficial to these highly social animals. For instance, the observation that a group member is in one location would suggest that the same individual could not be in another location at the same time. The perceiver could then use this information to advantage in a competitive situation.

COMPLEX COGNITIVE PROCESSES

In the past two decades, animal behaviorists have considered the possibility of even more complex cognitive processes in animals: intentionality, planning, self-recognition, theory of mind, and consciousness.

Intentionality and Planning

Having intentions and plans could provide clear fitness benefits; if animals could plan ahead and act on these plans, they could prepare themselves for various future contingencies. Do nonhuman animals have the capacity for such cognitions? One type of evidence of intentionality and planning ability may come from observations of social interactions. For example, a subordinate male primate may maneuver a female into a position out of sight of the dominant male before he attempts to copulate with her. Nonetheless, it is possible that the males simply learn this strategy by trial and error (Cheney & Seyfarth, 1991).

A more convincing example comes from a study of chimpanzees. As we shall see in Chapter 11, chimpanzee mothers observed in the wild often engage in behaviors that facilitate the learning of tool use in their offspring. The mothers leave objects to be used as hammers and anvils in close proximity to nuts; in some cases a mother will even leave a nut on the anvil. The relevance of this example is increased by the observation that females without young never leave these objects together or place nuts on the anvil (Boesch, 1991).

Perhaps the strongest evidence of planning and intentionality came from observations of Kanzi, the bonobo chimpanzee. Kanzi often signaled that he would engage in a behavior when he got to a particular place; upon arrival, he then engaged in the behavior (Savage-Rumbaugh & Lewin, 1994).

Despite the fact that critics can offer nonintentional explanations for each of the above examples, Frans DeWaal (1991) argues that we should consider the total pattern of evidence, especially evidence that comes from different sources. On these grounds, the support for intentionality and planning in nonhuman animals is strong. However, some types of experimental evidence would provide even stronger support.

Self-Recognition

The studies of search image and object permanence suggest that animals develop cognitions related to objects and other animals. But do animals have some cognition of themselves as distinct from their environment or from other animals? In 1970 George Gallup published the results of a simple demonstration that suggested chimpanzees have some kind of cognition that gives them a functional self-recognition. Gallup presented chimpanzees with mirrors and observed their reactions. At first the chimpanzees responded to their reflections as if the reflections were other chimpanzees. After a few days, however, the chimpanzees looked in the mirrors at regions of their bodies that they could not see without a mirror and groomed these areas—suggesting that the chimpanzees had some type of self-recognition. A critical test was then carried out: The chimpanzees were experimentally anesthetized and painted on the forehead and ears with nonirritating dye. When the chimpanzees woke up and looked in a mirror, they rubbed the painted spots as if they were trying to remove the spots (Gallup, 1970).

Self-recognition, as defined by attempts to remove spots after observation of the face in a mirror, has been identified in orangutans as well as in chimpanzees. However, it does not seem to be present in gorillas. In some senses this finding is surprising, because gorillas and chimpanzees are more closely related than are orangutans and chimpanzees. In other words, if the cognitive ability associated with self-recognition evolved before the ancestral orangutans split off from the chimpanzee–gorilla lineage, we would expect gorillas to have self-recognition. A plausible explanation for this gorilla limitation is that the ancestors of gorillas had the cognitive ability but "lost" it as they became specialized in other ways, particularly in the development of quadrupedal locomotion (Povinelli, 1993).

When given the opportunity, chimpanzees also seem to use video monitors to "inspect" themselves. For example, the chimpanzees Austin and Sherman glanced at a closed-circuit television monitor over a period of time and then, each at a different time, suddenly seemed to recognize themselves. They then began bobbing up and down and made "funny faces." The two chimpanzees also used the monitor to glean information about parts of their bodies that could not be inspected visually. For example, Sherman and Austin seemed to inspect the residue of an orange drink in their throats with considerable interest (Savage-Rumbaugh, 1986).

As in the case of planning and intentionality, there are critics who remain unconvinced that "mirror-directed body inspection" truly indicates self-recognition (see Heyes, 1994). Nonetheless, if we look at the sum total of findings as suggested by de Waal, the evidence for self-recognition is strong. Whether or not one agrees with Heyes's skepticism, her arguments can be taken as a challenge to search for more evidence in carefully controlled experiments.

Theory of Mind

Theory of mind, a powerful concept in the study of human cognition that emerged in the 1990s, has a name that is somewhat confusing. The term *theory of mind* refers to an ability to infer states of knowledge, intentions, and feelings in another that are different from one's own. The fitness advantages of theory of mind for social animals are clear. For example, individual humans possessing theory of mind have empathy for others' feelings and understand that they can learn something from (or teach something to) another person. They can use theory of mind to enhance alliance formation and also to develop deceptive strategies.

Do nonhuman animals have theory of mind? As with the other complex cognitions discussed, there is controversy on this question. Daniel Povinelli and his associates investigated the possibility by having experimenters take turns playing the role of "knower" and "guesser" in front of chimpanzees, which were tested one at a time on a simple apparatus. The "knower" hid food in one of two cups. In contrast, the "guesser" left the room before the food was hidden and presumably

had no knowledge of the location of the food. Because of a screen that blocked their view, the chimpanzees could not see which of the two cups contained the food. After the "guesser" returned, the "guesser" and the "knower" simultaneously pointed to different cups. (Of course, the "knower" always pointed to the correct cup.) The chimpanzees were then tested to see which cup they chose—and in most cases they chose the correct one (Povinelli et al., 1990).

The interpretation of these studies is uncertain, however, because of the possibility that the results may be explained as a simple type of learning. For example, the chimpanzees may simply have learned not to pay attention to the experimenter who left the room. Therefore, these results must be considered inconclusive.

However, there is evidence from the types of communications between Kanzi and his human companions that some aspects of theory of mind exist in chimpanzees (see Savage-Rumbaugh & Lewin, 1994). Furthermore, it seems reasonable to argue that if chimpanzees have self-reconition, this is a first step toward developing theory of mind; without a concept of self, theory of mind is inconceivable. On the basis of the evidence at this point, a reasonable conclusion is that certain apes have the rudiments of theory of mind but that this ability is limited.

The Question of Consciousness

Even if nonhuman animals are capable of humanlike cognitions such as self-awareness and planning, this does not mean that nonhuman animals experience humanlike consciousness, or awareness of existence. However, starting in the late 1970s, Donald Griffin, the psychologist who pioneered research on echolocation in bats, argued that scientists should consider the possibility that nonhuman animals have conscious awareness (Griffin, 1981, 1992). Griffin cited the evidence supporting complex cognitions in animals; he also argued that it was reasonable to assume that consciousness evolved by natural selection and thus must have had some beginnings in the ancestors of humans that were similar to animals living today.

Griffin's arguments met with considerable resistance. Some critics argued that human consciousness may be **epiphenomenal;** that is, consciousness may simply accompany problem solving, not have a causal link in the process. If indeed consciousness is incidental or epiphenomenal, it need not have evolved via natural selection; consequently, we would not expect any precursors to consciousness in nonhuman animals.

From a scientific standpoint, the question of consciousness in itself is not a fruitful one—because, at this point in time, consciousness cannot be measured either quantitatively or qualitatively. Even in humans, who can report verbally on their mental experiences, it is impossible to know for certain if one person's experience of consciousness is comparable to another's. Furthermore, there is considerable evidence that people are easily deceived about their conscious motivations (see Azar, 1996).

In conclusion, it is not possible to investigate the conscious minds of nonhuman animals with the research tools we have at present. Nonetheless, Griffin has made a valuable contribution by suggesting that we should not reject out of hand the *possibility* that certain animals have consciousness.

◆ HUMAN EVOLUTION

There has been a general resistance to conceptualizing human cognition as having evolved from cognitive processes in nonhuman animals. Even though many people have accepted the likelihood that human structural characteristics such as feet had an evolutionary basis, the hypothesis that human cognitive processes also had an evolutionary basis has been slower to gain acceptance (see Cosmides & Tooby, 1995).

Rather clearly, the secondary cognitive abilities (such as mathematical ability and reading, discussed in Chapter 3) are highly dependent on human cultural factors, do not have analogues in nonhumans, and are not directly affected by natural selection (Geary, 1995). Nonetheless, many of the human primary cognitive abilities—such as concept formation, memory, perception, communication, and planning—may very well have evolved by natural selection.

We will now consider evidence for the presumed evolution of human cognitive abilities. We'll begin by comparing some of the primary cognitive abilities of nonhumans with those of humans. Then we will speculate on the evolution of human cognition in general.

NONHUMANS COMPARED TO HUMANS

When the cognitive abilities of nonhumans are compared with primary cognitive abilities in humans, some nonhuman animals fare surprisingly well. For example, certain primates and birds are capable of a level of concept formation that resembles that of human children. Similarly, birds and primates can make judgments of relative numerosity; as mentioned earlier, one chimpanzee made pointing gestures similar to those of children while counting (Boysen & Berntson, 1995).

The memory and perceptual abilities of many nonhuman animals also compare favorably with those of humans. Several species of nonhumans show evidence of memory systems such as expectancy, the serial position effect, and chunking that are similar to those seen in humans. Certain primates and birds also exhibit evidence of search image and perception of object permanence similar to that found in humans.

Apes, marine mammals, and some birds can learn and utilize the rudiments of communication via language. There is also some evidence of intentionality, short-term planning, self-recognition, and the rudiments of theory of mind in apes. Roughly, the nonlinguistic cognitive ability of an adult chimpanzee approximates that of a 2½-year-old child. When we consider primary cognitive abilities in general, the gulf between our closest living relatives and ourselves is apparently more quantative than qualitative— a conclusion that is consistent with the theory of natural selection.

A significant difference between humans and chimpanzees is related to the degree of development of theory of mind. Clearly, the sophisticated theory of mind in humans enables us to engage in much more complex cognitions. Human developmental studies indicate that children normally acquire theory of mind starting between 2 and 3 years of age: At this time children begin to realize that people's feelings and thoughts differ, even when people are reacting to the same situation. Later, between ages 3 and 4, theory of mind becomes more sophisticated, and individuals understand that two people can reach different conclusions based on the same evidence (Basic Behavioral Science Task Force, 1996).

Children develop theory of mind relatively late, even after concept formation, counting ability, and language development have begun. Interestingly, autistic children develop some aspects of language and concept formation but do not develop theory of mind (Leslie, 1991). These findings suggest that theory of mind is an especially advanced cognitive function, even more advanced than some aspects of language. Such conclusions are consistent with the findings that chimpanzees and bonobos are limited in their development of theory of mind.

Scientists have also observed that humans lose empathy and sensitivity to other people's feelings under conditions of stress. The highest-level, most recently evolved cognitive abilities are among the first to be lost in response to stress; so these observations lend further support to the argument that theory of mind is a highly advanced cognitive ability.

THE EVOLUTION OF HUMAN COGNITION

Although the difference between the cognitive ability of humans and that of our closest relative, the chimpanzee, is not great in some respects, it is vast in regard to theory of mind and language ability. However, the development of this difference took place in a relatively short period of time from an evolutionary perspective. As I have mentioned, chimpanzees and humans had a common ancestor approximately 6 million years ago. A reasonable assumption is that our ancestors started out about 6 million years ago with a cognitive ability similar to that of a modern chimpanzee. That is, the differences that we now see between chimpanzees and humans probably resulted much more from increases in hominid cognitive ability than from decreases in the ability of chimpanzees as they evolved.

Although we cannot directly know the cognitive ability of any of our early ancestors, we can make reasonable assumptions about their ability by analyzing their artifacts and the size of their skulls, some of which are fairly well preserved. We have found fossils of hominids that date back more than 2 million years. The skulls of these hominids are not significantly larger than those of chimpanzees, suggesting that relatively little change in cognitive ability took place in the first two thirds of hominid evolution.

The earliest truly human (*Homo sapiens*) fossil dates back about 200,000 years. The skull suggests that the brain size was 1,600 cc, the same as that of humans today. Thus, in around 2 million years, our brains almost tripled in size—an amazing increase in such a relatively short period of time.

What accounts for such a rapid evolution? An earlier theory was that rapid evolution took place following the use of tools. However, there is evidence that early hominids used tools for more than a million years without producing a significant increase in brain size.

A more reasonable theory is that the development of complex social strategies drove the evolution of human cognitive ability. Once our ancestors developed a theory of mind, there would have been especially great advantages to more and more cognitive development. It was possible to gain fitness by doing such things as making complex alliances; sharing relevent information; and, of course, developing methods of deceit in competition with other humans.

The evolution of theory of mind meant that there would be a great advantage to sharing information with others. (There is much more to share when you can make the assumption that other people have information and feelings different from yours.) Consequently, the development of language would have especially great value. It seems likely that the evolution of language went hand in hand with the evolution of a complex theory of mind.

It also seems likely that the evolution of theory of mind facilitated the development of sophisticated concepts of the future and the past. No only could people assume that other people had different information; they could also understand that they themselves were different in the past and would be different in the future. Such cognitions could then give rise to religious and moral concepts.

◆ CHANGING PERSPECTIVES

PAST	PRESENT	FUTURE
Nonhuman animals are incapable of any type of cognition (nineteenth century, pre-Darwin).	Many nonhuman animals engage in simple cognitions that facilitate their survival and reproduction. Some animals appear to exhibit complex cognitions or at least the rudiments of such cognitions.	How well developed are the complex cognitions of birds and nonhuman mammals? How do these cognitions compare to those of humans?

SUMMARY

Certain birds and mammals are able to classify objects into functional categories (form object concepts) and extract general principles (develop abstract concepts). Concept formation has fitness benefits in that it enables animals to solve problems that are different in some way from problems encountered in the past.

Experiments with artificial language-learning systems suggest a rudimentary language-learning ability in certain apes, marine mammals, and parrots. Animals learn the receptive aspects of language before the expressive aspects. However, these animals do not develop language on their own, and their ability to learn syntax is very limited.

Similarly, certain birds and mammals develop a rudimentary concept of numerosity and can make judgments of "more" and "less." Nonhuman animals are limited in their quantitative ability, however.

Memory in animals has been tested in laboratory and in quasi-naturalistic settings. Cognitive processes, such as expectancy and the serial position effect, facilitate memory. Some types of memory, such as those exhibited by rats and food-caching birds, are highly specific.

Two types of perceptual processes—search image and awareness of object permanence—have been experimentally demonstrated in animals. These processes facili-

tate several functional behaviors, especially foraging.

Although research findings are somewhat controversial, there is evidence of complex cognitions such as intentionality and planning, self-recognition, and the rudiments of theory of mind in certain animals, especially apes. The question of consciousness in nonhuman animals cannot be answered by means of the scientific methods available at this time. However, the possibility of consciousness in nonhuman animals should not be ruled out.

When certain nonhumans are compared to humans in regard to primary cognitive abilities, these nonhumans fare surprisingly well, suggesting that the cognitive gulf between nonhumans and humans is more quantitative than qualitative. Many of the differences between humans and apes are related to the high degree of development of theory of mind in humans.

KEY TERMS

abstract concepts, p. 101
chunk, p. 112
Clever Hans phenomenon, p. 103
concept formation, p. 100
delayed matching-to-sample paradigm, p. 109
epiphenomenal, p. 117
expectancy, p. 111

intrinsic reinforcement, p. 107
object concepts, p. 100
object permanence, p. 114
search image, p. 113
serial position effect, p. 111
theory of mind, p. 116
trace theory of memory, p. 110

CHAPTER 6

FEEDING

◆ *Why do some animals move and feed in groups?*

◆ *Do animals choose food that is maximally nutritious?*

In response to the need for food, animals have evolved complex mechanisms that facilitate the location, capture, preparation, consumption, and digestion of food. Foragers have also evolved effective means of competing with other animals for limited supplies of food and strategies for feeding with maximum efficiency. Not only are adaptations for feeding interesting in themselves, but these adaptations have influenced the evolution of many other behavioral and cognitive systems. Thus, an understanding of feeding patterns is basic to an appreciation of the evolution of sociality and intelligence.

6

This chapter will begin by looking at how animals maximize the location and consumption of food. Then we will consider several types of competition in the quest for food. The third section will discuss a large variety of adaptations associated with feeding. Finally, we'll explore the relationship of feeding to human evolution.

MAXIMIZING FORAGING OPPORTUNITIES

Because fitness involves more than simply obtaining enough food, there are clear advantages to balancing the need for food with other, fitness-related needs. The optimal foraging theory, as suggested in Chapter 1, assumes that animals are naturally selected to forage efficiently and, as a result, are able to invest time and energy in other fitness-related strategies as well. As we shall see, there is support for the assumption of efficiency in several respects.

Finding the Optimal Place to Forage

When food is evenly and widely distributed, animals have little trouble finding it. When food is patchily distributed, however, animals must develop ways of locating and identifying the richest patches. Researchers tested a small

Eurasian bird known as the great tit in simulated food patches differing in density in order to discover the strategies the birds used. The researchers found that the birds spent the first few minutes searching randomly through several patches, a behavior known as the **sampling phase** of foraging. Subsequently, in what is called the **exploitation phase,** the birds spent most of their time foraging in the richest patch (Smith & Sweatman, 1974). Apparently the birds gained information regarding the density of food during the sampling phase and then decided where to spend the majority of their time.

In natural situations, however, food density is often in a state of flux. Consequently, it may be beneficial for an animal to sample food availability periodically in order to keep up with current conditions. In fact, fish occasionally choose smaller or less preferred prey even when optimal prey is available. This con-

TABLE 6.1 ◆ A Two-Phase Strategy for Feeding on Patchily Distributed Food

	Sampling Phase	Exploitation Phase
Behavior	Animal searches randomly through several patches.	Animal forages in richest patch.
Result	Animal obtains information about quality of patch.	Animal maximizes cost–benefit ratio.

tinuous updating of feeding conditions enables bluegills, for example, to make optimal decisions about when to give up on one feeding patch and move to another (Wildhaber et al., 1994).

Deciding When to Leave a Food Patch

In most instances, continued feeding from a patch depletes the food supply. At some point, an animal will do better to leave the patch than to continue feeding in the same area. At what point should an animal leave? In an attempt to find out how animals answer this question, E. L. Charnov (1976) developed the **marginal value theorem.** This theorem predicts that an animal will leave a food patch at the point when the net energy (calorie) intake drops to the level that approximates the average level for the habitat as a whole. In other words, it is best to stay until the food source is no better than the average of other sources.

Various predators as well as nonpredators that feed on patchily distributed food exhibit behavior that supports the marginal value theorem (see Davey, 1989).

But how do animals decide when to leave a patch? One simple explanation has to do with the **area-restricted search hypothesis.** Whenever an animal (a fish, for example) encounters food, it either decreases its speed of locomotion during the search or turns more sharply. Both of these response tendencies keep an animal in the same general area as long as the food source is rich (Thomas, 1974); conversely, when the food thins out, the animal moves faster and travels straighter.

Some foraging behavior, especially that of birds and mammals, cannot be completely explained by the area-restricted search hypothesis. For example, studies of starlings in semi-natural conditions indicate that these birds take into account the amount of time they will need to travel between food sources. The birds spend more time exploiting a patch when the travel time is long than when it is short. In this case, it appears that the optimal response requires some sort of learning and memory of travel time and an ability to integrate this information with information about the patch density.

Taking Risk of Predation into Account

To maximize their fitness while foraging, animals must do more than forage efficiently. In many cases animals are vulnerable to predation when they are eating, so they must balance nutritional considerations with the probability of meeting a predator.

Many animals feed in sheltered areas or leave the sheltered areas for only short bouts of feeding, during which they are especially vigilant. However, there is a trade-off; too much vigilance can drastically reduce feeding efficiency. Gray squirrels show a reasonable response to this trade-off by consuming small food items rapidly on the spot but carrying larger items, which take longer to eat, to a safe area (Lima, 1985).

Some animals take historical information into account. For example, if a rabbitlike animal known as a collared pika has had a recent encounter with a predator, it shows more cautious foraging behavior than if it has gone some time without running into a predator (Holmes, 1991).

Animals whose food is located in open areas where there is a high risk of predation may benefit from **central-place foraging**—taking food to an area from which there are several escape routes. Central-place foraging has been investigated extensively in rats, partly because it is relatively easy to test these animals in a laboratory situation that simulates a natural environment. Investigators use a radial maze similar to that depicted in Figure 5.3 in Chapter 5. The central area is "safest," because there are presumably escape routes available in each of the arms. In contrast, the arms, which lead to dead ends, are risky areas. Consistent with the behavior of gray squirrels, rats in the radial maze carry large pieces of food to the central area before consuming them, but eat smaller items when in the arms of the maze. The smaller items consumed in the risky areas are also eaten more rapidly than the items consumed in the safe area (Phelps & Roberts, 1989). When experimenters made travel more difficult by placing barriers at the arm entrances, rats in the maze began to carry several food items in one trip. One rat, in fact, filled its mouth with three food items and pushed a fourth item to the central area with its paws (Ash & Roberts, 1992).

In conclusion, it seems that animals at relatively high risk of being preyed upon take many factors into account in making decisions about eating in risky areas: the history of predation in the areas, the size of the food, how fast they can eat, and how much energy it would take to move the food.

COMPETITION

Because there is a limited amount of organic material that can function as food, a great deal of food competition exists. This competition takes place among members of the same species and, in many cases, among members of different species.

Intraspecies Competition

Individuals of the same species usually feed on the same type of food in much the same way. Consequently, there is considerable intraspecies (within-species) competition, which sometimes results in aggression. If there is a plethora of food, of course, aggression is minimal; why should animals put out the energy to fight when there is nothing to gain by winning? Similarly, grazing animals that live on food that is widely and evenly distributed are unlikely to engage in aggressive encounters related to food.

In contrast, animals that live on patchily distributed food are more likely to have aggressive encounters. As Chapter 13 will explain in more detail, the tendency to aggress often leads to the establishment of social hierarchies and territoriality. Once established, these systems reduce the expression of aggression between members of a group.

A different inhibition of aggression is related to **mutualism**—cooperation or coordination in the quest for food that directly benefits two or more members of a species. One type of mutualism is found when a group of animals is more efficient in locating patchily distributed food than are solitary ones. For example, flocks of birds are able to locate most types of food more quickly than individuals (Baird et al., 1991). Ravens, which feed on carcasses of large mammals during the harsh winter months in the northwestern United States, form roosts of many individual birds. Within these congregations the ravens exhibit behaviors that function to communicate the location of food sources. Although the food sources are rich, they are widely scattered, and individual birds would have difficulty locating them without this form of communication (Marzluff et al., 1996).

Another type of mutualism is seen when the coordinated effort of several hunters is capable of disrupting the prey's defenses. Thus, Eurasian black-headed gulls preying on fish are more successful when the birds are in a group than when they hunt singly, because fish attempting to escape from one gull often swim in the direction of another gull. Observations under controlled conditions indicate that gulls hunting in groups of two to six catch proportionally more fish than gulls hunting alone (Gotmark et al., 1986).

Still another type of mutualism occurs when cooperating members of a group can prey on larger animals than can individual members (Baird et al., 1991). For example,

groups of lionesses (Figure 6.1) may successfully hunt giraffes and buffalo, prey that are generally inaccessible to individual hunters (Schaller, 1972). In many cases, this group advantage is related to cooperation in the kill. Some lionesses have the role of circling the prey while others wait in tall grass. The roles of individual lionesses tend to be quite stable, suggesting that individuals become specialists for a particular role (Stander, 1992).

Because lions hunting in groups of two have a relatively high success rate, duos have the highest rate of potential food intake per individual (Schaller, 1972). Groups of lions larger than two may hunt together, however, despite the fact that with more than two lions, the rate of individual food capture diminishes. There may be a different type of benefit for a large group. Two lions may not be able to consume a whole carcass at one sitting; the remainder will be lost to scavengers. And if members of the lion group are related—as they frequently are—there will be indirect fitness value in providing food for relatives rather than for unrelated scavengers (Packer, 1986).

Cooperation and inhibition of fighting may also result from a type of reciprocity in the quest for food—one animal helping and the other animal returning the favor at a later time. Although favors are often returned, in many groups some individuals are highly cooperative while other individuals are scroungers—taking more than they give. Recent research indicates that even scroungers may make a contribution, however. Scroungers tend to be especially watchful for the approach of disapproving cooperators, so scroungers are also vigilant for the approach of predators—and therefore function as effective sentinels (Ranta et al., 1995).

FIGURE 6.1 ◆ **An illustration of the principle of mutualism.** By cooperating, a group of lionesses can prey on larger animals than can any one individual. The group can also effectively protect the carcass from scavengers.

Interspecies Competition

As we have just seen, there are numerous reasons why individuals of the same species may behave cooperatively while inhibiting aggressive competition over food. However, few if any of these factors are involved when interspecies competition—competition between members of different species—is involved. Elimination of competition from a different species virtually always increases fitness. Therefore, extreme conflicts develop when two species of animals compete for the same type of food at the same time; and eventually one species wins out. Such conflicts result in what is known as the **niche rule:** No two species can exist in the same locale and utilize the same resources at the same time. The unsuccessful competitor will either be driven to extinction or be forced to modify its feeding pattern.

Modification is the more common occurrence. An animal may switch to a different type of food, feed at a different time of the day (or night), or forage in a slightly different area. In essence, the competition promotes extreme variability in food choice and feeding patterns (Overmann, 1980). The results of a study of two closely related species of insect-eating warblers in New England illustrate how competition affects feeding. One species feeds near the top of the trees, while the other consumes insects on lower branches. These warblers have also developed specialized types of flight movements that facilitate feeding in their respective niches (MacArthur, 1958).

The competition displayed by the warblers, then, has led not only to different food preferences but to the evolution of different patterns of flight—probably made possible by structural (skeletal and muscular) adaptations. For many evolutionary patterns, it seems, competition leads to selection for divergent feeding behaviors, and the changes in feeding behavior influence structural adaptation. Thus, in many cases, behavioral evolution may precede and drive structural evolution (Wilson, 1975).

Two species of rodents, kangaroo rats and pocket mice, forage for exactly the same type of seeds at the same time in desert areas of the Americas. This similarity in feeding patterns may appear at first glance to be inconsistent with the niche rule. Careful observation indicates, however, that the two rodents have slightly different modes of foraging. The kangaroo rats feed in more open areas, while the pocket mice stay closer to shelter. This difference is apparently related to danger of predation. The kangaroo rats run faster and thus are less threatened by predators, so they can forage for clusters of seeds in the open desert, ignoring isolated seeds. Pocket mice, however, are more restricted in their range and pick up every seed they run across (Reichman, 1979). The fact that the two types of rodents move around and forage in slightly different ways minimizes competition and allows them to coexist.

ADAPTATIONS FOR FEEDING

Not only are animals in a continual state of competition with other animals for food; the plants and animals that serve as food change over time, and the environment is in a constant state of flux. Therefore, it is not surprising that animals have developed great diversity in the types of food they eat and the methods they use to obtain food. We will now consider some of the adaptations of the three major types of feeders—predators, herbivores, and omnivores.

Predators

Predators, obviously, have a negative effect on the individual animals they consume. Prey animals, in response, have evolved defenses against being consumed. Predators have then countered by developing more sophisticated predatory strategies. In essence, there is an **evolutionary arms race**—predators respond to their prey's strategies by adjusting and going one step farther, and the prey then compensates in the same general way. As a result, both groups evolve at a relatively fast rate. Put another way, the more effective the predator becomes, the more evolutionary pressure is placed on the prey animal to develop improved forms of defense. Conversely, the better the defense, the greater the evolutionary pressure on the predator to develop more effective predatory techniques.

The cost of failure, however, is clearly greater for the prey animal than for the predator. When a predator fails to catch its prey, the predator loses only its dinner. But when a prey animal fails in its attempt to escape, it loses its life. This asymmetry of costs is known as the **life/dinner principle** (Dawkins & Krebs, 1979). The life/dinner principle brings greater evolutionary pressure to bear on prey animals than on predators. With this strong evolutionary pressure, prey animals tend to evolve at a faster rate and generally to keep a step ahead of the predators. The life/dinner principle helps to explain why, under natural conditions, animals seldom drive their prey to extinction. We will consider the relationship between predators and prey again in Chapter 7 when we look at defensive adaptations.

The Motivation for Predation

Traditionally, animal behaviorists assumed that a predator's motivation to hunt was directly regulated by hunger. The relationship between hunger and predation is not as simple as it once appeared, however. In the first place, predators do not always eat animals they have just killed, and they may kill more prey than they consume. Second, predators will continue their predatory habits even when they are not allowed to eat their prey and are fed (by experimenters or by pet owners) from other sources. Finally, scientists have learned that different areas in the brain control eating and predation.

Fortunately (from the predator's standpoint), food deprivation and hunting become associated with each other as the result of classical conditioning. Consequently, predators living in a natural environment are typically in a position to learn to hunt for food. Also, in many mammalian predators, including cats, the mother is actively involved in her young's learning to hunt (see Bradshaw, 1992). We will examine the mother's role in this type of learning in more detail in Chapter 11.

Chasing Down Prey

Endotherms (warm-blooded animals) are particularly well adapted to chasing down their prey. For example, where chasing is concerned, endotherms such as wolves have an advantage over ectothermic (cold-blooded) crocodiles of the same approximate size, in that wolves can be active and maintain high levels of energy output over relatively long periods of time. In contrast, the crocodile is restricted to short bursts of activity. Consequently, large predatory endotherms often chase down their prey, whereas comparably sized ectotherm predators invariably sit and wait for their victims.

If prey animals are grouped together, a predator usually attempts to isolate an indi-

TABLE 6.2 ◆ Life/Dinner Principle

	Predator	Prey
Effect of Failure	Loss of meal	Loss of life
Natural Selection	Slow	Rapid
Result	Slow evolutionary adjustment to changes in prey	Rapid evolutionary adjustment to changes in predators

vidual. For example, an African cheetah will pick out an individual in a herd of antelope and concentrate its efforts on this individual, ignoring other antelope that may even be physically closer. This concentration on one individual may, in part, be an adjustment to the cheetah's particular abilities: A cheetah can run faster than an antelope but cannot sustain an output of energy for as long a period as an antelope.

Sit-and-Wait Strategies

There are many animals that, like crocodiles, lie in wait and ambush their prey. The strategy of ambushing prey may be facilitated by a mechanism that makes a predator difficult to detect. For example, **aggressive mimicry** allows the predator to resemble an inanimate object or another animal. Such mimicry, like a disguise or camouflage, enables the predator to get close to potential prey. The dung spider *Phrynarachne decipiens* of Malaysia places itself on white webbing on a leaf in such a way as to resemble a bird dropping. Another type of spider, *Cosmophasis,* is an ant mimic—it not only looks like an ant but walks like one, holding its two front legs in the air like antennae. This mimicry lets the spider ambush its prey and also affords some protection from the local East African insectivorous birds, which tend to avoid feeding on ants.

Still another spider, the trap-door spider, constructs a type of hideaway from which it can spring on its prey. After digging out a burrow, the spider builds a trap door of silk and hinges the door at the entrance of the burrow. The spider then stretches strands of silk along the surface of the ground, radiating out from the entrance of the burrow, and holds one of the strands with a leg. When a prey animal in-advertently displaces one of the strands, the predator responds by throwing open the door and seizing the intruder.

Using Lures

In some cases, sit-and-wait predators lure victims to their demise. The assassin bug, *Solenopsis geminata,* attacks a fire ant and sucks out the inner parts of its victim. It then places the shriveled body of its victim on its back. When other fire ants approach to inspect their dead nest mate, the assassin bug attacks them and adds their bodies to the increasing pile of corpses.

The bolas spider also lures its victims, but the attractant is chemical. The spider produces a scent that mimics the sex attractant of certain moths. The spider then fashions a sticky globule or bolas, soaks the bolas in the chemical attractant, and swings the bolas from a strand of silk. (The globule is named after a human weapon called a bola or bolas—a cord with rocks or iron balls at its ends.) Moths are attracted to the lure by the scent, then stick to the bolas, and the spider eats its prey at leisure.

Another type of sexual attractant is used by the female of the firefly genus *Photuris* to lure males of a related species. The attractant is a bioluminescent display—a pattern of flashing—that mimics one used by females of the related species. Thus, when the males approach the source of their natural sex attractant, they are met and eaten by a predatory female of the cousin species (Lloyd, 1975).

A major reason for the effectiveness of sexual attractants as lures is that animals are unable to evolve an ability to ignore these attractants. That is, animals that might have a

◆ UNUSUAL ADAPTATIONS

Catching Prey

At one time most people believed that only humans used tools. But if we define tools as objects found in the environment that are manipulated by an animal and result in the attainment of a goal, tool use occurs in several animals, including the ant lion. The ant lion—a larval insect in the family Myrmeleontidae—digs a funnel in loose sand and then waits at the bottom of the funnel for an ant to enter the trap. Once an ant starts to fall into the funnel, the ant lion tosses sand up from the base of its funnel, thwarting an escape. The predator then seizes and consumes its victim (Figure 6.2).

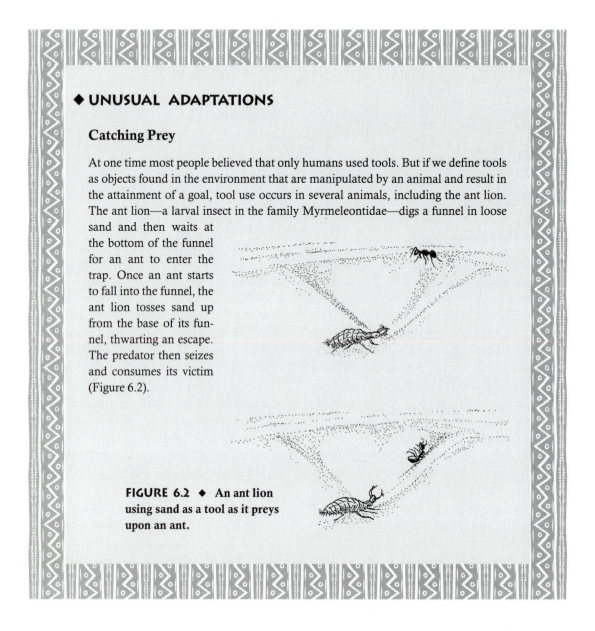

FIGURE 6.2 ◆ **An ant lion using sand as a tool as it preys upon an ant.**

genetic predisposition to ignore the attractants do not reproduce and, consequently, do not pass on the tendency to ignore the attractant. Humans have taken advantage of this sexual lure principle in developing certain pest-control strategies. For example, we can broadcast sexual lures of particular insects and then electrocute the insects when they approach the artificial source of the lures and the accompanying electrical apparatus.

In other words, the ant lion uses sand as a "tool." How could such an unusual predatory method have evolved? An analysis of the head-tossing movements the ant lion makes while digging its funnel provides clues about the origins of the natural selection process related to throwing sand at ants. Ant lion individuals that threw sand with unusual intensity—and incidentally struck some ants—would have had a selective advantage in catching prey. Consequently, a selection process would have favored the intense pattern of sand throwing (Alcock, 1972).

Another unusual use of a tool is seen in a small Asian freshwater fish known as the archerfish. The archerfish spits droplets at insects sitting on vegetation extending over the water. After a hit, the victim falls into the water and is immediately seized and eaten. The high degree of accuracy of the archerfish—which almost always makes direct hits on insects at distances up to 1.5 meters (5 feet)—is related to the structure of the fish's mouth. The roof of the mouth is grooved in such a way that when the tongue is pressed against it, a barrel is created through which the droplets of water can be propelled. (I have seen an archerfish in an aquarium that was able to put out observers' cigarettes with droplets of water.)

As in the case of the ant lion, an analysis of some of the subtle structures and behaviors of archerfish provides fairly substantial clues related to the evolution of this behavior. Archerfish are preadapted for spitting droplets of water because, during a phase of the respiratory cycle, they force water out through their mouth while their gill is closed. Perhaps, while feeding at the surface, an individual archerfish that had an unusually intense gill closure once inadvertently squirted an insect with water. This may have marked the beginning of a selection process that favored intense gill closing in the proximity of insects (Vierke, 1973).

Cannibalism

Predatory animals do not usually eat members of their own species. Some members of the same species, especially those that are living in the same area, are close relatives—so cannibalism would result in the loss of indirect fitness (Elgar & Crespi, 1992). Furthermore, scientists theorize that parasites specific to a particular species could be transferred from the victim to the cannibal as the result of cannibalism. Some support for this parasite transfer hypothesis comes from the finding that cannibalistic tiger salamander larvae are more likely to die from parasite infestation than are noncannibalistic larvae (Pfennig et al., 1991).

Nonetheless, as the above example indicates, cannibalism does occur in a few animals. Research evidence suggests that these animals are somewhat sensitive to the cost–benefit ratio associated with cannibalism. For example, larval marbled salamanders sometimes cannibalize siblings that are much smaller than themselves. Because these runts have a very poor chance of survival, there is little if any loss of indirect fitness (Walls & Blaustein, 1995).

A different type of cannibalism occurs in animals that sometimes eat the eggs of a conspecific—as in the case of the three-spined stickleback female. Sticklebacks are small fish, and it is the male sticklebacks that normally tend the eggs. In this case, the cannibalism seems to be an adaptation for bringing a potentially fit male back into breeding condition; after eating the eggs, the cannibalistic female then attempts to breed with the male (FitzGerald, 1993). But as we will see in Chapter 11 when we discuss parental behavior, this type of cannibalism is limited, because the male will try to protect the eggs.

Still another type of cannibalism, known as **sexual cannibalism,** is seen in certain spiders and in praying mantises: The female may eat the smaller male after mating, a strategy that provides food for the female but is obviously costly for the male. In response to this predatory possibility, male *Metellina segmentata* spiders have developed a strategy that reduces the possibility of their being eaten. The males typically wait until after the female has captured a fly and begun to bite it before they begin their courtship. An experimental study under field conditions indicates that such a strategy is indeed effective—at least most of the time (Prenter et al., 1994).

Herbivores

In contrast to predators, which have evolved specializations primarily related to the capture of prey animals, herbivores (plant eaters) are specialized for finding, digesting, and in some cases storing plant material. In addition, most herbivores have evolved mechanisms that protect them from predators when they are in the vulnerable position of eating. We will now look at some of these specializations.

Feeding on Grains and Seeds

A major benefit of feeding on grains and seeds is that these items have high food value; that is, they are high in nutrients in relation to their weight. Furthermore, grains and seeds can be stored with only limited spoilage, especially when kept in cool, dry places. A disadvantage faced by granivores (animals that eat grains and seeds), however, is that grains and seeds appear only during relatively short seasons of the year, and stored hoards or caches are vulnerable to thievery. In response to these disadvantages, many granivores have evolved complex strategies related to hiding and retrieving caches of food.

Chickadees in New England, for example, hoard seeds and are able to retrieve seeds hidden as long as 28 days previously with a high degree of accuracy (Hitchcock & Sherry, 1990). The Clark's nutcrackers of the Rocky

Mountain region hoard for even longer periods. These birds normally bury pine seeds in the fall and retrieve them during the winter and spring. Not only are they able to retrieve their seeds long after they have buried them, but they retrieve most of them by poking their heads through a thick snow cover (Balda, 1980).

There are two general hoarding strategies. **Scatter hoarding,** which is practiced by most hoarding birds, involves the wide spacing of caches. Because food thieves are likely to spend time searching in an area where they have just located a cache, this is an effective strategy. The disadvantage of scatter hoarding, however, is that caches are more difficult for the hoarder to retrieve. The second strategy is known as **larder hoarding**—placing all of the food in one site or in several closely placed sites. Mammals that are capable of defending their caches, such as chipmunks and squirrels, tend to be larder hoarders.

Cache thieves are generally more likely to find food if they have observed an animal in the process of hoarding. Consequently, animals are often secretive when hoarding food (Powlesland, 1980). Jays take a further precaution; if there are cache robbers in the immediate vicinity, the jays will sometimes retrieve and recache food items (Tomback, 1978). However, birds sometimes cache food in the presence of conspecifics if all the birds are engaged in caching behavior. It may be that danger of robbery is reduced when the other birds are preoccupied with their own caching activity (Kallander, 1978).

In temperate zones, hoarding animals are most likely to hide their food in the fall. What is the cue that sets off the tendency to hoard? Research findings suggest that there are several important cues, including falling body weight (Lucas, 1994), unpredictable supplies of food (Hurly, 1992), and changes in length of daylight (Shettleworth et al., 1995). Sensitivity to several types of cues enables animals to respond to a variety of predictors of future food shortage.

Grazing

In contrast to granivores, grazers (animals that feed on grasses) must take in a very large quantity of food in order to extract relatively sparse nutritive substances from a mass of indigestible vegetable material. Consequently, grass eaters spend a large portion of the day grazing.

In most cases, grasses are consumed on the spot. However, pikas—small rabbitlike mammals found in western North America—engage in a considerable amount of food preparation. Pikas pile up green vegetation near their burrows and then, as they add fresh vegetation to the pile each day, turn the material to assist in the drying process. During rains or snowstorms the pikas often protect the pile by placing it under an overhanging rock.

Grazers have typically evolved highly specialized digestive processes. For example, rabbits run certain vegetation through their digestive system twice. The first time, the rabbits take soft fecal pellets from their anus and consume them whole. The second time through the digestive system, hard pellets are produced but ignored by the rabbits.

Ungulates (hoofed animals) such as antelope and cattle also digest food in stages. However, ungulates have a highly specialized structure known as a **rumen** that greatly facilitates the breakdown of cellulose found in leaves and grasses. The rumen is a large chamber located between the esophagus and the stomach. It has several functions: It operates as a holding tank during predigestion, keeps the partially digested material close to the mouth so that it can be regurgitated and chewed (as the cud), and serves as a fermentation vat where microorganisms break down the cellulose. In addition, water is extracted from the vegetation in the rumen.

In African ungulates the pattern of grazing is closely related to the adult animal's size. For example, the small duiker lives in thick underbrush and eats leaves and berries; the moderate-sized impala is found at the forest's edge and consumes both shrub foliage and grass; and the large wildebeest dwells in the open savanna and feeds exclusively on grass. It seems that as ungulates became larger and their rumens more efficient, they were able to move out into the arid open plains and take advantage of extremely plentiful supplies of grass. This change of habitat became possible partly because the animals were large enough to face the increased danger of predation in

TABLE 6.3 ◆ Relationships among Size, Habitat, and Feeding Habits in Three African Ungulates

Size	Habitat	Food
Small (e.g., duiker)	Thick vegetation	Leaves and berries
Medium (e.g., impala)	Forest edge	Shrubs and grass
Large (e.g., wildebeest)	Open plains	Grass

open areas. Furthermore, their highly efficient rumens were able to extract water from the grasses and digest the relatively low-quality vegetation (Jarman, 1974).

Leaf-Eating Compared to Fruit-Eating Primates

Approximately 55 million years ago, after angiosperm forest spread across the surface of the earth, some small, insect-eating mammals resembling present-day tree shrews began to climb into the trees, presumably in search of insects that fed on pollen. The descendants of these animals began to feed on abundant plant parts in the forest canopy and gave rise to the great order of primates.

It seems that among primates two general evolutionary trends took place in regard to feeding. One trend involved adaptations for digesting leaves—which, like grasses, are widely available but relatively low in energy and nutrients. Howler monkeys are representative of leaf-eating specialists and have a digestive system specialized for the consumption of leaves.

The other trend, seen in spider monkeys, is toward greater behavioral adaptability. Spider monkeys search for ripe fruits and other vegetation that is available only in patches. Consequently, there is a selective advantage to cognitive abilities that help the spider monkeys remember the location of widely separated patches of fruit and anticipate when the fruit will ripen.

A comparison of the brain size of howler and spider monkeys, which have roughly the same body size, indicates that the spider monkeys have significantly larger brains. Apparently the feeding pattern of primates has an effect on the evolution of the brain, especially on the evolution of parts of the brain that are related to cognition (Milton, 1993).

The type of food an animal consumes, then, may have a strong effect on the evolution of both the animal's social system and its general cognitive ability. This generalization seems to hold for animals as diverse as food-caching birds, ungulates—and primates. Challenges associated with finding food are significant in the evolution of the relatively large brain and well-developed cognitive ability of certain primates, especially those of the ancestors of humans.

Omnivores

Omnivores, or animals that feed on a combination of both vegetable and animal material, are usually feeding **generalists**—they eat a wide variety of foods. An extreme generalist such as the ruffed grouse of North America may eat more than 300 kinds of plants and 100 varieties of insects (Edminster, 1947).

The feeding structures of generalists are less specialized than those of animals that eat only one type or a few types of food. For example, beaks of omnivorous birds are medium in size and shape as opposed to being unusually long, sharp, or curved. In a similar way, omnivorous mammals have a variety of teeth, including canines, molars, and premolars. Specialists, in contrast, typically have only one type of tooth, a type that is adapted to handle one particular type of food.

Ecological Plasticity

In unstable environments, feeding generalists such as rats tend to survive better than specialized feeders. This survival advantage is related to generalists' ability to shift from one type of food to another when there are fluctuations in food availability. In contrast, specialists such as Australian koalas, which feed exclusively on certain eucalyptus leaves and shoots, are typically found only in stable environments. Any significant change in the environment could result in a loss of their food source; consequently, specialists are relatively unlikely to survive in unstable environments. Arctic areas such as Alaska contain a relatively large number of feeding generalists, while specialists tend to be found in tropical regions with their more stable weather conditions.

The ability of generalists to adapt to changing food supplies and to a variety of habitats is known as **ecological plasticity.** This adaptability allows generalists to quickly utilize new resources when they become available. Plasticity is related not only to an ability to eat many different kinds of foods but also to an openness to new foods and surroundings.

To develop this openness, animals must overcome neophobia. (As you may remember from Chapter 4, neophobia is a general fear of new and unfamiliar objects.) Generalists have apparently evolved a tendency to overcome neophobia relatively quickly. For example, systematic observations of birds feeding in the wild and also under laboratory conditions indicate that generalist species show less neophobia than specialists (Greenberg, 1989, 1990).

Consistent with this lack of neophobia, generalist species tend to have **neophilia,** or an attraction to novel objects. For example, ravens are attracted to shiny objects that are never or only rarely seen in their natural environment. Laboratory experiments indicate that when given a choice of objects, juvenile ravens almost always choose objects they have not seen before. This curiosity apparently facilitates the identification of new food sources—a payoff that is particularly great for ravens, because these birds live in a great variety of habitats with many types of feeding opportunities (Heinrich, 1995).

Of course there is a trade-off. A complete lack of neophobia exposes animals to the risk of poisoning by toxic substances. Consequently, ground-dwelling primates, like all feeding generalists, must balance a tendency to sample new foods with a caution against subjecting themselves to toxic substances (Milton, 1993). Similarly, unrestricted neophilia can lead to a considerable waste of time. Thus, ravens fail to respond to shiny, novel objects if, after a period of time, the objects are not associated with reinforcement such as food (Heinrich, 1995).

Recent research with capuchin monkeys indicates that these animals make an optimal response by showing more of a tendency to overcome neophobia and sample new food in the presence of conspecifics than when they are alone (Visalberghi & Fragaszy, 1995). When other animals are eating the same food, there is an opportunity to observe the possibility that others are becoming ill. As Chapter 4 pointed out, observational learning in social settings is very important for providing information about food in feeding generalists.

When a novel food is found to be acceptable, there is an advantage to behavior that increases an animal's chances of finding that food again. Ground-dwelling Japanese macaque monkeys, which are also feeding generalists, alter their search patterns after an experimenter has introduced chocolate and nonnative bananas to their habitat. We saw in Chapter 4 that some animals can form search images, and it seems reasonable to assume

that the monkeys begin a search for the new food after they have found it enjoyable and nontoxic (Menzel, 1991).

Choosing a Balanced Diet

In addition to running a high risk of poisoning, generalists incur the risk of feeding on an unbalanced diet. In response to this possibility, generalists have evolved **nutritional wisdom**—the tendency to choose a well-balanced diet when different types of food are available. In a classic study, rats in a laboratory setting were given a wide choice of foods and were found to choose a reasonably well-balanced diet (Richter, 1943).

Nutritional wisdom in rats is related to the fact that when the animals are deprived of a specific type of nutrient, such as salt, they develop a preference for food that contains that nutrient. A physiological study suggests the neural basis of this preference. Normally, rats eat sugar but avoid salt; we may presume that sugar tastes good to them while salt does not. When a rat is deprived of salt, however, the pattern of neural firing in certain sensory neurons changes in such a way that a salt-deprived rat's neural pattern in response to salt is similar to that of a normal rat in response to sugar. Apparently, salt tastes good to salt-deprived rats in the same way that sugar tastes good to normal ones (Jacobs et al., 1988).

In contrast, protein-deprived rats must learn through experience to choose protein-rich foods (Simpson & White, 1990). Laboratory studies indicate that at least some of this learning is related to rats' "observation" of protein-efficient feeding behavior in adults and other group members (Galef & Wright, 1995). Apparently nutritional wisdom is related to a combination of factors, some of which are learned and some of which have an influence independent of learning.

Tool Use in Omnivorous Birds

Ant lions and archerfish use "tools," but in relatively stereotyped ways; tool use in certain omnivorous birds is more variable. In some instances there is evidence that a bird actually fashions a tool to meet a particular need.

The Egyptian vulture sometimes uses a stone to break an ostrich egg—which is too hard for the vulture to break with its beak. The bird holds a stone in its beak with its neck extended and then rapidly flexes its neck, propelling the stone at the egg (van Lawick-Goodall & van Lawick, 1966). Crows in the northwestern United States also use rocks as tools; in this case, however, the birds break the shells of whelks by dropping the whelks on a rocky beach. The crows climb to a height of about 16 feet before the drop and have a success rate of about 25 percent. In order to determine if the crows used an appropriate height for the drop, an experimenter climbed a ladder and systematically dropped whelks from various heights and evaluated the results. Indeed, the 16-foot height proved to provide the maximum efficiency (Zach, 1979).

Woodpecker finches of the Galapagos Islands use a different type of tool, breaking off twigs or cactus spines and inserting them in holes in the wood of dead trees or under bark, as shown in Figure 6.3. When the finches contact insects in these locations, the finches ei-

FIGURE 6.3 ◆ A woodpecker finch. The finch uses a stick as a tool to prod insects from beneath the bark of trees.

ther impale and withdraw their prey or chase them from their hiding place. Then the birds drop the tool and eat the insects (Eibl-Eibesfeld, 1970). In captivity, one of these finches has been observed shortening a twig or removing bits from a twig that apparently impeded the tool's insertion into a hole (Eibl-Eibesfeld & Sielman, 1962). This observation indicates rather clearly that these birds fashion their tools to meet their own needs.

Recently, Gavin Hunt (1996) reported some carefully documented examples of tool use in New Caledonian crows. These crows make two standard types of tools—a hooked twig and a stepped-cut barbed leaf. Each type of tool has a different, specific function in capturing insects. Christophe Boesch (1996), a specialist in the study of cultural heritage in nonhuman animals, suggests that the standardization of these tools represents a kind of cultural influence in these birds.

Tool Use in Mammals

As with birds, there are several examples of tool use in mammals. The California sea otter sometimes uses a rock to break open mussels. The otter gathers a rock and a mussel from the ocean floor and, after surfacing, balances the rock against its chest. The otter then holds the mussel with its forefeet and pounds its flat side against the stone several times. Periodically the otter bites the shell, apparently to determine if the shell is sufficiently cracked. If it is not broken enough for the otter to begin eating, the otter administers another series of blows against the rock (Hall & Schaller, 1964).

Otters may also use stones to loosen abalones from the substrate. One otter was observed pounding with a stone on an abalone attached to a rocky crevice. The otter surfaced

to breathe from time to time, then returned to the pounding until the abalone was detached (Houk & Geibel, 1974).

Much to the disgust of their trainers, otters in captivity sometimes use tools in mischievous ways, breaking glass or objects in their cages with rocks used as hammers. As in the case of the archerfish, it seems that the otters generalize the tool use to situations other than feeding.

Chimpanzees use tools, especially sticks, in several different ways: They separate ant nests from branches by using sticks as a lever, drive ants from inside a tree by inserting a stick into the cavity, and dig into subterranean bee nests with a stick (van Lawick-Goodall, 1970). The most celebrated example of chimpanzee tool use, termite fishing, was discussed and illustrated in Chapter 4—refer to Figure 4.4. Chimpanzees in Tanzania insert a probe such as a twig or blade of grass into a termite nest; when a termite worker seizes the probe, the chimpanzee withdraws the tool and eats the termite (Goodall, 1963). In some cases chimpanzees carry these tools a good distance from the spot where they are found to the termite nest. Everything considered, the chimpanzees require a fairly large amount of skill to locate workable termite tunnels with the probe, to select and modify the tools by trimming or removing bark, and to manipulate the tools effectively within the tunnels (Teleki, 1974).

The preadaptation for the skills needed for fashioning and using tools in termite fishing is considerably more complex than that needed by the other tool users we have considered. First, the animal must be structurally preadapted—the hands prehensile and flexible, the visual system capable of superior acuity and depth perception, and the nervous system capable of processing fine hand–eye coordination. Second, the animal must be capable of learning and retention that spans an extended period of time. Third, there must be a general predisposition to exhibit what has been termed curiosity or investigative manipulation, because the objects that will eventually be used as tools have to be manipulated generally before they can be put to use in a productive way. Furthermore, if the objects are manipulated in a large variety of ways, there is a better chance that trial-and-error learning will take place (Beck, 1980). In several respects, termite fishing is a remarkable food-acquisition technique.

Investigating the tool-related capabilites of apes in a seminatural setting, Nicholas Toth and Sue Rumbaugh (1993) attempted to teach the language-trained bonobo, Kanzi, to make stone tools similar to the ones made by the ancestors of humans. Toth, who is highly skilled in making these tools, served as a model. Kanzi was eventually able to produce stone chips, which he then used to cut a string and gain access to food. Although the tools were clearly inferior to those made by Stone Age humans, Kanzi demonstrated the ability to use one type of tool to make another—an ability thought to be exclusively human before this study was conducted.

◆ HUMAN EVOLUTION

This section will explore the effects of three food-related mechanisms quite surely found in early hominids—ecological plasticity, tool use, and nutritional wisdom. As we shall see, some of the insights gained by an increased understanding of the evolutionary bases of feeding have practical applications for us today.

ECOLOGICAL PLASTICITY

There is strong evidence that, before the time that hominids first appeared, our ancestors were fruit-eating primates. As I pointed out in connection with howler and spider monkeys, there were selective advantages to the development of cognitive abilities associated with memory for location of fruit trees and anticipation of future events such as when the fruit would be ripe.

Later, as our ancestors became hominids, they were almost certainly feeding generalists. Like other primate generalists, our early ancestors must have had relatively little neophobia and a general tendency to sample new foods. Furthermore, our ancestors must have had a neophilia that translated into a general curiosity. Not only were our ancestors likely to try new foods, but they were probably tempted to develop new and original ways of finding food and other resources. In other words, the evolution of some very basic human cognitive processes associated with ecological plasticity were related to our ancestors' feeding patterns.

This neophilia and curiosity, coupled with a tendency to live in small groups or bands, were essential to survival on the savanna lands of Africa. The challenge was great, because our early ancestors were not nearly as well adapted for life in this type of environment as were animals such as baboons and hyenas, which competed for some of the same types of food.

TOOL USE

Another factor that was undoubtedly important in the survival of our ancestors was the fashioning of tools for acquiring and preparing food. Researchers have found stones chipped in a regular manner in apparent campsites, indicating that our ancestors must have fashioned and used tools well over a million years ago. Furthermore, charred remains near apparent campsites indicate that our ancestors must have been able to control the use of fire. Fire was important not only for cooking food but for providing warmth. In addition, fire was an effective way of keeping potential predators at bay, because predator animals in the wild will not approach a campfire.

As important as tool use must have been, comparative fossil evidence indicates the brains of our ancestors did not increase significantly in size for more than a million years following the first signs of tool use. The strong natural selection process that resulted in the rapid growth of hominid brains must have come later. As suggested in Chapter 5, social cognition seems to have been of more importance than primitive tool use in the rapid evolution of the human brain in the past several hundred thousand years. During this time, humans also began to use tools in more complex ways.

NUTRITIONAL WISDOM

The classic study on human nutritional wisdom by Richter (1943) included a group of human infants. As in the case of rats, the infants tended to choose a balanced diet, a choice that was presumably independent of experience. Apparently humans have been naturally selected to practice nutritional wisdom. In fact, people who live in societies similar to the hunter–gatherer societies that shaped human evolution have generally healthier diets than those of most people in the United States and in many other Western nations.

Why do humans living in technologically advanced societies often fail to show nutritional wisdom? It seems that our ancestors did not need to

evolve the tendency to avoid overconsumption of fat and sugar. The wild game that they hunted did not have the high fat content of the domestic animals of today. (In recent decades humans have selectively bred domestic animals for high fat content.) Furthermore, fruit was relatively scarce; it was unlikely that anyone would get a more than optimal amount of sugar living off food found in the wild. Finally, the natural food of early humans contained a large amount of fiber (see Allman, 1994).

In technological societies, by contrast, foods that contain excessive amounts of fat and refined sugar with little or no fiber are abundant. Advertisements, attractive packaging, artificial flavorings, and convenient processing promote the sale of many foods that have less than optimal nutritional value. Furthermore, many people eat under stressful conditions or when they are in a hurry. Studies of contemporary American homes indicate that meals are often eaten while family members watch television or are engaged in other tasks (see De Angelis, 1995). Haste and distraction tend to interfere with digestion, so such conditions are deleterious to nutrition.

Nonetheless, nutritious foods are available in modern Western societies and opportunities to eat under pleasant conditions abound. Eating properly is certainly possible in technologically advanced societies. It probably takes more commitment and conscious effort than in the past, however, because we are often hurried as well as exposed to media messages that may be antithetical to good nutrition.

◆ CHANGING PERSPECTIVES

PAST	PRESENT	FUTURE
Feeding strategies are simple and inflexible (early twentieth century).	Feeding strategies of most animals are complex, flexible, and predictable in accordance with optimality theory.	Will optimality theory continue to explain feeding strategies effectively? Will new theories be needed to address the extreme complexity of certain feeding strategies?

SUMMARY

Animals maximize foraging opportunities in a number of ways: by locating an optimal place to forage, by moving strategically within a food patch, and by making optimal decisions about when to leave a patch. Animals also take into account the risk of predation.

Intraspecies competition is greatest when food is patchily distributed. In some cases intraspecies aggression is reduced by dominance hierarchies and territorial systems. In other cases mutualism develops.

Interspecies competition for food is less likely to result in compromise. The competition either drives one species to extinction or forces that species to modify its feeding pattern (and other aspects of its behavior).

Predators and prey are in an evolutionary arms race. In a pattern related to the life/dinner principle, prey animals are usually one step ahead of predators.

Predators use a variety of strategies, including chasing down prey, lying in wait, using lures of various kinds, and, in a few cases, using tools. Cannibalism is rare, because it may result in loss of indirect fitness and increased risk of parasitism. However, it occurs in some animals when there is a favorable cost–benefit ratio associated with cannibalistic activity.

Herbivores are specialized for finding, digesting, and in some cases storing plant material that serves as food. Granivores in particular are often adept at storing and retrieving food. Grazers are specialized for digesting cellulose found in leaves and grasses. Fruit-eating primates are of special interest because they have evolved cognitive capacities that allow them to anticipate when fruit will ripen.

Omnivores are usually feeding generalists and accordingly have evolved ecological plasticity, the possibility of social learning, and nutritional wisdom. Some omnivorous birds and mammals use tools to gain access to food; the most highly developed example of tool use in nonhumans is seen in the termite fishing in chimpanzees.

Two significant factors in human evolution are strongly related to feeding—ecological plasticity and tool use. Like many other omnivores, humans have nutritional wisdom; but this wisdom is compromised in technologically advanced societies.

KEY TERMS

aggressive mimicry, p. 131
area-restricted search hypothesis, p. 125
central-place foraging, p. 126
ecological plasticity, p. 137
evolutionary arms race, p. 129
exploitation phase, p. 124

generalists, p. 137
larder hoarding, p. 135
life/dinner principle, p. 130
marginal value theorem, p. 125
mutualism, p. 127
neophilia, p. 137

CHAPTER 7

DEFENSE AGAINST PREDATION

◆ *Why are some animals
conspicuously marked?*

◆ *Why are other animals
camouflaged?*

DEFENSIVE TECHNIQUES AND STRATEGIES

Concealment

Warning Strategies

Defensive Aggression

Escape

Inhibition of Consumption

MAXIMIZING DEFENSIVE EFFICIENCY

Adjustment of Strategies

Risk Taking

GROUP DEFENSES

Predator Detection

Pooling of Resources

The Confusion Effect

The Dilution Effect

THE RELATIONSHIP BETWEEN PREDATORS AND PREY: A REPRISE

HUMAN EVOLUTION

Fear Responses

Risk Taking

Sociality

*E*ver since some animals first began preying on other animals, there has been strong evolutionary pressure to develop defenses against predation. This prolonged evolutionary pressure has resulted in great complexity and variation of defensive adaptations— some of which have only recently been identified.

7

We will begin by looking at a variety of defensive mechanisms and strategies. Then we will consider how animals maximize the effectiveness of their strategies as well as the evolution and functions of various social defenses. Next, we will look once more at the relationship between predators and prey. Finally, we will discuss human evolution as it relates to defense against predation and other dangers.

DEFENSIVE TECHNIQUES AND STRATEGIES

Predation, as we saw in Chapter 6, involves three general stages: locating the prey, overcoming the prey's defenses, and consuming the prey. Prey animals have evolved strategies to counteract predation at each of these stages. To reduce the possibility of being located, prey attempt to conceal themselves. To defend themselves, prey try to warn predators, fight against them, or escape from them. Finally, when all else fails, prey animals may resort to methods that inhibit consumption by the predator. Let us now consider defensive adaptations at each of these stages.

Concealment

The first line of defense may be considered concealment or avoiding detection by a predator. To facilitate the effectiveness of structural adaptations (such as camouflage), animals often suppress movement and maintain a particular stance or position for the period of time that the danger of predation exists. The adopted posture typically maximizes their concealment.

Protective Coloration and Form

Animals in danger of predation have evolved several types of structures and behaviors that promote camouflage. Perhaps the simplest type of camouflage is **color resemblance,** in which an animal's color matches the color of its background. Color resemblance is illustrated by green aphids that live on vegetation, gray-brown lizards inhabiting sandy areas, and black beetles that cling to the bark of trees.

When given a choice of backgrounds on which to sit or perch, animals with color resemblance usually maximize their camouflage by choosing the appropriately colored background. For example, Australian lizards that are lightly colored spend most of their time perched on lightly colored rocks, while darkly colored lizards of the same species tend to perch on dark rocks (Gibbons & Lillywhite, 1981).

Although most animals that utilize color resemblance as a defensive mechanism must select an appropriate background, there are exceptions to this rule. The chameleon and the flounder are able to change their colors to match those of their backgrounds. In the flounder this adaptation is related to the fact that the flounder's chromatophores (pigment cells) are under neural control and can be redistributed in less than a second. Consequently, the flounder is able to change color immediately after it selects a place to lie on the ocean floor.

Another aspect of camouflage is **counter-shading.** Without markings, an object will reflect more light—and appear lighter—on its top surface than on its bottom surface. This difference in reflectance between top and bottom functions to give the appearance of depth and makes an animal stand out against its background. Countershading, or the placement of darker markings on the top of the animal, reduces the differences in reflectance and creates an illusion of flatness. For example, most fish are darkest on their top sides and consequently less visible when alive than when dead and floating belly up.

Still another aspect of camouflage is **disruptive coloration,** or irregular patches of contrasting colors. When one or more of these patches match the color of the background, part of the animal's body fades from view and the rest is seen as an irregular, non-animal-shaped object (Cott, 1957). In brook trout, for example, the spots on the fish's body seem to disappear when viewed against the pebbles on the bottom of a stream.

Some animals are concealed not because of camouflage as such but because they resemble objects normally found in their habitat.

For example, the stick shape of mantids disguises them from predators as well as from the insects on which they prey. Certain species of mantids facilitate their resemblance to twigs by moving back and forth slowly as if swaying in the wind. As Chapter 6 mentioned, the dung spider shows object resemblance with the assistance of its web. It spins a white web on a leaf and places its black-and-white body in such a way that the whole arrangement resembles bird droppings on a leaf.

The effectiveness of protective coloration or form varies greatly. Part of the reason for this variation has to do with whether the defense is utilized against a homogeneous group of predators or against predators that differ in their color discrimination and visual acuity. If the predators differ, the prey's adaptation will probably represent a compromise. And this compromise will be less effective in any one specific situation than will an adaptation directed specifically against one type of predator (Endler, 1986).

Removal of Telltale Evidence

Even though animals may have effective methods of camouflage or object resemblance, predators are sometimes able to locate them on the basis of telltale evidence. Thus, a caterpillar-eating bird learns to spend more time searching for its prey in trees with damaged leaves than it does in undamaged trees. The caterpillars have, in turn, evolved a tendency to snip off partially eaten leaves, thereby removing cues that would indicate their location (Heinrich & Collins, 1983).

Another example of eliminating telltale evidence involves birds' removal of eggshells from the nest. The young of most birds—and sometimes the adults too—are camouflaged as they sit in their nests. However, the inside of an eggshell is typically white and easy for a predator to spot, so the presence of a shell from an egg can give away the nest's location. Researchers tested the hypothesis that birds remove eggshells to reduce the possibility of predation by experimentally scattering broken eggshells near the unhatched eggs of gulls. Results indicated that eggs near broken shells are more likely to be taken by predatory crows than eggs that are not near broken shells (Tinbergen, 1963). Apparently, then, the removal of broken eggshells, which is found in many species of birds, is a defensive adaptation for protecting the young.

The Use of Protective Armor

Most forms of concealment rely in part on the external environment. In contrast, mollusks such as clams and snails manufacture their own protective shells. There is also an example of a type of protective armor in a rare spider found in the southeastern United States, *Cyclocosimia truncata.* This spider has a leathery shield on the posterior part of its abdomen. When *Cyclocosimia* is disturbed, it retreats to the lower part of its burrow and wedges itself into the narrow space with only its leathery shield exposed.

The hermit crab does not manufacture its own protective armor but crawls into a snail shell after the former resident has died. The crabs are able to discriminate among shells that are very similar and choose an appropriate shell on the basis of a combination of factors, including vision, touch, and past experience with shells. As the crab grows, it discards one shell and chooses another slightly larger one. In some cases two hermit crabs will exchange shells, after a "negotiation" session involving a series of raps made by one crab on the other crab's shell (Hazlett, 1996).

Shells or armor plates were common in the early evolution of vertebrates and were the hallmark of long-extinct fishes known as placoderms. Protective armor is rare among living vertebrates, however—with the exception of turtles and a few primitive mammals such as pangolins and armadillos. Perhaps the reason for this decline in the prevalence of armor is related to the fact that shells are energy-expensive to produce and greatly limit the animal's speed and maneuverability.

Warning Strategies

If an animal is detected, a second line of defense is to warn the predator. Most animals that engage in a warning strategy have an effective means of defense to back up their warning. By warning the predator first, an animal may avoid the risk of an encounter and save energy and other resources for a later time. For example, the rattle of a rattlesnake functions specifically as a warning device and enables the snake to save its poison for prey capture. The snakes rattle when they are threatened, but they do not rattle before they strike at prey.

Aposematic Coloration

Several poisonous insects and frogs have bodies conspicuously marked with red, orange, and yellow. This conspicuous or **aposematic coloration** functions to protect the animals by warning potential predators.

Laboratory experiments suggest that the effectiveness of aposematic coloration is related to the fact that at least some predators quickly learn to avoid brightly colored objects. For example, chicks (of domestic hens) were given a chance to eat foul-tasting colored food that was placed either on a background with similar coloration (inconspicuous coloration condition), or on one with contrasting coloration (conspicuous coloration condition). The chicks soon avoided the food in all conditions, but they learned to avoid the food fastest in the conspicuous color condition (Gittleman & Harvey, 1980).

There is also evidence, however, that aposematic coloration may inhibit attack independent of experience. In a laboratory setting, hand-reared predatory birds, presumably lacking any relevant experience with prey, were presented with two types of prey, identical except that one was experimentally colored to resemble an aposematic food stimulus. The predators were less likely to take the aposematically colored prey (Sillén-Tullberg, 1985). It seems, then, that the effectiveness of aposematic coloration is due to a combination of a genetically influenced tendency to avoid brightly colored prey and a learned avoidance of the prey. This combination of factors makes aposematic coloration an especially effective defense.

At least some of the great diversity of color and color patterns of animals—such as fish and insects—that are preyed upon by color-sensitive predators is probably related to aposematic coloration. For example, reds, yellows, and oranges that are especially intense are most likely to evolve as warning signals. In addition, repeating patterns such as spots and stripes enhance the regularity of a design and make the animal look similar from all possible angles of attack (Guilford & Dawkins, 1991).

Mimicry

The success of aposematic coloration has led to the evolution of **Batesian mimicry**—the resemblance of some harmless animals to ani-mals that are able to defend themselves or are toxic. For example, some nonvenomous snakes resemble the highly poisonous coral snake. Experiments in both the field and the laboratory indicate that the mimics gain protection from predators as a result of their mimicry (Brodie, 1993; Brodie & Moore, 1995).

In a second type of mimicry, **Mullerian mimicry,** both model and mimic are harmful. For example, both monarch and queen butterflies are toxic after eating certain plants, and each gains from their mutual resemblance.

The most common examples of mimicry are visual, but there are also a few cases of auditory mimicry. For example, an owl that nests in a burrow makes a noise that resembles the rattle of a rattlesnake. Taped recordings of the owl's "rattle" discouraged ground squirrels from entering a burrow. Other types of sounds made by the owl had no deterrent effect, so there is a clear suggestion that the rattling sound was indeed the critical variable in inhibiting the ground squirrels from entering the burrow (Rowe et al., 1986).

The Defensive Use of Tools

We have already seen how some animals use tools to obtain food; and in a few cases animals may also use tools to accentuate a warning to potential predators, including humans. A raven, standing on a cliff above its nest site, threw several golf ball–sized rocks from its beak down to the vicinity of a scientist–observer—who reported one direct hit and several near misses (Janes, 1976).

The apparent throwing of objects is more frequently reported in mammals. Captive elephants have been seen to throw objects at human observers with their trunks and, moreover, to increase their accuracy with experience (Kuhme, 1963). A large Asian bull elephant named Ziggy, who was a resident at Chicago's Brookfield Zoo, became noted for picking up and hurling feces at janitors attempting to clean his cage. Unfortunately, from the janitors' point of view, Ziggy was quite accurate in his aim (Beck, 1980).

As in the case of obtaining food with tools, primates exhibit the greatest variability in the defensive use of tools. Several monkey species occasionally drop or throw stones and branches. Tree-dwelling monkeys usually drop objects, while ground-dwelling monkeys such as baboons typically throw objects backhanded with a rapid extension of the wrist and forearm. Apparently these monkeys are anatomically incapable of a more accurate and forceful throwing motion (Washburn & Jay, 1967). Chimpanzees, however, can throw stones overhand with a moderate degree of accuracy (Goodall, 1986).

Chimpanzees have also been observed using sticks in response to the experimental presentation of an animated model of a leopard. The chimpanzees may wave sticks or branches about, throw the sticks, or use the sticks as clubs (Kortlandt, 1967). There are also a few observations of chimpanzees using sticks against live leopards and lions, but such usage is unusual (Goodall, 1986).

Defensive Aggression

If warnings fail, many animals are prepared to fight in order to protect themselves. The tendency to fight against a predator, referred to as **defensive aggression,** may seem superficially similar to other types of aggression—but there are important differences. For example, a cat that is defending itself typically places its ears back against its head, hisses, and attempts to

bite or scratch the potential predator at any point on its body. When the cat is exhibiting predatory aggression, however, it does not hiss or retract its ears (Archer, 1988). Another difference between defensive and predatory aggression is physiological. The neural mechanisms involved in predatory and defensive aggression are distinct; stimulation of a certain area of the cat's brain produces ear flattening, hissing, and growling, behaviors that are related to defense but not predation (Shaikh & Siegel, 1989).

Defensive aggression is also different from aggression against conspecifics. Defensive aggression may include attempts to inflict serious damage or even death. Aggression against conspecifics, in contrast, is rarely seriously damaging or lethal; one of the reasons for not seriously injuring a conspecific is that it may be a relative.

The Use of Chemical Defenses and Projections

Animals such as wasps and bees defend themselves and their colonies by injecting poison into a potential predator. Wasps can use their stingers several times, but bees leave their stingers and the apparatus that drives the mechanism in their victims as they fly away. Although this adaptation costs the bee its life, there is a defensive benefit. That is, the stinger continues to drive into the victim and deliver venom after the bee has retreated, because the motor program is contained in a ganglion (a mass of nerve cells) that is attached to the stinging apparatus. This increased effectiveness of the sting may provide a significant indirect fitness benefit. Worker bees are sterile and have no chance of passing on their genes directly. However, the worker bees share 75 percent of their genes with the queen, so saving the queen and the colony has a large indirect fitness payoff.

In certain insects and amphibians, defensive toxin is contained within the prey's body and is effective only when the predator attempts to eat its quarry. In many cases the toxin saves the prey's life. Monarch butterflies, for example, are usually released by predatory quails before they are fatally damaged (Wiklund & Sillén-Tullberg, 1985). Even if the prey animal is killed, however, it may gain some indirect fitness benefits. The predator will most likely avoid this type of prey in the future, including the prey animal's relatives, as the result of its negative experience. For example, birds fed a toxic monarch butterfly later refuse to feed on monarchs (see Brower & Calvert, 1984).

Most animals manufacture their own toxins. Monarch butterflies, however, consume poisonous milkweed during their larval stage and store the toxin in their tissues, retaining the toxin even after they undergo metamorphosis. An experiment utilizing predatory jays illustrates the effectiveness of this technique. Jays introduced to monarchs raised on nonpoisonous cabbage showed no aversive reaction. However, jays fed monarchs reared on

milkweed consistently vomited a short time after the experience (Brower et al., 1968).

The large, slow-moving bombardier beetle (Figure 7.1) is one of the few animals that are able to project poison. The beetle gets its name from its ability to aim and "fire" toxic chemicals from flexible abdominal ducts with considerable accuracy at potential predators. Three chemicals are mixed in a hard-walled reaction chamber inside the body of the beetle. When a catalyst is added, an explosion takes place, complete with sound and what appears to be a puff of smoke. If a potential predator is hit directly, it is usually killed or disabled (Eisner, 1966).

Escape

An alternative to concealment, warning, or fighting a predator is to attempt an escape. Large prey animals that inhabit wide, open areas, such as antelope and giraffe, are often able to outrun their predators. However, many prey animals are considerably smaller than their predators and are not able to generate as much speed as the hunters. Consequently, some relatively small prey animals rely on quick starts and maneuverability—as

FIGURE 7.1 ◆ **A bombadier beetle "firing" a noxious chemical at a potential predator.**

illustrated by the ability of a rabbit or a sparrow to turn suddenly and thus avoid the onslaught of larger and faster predators.

Certain marine animals have evolved unusually large nerve fibers that facilitate quick responses. For example, the giant nerve fibers in the squid's nervous system and in the tails of fishes conduct nerve impulses extremely rapidly, thereby reducing the response time necessary before the animal can make an evasive maneuver.

Startling Predators

Some animals gain valuable time by startling a predator. For example, several species of moths and butterflies have markings known as **eye spots** on their hind wings. These spots resemble the eyes of predatory owls or hawks. When the forewings are quickly withdrawn, the eye spots are suddenly presented and induce a startle reaction. The attack is inhibited—or at least delayed long enough for the potential victim to move off (Blest, 1957).

One of the most dramatic startle displays is made by a tropical caterpillar. Upon tactual contact the caterpillar transforms its anterior (front) end into a mock snake head. This response seems to be particularly effective against birds in areas where there is a danger of predation by snakes.

The Use of Decoys

Another escape strategy is to direct a predator's strike to some relatively nonvulnerable part of the body. We saw an example of this strategy in the blue-tailed skink, discussed in Chapter 1. In some other lizards, the tail breaks off and continues to twitch after having been grasped by a predator. (The tail later regenerates, so the loss is only temporary.) Research on predatory snakes' responses to twitching versus nontwitching lizard tails indicates that the tail's continued movement holds the snake's attention long enough to give the lizard time to escape (Dial & Fitzpatrick, 1983).

The hairstreak butterfly also uses a decoy, but in this case it is a false head located on the butterfly's hind wings. This false head directs a predator's attack toward an expendable part of the body. To test the effectiveness of this decoy, rather than removing false heads from the wings of the butterflies (which is the typical experimental approach), researchers painted false heads on the hind wings of white butterflies. The researchers then presented normal (control) and experimentally painted white butterflies to captive blue jays. The painted butterflies escaped more often than did the controls, suggesting that the decoy was indeed effective (Wourms & Wasserman, 1985).

Inhibition of Consumption

Even if a prey animal has failed to hide, defend itself, or escape, there are some last-ditch strategies that may prove effective, at least under some circumstances.

Altering the Body

Some animals alter their bodies in such a way that it becomes difficult for predators to grasp or swallow them. The hagfish, for example, secretes a slimy cocoon that makes it virtually impossible to grasp. After a potential predator departs, the hagfish wipes off the slime by looping itself into a half hitch and pulling its body through the loop (Jensen, 1966).

An insect known as the lacewing (*Palmipenna*) does not have the ability to make itself more difficult to swallow but merely creates an illusion of large size. The lacewing has hind wings that, when folded, extend far out beyond its body, making the body appear larger than it actually is. Experiments in semi-natural surroundings indicate that this illusion is great enough to deter some predators. The experimenters tethered two groups of lacewings in an area exposed to predation by robber flies. The hind wings of the insects in one group (the experimental group) were removed, while the other group (the control group) was left intact. As predicted, the experimental lacewings were taken more often by the robber flies than the control lacewings in the test situation (Picker et al., 1991). It is not

so much an animal's actual size as predator's (or competitor's) perception of the animal's size that is important.

Becoming Immobile

I mentioned earlier that animals often facilitate the effects of their camouflage by remaining immobile for periods of time. When an animal is threatened with attack, however, a type of immobility called **death feigning** is effective for a different reason: Animals that feign death, such as the opossum, are not attractive to predators that take only live prey and do not scavenge. The opossum not only becomes immobile but draws back its lips in what appears to be a dying grimace (Figure 7.2).

Perhaps the most dramatic example of death feigning occurs in the toadfish. When first confronted, the fish makes a noise that re-

FIGURE 7.2 ◆ **An opossum showing a type of immobility known as death feigning.**

sembles a sad honk. It then gives the appearance of asphyxiation and gradually loses its color. The fish remains in this deathlike condition for 2 to 3 minutes before it returns to its normal state (Gunter & McCaughan, 1959).

A different type of immobility, **freezing,** is temporary and involves a tenseness that can be converted into sudden action. For example, a deer mouse may freeze in the presence of a gopher snake. Then, if the snake detects the mouse and starts to strike, the mouse explodes into a sudden leap at the last possible second, sometimes avoiding the strike (Hirsh & Bolles, 1980).

In still another type of immobility, prey animals become extremely tranquil when they are about to be consumed. The possible advantage to this reaction is that a predator may become distracted by some type of movement in its environment. Predators are adapted to attend to movement, so the tranquil animal may benefit if another animal comes along at the critical time (Halonen & Denny, 1980).

When a mammal is in dire straits—for example, about to be eaten by a predator—it secretes endorphins, opiumlike brain proteins that have an analgesic (pain-killing) effect. The endorphins prevent pain and possible distraction from injuries the animal may incur during the initial encounter. The analgesic effect enables the animal to ignore an injured part of its body, to remain tranquil, and in some cases to fight back vigorously (Bolles & Fanselow, 1980).

If a predator injures an animal but does not kill it, the victim enters a recuperation phase in which the analgesic effects of the endorphins wear off and the animal experiences pain in the part of the body that has sustained injury. At this point the pain and general stress have an adaptive effect, inducing the victim to hole up, pay attention to the injury by doing such things as licking it, and rest. These recuperative behaviors promote healing and also discourage the animal from engaging in risky behaviors (Fanselow & Sigmundi, 1982).

MAXIMIZING DEFENSIVE EFFICIENCY

Animals cannot spend too much time engaged in any one activity without sacrificing in some other aspect of their lives. If an animal devotes excessive time and energy to protecting itself, it may not be able to find enough food or reproduce optimally. Therefore, maximizing defensive efficiency is crucial.

Maximizing defensive efficiency has two key aspects—engaging in the most effective strategies for the situation at hand, and adjusting the amount of risk taken to the general circumstances.

Adjustment of Strategies

Although some animals have only one way of protecting themselves against predators, others, especially vertebrates, are capable of adopting the strategy that is most efficient for the situation at hand. We will look at strategic adjustments in two representative groups of vertebrates—lizards and mammals.

Lizards

Lizards remain motionless until a predator comes within a certain distance, basically relying on their camouflage for evasion. If a predator comes close enough, however, the lizard will run toward a burrow or crevice. Finally, if a lizard is cornered, it will engage in defensive aggression; it will issue a warning and, as a last resort, attack. In essence, the lizard uses the most risky, energy-consuming defense only if it is absolutely necessary.

Anole lizards of the West Indies have two general strategies to avoid predators—freezing and running. Like most lizards, they rely on the energy-efficient freezing strategy when a predator is at a distance; but they run when a predator gets within striking distance. Interestingly, these lizards are able to adjust to temperature conditions that affect their running speed. The lizards are able to run faster as the temperature increases—so they start running sooner in cool weather than in warm weather (Ydenberg & Dill, 1986).

Some lizards escape by either jumping or running. Recent research indicates that they use the most effective method, depending on the immediate circumstances. When the lizards are caught on a narrow perch that compromises their running speed, such as a thin twig, they tend to jump. When on a wider substrate, however, the lizards usually run in order to escape (Losas & Irschick, 1996).

An adjustment in defensive strategies also occurs after a lizard has shed its tail. Once its tail has been lost, the lizard loses some of its speed of escape—and, of course, it no longer has the defensive option of shedding its tail. Experiments with tailless lizards indicate that the tailless animals show a reduced general level of activity and flight distance; that is, they wait longer before fleeing an approaching predator. Apparently, after the lizards lose their tails, they adopt a defensive strategy more consistent with their best defense of the moment—hiding as opposed to fleeing (Formanowicz et al., 1990).

At one time people made the assumption that lizards responded to predators in a very stereotyped way. Thanks to careful research, we now understand that lizards have a remarkable ability to adjust their defensive strategy according to principles of optimality.

Mammals

Baby rhesus monkeys also adjust their defensive strategies as the situation changes. When an adult human (a potential predator) is present but not looking at the monkeys, the monkeys tend to freeze and remain motionless for prolonged periods of time. Such a response presumably reduces the probability of their being discovered. Then, if the human stares at them as if they have been discovered, the monkeys "bark," bare their teeth, and make other threatening gestures (Kalin, 1993; Figure 7.3).

As you can imagine, experiments involving a realistic threat of predation are hard to conduct with adult mammals. These animals are difficult to deceive; besides, if a live predator is used experimentally, the predator's actions are virtually impossible to regulate. Therefore, experimenters have often used electric shock to simulate the effects of an encounter with a predator. This simulation seems reasonable, because the physiological reactions of prey animals to shock are similar to their reactions to a predator. For example, the hormonal response to shock is very much like the hormonal response to the experimental presentation of a predator.

Experimenters also assume that the probability of a shock occurring is comparable to

FIGURE 7.3 ◆ **A monkey protecting itself by making a threatening gesture.**

the probability of the arrival of a predator in a given situation. That is, the anticipation of a predator's arrival and the anticipation of the onset of shock produce similar hormonal reactions.

Experimenters have found that rodents shocked frequently in open areas leave their secure home areas to feed less frequently than do rodents shocked infrequently. The frequently shocked rats eat larger amounts at one time, however. Apparently rodents in danger of predation expose themselves less often in open areas, but compensate by eating larger amounts of food at one sitting (Fanselow & Lester, 1988).

When entering novel environments, rats and other rodents immediately engage in ex-

ploratory activity that enables them to learn possible escape routes. If a predator is detected and there is an accessible escape route available, a rat will usually flee. If an escape route is not accessible, however, the rat will freeze next to a wall, in a corner, or in a dimly lit area. In simulated conditions with shock as the aversive stimulus, the rat will freeze in an area that has formerly been associated with the termination of the shock (LeClerc & Reberg, 1980). It seems that freezing in an area previously associated with escape from predation is adaptive in the sense that what worked once is liable to be effective a second time.

In the 1940s and 1950s, the findings of many laboratory experiments using shock with rodents did not seem to make much sense. Some experimenters assumed that the animals were behaving nonadaptively. Today, however, scientists have been able to interpret these studies' findings in the light of the optimality model—with the assumption that the animals evolved the responses under natural conditions—and realize that they make a great deal of sense. Furthermore, the studies point out the durablity of evolution-based mechanisms, which tend to persist under conditions vastly different from those found in the natural environment.

Risk Taking

Another factor that animals take into account in making a maximally efficient defensive response is how much they have to lose by taking a chance. From an optimality model standpoint, an animal has relatively little to lose by taking risks if its quality of life is poor and there is only an outside chance of passing on its genes. In contrast, an animal has a lot to lose by risk taking if the quality of its life is good and there is a high probability of passing on its genes. It follows that animals should take more chances when their circumstances are desperate. Even though there is a chance that things could get worse as the result of risk taking, the chance that they could get better offers an attractive payoff (Caraco, 1980).

And indeed, there is evidence that animals in poor circumstances take greater risks in regard to predation. For example, in an experimental situation stickleback fish parasitized by a cestode worm take more risks with a predator than do healthy fish (Milinski, 1984). Similarly, yellow-eyed juncos that are hungry are more likely to take risks than are well-fed juncos (Caraco et al., 1980).

There is also evidence that animals in negative circumstances will take relatively large risks to obtain a substantial reward. For example, juncos experimentally housed under the negative condition of low temperature are more likely to gamble (choose a variable reward condition) than birds housed in normal temperatures (Caraco et al., 1990).

There are sometimes gender differences in the tendency to take risks. In polygynous species, males tend to take greater risks than females. An evolutionarily based explanation for this difference is related to reproductive potential. Polygynous males have a great deal to gain by taking risks when the reward is an opportunity to win male–male competition and inseminate several females.

GROUP DEFENSES

In addition to optimizing individual defense strategies, animals sometimes optimize their defense by gathering in a group. Sociality has its costs, however. Competition with other group members can lead to destructive aggression. Close contact may facilitate the transfer of parasites. Also, grouped animals may be easier for a predator to locate than lone individuals.

On the other side of the cost–benefit ratio, group living can provide a variety of benefits for the species—as we shall see shortly. Yet animals are unlikely to have evolved sociality simply because living in groups benefited the species. There must have been some immediate advantage for individuals remaining in a group, at least under certain circumstances.

To explain the possible early evolution of sociality at the individual level of selection, William Hamilton (1971) proposed the **selfish**

herd hypothesis. This hypothesis assumes that some animals develop a tendency to come close together because they use each other as a shield. Because predators usually take the animals on the outside of a group first, there would be a selection for the tendency of the prey animals to move toward the center of the group. In essence, this centripetal movement induces the formation of tight groups of animals, especially when the animals are faced with the danger of predation (Hamilton, 1971).

Once the basic tendency to form groups is established, other factors influence the strengthening (or weakening) of social bonds. We will now look at some of these factors, particularly those on the benefit side of the cost–benefit ratio.

Predator Detection

Predator detection is basic to most group defensive strategies. The **many-eyes hypothesis** sugggests that as group size increases, there are more eyes (or ears or noses) on the lookout for predators, and predator detection is therefore more rapid (Lima, 1990, 1995). In fish, for instance, the individual that first becomes aware of danger reacts with a fright response or a rapid turn, which communicates alarm to the other members of the school. The more fish present, the greater the probability of early predator detection.

In some cases recognition of a predator is passed on from one fish to another; there is a "cultural transmission" of information about the defining characteristics of a predator. For example, the fright response of an experienced minnow to chemical stimuli from a northern pike is passed on to a naive (inexperienced) minnow so that the naive minnow develops a fear of pike without ever having been chased by a pike. Such cultural transmission may even take place between minnows of different species (Mathis et al., 1996).

Flocks of birds are also able to identify predators faster than individuals can. The larger the group, the greater the defensive advantage. For example, individual redshank birds in large groups are more likely to avoid predation by hawks than individuals in small groups, even though the large groups are attacked more often than the small ones (Cresswell, 1994). In addition to benefiting from an early warning system, individual birds can afford to be somewhat less vigilant, relying partly on detection by other members of the flock. Research indicates that as group size increases, each bird devotes less time to vigilance (McNamara & Houston, 1992).

Monkeys such as white-faced capuchins also show the many-eyes effect, especially around water holes. (Water holes are dangerous because predators tend to hide in the vicinity.) High-status males are more vigilant than low-status males or females, however. The high-status males are also particularly watchful for males from other capuchin groups. These high-status individuals, who tend to sire most of the offspring, have more to lose if one of the group members is lost or if another male comes into the group and tries to displace them (Rose & Fedigan, 1995).

When prey animals live in open areas relatively close to predators, there is another type of detection advantage associated with groups: A small number of the prey animals may assess the predator's motives by conducting what is called **predator inspection.** For example, two or more small fish such as minnows will approach a predatory pike and "inspect" the pike from a relatively close distance, avoiding the area in front of the pike's mouth (Magurran & Pitcher, 1987). Although the inspection involves obvious dangers, it apparently enables the other prey fish in the area—including individuals observing from a distance—to identify the predator and predict immediate future consequences. If the predator doesn't turn to attack the inspectors, the situation is not critical (Milinski, 1992; Turner & Robinson, 1992).

Fish inspecting a predator are in a situation where cooperation is required for the behavior to be effective. For example, if two fish start out to inspect and one fish defects (turns and bolts), not only is the inspection ineffective, but the other fish is left in a vulnerable position. Research using models of predators indicate that pairs of stickleback fish will adopt a general **tit-for-tat strategy** over a series of inspections; this strategy involves cooperating on the first move (moving forward) but then matching the other individual's moves on succeeding occasions (moving forward when the other fish moves forward and defecting when the other fish defects) (Huntingford et al., 1994).

Before a tit-for-tat strategy can be effective, an animal must be able to identify other individuals and associate past interactions with those individuals; that is, "remember" who has cooperated in the past. A laboratory experiment involving pairs of guppies in a simulated predator inspection situation indicated that an individual guppy could remember for up to 4 hours which of two conspecifics was the most cooperative in the past (Dugatkin & Alfieri, 1991).

Predator inspection also takes place in Thompson's gazelles on the plains of Africa. Groups of gazelles may approach and follow a cheetah or lion for an hour or longer. This inspection behavior takes into account general risk factors such as the height of vegetation and how many gazelles are in the inspection group. In addition to providing information about the particular predator's intentions, the inspection behavior causes some predators to leave the area and apparently also enables young gazelles to learn something about predators (Fitzgibbon, 1994).

Pooling of Resources

Once a predator is detected and identified as dangerous, a group may act in concert, pooling its resources. A single worker bee may be unsuccessful in deterring an enemy, but a large group of workers can be very effective in protecting a hive—as some of us have unfortunately discovered when we have inadvertently stumbled on a beehive in an open field. Musk oxen also defend against predators cooperatively, but in a different way. When confronted by a pack of wolves, the musk oxen form a ring, allowing their horns to form a protective shield.

Some birds engage in a group defense known as **mobbing,** in which adult birds leave their nests and cooperatively attack or make dives at a predator. The birds also make loud calls that attract other adult birds to the mobbing group. In addition to causing general harassment, mobbing functions to confuse the predator; it may also provide an opportunity for young birds to learn to identify the predator (Curio, 1978).

Mobbing is quite effective, especially in protecting birds' eggs. For example, as the number of mobbing attacks by gulls against a predator increases, the number of gull eggs taken by the predator decreases. Because intrusions by predators in the center of the colony evoke more consistent and vigorous attacks than intrusions at the periphery, there is an advantage for nesting birds to obtain a central location.

The Confusion Effect

In some cases, prey animals gain benefits from being in a group because a predator becomes confused when entering a group of rapidly moving animals. This **confusion effect,** common in schooling fish, results primarily from the difficulty a predator has visually fixating on and pursuing a single individual amidst the throng. Members of a school of fish will sometimes facilitate the confusion effect by surrounding the predator, leaving a distance of approximately 10 body lengths between the school of prey fish and the predator. Such a distance maximizes not only the confusion effect but the prey fish's advantage of maneuverability and acceleration (Magurran & Pitcher, 1987).

African gazelles also create a confusion effect when they run from a cheetah in a herd. Consequently, gazelles in large groups are victims of cheetahs less often than are solitary gazelles or gazelles in small clusters. This difference in vulnerability to predation helps to explain the sex bias in gazelles that fall prey to cheetahs: Even though males are more effective than females in eluding a cheetah in a one-on-one situation, males are more likely to

fall prey to cheetahs. The males' vulnerability seems to be related to their tendency to be solitary (Fitzgibbon, 1990).

The Dilution Effect

Individuals in a large group may gain defensive benefits simply because the predators present can take only a small percentage of the total group. This benefit, associated with a number of prey animals vastly greater than the number of predators, is known as the **dilution effect.**

The dilution effect is most pronounced when a large number of prey animals appear rather suddenly on the scene. For example, mayflies synchronously emerge as adults in great numbers, living just long enough to mate and lay their eggs in a period of a day or two. (These insects do not even take time to feed as adults.) In some areas in the Great Lakes region, the flies congregate by the thousands around streetlights. The dilution effect is particularly advantageous for mayflies because they are highly vulnerable to predation during their transition to the adult state—when they are unable to fly. Field research indicates that when a very large number of adult mayflies emerge in a short period, a high percentage of the insects survive long enough to mate and lay their eggs. Conversely, when there are fewer adults emerging, the percentage of adults surviving and laying their eggs is smaller (Sweeney & Vannote, 1982).

Monarch butterflies also benefit from the dilution effect. These insects spend the winter in huge clusters in the highlands of Mexico. More than 10,000 may be found in a semidormant condition on a single tree; a total of perhaps 20 million butterflies overwinter in a relatively small area. The success of the local bird predators in significantly reducing the butterfly population is hampered not only by the sheer number of these insects but also by the fact that some of the monarchs are noxious, having consumed milkweed as larvae (Brower, 1985).

THE RELATIONSHIP BETWEEN PREDATORS AND PREY: A REPRISE

As Chapter 6 pointed out, predators and prey are in an "evoutionary arms race," but in general prey animals tend to keep a step ahead of the predators. Nonetheless, there are certain predators that have a tendency to eliminate prey in localized areas. For example, the mosquito fish, when introduced into freshwater ponds and streams, often eliminates mosquitoes completely by feeding on the larvae. A major reason for the mosquito fish's success is that this fish is a predatory generalist; that is, it preys on a variety of animals. In contrast to specialized predators, which are dependent on their prey and which therefore suffer population plunges when the prey population drops, the mosquito fish is able to survive on other prey. Consequently, the fish's population does not fall when the larval population has fallen to a low level; the fish continues to prosper and remains on hand to prey on the next hatch of mosquito larvae.

This finding is of interest not only from a theoretical but from a practical standpoint. Mosquito fish have been very effective in controlling mosquitoes in certain areas, whereas specialized predators have generally failed.

(Mosquitoes are in no danger of extinction, however, because they are able to thrive in areas uninhabited by mosquito fish.)

If prey animals are typically ahead of predators in the evolutionary arms race, why don't prey animals evolve impregnable defenses? There seem to be several reasons. First, it is difficult for a prey animal to evolve defenses against many different predators. With finite resources, an animal cannot be a specialist for all eventualities, so a prey animal is likely to remain somewhat vulnerable.

Second, from the standpoint of the prey animal, there is a reduced selective pressure to increase the effectiveness of a defense once it has become extraordinarily effective. As we have seen, animals allocate their resources in such a manner that the most important matters are taken care of first (Staddon, 1983). In other words, when the probability of being captured falls to a very low point, resources tend to be allocated to functions other than defense.

Finally, when populations increase to the point that there is not enough food for all of the prey animals, some of them become risk-prone and especially open to predation. Similarly, population pressure may force some individual animals into areas where there is less natural protection against predators.

In conclusion, predators and prey tend to act as population checks on one another. Predation tends to be greatest when prey populations become large. Conversely, when prey populations are low, predators take relatively few prey. For example, it is easier for a few individuals to hide in a given area than for a large number of individuals. We will return once more to the complex interactions between populations of predators and prey when we discuss population control in Chapter 20.

◆ HUMAN EVOLUTION

Human evolution has been greatly affected by a need for vigilance and defense against predators, aggressive conspecifics, and natural disasters. Let's consider first how this need has resulted in the evolution of some rather specific fear responses. We will also examine the relationship between risk taking and our need for safety and security. Finally, we will look at how the threat of predation and other dangers have resulted in a natural selection for strong social bonds in humans.

FEAR RESPONSES

The response of fear is important to defense against predation in that it alerts an individual and provides the quick energy needed for escape. Humans give basic startle and fear responses to loud noises and quick movements that, under natural conditions, predict danger. In addition to providing defensive benefits, such responses function to prepare people for adverse environmental conditions such as the beginning of a storm or the approach of a threatening fellow human.

Humans also give fear responses to the sight of a spider or a snake. At one time we assumed that these responses were learned, in the same general way as we learn responses to other noxious stimuli such as live electric wires or guns. However, children learn avoidance to snakes and spiders much more rapidly than they learn fear responses to live wires or guns, even though these man-made objects present a greater danger to most modern humans. Apparently there was a natural selection for a predisposition to learn avoidance of snakes and spiders, which were real threats during our early evolutionary history. But there has not been time for us to evolve a similar propensity to learn aversion to the dangerous man-made objects in our modern world (Marks, 1987).

A similar evolutionarily based argument can be made for the development of fear of the dark in young children. The danger associated with darkness was very real for much of our evolutionary history, so it is not surprising that children in virtually all cultures develop a fear of being alone in the dark (Marks, 1987). In many non-Western cultures today, children sleep in close proximity to their parents; fear of the dark may not be activated as much in these cultures as it is in Western societies in which children tend to sleep alone at night.

From a commonsense standpoint it might seem that humans facing mortal danger would experience high levels of fear. However, many people who have gone through near-death experiences report a feeling of well-being and extreme calm. The studies of prey animals that secrete endorphins moments before a predator attempts to consume them suggest that endorphins' pain-killing and euphoric effects are adaptive as a last-ditch mechanism because the reactions are associated with tranquil immobility. It may be that the calm that humans experience in the face of impending death reflects this once adaptive advantage.

RISK TAKING

Humans, like nonhumans, tend to take relatively great risks when they are in a suboptimal situation or when they perceive things to be going poorly. Thus, people are more willing to take large risks when they are in a negative mood than when in a positive one (Arkes et al., 1988). As in the case of nonhuman animals, humans have less to lose when in a bad or precarious situation.

Unfortunately, this risk-taking strategy can have some negative social consequences. For example, people are more likely to take dangerous risks when they are angry or emotionally upset. Another example: Poor people, who can ill afford to lose the little money they have, may be inclined to gamble in situations with poor odds of winning. The fact that we evolved in a situation very different from that found in highly technological societies is reflected in both irrational fears and a tendency to take foolish risks.

Another human analogy to risk taking in nonhuman animals is seen in gender differences. Men in many societies, especially men between the ages of 16 and 24, tend to take greater risks in a large variety of situations than women (Wilson & Daly 1985). The ages of the men putting themselves at high risk correspond to the period when mate competition is most intense. It seems that the same natural selection processes that operate on polygynous nonhuman males have influenced men. When there is a great deal of fitness at stake—such as during competition for a mate—there is an advantage to risk taking. Once again, it is not difficult to generate examples of how this evolutionary adaptation has become inappropriate in many ways in technologically advanced societies.

SOCIALITY

Like other ground-dwelling primates, the early ancestors of humans moved from forested areas into open savanna lands, where they were not well adapted for defense against predation. Consequently, there was a strong evolutionary tendency to develop social bonds and complex ways of communicating. As in the case of many other animals, groups of cooperating humans are better able to defend themselves than solitary individuals. And because there have been important fitness benefits associated with social

life, there has been strong evolutionary pressure to thrive and feel good in positive social situations. In other words, we have a deep-seated tendency to need other people.

Unfortunately, a variety of factors tend to make people in highly technological societies socially isolated from one another, especially in urban settings. For example, economic factors may force people to move frequently, resulting in the breakup of friendships and romantic relationships. In some cases crowded conditions produce an atmosphere of anonymity that results in feelings of isolation. Television may also function to isolate individuals, especially if television viewing is passive and functions as a substitute for social interaction (see De Angelis, 1995). Nonetheless, crowded conditions and television do not necessarily produce social isolation. When people have good social skills, optimism, and a sense of control over their lives, they tend to form good social relationships even under difficult situations. And countless organizations and programs exist to help people develop these skills and perceptions (see Seligman, 1995).

◆ CHANGING PERSPECTIVES

PAST	PRESENT	FUTURE
Defensive strategies are simple and inflexible (early twentieth century).	Defensive strategies evolve in response to evolving predatory strategies. There tends to be a stable balance in populations of predators and prey animals.	How do defensive strategies and predatory strategies interact with one another?

SUMMARY

Animals have developed mechanisms and strategies that counteract predation in a variety of ways. Concealment is facilitated by protective coloration and form, the removal of telltale evidence, and/or the use of protective armor. Warning of predators may take place through aposematic coloration, via mimicry, or by bluffs involving tool use. Defensive aggression, which differs from other types of aggression, may include the use of toxins. Escape may be facilitated by devices that startle predators or function as decoys. As a last resort, animals may inhibit consumption by altering their body shape or becoming immobile.

Animals that have more than one defensive strategy maximize efficiency by appropriately adjusting their defensive strategies to the situation at hand. Another method of maximizing efficiency is to increase the tendency to take risks when in a precarious situation.

Animals may benefit from group defenses in several respects. The many-eyes effect and predator inspection strategy promote increased predator detection by groups. Groups of animals may pool resources to mob preda-

tors or coordinate defenses in some other way. Groups may also have defensive advantages because large numbers of prey animals confuse predators or because predators become overwhelmed (the dilution effect).

Although prey animals are usually a step ahead of their predators in the evolutionary arms race, certain predatory generalists may eliminate prey in localized areas. Predators rarely drive prey to extinction, however. For several reasons, prey animals seldom if ever evolve impregnable defenses.

As in the case of many nonhuman animals, the danger of predation has had a significant effect on human evolution and has helped shape our fear responses, risk-taking behavior, and sociality.

KEY TERMS

aposematic coloration, p. 150
Batesian mimicry, p. 151
color resemblance, p. 148
confusion effect, p. 162
countershading, p. 149
death feigning, p. 155
defensive aggression, p. 152
dilution effect, p. 162
disruptive coloration, p. 149

eye spots, p. 154
freezing, p. 156
many-eyes hypothesis, p. 160
mobbing, p. 161
Mullerian mimicry, p. 151
predator inspection, p. 160
selfish herd hypothesis, pp. 159–160
tit-for-tat strategy, p. 161

BASIC REPRODUCTIVE PROCESSES

◆ *Why do male frogs clasp females for extended periods of time?*

◆ *Why does fertilization take place outside the female in some species but within the female in others?*

REPRODUCTIVE TECHNIQUES AND STRATEGIES

Asexual–Sexual Processes

Hermaphroditism–Dioecism

External Fertilization–Internal Fertilization

EVOLUTION OF REPRODUCTIVE PROCESSES AND STRUCTURES

The Dawn of Sex

The Evolution of Distinct Gametes

The Evolution of Sex Organs

ECOLOGY AND REPRODUCTION

Number of Offspring Produced

Age of Sexual Maturity

Timing of Reproduction during the Season

HUMAN EVOLUTION

Gender Ratio

Reproductive Maturity

Copulatory Patterns

Orgasm in Women

Menstruation and Menopause

Successful reproduction is basic to fitness. However, simply producing offspring is no guarantee that an animal's genes will be passed on. The young must survive and, in turn, reproduce. And there is always competition with other animals that are also selected to pass on their genes. Consequently, for every species there has been a natural selection process to pass on genes in an optimal manner, taking into account a great

169

8

number of factors—including what the competition is doing, the dangers of predation, and various constraints imposed by the physical environment.

As we shall see in this and the following three chapters, the long evolutionary history of reproduction and the great variety of ecological conditions has resulted in tremendous diversity in reproductive patterns and strategies. For example, a few animals are entirely asexual. Others reproduce sexually at certain times and asexually at others. Most animals, however, are sexual reproducers. Within the category of sexual reproducers we find enormous variation, and some patterns appear to be quite bizarre. Nonetheless, virtually all of the patterns make sense in light of optimality theory and the principles of natural selection.

We will begin this chapter by considering the major types of reproductive techniques and strategies. Then we will speculate on the evolution of reproductive processes, and we'll look at the relationship between ecology and reproduction. Finally, we will survey aspects of sexuality as they relate to human evolution.

REPRODUCTIVE TECHNIQUES AND STRATEGIES

Animals not only live in varying environments but differ greatly in evolutionary history, size, behavior potential, and the types of constraints they face. And there is a close relationship between these numerous variables and animals' reproductive techniques and strategies.

Asexual–Sexual Processes

Many people are inclined to think of sex and reproduction as being linked together. However, there are some cases in which sex occurs independent of reproduction; also, reproduction may take place asexually (without sex). To gain a better understanding of why reproduction is sometimes asexual and at other times sexual, let us begin by considering the advantages of the two general types of reproduction.

The Advantages of Asexual Processes

Perhaps the greatest advantage of asexual reproduction is its efficiency. An animal that reproduces asexually does not spend time and energy looking for a partner, courting, or cop-

◆ UNUSUAL ADAPTATIONS

Parthenogenesis in Fish and Lizards

Species that reproduce asexually and never engage in sexual processes are extremely rare. However, a few fish and lizards reproduce asexually by a process known as **parthenogenesis,** in which eggs laid by the female develop even though they have not been fertilized.

The first reported example of a parthenogenetic vertebrate was an all-female species of fish: the Amazon mollie, found in freshwater streams in southeastern Texas and northern Mexico. The Amazon mollie females mate with males of a closely related species called sailfin mollies. However, the chromosomes in the males' sperm do not fuse with those in the eggs. Instead, the sperm merely serves to activate parthenogenetic development of the eggs. Consequently, the young are genetic duplicates of the mother.

Following the report of this phenomenon, animal behaviorists asked the question, What fitness benefits did the sailfin mollies gain by engaging in a type of sexual interaction in which their sperm did not fertilize an egg? More recently, careful observations have provided an answer. When a sailfin male sexually interacts with an Amazon mollie, he is often observed by sailfin females. Laboratory studies indicate that the females are then more likely to choose this male than to select a male that they have not observed mating (Schlupp et al., 1994). Thus, both Amazon females and sailfin males benefit from the encounter.

Whiptail lizards of the southwestern United States are also parthenogenetic and unisexual. Unlike Amazon mollies, however, the lizards interact sexually (or, strictly speaking, pseudosexually) with members of their own species. Some individual females court and mount other females. This pseudosexual interaction stimulates parthenogenetic development of the eggs in the mounted lizard (Crews, 1989). In essence, the female whiptail lizards engage in both female and male roles, eliminating the need for males.

Apparently these parthenogenic vertebrates evolved from sexually reproducing ancestors. The advantages that the females gained from passing on 100 percent of their genes was probably a factor in this unusual adaptation. As we will see, however, the benefits of sexual reproduction tend to outweigh the relatively short-lived advantages of asexual reproduction; so parthenogenesis in vertebrates is extremely rare.

ulating. Furthermore, asexually reproducing animals do not invest energy in the production of gametes—that is, of eggs or sperm. The cost of producing gametes is reflected in the fact that many never enter into the process of fertilization; in virtually all sexually reproducing animals, only a very small percentage of sperm fertilize an egg, and even under optimal conditions many eggs remain unfertilized.

Even more important in terms of efficiency is the fact that the asexual parent is able to pass on 100 percent of its genes to each offspring—as opposed to the 50 percent that the sexual parent passes on. This means that an asexually reproducing parent need generate only half as many offspring to have the same fitness benefit as a sexually reproducing one. Also, all offspring of asexual parents are able to bear young, whereas only the females of sexual reproducers may bear young.

Asexually reproducing animals have another advantage in that they are not exposed to the danger of predation while reproducing, as are many animals that engage in sexual interaction. Not only does the act of copulation expose an animal to predation, but sexual readiness may increase vulnerability. For example, male moths show a peak in flight activity in the middle of the night, a time when moth-eating bats are most active in their feeding. Consequently, the male moths are more likely to be preyed upon than females, who either are flightless or take short flights early in the evening (Acharya, 1995).

The Advantages of Sexual Processes

As we saw in Chapter 2, the genetic variability associated with sexual reproduction results from the mixing of chromosomal material that occurs during meiosis. The advantages of genetic variability are so great that most species of animals, invertebrate as well as vertebrate, exhibit sexual processes at one time or another.

There are several reasons why genetic variability is advantageous. These reasons are represented by three separate—but not mutually exclusive—hypotheses. The **lottery hypothesis** draws an analogy to a lottery. The optimum strategy for a gambler is to buy tickets that maximize the chance of winning the lottery; the gambler does this by placing bets on a variety of numbers as opposed to betting everything on one number. In a similar way, there is a better chance of at least some of the offspring surviving in a variable environment if offspring are different from one another than if they are all extremely similar (Williams, 1975).

The second hypothesis related to the advantages of sexual reproduction is the **coevolution hypothesis.** This hypothesis assumes that animals are most likely to benefit from genetic variability when they are significantly affected by another group of animals, such as predators. If the predators change, sexual processes enable the prey to adapt rapidly to these changes (Hamilton et al., 1981). As Chapters 6 and 7 explained, the struggle between predators and their prey is an "evolutionary arms race"—and both predators and prey benefit from the variability associated with sexual reproduction. (The same argument can be applied to the relationship between hosts and parasites, which, as we shall see in Chapter 15, also features an evolutionary arms race.)

A third hypothesis related to the advantages of sexual reproduction is the **repair hy-**

pothesis. This hypothesis suggests that there is a selective advantage to sexual processes for reasons independent of genetic variability: The recombination of genetic material that takes place during meiosis provides for repair of possible damage to the DNA. In light of the fact that significant mistakes do occur occasionally—such as breaks in the structural regularity of DNA—this provision is highly adaptive (Bernstein et al., 1985).

A combination of these three hypotheses effectively accounts for the almost universal expression of sexual processes. It is of particular significance, from an evolutionary perspective, that no *class* (see Appendix) of strictly asexual animals exists. That is, exclusive asexuality occurs in only a few isolated species. It seems that asexual animals eventually lose out and become extinct rather than giving rise to new evolutionary trends (Trivers, 1985).

TABLE 8.1 ◆ Advantages of Asexual and Sexual Reproduction

Asexual Reproduction	Sexual Reproduction
Highly efficient.	Produces genetic diversity in offspring. (Particularly advantageous for animals that live in rapidly changing environments or are coevolving with other animals.)
Less likely to cause vulnerability to predation.	
Not dependent on availability of a mate.	
	Provides for repair of DNA during meiosis.

The Best of Both Worlds: Combining Asexual and Sexual Processes

Because both asexual and sexual processes have unique advantages, it is not surprising that some organisms have evolved an ability to utilize both processes. For example, when food is plentiful and the surrounding conditions are generally favorable, the single-celled *Paramecium* reproduces by binary fission—an asexual process involving division into two separate parts. When conditions deteriorate, however, the organism engages in a process known as **conjugation:** Two paramecia come together and exchange their small nuclei while retaining their large nuclei. As a result of this interaction, both individuals are modified genetically; but there is no increase in the number of organisms. This double-barreled strategy enables the *Paramecium* to reproduce rapidly when conditions are conducive to the survival of a large number of offspring, and to prepare for changing conditions by promoting genetic variability when survival is difficult (see Anderson, 1988).

Bees, ants, and wasps also utilize both sexual and asexual processes, but with a different effect. Among these insects the queen is able to determine the sex of her offspring. She is able to do this because she stores sperm and can regulate whether or not sperm is released when she lays the eggs. When sperm are released and the eggs are fertilized, the offspring are female. When sperm are retained, however, the unfertilized eggs develop as males. For highly social insects such as honeybees, control of sex assignment is particularly advantageous, because males can be produced selectively when needed for sperm deposition. Because males perform no nest duties, their presence at other times would be counterproductive; imagine large numbers of males being on hand but having no real purpose. In contrast, females, which under most conditions develop into workers, can be produced on a regular basis.

Hermaphroditism–Dioecism

Although sex often involves interaction between a male and a female, two separate genders are not a necessary requisite for sexual reproduction. Some species of animals are **hermaphroditic;** that is, the same individuals produce both sperm and eggs.

The Advantages of Hermaphroditism

There are two types of hermaphroditism, each with its own particular advantages. In the first type, **simultaneous hermaphroditism,** an individual produces male and female gametes at roughly the same time. The advantage of this arrangement is that an individual is always assured of a sexually appropriate partner when encountering a member of the same species. This certainty of mating compatibility is particularly advantageous when the population density is low, as it is in deepwater fishes—and these fishes are often simultaneous hermaphrodites.

Another advantage of simultaneous hermaphroditism is seen in animals that are sometimes isolated from all other members of the species. For example, if there is only one tapeworm in a host's gut, the worm may engage in self-fertilization. Because self-fertilization has the same limitations in terms of genetic variability as asexual reproduction,

animals often have adaptations that reduce the probability of self-fertilization. However, as Darwin pointed out many years ago, even a suboptimal form of reproduction is preferable to no reproduction at all (Darwin, 1871).

In most simultaneous hermaphrodites, simultaneous copulation takes place; that is, sperm are exchanged between partners at the same time. In the sea slug (*Aplesia*), however, there is unilateral copulation: One individual performs the male role while another assumes the female role; then, shortly thereafter, the roles are reversed. Sometimes a group of sea slugs will form a copulation chain, with the individual at one end acting as a male, the individual at the other end acting as a female, and those in the middle functioning as both males and females (Leonard & Lukowiak, 1991).

The second type of hermaphroditism is **successive hermaphroditism,** or changing from one sex to another at some point in the animal's life. The major advantage of this adaptation is that an animal may benefit from being a female at one time and a male at another. For example, in some species of parrotfishes, a male lives with a harem of females. A male that is large and strong enough to attract a harem accrues great fitness benefits. In contrast, small males are unlikely to attract any females at all and suffer from the shortage of available females. Thus, the optimal strategy is for young parrotfish males to be female and then, as they grow relatively large, to turn into males.

In an aquarium of parrotfishes, there is always only one male and several females. If the male dies or is experimentally removed from the group, one of the females—typically the largest one—changes into a male and "inherits" the harem (Shapiro, 1984).

A sex change in the opposite direction is also seen in a few cases. As they grow to a relatively large size, anemone fish change from male to female. Large female anemone fish live in a mutualistic relationship with a flowerlike sea anemone and establish a territory surrounding the anemone. One large female may monopolize several sea anemones and set up multiple territories to attract males. She then mates with a male in each territory and lays her eggs, which are then tended by her several male partners (Turner, 1986). Because large size is a particularly advantageous attribute for female anemone fish, it makes fitness sense that the largest anemone fish are females.

A sex change in parrot and anemone fish is relatively simple, because the individuals have no external genitals. The change simply involves a shift from functional ovaries to functional testes or vice versa. The only sacrifice is that the animals are nonreproductive during the time that the change is taking place. But in animals with external genitals, such as mammals, the constraints against sex change are so great that such changes are never found under natural conditions.

The Advantage of Dioecism

Dioecism, the condition in which an animal is either a male (producing sperm) or a female (producing eggs), is more common than hermaphroditism. Dioecism has an important advantage in that the development of male and female parts in separate individuals allows the species to develop a division of labor. This division is especially important for the survival of the young. In dioecious species, for example, one parent may nurture the young while the other provides protection from predators. The advantage is even more pronounced in animals that engage in complex behaviors and interactions, such as birds and mammals.

In a classic paper, R. A. Fisher argued that under most circumstances it is advantageous for parents to produce approximately equal numbers of male and female offspring (Fisher, 1930). If there were significantly more individuals of one gender than the other, the gender in the minority would have a relatively easy time finding partners. Fitness benefits would accrue, in turn, to parents that produced offspring of the minority gender. But once the minority gender surpassed the majority gender, there would be a reversal in which gender would be most advantageous to produce. Consequently, asymmetry in gender ratio tends to disappear, and there is a general evolutionary trend for the sex ratio to hover around 50–50.

The advantages of a 50–50 sex ratio do not hold for all animals under all circumstances, however. Parasitoid wasps lay eggs on a host, after which the wasp larvae feed on the host. The female parasitoid wasps can easily control the sex of their offspring, because they can lay either fertilized or unfertilized eggs. (The fertilized eggs develop into females, while the unfertilized eggs develop into males.) When there are no eggs of other wasps on the host, a given wasp gains maximally by producing predominantly female offspring; the females can successfully reproduce and colonize the host. Thus, parasitiod wasps maximize their fitness by producing female-biased sex ratios when no other eggs are on the host, but move toward a 50–50 sex ratio when the host is parasitized by other wasps (Antolin, 1992).

The Mechanism of Gender Determination in Vertebrates

What determines whether the offspring of a vertebrate is male or female? Some of the ancient answers to this question seem far-fetched. For example, Aristotle suggested that it was the heat of passion of the father that determined the sex of offspring, with the hottest passion resulting in sons. Interestingly, evidence from research in recent decades indicates that for certain reptiles there is some truth to this hypothesis. Environmental temperature does determine the gender of crocodiles—but it is the temperature at which the eggs are incubated that is critical. Crocodile eggs incubated at a relatively high temperature become male hatchlings, while those developing at a lower temperature become females. Eggs incubated at an intermediate temperature develop into an approximately equal distribution of males and females (see Bull, 1983).

A similar temperature-dependent gender determination is found in lizards known as leopard geckos. In this case, extremely high or extremely low temperatures produce females, while intermediate temperatures yield males; moderately high or low temperatures result in an approximately even number of males and females. Under incubation temperatures that produce exclusively females, the females develop faster and are more attractive to males than under temperatures that produce both males and females (Crews, 1994). It seems that not only the gender but the fitness of the female geckos is temperature dependent.

In most mammals, however, as discussed in Chapter 2, gender is not temperature dependent but is chromosomally determined. One half of all mammal sperm are X chromosome–bearing and the other half are Y-bearing, so it might seem that the sex ratio of mammalian zygotes (fertilized eggs) would be 50–50. However, Y-bearing sperm swim faster than their X-bearing counterparts, so most mammalian zygotes are male. But by the time the zygotes develop into adults, the gender ratio approaches 50–50, because male zygotes have a higher mortality rate.

Mammals are also able to control the gender ratio. In an experimental study, researchers removed large numbers of female woodchucks of all ages from a study site. A year after this manipulation, the sex ratio of the young was found to be strongly biased in a female direction. The woodchucks were, in fact, able to compensate for the loss of females (see Trivers, 1985).

If the gender ratio can be adjusted to account for variations in the deviation from a normal 50–50 ratio, can the ratio be varied under other circumstances? A study of opossums suggests that it can. Females that have access to large amounts of food produce more sons than daughters, although under normal conditions opossums have equal numbers of sons and daughters (Austad & Sunquist, 1986). Because mothers with large amounts of food produce larger than normal offspring, both sons and daughters are large. Large size is particularly beneficial for males, however, because bigness provides fitness advantages in intermale competition—and these fitness advantages are realized by the mother as well. In other words, these findings are consistent with the theory of parental investment. When opossum mothers can produce large offspring, they predictably invest more in sons than in daughters (Trivers & Willard, 1973).

External Fertilization–Internal Fertilization

In most aquatic animals, including frogs and most fishes, fertilization occurs outside of the female's body. This process of **external fertilization** takes place in the water as the eggs are deposited or shortly thereafter. In contrast, the familiar avian (bird) and mammalian process of **internal fertilization** occurs while the eggs remain in the female's reproductive tract.

The Advantage of External Fertilization

The primary advantage of external fertilization is its relative simplicity. In salt water, as long as eggs and sperm are deposited at about the same time, it is not necessary to have complex interaction between males and females for fertilization to take place. For example, sexually mature tuna fish gather in a large group and swim in frenzied, swirling masses. Chemicals produced by the sperm stimulate the females to release their eggs, and fertilization takes place in the open ocean.

If the eggs are released in fresh water, more coordination is necessary, because fertilization must take place within a short time. The reason is that the environment inside the female that produced the eggs is more similar to salt water than to fresh water, so unfertilized eggs exposed to fresh water for long periods will die as the result of osmotic imbalance.

Freshwater vertebrates show a variety of adaptations that promote rapid fertilization of the eggs. For example, a male stickleback fish prods the female with his snout at the base of her tail, stimulating her to deposit her eggs in his nest site. Immediately afterwards, he fertilizes the eggs.

The bitterling, another freshwater fish, has a truly unique method of fertilization. The female has a long ovipositor (egg-depositing organ) that enables her to lay her eggs inside a clam. The male bitterling then sprays his sperm over the clam, and the clam sucks the sperm into its shell with its feeding current. As a result of this bizarre technique, fertilization takes place—inside the clam—without the male contacting either the female or the eggs.

Frogs have a still different method of promoting rapid fertilization of eggs. The male grasps the female with his front legs and holds her in an embrace called **amplexus** until she releases her eggs. In many frogs, the male's grasp of the slippery female is facilitated by the growth of nuptial pads on his digits during the breeding season. These pads pierce the female's skin and allow the male to retain his grasp as long as necessary. Because the pair are in close physical contact during amplexus, the male can feel the female's abdominal contractions, which precede egg release. Consequently, he is stimulated to release his sperm at the time she sheds her eggs (see Stebbins & Cohen, 1995).

The Advantages of Internal Fertilization

Internal fertilization, unlike its external counterpart, does not depend on the presence of water, because the fusion of gametes takes place inside the female's body. Consequently, internal fertilization may take place on land, in water, or even in the air. Internal fertilization also benefits aquatic animals that live in fast-moving streams or turbid waters; the eggs and sperm cannot be separated from each other by water currents as they might be in the case of external fertilization.

Internal fertilization has other advantages as well. First, an egg that is fertilized within the female's reproductive tract may be retained and protected. In fact, virtually all species in which the females retain their eggs after fertilization and produce live young are internal fertilizers.

Another advantage of internal fertilization is that sperm may be stored inside the female for a period of time before fertilization takes place. Sperm storage allows a female to produce several batches of fertile eggs after only one mating. For example, a queen bee can produce great numbers of offspring without experiencing the risks or time involved in multiple nuptial flights and matings.

Still another advantage of internal fertilization is that implantation (attachment of the zygote in the uterus) may be delayed. Delayed implantation puts embryonic development on hold, allowing animals to time the arrival of their offspring. Through this mechanism the female sea lion, for example, can deliver her pup from the previous year's mating in the early spring, a time that corresponds with her arrival at the mating grounds. Hundreds of females arrive at the same place at about the same time, so the young can be raised in communal rookeries. Although the crowded conditions might appear, on the surface, to be detrimental to the young, research indicates that the offspring survive much better in breeding groups than when they are placed alone with their mothers (Campagna et al., 1992).

Passive Spermatophore Transfer

In some species the male deposits a packet of sperm known as a **spermatophore** on the ground or at the bottom of a body of water,

TABLE 8.2 ◆ Advantages of External and Internal Fertilization

External Fertilization	Internal Fertilization
Relatively simple.	Fertilization may take place in any environment: water, land, or air.
Rapid fertilization possible.	
Female may leave eggs after fertilization.	Fertilized egg may be protected.
	Storage of sperm possible.
	Implantation may be delayed, allowing timed arrival of offspring.

and the female picks up the spermatophore with her cloaca (her genital opening). Once inside the female's reproductive tract, the packet absorbs fluids, swells, and eventually bursts and releases the sperm.

Although the transfer of the spermatophore is passive, in the sense that the male simply leaves his spermatophore, the male usually engages in behaviors that promote the female's acceptance of the spermatophore. For example, when a male scorpion approaches a receptive female, the two face each other, extending their long abdomens high in the air and beginning to move around in circles. The male then grasps the female with the pincers on his anterior appendages, and the pair move back and forth together in a type of dance. This dance may last for a day or more before the male deposits his spermatophore on the ground. The male then appears to maneuver the female in such a way that her genital area comes in contact with the sper-matophore. When contact is made, tiny hooks on the spermatophore fasten it to the genital area, and as the female moves about, the sperm-bearing package works its way into her genital opening (see Savory, 1965).

Male American dusky salamanders also engage in passive spermatophore transfer. A receptive female typically places her nose against the base of the male's tail. The male then deposits a spermatophore and begins to walk away, leaving a mucous thread extend-ing from his cloaca to the spermatophore. This thread probably helps the female move along the mucous path and position her cloaca directly above the spermatophore (see Halliday, 1982).

In some cases the spermatophore not only transfers sperm but provides an important benefit for the female, because she eats part of the spermatophore. For example, the large spermatophore of the bush cricket includes protein-rich substances that significantly in-crease the size and number of the female's eggs. Accordingly, the males with the largest spermatophores are the most attractive to fe-males (Gwynne, 1984).

Copulation

The direct placement of sperm into a female receptacle, referred to as **copulation,** is the most common method of achieving internal fertilization. The male octopus copulates with the aid of a hooklike adaptation on one of his eight arms. After stimulating a female with one or more of his other seven arms, he reaches into his body cavity with his hooklike mechanism and retrieves a spermatophore. He then places the spermatophore far into the female's body cavity. Since the ovaries are lo-cated deep inside the female, this method of placement ensures that the sperm are de-posited near the site of her eggs—a task that would be extremely difficult to accomplish with a more conventional intromittent organ such as a penis.

In some species of octopus, the couple en-gages in prolonged copulation and the male transfers several spermatophores to the female (see Wells & Wells, 1972). Research evidence suggests that males are sensitive to the mating history of the female. If the female has copu-lated with another male in the last 24 hours, the most recent male partner removes or dis-places previously deposited sperm (Cigliano, 1995). (I will return to this and other methods of a male's promoting the postcopulatory suc-cess of his own sperm when we consider sperm competition in Chapter 10.)

In contrast to the octopus method, most examples of copulation involve the insertion of a male intromittent organ or penis that de-livers the sperm directly into the female's body. Females of copulating species typically have a receptacle or vagina that receives the male organ. Nevertheless, there are several ex-ceptions to this arrangement.

Patterns of Copulation

Most animals copulate in a consistent, stereo-typed manner. For example, male rats always mount the female from behind in a species-specific sequence of movements. Apes, how-ever, show more variability in copulatory pat-terns. Gibbons (small tailless apes) sometimes mate on the ground but at other times copu-late while hanging from tree branches. Bonobo chimpanzees exhibit an exceptionally large variety of copulatory positions. They have been observed mating with one partner

◆ UNUSUAL ADAPTATIONS

Pseudocopulation, Exceptionally Large Organs, and Variations in the Number of Intromittent Organs

Spiders are exceptional in that the intromittent organ—a hollow enlargement at the tip of appendages located beside the jaws—does not initially contain semen. In order to fill the organ with sperm, the male ejaculates semen into a web and then sucks it up into his organ. He then empties the semen into the female's receptacle.

In some cases the male spider intromits his organ without having filled it with sperm, thereby engaging in a nonreproductive behavior known as **pseudocopulation.** Pseudocopulation serves an important function for the males of the spider *Frontinella pyramitela.* By intromitting his organ before filling it with sperm, the male is able to test a female and determine if she has had a recent previous mating. If he determines that the female is recently mated, he then withdraws his organ and leaves. If he finds she is a virgin, however, he fills his organ with sperm and proceeds with true copulation. This strategy is adaptive for the male spider because mating with a female that had already received another male's sperm would be a poor investment; the second male's sperm would not fertilize many of her eggs (Suter, 1990). From the female's fitness standpoint, pseudocopulation is not too costly, because females that are rejected still retain some of the first male's sperm for a long period of time and may continue to lay fertilized eggs.

In most animals the male has an intromittent organ that conveys sperm to a female when the two animals are in close proximity. Some barnacles, however, have intromittent organs adapted for a sessile (nonmoving) existence. The barnacle organ is long enough to reach a sex partner without any movement on the part of either animal (Figure 8.1). Because these animals are hermaphroditic, they typically engage in mutual copulation; and in

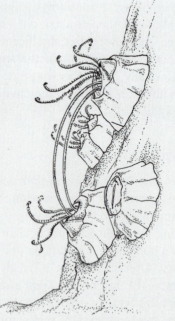

FIGURE 8.1 ◆ Copulation in hermaphroditic barnacles. Each individual is both sending and receiving a long intromittent organ to and from another barnacle.

some cases intromittent organs from three or four males will enter a female receptacle at the same time.

In most mammals, erection of the penis results from blood flowing into spongy tissue in the penis. Some mammals, however, have a bone known as an **os penis** that supports the penis. The walrus is an example; the penis of the walrus male may exceed two feet in length and is withdrawn into the body cavity when the animal is not sexually aroused. This protects the organ from sharp objects and reduces hydrodynamic resistance. Incidentally, the os penis of the walrus is so large and sturdy that it has been used as a war club by certain Eskimo tribes.

The usual number of intromittent organs per individual is one. Snakes and lizards have two intromittent organs, however, one on each side of the body. The organs, which are called **hemipenes,** are held flush against the body when the male is relaxed, which prevents possible injury to the hemipenes. When the male is sexually aroused, the hemipenes protrude like the fingers of a rubber glove when air is inserted.

Despite the physical possibility, no male has been observed with two females at one time. Rather, the two hemipenes alternate in usage when lizards such as *Anolis sagrei* mate more than twice in 24 hours. This alternation seems to be an adaptation for increasing sperm transfer in successive copulations; when the lizard is experimentally forced to use the same hemipenis twice in succession, fewer sperm are transferred than when the hemipenes are alternated (Tokarz & Slowinski, 1990).

At the other extreme, most male birds lack an intromittent organ. In 97 percent of bird species—including the songbirds—the male simply places his cloaca close to and above that of the female, stimulating her to open her cloaca and receive his sperm (Figure 8.2).

FIGURE 8.2 ◆ **Copulation in a pair of dunnocks (English songbirds).** The male jumps above the female and "dumps" his sperm into the female's open cloaca.

(continued)

Thus, in the vast majority of avian species, males are unable to copulate forcibly with a female; males are highly dependent on female cooperation in order to achieve insemination (Birkhead & Moller, 1992).

Some ancestral types of birds, such as ducks, do have an intromittent organ. Significantly, two mallard ducks have been observed raping a female (see Barash, 1977). It seems likely that more recently evolved birds were selected for smaller and lighter intromittent organs to the point that the organs were lost entirely. This adaptation for light weight, along with several other weight-reducing adaptations, was clearly important in the development of birds' ability to fly long distances with relatively little expenditure of energy. And as a side effect, the loss of the intromittent organ also resulted in a reduction in the amount of reproductive control that male birds could exert over females.

hanging from a tree branch, using the rear entry position, and copulating face-to-face with the male on top (DeWaal, 1989).

When coital positions of mammals are considered, the most important factor appears to be the development of the brain. Relatively large and well differentiated brains are associated with the ability of an animal to vary its coital position (Beach, 1965).

Large brain size in mammals is also associated with an increase in functions associated with copulation. Although the function of copulation in relatively small-brained mammals is almost exclusively reproductive, copulation in large-brained primates serves nonreproductive functions. For example, bonobos often copulate at times when the female is infertile. Female bonobos also engage in same-gender sexual activities such as mutual genital stimulation. The sexual interaction appears to reduce social tension and build social bonds between the partners (Kano, 1992).

Another example of nonreproductive sex occurs in bonobos. Females have been observed offering males copulation in exchange for a piece of fruit. It seems likely that the nonreproductive functions of sexual interaction in these large-brained primates have been important in the evolution of extended female receptivity throughout the reproductive cycle.

EVOLUTION OF REPRODUCTIVE PROCESSES AND STRUCTURES

Now that we have considered some examples of the great diversity of reproductive techniques, it is interesting to speculate on how reproductive processes evolved. Because by definition reproduction is part of all life, the beginning of reproductive processes is obviously extremely ancient. Nonetheless, we are able to make some reasonably educated guesses, based on several different types of evidence, about the evolution of certain reproductive processes and structures.

The Dawn of Sex

The evolution of sexual processes seems to occurred separately in **prokaryotes** and **eukaryotes.** Prokaryotes are primitive bacteria that do not have a clearly differentiated cell nucleus; eukaryotes are all other organisms—including certain protozoans and all multicellular animals—and have a distinct cell nucleus.

Prokaryotes

The first type of reproduction probably involved simple fission. However, the fact that sexual processes exist in present-day bacteria suggests that sex may have evolved in prokaryotes at a very early time—long before the evolution of eukaryotes.

Experiments with present-day bacteria indicate that a primitive type of sexual process could have occurred in the earliest bacterialike cells as a response to life-threatening ultraviolet radiation. Because there was, quite surely, no free oxygen in the earth's early environment, the ozone layer that protects organisms today from ultraviolet light was not in place, and the early bacterialike organisms would have benefited greatly from genetic repair (Bernstein et al., 1984). Essentially, the organisms could have taken up DNA from other

bacterialike cells and from viruses. This DNA would then have served to replace DNA damaged by the radiation.

This hypothesis of the origin of sex in bacteria is essentially an elaboration of the genetic repair hypothesis discussed earlier in this chapter. According to this theory, after the origins of sex as a genetic repair mechanism, it was possible for organisms to accrue the advantages of genetic variability. This variability could have then become a driving force in the evolution of sexual processes.

Eukaryotes

The genetic repair hypothesis may account for the evolution of a very primitive sexual process in bacteria, but it cannot explain the evolution of sexual processes in eukaryotes. The type of sex found in eukaryotes requires a fusion—first of cell membranes, then of the nuclei. A reasonable, though somewhat bizarre-sounding, hypothesis is that the primordial fusion occurred when one single-celled animal attempted to cannibalize another. Instead of complete consumption, fusion took place; the animals became a double organism, then later split apart and divided the genetic material (see Margulis & Sagan, 1988).

Evidence for the fusion hypothesis comes from the fact that fusion takes place in certain present-day protozoans. For example, shelled amoebas engage in sex when one individual leaves its shell to enter the shell of another. The two individuals then fuse and mix their genetic material. At a later time the animal divides, producing two individuals. Each individual has genetic material that is a mixture of material contained in the original amoebas.

Once the basic sexual process was in place, the next evolutionary step was probably the formation of gametes that contained the haploid number of chromosomes (refer to Chapter 2). The gametes, rather than the whole organism, could then fuse and their nuclei meld together.

The Evolution of Distinct Gametes

Not all gametes are distinctly male and female. For example, flagellate protozoans (protozoans with whiplike tails) include species that vary from having identical gametes to having extreme differentiation of gametes (see Anderson, 1988).

The ancestral condition was probably that of having identical gametes. Then the evolution toward extreme differentiation of gametes—eggs and sperm—may have taken place by degrees. This evolutionary development is likely to have involved two concurrent trends. The first was a trend toward the production of large gametes that carried nutrients (such as eggs). The second was a trend toward smaller, less energy-expensive gametes (such as sperm). In the latter trend, energy could be invested in producing large numbers of gametes that were motile. But the fusion of two small gametes would not produce enough resources, so there would be a selection for small gametes to reject other small gametes and pursue large ones. Although there would have been no disadvantage to large gametes fusing, the strong selection pressure for small gametes to pursue large ones would eventually prevail; at some point it became impossible for either two small or two large gametes to fuse (see Daly & Wilson, 1983).

The Evolution of Sex Organs

Which organ evolved first, the penis or the vagina? In some cases, the male organ appears to be ancestral. For example, one primitive type of flatworm has a male organ but no specialized female receptacle. The male inserts his intromittent organ, which is typically armed with sharp stylets or probes, into the female at any point; the sperm are then deposited freely into her body cavity.

In other, more recently evolved flatworms, the females have evolved a receptacle that receives the intromittent organ during copulation. It seems that as flatworms and other organisms evolved a larger size, there was an advantage to having a female receptacle that accepted the male organ and allowed the sperm to be deposited in close proximity to the eggs.

In contrast to flatworms, however, some female animals have receptacles that seem to have evolutionary origins earlier than those of the males' intromittent organ. Like ancestral species of fish, the female guppy has a receptacle through which her fecal material as well as her eggs pass. The female receptacle in guppies takes on the additional function of receiving the male guppy's intromittent organ—a structure known as a gonopodium that is derived from his anal fins. The anal fin of male guppies develops into the organ when the male reaches sexual maturity and produces large amounts of the hormone testosterone. In this instance, evidently, it is the female's receptacle that is ancestral and the male organ that has a relatively recent evolutionary origin.

In conclusion, it appears that sex organs in different groups of animals have had a variety of evolutionary origins. In some cases the male organ evolved first; in other cases the female organ has a longer evolutionary history. And once the male and female organs evolved to a certain extent, they clearly influenced one another's evolutionary development.

Genital Locks

In most animals the male organ fits into that of the female and is removed immediately after ejaculation. In some cases, however, the male and female organs have evolved in such a way that the male organ becomes locked inside that of the female for a period of time. For example, the penis of the male dog becomes locked in the female's vagina, and the couple remain together even after the male has ejaculated and dismounted. Because dogs typically mate while they are running, this **genital lock** functions to keep the penis inserted long enough for all or at least most of the semen to enter the vagina.

Genital locks also occur in certain rodents, but in rodents the lock seems to function primarily to prevent the possibility of sperm competition. When the male remains intromitted for an extended period, the possibility that another male will copulate with the female is reduced. However, the prolonged copulation makes the pair especially vulnerable to predation. Thus, it is not surprising that rodents that utilize genital locks tend to live and copulate in elaborate nests or burrows where the exposure to predators is minimal (Dewsbury, 1972).

Induced Ovulation

Cats do not exhibit genital locks. However, male felines have evolved special barbs on the penis that are pointed backwards in such a way that the male provides strong stimulation to the vagina as he withdraws his penis. (As many cat owners have noted, females often let out a screech and attempt to bat at the male as he withdraws.) This strong stimulation is necessary to evoke the release of the luteinizing hormone (LH), which in turn induces ovulation. Mammals that ovulate only when they are mated, such as felines, are known as **induced ovulators;** they are highly efficient reproducers, because the female almost always becomes pregnant following bouts of copulation.

Female Orgasm

In rare cases, prolonged genital stimulation by a male results in female orgasm in nonhuman animals. For many years the existence of female orgasm in nonhuman animals was unknown. However, laboratory research indicates that female stump-tailed macaque monkeys show orgasmic responses—including uterine contractions, increases in heart rate, and distinctive facial expressions and grunts—during prolonged sexual stimulation (Goldfoot et al., 1980).

Because the stimulation that is normally applied by male monkeys during intercourse is of short duration, female orgasm is relatively infrequent. Nonetheless, the uterine contractions can function to transport some of the sperm to the opening of the fallopian tubes and reduce the time span between male ejaculation and fertilization. This transport of sperm can function as a sperm competition mechanism if the female copulates with two or more males within a short period of time, because the sperm from a male that induces orgasm is most likely to impregnate the female.

ECOLOGY AND REPRODUCTION

The example of genital locks in rodents illustrates how the threat of predation can influence the evolution of reproduction. Let's now consider some other examples of the relationship between ecology—the impact of the environment—and the evolution of reproduction.

Number of Offspring Produced

The stability of an environment has a strong influence on reproduction. Unstable environments are usually populated by less than the optimum number of individual animals, because catastrophic events periodically reduce the population to a point below the saturation level. Species that inhabit these below-saturation-point habitats are called *r*-selected species. (The *r* stands for the beginning letter in the last word of the phrase "species-specific growth rate.") In contrast, animals living in stable environments that are at or close to the saturation point are called *K*-selected species. (The *K* stands for the carrying capacity of the habitat.) Although we will focus on differences between *r* and *K* selection, remember that the differences are distributed on a continuum. Most species fall somewhere between the two extremes.

One way to conceptualize the distinction between *r*-selected and *K*-selected species is to think of the contrast between people in a gold-rush town and in an old, established community. Gold-rush types—"rough and ready" or *r* selected—live in an unstable environment and are liable to move in and out quickly. In contrast, people living in established environments are "cool" or *K* selected. They are much more likely to remain in the community for long periods.

As we would predict on the basis of the above analysis, strongly *r*-selected mammals such as rats produce relatively large numbers of offspring in a short time: Their environment is generally below the carrying capacity, so there is a "race" to fill the void. In contrast, strongly *K*-selected mammals such as elephants do not produce many offspring. Because there is typically little room for an increase in an elephant population in a particular habitat, producing few offspring and investing time in caring for each one is a more beneficial strategy. In addition to producing more young, *r*-selected animals tend to be smaller, have shorter life spans, reach maturity earlier, and produce young that mature faster than those of *K*-selected animals (MacArthur & Wilson, 1967; Pianka, 1970). All of these factors tend to facilitate gold-rush strategies.

TABLE 8.3 ◆ Some General Correlates of *r* Selection and *K* Selection

Type of Species	Environment	Reproduction Rate	Growth	Life Span
r-selected	Unstable	High	Rapid	Short
K-selected	Stable	Low	Slow	Long

Arctic or mountain regions are good examples of unstable environments inhabited by *r*-selected species. Periodically, populations of land animals in these regions are greatly reduced by extended cold spells, floods, or droughts, and any given population is often below the carrying capacity; consequently, there is relatively little competition from conspecifics. Under these conditions, producing large numbers of offspring during the relatively short periods of favorable weather is most beneficial.

In contrast, *K*-selected animals in stable environments such as the tropics tend to face great intraspecific competition; investing in activities that increase the offspring's chances of competing effectively is of more benefit than simply producing large numbers of offspring. Thus, parrots that live in the tropics produce fewer offspring in a given period of time than do birds that inhabit temperate or arctic regions (MacArthur & Wilson, 1967; Pianka, 1970).

A comparison of the number of eggs produced by the same or closely related species of birds living in different environments illustrates this environmental effect. A house wren may lay two or three eggs in the stable environment of the tropics but as many as seven in a less stable temperate zone. Similarly, populations of birds on offshore islands—which tend to have stable habitats—lay fewer eggs than do birds of the same species on the mainland (Faaberg, 1988).

Age of Sexual Maturity

Ecological factors have also influenced the evolution of the timing of sexual maturity. This timing effect is clearly seen in female fish.

Most species of fish continue to grow throughout their lives, and the greater the female's size, the greater her **fecundity,** or the number of eggs she produces. Thus, female fishes living in favorable environments—where they are likely to survive for several years—may maximize their reproductive potential by delaying the production of eggs until they have achieved a relatively great size. In contrast, females living in unfavorable environments benefit from reproducing early in life, because their chances of becoming old are limited.

Male fish show a similar timing effect, but the fitness advantages are somewhat different. There is often strong competition for the establishment of a territory—an area that is defended against other males and that attracts females. Consequently, in favorable environments the males of territorial species often delay the onset of sexual maturity until they are relatively large and capable of successfully competing with other males for a territory.

In the case of the Pacific salmon, reproductive maturity of both sexes is delayed for an extremely long time; these fish do not reach sexual maturity until they are several years old. Then they reproduce just once— shortly before they die. This strategy of building up to one large reproductive bout, known as the **big bang strategy,** occurs only in stable environments.

The age of sexual maturity in rodents is also influenced by ecological factors, but in a different way than in fishes. At least part of this difference is due to the fact that female rodents do not gain a significant increase in fecundity with increasing age; nor are old adult male rodents better able to establish territories than young ones. Another difference is that in the rodent's environment conditions are liable to fluctuate within relatively short periods of time. Thus, in contrast to fishes, rodents gain clear advantages by delaying reproduction under unfavorable conditions, given the reasonably good probability that conditions will improve within a short time or that the rodents may move to a new location (Bronson & Rissman, 1986).

Timing of Reproduction during the Season

The young of animals, especially birds in temperate climates, typically arrive in late winter or early spring. Although parental care does not seem to differ in early- and late-reproducing parents, experiments manipulating the time of breeding indicate that the young of parents reproducing early in the reproductive season survive more consistently than those reproducing later in the season (Norris, 1993).

Nonetheless, there are certain dangers in early breeding. For example, the possibility of unfavorable weather and subsequent food shortages represents a significant risk factor, especially if birds reproduce only once per season (Nilsson & Smith, 1994). In other words, early breeding is most risky for birds that produce only one batch of eggs—or, figuratively speaking, put all of their eggs in one basket. A study of the timing of reproduction in several species of birds has indicated that one-time breeders are later reproducers than several-time breeders, supporting the hypothesis that one-time breeders tend to be more "prudent" about the timing of egg laying (Svensson, 1995).

In conclusion, ecological factors influence reproductive strategies in a variety of ways. In the following three chapters, we will continue to see many instances of the strong relationship between ecology and reproduction.

◆ HUMAN EVOLUTION

In some respects humans are typical mammals in regard to reproduction. In other respects, however, we are unusual or at an extreme, even when compared to other primates. We will now look at the probable evolution of our sexuality in an attempt to explain both our similarities to and our differences from other animals.

GENDER RATIO

In the past many people assumed that the human gender ratio was fixed at 50–50. However, there is some evidence that the gender ratio in human births may be influenced by a deviation from the normal 50–50 ratio in the population at large. Birth records show a temporary increase in the proportion of males born in countries that were involved in World War I, in which enormous numbers of soldiers were killed. A similar short-lived increase in the proportion of male births occurred after World War II, as shown in Figure 8.3.

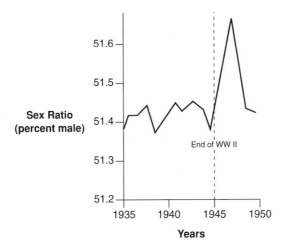

FIGURE 8.3 ◆ **The gender ratio of male births in the United States over a 15-year period.** Note the significant increase in male births immediately following World War II.

This apparent gender ratio adjustment in humans is not well understood. It may result, however, from the high frequency of copulation that is typical after couples are reunited following a period of separation. This high frequency of copulation is associated with a slight increase in the relative number of male births (see Trivers, 1985). At any rate, humans seem to be similar to other vertebrates studied in that we have a mechanism allowing us to adjust to imbalances in the gender ratio.

REPRODUCTIVE MATURITY

As in the case of many other vertebrates, environmental factors have an effect on human reproductive maturity. For example, a starvation diet that results in a low fat content in a woman's body inhibits menarche (first menstruation). Consequently, food shortages function to delay human reproductive potential—an adaptive response in the sense that infants are not likely to survive during times of extreme food shortage.

Research has also identified a different type of environmental influence on menarche and pregnancy. Girls that grow up under conditions of family stress experience an earlier menarche and reproductive maturity than girls raised in relatively stable family conditions; these early-maturing girls then tend to engage in sexual intercourse and give birth at an earlier age than later-maturing girls (Moffit et al., 1992; Stattin & Magnusson, 1990).

Leaving aside the many social and psychological reasons why stress may increase the probability of early pregnancy, the finding that the biology of menarche is affected by family stress raises the question of adaptiveness. Why would the relationship between early stress and early reproductive potential have evolved? It seems that girls raised under stressful conditions are, at a certain level, investing in a kind of *r*-selected strategy—that is, they are getting an early start on reproduction, even at the cost of sacrificing quality in parenting potential (Belsky et al., 1991). Under natural conditions, stress-related environmental factors were probably correlated with a short life expectancy. With a short life expectancy, an early start to reproduction would have been a good strategy for passing on one's genes. In our modern technological society, of course, early reproduction often produces serious social problems. However, as we have already seen at several points, our genes have not had time to adjust to modern life.

COPULATORY PATTERNS

Although face-to-face coition is uncommon among animals, it is not unique to humans. We have seen that, on occasion, some male and female apes copulate facing each other. The evolution of a general preference for face-to-face coition in humans was probably driven, at least in part, by the somewhat modified angle of the woman's vagina compared to that of other primates. This modification represents an adaptation to bipedal locomotion, or walking upright.

The elaboration of nonreproductive aspects of human sexuality is also unusual, but not unprecedented. Bonobos engage in nonreproductive sex, apparently to relieve social tension, and female chimpanzees sometimes exchange copulations for resources.

Generally speaking, variability of sexual behavior, like variability of other behavior patterns, is associated with the development of a relatively large brain and an advanced level of cognition. This advanced level of cognition is seen in apes and was probably present in our ancestors. Thus, nonreproductive sex and general variability in sexual expression may be considered extensions of evolutionary trends present in our primate ancestors.

ORGASM IN WOMEN

Although female orgasm is not uniquely human, it is much more prevalent in humans than other primates. The proximate explanation for the higher incidence of female orgasm in humans is related to the fact that humans copulate for relatively long periods of time; copulation usually lasts less than 10 seconds in other primates. Furthermore, humans often engage in foreplay that tends to heighten sexual arousal.

Historically, there have been several ultimate explanations given for the evolution of orgasm in women. One theory is that female orgasm tends to increase emotional bonding between partners (see Morris, 1967). A less romantic explanation is related to the finding, discussed earlier, that female orgasm greatly increases the speed of transmission of the sperm to the ovaries. If a woman has intercourse with more than one man within a short period of time, the man who is associated with an orgasm has an advantage in terms of sperm competition (see Baker & Bellis, 1993). This explanation is of interest not only because it makes sense in terms of how female orgasm could be influenced by natural selection, but also because it suggests how a female can be more than simply a passive recipient of male semen: A woman can presumably influence which of two or more partners will father her child by being especially responsive to one of the partners. We will consider the possible role of female orgasm in sperm competition in more detail in Chapter 10.

MENSTRUATION AND MENOPAUSE

Menstruation and menopause, like female orgasm, were thought at one time to be uniquely human. However, research evidence now suggests that certain nonhuman female animals also menstruate and experience menopause.

Menstruation (the passing of blood and the remains of the outer layer of the uterus) occurs in several primates and in a few nonprimate mammals. The amount of bleeding is relatively small in these animals, and the females clean their vulvas before the blood becames noticeable. Margie Profet (1993) has proposed that menstrual bleeding functions as a defense against parasites frequently introduced by semen. The relatively great menstrual flow in human females is related to women's relatively low probability of pregnancy with each copulation and long period of sexual receptivity during each menstrual cycle. Because of these factors, women have a relatively great need for defense against parasites introduced by semen (Profet, 1993).

Menopause, the cessation of menstruation and of a woman's ability to bear offspring, is highly unusual in the animal world. It has been found in only one other species of animal besides humans—the whale. Why was menopause naturally selected to evolve in humans but not in other primates? Jared Diamond (1996) suggests that a combination of several factors were involved. First, the human baby's head is larger at childbirth than that of other primates, resulting in a significantly greater risk of death at childbirth than exists in any other primate mother. And in a natural state the mortality risk is 3 times greater for women over 40 than for women in their 20s.

Another factor is the length of dependency of human children compared to the dependent period of the young of other primates. A mother may gain fitness by providing long-term help in the care of her children as well as of her sisters' and her children's children.

Still another factor is that in preliterate societies older women—and older men as well—were sources of important knowledge, a fact that is related to the reverence still shown to older people in many nontechnological societies today. In short, women have clearly gained more inclusive fitness benefits by giving up their reproductive potential at an age when the risk of death outweighs the potential indirect fitness benefits associated with a long life (Diamond, 1996).

◆ CHANGING PERSPECTIVES

PAST	PRESENT	FUTURE
Human sexual processes are very different from those in nonhuman animals (nineteenth century, pre-Darwin).	Natural selection influenced the evolution of sexual processes in all animals. Consequently, the basic processes are very similar in humans and other mammals, especially apes.	How is the cultural evolution of reproductive processes related to the process of natural selection?

SUMMARY

A large variety of reproductive techniques and strategies exist in animals. Reproduction may be either asexual or sexual. Compared to sexual reproduction, asexual reproduction is more efficient and exposes an animal to less danger. A major advantage of sexual reproduction is that it results in genetic diversity in the offspring.

Sexual processes are particularly beneficial to animals that live in a changing environment (the lottery hypothesis), are strongly affected by other rapidly evolving organisms (the coevolution hypothesis), and have a need for genetic repair (the repair hypothesis). In some cases individuals exhibit both sexual and asexual processes.

Although some animals are hermaphroditic (either simultaneously or successively), most are dioecious. When the gender ratio fluctuates, there is a strong tendency to return to the evolutionarily stable 50–50 ratio. Therefore, the sex ratio for most animals remains at approximately 50–50.

External fertilization is characteristic of most aquatic animals. In contrast, internal fertilization takes place in terrestrial vertebrates and in a few aquatic vertebrates. The benefits of internal fertilization can include the possibility of live birth, the ability to store sperm, and the chance to postpone birth by delaying implantation.

Internal fertilization is accomplished by either spermatophore transfer or copulation. There are a wide variety of adaptations associated with copulation, including pseudocopulation, the use of hemipenes, and the development of an os penis. The earliest sexual process in bacteria possibly evolved as a type of genetic repair. Later, sexual processes in eukaryotes may have evolved in the following steps: fusion of complete organisms, resulting from attempts at cannibalism; formation of gametes; and the development of extreme differentiation of gametes (eggs and sperm). Copulatory organs have a variety of evolutionary origins. Some animals have evolved special mechanisms such as genital locks and induced ovulation.

Ecological conditions are related to several aspects of reproduction. Animals living in unstable environments tend to be *r* selected and produce many offspring in a short time, while those in stable environments are generally *K* selected and produce relatively few offspring. Environmental factors are also related to the age of sexual maturity and to the timing of reproduction during a season.

A consideration of the probable evolution of humans helps to explain both similarities and differences between basic reproductive processes in humans and nonhumans. Evolution has played a part in human gender ratio adjustment, age of reproductive maturity, copulatory patterns, orgasm in women, menstruation, and menopause.

KEY TERMS

amplexus, p. 177
big bang strategy, p. 187
coevolution hypothesis, p. 172
conjugation, p. 173
copulation, p. 179
dioecism, p. 175
eukaryotes, p. 183
external fertilization, p. 177
fecundity, p. 187
genital lock, p. 185
hemipenes, p. 181
hermaphroditic, p. 174

induced ovulators, p. 185
internal fertilization, p. 177
lottery hypothesis, p. 172
os penis, p. 181
parthenogenesis, p. 171
prokaryotes, p. 183
pseudocopulation, p. 180
repair hypothesis, pp. 172–173
simultaneous hermaphroditism, p. 174
spermatophore, p. 178
successive hermaphroditism, p. 174

CHAPTER 9

ATTRACTION AND COURTSHIP

◆ *Why do male bowerbirds build structures known as* bowers?

◆ *Are females generally more discriminating than males in their choice of mates?*

In contrast to a popular misconception, most animals do not simply mate at random with individuals of the opposite sex. On the contrary, because there is great advantage in an animal's obtaining the "best" partner available, there has been a strong evolutionary trend toward maximizing the possibility of obtaining a partner that will promote reproductive success.

9

An especially important factor in a partner is "good genes"—that is, the genetic potential to contribute genes associated with fitness to the offspring. Genetic potential cannot be assessed directly, so evolution has tended to promote sensitivity to factors that reflect good genetic potential. On the other side of the coin, there has been a comparable evolutionary trend toward prominent display of structures and behaviors that are indicative of good genes.

There has also been a evolutionary trend encouraging development of sensitivity to resources that contribute to the reproduction process, particularly to the survival of the offspring. Thus, factors related to attraction often include evidence of both good genes and appropriate resources—or at least the potential to supply resources.

Because the factors that promote survival and successful reproduction differ greatly from species to species, the determinants of attractiveness are also extremely varied. At first glance, some of the attributes associated with attractiveness seem strange and incomprehensible. As with the reproductive processes discussed in Chapter 8, however, many of these "strange" attributes make sense in light of the principles of natural selection.

We will begin by considering the factors that determine sexual attraction and how attraction is communicated. Then we will discuss courtship, the interaction that facilitates a mutual evaluation process and prepares the partners for mating. Finally, we will examine attraction and courtship in human evolution.

ATTRACTION

How do animals evaluate one another's attractiveness? First, animals tend to respond to attractiveness cues that are an "honest" representation of good genes and resources. If an unfit animal is able to produce the same cue as a fit animal, then there will be a natural selection against responding to this type of cue. Second, it is important that an attractiveness cue be easily perceptible. It accomplishes little

for an animal to present cues that cannot be evaluated quickly and accurately under the appropriate circumstances. A third important factor is predation: A cue that indicates fitness but that also attracts predators has obvious costs.

There are also differences in the cost of making a poor choice of a partner. A hypothesis derived from Trivers's (1972) "theory of parental investment" is that one gender will usually pay a higher cost for a poor choice than the other. In most species, females bear the brunt of reproductive costs. For example, oviparous (egg-laying) females such as birds must wait for some time after depositing a clutch of eggs before they can produce eggs again. Similarly, live-bearing females such as mammals must wait until after the young are born before they can become fertile again. Also, female birds and female mammals both invest time and energy in parental behavior. For these females, in other words, a choice of an unfit partner cannot be immediately rectified. Males, which can typically inseminate more than one female within a very short time, have less to lose by choosing an unfit partner. Consequently, females tend to gain a relatively large amount of fitness by being choosy and are usually more sensitive to cues indicative of reproductive success than males (Sargent & Gross, 1985). This question of gender differences in the relative costs of making a poor choice of partners will come up again when we discuss courtship later in this chapter.

Attractiveness Cues

The types of cues an animal uses to communicate attractiveness obviously depend on the species' sensory capabilities. An animal's environment is also an important factor. For example, birds that live in forested areas cannot see other birds at a distance. Thus, songbirds in forest habitats use vocal cues to attract mates, while aquatic birds rely on visual cues. Another example: Small mammals are usually in more danger of predation than larger ones. Consequently, small mammals often rely on chemical cues that can be effective at night, when the risk of predation is relatively low. With these considerations in mind, let's now examine various types of cues related to attraction.

Auditory Cues

Auditory signals have distinct advantages over other types of signals that are used to communicate attractiveness: Under most conditions sound waves travel a great distance, and sound can be as effective at night as during the day.

In male frogs, large size is an important fitness characteristic. However, female frogs have relatively poor form vision; so the female gains information about the male by analyzing his calls. Females of different frog species have evolved sensitivity to different aspects of the call. A study of tungara frogs indicates that females prefer males that call with great intensity, especially at the higher frequencies (Wilczynski et al., 1995). Such a high-intensity call is associated with large size; small tungara frogs cannot produce a high-intensity call.

In addition to frequency and intensity, frogs that call from burrows are responsive to the acoustics of their burrows. Thus, leptodactylid frogs call from burrows that resonate sympathetically with the dominant frequency of their calls, thereby promoting the broadcast of their calls. Some frogs even choose burrows whose acoustic properties enable the frogs to accurately detect the calls of their competitors (Penna & Solis, 1996).

As effective as auditory communication can be, there is a major drawback: Producing sound may expose an animal to predation. For example, the fringe-lipped bat preys on the tungara frog by zeroing in on the frog's call. Although a frog typically stops calling when it detects a bat approaching, a certain percentage of frogs still fall victim to the bats (Tuttle et al., 1982; see Figure 9.1).

Male songbirds, too, rely on auditory cues to attract females. Male singing begins early in the mating season and initially functions to threaten other males that impinge on the male's territory. Thus, the same songs that serve to threaten other males are also attractive to females. As in the case of other animals that use sound as a courtship signal, the female bird is attracted only to males that sing the species-specific song.

Many male songbirds sing a variety of forms of the species-specific song, however,

not just a stereotyped version. Because older males are capable of singing a larger variety of songs than young males, song variability is a legitimate sign of age. Age and experience, in turn, are related to good parental ability and a superior ability to defend the territory. Thus, it is not surprising that singing a variety of songs increases the male's success in both territorial defense and attraction of females. Similarly, recent research indicates that singing complex songs increases the male's attractiveness (Mountjoy & Lemon, 1996); like variety, complexity is associated with age and, to a certain extent, with physical condition.

Among mammals, as with birds, the same male courtship gestures that threaten other

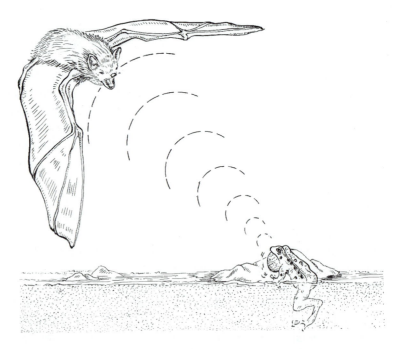

FIGURE 9.1 ◆ A frog-eating bat about to prey on a frog. The bat locates the frog by zeroing in on the frog's courtship call.

males tend to attract females. For example, male red deer emit loud roars during the mating season. The males that give the loudest and longest roars are generally successful in intimidating other males and are most successful in attracting females. Since roaring ability is correlated with size and strength, roaring is a legitimate measure of desirable male characteristics (McComb, 1991).

Elephants also communicate with sounds, especially low-frequency signals. The great advantage of such signals is that they travel relatively long distances. Calls of Asian elephants are apparently important in coordinating the behavior of widely separated elephant groups and may also function in courtship (Payne et al., 1986).

Visual Cues

A very large amount of information regarding attractiveness may be communicated visually; and, we might expect, many animals evaluate the visual appearance of a potential partner. However, the specific cues that experimenters have found to affect attractiveness are often quite unexpected. For example, female scorpion flies choose males with symmetrical wings over males whose wings are even slightly asymmetrical. Apparently the symmetry reflects a resistance to parasites and an ability to withstand attacks from predators or conspecifics that might cause damage to one of the wings. Since at least some of this resistance is related to genetic factors, the female's sensitivity to symmetry has a definite fitness advantage (Watson & Thornhill, 1994).

Animal behaviorists have known for many years that males with large, colorful visual displays, such as peacocks and widowbirds, are more successful in mating than comparable males with less gaudy characteristics (Petrie et al., 1991). However, it was difficult to know whether the females were responding to the visual display or to some other factor that was coincidently associated with the display. In a classic experiment with widowbirds, Malte Andersson (1982) was able to demonstrate that visual cues were basic to a female widowbird's mating decision. When Andersson made the tails of some males even longer by gluing additional feathers to them, these males were able to attract more females than males whose tails were left unaltered. Clearly, if males could develop these extra-long tails under natural conditions, they could experience significant fitness benefits with regard to mating.

Sexual selection is a major factor in the evolution of exaggerated characteristics such as extra-long tails (recall Chapter 1). Exaggerated characteristics are very expensive to produce from the standpoint of energy expenditure, however. Also, males with long tails or bright colors are more open to predation than less showy males (Rodd & Sokolowski, 1995). Thus, there is a balance between costs and benefits; but polygynous males such as widowbirds gain such great fitness advantages from mating with several females that they can "afford" large costs.

R. A. Fisher (1930) proposed an interesting corollary to sexual selection. Fisher's **runaway selection hypothesis** attempts to explain exaggerated characteristics in males by suggesting that the tendency of females to choose a particular attractiveness trait will be passed on to their daughters. In addition, the female's sons will be likely to have this trait. Consequently, both male and female offspring will then have a fitness advantage—males, because they possess the trait that females prefer, and females because they produce sons that possess the trait. This process will continue until the costs of producing the exaggerated characteristic become too great. Considering the great fitness advantages hypothesized, the runaway selection process can operate for long periods of time.

It is even possible that some traits developed through these sexual selection processes never had any survival value. These traits may originally have attracted females by chance; then, once the runaway process became established, the trait would continue to be exaggerated. Mathematical models demonstrate that such selection processes are indeed possible (Kirkpatrick, 1982). However, the possibility of a trait becoming established is even greater if the trait is a legitimate honest signal of favorable genes.

Experimental Manipulation of Visual Cues

While routinely banding zebra finches—songbirds indigenous to Australia—Nancy Burley (1982) made a startling discovery. She noted that the color of a band placed on the birds' legs strongly affected their attractiveness to the opposite sex. For example, males with red leg bands became highly attractive to females, and females with black bands appeared irresistible to males. The colors of the leg bands that influenced mate choice were similar to colors found on other parts of the zebra finches' bodies, suggesting that band color functioned to enhance naturally attractive characteristics.

This discovery proved to be particularly important because it enabled Burley and later researchers to experimentally manipulate the attractiveness of zebra finches. One of the most unexpected findings emerged when researchers mated attractive finches with individuals that had been experimentally made unattractive. Because certain colors were found to reduce attractiveness, experimenters were able to produce both very high and very low attractiveness in both sexes. And after mating, the unattractive birds provided most of the parental care. At some level the birds were following a principle of equity. Those low in attractiveness apparently compensated for their shortcoming by investing more in parental care (Burley et al., 1982).

Another unexpected finding was that when a male was made highly attractive, more sons were produced than daughters. Conversely, when a female was made highly attractive, more daughters were produced than sons (Burley, 1981). If we assume that, under natural conditions, zebra finches are especially likely to pass on attractive traits to their same-sex offspring, these results make sense. But how the birds manipulate the gender ratio is not clear at this time.

The sensitivity of females to asymmetry has also been tested in zebra finches through the colored banding technique. As in the case of scorpion fly females, zebra finch females chose males with symmetry: Males with same-colored bands on both legs were definitely preferred to males wearing a different-colored band on each leg. Furthermore, males with symmetrical leg bands gained reproductive advantages under controlled laboratory conditions (Swaddle, 1996). Apparently there is some generality of the symmetry effect.

Despite the dramatic effects in zebra finches, experiments with colored bands have not produced significant effects on the attractiveness of other species of songbirds tested (see Hannon & Eason, 1995). In fact, male red-winged blackbirds with red leg bands that match the color of the birds' epaulets (markings on the wings) experience a negative effect. In a natural setting, the red-banded males lose their territories much more frequently than birds without bands or those wearing black bands (Metz & Weatherhead, 1991). It seems that the red leg bands exaggerate the aggressive signal of the red epaulet. Neighboring males are then challenged to test the reliability of the signal and end up expelling those with illegitimate displays.

Chemical Cues

Chemical signals have important advantages over visual signals in that they may be transmitted day or night, are unimpeded by obstacles, and can travel a great distance. The female gypsy moth appears to be the most effective long-distance chemical communicator in the animal world; she produces a chemical signal that attracts males from a distance of several kilometers.

Chemical signals that function to attract members of the opposite sex are known as **sexual pheromones.** The female gypsy moth broadcasts her pheromone at night and, consequently, is able to take advantage of consistent nocturnal breezes (Bossert & Wilson, 1963). Not only does such a pheromone travel a great distance, but the pheromone takes relatively little energy to produce. Furthermore, a pheromone that communicates sexual availability is not usually detected by predators or even by members of closely related species. This "private channel" effect is possible because relatively large chemical molecules pro-vide great opportunities for chemical diversity (Wilson, 1963).

Mammals often communicate attractiveness via sexual pheromones released in their urine. Males are maximally attracted to female pheromones emitted during estrus (a period of sexual receptiveness) or when the female is in season (Ziegler et al., 1993). In a complementary way, females in estrus are most sensitive to male pheromones (see Johnston, 1983). As we shall see in Chapter 17 when we discuss pheromones in more detail, these chemical triggers may also affect reproductive physiology.

Male white-footed mice communicate considerable amounts of information about themselves via pheromones. On the basis of odor cues, a female mouse can differentiate sexually mature from immature males and can also assess how closely a male is related to her. In controlled mating tests, female white-footed mice show the greatest preference for males that are moderately related, such as first cousins (Keane, 1990). This preference is generally beneficial, in that distantly related individuals may not be as well adapted to local conditions as closer relatives. At the other extreme, the female can avoid inbreeding with close relatives—which, as explained in Chapter 2, can lead to deleterious expressions of recessive genes.

Attraction Based Primarily on Good Genes

When a female chooses a male on the basis of some characteristic such as size, one possibility is that she is basing her choice on the probability that a large male or one with exagger-

◆ UNUSUAL ADAPTATIONS

Attraction via Surface Waves and Electrical Fields

Some animals have evolved unusual abilities and have then used some aspect of these abilities to attract mates. For example, certain long-legged insects known as water striders are light enough to "walk" on the surface of water without breaking the surface tension. Males of the water strider *Rhagadotarsus* utilize surface waves as communication signals. The males signal nearby females by grasping an object in the water and vibrating it in such a manner that it sends out surface waves at a frequency of about 25 per second. Receptive females approach this source of stimulation and, when they get within a few inches, make waves of their own that communicate either acceptance or rejection of the male (Wilcox, 1988).

Some tropical fish produce electric fields that allow them both to avoid obstacles and to find food, because objects disrupt the electric fields in predictable ways. Being able to vary the waveform of the signal, the fish also communicate electrically. For example, *Pollomyrus isidori* can recognize an opposite-sex conspecific on the basis of electrical output (Crawford, 1991).

In both of these examples, it is clear that these unusual signaling methods are effective in helping animals locate mates. It is not clear, however, how much information these methods can communicate about specific factors related to attractiveness.

ated characteristics has "good genes"—that he will help her produce large and attractive male offspring. However, it is also possible that she chooses a large male because his size or some other characteristic is related to providing good resources such as a favorable territory, as we will discuss shortly.

How can we test the good genes hypothesis? One way is to experimentally present males to females apart from the males' territory (and the attractive resources). When swordtail fish males are presented to females in a neutral area and the females are given a choice between two males, the females consistently choose the males with the longest tails. These results suggest that individual characteristics reflecting good genes are of prime importance for these fish (Basolo, 1990).

Sometimes, incidentally, females interact with males in ways that indirectly help the females obtain information related to males' fitness and genetic potential. For example, female pronghorn antelopes may move away from a male after spending time in his harem group, thus provoking a fight with another nearby male. Immediately after the fight the females mate with the winning male (Byers et al., 1994).

We have already seen how symmetry seems to indicate good genes. William Hamilton and Marlene Zuk (1982) hypothesized that bright coloration may also be a reflection of good genes, especially in bird species that are open to parasitism. In natural environments bright coloration indicates a resistance to parasites, because parasite-infested animals cannot produce the bright coloration. Presumably, this resistance to parasitism is related to genetic factors. Therefore, bright coloration may serve as an honest signal of fitness in bird species that are subject to parasitism. This hypothesis is known as the **bright bird hypothesis.**

To test the bright bird hypothesis at the species level, experimenters independently ranked several different species of birds in order of brightness of plumage coloration. As predicted, the most brightly colored species of birds were those most open to parasitism (Hamilton & Zuk, 1982). A later study tested the hypothesis at the level of individual birds. Barn owl males with a characteristic analogous to gaudy coloration—long tail feathers—were found to be more free of parasites than individual males with shorter tail feathers (Moller, 1990).

Not all bright coloration in birds or other animals can be explained by the bright bird hypothesis, and there are several other hypotheses capable of explaining the evolution of gaudy characteristics (see Zahavi, 1975). Furthermore, the indicators of parasite infestation in males may be less important under conditions where immunity to parasitism is rare (Poulin & Vickery, 1996). Nonetheless, it seems that advertising resistance to parasitism has a large payoff for many animals. Not only does advertisement of parasite resistance provide cues related to fitness, but it is in females' best interest to avoid mating with parasitized males, because some of the parasites may be transferred during physical contact. It seems likely, then, that good genes responsible for resistance to parasitism may start an evolutionary trend. This trend can then be carried to extremes as the result of runaway selection. In other words, gaudy characteristics may be a result of both attention to good genes and runaway selection.

Attraction Based Primarily on Resources

Females do not always give primary attention to individual genetic characteristics; in some cases resources are more important to the female than good genes. For example, several species of male fishes establish territories. Because territories must be obtained through competition with other males, the strongest and fittest males tend to establish mating territories in the most desirable locations. Thus, it is clearly to the female's advantage to consider a male's territory.

The male stickleback establishes a territory that features a nest of weeds in a shallow pit. When a **gravid female** (a female carrying eggs) swims by, she inspects the territory—as well as the resident male, which engages in a zigzag dance—and decides whether or not to accept the male and his territory (Tinbergen, 1951).

Some animals assess resources in indirect and surprising ways. For example, female red-backed salamanders squash male fecal pellets.

They prefer to associate with males whose pellets have a quality that reflects a good diet. Males, in turn, adjust their foraging tactics to include a diet that makes their pellets attractive to the females (Jaeger et al., 1995).

Picking males that are good providers not only gives immediate benefits but may provide long-term advantages. An ability to provide is a reasonably good sign of the male's fitness, especially in regard to male–male competition and to future contributions as a parent. Thus, a female can make a reasonably good choice by attending to either the male or his territory.

Attraction Based on Other Considerations

Although most attraction of females to males is based on good genes and resources, some females have evolved a sensitivity to other fitness-related factors. Let's look at a few examples.

The "Copycat Effect"

Male sailfin mollies, as we saw in Chapter 8, are more attractive to females if they have been observed mating with Amazon mollies. A comparable "copycat effect" has been observed in guppies. Females tend to choose males that have mated successfully with other female guppies. By using information about fitness gathered by others, an individual may save herself time and effort in making assessments. Not all females are equally imitated, however. Young, inexperienced females—who may be relatively poor judges of fitness—

are not imitated as much as older, experienced females (Dugatkin, 1992; Dugatkin & Godin, 1993).

Copying of mate choice has also been identified in a polygynous bird species, the black grouse. After females have observed a male being chosen by one female, other females show an increased probability of choosing that male. In an experiment that involved the presentation of female dummies, females that observed a male copulating with a dummy were increasingly likely to choose that male (Hoglund et al., 1995). These results suggest that observing the act of copulation—over and beyond the act of choosing a partner—increases attraction. (The fact that the black grouse males would copulate with a dummy also supports the conclusion that males in polygynous species are not very choosy in their selection of partners.)

Potential for Parenthood

In species where the male provides some parental care, the females may take into account factors that predict good parental behavior. For example, certain female fish apparently test a male's tendency to care for eggs by laying a few eggs and observing whether or not the male guards them. Only when he shows parental guarding behavior does the female continue to lay eggs (Kraak & van Den Berghe, 1992).

Another tactic for assessing potential parental ability in fishes is to consider the age of a male: Older males exhibit more parental care than young ones. From a research standpoint, it is often difficult to be sure of the reason for a female's choice, because older male fish tend to be larger than young ones; so the female may be responding to size rather than to age. In redlip blennies, however, older males are not necessarily larger than young ones. Because female redlip blennies choose the older males, the hypothesis that females are responding to age—and potential for parental caretaking—gains support (Cote & Hunt, 1993).

In the European moorhen, small size in the male is a predictor of good parental care—for an unusual reason. Small males need less food than larger males. This characteristic, in addition to adequate fat reserves, may prove to be critical to the ultimate survival of the male and of the eggs in a habitat with limited food resources. At any rate, female moorhens show a preference for small, plump males (Petrie, 1983).

Friendship

In some primates, what could be called friendships influence the female's choice of a sexual partner. Barbara Smuts (1987) carefully observed a troop of olive baboons in Kenya and found that individuals tended to form friendships that were independent of any sexual activity. Friends remained generally close to one another and spent considerable time grooming one another. In many cases the friendships involved opposite-sex pairs, and some older males developed friendships with several females.

One of the advantages of such friendships for females was that the males protected their female friends against aggression from other males. Then, when the females came into estrus, they would solicit copulations from their male friends—although they might copulate with other males, as well. Thus, like the bono-

bo chimpanzees discussed in the last chapter, the baboons engage in a type of reciprocity involving sex.

COURTSHIP

This discussion of attraction has focused on attributes associated with fitness that may be assessed relatively quickly, without too much interaction between the sexes taking place. In some cases, however, it is necessary for animals to observe behavior in addition to physical characteristics before a reasonable choice can be made. Consequently, some animals go through a courtship period before finally deciding on a mate.

Male Courtship of Females

Because females tend to be more choosy about their partners than males, males have been naturally selected to invest more energy in courtship activities than females. Females, in turn, have been especially selected for sensitivity to cues predicting reproductive success.

Bateman's Principle

A classic example of sex differences in courtship and choosiness is seen in the fruit fly. Males will court almost any female in the area, including females from a different species. In contrast, females reject numerous males before they allow one to mate (Bateman, 1948).

As a result of this sex difference, almost all female fruit flies are successful in attracting a mate. Furthermore, copulating with more than one male does not usually lead to producing more young, so one mate typically provides optimal reproductive success for the female. In contrast, males vary from attracting no mates to attracting several mates (see Figure 9.2). When a male attracts several mates, his reproductive success can be very high. Consequently, there is more variability in the reproductive success of males than in that of females, a pattern known as **Bateman's principle.**

Although females clearly have something to gain by being choosy, how much difference does female choosiness actually make? Darwin argued that the male's courtship behavior provides information directly relevant to his fitness and, consequently, that the female's choosiness is a very important factor in evolution. But for many years after Darwin, there was controversy concerning how much difference the females' choices made; some scientists even suggested that most animals mated randomly. Since the 1970s, however, growing evidence has strongly supported Darwin's argument. Most evidence indicates that the females' choosiness does in fact reflect an important sensitivity to male fitness. An example of this fitness benefit is provided by the results of another experiment with fruit flies. When females are allowed to choose their mates, their offspring show a significantly higher survival rate than when the females are forced to mate randomly (Partridge, 1980).

Male–Male Competition

Competition between males is the hallmark of courtship in many species of animals. If there are a limited number of females in reproduc-

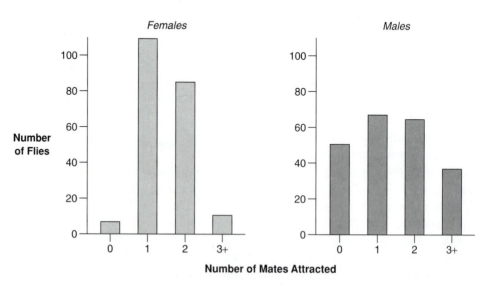

FIGURE 9.2 ◆ **Variance in reproductive success in fruit flies.** Success is measured by number of mates per fly; note that males show greater variance.

tive condition at any one time, competition among males may become intense. Competition in wood frogs is particularly intense, because the females are receptive only during one night of the year. During this special night, males patrol the surface of a pond in search of females. The males are relatively indiscriminate and will grab onto almost anything they come across, including the foot of a researcher who might be in the pond at the time. Male frogs also grab other males, but the accosted ones typically obtain their release by croaking.

After males embrace gravid females, the males then maneuver their prospective mates into the amplexus position. The males can distinguish gravid females from females that have already released their eggs on the basis of the gravid females' egg-swollen girth and firmness.

Even though a male has obtained amplexus with a female, he is not assured of mating success. Other males attempt to dislodge him; and if he is relatively small, he has difficulty retaining his grasp. Females also tend to dislodge smaller males, with the result that mating pairs tend to be similar in size. This matching according to a significant trait is known as **assortative mating.** The frogs' assortative mating by size occurs primarily because large males cannot be dislodged even by large females, while smaller males are successful only with smaller females (Woolbright et al., 1990).

Male salamanders such as the red-spotted newt also interfere with the success of conspecific males, but they use a different tactic. One male may imitate the behavior of a female, inducing another male to deposit his spermatophore. Once the deceived male has depleted himself, he is no longer a threat to the imitator, who then has open access to females in the area (Massey, 1988).

Males also compete with other males to establish the mating territories that are often necessary to attract females. As we shall see in Chapter 13, male competition either for direct access to females or for territories that attract females is basic to the evolution of male–male aggressiveness—and of social systems that tend to keep the aggressiveness from being too disruptive.

Alternative Male Courtship Strategies

The examples considered so far may give the impression that in any given species all the males always exhibit the same courtship strategy. However, there are several species in which two or more strategies exist—a primary strategy and one or more alternative strategies. In some cases, these alternative approaches are **conditional strategies;** that is, the males exhibit a primary strategy under some conditions but an alternative strategy under other conditions.

In other cases, both primary and alternative approaches are **nonconditional strategies;** that is, the strategies are strongly influenced by genetic factors. In other words, an animal inherits a tendency to develop either a primary or an alternative strategy but cannot switch from one to another.

Conditional Strategies

Conditional strategies have the advantage of flexibility. When possible, an animal can adopt the strategy with the largest fitness payoff. When that is not possible, the animal has

◆ UNUSUAL ADAPTATIONS

Courtship Involving Decorative Structures and Worthless Gifts

In New Guinea, drab-colored male bowerbirds clear an area on the jungle floor and build structures known as bowers to attract females. In some respects these structures act as a substitute for the brilliantly colored feathers of many species of birds found in the area. The males decorate their bowers with colorful objects such as flowers and fruits. In addition, some species paint the walls of their bowers with a mixture of saliva and chewed-up fruits and grass, smearing on the "paint" with wads of fibrous bark.

The importance of the ornamentation of the bower has been demonstrated by a simple experiment: Removal of the decorations significantly reduced the attractiveness of males (Borgia, 1985). The birds obviously have a sensitivity to the importance of decorations. Some males pilfer prize objects such as broken bits of blue glass from a rival's bower and add them to their own.

When a female approaches the bower, males exhibit behaviors that further enhance the overall effect. For example, a male spotted bowerbird raises and lowers his mantle feathers, contorts his body, and leaps up and down. In addition, he may fling about decorations from the bower. The female then either rejects his display or accepts him and mates. Shortly thereafter, she leaves. The male calms down, replaces objects in his bower, and waits for another female.

Why did females develop this seemingly strange attraction to elaborate bowers? It seems that building an elaborate bower requires a certain amount of success in intermale competition; as we have seen, males steal ornaments from one another. Thus, choosing a mate on the basis of the bower quality may maximize the female's prospects of passing on genes related to dominance or success in intermale competition (Borgia, 1995).

an alternate option to make the best of a bad situation (Dawkins, 1980).

For example, the primary courtship strategy for male scorpion flies is to establish a territory around carrion such as dead insect, a morsel that is especially attractive to females. One alternate strategy is for the male to secrete saliva as a type of nuptial gift. As a female approaches to accept the gift, the male then attempts to mate with her. This strategy

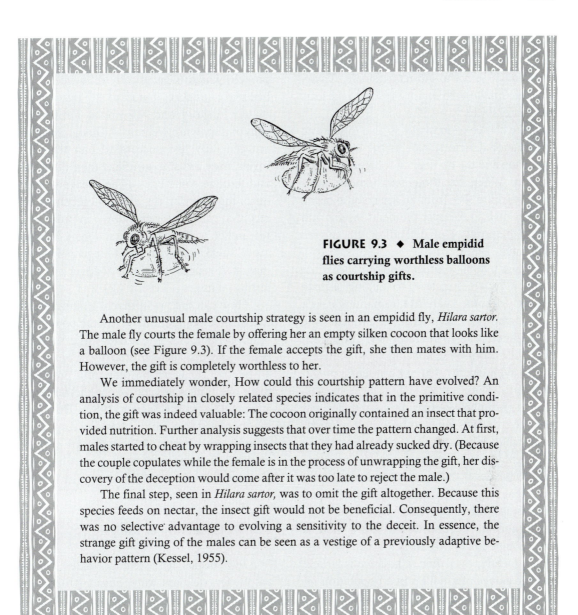

FIGURE 9.3 ◆ Male empidid flies carrying worthless balloons as courtship gifts.

Another unusual male courtship strategy is seen in an empidid fly, *Hilara sartor.* The male fly courts the female by offering her an empty silken cocoon that looks like a balloon (see Figure 9.3). If the female accepts the gift, she then mates with him. However, the gift is completely worthless to her.

We immediately wonder, How could this courtship pattern have evolved? An analysis of courtship in closely related species indicates that in the primitive condition, the gift was indeed valuable: The cocoon originally contained an insect that provided nutrition. Further analysis suggests that over time the pattern changed. At first, males started to cheat by wrapping insects that they had already sucked dry. (Because the couple copulates while the female is in the process of unwrapping the gift, her discovery of the deception would come after it was too late to reject the male.)

The final step, seen in *Hilara sartor,* was to omit the gift altogether. Because this species feeds on nectar, the insect gift would not be beneficial. Consequently, there was no selective advantage to evolving a sensitivity to the deceit. In essence, the strange gift giving of the males can be seen as a vestige of a previously adaptive behavior pattern (Kessel, 1955).

is somewhat less successful than the primary one. Another alternate strategy is for the male to attempt a mating by force. This force-related strategy is less successful than either of the others.

Research indicates that the size of the male determines which of these strategies is chosen. Large males are capable of defending carrion or secreting saliva; medium-sized males are less capable of defense, but are able to secrete saliva; and small males have difficulty with both defending carrion and secreting enough saliva to attract a female. Therefore, the smallest males must resort to the least successful strategy.

The choice of strategies is also influenced by situational factors, such as the availability of carrion and the number of competing males present. When experimenters remove large male scorpion flies from an area, some of the smaller males take over the dead insects and adopt the strategy of defending the carrion (Thornhill, 1981).

Frogs exhibit another type of conditional strategy. As an alternative to singing, a male frog may become a **satellite,** remaining near a singing male and, as a female approaches the singer, attempting to intercept her. The advantages of becoming a nonsinging satellite include saving energy and not attracting predators (Perrill et al., 1978).

The ratio between primary strategies and satellite strategies tends to become evolutionarily stable. When one strategy becomes more prevalent, there is an advantage to adopting the other one. If there are a large number of frogs that sing, for example, possibilities open up for nonsingers. Conversely, when the number of nonsingers becomes too great, there is not enough singing to attract many females. Consequently, over time, a balance is struck; the percentage of satellites in a population remains stable (Dawkins, 1980).

Nonconditional Strategies

An example of nonconditional strategies is found in bluegills. The primary courtship strategy for the males of these fish is to establish a territory and court females when they enter the territory. Not all bluegill males become territorial, however. The alternate approach, which is genetically influenced, is to become a **sneaker;** that is, to slip into a larger male's territory and attempt to fertilize the eggs of a spawning female. Although sneakers are generally less successful than territorial males, they are able to utilize their quickness and fertilize some eggs. (The sneakers are so quick that the film on which their behavior is recorded must be slowed down in order for a researcher to follow their actions.) Furthermore, sneakers have an advantage in that they may start reproducing at a younger age than territorial males (Gross, 1982).

How can the two different strategies exist in the same population? When the population of territorial males is relatively large, there are benefits in the sneaker strategy. Conversely, when the sneakers become too prevalent, there are fitness advantages to the territorial strategy (Gross & Charnov, 1980). Thus, evolutionarily stable ratios may develop when primary and alternative strategies are strongly affected by inheritance as well as when they are conditional.

Female Courtship of Males

In a few species, females court males. For example, female giant water bugs approach and attempt to attract males (Smith, 1979). Similarly, in a small species of shorebird called the red-necked phalarope, the brightly colored females fight one another and aggressively pursue the more docile and choosy males (Reynolds, 1987).

Significantly, the males of both giant water bugs and red-necked phalaropes provide more in the way of parental care than do their female counterparts. The giant water bug male carries the fertilized eggs around with him until they hatch, and the red-necked phalarope male incubates the eggs after the female lays them. In fact, a female may leave three or four batches of eggs for different males to incubate.

As with the examples of male-dominated courtship, these findings on female-dominated courtship are consistent with parental investment theory. In other words, when males invest more in parental behavior than females—and when, as a result, the males must wait longer to reproduce again if they have made a poor choice of a sexual partner—there is stronger evolutionary pressure on the males to be choosy than there is on the females. And because the males are more choosy, there is pressure on the females to attract the males; this pressure produces active courtship displays and interfemale competition.

Mutual Courtship

The males and females of some species may benefit equally from being choosy if they both invest a great deal of time and energy in the care of offspring. More than 90 percent of birds are monogamous, and most bird parents cooperate in the rearing of the young. In these species there has been an evolutionary trend toward extended courtship interaction, during which the individuals are able to evaluate the fitness of their potential partners. The prolonged interaction before mating also establishes a **pair bond**—that is, a tendency to stay together. This bond functions to keep the couple together in a more or less monogamous relationship during at least one breeding season.

Monogamous pairs of birds sometimes court one another for weeks before they mate. This togetherness not only allows the birds to evaluate each other thoroughly, but provides additional benefits as well. For the male there is a reduced probability that other males have copulated with the female and **cuckolded** him—put him in the position of investing in the rearing of another male's offspring. For the female the prolonged togetherness provides evidence that the male is not investing time and energy in another relationship (Daly & Wilson, 1983).

Most primates are not monogamous, and male primates generally provide little or no parental care. An exception is the cotton-top tamarin—a small monkey found in tropical forests of Central and South America. The males of this monogamous species cooperate with the females in caring for the young, and the young cannot survive without the care of both parents. As in the case of monogamous birds, there is an extended period of courtship and mutual evaluation.

Courtship and the Danger of Predation

Although animals benefit from mating with the fittest partner available, there are certain constraints on the courtship process. Elaborate courtship behaviors do not take place at times when the danger of predation is high. Furthermore, animals may compromise their standards and accept a mate that is readily available rather than risk their lives in order to contact a preferred partner. Thus, experiments with female crickets of the species *Grillus* indicate that if there is a danger of predation associated with approaching a distant male, females will accept a less fit nearby male (Hedrick & Dill, 1993). Similarly, male pipefish are less choosy under conditions that simulate the presence of a predator; in these conditions the males also spend less time in attempts to court females (Berglund, 1993).

Because threat of predation affects female choice, different natural selection processes occur in populations where the threat of predation is great than in populations where there is little threat. For example, researchers recently found that female guppies responded more positively to bright-colored males in a river where predation levels were low than in a river where predation levels were high (Godin & Briggs, 1996).

Not only does danger of predation influence how courtship is expressed; predatory risk has undoubtedly been important in the evolution of courtship patterns. For example, some animals probably evolved courtship patterns that involved auditory and olfactory cues because visual cues would be more easily detected by predators. Also, the danger of predation must have acted as a constraint in sexual selection processes. Even if distinctive characteristics increased mating success, sensitivity of predators to these characteristics could halt or reverse the selection process.

Additional Functions of Courtship

I have described how courtship interaction provides an opportunity for potential partners to display their attributes and, in some cases, to emphasize certain aspects of their territory. Courtship has additional functions as well; indeed, some courtship behaviors have multiple benefits.

Species Differentiation

Sexual attraction to a member of a different species wastes time and energy and may even provoke aggression. Consequently, many animals have evolved courtship signals that are highly specific to their own species. For example, male fiddler crabs court females by moving their large claws in what resembles a beckoning gesture. The males of each particular fiddler crab species have a species-specific pattern of movement that attracts only females of the same species.

Fireflies exchange courtship signals produced by their bioluminescent organs. Each firefly species produces its own particular rate of flashing, so the males and females are usually attracted only to their own kind. But because males of certain species are subject to deception and predation by females of a predatory species (as discussed in Chapter 6), these particular males have evolved a tendency to approach the flashing female with great stealth (Lloyd, 1975). Consequently, the males sacrifice courtship exuberance but increase their chance of survival.

Appeasement of Aggression

Although the vast majority of species are not preyed upon by their mates, close contact by a conspecific does evoke an aggressive reaction in many animals. This aggressive tendency results in the development of **personal space:** an area surrounding an animal that the animal protects against intrusion. In order for mating

◆ UNUSUAL ADAPTATIONS

"Suicidal" Courtships in Male Praying Mantises and Redback Spiders

Male praying mantises also face a danger of predation, but from females of their own species. To minimize the possibility of getting eaten, a courting praying mantis male approaches a female slowly and, when he is close enough, leaps onto her back and attempts copulation. Sometimes she pays little attention to him and may even continue to move around and feed while he copulates with her. But at other times she wheels around, seizes him, and begins to eat him head first.

The male is physiologically adapted for this carnivorous possibility, however. Without his head, he is still able to achieve intromission and copulate effectively. As a matter of fact, copulatory movements speed up when the male loses his head, because inhibitory neural centers in the head are eliminated by the female's cannibalism. In contrast, neural centers that control copulation are located in the body behind the head and are temporarily spared (Roeder, 1970).

The sexual cannibalism of praying mantises developed into somewhat of a controversy, because some scientists suggested that the cannibalism was an artifact of laboratory conditions and did not occur regularly under natural conditions. However, careful field research indicated that in the wild 31 percent of the males are normally cannibalized (Lawrence, 1992).

The cannibalism is obviously beneficial to the female mantid, because she gets a meal. And indeed, females that are experimentally starved under laboratory conditions are much more likely to consume their mates than are well-fed females (Kynaston et al., 1994). But what about the male? He seems to pay a high price for a copulatory experience. However, some males, especially older or feeble ones, may not have much of an opportunity to mate again; these males may actually gain fitness, in that the speeded-up copulatory movements associated with the loss of their heads increase the probability of successful insemination.

Maydianne Andrade (1996) has discovered that male Australian redback spiders also face the strong possibility of being consumed by their mates. In contrast to praying mantises, however, the male spiders actually encourage mate cannibalism by positioning themselves above the female's jaws. Why do the males act in this suicidal manner? Andrade suggests that there has been a natural selection for this self-sacrificing behavior because males that are cannibalized fertilize more eggs than those able to escape. Furthermore, females that have consumed their first mate are less likely to accept a second mate. Because females of the species are likely to mate with many males, this ultimate nuptial gift of oneself seems to have a large fitness payoff.

to occur, the barriers of personal space must be overcome.

Thus, many male courtship behaviors function to appease the aggressiveness of the female. The courtship rituals of many male animals include behaviors that indicate submission and, consequently, reduce the female's natural tendency toward aggression when approached. Submissive gestures such as bowing and presenting the neck in a vulnerable position have become part of courtship in many species of birds and mammals.

Coordination of Reproductive Activities

In addition to communicating information about fitness and appeasing aggression, courtship tends to coordinate levels of sexual readiness between male and female. We have seen how female sticklebacks inspect male territo-ries before they mate with the male; by the time the female enters the male's nest and lays her eggs, the male is highly aroused by the courtship "dance" and responds by fertilizing the eggs.

Similarly, some bird courtship tends to coordinate reproductive activities. For example, ring dove females will not reach complete sexual maturity unless they have observed a male making courtship gestures. Courtship interaction in monogamous species also, as explained earlier, functions to keep the pair together during the mating season. In summary, courtship may have multiple functions in some species. It seems likely that after the evolution of a courtship pattern associated with one function, the courtship took on other functions. As demonstrated in other chapters, the evolution of multiple functions is quite common.

◆ HUMAN EVOLUTION

Historically, many people believed that standards of human attractiveness and patterns of courtship were culturally determined and showed unpredictable variation across cultures. There was also a tendency to think of principles related to human attractiveness and courtship as being uniquely human. However, we now understand that many evolutionarily based principles of attraction and courtship are as basic to humans as to nonhuman animals.

ATTRACTIVENESS

The fact that human definitions of attractiveness reflect fitness considerations can be seen both in general definitions of attractiveness and in gender differences in perceived attractiveness.

General Definitions of Attractiveness

An analysis of definitions of attractiveness in a large number of different human societies indicates that good complexion and cleanliness, which are reliable indications of favorable health and fitness, are almost always considered attractive. Conversely, indications of disease or deformity are typically evaluated negatively (Symons, 1979).

Humans also seem to be sensitive to symmetry. In nonhuman animals, as we have seen, symmetry can reflect health (in regard to resistance to parasites) and self-defense capability. After carefully measuring the degree of symmetry in photographs of human faces, researchers asked people to judge the attractiveness of the faces. The male and female faces named as most attractive were the ones with the greatest symmetry (Grammer & Thornhill, 1994). These attractiveness ratings were consistent across several cultures (Jones & Hill, 1993), indicating the generality of this symmetry effect.

In relation to a potential mate's personality, traits indicative of cooperativeness and fair play are evaluated positively in virtually all cultures studied. For example, honesty and kindness are highly evaluated by individuals of both genders in anticipation of a long-term relationship (Buss, 1989).

Gender Differences in Perceived Attractiveness

Despite the several gender similarities in qualities considered attractive in a mate, women and men benefit, in fitness terms, from somewhat different characteristics in their mates (see Buss, 1993; Symons, 1979). For example, women gain maximally from mate characteristics correlated with a man's ability to provide resources for himself and his offspring. Women perceive male assertiveness and social power, which are good predictors of present or future success in resource provision, as highly attractive. Women also rate men somewhat older than themselves as most attractive; in most societies, older men are likely to provide more resources than younger men.

In contrast, from a fitness standpoint men are primarily concerned with reproductive potential, so men tend to value youthfulness in women. Furthermore, men prefer women with a hip-to-waist ratio of 3 to 2. Although there are considerable cultural and historical differences in preference for height and bust size, this hip-to-waist ratio preference is highly consistent throughout the human species—and, significantly, is the dimensional measurement that best predicts reproductive success (Singh, 1993).

There are also gender differences in sexual jealousy that make sense from an evolutionary standpoint. Although the magnitude of jealousy tends to be similar for the two genders, men experience more intense jealousy associated with physical infidelity, whereas women report the highest degree of jealousy associated with their partner's forming a new emotionally intimate relationship. These findings are consistent with an analysis of potential loss from a fitness standpoint. Males have a great deal to lose if their parental care is invested in some other man's child, while women lose maximally if their mate leaves to invest in another relationship (Buss et al., 1992).

Matching of Attractiveness

As among nonhuman animals, not every human individual can obtain the most attractive mate. Consequently, there is a **matching of attractiveness** phenomenon; that is, members of a couple tend to be approximately equal in levels of attractiveness. This phenomenon is analogous to assortative mating, discussed earlier. If both physical attractiveness and resources provided are taken into account, there is a highly significant correlation of attractiveness ratings for the male and female in both dating and married couples. Furthermore, couples who are—and also perceive themselves to be—closely matched in attractiveness tend to have the most satisfying relationships.

This matching of attractiveness phenomenon probably results from individuals' attempting to obtain the most attractive partner they can, given their attributes and resources. After a series of rejections, for example, people low in attractiveness ultimately tend to settle for less attractive partners. Thus, there is a type of equity in the mating transaction, in the sense that one receives his or her "worth." And we will see in later chapters that this principle of equity applies to friendships and coalitions of various kinds as well as to romantic relationships (see Clark & Reis, 1988).

COURTSHIP

Several evolutionary principles related to courtship also apply to humans. For example, men, like many nonhuman males, make gestures or bear gifts that are indicative of fitness or social status. As a musician, I am particularly interested in the observation that music is a part of courtship in many different societies (see Ford & Beach, 1951). In some respects a human love song has a function similar to a frog's croak or a bird's song.

There are other analogies between bird courtship and that of humans. People exhibit an equity principle that is similar to that observed by Nancy

Burley (1982) in zebra finches. If one person in a relationship is more attractive than the other, the other may compensate for the inequity by contributing more in the way of courtship rewards such as money. The less attractive partner may also compensate by taking on a relatively large part of the shared workload (see Hatfield & Walster, 1981). Furthermore, relationships between individuals whose attributes are inequitable are unlikely to endure. As might be expected, perceived equity is even more important than some objective measure of equity in predicting the success of a relationship.

Similarities related to the length of courtship also exist between monogamous songbirds and humans. In both groups, a long courtship facilitates a good choice of partners. Qualities that predict couples' working well together over a long period of time cannot be evaluated as quickly as good genes or adequate resources. Finally, human courtship that is very brief is related to an early breakup of the relationship.

THE ROLE OF TECHNOLOGY

In contrast to nonhuman animals and humans in preliterate societies, humans in highly technological societies learn a great deal about courtship and attraction from observing role models on television, in the movie theater, and at musical events. Unfortunately, because producers of these media are often trying to attract the immediate attention of the audience—and to sell products that putatively increase attractiveness—the portrayal of attractiveness in technological media is unrealistic. For example, movies, TV, and popular music frequently overemphasize aggression and the importance of physical factors in attraction.

Clearly, these presentations can have a negative social effect. There is a message that physical violence in a relationship is acceptable. Also, advertising models, actresses shaped by plastic surgery, and the use of "body doubles" in most films tend to create distorted ideals of attractiveness that can have a destructive effect on women's body image. Unfortunately, many young women feel disappointed with their bodies, and many young men believe violence and sexual aggressiveness are acceptable behaviors (see Heinberg & Thompson, 1992).

Once again we see that technology has produced mixed results. Balanced against these negative effects, our technology has promoted research and has disseminated information to facilitate knowledgeable decisions in regard to mate choice and to help improve the quality of intimate relationships. We have also developed therapeutic techniques that can help people in troubled relationships—and the children who are often the helpless victims of these relationships. Fortunately, we have the choice of accepting the more positive effects of technology while rejecting or minimizing its negative effects.

◆ CHANGING PERSPECTIVES

PAST	PRESENT	FUTURE
Most nonhuman animals are indiscriminant in their choice of sexual partners (early twentieth century).	Most animals, especially females, show discrimination in their choice of partners. The choice reflects fitness considerations related to the production of offspring.	How do animals process information related to fitness potential in prospective mates?

SUMMARY

Sexual attractiveness is typically linked to attributes that are associated with good genetic potential. Other factors of importance include the quality of resources, success in intrasexual competition (e.g., male–male competition), and attributes that predict success as a parent.

Females tend to be more discriminating in their choice of partners than males, because a poor choice by a female generally results in a greater delay in future reproduction than does a poor choice by a male. In contrast, males have tended to evolve elaborate behaviors and physical attributes that facilitate success in intermale competition and that also advertise fitness.

Animals tend to be specialized for communicating attractiveness on the basis of audi-

tory, visual, or chemical cues. A few species utilize water-surface waves or electrical fields. In some species males have evolved extreme or gaudy characteristics. At least part of the explanation for the evolution of these characteristics is the runaway selection hypothesis. The bright bird hypothesis helps to explain the role of resistance to parasites in the evolution of bright coloration.

Courtship enables animals to observe each other's behavior before deciding to mate. Because females tend to be more choosy, the most common courtship pattern is one in which males court females. Some males exhibit multiple courtship strategies. Whether an alternative strategy is conditional or nonconditional (influenced by genetic factors), an evolutionarily stable ratio tends to develop between the primary and alternative courtship strategies.

In a few species of animals, males make a larger parental investment than females. Here, the males are more choosy and the females court the males.

Under certain conditions a poor mate choice is costly for both sexes. In such cases courtship tends to be prolonged and mutual and develops into a more or less monogamous relationship.

When risk of predation is great, animals spend less time courting and may settle for less attractive partners. Risk of predation may also influence the evolution of courtship behaviors and the evolution of extreme characteristics.

In addition to facilitating the choice of sex partner, courtship may function to differentiate species, reduce aggression, synchronize sexual responses, and facilitate development of a pair bond.

Several aspects of sexual attraction and courtship in humans can be viewed in an evolutionary context. These include general definitions of attractiveness, gender differences in perceived attractiveness, matching of attractiveness, courtship patterns, and the role of technology.

KEY TERMS

assortative mating, p. 207
Bateman's principle, p. 206
bright bird hypothesis, p. 203
conditional strategies, p. 207
cuckold, p. 211
gravid female, p. 203
matching of attractiveness, p. 216

nonconditional strategies, p. 207
pair bond, p. 211
personal space, p. 212
runaway selection hypothesis, p. 199
satellite, p. 210
sexual pheromone, p. 201
sneaker, p. 210

CHAPTER **10**

MATING SYSTEMS AND POSTCOPULATORY COMPETITION

◆ *Why are some species of animals monogamous?*

◆ *Why do other species typically mate with a variety of partners?*

*B*ehaviors that precede mating were the topic of Chapter 9; in this chapter we will examine behaviors and mechanisms that follow the choice of a partner, including decisions about whether to remain in association with the partner or to look for another partner. Systems that determine how many sexual partners an animal has and how long the partners stay together are known as **mating systems,** and we will focus on mating systems in the first part of the chapter.

Then we will look at postcopulatory competition. Male competition continues after mating, as males engage in various types of competition to increase the probability that they alone have fertilized the eggs. As we shall see, mating systems and postcopulatory competition are closely related, because one often drives the evolution of the other.

10

MATING SYSTEMS

There is a large variety of mating systems, and their evolution is driven by ecological conditions. For males there are clear benefits from mating with as many females as possible. If the young can survive on their own or with the parental care that the female can provide by herself, there is a definite fitness advantage for the male to fertilize the eggs of several females. But if females are in short supply, or if it takes the combined efforts of two parents to effectively promote the survival of the young, the male may gain more fitness advantages from staying with the female. The male can then reduce the possibility that other males will inseminate the female's eggs, and he may also contribute parental care.

For females the advantages of mating with several males are minimal. In rare circumstances matings with multiple partners may provide benefits for certain females, but the benefits are clearly less for females than for males.

Polygyny

Polygyny (mating with many females) is a type of polygamous (multiple-mate) system in which one male mates with several females while female matings are restricted to one or relatively few partners. Because males often benefit from mating with multiple partners, and because the young of many species can survive without male parental care, polygyny is a very common type of mating system.

Animals differ greatly in the degree of polygyny they express, ranging from the moderate polygyny of the male gorilla, who usually mates with the 4 to 6 females in his group, to the high degree of polygyny of the male elephant seal, who may have more than 100 partners in a breeding season. In some animals, such as fruit flies, both males and females mate with multiple partners—but because the most active males mate with a greater variety of partners than the most active females, the system is classified as polygynous. Let's consider the various different polygynous arrangements.

Resource Defense Polygyny

A very common polygynous arrangement, occurring in a great variety of animals, is **resource defense polygyny.** In this arrangement, males gain sexual access to multiple females by establishing a territory that includes some type of resource needed by females. The males then protect the resource and in the process establish a harem of females with whom they have exclusive rights to mate.

Several different types of resources are defended by males. For example, black-winged damselfly males establish territories on strips of floating vegetation. The larger the strip, the greater the number of females attracted. Consequently, males with large territories are more successful, at least temporarily. But because large strips also attract more competing males, it is difficult for a male to retain the territory, and males with large territories may be displaced after a relatively short time (Alcock, 1987).

In fur seals and sea lions, the guarded resource is not food but simply a small area on a rocky beach, where, huddling together, the animals can provide warmth for one another. In this territory the animals mate and the young from the previous year's mating are raised. Males arrive at their traditional island mating grounds several days before the females and fight to establish their territories. When the females arrive, they choose one of the territories and mate exclusively with the resident male. There may be six or more females with their young in each territory. However, the male does not provide any care for the young, nor does he protect the females; he simply fights to keep other males out of the territory (Campagna et al., 1992).

The mating system and territorial arrangement are similar in elephant seals, except that the harem size may be much larger. One of the disadvantages of a large harem is that some of the young may be crushed by the movement of the very large males. However, a recent study indicates that southern elephant seals in Patagonia breed on long continuous beaches where the harem groups tend to be smaller and more spread out than in other areas. This spacing, which is controlled largely by the females, results in a relatively low infant mortality for the Patagonian elephant seal pups (Baldi et al., 1996).

Generally speaking, the quality and distribution of required resources is of overriding importance in resource defense polygyny. When resources are clumped together, it is possible for a male to monopolize them, and females that need the resources will benefit from entering the male's territory. The smaller the area containing the resources, the larger and more tightly packed the harem group.

Female Defense Polygyny

In contrast to resource defense polygyny, **female defense polygyny** involves a male's defending the females to which he has gained access against other males. Female defense polygyny is most often found among large ungulates and ground-dwelling primates. The resources these animals need are plentiful and widespread, and females can gain access to the resources on their own. Consequently, the females are not likely to be enticed into a territory. Instead, females often form groups and forage within a relatively large range. The optimal strategy for a male in this case is to join one of these groups and establish a harem, which he can then defend against other males.

A study of red deer demonstrates how food distribution drives the evolution of female defense polygyny. In parts of Europe where resources are evenly distributed over a wide area, red deer tend to form harem groups. However, in places where resources are clumped, males usually form territories (Carranza et al., 1990).

Red deer males that engage in female defense polygyny typically gather a harem of females during the rutting or mating season in the fall, and the group moves together over a relatively large range. The European red deer males frequently have aggressive encounters with other males in the process of maintaining their harem, and in some cases one of the males is severely injured as the result of antler clashes. However, encounters are frequently settled by competitive roaring; these matches demand a large amount of energy, so the male that can roar loudly for the longest period of time displays a legitimate measure of strength and projects accurate information about his fighting potential. As explained in the previous chapter, the roars also function as courtship signals. In addition, experimenters have found that female red deer exposed to the recordings of male roars have an earlier than usual period of estrus. Thus, the male roars appear to have multiple effects: to facilitate the establishment of male dominance, to attract females, and to speed up the reproductive process (McComb, 1991).

In primates, female defense polygyny is found in a variety of species, including gorillas and gelada monkeys—ground-dwelling African monkeys related to baboons. As in all harem groups, the primate male is constantly faced with other males trying to take over his harem. Generally, the larger the number of males in the area, the greater the competition, and the shorter the reign of the harem master. The master is likely to lose his harem when he is challenged by a series of males in rapid succession (see Dunbar, 1988).

Male primates typically take over a harem by attacking and defeating the harem master. In gelada monkeys, however, the females have an influence on takeover attempts. A challenging male will often attempt to form a relationship based on mutual grooming with several females in the harem. If the females accept the challenger, he is more likely to be successful in his takeover attempt. Thus, the females, who may fight among themselves in an apparent attempt to arrive at a consensus, have a definite "vote" in the determination of the outcome of the takeover attempt (see Dunbar, 1988).

Lek Polygyny

Lek polygyny is relatively rare but is found in a few isolated species of insects, birds, and mammals. A *lek* is an assembly area that functions as a special setting or stage where a group of males display flashy characteristics. Males within the lek establish small territories in close proximity. Females then visit the lek and mate with one of the males. In contrast to the territories considered earlier, territories within the lek are devoid of any valuable resources. Furthermore, the lek itself is indistinguishable from the surrounding terrain. Even though a lek's boundaries are indistinct and the lek is apparently valueless, the animals remember its location and return every year.

Lek polygyny was first identified in sage grouse of the western United States. The male birds arrive at the lek several weeks before the females. The males on the lek adopt exaggerated postures, standing with their tail cocked and white neck feathers raised (see Figure 10.1). The males also make a loud popping sound by suddenly expelling air from a specialized air sac in the throat. As the females arrive in the area, they make their way to the center of the lek. Most of the females mate with the same cock; however, a few males in close proximity with the successful male are able to mate at some time during the season (Johnsgard, 1967).

FIGURE 10.1 ◆ **Sage grouse on a lek in Montana.** The males, identified by their white breasts, are displaying in front of the less colorful females.

The lek polygyny of an African antelope, the Uganda kob, is similar to that of the sage grouse. The male kobs arrive first in the area and compete for a spot in the center of the lek. When a female approaches, the males begin to display vigorously, adopting a variety of postures. The female then moves to the center of the lek, generally ignoring the displays of males along the periphery, and almost always mates with the dominant male. Only when he tires from multiple matings and from fights with other males to maintain his position does the dominant male move from the central spot and allow another male to take his place. In this as in most lek species, the vast majority of offspring are fathered by a small minority of the male kobs.

How did this mating system evolve? It may have had its origins in situations in which females became widely and evenly distributed, causing other polygynous systems to lose effectiveness. Lekking may have developed when ecological conditions changed and the resources became scattered. Females then would become widely distributed, and both female defense and resource defense polygyny would fail (see Bradbury & Gibson, 1983). There is some evidence supporting this hypothesis. The topi, an African antelope, practices both resource defense and lekking. Resource defense exists in some regions without lekking, but lekking never occurs independent of resource defense polygyny. These findings suggest that resource defense polygyny is the more primitive of the two systems and that lekking probably evolved out of resource defense polygyny (Gosling & Petrie, 1990).

Why do animals develop a fidelity to a valueless area? The **spillover hypothesis** predicts that if an area becomes associated with frequent successful copulations, other males will be likely to go to that area in the future. Going to that area would be a good male strategy in that, as we have seen, proximal bystanders are sometimes successful. Furthermore, it is always possible that the most successful male from the previous year will not return and that another male can then occupy the territory.

The spillover hypothesis is indirectly supported by observations of black grouse. While the most successful male grouse stays in his central territory, the less successful males compete with each other and tend to move toward the center (Rintamaki et al., 1995).

Females also play a role in the development of lek polygyny. They benefit from going to an area that includes a large number of males clustered in a small space. The females may have a chance to compare males more easily than if they are dispersed; in addition, the clustered males may reduce the female's chances of being taken by predators (Bradbury, 1982).

Scramble Competition Polygyny

The types of polygyny we have considered up to this point are fairly well organized and predictable. **Scramble competition polygyny,** in contrast, lacks structure and organization. In this rare type of arrangement, illustrated by the wood frogs described in Chapter 8, males simply scramble about in an attempt to obtain as many matings as possible within a short period of time. There is relatively little active choice of partners on the part of either males or females. However, selective processes do take place; large male wood frogs are generally more effective in the scramble than small ones.

An advantage to scramble competition in frogs is that, since all females come into breeding condition at the same time, all eggs develop at about the same time, and the tadpoles in the pond are all about the same age. This synchrony in breeding reduces the possibility of cannibalism by older tadpoles on younger ones (Petranka & Thomas, 1995). As mentioned in Chapter 6, cannibalism is fairly common in tadpoles.

Scramble competition also occurs in the North American thirteen-lined ground squirrel. Female ground squirrels, like female wood frogs, are sexually receptive for a relatively brief time each year. During the 2-week mating period, males move about rapidly, mating with as many receptive females as they can find (Schwagmeyer & Parker, 1990). It seems that when a large number of females are available for only a short period of time, male strategies such as resource defense and female defense are too time-consuming. Scrambling is the most profitable alternative.

Polyandry

Polyandry is the opposite of polygyny: A polyandrous female has several partners, while the male has one (or at least fewer partners than the female). Polyandry is relatively

TABLE 10.1 ◆ Types of Polygyny

	Resource Defense	Female Defense	Lek	Scramble Competition
Defining Characteristics	Resources (such as food) are defended against other males.	Females are defended against other males.	Males congregate at traditional mating sites. Females choose males.	Males scramble about to obtain mates.
Ecological Conditions	Resources are clumped.	Resources are spread evenly.	Females are widely distributed.	A large number of females are available for only a short time.

uncommon, but we have already seen one example of polyandry in the anemone fish discussed in Chapter 8; the female anemone fish leaves her eggs with each of several males who then fertilize and tend the eggs (Turner, 1986).

Polyandry is also found in a few species of birds. For example, the female spotted sandpiper of North America mates with two or three males and then leaves clutches of eggs for the males to incubate (Oring, 1985). The species of birds that exhibit polyandry have certain things in common with each other. The males are the parental gender and are smaller than the females. The females are more active during courtship and arrive first at the breeding ground. And in contrast to most other birds, polyandrous females are able to produce more than one clutch of eggs during a short period of time (see Trivers, 1985).

Many of these factors interact and probably were important in the evolution of polyandry in birds. For example, when males exhibit most or all of the parental care, female–female competition for access to males is likely to develop. When female–female competition exists, sexual selection for size takes place and females are likely to initiate courtship. When females initiate courtship, they benefit from arriving first at the breeding grounds.

Polygynandry

In **polygynandry** animals live in groups in which both males and females mate with a variety of partners. This mating system is fairly uncommon but occurs among some mammals. For example, two or three male African lions share sexual access to all of the females in the pride. The most dominant male does most of the copulating. The males are often related, however, so even those that do not sire many of the offspring gain some fitness benefit (Bertram, 1978).

Primates such as chimpanzees, rhesus monkeys, and baboons also live in multimale groups or troops. The female's advertisement of fertility—sexual swelling—is more common in multimale primate groups than in single-male groups or monogamous pairs. Primatologist Sarah Hrdy (1988) suggests that this advertisement promotes mating with several males, which may be of some advantage to the female. Presumably, primate males remember the females with whom they have recently had sexual relations; and there has undoubtedly been a selection process favoring tolerance and helpfulness toward females that have been recent sexual partners, even if the males do not "know" which male fathered a female's young.

The dominant primate males do most of the mating, especially when the females are ovulating. To heighten their advantage, dominant males often interfere with attempts of other males to copulate. However, subordinate males are not powerless. For example, male chimpanzees will often retire with a female to an inconspicuous area, out of sight of the dominant male. During such encounters, the female typically inhibits the high arousal vocalizations that accompany less secretive matings (see Dunbar, 1988).

Primate groups, then, may be either polygynous or polygynandrous. Polygyny is probably the ancestral system. As groups became larger, however, it seems likely that they became multimale, because it would have been difficult for one male to monopolize all the females in a large group, especially if the females' fertile periods were synchronized.

The size of a group is often determined by the grouping patterns of females—which in turn are related to availability of food. Large groups of primates may also evolve because they are more effective in establishing a defense against predators (DeVore, 1963). Thus, with increasing numbers of females, it seems likely that groups contained more males. If the males were related, there would be inclusive fitness benefits (refer to Chapter 1) for each male. Support for this hypothesis that the size of the primate drives the evolution of polygynandry comes from the observation that small groups of primates virtually always contain only one male; groups of intermediate size may have one or two males; and groups with more than 10 females invariably contain more than one male (Altmann, 1990).

Monogamy

As suggested earlier in the chapter, a monogamous relationship often proves beneficial because the male may help with care of the young and provide some protection from predators or aggressive conspecific males. These behaviors can significantly increase the probability that the young will survive. The male gains further benefits: He has ready access to a female when she is fertile, and he is highly likely to be the father of the offspring. As we shall see later, monogamous males typically engage in mate-guarding activities that reduce the possibility of their being cuckolded—that is, of their investing in young fathered by another male.

Chapter 3 explained that young are born or hatched in varying stages of development ranging from altricial states (not fully developed) to precocial states (highly developed). In birds, the stage of development of the young is related to what type of mating system is adopted. Because altricial young require more parental care, altricial species of birds are most likely to be monogamous and to provide the young with biparental (two-parent) care. More than 90 percent of bird species are altricial, and most of these, including the great majority of songbirds, are monogamous.

The availability of food is another factor related to monogamy in birds. When food is scarce, it is difficult for one parent to gather enough by itself to feed the offspring. Consequently, there is a strong advantage to monogamy and biparental care. This relationship between food and biparental care is illustrated by the European wren. On the northern island of Saint Kilda, where food is scarce, this wren is monogamous and both parents feed the young. In England, however, where food is more abundant, the species is polygynous and only the female feeds the young (see Welty & Baptista, 1988).

Female mammals, under natural conditions, are usually able to provide enough milk and protection for the young. Even in species where the young receive parental care after weaning, the mother is generally able to care for them on her own. Therefore, it is not surprising that only about 10 percent of mammalian species are monogamous. The monogamous mammals include wolves: Wolves produce an unusually large litter of offspring, so it would be difficult for the female to be the sole provider. Thus, there is a definite advantage to monogamy and biparental care.

Monogamy is extremely rare in primates. However, it is found in two types of monkeys—marmosets and tamarins (discussed in Chapter 9). The males of these monkeys provide considerable parental care and facilitate the survival of the young. Interestingly, twin-

ning, which is very rare in other primates, occurs regularly in these monkeys. On the basis of an approach examining the costs and benefits of twinning, R. I. M. Dunbar (1995) suggests that a tendency toward monogamy must have preceded the evolution of twinning. One parent could not care effectively for two primate babies.

The only case of monogamy in an ape is seen in gibbons. Gibbons in Borneo form a monogamous relationship, but the male does not help feed the young and contributes very little to their overall survival. Monogamy in this species seems to have more to do with the defense of a feeding territory. In contrast to mates in the many species in which the territory is defended entirely by the male, both gibbon partners aggressively defend their joint territory against other gibbons. When an intruder is a female, the female member of the pair initiates the defense. The male partner takes the initiative when the intruder is male (Mitani, 1984).

Extrapair Copulations

In a monogamous system, infidelities, or extrapair (outside of the pair) copulations, on the part of one partner are potentially destructive to the other. If a female copulates with a male other than her partner, her partner may invest time and energy helping to rear offspring that are not his. Infidelity on the part of the monogamous male leads to a different type of problem: A male that spends time with another female will reduce the time and energy he has available for providing optimal parental care and protection for his mate.

Considering the loss that both males and females suffer as the result of infidelity, it is

◆ UNUSUAL ADAPTATIONS

Monogamy in a Shrimp and a Fish

Monogamy is extremely rare among invertebrates. The shrimp *Hymenocera picta* is monogamous, however, because of an unusual condition. In contrast to the usual one-to-one sex ratio in animals, there are many more males than females among these shrimp. Furthermore, females are widely scattered and become receptive for only a few hours every several weeks. Under these conditions it is very difficult for a male to find several receptive females. Monogamy in this animal probably represents an instance of a male making the best of a very limiting situation (Wickler & Seibt, 1981).

Monogamy is also rare in fish, especially in species that live in sea-grass habitats. Sea horses, however, engage in a highly unusual form of monogamy. The female places her eggs in a male's specially adapted brood pouch (see Figure 10.2). After he fertilizes the eggs, he continues to carry them in his pouch. The male would not gain fitness by sexually interacting with other females during his "pregnancy," and so it is not surprising that he does not seek out other partners. Once the eggs have been fertilized, they expand and the pouch becomes sealed shut, preventing other females from adding eggs and, in effect, "cuckolding" the female. Because the female cannot produce additional mature eggs before the male's "pregnancy" is terminated, the female is not likely to seek other partners either.

During the sea horse male's extended "pregnancy," the eggs are protected and nurtured. Each morning, male and female partners perform a greeting ceremony in

not surprising that females of many monogamous species chase other females out of their male's territory and that males guard their partners closely, especially during their fertile period (Kempenaers, 1995). Nonetheless, infidelity sometimes occurs in monogamous birds. Extrapair copulation appears to be most likely when the territories of several males are in close proximity, creating opportunities for males and/or females to mate with different partners (Alatalo et al., 1984).

DNA analysis (see Chapter 2) has now made it possible for scientists to accurately determine parentage of offspring. In some

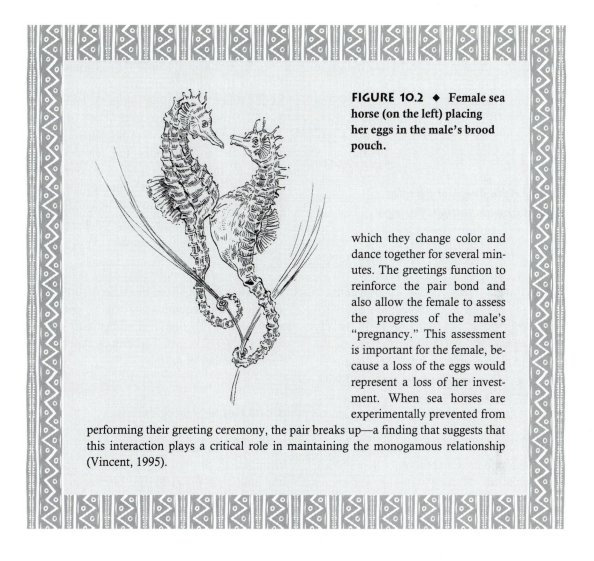

FIGURE 10.2 ◆ **Female sea horse (on the left) placing her eggs in the male's brood pouch.**

which they change color and dance together for several minutes. The greetings function to reinforce the pair bond and also allow the female to assess the progress of the male's "pregnancy." This assessment is important for the female, because a loss of the eggs would represent a loss of her investment. When sea horses are experimentally prevented from performing their greeting ceremony, the pair breaks up—a finding that suggests that this interaction plays a critical role in maintaining the monogamous relationship (Vincent, 1995).

monogamous species of songbirds, extrapair paternity is quite high, surpassing 30 percent. In contrast, extrapair paternity is less than 4 percent in a species of European songbird known as the dunnock (Burke et al., 1989). As we will see later in this chapter, certain adaptations that promote effective sperm competition in dunnocks tend to keep extrapair paternity low when these birds are in monogamous relationships.

Some species apparently remain monogamous despite opportunities for extrapair matings. For example, an African antelope known as a dikdik was experimentally tested in a field setting. Males that were previously unmated left their territories to search for a presumably available female. Mated males, in contrast, did not leave their territories to search for other females, even under tempting conditions. Interestingly, monogamy in these antelopes occurs even though the male provides no parental care (Komers, 1996).

Possible Advantages for Females That Mate with Multiple Partners

As indicated earlier, females have less to gain by accepting multiple partners than do males. However, research has identified some advantages accrued by females that are polygamous (that is, they mate with more than one partner). Despite the fact that one male usually produces enough sperm to fertilize all of the eggs a female is able to produce, certain female insects, such as *Zorotypus barberi* females, lay more eggs after copulating with several partners than after copulating with only one (Chloe, 1995). Furthermore, as we saw in Chapter 9, certain female insects are sometimes able to collect nuptial gifts in exchange for copulation. Mating with several males could provide significant material benefits for these females. Finally, mating with several males is likely to promote more genetic diversity in the offspring than mating with just one male (Birkhead & Moller, 1992).

At any rate, a study with snakes indicates that mating with several males does indeed have fitness benefits in terms of the rate of offspring survival. The viability of offspring from female European adders that had mated with several males was compared to that of offspring from females that had mated with a single male. The offspring of the multiple-mated females were much less likely to be stillborn (Madsen et al., 1992).

There is also evidence that in some birds, females choose to mate with more than one male. When jungle fowl females were given an opportunity to mate with more than one male—and the males were restrained so that they could not interfere—the females often chose to mate with more than one. This choice occurred even when one of the males had a characteristic that female jungle fowl find very attractive—a large comb—and the other males lacked it (Ligon & Zwartjes, 1995).

Nonetheless, males typically gain more fitness advantages from multiple matings than females. Consequently, when animals are polygamous (engage in matings with several individuals), it is usually the male that has the largest number of partners.

Conditional Strategies

It may be advantageous for animals to shift from one mating strategy to another, choosing the one that provides the best cost–benefit ratio under certain conditions. Since the maximum cost–benefit ratio may not be the same for both genders, gender conflicts may arise in these conditional strategies.

Shifting from Monogamy to Polygyny

Indigo buntings are usually monogamous, but sometimes these birds live peaceably in a relationship that includes two females and a male. This polygynous relationship is most likely to be found when a territory is rich in resources

(Carey & Nolan, 1979). There seems to be a **polygyny threshold;** that is, a point at which a female does better to shift from a monogamous to a polygynous relationship (Verner, 1964). With some modification, the polygyny threshold model has generated several hypotheses that have gained support. For example, a female may engage in polygyny even if she obtains immediate fitness benefits slightly below those that could be provided by monogamy. Her behavior is reasonable if you take into account the probability that a polygynous male will carry superior genes. In other words, the sons of a father attractive or strong enough to gain more than one mate may themselves be relatively successful in reproduction.

It is also possible that a female will choose an already mated male because he acts as if he is unmated. There is some experimental evidence that this type of deception does indeed take place in pied flycatchers. Experimenters placed mated and unmated males in a semi-natural condition that contained a nest box and a simulated territory. A male with a partner behaved much more like an unmated male when there was a caged female present than when he was alone (i.e., the cage was empty). Apparently the presence of a female evoked functionally deceptive behaviors (Searcy et al., 1991).

A primary female (one that is already in a monogamous relationship with a male) is not always willing to allow a secondary female into the group. Research indicates that a primary female blue tit will fight especially hard if she has been recently mated. This high level of aggression makes sense, because the male is more likely to divide his parental care between the two females' young if the females lay their eggs within a short interval. In other words, the primary female has more to lose if her young and her rival's young arrive about the same time (Kempenaers, 1995).

Shifting from One Polygynous Strategy to Another

There is also evidence that animals may shift from one form of polygyny to another in response to changing environmental conditions. When a population of breeding wood frogs is only moderately dense, however, the males are territorial and move around very little. When the population of fertile females and competing males becomes more dense, males move around and engage in scramble competition (Woolbright et al., 1990). The superior strategy under these crowded conditions is apparently to mate with as many females as possible during the short time they are available.

An experimental study of red deer also illustrates a tendency to shift from one polygynous strategy to another. Researchers placed clusters of food in small, scattered areas within the range of a herd of red deer. Within a short time, the male deer changed from a female defense mating system to a resource defense system (Carranza et al., 1995). In addition to demonstrating the deer's ability to shift strategies, this study further supports the hypothesis that ecology is basic to the evolution of mating strategies.

Perhaps the greatest tendency to shift mating systems is found in the dunnock. These birds exhibit polygyny, polyandry, polygynandry, or monogamy, depending on environmental factors (Davies, 1992). Such flexibility in choice of mating systems allows dunnocks to adjust optimally to a variety of ecological conditions. Control on the part of females is a likely requisite for such a variable mating system. If males were the only ones making the choices, stable polygyny would probably be the general rule (Davies et al., 1995).

POSTCOPULATORY COMPETITION

Competition between males to fertilize a large percentage of a female's eggs does not end with copulation. A male faces the possibility that another male will copulate with the female and that the rival's sperm will fertilize her eggs. There is also the possibility that the female has previously copulated and the male's effort will be wasted. In response to these threats, males have evolved both behavioral and physiological mechanisms that increase the probability that their sperm will indeed fertilize the female's eggs.

Mate Guarding

One of the most straightforward methods of ensuring paternity is a behavioral approach: mate guarding, or chasing off other males that approach during the female's fertile period. In both insects and birds, a female is able to store sperm for several weeks or more after copulation, until her eggs are ready to be fertilized. The sperm of the last male to mate with the female will usually fertilize the largest share of her eggs, a phenomenon known as the **recency effect** (Birkhead & Moller, 1992). Because of

this effect, mate guarding is a particularly beneficial strategy for male insects and birds.

Species of birds that nest in colonies, such as bank swallows of North America, are especially likely to practice mate guarding. The male swallows guard their females most vigorously during the females' fertile period (Beecher & Beecher, 1979). Mate guarding is less common among bird species in which the male establishes a territory. Apparently other males are not likely to enter the defended territory, an area in which the female spends much of her time. Furthermore, when she does leave the territory, the male does not usually follow her, because his priority is to defend the territory (Leffelaar & Robertson, 1984).

In contrast to insects and birds, mammals exhibit a **primacy effect:** When several males copulate with a female within a short time, it

TABLE 10.2 ◆ Primacy and Recency Effects in Fertilization

	Recency Effect	Primacy Effect
Definition	The last male to mate has the best chance of fertilizing the eggs.	The first male to copulate has the best chance of fertilizing the eggs.
Examples	Insects and birds.	Mammals.
Effect on Mate Guarding	Strong natural selection for males to mate guard after mating.	Weak natural selection for males to mate guard after mating.

is usually the first male's sperm that fertilize the eggs (Foltz & Schwagmeyer, 1989). The primacy effect is related to the fact that fertilization of mammalian eggs takes place shortly after copulation. By the time subsequent males deposit their sperm, most of the eggs may already be fertilized. Consequently, mate guarding is usually less common in monogamous species of mammals than in monogamous species of birds.

Prolonged Copulation

Another method of mate guarding is for the male to remain joined in copulation with the female for a long period of time. Damselflies sometimes remain joined for as long as 6 to 7 hours, especially when there is intense competition among males for access to females.

An experimental study of millipedes provides more direct support for this hypothesis that prolonged copulation is a type of mate guarding. Experimenters manipulated conditions so that competition among the millipede males was more intense in some circumstances than others. Under the most intense competition, the millipedes copulated for the longest period of time (Telford & Dangerfield, 1990).

Prolonged copulation also takes place in some species of mammals (although less commonly than is the case for insects). For example, a pair of sables has been observed joined together for 8 hours (Ford & Beach, 1951). But because mammals in copulation are particularly open to predation and, in some cases, harassment from other males, prolonged copulation is less common when copulation occurs in open areas.

Mate Guarding by the Female

I have already mentioned that female blue tits will sometimes express strong aggression against other females that enter their mate's territory. Strong aggressive responses that function as mate guarding occur in females of other species of birds as well (Slagsvold & Lifjeld, 1994).

Because a male copulating with one female is at least temporarily prevented from soliciting copulations with other females, females soliciting frequent copulations with a male are engaging in a form of mate guarding. Thus, a high level of sexual activity in females functions as a mate-guarding strategy as well as a method of increasing the probability of fertilization (see Eens et al., 1995; Whittingham et al., 1995).

Sperm Competition

Another "strategy" to reduce the probability that a rival male will fertilize female's eggs consists of physiological adaptations that enable a male's sperm to compete successfully with sperm of a rival.

At one time animal behaviorists believed that a **vaginal plug,** or viscous material left in the vagina of a female mouse after the male has copulated, functions as a barrier to prevent another male's sperm from entering the female's vagina. But when the plug is experimentally removed after copulation, deer mice females are no more likely to become inseminated by a second male than when the plug is left in place. It seems that the plug acts more to prevent leakage than to form a barrier (Dewsbury, 1990).

In honeybees, the male utilizes a different type of plug: namely, the intromittent organ is left in the queen bee after the male copulates. The male then falls and dies as the result of his loss (Thornhill & Alcock, 1983). At one time the abandoned organ was thought to act as a barrier against sperm from other males. More recent research, however, suggests that the remains of the copulatory organ, or mating sign, does not serve as a mating deterrent. Experiments indicate that males are actually more attracted to a queen carrying a mating sign. The latest suitor is easily able to remove the sign with a special set of hairs on his own intromittent organ (Koeniger, 1990).

Over a period of time, bees probably evolved an ability to remove the mating sign and reduce or eliminate its deterrent effect. Recent evidence indicates that the mating sign functions to prevent semen from flowing out of the female rather than as a sperm competition device (Woyciechowski et al., 1994).

Nonetheless, males have evolved several behaviors and structures that do function effectively in sperm competition. And in many cases females cooperate in promoting sperm competition, because the results of sperm competition may be of benefit to females. Let's consider some examples of these competitive physiological adaptations.

Frequent Ejaculations

Some males that face stiff competition from other males ejaculate several times within a short period when with a female. For example, a male Shaw's jird (a small rodent in the Sahara Desert) is capable of more than 200 intromissions and more than a dozen ejaculations within a 2-hour period (Bourlière, 1954).

In a large colony of stump-tailed monkeys, noted for their sexual potency, a male named Sam was observed completing 59 matings in 6 hours, each with an ejaculation (DeWaal, 1989).

These observations do not clearly indicate that it is competition that drives the frequent ejaculations, but more convincing evidence comes from a study comparing the copulatory frequency of African marsh harriers (hawks) under various conditions. The investigator found that mated pairs of these birds copulated twice as often when nests were clumped as when they were isolated. In the clumped condition there is an increased possibility of another male copulating with the female (Simmons, 1990).

Another study provides further support for the hypothesis that frequent ejaculations play a role in sperm competition. Pairs of male Mongolian gerbils were allowed to copulate with a female. In each pair of males, the gerbil with the greatest number of ejaculations sired the larger proportion of the offspring (Agren, 1990).

At this point it is unclear why frequent ejaculations increase the probability of paternity. One possibility is that frequent ejaculators introduce a larger number of sperm than infrequent ejaculators. Another possibility is that frequent ejaculation increases the likelihood of at least one of the ejaculations' occurring at a time that is optimal for fertilization. Still another possibility is that frequent ejaculation is correlated with sperm viability. More research is needed to determine which of these factors—or what combination of these factors—is basic to the relationship between ejaculatory frequency and sperm competition.

Sperm Removal

J. K. Waage (1973) identified a surprising adaptation on the male damselfly's intromittent organ. The organ has horns and spines on its sides, allowing the male to use it as a scrub brush. Before he copulates, the male is able to remove more than 90 percent of the sperm deposited by previous partners in the female's spermatheca (the sac where the sperm are stored). In the decades since this discovery, researchers have identified adaptations for removing sperm in other animals as well. Some shark males forcefully spray seawater into the female, which apparently washes out some of the sperm from a previous mating (Eberhard, 1985). Because sperm can be stored by both female damselflies and female sharks, direct sperm removal appears to be an effective strategy in these species.

The male dunnock (the European songbird discussed earlier) also uses a sperm removal strategy. He pecks at his female partner's cloaca just before he attempts copulation. This stimulates the female to expel sperm deposited by a previous suitor. The observation that males are more likely to peck at the female's cloaca if there has recently been another male in the vicinity supports the conclusion that the pecking behavior is related to sperm competition (Davies, 1983). The fact that dunnocks experience an extremely low rate of extrapair paternity testifies to the effectiveness of this sperm competition technique.

Production of an Abundance of Sperm

Perhaps the simplest method of increasing the chance of paternity is for the male to ejaculate copious amounts of semen and sperm. This increases the probability that some of the sperm will fertilize eggs. Although all male mammals produce a large number of sperm, the male pig is at the extreme, ejaculating as much as a pint of semen containing more than 100 million sperm (Dewsbury, 1972). At least part of the reason for this apparent overabundance is related to the strong possibility that a female of this species will mate with more than one male (Dewsbury, 1990).

If a female mammal has spent time with another male, there is a possibility the pair has copulated. Interestingly, male rats that receive information about this possibility show appropriate adjustments to increase their chances of winning in sperm competition. In a carefully controlled study, male rats had an increased sperm output after they had observed their partner in the presence of another male (Bellis & Barker, 1990).

Introduction of Antiaphrodisiacs

Another physiological adaptation related to sperm competition is for the male to leave an **antiaphrodisiac**—a substance that reduces the attractiveness of a female to males who might try to mate with her after one male has already inseminated her. Evidence of a male-produced olfactory antiaphrodisiac has been found in certain butterflies (Gilbert, 1976).

In the fruit fly, the female herself produces an antiaphrodisiac, discouraging other males from courting her after she has been mated. Although multiple matings are advantageous for some female animals, female fruit flies are often in the company of a large number of highly aggressive males, and multitudinous matings under such conditions involve a significant risk of injury.

Certain male fruit flies utilize this female-produced antiaphrodisiac. After mating, some males produce a chemical substance that stimulates the female's release of the antiaphrodisiac (Scott & Jackson, 1990). This serves as another example of how animals have evolved the ability to take advantage of unusual opportunities.

Production of Kamikaze and Altruistic Sperm

There is interesting evidence that in species that perform internal fertilization, sperm themselves compete with one another in an aggressive manner. Certain sperm, perhaps more than 99 percent of them, act as **kamikaze sperm.** Kamikaze sperm reduce the viability of sperm from other males' copulations—and, in the process, fail to reach the egg themselves. Among the kamikaze sperm there appear to be at least two distinct types. Low down in the female reproductive tract, type A sperm hinder the passage of sperm from subsequent males' matings. Higher in the tract, type B sperm are involved in a "seek and destroy" tactic, attacking sperm from a previous male's mating (see Baker, 1996).

An experimental study with rats lends support to the kamikaze sperm hypothesis. Male rats in one group accompanied a female for 5 days before estrus and were then allowed to mate with her (the guarded female condition). Males in another group were introduced to estrous females after they had been in the company of, but not copulated with, another male (the unguarded condition). Consistent with the kamikaze sperm hypothesis, examination of the females showed that females in the unguarded condition had more sperm in the upper portion of the reproductive tract (type B sperm) than those in the guarded condition (Bellis & Baker, 1990). As in the case of sperm count, the male's ejaculate seems to vary in terms of the number of type B sperm as an adaptation to possible sperm competition.

While sperm from different males seem to compete with one another, there is evidence that in some cases sperm from the same male cooperate, or function as **altruistic sperm.** In certain mollusks, for example, a very large "helper" sperm carries hundreds of fertilizing sperm on the journey toward the egg. In other mollusks, short wormlike sperm apparently do not fertilize the egg but serve a nutritive function. Because all sperm from the same male carry the same genetic material, it does not matter, from a fitness standpoint, which particular sperm reaches the egg. Thus, altruistic sperm can have a significant beneficial function if they increase the probability of fertilization (see Trivers, 1985).

◆ HUMAN EVOLUTION

Like many species of nonhuman animals, humans have what could be called a mixture of mating strategies. Similarly, some of the same types of sperm competition take place in humans as occur in certain nonhuman animals. We will now look at the evidence for these general observations as well as at the possible evolutionary history of mating systems and sperm competition in humans.

MATING SYSTEMS

Did the ancestors of humans live in multimale groups similar to those of chimpanzees, or in single-male groups such as those of gorillas? Evidence from comparative anatomy suggests that our early ancestors probably lived in groups that more closely resembled those of the gorilla. Chimpanzees and other primates in multimale groups have relatively large testicles. There was apparently a selection for large testicles in these animals because the large testicles produce large amounts of sperm, advantageous in the intense sperm competition associated with multimale groups. Humans, like gorillas, have relatively small testicles, which suggests that early hominid systems probably contained a single sexually active male (Hrdy, 1988). At a later time, reduced sexual dimorphism (refer to Chapter 1) indicates that early humans probably developed less polygyny and perhaps a certain degree of monogamy.

Like their early ancestors, modern humans have a tendency to engage in both polygamous and monogamous mating systems. In their survey of human societies that are culturally independent of one another, Ford and Beach (1951) reported that more than 50 percent of societies sanctioned polygamous marriages.

As with certain nonhumans, the type of mating system adopted by a human society sometimes correlates, to a certain extent, with the availability of females. In preliterate societies in Paraguay, for example, one society containing more women than men is primarily polygynous, while another society containing relatively few women is highly monogamous (Hill & Hurtado, 1989). Apparently the relative availability of mates has influenced the type of mating system adopted in both nonhumans and humans.

Why do many humans in all societies exhibit a combination of monogamous and polygamous mating tendencies? David Buss and David Schmitt (1993) looked at several variables related to the type of mating system human behavior reflects. Buss and Schmitt classify individuals' polygamous *tendencies* (as opposed to culturally sanctioned polygamous marriages) as short-term mating strategies, and monogamous *tendencies* as long-term mating strategies. Short-term strategies imply mating with no commitment for the future, while long-term strategies reflect concern for the future and a commitment to one person and the offspring.

The advantages and constraints associated with these two strategies differ for the two genders. From a direct fitness standpoint, men have more to gain following short-term mating strategies than women, because it is possible for men to sire many children with little investment of time or resources.

In many situations, however, long-term mating strategies actually have superior fitness benefits for men. As compared to men adopting short-term strategies, men engaged in long-term strategies are more likely to attract women who will be good mothers, to form mutually beneficial alliances with their partners, to have an opportunity to contribute to the fitness of their offspring by providing parental care, to form beneficial alliances with friends and relatives of their partners, and to be reasonably assured of paternity.

For women, long-term strategies are generally more beneficial than short-term ones. By following a long-term strategy, a woman can attract a man who protects and provides for her in the long run and helps provide parental care. In certain circumstances, however, short-term strategies may have benefits for women. A woman may be able to attract a wide variety of men, including some with unusually good genetic potential who would not be willing to make a long-term commitment. In addition, a short-term relationship may have the chance of developing into a long-term relationship.

In contrast to evolution-based conceptualizations that implied biological determinism in human mating systems, Buss and Schmitt's analysis suggests that contextual and cognitive factors are important in the mating system adopted. For example, under stressful conditions such as war or social breakdown—or under conditions perceived as stressful—both genders are inclined to adopt short-term mating strategies.

SPERM COMPETITION

Is there any evidence that sperm competition exists in humans? Interestingly, the answer is a qualified yes. For example, English couples who volunteered to participate in a study of human sexuality collected sperm in condoms during intercourse and then allowed researchers to analyze the sperm count along with questionnaires the couples completed after intercourse. The researcher, Robin Baker (1996), found a positive correlation between the sperm count and the amount of time the couple had been sepa-

rated before intercourse. In other words, the men ejaculated more sperm if they had been separated for a period of time from their partners—and the possibility of infidelity existed—than if they had been with their partners and the possibility of infidelity did not exist.

Robin Baker and Mark Bellis (1993) also looked at the role of female orgasm in sperm competition. When a woman is nonorgasmic, she ejects up to 3 ml of seminal fluid from her vagina after copulation. However, if she is orgasmic at any time from 1 minute before to 45 minutes after the man ejaculates, she retains a much higher percentage of the man's semen. The contractions of the orgasm propel the contents of the upper vagina into the cervix. Therefore, as noted in Chapter 8, if a woman has intercourse with two or more men within a short period of time, the sperm from the man associated with her orgasm has a competitive advantage over the sperm of a man associated with a nonorgasmic encounter.

The findings of Baker and Bellis are certainly interesting and contribute in some unexpected ways to our conceptualizations of human sexuality. These are preliminary findings, however, and confirmation based on additional research is necessary before firm conclusions can be drawn.

◆ CHANGING PERSPECTIVES

PAST	PRESENT	FUTURE
Mating systems are randomly selected or related to phylogeny (the general biological grouping of animals). Postcopulatory competition does not exist (early twentieth century).	The evolution of mating systems is related to various ecological factors, including availability of food and of sexual partners. A large variety of postcopulatory techniques and strategies have evolved, particularly in those species in which females mate with many males.	What ecological factors influence the evolution of mating systems? Are there still methods of postcopulatory competition to be identified?

SUMMARY

Polygyny is a mating system in which a male mates with several females. There are several types of polygynous systems: resource defense polygyny (the males defend a resource that is attractive to females); female defense polygyny (the males defend a harem of females); lek polygyny (the males assemble at a lek, a small area where females go to choose a mate); and scramble competition polygyny (the males attempt to copulate with as many females as possible in a short time).

Polyandry—a system in which a female mates with several males—features sex-role reversals. In polyandrous birds, the female mates with each of several males, then lays her eggs and leaves them in the care of the males.

In polygynandrous systems, the males and females in a social group mate with each other. Multimale polygynandrous groups—which are typically larger than single-male groups—occur in lions and in several species of primates.

Monogamy, in which the male and female mate with each other more or less exclusively, is strongly associated with biparental care. Thus, monogamous systems tend to evolve when the young are altricial, especially in birds, and when food is scarce. Monogamy not associated with biparental care is also found in a few cases.

Ecological factors such as the distribution of food and the presence of predators have a strong effect on the evolution of conditional mating strategies. In response to changing environmental factors, some animals have developed the ability to shift from one mating system to another.

Competition between males continues even after copulation. One form of postcopulatory competition is mate guarding, which may occur in females as well as males.

Another type of postcopulatory competition is sperm competition. Sperm competition strategies include frequent ejaculations, sperm removal, the production of an abundance of sperm, the introduction of antiaphrodisiacs, and the production of kamikaze and altruistic sperm.

Some aspects of human sexual motivation can be understood in terms of our evolutionary history. Examples include the choice of long-term or short-term mating approaches and how much sperm a man produces.

KEY TERMS

altruistic sperm, p. 238
antiaphrodisiac, p. 237
female defense polygyny, p. 223
kamikaze sperm, p. 238

lek polygyny, p. 224
mating systems, p. 221
polyandry, p. 226
polygynandry, p. 227

CHAPTER 11

PARENTAL CARE

- ◆ *Why do emperor penguin males provide most of the care for the young?*

- ◆ *Why do these penguins breed during Antarctic winters?*

When an animal passes on its genes to its offspring, this alone does not ensure reproductive success. The offspring must survive until they, in turn, reproduce. As you may recall from Chapter 8, there are two general strategies for increasing the probability

11

that the young will survive to reproduce. One approach is to produce a very large number of offspring and rely on the probability that a few will survive (r selection). The other strategy, which will be the focus of this chapter, is to invest time and energy in promoting the survival of the young (K selection).

We will begin by discussing parental investment theory as it applies to the evolution of parental strategies. Then we will look at which gender provides the parental care and at factors that promote biparental care. Next, we will explore the various types of parental care and the mechanisms that facilitate this care. Finally, we will consider aspects of human parental behavior as they relate to human evolution.

PARENTAL INVESTMENT THEORY

Animals vary greatly in how much parental effort they display. Parental investment theory, as outlined by Robert Trivers (1972), proposes that sexually reproducing animals must balance the cost of investing in their offspring against the cost of delaying or forgoing the production of future offspring. For example, the longer a mother mammal continues to nurse her young, the longer she has to wait before she can reproduce again. As suggested in Chapter 1, one of the marks of a fruitful theory is that it can generate testable hypotheses. And indeed, researchers have been able to generate and test numerous hypotheses generated by Trivers's theory.

Number of Offspring

One of the most straightforward hypotheses derived from Trivers's theory is: The greater the number of offspring present at one time, the greater the "value" of the offspring to the parent and the greater the investment in parental care. Although an individual animal typically invests more energy in caring for several offspring than for one or a few offspring, it is difficult to assess what determines this differential output. Several young may require more attention because their individual demands cumulatively produce high levels of stimulation.

It is possible, however, to assess parents' perception of the evolutionary "value" of their young by examining the guarding of eggs in fish. Large numbers of eggs do not produce more intense stimulation than small numbers, and a parent can guard a large number of eggs with the same amount of energy it takes to guard few eggs. Researchers have experimentally varied the number of eggs of stickleback fish by removing or adding clutches of eggs— and have found that parental males show more vigorous defense for large numbers of eggs than for small numbers (Sargent, 1981). This finding lends support to the hypothesis that differential "value" affects parental investment.

Parent–Offspring Conflict

Both parents and offspring gain in fitness if the offspring survive. In addition, both parents and offspring can benefit from the parents' production of additional offspring. The parents experience direct fitness benefits, while the offspring gain indirectly because siblings share 50 percent of their genes. In a 1974 paper, Trivers argued that the point at which parents gain optimally from turning to the production of more offspring is different from the point that is optimal for the offspring. This difference results from the fact that parents are genetically related by the same amount to all of their offspring and therefore benefit from distributing their parental investment. Offspring, on the other hand, have more to gain by promoting their own survival than by tolerating parental investments in their siblings.

Following this logic, a basic prediction is that in mammals the cost of nursing the young would become prohibitive for the mother, in terms of delaying further reproduction, before it would be prohibitive for the offspring. In other words, offspring would be selected to take nourishment for a longer period of time than the mother would be selected to provide it. This difference between parents and offspring would lead to a weaning conflict when the offspring reached a certain stage in development. And a significant amount of weaning conflict has indeed been observed in a great variety of species (Trivers, 1974). For example, older kittens often try to nurse from the mother, but the mother pushes them away or hisses at them.

Future Full Siblings Compared to Future Half Siblings

If the future siblings are likely to be half siblings, fitness theory predicts, there should be more prolonged weaning conflicts than if the future siblings are likely to be full siblings. Since half siblings share only 25 percent of the existing offspring's genes, there is less indirect fitness advantage to half siblings' arrival than to full siblings' arrival. Consequently, offspring should be selected to be more ready to give up nursing for the future benefit of full siblings than for half siblings.

A comparison of weaning conflicts in two species of monkeys lends support to this hypothesis. Langur monkeys, whose offspring are likely to be half siblings because of the frequent replacement of dominant males in the troop, have relatively long-lasting weaning conflicts. In contrast, rhesus monkeys, which live in stable hierarchies and are likely to produce full siblings, have shorter weaning conflicts (see Trivers, 1985).

Old Mothers Compared to Young Mothers

Another testable hypothesis generated by Trivers's theory is that older mothers, who have a reduced possibility of future reproduction, will wean their offspring later and therefore will have fewer weaning conflicts than younger mothers. Observations of baboon mothers indicate that indeed older mothers are significantly slower to wean their offspring (Nicholson, 1982).

Parental investment in general should also be greater for older than for younger parents. The findings of a study of parental investment in California gulls clearly support this prediction: Rates of nest attendance, territorial defense, and feeding of chicks all increase as the parents grow older (Pugesek, 1981). Comparable findings have been reported for red deer. In this case, the degree of parental care was inferred from the condition of the young, and the calves of older red deer in their first winter were found to be in better condition—relative to the condition of their mothers—than the calves of younger mothers (Clutton-Brock, 1984).

Parents with Short Life Spans Compared to Those with Long Life Spans

If an animal lives a relatively long time, it has another chance to reproduce if its young are lost; animals with a short life expectancy are less likely to have a second chance if their offspring die. Thus, another hypothesis derived from parental investment theory is that, other things being equal, parents in short-lived species should invest more of their energy in parental care than long-lived species. More specifically, when extra effort is required, parents in short-lived species should be more willing to make the additional investment in their offspring than parents in long-lived species.

Experimental tests with certain species of birds provide support for this hypothesis. When parents of short-lived species (e.g., blue tits and coal tits) were experimentally handicapped, the parents worked overtime and lost weight while investing in their young (Slagsvold & Lifjeld, 1990). In contrast, long-lived petrel parents, when handicapped by an experimental reduction of their wingspan, shunted the experimentally increased "costs" to their offspring; that is, the petrel parents fed the offspring less. Consequently, the offspring gained weight relatively slowly, while the parents showed no ill effects from the handicapping (Mauck & Grubb, 1995).

Toleration of Infanticide

Parental investment theory also helps to explain a phenomenon that has traditionally been difficult to understand—the fact that in some circumstances, one or both parents will tolerate another animal's killing their offspring.

Infanticide by a "Stepparent"

An African lion male will often take over a pride of females from another male or males. (We will examine the social structure of African lions in more detail when we discuss social groups in Chapter 14.) The male then typically kills the young cubs. Why? First, the offspring are not related to the new male, so the infanticide does not result in any loss of his fitness. Also, the mothers of the victimized

TABLE 11.1 ◆ Parent–Offspring Conflict

Factors That Contribute	Most Conflict	Reasons
Age of offspring	Older offspring	Nursing older offspring can delay further reproduction.
Age of parents	Younger parents	Younger parents have more to lose because they have a greater reproductive potential.
Degree of relatedness of future siblings	Future half siblings	If future siblings are full siblings, the offspring gains more from the parents' future reproduction.
Life span of parents	Parents with long life span	Parents with short life spans can lose much of their reproductive potential if present offspring die. Therefore, they tend to invest greatly in present offspring.

young come into estrus quickly after lactation has ceased, so the male may become a parent earlier and gain fitness from this seemingly senseless killing (Schaller, 1972).

But why do the females tolerate their loss of parental investment? Lion males are larger and more powerful than the females, so the females would have difficulty preventing the eventual occurrence of the killing. By tolerating the infanticide and coming into estrus rapidly, the females get a fast start on the production of new offspring. The male then accepts the new offspring and even treats them with apparent affection.

Langur monkey males may also commit infanticide when they take over a group of females. In this case, however, the females are sometimes able to protect their offspring; a group of females may even work together to protect their young (Hrdy, 1977).

Infanticide by females has been regularly observed in a polyandrous bird called the jacana, which inhabits tropical lakes and pools overgrown with low-water vegetation. The jacana female may approach and begin to court a male who is incubating eggs or caring for young that are the offspring of another female. The new female then destroys the eggs or kills the young. This infanticide may have a comparable function to that observed in lions and langur monkeys. If the female kills another female's young, she can induce the male to mate with her and care for her eggs. In this sex-role reversal, the male is smaller than the female and apparently unable, at least in many cases, to defend the offspring (Stephens, 1982).

Female infanticide of a mother's own offspring sometimes occurs in mice when there is an extreme shortage of food (Bronson & Marstellar, 1985). Infanticide or abandonment by the mother mouse may also occur if young mice are deformed or unresponsive to the mother. In these cases the probability that the young would survive and reproduce is very low. In light of the theory of parental investment, continued parental care would be a poor investment.

Siblicide

Among certain birds one sibling will kill another sibling, even in the presence of the parents. For example, the larger of two great egret siblings will sometimes kill the smaller sibling in a fight over food that the parents deposit in the nest (Mock, 1984). Why does this siblicide occur, and why is it tolerated by the parents?

A fitness-oriented explanation is that when there is a scarcity of food (as in the mouse infanticide example), the larger egret sibling is making an adaptive response. The siblings could not be fed enough food for both to survive, so the elimination of the weakest one increases the probability that the stronger one will live. The larger sibling is then providing fitness benefits for itself as well as for its parents.

The fact that great egret parents begin incubating their first egg before a second egg is laid contributes to the size and strength difference between the siblings. One egg hatches earlier than the other, and the first offspring gets an early size and strength advantage. (In most birds, incubation does not begin until all the eggs are laid.)

An experimental study of cattle egrets, which also incubate a first egg before a second is laid, provides support for the hypothesis that the conditions associated with siblicide have fitness benefits. Eggs were experimentally incubated at the same time, and the fledg-lings that resulted from this arrangement were similar in size. The researchers then compared the efficiency of the experimental system (similar-sized offspring together with parents) with that of a natural system (different-sized chicks with parents). The natural system was clearly the most efficient when the amount of food necessary to produce a surviving offspring was taken into account (Mock & Ploger, 1987).

Ecological Factors

While much of the variation in parental investment can be explained by Trivers's theory, ecological factors may also contribute to variability in parental investment. As discussed in Chapter 8, *r*-selected animals (following the gold-rush strategy) produce relatively large numbers of offspring and invest relatively little time and energy in each individual. In contrast, *K*-selected animals (which live in habitats at or near their carrying capacity) produce relatively few offspring and invest a considerable amount of time and energy in each individual.

These differences make sense in terms of fitness benefits. An *r*-selected animal such as a rat lives in an environment that is unstable but below carrying capacity, so the rat has an opportunity to reap benefits quickly. Getting a jump on the competition by producing many young in a short period of time can have a large payoff. In contrast, *K*-selected animals such as gorillas live in an environment that is stable but cannot support many additional gorillas. Therefore, a conservative approach—investing large amounts of time and energy in a few offspring—is the best strategy for these animals.

Another ecological factor, predation, also has a strong effect on the amount of parental care invested. When the danger of predation is high, it is especially important to invest in parental behaviors that function to protect the young. In fact, animals often adjust the amount of parental care they invest to the threat of predation. For example, male members of the cichlid fish family guard the eggs when predatory pressure is high, but not when it is low (Townshend & Wootton, 1985).

Finally, as we shall see throughout the rest of this chapter, not only the amount of parental investment but the nature of parental care depends on the type of environment in which an animal lives and the type of predation or parasitism that is most threatening. In addition, the parental care must be able to help the young survive in environmentally threatening conditions such as extreme temperatures, lack of oxygen in the water, or shortages of food.

WHICH GENDER BECOMES PARENTAL?

Successfully rearing offspring has the same fitness payoff for both males and females. However, when one parent can provide enough care to promote the survival of the offspring, one parent alone—usually the female—often provides the parental care. Several factors affect which parent is most likely to become parental in a given species. The **association hypothesis** states that the gender present when the eggs or young first appear will be most likely to become parental. (If a potential parent is absent for even a brief time, the offspring may arrive and die before parental care can take place.)

A second factor of presumed importance is reflected in the **certainty of parenthood hypothesis.** This hypothesis states that the greater the certainty that an animal is the true biological parent, the greater will be the probability that the animal will provide parental care.

A third factor that apparently makes a difference is the relative cost of parenting to each gender. If one gender incurs a greater cost associated with its investment—and if the payoffs are the same for both genders—the gender incurring the lesser cost should be more likely to become parental.

Finally, there is a physiological constraint on the relationship between gender and parental behavior in mammals. Because only female mammals are capable of supplying milk, females are the only gender that can provide nutrients to newborn mammal offspring.

The operation of these and other factors is quite different in oviparous and viviparous animals, so we will consider these groups separately.

Oviparous Animals

Oviparous animals, including most fish, produce eggs that hatch after the eggs are extruded from the mother's body. As we saw in Chapter 8, the males and females of external fertilizers are both present when the eggs are extruded. Thus, according to the association hypothesis, it is just as likely that males will evolve parental behavior as females. Furthermore, both parents have high certainty of parenthood; the female has produced the eggs and the male is present when the eggs are fertilized. However, in species that provide parental care, male fish are more likely to be parental than females. This gender difference seems to be related to biological costs. As Chapter 9 described, many male fish attract females by establishing a territory. If the male is parental, the cost to him is relatively small, because it takes little or no additional energy to guard the eggs as well as the territory. Furthermore, the male can still attract other females to his territory.

In contrast, the cost of caring for the young is relatively high for a female fish, because the energy she invests in parental behavior limits her growth. This limitation is significant because size is related to fecundity (the number of eggs the female produces); as a matter of fact, fecundity increases exponentially with body size. Consequently, a male fish pays a lower price for becoming parental than a female (Balshine-Earn, 1995).

Birds, like most fish, are also oviparous. However, because birds practice internal fertilization, females should be more likely to become parental than males according to both the association hypothesis and the certainty of parenthood hypothesis. Females are always present when the eggs are laid, and females have absolute certainty that they are the mothers of the embryos in the eggs. In fact, in almost all species of birds in which only one gender cares for the eggs and young, it is the female that is parental. (Chapter 10 explained the reasons for male parental behavior in exceptional birds such as the spotted sandpiper.)

Viviparous Animals

In **viviparous** animals, the young are born alive. Until the live birth of her offspring, the mother retains the eggs in her reproductive tract, where they are protected and nurtured. Thus, the female has already made a considerable parental investment before the young are born.

The most highly evolved way of supplying nutrients to the unborn young is via the mammalian placenta, through which there is an exchange of nutrients as well as waste products between the mother and the fetus. The most efficient placenta with regard to exchanges between fetal and maternal blood is found in chimpanzees, gorillas, and humans.

Primates are extremely K selected in regard to parental care. One of the major differences in the parental care of primates relative to other mammals has to do with the small number of offspring primates deliver with each pregnancy. Typically, only one baby is delivered at a time, although twins and other multiple births do occasionally occur. Several structural and physiological changes are associated with this reduced number of offspring: Primates have only two mammaries; the primate uterus is a single, medial structure (nonprimates have two uterine horns); and, as we have seen, the placenta of primates provides the most efficient direct contact between fetal and maternal blood of all mammalian placentas. Thus, the large investment in each individual offspring begins in utero; and parental care continues for an extended period after birth (see Pianka, 1970).

Significantly, live-bearers always practice internal fertilization. Therefore, the association hypothesis and the certainty of parenthood hypothesis both predict that if only one gender is parental, it will be the female. In mammals there is another consideration, too: Only the female can produce milk to nurture the young (Sargent & Gross, 1986). No mammals exist in the natural world where only the male is parental.

TABLE 11.2 ◆ Gender That Provides Care When Only One Parent Provides

Animal	Gender of Parent	Explanation
Fish	Usually male	Parental care is usually less costly for males.
Birds	Usually female	Females are most likely to be present at hatching and are certain of parenthood.
Mammals	Always female	Females are present at birth, are certain of parenthood, and are the only gender to provide milk.

Biparental Care

As suggested earlier, **biparental care,** or care provided by both the mother and the father, is related to the needs of the young. When the young are highly dependent at birth or hatching, there is a tendency for both parents to contribute parental care. Furthermore, limited resources may place an impossible burden on one parent, so biparental care is more likely to develop when resources are scarce than when they are abundant.

In fishes, birds, and mammals, biparental care is almost always associated with monogamy. However, when certainty of parenthood is relatively high in a polygamous system, certain male mammals may contribute limited amounts of parental care and contribute to the survival of their offspring. For example, goril-

las, which live in single-male groups, are more likely to be parental than chimpanzees, which live in multimale groups (see Dunbar, 1988). This species difference can be explained by the fact that certainty of paternity is relatively high in single-male gorilla groups, because the females all mate with the single male. In chimpanzee groups, by contrast, the polygynandrous mating system makes certainty of parenthood relatively low for the males.

TYPES OF PARENTAL CARE

Up to this point we have looked at parental care in terms of parental investment theory and in relation to which gender takes on parental responsibilities. Now we will consider the various types of parental care that animals exhibit together with the mechanisms involved.

Care of the Eggs

Some animals simply extrude their eggs into a generally favorable environment; others, however, continue to provide for the eggs after they have been deposited. And as we shall see, it is often a small transition from caring for the eggs to caring for the young. Parental behaviors such as territorial defense and mobbing of predators continue in much the same way after the eggs hatch. Furthermore, responses given to the young may be very similar to responses given to eggs. The fighting fish male retrieves eggs in his mouth and later, after the eggs hatch, retrieves the young in the same manner. The domestic hen incubates her eggs by sitting on them and then provides warmth and protection for the chicks by sitting or crouching over them. At least part of the proximate reason for the similarity between care of the eggs and behaviors directed toward the young is due to the fact that some of the same hormones are involved in both stages of parental care.

Providing Protection

There are several ways in which an oviparous parent may protect the eggs. One of the simplest is to carry the eggs with her or him. For example, the male giant water bug maneuvers himself into a position underneath the female. Then, as the female lays her eggs, they stick to the male's back (see Figure 11.1). The male then carries the eggs with him, adjusting his position so that the eggs are at or above the surface of the water

Another site for carrying eggs is the mouth. Freshwater fishes of several different families known as **mouthbreeders** carry their eggs until the eggs hatch. Usually it is the male that carries them; but sometimes it is the female, and in certain cases both parents carry the eggs.

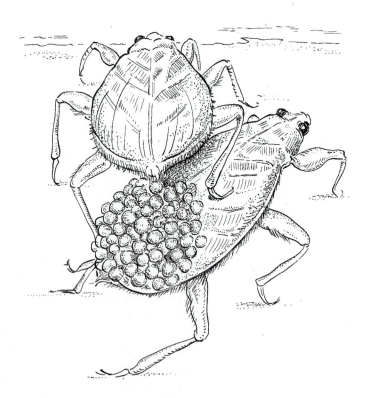

FIGURE 11.1 ◆ Female giant water bug laying her eggs on the back of the male. The eggs stick to the male's back; he then carries them with him, providing protection from predators.

A female Australian frog carries this behavior one step farther; shortly after fertilization, she swallows the eggs and retains them in her stomach. All through the period of development of the eggs and their hatching and metamorphosis into frogs, the mother frog refrains from feeding, inhibits the secretion of stomach acids, and shuts down the digestive system. Then at last she opens her mouth and extrudes her miniature frog offspring.

The carrying of eggs by a parent has a large payoff. Research indicates that 97 percent of giant water bug eggs survive when carried by the male, while none survive if experimentally detached from the male and placed in the water (Smith, 1976). However, the cost is also great. The giant water bug is especially open to predation and has difficulty feeding while carrying the eggs. In the case of mouth-breeding fish, the parent does not feed at all while tending the eggs. Thus, it is not surprising that parental protection provided by egg carrying is limited to relatively few species.

A more common method of protecting eggs is to stay in the vicinity of the eggs and to direct aggression toward intruders. We have already seen an example of this strategy in stickleback fish. In some cases a parent not only will stay in the vicinity but will build a protective structure. For instance, the male Siamese fighting fish constructs what is called a bubble nest at the surface of the water by blowing air into secretions produced by glands in his mouth. He fertilizes the female's eggs as she extrudes them, then retrieves the fertilized eggs in his mouth. Finally, he places the eggs in the bubble nest and stands guard in the vicinity.

American alligator females dig a nest hole; they deposit their eggs in the hole and cover them with grass and mud. Not only are the eggs hidden from predators, but the heat produced by fermentation of the decaying vegetation speeds up the development of the embryos. Furthermore, the mother alligator is able to influence the sex of the offspring by manipulating the temperature surrounding the eggs: The warmer the nest hole, the higher the ratio of male to female hatchlings.

Distracting Predators

Many species of birds build nests in trees that are difficult for predators to climb, thus providing considerable protection. In contrast, some ground-nesting birds protect their eggs or newly hatched young by exhibiting behaviors that function to distract predators and to lead them away from the nest area. Distraction displays come in many forms, but one of the most common is what has been termed **injury feigning.** For example, an avocet flies conspicuously in front of an intruder, then drops to the ground at some distance from the nest with a wing drooping as if injured (see Figure 11.2).

Consistent with parental investment theory, the intensity of the distraction display varies according to risk of predation, brood size, and amount of protective cover. Furthermore, the risk of predation on a parent seems to be a factor of importance. When the male is absent and therefore unable to protect the female, her level of injury feigning is at a lower level than when he is present (Hudson & Newborn, 1990).

Providing Food

Certain insects not only build protective structures but provide food that nourishes the larvae after they hatch from the eggs. For exam-

FIGURE 11.2 ◆ **American avocet engaged in a "broken wing" display.** The display functions to protect the young by luring potential predators from the nest site.

ple, dung beetles (so named because of their taste for animal droppings) spend as much as a month preparing for the arrival of their young. The female beetle sinks a shaft and then fashions several small chambers in the ground; the male carries the dirt to the surface. Later on, the male collects pellets of dung, dropping them down to the female at the bottom of the shaft. The female then kneads the dung into sausage shapes and places them in the chambers. Finally, she lays her eggs near the dung (Heinrich & Bartholomew, 1979). The dung beetle acts as such an effective scavenger that at one time it was imported to Australia in large numbers to handle a plethora of dung from imported cattle.

Burying beetles also invest considerable time and energy in preparing resources before oviposition (i.e., egg laying). Male and female burying beetles are attracted to dead birds and small mammals and even fight others for control over the carrion. Typically, the largest male and female win the competition and dig around the carcass in such a way that it sinks into the ground. Once the corpse is underground, the beetles roll it into a ball, clean it of fur or feathers, and treat it with oral and anal secretions. The female then lays her eggs nearby; and when the larvae emerge, they feed on the carrion (Scott & Traniello, 1990).

Insects, especially parasitoid wasps, may deposit their eggs inside a specific type of animal that later serves as food for the larvae after they hatch. We will examine this strategy in more detail in Chapter 15.

Providing Oxygen

Eggs deposited in still water do not receive enough oxygen to develop. In response to this problem, parental animals that live in such an environment often agitate the water and produce the currents necessary to supply the oxygen. The female octopus—one of the most remarkable parents among invertebrates—oxygenates her eggs constantly for as long as 6 weeks; she does this by periodically ejecting water from her funnel. Shortly after the eggs hatch, the mother octopus, who has not eaten throughout the period of egg development, dies.

Most fish, however, continue to live after oxygenating their eggs. The female fish typically agitate the water by fanning it with their tails. Some fish, including convict and rainbow cichlids, fan their eggs around the clock. During daylight hours the fish can see where the eggs are, but at night the parental females rely on tactile and olfactory cues to locate their eggs (Reebs & Colgan, 1991).

Incubating the Eggs

Mammals and birds must keep their eggs at a warm, constant temperature in order for the embryos to develop. The warmth is typically provided by a behavior known as **incubation**—the transfer of heat from a heat source (usually the parent's body) to the eggs. The most common method of incubation is to keep the eggs in contact with the breast area. In many birds, this area functions effectively as a heat-radiating surface because it becomes highly vascularized (densely supplied with blood vessels) and bare of feathers during the incubation period.

Throughout the period of embryonic development within the egg, the bird parent is sensitive to fluctuations in the temperature of the eggs. The parent typically adjusts to these fluctuations by moving away from the eggs or pressing its body closer to the eggs.

For many years scientists believed that the developing fetuses within birds' eggs were passive. Fetuses of the American white pelican, however, take an active role in the stabilization of the eggs' temperature. When the temperature drops, they make a piping sound, to which the parent responds by increasing the amount of heat transfer (Evans, 1990a, 1990b).

In contrast to most birds, the emperor penguin male incubates his one egg by placing it on its feet, covered by highly vascularized fatty tissue hanging down from his belly. This method allows the male to move around slowly while protecting the egg from frigid temperatures. Because penguin incubation takes place during the Antarctic winter, when temperatures drop to minus 80°F, this adaptation is of considerable importance. During the 64-day incubation period, the male penguin does not eat, living off large amounts of stored fatty tissue.

Incubation in the winter rather than the spring (which is the usual time for incubation in birds) seems to be related to the unusually long incubation and growth period of emperor penguins. That is, if the penguins incubated in the spring, the eggs would hatch in the summer, and the chicks would not have time to grow to the size necessary for survival of the

◆ UNUSUAL ADAPTATIONS

The Egg-Incubating Nests of Mallee Fowl

A few birds do not transfer their body heat to their eggs but, like the alligator, rely on environmental factors to supply heat. The mallee fowl of Australia excavates a large pit and fills it with leaves that will decay and provide heat. Then the bird adds a layer of sand that will eventually function as insulation. Over a period of several months, the female digs into the nest and lays her eggs.

In contrast to alligators, however, the mallee fowl maintain a constant temperature. The male periodically tests for the temperature near the eggs by picking out material from inside the nest with his beak. If the temperature is above 91°F, he reduces it by removing some sand; if it is below the critical temperature, he adds more sand. Because the eggs take 2 months to incubate—and eggs are laid at intervals over a period of several months—the mallee fowl spends up to 11 months a year in various aspects of the incubation process (Frith, 1957).

Why do these birds retain such a complex, inefficient, and energy-expensive way of providing heat for their eggs when incubation is clearly a superior method? The mallee fowl's strategy is related to this bird's evolutionary history. Indirect evidence suggests that the ancestors of the mallee fowl lived in an area where an environmental supply of heat was constant, dependable, and easily accessible. In fact, there are relatives of the mallee fowl living today that inhabit such an environment. For example, the maleo fowl digs a pit in a sandy beach and lays its eggs at a depth where the temperature is constant and appropriate for the eggs' development.

This weather constancy was probably the condition that fostered the evolution of the use of environmental heat instead of incubation. Once the birds' tendency to incubate was lost, it could not be recaptured. Rather, as the ancestral types moved into more variable climates, they seem to have evolved more and more adaptations consistent with the use of the environmental heat (see Burton, 1985). As inefficient as the system became, there was no turning back to the tendency to incubate. To turn back would have required a large step, whereas continuing the use of environmental heat could take place in a series of small steps. Thus, despite its inefficiency, the use of environmental heat continues in certain birds living in variable environments.

antarctic winter. An additional advantage of winter incubation is the absence of predators and parasites during these frigid times.

Adult emperor penguins also show an adaptation for helping the young survive the winter, especially when there is a storm. A large number of adults huddle together in a tightly knit cluster, surrounding the younger penguins. The temperature in the middle of the group is as much as 20°F warmer than on the outside. During the storm the penguins on the windward side slowly work their way around to the leeward side, with the result that no individual faces the brunt of the storm for too long a period of time (see Burton, 1985). Extreme environmental conditions, then, have clearly had a strong effect on the evolution of several aspects of parental care in the emperor penguin.

Care of the Young in Fish

Most oviparous animals other than birds do not pay much attention to the young after the eggs hatch. However, parental responses toward the young do occur in some fish, especially freshwater species. As we have seen, mouth-breeding fish carry the eggs in their mouths. Then, after the eggs hatch, one or both of the parents take the young into their mouths when danger threatens. Once the danger passes, the parents spit out their young; but they continue to stay in the vicinity in preparation for possible danger in the future. Classic experiments with models of a parent fish indicate that the young of mouth-breeding fishes find the parent's mouth by swimming to contrasting dark spots on the parent's body—which would normally indicate an

open mouth (Baerends & Baerends-van Roon, 1950).

In a few fish species, the parents are able to provide food for the young. Discus fish parents produce large amounts of mucus, and the young feed by nibbling at the mucus on the sides of their parents' bodies (Hildemann, 1959). Convict cichlid fish parents provide food for the young by digging in the floor of a pond with their fins and lifting leaves with their mouths. Careful observations indicate that these behaviors occur with maximum frequency in the presence of free-swimming young, suggesting that fin digging and leaf lifting do in fact perform parental functions (Wisenden et al., 1995).

Care of the Young in Birds

Birds often continue to provide large amounts of parental care after the eggs hatch. Because birds are warm-blooded, the young must be provided with warmth, especially altricial young that do not stabilize their body temperatures until some time after hatching. Most avian parents also protect their young and provide them with food.

Recognizing and Accepting the Young

There are significant differences in the ability of parents to recognize young in precocial as compared to altricial bird species. In precocial species of birds (such as ducks, geese, and fowl), the young are able to locomote at an early age. Without a rapidly developing ability to recognize each other, the young and parents could easily become separated. We saw in Chapter 3 how imprinting facilitates the infant's recognition of the mother. The mother in a precocial species also learns very quickly to identify her own young. Experimental tests of domestic fowl indicate that the mother uses a combination of visual and auditory cues in making the appropriate discriminations between her own chicks and others (Maier, 1963a).

In contrast, the young of altricial species of birds, such as songbirds, do not leave the nest until they are ready to fly. Consequently, there has been little or no advantage for songbird parents to learn to identify their eggs or their young. Unfortunately for the parents, this limited ability of altricial birds to recognize their own young has resulted in the tendency of certain birds to become opportunistic as nest parasites.

Providing Warmth and Protection

As in the case of mouth-breeding fish, the transition from caring for the eggs to caring for the young is not great for many birds. For example, birds that have incubated their eggs typically provide heat and protection for the young by placing their warm undersides over their young. Brooding—the domestic hen's placement of her warm undersides over her chicks—occurs regularly at night while the chicks sleep. If a hen is experimentally confined in a cage, but the chicks are allowed to run free, the hen may brood chicks other than her own. Under natural conditions, however, the hen always broods her own chicks. Apparently, given freedom of movement, the hen responds selectively toward her own chicks, a behavior that helps ensure that she does not invest energy in parental responses to nonrelatives (Maier, 1963a).

During the day the mother hen makes an alarm call when danger threatens. This alarm call functions to attract the chicks and to induce them to get into the brooding position (Maier, 1963b). In this position the chicks gain a certain amount of protection. We will look at alarm calls in more detail in Chapter 12.

Providing Food

Songbirds spend a great percentage of their time feeding the young after they hatch, making up to 900 feeding visits a day. The young of songbirds make begging responses as the parents return to the nest. Nestlings make begging calls, open their beaks, and present visual "targets" (markings inside their mouths) that stimulate the parents to provide food (see Figure 11.3). A classic experiment systematically varying the intensity and duration of begging calls indicated that songbird parents can be tricked into bringing more food than usual by the experimental presentation of continuing begging calls after the young have been satiated (von Haartman, 1949). Apparently the young normally influence the amount of food they are given by regulating the intensity and duration of their begging.

Under most circumstances, parent songbirds give highest priority to the young that give off the most intense cues. When food is plentiful, all of the nestlings receive enough food to survive. If there is a shortage of food, however, the smaller and weaker young will not be fed and will fail to survive. This system might appear to be cruel by some human standards, but it makes sense in terms of optimal reproduction. Under difficult conditions only a few can survive, and those with the best chance of surviving will receive the parental investment.

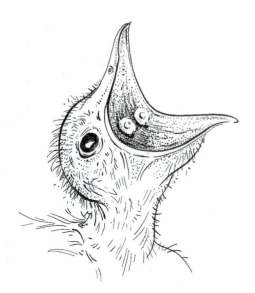

FIGURE 11.3 ◆ **Conspicuous "targets" on the inside of a nestling bird's mouth.** These targets stimulate the parents to provide food for the nestlings.

In most altricial species the two parents cooperate in feeding the young and performing other nest duties. What happens if one of the parents doesn't contribute his or her share? Field observations indicate that as one partner decreases the amount of care given, the other increases it, thereby adjusting its behavior to the increased needs of the offspring. An experimental study with starlings provided support for this observation: A forced decrease in one parent's contribution resulted in an increase in the contribution of the other parent (Wright & Cuthill, 1990).

In contrast to parents in altricial species, parents of many precocial young do not feed the young directly. Rather, the mother leads the young to areas in which food is abundant. Once in a food-rich area, a mother domestic hen makes scratching movements with her feet on the ground; when she locates food such as seeds, she emits a specific type of call that functions to attract the chicks to the area.

Care of the Young in Mammals

In terms of duration and intensity of parental care, mammals make a greater investment than any other class of animals. This aspect of *K* selection is most pronounced in primates, and the selection process for increased parental investment becomes apparent when we compare ancestral primates to those that are more highly evolved. Prosimians (ancestral primates such as lemurs) are relatively short-lived, while monkeys have an intermediate life span and apes have the longest life span. Consistent with this evolutionary trend toward expansion of the life span, there is an increase in the period of gestation: Prosimians gestate for 3 to 4 months; monkeys carry their young for 5 to 6 months; great apes are pregnant for up to 8 months. The period of parental care also increases, lasting just a few months in the smaller prosimians but up to several years in apes.

Recognizing and Accepting the Young

As Chapter 3 described, mother sheep develop a remarkable ability to recognize and accept their lambs on the basis of smell. Similarly, rat mothers learn the smell of their pups during a sensitive period as the pups are being born. Thereafter, the mothers selectively provide parental care for their own young. The mother rats apparently develop an attraction to odor

◆ UNUSUAL ADAPTATIONS

Finding Offspring within a Large Group

In some species of mammals, the young of a large number of parents are kept in a group during the temporary absence of their mothers. For example, mother California sea lions leave their pups on the shore and go into the ocean to feed. After more than a day, the mothers return. The mothers must then search in an area containing hundreds of adult animals and pups of a similar age. During a sea lion pup's first days, much of the recognition of the pup by the mother depends on her ability to recognize her pup's voice. After a week or more, however, the pup can accurately distinguish its mother's vocalizations from those of another female. As a result of this ability, the pups are able to contribute actively to the reunion. When the pups grow older, they move around and play an even more active role in the reunion with their mothers (Gisiner & Schusterman, 1991).

Parental reunion in bats is even more remarkable; the mother bat must find her own baby in an enormous "nursery" of offspring, or **crèche,** that may contain more than 10,000 infant bats. Research using genetic markers indicates that Mexican free-tailed bat mothers, who roost some distance from the crèche, are able to locate and selectively feed their own offspring. The recognition by the mother seems to be based on a combination of cues: unique odors produced by the young, a special odor that the mother transmits to mark her baby, and distinct calls that the baby makes when separated from its mother. Also, the mother bat is able to remember the specific place in the crèche where she last nursed her infant (McCracken, 1993).

that originates primarily in the pups anogenital region (Brouette-Lahlou et al., 1991).

Olfaction is also important in subtle aspects of the rat's parental response. A virgin rat will retreat from a newborn pup. However, if a virgin female is forced to live with young pups, she will begin to exhibit parental responses. Once this tendency toward parental behavior has developed, it continues for the rest of the animal's life.

Feeding the Young

Female mammals are the only animals that nurse their young. Once the hormone oxytocin stimulates a let-down of milk, or milk flow, various cues from the young induce the mother to assume a nursing position. Mother cats respond to vocal, tactile, and olfactory cues from the babies by lying down and presenting their ventral (abdominal) surfaces to the babies. The young kittens, which are blind, usually locate the nipple by orienting to olfactory and tactile cues from the mother. The kittens root in the hair on the mother's belly until they find a nipple.

Tactile cues are also important in the nursing and parental interaction of rats. If the region around the mouth of the mother rat is experimentally desensitized, she is less likely to lick and retrieve the pups. The pups, in turn, depend on tactile cues in their response to the mother. The experimental elimination of tactile sensitivity around the mouths of the pups reduces the tendency of the pups to root against the mother. Without this rooting, the mother fails to get into the crouching position that is necessary for nursing (Stern, 1989).

Most mammals nurse only their own babies and, as we have seen, show an ability to recognize their own offspring even under difficult conditions. Fallow deer, however, sometimes nurse young that are not their own, a behavior known as **alloparental care** (Birgersson et al., 1991). It may appear at first that this example of alloparental care represents an exception to the rule that animals must gain fitness when they provide parental care. In fallow deer, however, the suckling young are almost always of the same age as the female's own young and are relatives of the nursing female. Consequently, the cost of alloparental care is small, and there is an indirect fitness advantage for the female because the young are relatives.

Transporting and Retrieving the Young

Because mammals' young must be nursed regularly, altricial mammalian young are often carried by the mother as she moves from place to place. In marsupials the young are trans-ported in a pouch (marsupium). In the case of large kangaroos, the young are born at a very early stage of development and consequently must remain in the pouch for as long as 6 months. The older young leave the pouch and wander about when the mother kangaroo is grazing, but return to nurse or to be transported when the herd travels from one general location to another.

Rodents and carnivores retrieve and carry their young with their mouths. Rat mothers, for example, retrieve the pups with their mouths if the pups wander from the nest. Or if there is a disturbance of some kind, the mother moves the whole litter to a new nest site. The mother picks up each pup with her mouth, moves it, and keeps returning until there are no more pups left at the former nest site. During retrieval of the young, an especially strong bite by the mother on the neck of a pup evokes an ultrasonic call (a call so high-pitched that it is inaudible to humans) by the pup; this call, in turn, stimulates the mother to pick the pup up more gently. Rat pups give another type of ultrasound when they are cold, inducing retrieving behavior by the mother (Noirot, 1972). The pups stop emitting this sound when they reach 2 weeks of age, making themselves less conspicuous at a time when they are vulnerable to predation, or to hostile male rats they may encounter outside of the nest (Takahashi et al., 1990).

Primates, like marsupials, keep their young with them at almost all times, but primates' method of transport varies with the age of the infant. After birth, young baboons cling to the underside of the mother; at about 2 months they begin to spend some time lying along the mother's back; then, after the 4th or 5th month, the baby rides the mother's back like a jockey on a horse (DeVore, 1963; see Figure 11.4). Older gorilla babies also ride on

FIGURE 11.4 ◆ **Young baboon riding on its mother's back.**

their mother's back; but newborn gorillas, which are unable to cling to the mother, are carried like human babies—in one arm.

Cleaning and Providing Warmth

Mother mammals lick and clean their young as they emerge from the birth canal. Then, periodically, mothers continue to lick and clean the offspring, particularly during the nursing period.

In rodents and carnivores, the licking has the additional effect of inducing elimination. Urination into the mouth of the mother as the result of this stimulation also functions to re-

cycle liquid, which is needed by the mother during lactation. For example, a mouse mother recycles approximately two thirds of the water she gives to the pups in the form of milk. Because the mother stays with the pups most of the time and does not have much chance to look for water, this recycling represents a significant adaptation for conservation of water (Friedman & Bruno, 1976).

In addition, the parent or parents provide warmth for mammalian young, especially in early stages of development—when the young have a large percentage of their body surface exposed to the environment and, in some cases, very little fur.

In most mammals only the mother exhibits parental behavior; but in the monogamous California mouse, *Peromyscus californicus,* the male is also parental. He typically licks a pup during or right after birth and huddles over it as the female gives birth to another pup. He also retrieves pups that stray from the nest and remains in the nest when the female is out foraging, providing warmth and protection from predators.

Male meadow voles are also monogamous and parental. However, the male and female meadow vole nest together only during fall and winter. That is, the male's parental investment is specially adapted for providing warmth during the cooler seasons (Storey & Joyce, 1995).

Providing Opportunities for Learning

Because the young of certain mammals remain with their parents for a long period of time, there are many opportunities for a special type of interaction—observational learning, as discussed in Chapter 4. Kittens, for example, learn how to kill their prey by observing their mother's response to prey.

Many exchanges of information seem to take place between mother and offspring in chimpanzees. We have already seen some examples of communication about tools for termite fishing. Chapter 5 also described a study of how mother chimpanzees facilitate the development of nut cracking in their offspring. First, the mothers leave objects used as hammers and anvils in close proximity to nuts, sometimes even leaving a nut on the "anvil." (Females without infants never behave this way.) Second, mothers often directly provide their young with efficient hammers. Finally, mothers discourage their offspring from begging for nuts that have already been cracked, thereby increasing the probability that the babies will learn the nut-cracking skill (Boesch, 1991).

Clearly, a large amount of information may be passed from one generation to another—especially in apes, with their extended relationship between the mother and her young. Can an ape mother's behavior be called teaching? If teaching is defined as the passing on of information without reference to intent on the part of the mother, the term is certainly appropriate for many apes.

It is difficult to assume a conscious attempt to teach, however, as there is no way of knowing for certain the intent of the mother—even in chimpanzees. After all, a conscious attempt is difficult to analyze even in other humans. When someone else says they tried to do something, can we be sure that this means the same thing as when we try to do something? Judges and juries have been asking this question for centuries.

At this point, the best we can do is to say that the data on chimpanzees' passing on information are highly suggestive of teaching with intent. New experimental techniques may well shed more light on this issue in the future.

◆ HUMAN EVOLUTION

Humans have traditionally been considered very different from nonhuman animals in regard to parental care. However, some principles of parental behavior apply to virtually all animals, including ourselves. Let's look briefly at three aspects of human parental care that have clear analogues in nonhuman animals and consider these in light of evolutionary theory.

RESPONSE TO CUES ASSOCIATED WITH NORMAL OFFSPRING

In accordance with parental investment theory, nonhuman animals typically refrain from giving parental assistance to abnormal offspring, which have a poor chance of surviving and reproducing. Although humans in most societies do not routinely abandon offspring that are abnormal in some way, research indicates that parents show less-positive responses to premature babies than to full-term infants. Research using drawings of infant faces suggests that at least part of this tendency is related to the fact that premature babies do not present cues such as a round face, large eyes in the middle of the face, and fat cheeks (Maier, 1983). Furthermore, premature babies do not respond as vigorously to stimulation from the parents as full-term babies. These findings suggest that humans have evolved a tendency to respond less positively to cues indicative of poor health than to cues that reflect vitality. Fortunately, from a humanitarian standpoint, health professionals can help parents adjust their responses to babies that do not give off positive and vigorous cues.

On the other side of the coin, it appears that humans have evolved a very strong general tendency to respond positively to characteristics associated with healthy offspring. Many years ago Konrad Lorenz (1942) pointed out that we have a tendency to respond positively to characteristics in animals that are similar to those of human babies, such as large eyes and a snub nose. The highly popular teddy bear possesses exaggerated characteristics that are especially close to those of a human baby.

But why would teddy bears be popular with young children? Shouldn't the teddy bear's babylike characteristics be most popular with older children who are closer to reproductive age? By experimentally varying the characteristics of teddy bears, researchers have found that 8-year-old children do in fact react more positively to teddy bears than 4-year-olds (Morris et al., 1995). It seems that the liking for teddy bears, certain pets, and cartoon characters with childlike characteristics is driven by the development of nurturant feelings in late childhood.

RESPONSES TO UNRELATED CHILDREN

It is difficult to analyze human responses to unrelated young by comparing the reactions of parents who adopt children with those who have biological children. Adoptive parents are, as indicated by their desire to adopt, highly motivated to become parents. In contrast, not all individuals who become parents desire to have children, at least at the time the offspring are conceived.

It is possible, however, to consider other aspects of humans' responses to unrelated children. For example, families in Trinidad sometimes consist of a man living with his wife and his own children as well as the wife's children fathered by another man. There is typically more conflict between the father and his stepchildren than between the father and his own children (Flinn, 1988).

In North America, reported child abuse is as much as 40 times more common in families with a stepparent or live-in boyfriend/girlfriend than in families where both biological parents are present (Daly & Wilson, 1987). There are many and complicated reasons for this difference in the level of reported child abuse, including economic frustration and the stress associated with a sudden increase in family size in "blended families." However, the magnitude of the difference is striking and suggests that part of the reason may be related to adults' evolutionarily developed difficulty in responding parentally to children that are unrelated to them.

PARENT–CHILD CONFLICT

The period of offspring dependency is greater for humans than for any other animal, even greater than that for chimpanzees and gorillas. This long period of dependency is especially protracted in highly technological societies, because it takes longer for children to develop the skills necessary to make a living in these societies than in preliterate societies. All in all, raising offspring in technological societies demands a tremendous output of time, effort, and resources. According to parental investment theory, this increased dependency should create a relatively long period of parent–offspring conflict—a hypothesis that has considerable indirect support.

In Western industrial societies many children are raised by a single parent and/or by a mother who spends much of the day working outside of the home. Furthermore, there is less of a community in which parents include the children in work-related activities with relatives, friends, or close associates. It has been argued that this movement away from a sense of community is responsible for the rapidly increasing incidence of children's problems, such as high rates of depression and suicide. While the reasons for these problems in children are complex and varied, it is unquestionable that parent–child relationships are now very different from the ones for which we are adapted by natural selection. For example, children are now more of an economic liability than they were in hunter–gatherer societies.

In conclusion, it seems that research testing evolution-based hypotheses can make a major contribution to an understanding of human parental relationships. Hopefully, such hypotheses will also be used to help identify children at risk and develop effective intervention techniques.

◆ CHANGING PERSPECTIVES

PAST	PRESENT	FUTURE
Parental behavior in nonhuman animals is inflexible and insensitive to shifting environmental conditions. Parental behavior in humans is very different from that of nonhumans (early twentieth century).	Many aspects of parental behavior in nonhumans and humans are similar. Parent–offspring conflict can be explained by parental investment theory in many cases.	Can parental investment theory be revised or extended to explain all parental behavior, including that of humans?

SUMMARY

Animals vary greatly in the amount of parental investment they display, the type of investment they make, and the length of time they engage in parental behavior. Much of this variability can be explained by the theory of parental investment and ecological factors. Hypotheses developed from parental investment theory also help to explain parent–offspring conflict and, in certain cases, the tolerance of infanticide.

If one parent can provide enough care for the offspring to survive, it is usually the female that is parental. This gender bias may be explained by the association hypothesis and the certainty of parenthood hypothesis. Nonetheless, male fish are more likely to become parental than females—for reasons related to differential gender costs in parenting. Some species exhibit biparental care, which is usually associated with monogamy.

Oviparous species may invest in care of the eggs by providing protection, distracting predators, providing food, providing oxygen, and/or incubating the eggs. Although some fish care for the young after they hatch, the most extensive parental care is provided by birds and mammals.

Parental responses toward young birds and mammals after they hatch or are born include recognition and acceptance, feeding, providing warmth and protection, transporting and retrieving the young, cleaning and providing warmth, and providing opportunities for learning.

Evolutionary theories basic to our understanding of parental responses in nonhumans apparently apply to humans as well. Humans, like nonhuman animals, may give reduced parental care to abnormal offspring. Some of the principles related to responses to unrelated young and to parent–offspring conflict apparently apply to both humans and nonhuman animals.

KEY TERMS

alloparental care, p. 263
association hypothesis, p. 251
biparental care, p. 253
certainty of parenthood hypothesis, p. 251
crèche, p. 262

incubation, p. 257
injury feigning, p. 255
mouthbreeders, p. 254
oviparous, p. 251
viviparous, p. 252

CHAPTER 12

COOPERATION AND COMMUNICATION

◆ *Why do animals sometimes help others in their groups?*

◆ *When are animals more likely to compete with one another versus help or cooperate?*

As we have seen in previous chapters, cooperative social behavior can be highly beneficial, especially in relation to feeding and defense against predators. Furthermore, even animals that are solitary for most of their lives must be cooperative long enough to mate and, in many cases, to rear the young. Basic to effective cooperation is an effective communication system. Consequently, animals that engage in complex social interactions tend to have well-developed systems of communication.

12

We will begin by considering the bases of cooperation. Then we will turn to various types of communication systems and how they may have evolved. Finally, we will look at human cooperation and at the evolution of friendships, laughter, and humor as social strategies in humans.

COOPERATION

Cooperation among individuals in a group may be advantageous for a variety of reasons. In the first place, all group members may obtain direct benefits from the group association, the effect known as mutualism (recall Chapter 6). Second, as we saw in Chapter 1, **kin selection,** or animals' tendency to help their close relatives, may cause an animal to gain indirect fitness (Hamilton, 1964). Third, **altruism,** or helpful behavior, is sometimes reciprocated later; this **reciprocal altruism** is especially likely to develop when the cost of helping is small and the benefits of being helped in return are relatively large (Trivers, 1971).

When animals cooperate, it is often difficult to determine by casual observation which of these three factors is of primary importance. However, it is sometimes possible to analyze their relative contributions. Let's look more closely at all three factors.

Mutualism

African lions hunting in pairs are more successful than lions hunting singly in terms of food intake per individual, probably because paired lions can bring down prey inaccessible to single lions. Interestingly, however, lions often hunt in groups of three or more, even though the food volume per individual drops in these larger groups. Why? Three or more lions can effectively protect their kill from scavenging hyenas or wild dogs, so each individual derives mutualism benefits from being part of the group (Packer et al., 1990).

Kin Selection

Lions, like other social hunters, show kin-selected altruism; that is, they often cooperate with relatives. Consequently, a combination of mutualism and indirect fitness may contribute to the size of the group. However, as we will see, there are also some examples of indirect fitness from kin selection in the absence of mutualism.

Kin Recognition Mechanisms

If animals behave selectively toward their kin, they must be able to recognize kin and differentiate them from nonrelatives. In many cases individuals identify relatives on the basis of chemical cues. As I will discuss further in Chapter 17, social insects recognize nest mates, which are always close relatives, on the basis of an odor specific to the colony. This odor is spread from one individual to another by trophalaxis (mutual feeding) or bodily contact.

Rodents also use olfactory cues in kin recognition. For example, thirteen-lined ground squirrels lose their ability to recognize kin when their olfactory sense is experimentally impaired with zinc sulfate (Holmes, 1984). At least part of this recognition in ground squirrels is related to early olfactory experience. Thus, ground squirrels experimentally reared with nonrelatives fight less with these "adopted" relatives than with nonrelatives who are strangers (Holmes & Sherman, 1983).

Early experience is only part of the story, however. In another study, female ground squirrels were again reared with nonrelatives (they were never exposed to their sisters during rearing). At 8 months of age, the squirrels were tested under two conditions: with strange nonrelatives and with sisters who, of course, were also strangers. The squirrels fought most vigorously with the nonrelatives (Holmes &

Sherman, 1982). Apparently there is an ability to recognize kin independent of early experience. This ability is presumably related to **self-matching**—the process of comparing a quality of another individual, such as smell, with the same quality in oneself.

Helping Kin Reproduce

Much kin-selected altruistic behavior in animals is related to reproduction. There are especially great advantages to kin selection in most **eusocial** insects (highly social colonizing insects); as Chapter 2 explained, sisters among ants, bees, and wasps are very closely related genetically, with 75 percent identical genes.

Even though the indirect fitness advantages to be obtained through altruism are not as great for vertebrates as they are for eusocial insects, there are certain situations where the indirect advantages are significant. For example, there are sometimes as many as six helpers in the nest of a pair of Florida scrub jays. These "helper" birds, which are often the adult male offspring of the breeding pair, are physiologically capable of reproducing on their own, but instead they devote their energy to feeding the young and defending their parents' territory.

Although the helpers gain some indirect fitness benefit by aiding their relatives, the fitness gain is not as great as if they raised their own offspring. Why, then, do these jays choose the helping option? Analysis of population density and availability of territories indicates that unless the male jay is high in dominance, he will be unsuccessful in obtaining a territory. Only the helpers highest in dominance in their particular group abandon their helping role and obtain a territory when a neighbor or one of the parents dies (Wool-fenden & Fitzpatrick, 1984). In other words, helping in these birds is a conditional strategy. The strategy dictates: Be a helper when it is the only option, but establish a territory and mate if an opportunity becomes available.

The offspring of certain mammals also provide some help in rearing their siblings. For example, prairie vole young often show parental-like responses to their newborn siblings—such as huddling over and grooming the younger siblings. The juveniles of these monogamous rodents are more likely to exhibit parental responses when housed with both parents than when housed only with the mother (Wang & Novak, 1994). It may be that the father serves as a model for helping behavior.

Warning Kin of Danger

There are also examples of indirect fitness advantages related to warning kin of the danger of predation. Many species of birds emit calls that warn conspecifics of danger. In some cases the caller may benefit as much as the recipients of the warning, and the calling may be considered a type of mutualism. In other cases, however, the callers expose themselves to an increased risk of predation, so the calling may be viewed as altruistic.

In keeping with the principles of kin selection, some individual animals may have more to gain by making warning calls than others. For example, if an individual is in the presence of several relatives, a warning call can produce more fitness benefits than if only a few relatives are in the area. Spider monkeys alter their calling behavior depending on the number of relatives present. As the number of relatives present increases, the duration of the warning calls also increases (Chapman & Chapman, 1990).

In some species dominant animals have more to gain by making warning calls than less dominant animals, because the dominant males father most of the offspring present. In an experiment with captive willow tits, the birds were exposed to models of sparrow hawks. The older, more dominant males gave more warning calls than did young males or females (Alatalo & Helle, 1990).

Reciprocity

For reciprocity to develop between conspecifics, individual recognition is important. If individuals could not recognize and remember one another, an animal would not be able to identify the altruist and reciprocate. Furthermore, the system could be exploited by animals that accepted help and did not repay (Axelrod & Hamilton, 1981). Consequently, reciprocity is most clearly represented in mammals.

Direct Reciprocity

A classic example of reciprocal altruism is seen in vampire bats. These tropical Western Hemisphere bats feed on the blood of cattle and horses; then, after they return to the roost, they regurgitate some of the blood they have collected to other bats. Because the cattle and horses are able to fight off the bats fairly effectively, many bats are unable to obtain a meal, so the blood sharing helps keep many bats from starving. G. S. Wilkinson (1984) marked individual bats in order to observe the individual interactions among a group of bats. He found that bats closely associated with one another tended to share blood most often, and that they remained in association long enough for the recipient to repay the donor. He also calculated that, because the bats obtained a large amount of blood from their victims, the cost of sharing was significantly less than the benefits of receiving.

Another study investigating reciprocal altruism in vampire bats was conducted over a 7-month period in a captive colony. Investigators found that even males, which are normally highly competitive with one another, will participate in reciprocal food sharing (De Nault & McFarlane, 1995).

Impala also show a type of reciprocity. Within the social group, impala groom one another with their tongues. The cost of grooming—a small amount of saliva and a somewhat reduced predatory vigilance—is relatively small. In contrast, the payoff for the individual being groomed is large, because the grooming removes parasites. As individuals cannot groom each other simultaneously, there is a reciprocity; an individual that is groomed returns the grooming favor at a later time (Connor, 1995; Hart & Hart, 1992).

Reciprocal grooming is also important in several types of primates, including chimpanzees. The chimpanzees run their fingers through one another's fur. At one time it was thought that the basic function of this **social grooming** was to remove parasites from group members' bodies. It is now clear, however, that the grooming has a calming effect and that social grooming has the effect of reinforcing social bonds between group members (see DeWaal, 1989). Thus, grooming has an important function in primates even when the animals are not removing parasites (see Figure 12.1).

The social grooming of chimpanzees illustrates a tit-for-tat strategy analogous to the inspection strategy of fishes that we discussed in Chapter 7. A common procedure among chimpanzees is for one individual to attempt to groom a second one—or to present itself for grooming. If the other individual is unresponsive, the first chimpanzee backs off and tends to avoid other social encounters with that individual. After some time, however, the second individual can usually reestablish friendly relations with the first by initiating grooming. Thus, grooming is a way of regulating what might be called friendships. In fact, animals that have friendly relationships with each other spend a relatively large amount of time grooming each other (Boccia, 1986).

Another example of a tit-for-tat stategy occurs in olive baboons. Two unrelated males may interrupt a male in consort with a female in estrus, and one of the males will then copulate with the female. At another time the two males will again attack a sexually interacting couple, but this time the other male will copulate (Packer, 1977).

Indirect Reciprocity

In some cases reciprocal altruism may develop even when the helper gains future rewards from individuals different from those that received the help. For instance, H. U. Reyer (1984) identified unrelated birds in the nest of East Asian pied kingfishers. He found that male nonrelatives or secondary helpers that live in the nest of a reproducing pair of

FIGURE 12.1 ◆ A juvenile vervet monkey grooming another juvenile.

birds gain benefits the season following their helping behavior. The helpers have a better chance of attracting a mate than do bachelor males that have not engaged in helping behavior.

The long-tailed manakin of the American tropics is another bird that engages in helpful behavior and apparently reaps the rewards at a later time from different individuals. As we have seen, most birds court in male–female pairs. The manakin is an exception, however, in that two male birds may cooperate in the courtship of a female. The males start off by singing in synchrony. They then take turns doing cartwheels beside the female; and, if she does not leave the scene, the males begin a series of rapid flights over her head. When the female gives a signal that she is ready to mate, one of the males leaves and the other copulates with her. Finally, the mated female flies away and the male gives a call that brings about the return of his partner. The two suitors then begin another duet.

By marking the individual males, D. B. McDonald (1989) determined that one of the males does the vast majority of the mating. The other, who is apparently not a brother, simply functions as a helper. At a later time,

TABLE 12.1 ◆ Factors Related to the Development of Cooperation

Factors	Advantage to the Cooperating Individual
Mutualism	Participation in group enhances efficiency.
Kin selection	Altruism toward close relatives provides indirect fitness benefits.
Reciprocity	Low-cost helping behavior may result in relatively great benefits in return.

however, the male helper is more likely to attract a mate than males who did not engage in this type of altruistic behavior.

COMMUNICATION

Cooperating animals must be able to coordinate their activities by means of some type of communication system. Formally defined, communication is action on the part of one animal (the sender) that alters the behavior of a second animal (the receiver). In order for a communication system to evolve, the sender must derive some benefits from alteration of the receiver's behavior. The signal sent must also offer some benefit to the receiver, or the receiver would develop a tendency to ignore it.

We have already encountered some forms of communication in relation to courtship and in the relationship between parent and offspring. Building on this background, let's now look at some aspects of animal communication in general.

Channels of Communication

Communication may take place via a variety of channels. Each channel has certain advantages as well as limitations. As I indicated in discussing courtship in Chapter 9, the communication channel utilized by an animal depends on both ecological conditions and the animal's sensory and physiological capabilities.

Chemical Channels

Chemical communication is highly developed in a large variety of animals. For example, we saw in Chapter 9 that certain insects and mammals communicate their sexual readiness via pheromones; and we will consider various other types of pheromonal communication in Chapter 17.

Chemical cues are used for individual recognition by several species of mammals. For example, hamsters recognize individual conspecifics on the basis of odor (Johnston & Robinson, 1993). Pipistrelle bats identify individuals in their own group by odor—and can also distinguish whether an individual bat is from their own colony or from a different colony (de Fanis & Jones, 1995). This discrimination may be important in the bats' ability to exclude strange bats from the cave in which the colony roosts.

Visual Channels

In contrast to chemical signals, which travel slowly, visual signals travel at the speed of light. Visual signals are particularly effective for diurnal animals' communication of fluctuating emotional and motivational states. For example, African elephants communicate various levels of aggressiveness with their head, trunk, and ears (Brown, 1975). Similarly, wolves communicate hostile intent as well as various degrees of dominance and submission with their tail position and general body posture (Schenkel, 1967).

In some male mammals the display of an erect penis functions as a display of aggressiveness and status. Dominant males of several species of monkeys not only present an erect penis but mount a submissive male in a display of dominance. Interestingly, the female spotted hyena is unique in that she has a greatly enlarged clitoris called a **pseudopenis.** As we shall see when we discuss hormones in Chapter 17, the pseudopenis develops in fetal hyena females as the result of high levels of testosterone in the mother. When the females become adults, they erect and inspect one another's organs. Apparently, once the very large clitoris evolved in these hyenas, it became involved in social communication very much the way the male organ is involved in the communication of other species of mammals (Kruuk, 1972).

A few species of animals use visual signals to communicate with a possible predator. For example, gazelles exhibit a behavior known as **stotting:** When a cheetah approaches and is spotted, a gazelle repeatedly leaps about 20 inches off the ground with its legs held stiff and straight. An analysis of when the behavior occurs and its effects on other gazelles suggests that this behavior is not important for communication between gazelles; rather, the stotting signals to the predator that it has been identified. In essence, the gazelle warns the predator that the pursuit will most likely be fruitless and not worth the trouble (Caro, 1986).

This type of communication is particularly appropriate on the plains of Africa where there are predators and prey in abundance. The energy both predators and prey save by not running or chasing every time they sight one another could be significant.

Auditory Channels

Auditory communication has several advantages over other types of communication systems. Under favorable conditions sound waves are carried a relatively great distance, circumvent obstacles, are effective at night, and travel efficiently in both water and air.

The lower the frequency of sound, the greater the distance it travels. Whales—which are large enough to produce and receive high-energy, low-frequency sounds—are the longest-distance communicators in the animal world. Humpback whales, whose individualized "songs" last up to 30 minutes, apparently communicate with one another across thousands of miles of ocean. For some reason these "songs" vary from one season to the next (Payne & McVay, 1971).

Kangaroo rats also use acoustic signals to communicate, but these signals are produced with the aid of part of the environment. The rats drum their hind feet on the ground to produce vibrations that are carried in the air as well as along the ground. The foot drumming functions primarily to advertise a territory (Randall, 1989). Research observations indicate that the rats change the signature of the signal when they change territories, much the way whales change their songs from one season to the next (Randall, 1995).

As mentioned in the discussion of defensive behavior in Chapter 7, many animals communicate alarm via calls. In some cases alarm calls may attract a predator's attention but still benefit the caller. For example, Belding's ground squirrels give high-pitched whistles that signal other ground squirrels to seek cover. The squirrel that makes the original call, however, is not risking its own life. The caller gains an important benefit, in that it gets lost in the chaos created by numerous animals rushing for cover. Consequently, all of the ground squirrels, including the caller, seem to benefit directly from the alarm call (Sherman, 1985).

Eastern chipmunks, like several other species of mammals, give a different type of call in response to an aerial predator than in response to a terrestrial predator. This differentiation of calls increases the probability that conspecifics will make appropriate escape responses. Chipmunks are also sensitive to environmental conditions. For example, experiments involving playbacks of recorded alarm calls indicate that the chipmunks have a higher probability of fleeing and a longer period of alert when visual and auditory cues associated with the approach of a predator accompany the alarm calls than when no cues are present (Weary & Kramer, 1995).

Finally, animals may use auditory signals to attract others to feeding sites. For example, Eurasian house sparrows typically forage or search for food in large groups. They attract other individuals to the group with a "chirrup" call—but call only when there is an excess of food. At other times, when there is not enough food for a large group and attracting others would lead to severe competition for the food, the individual birds feed silently (Elgar, 1986).

Tactile Channels

Mammals often communicate with touches of various kinds. For example, black-tailed prairie dogs, which live in large groups in the hills of South Dakota, may touch mouths in what is called a kiss as they pass one another or enter one another's burrows. The kiss serves as a greeting and also seems to facilitate recognition of kin (see Hoogland, 1995).

Chimpanzees also kiss; but the kiss is a different type of signal, marking the end of a quarrel. Gestures such as kissing to mark the end of a disruptive encounter are basic to the control of aggression in chimpanzee groups. Like kissing, grooming may also function as a signal of reconciliation. The level of tension in a group of primates is generally reduced during times when grooming is taking place (DeWaal, 1989).

Integration of Information from Several Communication Channels

In the 1960s a controversy over bee communication surfaced. Several researchers argued that the fact that various aspects of bee dancing were correlated with the worker bees' flying a certain distance in a certain direction did not prove a cause-and-effect relationship. In other words, it was possible that the dancing observed by von Frisch was a side effect and that the real communication took place through sound or smell (Wenner, 1971).

◆ UNUSUAL ADAPTATIONS

Tactile Communication in Honeybees

When a honeybee returns to the hive after foraging, she performs a dance that indicates the direction, distance, and quality of a food source. Because the hive is too dark for visual cues to be effective, the bees seem to pick up the cues by rubbing against the dancing bee.

In a classic series of studies, Karl von Frisch determined that when a worker bee returns from foraging at a food source less than approximately 25 meters away (the cutoff point varies with the strain or race of the bee), she performs a **round dance** consisting of two superimposed circles. Bees in the hive then go out and search for the nectar in the immediate vicinity of the hive.

If, however, the food source is more than 25 meters away, the returning forager performs a **waggle dance.** In this dance she waggles, or rapidly moves her abdomen from side to side, while she locomotes in one direction; then she moves in the pattern of a figure 8, returning at the end of each loop to the general area where she began her waggle (see Figure 12.2). The direction in which the bee moves during the waggle part of the dance indicates the direction of the food source; the time taken to perform the waggle represents the distance (the longer the waggle, the greater the distance); and the vigor with which the bee dances reflects the quality of the source. When the dance is performed on the vertical face of the comb, as it typically is among bees that live in temperate regions, the waggle part of the dance is at an angle to gravity equivalent to the angle of the sun in relation to the food source. As an example, if the waggle part of the dance is 20 degrees off the vertical direction, the food source is at an angle 20 degrees to the right of the sun (von Frisch, 1971).

There was some support for the hypothesis that bees use both sound and smell in communication. During the waggle part of the dance, bees make sounds that are correlated with the distance from the food source and the quality of the source; the average length of the train of sound is proportional to the distance from the food source; and the rate of pulse production of the sound is related to the strength of sugar concentration. Furthermore,

The communication system of bees is even more remarkable when we realize that the bees are able to compensate for the movement of the sun in the sky; they fly at a predictably different angle relative to the sun after an interval of time. This compensation allows them to find the hive after they have spent considerable time away from it. The bees are also able to navigate even when the sun is not visible and there is only a patch of clear sky. Any patch of sky provides useful information, because the bees are sensitive to the pattern of polarized light in the sky; this pattern indicates the position of the sun. And when the sky is completely overcast, the bees have a functional backup system: They are sensitive to directional cues based on the earth's magnetic field (Gould, 1980).

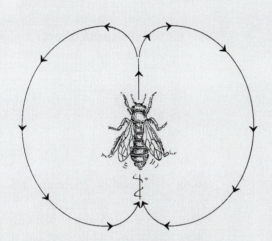

FIGURE 12.2 ◆ **The figure-8 pattern of a honeybee's waggle dance.** The direction of the bee's movement during the waggle part of the dance indicates the direction of the food source.

bees are influenced by the smell of the nectar on the body of the returning forager (Esch, 1967)

Finally, in the 1980s, researchers were able to construct a computer-controlled robotic bee that helped resolve the controversy. The robot danced, carried a scent, and emitted beelike sounds. The robot behaved so realistically that it was capable of fooling the bees inside the hive. (Deceiving bees is not easy; it took many attempts before any success was achieved.) Using the model, the researchers could systematically vary cues and assess the different cues' relative importance in communication. Results indicated, as von Frisch had hypothesized, that the waggle part of the dance was the "master component": The figure-8 part conveys little or no information. Both sound and the waggle part of the dance must be present, however, or the bees will not respond to the model.

It seems that both the sound and the tactual cues associated with waggling convey information about the food source. It is not that the bees pay attention to one cue and ignore the other; rather, the multiple channels provide information that is redundant, thus increasing the accuracy of the communication (Michelsen et al., 1992). At any rate, the precision of this communication system allows bees to locate the general area of a designated food source situated several hundred meters from the hive. Once the recruited bees are in the general area, they begin a search for food that smells like the food that was present on the recruiting bee's body. This task is not difficult for bees, because they have a well-developed ability to learn various scents and can differentiate as many as 700 different odors (von Frisch, 1971).

The integration of information from several channels of communication is probably more the rule than the exception in animal communication. For example, elephants and wolves generally accompany their visual signals with trumpeting and growls. The use of multiple channels provides an adaptive type of redundancy and enables certain animals to produce a relatively great range of signals.

Types of Signals

In addition to classifying communication signals on the basis of the channel utilized, we can decribe signals according to their degree of generality and amount of variability. Each type of signal has certain advantages and disadvantages, depending on the content communicated and the context in which it is communicated.

Specific versus General Signals

Specific signals are ones that have an effect only on members of the same species. This species specificity is particularly important in attraction and courtship, because attracting and mating with a partner from a different species can have serious disadvantages (refer to Chapter 2). Consequently, there has been a strong evolutionary trend toward extreme specificity in attraction signals. Thus, female gypsy moth pheromones attract only males of the same species, and the blue feet of the male blue-footed booby interest only blue-footed females (the female of the red-footed species is unresponsive to the display.)

In contrast, alarm signals are very general in their effect and may attract the attention of a variety of animals—including, in some cases, the predator. As we have seen, the stotting of antelopes may be beneficial to a predator, because the predator becomes aware of being identified; it does not waste time chasing an animal that is forewarned and has a good chance of escape. Prey animals of other species are also warned by the antelope's stotting behavior and may increase their vigilance.

When we compare specific and general signals, it is clear that specific signals are more complex. For example, species-specific courtship songs in birds are longer and more variable than alarm signals. Species-specific chemical signals that function as sex attractants consist of heavier and structurally more complex molecules than do general alarm signals. The complexity is required to make the signal unique. Nonetheless, there are costs in producing and broadcasting specific signals. A complex signal can take more energy to produce and may take longer to broadcast than a simple one. As a result, specific signals tend to evolve only when there are strong advantages associated with the specificity (Wilson, 1975).

Discrete versus Graded Signals

Discrete signals are signals that are either present or absent; they do not vary along a continuum. Examples of these types of signals are sexual attractants such as the flashes of fireflies or the chemical signals of gypsy moths. Discrete signals may also include sounds that identify members of a flock of birds and serve to keep the flock together. The message conveyed by a discrete signal is very simple, such as "I am a particular type of animal and I am here." The evolutionary path of a signal that is discrete is in the direction of clarity. Thus, there has been an evolutionary trend toward reduced variability in the expression of—and in the response to—discrete signals (Morris, 1957).

In contrast, a **graded signal** is variable, and its variations convey information about the level of the sender's motivation. Gener-ally, the higher the level of motivation, the more intense the signal and the longer its duration. Graded signals are most likely to be used when there is interaction between individuals. For example, when two males are displaying aggressive signals toward each other, the signals are likely to be graded. As one male red deer increases the level and duration of his roar, a competing male either escalates his own roaring intensity or backs off. The first male then faces different options, depending on the ability and level of motivation of the second one (Maynard Smith, 1974).

Generally, mammals and birds are more likely to use graded signals in their communication than are ectotherms (cold-blooded animals) such as insects. The honeybee dance is exceptional, however, not only because it is a unique form of communication but because it conveys graded information. The graded as-

TABLE 12.2 ◆ Types of Communication Signals

Type	Characteristic	Primary Function
Specific	Affects only conspecifics	Attraction display
General	Affects both conspecifics and other animals	Alarm signal
Discrete	On/off	Sex attraction
Graded	Variable in intensity and/or duration	Communication of different levels of motivation

pects of bee communication apply to three aspects of a food source—quality, direction, and distance of the food source.

Amount of Information Communicated

Like other aspects of communication, the amount of information communicated between animals varies greatly. As we have seen, the flash of a male firefly communicates only the simple message that he is in the area and is a male member of a particular species. In contrast, the honeybee dance communicates considerable information about the direction, location, and quality of a food source. What are the factors that account for these differences?

It was originally thought that animals that communicate large amounts of information must use a large variety of **displays;** that is, signals or behavior patterns that are specialized to convey information. However, comparative research indicates that animals do not vary significantly in the number of displays they use. For example, a mouth-breeding fish, a green heron, and an elk all exhibit 26 different displays. Even the highly social rhesus monkey shows 37 displays—a number not very different from the number of displays in less social animals. There seems to be an upper limit to the ability of animals to process signal diversity; this limit prevents the continued increase in number of displays in a given species (Moynihan, 1970).

If animals are limited in the number of distinct displays that they can use, what enables some animals to exchange such a vast amount of information? The answer seems to lie in the development of enrichment devices, or signals that modify the meaning of another signal.

Enrichment Devices

One type of enrichment device is **metacommunication,** or communication about the meaning of communication. For example, the "play face" of the chimpanzee (illustrated in Figure 3.3 in Chapter 3) indicates that communication that will follow will be related to play. A similar type of metacommunication is seen in dogs; the lowering of the forequarters serves as an invitation to engage in playful activities. The dog implies that the aggressive-looking behaviors that will follow are not to be taken as signs of aggressive intent (see Figure 12.3).

Another enrichment device is a composite signal or **medley:** Two or more signals are presented together, and the mixture conveys a message different from that of either signal alone. For example, one fire ant chemical signal stimulates general alarm behavior; another produces attraction; and presented in combination, the two signals stimulate a distinct type of oriented alarm reaction (Wilson, 1970). Other medleys are seen in the visual displays of zebras. An open mouth in combination with the ears *forward* indicates an enthusiastic, friendly greeting. However, an open mouth with ears *back* is a strong threat display (Trumler, 1959).

Still another way of enriching communication displays is to regulate the intensity or duration of a display. In a dog, for example, a loud bark or a series of barks has a very different meaning than one soft bark, even if all

FIGURE 12.3 ◆ **Metacommunication in dogs.** The "bow" of the dog on the left is an invitation to play.

other aspects of the bark are similar. Varying intensity and duration also convey different meanings in chemical communication. Harvester ants react to small concentrations of a particular signal by simply moving toward the odor source; at higher concentrations the ants show an alarm frenzy; and at the highest concentrations some ants begin digging (Hölldobler & Wilson, 1990).

Finally, the context in which a signal is given can enrich the message, a phenomenon known as the **contextual effect.** For example, many male displays—including singing in songbirds, claw waving in fiddler crabs, and roaring in red deer—have aggressive meaning when expressed toward other males but express sexual intentions in the presence of females. The lion's roar may have as many as four different functions, depending on context: It can be an attractiveness cue for pride members; a spacing device for neighbor-

ing prides; a threat during aggressive encounters; and/or a way of locating members of the pride during periods of separation (Schaller, 1972).

Redundancy

While one evolutionary trend tends to select for ability to communicate a large amount of information through enrichment devices, an opposite evolutionary trend tends to promote behavior that presents information redundantly. Redundancy may be accomplished by the repetition of a signal or by the presentation of two or more signals with identical meaning. Because the presentation of a signal has a cost, in terms of both expenditure of time and energy and vulnerability to predation, you may well ask, What is the function of redundancy? And if you have ever been awakened by the yelling of crows on a camping trip or the barking of dogs in your neighborhood, you may ask, Why does redundancy occur to such an extreme degree?

Redundancy appears to have several functions. Signals may be missed or misinterpreted, so redundancy increases the probability that a message will be received correctly. The need for redundancy is particularly great when the conditions for reception are poor, as in dim light or in situations involving background noise, or when the receiver might be distracted.

Redundancy may have a different function if the two animals communicating with each other are likely to alter their motivation in some way. For example, if two animals are competing with each other—as in crows' yelling or dogs' barking—their motivational states are likely to shift as one animal becomes tired or develops an interest in something else. Thus, the repeated communication may enable the animals to periodically reassess or restate the immediate situation.

Redundancy may also function to coordinate animals' states of sexual arousal and, once these states are at a high point, to sustain them. Consequently, courtship displays may be presented over and over or maintained for a long period. In lek species, the male courtship and competition between males take place simultaneously, so it is not surprising that the displays have a great deal of redundancy (Wilson, 1975).

Finally, it is possible that one form of redundancy—simultaneous presentation of multiple signals that have the same meaning—may enhance **memorability,** or the likelihood that the display will be remembered by its audience. The animal that is most memorable may then have a better chance of being chosen as a mate than less memorable competitors. This benefit of memorability helps explain why animals such as male birds of paradise present dramatic sounds, colors, and movements, all at the same time (Guilford & Dawkins, 1991).

Honesty and Dishonesty in Communication

As we have seen, communication usually benefits both the sender and the receiver. For example, a courtship signal such as a peacock's display is advantageous for the broadcasting male because it advertises his fitness; the female also benefits from the display, because she receives information that helps her make a decision as to whether or not to mate with the male. Similarly, an alarm call may provide indirect fitness benefits for the sender as well as a forewarning of danger for the receiver.

Nonetheless, as is true for many processes, communication is unlikely to have evolved for the "good of the species." Consequently, some communication develops that benefits the sender but exploits the receiver. For example, a study of red jungle fowl (which are the ancestors of domestic chickens) indicates that some males make deceptive food calls. When a female receiver goes in search of the food source, the male then attempts to mate with her (Gyger & Marler, 1988). Similarly, an individual vervet monkey will sometimes make an alarm call; then, when the other monkeys flee, the deceiver has lone access to the food source (Cheney & Seyfarth, 1990).

A question you might very well ask is, If there is a selective benefit to dishonest communication, why isn't every communication system dominated by "liars"? One answer is that there is usually more than one way to communicate. When a system becomes riddled with dishonest communicators, receivers will focus on an alternate system to obtain information. For example, if the male of a species is able to advertise fitness in a variety of ways but may use some of the signals for deception, the female will be selected to attend to the signals that have has not been used dishonestly (Parker, 1974).

Another method of avoiding deception is to develop an ability to discriminate honest from dishonest signals. For example, despite the generalization that songbirds are unable to discriminate their own eggs from those of other birds, some species have evolved the ability to discriminate a parasitic cowbird egg from their own eggs (Rothstein et al., 1988). Some birds, too, are able to discriminate legitimate from illegitimate food calls. For example, jungle fowl hens can learn to ignore food calls from exploitative males (Moffatt & Hogan, 1992). In vervet monkeys, an even more sophisticated method of avoiding deception has been reported. The monkeys remember an individual that was deceptive in the past, and later they ignore this individual's calls (Cheney & Seyfarth, 1990).

The Evolution of Communication Signals

We have already seen how the constraints and advantages of different communication channels are basic to the type of communication system that can evolve. We have also considered factors that influence the evolution of honest and dishonest communication. Now let's look in more depth at the interacting roles of the sender and receiver in the evolution of a communication system.

Building on Behaviors Already Present

Almost any behavior that is conspicuous and consistently predictive of relevant subsequent behavior may serve as a building block for a communication signal. Some signals arise from **intention movements**—movements that normally precede a behavior pattern and reflect what an animal "intends" to do. The gaping mouth of a gull and the raised paw of a cat are examples of intention movements that have come to signal aggression. In some cases, however, communication signals have evolved to the extent that it is not clear to the casual observer that they began their evolutionary trek as intention signals. Only after careful observation and a comparison of the signals of closely related species can we make reasonable hypotheses.

For example, after analyzing patterns of communication in several types of bees, Martin Lindauer (a student of von Frisch) hypothesized that the primitive communication of direction was very simple: A forager that had just returned from a rich food source would show excitement, gain the attention of other workers, then fly to the source with the other workers following. The next step was probably to fly out of the nest headed in the appropriate direction but to lead the others only partway to the source. The third step was probably simply to point in the appropriate direction on the horizontal surface of a nest after gaining attention with a dance of excitement.

Finally, in temperate-zone bee species, the last step must have involved substituting a vertical surface for a horizontal surface. As bees moved into temperate zones and built nests whose inside surfaces were dark and vertical, they used gravity instead of the sun as the point of orientation. In other words, the bees translated information based on the angle to the sun into comparable information expressed as the angle to maximum gravitational pressure (Lindauer, 1961).

Autonomic (reflexive) responses may also function as the building blocks for communication signals. For example, at high levels of excitement and stress, many animals lose control of their bladder function. The tendency to use urine as a communication signal may have begun with an association between autonomic arousal, urination, and the need to communicate with others about the source of the arousal (Morris, 1957).

Finally, there is clearly a natural selection for certain types of male courtship signals that function to appease the aggressiveness of the female. (If threat associated with physical closeness cannot be reduced, the probability of successful mating is very low.) Thus, some courtship signals include gestures that resemble the responses of low-status subordinate animals to higher-status conspecifics. For example, the "bowing" of a male penguin to a female probably evolved out of the tendency of subordinate males to bow to dominant ones.

Applying an Accent

Communication signals often add an accent to an existing characteristic that has relevance for the species. In many cases this accent takes

the form of exaggeration. For example, when confronting another male, a male stalk-eyed fly spreads its eyes (located on stalks) apart as far as it can. Because all the flies exaggerate in the same way, the distance between eyes is an accurate estimate of the male's size and is a legitimate signal of potential fighting ability (Burkhardt & de la Motte, 1983). Similarly, many fish have evolved horizontal stripes that create the illusion of greater body length and thus make the fish appear larger (i.e., more attractive and/or more intimidating; Zahavi, 1987).

Novelty may be a significant factor in the evolution of certain communication signals, because novel stimuli are most easily remembered. For example, the varied songs of some species of songbirds and the individualized coloration of male birds such as the ruff (a European relative of the sandpiper) may function to enhance memorability and so increase the probability that females will seek out a particular male (Guilford & Dawkins, 1991). However, there are also constraints on novelty. A stimulus that is too novel may lose its effectiveness. Accordingly, it seems that the degree of novelty that can develop is limited, especially in animals with relatively simple nervous systems.

Ritualization

As suggested in some of the examples just given, a signal may change once it has become part of a pattern of communication. More than 70 years ago, Julian Huxley (1923) pointed out that communication signals tend to evolve out of behaviors not originally involved in communication. As they take on communication functions, the behaviors become more stereotyped, a process Huxley called **ritualization.** This stereotypy performs an important function by increasing the attention-getting aspects of the signal.

Gaining attention is particularly important in courtship where several males are competing for the available females. The movements of lek-polygynous males such as the sage grouse described in Chapter 10 are good examples of this extreme stereotypy. In many cases an animal makes noticeable sounds or movements that increase the attention-getting properties of a ritualized signal. Lek birds, for instance, typically utter loud vocalizations that call attention to their visual displays as well as attract females from relatively great distances. Similarly, many male lizards make head-bobbing movements that call attention to the bright color and ornamentation in their head regions.

In addition to increasing attention-getting aspects of a signal, ritualization also helps to distinguish one signal from another. The distinctness of a particular courtship signal is especially important if there are several closely related species in the same area. For example, birds in the jungle and fish in coral reef communities tend to evolve highly elaborate and stereotyped courtship signals.

How does the process of ritualization take place? One evolutionary trend is to alter general movement patterns. For example, the waving of the claw of a fiddler crab may have begun as a single thrusting of the claw associated with aggression; this thrust may have become repeated and exaggerated as the signal became incorporated into courtship. In certain moths the change in the type of movement pattern apparently went in the opposite direction; wing-movement patterns used in flight

were slowed down as the moth began to beat its wings at a more leisurely pace while remaining stationary (Blest, 1957). These movement changes then became reinforced by the process of sexual selection (Eibl-Eibesfeld, 1975).

Another trend is for a communication signal to combine elements of two separate behavior patterns. For example, a courtship signal may develop from a conflict between incompatible behavioral tendencies. If a bird is in a conflict between fighting or taking flight, it may express a behavior that has elements of both patterns—such as jerking its head forward and raising its wings —but the behavior sequence may be unique. When this behavior is conspicuous and appears consistently, it can then become a courtship signal (Tinbergen, 1959).

TABLE 12.3 ◆ Processes in the Evolution of Communication Signals

Process	Manner of Expression
Building on behaviors already present	"Intention" movements; autonomic responses; appeasement of aggression
Applying an accent	Exaggeration; introduction of novelty
Ritualization	Attention-getting behaviors; stereotyped behaviors; alteration of movement patterns; combination of elements of different patterns

The evolution of courtship signals, in sum, seems to involve several different types of processes. It is likely that combinations of these processes explain the evolution of many courtship behaviors that at first glance appear bizarre and difficult to understand.

◆ HUMAN EVOLUTION

Several of the principles apparent in the evolution of cooperation and communication in nonhuman animals are also at work in human evolution. We will begin by looking at the roots of human cooperation. Then we will consider the tit-for-tat strategy in the development of human friendships. Finally, we will discuss the evolution of laughter and humor—factors that are basic to human communication.

COOPERATION

As in many nonhuman species, human cooperation is based on mutualism, kin selection, and reciprocity. The mutual advantages of group formation and cooperation were great for the ancestors of humans, because early hominids were not well adapted for life on open savanna lands. As we shall see in Chapters 13 and 14, living in a cooperative group provided our predecessors with many advantages, especially in regard to feeding, defense against predators, and competition with other groups of hominids.

Similarly, kin selection is an important principle in the formation of human groups: In virtually all cultures that have been studied, people are more likely to make sacrifices for close relatives than for strangers. Furthermore, people through the millennia have tended to live with or near kin. In some present-day technological societies extended families become widely separated, because individuals frequently move around the country for better economic opportunities. Unfortunately, the resulting lack of contact with family members appears to be a major cause of feelings of loneliness and alienation (see De Angelis, 1995). We seem to have a very basic need to feel close to our kin.

Reciprocity is also an extremely important factor in human cooperation. Phrases such as "I owe you one" and "it's my turn" are commonly used in all cultures. Reciprocity is also important in business and political exchanges. For example, a very effective strategy in a negotiating session is to present a relatively low-cost gift or to begin by making a small concession. This ploy is likely to begin a tit-for-tat exchange. If the other side co-operates, concessions and exchanges can escalate. If the other side fails to cooperate, the loss is minimal.

Because of the considerable mutual benefit provided by reciprocity, the tit-for-tat strategy is extremely effective in the many situations marked by a choice between cooperation and competition. For example, Robert Axelrod (1984) consulted with various experts on a game known as the Prisoner's Dilemma, which has been traditionally used to pit cooperative strategies against competitive strategies. Essentially, the game involves trying to maximize winnings in a series of encounters between two players. Player A can win the maximum amount during each encounter if he or she elects to compete when player B elects to cooperate. However, player A loses large amounts if both A and B elect to compete, whereas both players win a small amount if they both elect to cooperate.

If neither player knows what the other is about to do, which strategy is best? Axelrod had a group of experts write computer programs that each believed would maximize winnings. He then tested every program against all the others by computer simulation. The program that was most effective in the long run was a simple tit-for-tat strategy: Always begin by cooperating, then match the strategy chosen by the other player on the preceding move. This strategy—to begin with good faith but to stay cooperative only when the other player also shows good faith—was successful whether the other player was predominantly cooperative or predominantly competitive.

As with nonhuman animals, the tit-for-tat strategy is evolutionarily stable, because it cannot be replaced by other strategies. However, if there is only one encounter between players—and if the other player tends to begin by cooperating—a competitive strategy can be effective. In other words, if a person can avoid future meetings with the initial opponent, a hit-and-run strategy can have a positive payoff. In large cities, unfortunately, this type of situation often exists. This basic anonymity is a major factor in promoting crime and exploitation in cities as compared to small, stable communities.

FRIENDSHIPS

Several similarities or analogies exist between associations or friendships in chimpanzees and friendships in humans. Like those of chimpanzees, human friendships are reinforced by physical contact such as hugging. Furthermore, non-goal-oriented conversation or chat tends to maintain relationships among humans in much the same way as grooming does in chimpanzees.

Friendships often develop in both chimpanzees and humans as a function of reciprocity. There is a tit-for-tat type of arrangement as a friendship builds or is maintained. Reciprocal cooperation promotes a strengthening of the bonds of friendship, while a failure to reciprocate results in a weakening of the bonds. Evidence of the importance of reciprocity is the fact that individuals who do not reciprocate in some way cease to be friends.

Reciprocity in humans can be seen in verbal interactions as well as in behavioral interactions. As many of us have observed, when one of two individuals self-discloses, the other tends to self-disclose to a comparable extent. If the second person does not reciprocate, however, the first person pulls back and does not continue to self-disclose.

For both chimpanzees and humans, friendships provide social support systems that reduce the effects of stress. Chimpanzees typically increase their rate of grooming and physical contact following stressful events. Similarly, humans are likely not only to increase physical contact after stress but to increase their liking for one another (Dutton & Aron, 1974). Clearly, the effectiveness of social support systems in reducing the harmful effects of stress in humans has deep evolutionary roots.

THE EVOLUTION OF LAUGHTER AND HUMOR

Glen Weisfeld (1993) has proposed that human laughter and humor have evolved, consistent with principles of natural selection, as important aspects of human communication. In virtually all human societies, fitness-related behaviors and characteristics such as aggression, social poise, and sexuality are potentially humorous topics, especially in relaxing circumstances. Lighthearted or humorous approaches to these topics may function to reduce some of their potential threat. For example, roughhousing and tickling enable children to explore basic aspects of aggression in a safe atmosphere, much the way puppies engage in play fighting.

In both children and adults, laughing and smiling provide a release in tension and are therefore reinforcing. In fact, controlled studies indicate that when people utilize the muscles used in smiling and laughing independent of conscious thought, they experience uplifting feelings (Zajonc, 1985). Furthermore, mutual laughing and smiling signal liking and agreement—a signal that is reinforcing and also promotes social bonding. Finally, humor and laughter reduce feelings of aggression and may contribute to the effectiveness of the immune system (see Baron & Richardson, 1994).

Robert Provine (1995) has suggested that laughter evolved as a form of social signaling. He points out that in many respects laughter is more

closely related to nonhuman animal calls such as bird songs than it is to human speech. Furthermore, Provine proposes that because laughter tends to be contagious, we may have "auditory feature detectors," or a set of neural circuits that promote laughter even when we consciously try to inhibit it. Researchers have found that chimpanzees in the wild exhibit behavior similar to laughing, especially when they tickle and wrestle with one another. And captive chimpanzees that have been trained to signal "funny" in situations marked by incongruity, such as when they are presenting incorrect signs. Some of these chimpanzees also signal "funny" when attempting to urinate on people. The evolutionary roots of humor and laughter may go back to the common ancestors of chimpanzees and early hominids.

◆ CHANGING PERSPECTIVES

PAST	PRESENT	FUTURE
Helping behavior in animals can be explained by group natural selection. Communication in nonhuman animals is simple and stereotyped (early twentieth century).	Helping behavior evolves at an individual level, by such processes as kin selection and reciprocal altruism. Communication in some animals is highly complex and involves several channels and types of signals.	What ecological conditions promote the evolution of helping behavior? How did human language evolve out of simpler communication processes?

SUMMARY

Much cooperative behavior is based on kin selection: Social animals are generally capable of kin recognition and tend to make altruistic responses to close kin. Helping relatives reproduce and making alarm calls in the presence of relatives are two common examples of altruism based on kin selection.

Another type of helping behavior, based on reciprocity, is seen in social animals. For reciprocity to develop, individual animals must be able to recognize other individuals and have a well-developed social memory. Reciprocity is most likely to develop when the cost of helping is less than the benefit of being helped.

A variety of communication channels exist, including chemical channels, visual channels, auditory channels, and tactile channels. Animals generally specialize in one channel of communication, but many communicate via multiple channels.

Communication signals may be divided into general types. Specific (as opposed to general) types of signals are typically used in sexual communication. Graded (as opposed to discrete) types can indicate varying levels of motivation.

Enrichment devices greatly increase the amount of information that may be communicated. Enrichment devices include metacommunication, medleys, regulation of intensity and duration of signals, and contextual effects.

Redundancy in communication systems increases the probability that messages will be received correctly. Redundancy may also enable animals to communicate or monitor

shifts in motivation, to coordinate states of sexual arousal, or to enhance the memorability of an animal's display.

There are limits to the degree that communication systems may be exploited dishonestly; when dishonest signaling reaches a certain frequency in a population, alternative communication systems tend to evolve. Furthermore, receivers may learn to discriminate honest from dishonest signalers.

Behaviors that conspicuously and consistently predict relevant subsequent behaviors can act as the building blocks for the evolution of communication signals. Behaviors that accentuate relevant attributes or are somewhat novel are also good candidates for communication signals. Over time, the nature of communication signals—particularly courtship signals—tends to evolve by the process of ritualization.

As in the case of many nonhuman animals, mutualism, kin selection, and reciprocity affect cooperation and the development and maintenance of friendships in humans. There is some evidence that human laughter and humor evolved as social strategies.

KEY TERMS

CHAPTER 13

COMPETITION, AGGRESSION, AND PEACEMAKING

◆ *What are the major causes of aggression in animals?*

◆ *In what situations do animals fight most viciously?*

COMPETITION AND AGGRESSION

The Fighting Styles of Animals

Game Theory and Fighting Strategies

Gender and Aggression

Aggression in Ground-Dwelling Primates

LIMITATIONS ON AGGRESSION

Dominance Hierarchies

Territorial Systems

PEACEMAKING

Reconciliation

Incompatible Responses and Mediation

HUMAN EVOLUTION

The Expression of Aggression

Dominance Hierarchies and Territorial Organizations

Peacemaking

*C*hapter 12 emphasized that altruism and communication are often basic to the development and maintenance of groups. In contrast, disputes over resources—which often lead to aggression—can be disruptive to a group. Consequently, there has been a strong evolutionary trend, particularly in social animals, to develop ways of countering the negative effects of competition and aggression within species.

In this chapter we will begin by considering several aspects of intraspecies competition and aggression in general. Then we will examine two systems commonly seen in

13

~~~~~~

*animals that reduce the direct expression of aggression—dominance hierarchies and
territoriality. Next, we will look at the findings of research on peacemaking gestures
that tend to ameliorate the consequences of aggression among primates. Finally, we
will discuss aggression and peacemaking in humans.*

COMPETITION
AND AGGRESSION

As I have pointed out in earlier chapters, intraspecies aggression is very different from other types of aggression. In a battle with a predator, there is a great deal at stake: An animal's failure to effectively defend itself or its offspring is disastrous. In intraspecies aggression, however, winning is not always necessary; the decision to withdraw from an encounter may enable the animal to fight another day or to compete in some other way for the needed resource. Thus, a withdrawal from an intraspecific (within-species) encounter may sometimes be an adaptive response.

Disputes over limited resources such as sexual partners, food, and shelter are primary causes of intraspecies aggression. The expression of aggression is especially intense among strongly polygynous males that have the opportunity to mate with several females. For example, male elephant seals fight more violently than males of species that protect smaller harems or are monogamous. In fact,

elephant seals sometimes engage in fighting that results in serious injury or death. In these animals the "resources" (the harems) are rich, and so the risks are often extreme (Enquist & Leimar, 1990).

The generalization that animals fight most vigorously to defend rich resources applies to both abundance and quality of food. For example, red-backed salamanders fight more strenuously over territories if they have recently eaten rich food (in an experimental setting) than if they have recently eaten moderate or poor food (Gabor & Jaeger, 1995).

There is a limit to this generalization regarding the richness of a food resource, however. When the food resource is copious enough to supply enough food for all of the animals in a group, there is less fighting and more sharing. In this case the advantages of sharing and avoiding confrontations outweigh the possible advantages of fighting (Archer, 1988).

Another cause of aggression, disputes over status, is indirectly related to competition over resources. High status often helps an animal attain valuable resources such as food, shelter, or (in the case of polygynous males) access to females. And as with direct access to resources, the greater this indirect benefit of status, the greater the intensity of aggression. For example, domestic hens in a group fight much more fiercely among themselves than do pigeons in a group. The reason is that the high-status domestic hens have primary access to resources such as as food, water, and shelter, whereas status confers relatively few benefits on pigeons (Guhl, 1956).

The Fighting Styles of Animals

In contrast to predatory aggression, where there are obvious advantages to a lethal attack, such an attack against a member of the same species involves some real disadvantages. The rival may be a relative, and killing a relative would reduce indirect fitness. In addition, fighting in a style that is directed toward killing could result in death or serious injury to the initiator. Consequently, most fights between conspecifics have become ritualized in such a way that lethal weapons are not used. For example, rattlesnakes raise the upper parts of their bodies and attempt to push one another rather than relying on their deadly fangs (see Figure 13.1). Similarly, deer and antelope attempt to push one another and refrain from spearing their opponent with their antlers or horns.

Animals have also developed ritualized submissive gestures that inhibit aggression among conspecifics. In the vast majority of cases, the presentation of a submissive gesture will allow the loser of an encounter to slink away without further attack by the winner. Afterwards, further encounters between the winner and the loser will evoke subtle expressions of dominance and submission, and both animals can save the energy they might otherwise waste on fighting.

Why have animals in a wide variety of species developed the tendency to follow the "rules" of the dominance–submission ritual game? Essentially, it is the only evolutionarily stable strategy. In many different types of situations, other strategies—such as attacking an animal that has given a submissive gesture—would have a less successful overall payoff and would consequently be unstable (Maynard Smith, 1982).

Game Theory and Fighting Strategies

One of the most important considerations in the decision to fight is the behavior, or anticipated behavior, of the competing animal or animals. John Maynard Smith (1974) developed a game theory model that generated several fruitful hypotheses to explain fighting strategies. In Chapter 12 we looked at competition versus cooperation and the tit-for-tat strategy; now let's consider some related hypotheses.

Hawk and Dove Strategies

There are two general strategies related to intraspecies confrontations over resources: The **hawk strategy** is to fight, and the **dove strategy** is to back off. If all animals acted like

FIGURE 13.1 ◆ **Male rattlesnakes in an encounter to establish dominance.** The weaker individual eventually yields and allows the stronger one to express domination by pushing his (the weaker one's) head to the ground.

doves, there would be an advantage to becoming a hawk. Being the only hawk, an animal could win every encounter. As the number of hawks increased, however, the chance of meeting another hawk would increase; and there would come a point where the probability of meeting another hawk—and possibly losing a costly fight—would become relatively large.

At the point where the probability of meeting another hawk becomes prohibitively large, there is an advantage to remaining a dove. Encounters with another dove will sometimes yield a positive payoff, and an encounter with a hawk will involve only a minimal loss; the animal will lose the resource but will not be injured or spend time fighting. Thus, if hawk and dove strategies are genetically influenced, the population will reach a point where there are stable percentages of hawks and doves. As soon as one strategy begins to appear at a frequency higher than the stable point, there will be a shift back in the other direction. And as we have seen, this kind of stable balance does develop. The relationship—in this case, between hawks and doves—is known as **stable polymorphism** (Maynard Smith, 1973).

This concept of stable polymorphism helps to explain not only why two diametrically opposed strategies can exist in the same population of animals, but also why it is unlikely that a selection process will produce an extreme and reckless tendency to fight. (Reckless tendencies to fight are found in gamecocks and male Siamese fighting fish, but these animals have been selectively bred by humans.)

Conditional Strategies

When an animal's tendency to fight is not rigidly influenced by genetic factors, as in the hawk/dove example, an animal may develop a conditional strategy; that is, it may fight when there is a reasonably good chance of winning, but back off when there is a significant chance of losing. The effectiveness of a conditional approach is enhanced by threats and bluffs, which prevent an opponent from anticipating at what point the animal will back down.

There is considerable evidence that conditional strategies are evolutionarily stable. In the first place, as we shall see, a wide variety of animals use threats and bluffs. Furthermore, animals are much more likely to fight if they are equally matched. If there is a mismatch, the smaller or otherwise disadvantaged animal is very likely to back down (Dawkins, 1977).

How do animals know, before a fight starts, how they match up against each other? The intensity of the threats and displays may very well indicate each animal's motivation and fighting potential. In red deer, two types of displays enable the males to make judgments about their rivals' fighting ability: a parallel walk, which enables the two animals to make a determination of relative size; and competitive roaring, which provides informa-

tion about physical stamina (Clutton-Brock et al., 1979; see Figure 13.2).

As we saw in Chapter 12, there is a selection for sensitivity to good indicators of strength and size. Animals also benefit by broadcasting their strong points in a clearly perceptible manner. Thus, it is not surprising that aggressive displays tend to be accurate, clearly perceived indicators of fighting potential. In the case of the red deer, not only is the roar an accurate representation of the male's overall strength and condition, but the intensity of the roar is difficult to ignore (Clutton-Brock et al., 1979).

Wars of Attrition

In some cases animals do not fight vigorously over a resource but engage in a **war of attrition**—a battle in which the "winner" is the animal that stays the longest time at the point of

FIGURE 13.2 ◆ **A red deer stag roaring in an attempt to establish dominance.**

encounter. In such a battle it is possible for both animals to lose more than they gain if they invest an amount of time that surpasses the value of the disputed resource. In response to this possibility, animals have evolved the ability to take into account the value of the resource and to determine in some way how long they should stay in competition. The value of the time each animal is willing to invest should approach, but not significantly exceed, the value of the resource.

Let us suppose that two males, A and B, are competing for a female by trying to outstay each other. If A's behavior were to indicate how long he planned to stay, this would give B a large advantage. B could then decide to leave right away, or to continue if the wait were not going to be too long. This strategy of A—either to give away his plan with a gesture or to be highly predictable—would be ineffective, and thus unstable.

In contrast, an evolutionarily stable strategy would be for an animal to be somewhat unpredictable and act as if it would never give up. Furthermore, the amount of time spent should, on the average, match the value of the resource. In other words, animals should spend, on the average, a large amount of time in wars of attrition involving valuable resources and a small amount of time trying to outstay competitors over relatively poor resources (Maynard Smith, 1982).

In the hawk/dove and war of attrition models just presented, we assumed that the animals were equal in strength and/or that the resources were of equal benefit to each animal. However, game theory models are also capable of making predictions about asymmetrical relationships—situations in which one animal is a better fighter than another or in which one animal can benefit more than the other from the contested resource. Both symmetrical and asymmetrical models have been successful in accounting for the nature of aggressive encounters in a wide variety of animals (Maynard Smith, 1982).

Gender and Aggression

There are no consistent gender differences in the aggressiveness with which animals protect themselves from predators or other outside threats. Female rats, for example, are just as vigorous in their self-defense as males are (Adams, 1983). Gender differences in aggressiveness, when they exist, tend to be specifically associated with intraspecies encounters. For example, male mice fight with other male mice much more often than female mice fight with females. As Chapter 17 will explain, the greater aggressiveness of males in mice and in many other species of animals is related, at a proximate level, to testosterone.

From a functional standpoint, greater male aggressiveness in competitive same-sex situations is related to the intense competition between males in many species for access to females. Sexual selection may have a strong effect on the evolution of aggressiveness, especially in polygynous males. And because males have little or nothing to gain by fighting with females, it is not surprising that males usually inhibit their aggressiveness toward females.

Recognition of Gender

In order for males to inhibit aggression against females and to avoid unnecessary encounters with potentially aggressive males, the males must be able to tell the diffence between females and other males. In a similar way, females, too, benefit from accurate gender recognition. How do animals recognize gender, especially in species where males and females look very much alike?

In several species of mammals, olfactory cues are basic to gender recognition. For example, in a laboratory study of rats, experimenters painted the urine of a female onto a male; and when the urine-soaked male was introduced into another male's cage, the resident male did not attack (Dixon & Mackintosh, 1971).

More direct evidence that the gender-recognition cue is olfactory comes from a study of mice in which the nerve carrying olfactory information to the brain was experimentally severed. As predicted, when male mice with nonfunctional olfactory systems were placed together, they failed to aggress against each other (Bean, 1982). We will return to the relationship between olfactory cues and gender recognition when we discuss the olfactory system in Chapter 18.

High Levels of Aggression in Females

In a few species the female has a very high level of testosterone and is more aggressive than the male. Spotted sandpipers, which are polyandrous, are one such species. The aggressiveness of the female sandpiper facilitates her establishment of a territory and competition for a mate, responses that are basic to her reproductive success (Oring, 1985).

Female spotted hyenas are also extremely aggressive and have high levels of testosterone. However, their aggressiveness is related to food competition rather than to competition for a mate. After the hyena clan has killed a large animal, female spotted hyenas compete intensely for food with one another, with males, and with scavengers. Female hyenas' aggressiveness has another benefit as well. Aggressive, dominant females produce highly aggressive sons—and only the most dominant male in the clan reproduces. Therefore, there is an unusually strong selection pressure for dominance and aggression in female spotted hyenas; the sons' mating success strongly affects their mothers' fitness (Stewart, 1987).

Aggression in Ground-Dwelling Primates

Ground-dwelling primates are of special interest because they express high levels of aggression toward conspecifics under certain circumstances. Because primates are poorly adapted structurally for life on the ground, ground-dwelling primates have evolved high levels of social organization that enable them to compete successfully with other ground-dwelling animals as well as with other groups of their own species. But much of this social organization is based on aggression or threats of aggression. Ground-dwelling primate species are not only more social but more aggressive than their tree-dwelling cousin species. Much to her dismay, Jane Goodall (1986) found that chimpanzees occasionally even killed conspecifics from another troop.

Jane Goodall (1986) has identified several apparent motivations for aggression based on her own extensive observations of wild chimpanzees. Much aggression seems to stem from interventions into the affairs of other chimpanzees. For example, if two individuals are in conflict, a third may intervene in support of one of them. There are also instances of intervention into a friendly contact between two other individuals. Although it is impossible to know for certain whether any animal is capable of intentional behavior, both the contexts of these interventions and later interactions suggest that the intruder is trying to break up an alliance.

Fear of the unfamiliar may also evoke aggression. In 1966 a polio epidemic struck Goodall's research area, and three chimpanzees developed an abnormal appearance as well as bizarre movements resulting from partial paralysis. Other chimpanzees reacted at first with fear; then, as the fear began to subside, some began to hit the victims. This fear of the unfamiliar also applies to strangers. When chimpanzees encounter other, unfamiliar chimpanzees, there is often a fear-turning-to-aggression reaction.

Sometimes, too, aggression seems to spread by contagion. An individual may join a group of fighting chimpanzees for no apparent reason; or it may attack an innocent bystander after observing two other individuals fight. When chimpanzees attack strangers, the aggression is usually initiated by one individual and then adopted by the whole group.

Finally, there is aggression that seems to be aberrant. An adult chimpanzee female and her daughter killed several baby chimpanzees. Despite the attempts of the mothers to save their babies, the cooperative efforts of the mother-and-daughter team were overwhelming. Unlike the infanticide discussed in Chapter 11—which produced some fitness advantage for the aggressors—these killings afforded no apparent fitness advantage (Goodall, 1986). It seems that, with the evolution of large brains and highly variable behavior in the great apes, some individual behavior patterns develop that are destructive to the group as a whole and of no advantage to the individual.

LIMITATIONS ON AGGRESSION

As game theory models make clear, unchecked intraspecies aggression has serious negative consequences—not only for losers but also for winners, who spend time and energy that could be invested in other activities. Consequently, there has been strong natural selection for the development of systems that minimize the amount of fighting that occurs between conspecifics. We will now consider two related social systems that function to limit intraspecies aggression: dominance hierarchies and territoriality.

Dominance Hierarchies

A common strategy related to minimizing the potentially harmful effects of aggression is for one animal to make appeasement gestures which, in effect, signal submissiveness. Once established, a dominance–submission relationship tends to persist, reinforced by the tendency of animals to make gestures that signify dominance or submission. For example, a dominant domestic hen typically holds her head high as she approaches a subordinate hen. The subordinate hen usually responds by making submissive gestures such as turning away or lowering her head (see Figure 13.3).

The continued expression of this kind of dominance–submission ritual is basic to the

FIGURE 13.3 ◆ **A ritualized expression of submissiveness.** The hen on the right is lowering her head in the presence of the more dominant hen on the left.

maintenance of the social ranking system, or hierarchy; and the hierarchy, in turn, functions to help keep the peace. For example, after two hens are allowed to establish a dominance–submission relationship, they will live peaceably together, periodically expressing the dominance–submission ritual. However, if they are caged next to each other for 3 weeks—so that they can see and hear each other but cannot express the ritual—they will fight like strangers when they are released from their cages (Maier, 1964). Apparently, seeing and hearing one another is not enough; the hens must have the freedom to express the ritual in order for the hierarchy to be maintained.

The more that is to be gained by being dominant, the more vigorously animals are likely to struggle for dominance. This relationship between possible gain and energy invested in competition for dominance is illustrated by the results of a experimental study of dark-eyed juncos. The experimenter made a food source available to two groups of these birds. One group consisted of dominant birds that had been fed normally; the nondominant birds in the other group had been deprived of food. Competing one-on-one for food, the food-deprived juncos fought with great vigor and were likely to become dominant over the previously dominant nondeprived birds. Incidentally, this new dominance hierarchy remained stable for a day or so after the food fight but then shifted back to the old relationship after food was made plentiful for all the birds (Cristol, 1992).

Linear Dominance Hierarchies

Animals that live in large groups typically establish a hierarchy in which there is a more or less **linear dominance hierarchy**—a social structure in which one animal is dominant over all others, a second is dominant over all others but the first, and so on.

Linear dominance hierarchies are established by a series of encounters in which each animal fights or threatens all of the other members of the group, one at a time. In each encounter the winner becomes dominant over the loser. After some time, a social hierarchy takes shape in which the big winner (or alpha individual) dominates all other animals, a beta individual dominates all but the alpha, and so on down the line. At the bottom of the hierarchy is the omega animal that has lost to every other animal. Sometimes there are circular arrangements: A dominates B, B dominates C, but C dominates A. These are rare, however, and when they do occur, they usually develop into a linear hierarchy over time.

The stability of dominance hierarchies is explicable in terms of game theory; that is, the strategy of fighting those that one has beaten previously but retreating from fights with those to whom one has lost will always be the superior and evolutionarily stable strategy (Maynard Smith, 1982). Therefore, it is not surprising that social hierarchies have evolved in such a wide variety of animals, especially in those that have a memory for previous encounters.

Even animals that do not have an ability to recognize individuals and remember the outcome of previous encounters are able to establish a quasi-dominance relationship. After losing a fight with another male, for example, a male field cricket will move off and refrain from engaging in another fight with any male for a period of approximately an hour. This period of fighting inhibition leads to a quasi-dominance hierarchy, because the loser is unlikely to encounter and challange the winner (Adamo & Hoy, 1995).

Dominance Hierarchies and Fitness

Dominant males have relatively great access to females, so dominance offers clear fitness advantages in terms of the reproduction of polygynous males. For example, dominant males of a Panamanian insect, *Zorotypus gurneyi,* engage in the most frequent copulations (Chloe, 1994). In baboons the dominant male does not necessarily copulate more frequently than the other males, but he is likely to copulate with females when they are ovulating. Therefore, he tends to sire the greatest number of offspring (Hausfater, 1975).

Animals that are dominant also tend to live longer than subordinate individuals. This longevity effect is related to the fact that dominant animals have relatively great access to resources such as food, water, and shelter (Guhl, 1956). In addition, dominant animals experience less social stress than subordinate ones. For example, low-ranking cockroaches that are repeatedly exposed to the stress of encounters with dominant roaches show an unusually high death rate, even though they do not sustain significant physical injuries (Ewing, 1967).

If low-ranking animals are at such a disadvantage, why don't they leave the group? There seem to be several reasons. First, low-ranking animals often have the opportunity to work their way up in the hierarchy, especially when higher-status animals die or become feeble. Also, even animals that do not rise to the top of the hierarchy may derive some benefits from the system. As we have seen, the dominance hierarchy provides a structure that reduces disruptive conspecific fighting and promotes cooperation. For example, when a group of domestic hens are first introduced, individuals eat less and suffer more wounds than when the group becomes established and a stable social hierarchy is formed (Guhl, 1956). Finally, under certain conditions subordinate animals are reasonably successful. If the density of females is high in fish known as the dark chub, the dominant male becomes exhausted and many subordinate males are successful in mating (Katano, 1990).

The Role of Size and Level of Aggressiveness

In many species size has a strong effect on dominance, because size is often correlated with strength and fighting ability. Gender is also a factor; males tend to be dominant, partly because males are generally larger than females in polygynous species. This gender-related dominance is clearly illustrated in domestic fowl, where virtually all males rank socially above the most dominant female. There is little interaction between males and females apart from mating, however, so the status differential between genders is not a significant cause of conflict in these birds.

Males also tend to be more dominant because there is sexual selection for male aggressiveness associated with intermale competition and female choice. Aggressive males tend to be most successful in establishing territories and attracting females.

Another, more subtle factor tends to link aggressiveness and male dominance. If a male such as a rooster were less aggressive than a hen, a successful mating could not take place and the genes associated with the male's submissiveness would not be passed on. Similarly, a female that was extraordinarily high in aggressiveness would not be able to pass on her genes related to aggressiveness, because such a female would be very difficult for most males to mate.

There are exceptions to males' general dominance over females, however. In brown hyenas, the highest-ranking female is highly aggressive and is equal to the highest-ranking male in the dominance hierarchy. The dominant female gains advantages in terms of access to food (Owens & Owens, 1996). Spotted hyena females, who compete especially fiercely over food, are even more dominant than males. The female hyenas benefit from this dominance during the competition for access to a kill on the open plains of Africa (Kruuk, 1972). In some animals, intense competition over food can apparently mitigate the usual male dominance system.

The Role of Experience

J. P. Scott and E. Fredericson (1951) conducted a classic study of mice in which they presented strong evidence for the role of experiential factors in aggression. After a few weeks of social isolation, mice were divided into two groups. Each mouse in one group was paired with less aggressive mice and won a few paired encounters with ease. The mice in the other group were paired with highly aggressive mice and lost their encounters. Thereafter, the winners became highly aggressive and obtained considerable social status, while the losers retreated from fights and ended up with low status. It appears that the experience of winning increased the confidence levels—and possibly also the skill levels—of the mice.

The percentage of wins compared to losses in the past is a good predictor of success in the future. Therefore, the tendency to fight vigorously if one has a winning record is a reasonable strategy and is likely to become evolutionarily stable (Maynard Smith, 1982).

Chimpanzees may use general experience to develop higher-order strategies that can increase their status. For example, a wild male chimpanzee named Mike was able to move up in the social hierarchy by clattering two or three empty kerosene cans in front of him and occasionally throwing them during his charging displays. After having been hit a couple of times by the cans, the human observers hid the cans. However, Mike then began to take other objects and throw them, as well as natural objects, at the observers (Goodall, 1986).

Seniority and Prior Residency

Animals that have been members of an established group for a period of time are almost always higher in social rank than newcomers. It takes newcomers a while to work their way up the social hierarchy. For example, senior members of rhesus monkey groups are usually dominant over junior members (Drickamer & Vessey, 1973). This seniority effect provides a certain degree of stability to dominance hierarchies. Newcomers to a group are not likely to be as disruptive as they would be if they could immediately obtain high status.

There is also evidence that prior residency—independent of seniority—is related to dominance. Experiments with great tits, in an aviary where prior residency can be manipulated, indicate that prior residency is more important than age or size in determining dominance among these birds (Sandell & Smith, 1991). Apparently, some animals benefit from both the seniority and the prior residency effect.

Kinship Ties

In rhesus monkeys the status of a daughter in the social hierarchy is highly correlated with that of her mother. Although some of this correlation may be associated with inheritance, at least part of it is attributable to experience. If daughters are raised by foster mothers, a correlation between the status of mothers and daughters is still found (DeWaal, 1989).

At any rate, monkeys and apes are sensitive to kinship ties. For example, fights sometimes involve a monkey attacking the innocent kin of a monkey with whom it was previously in conflict. In one study, a rhesus monkey that had just had an altercation with another monkey was seen to walk over to the other monkey's sleeping sister and grab her aggressively (DeWaal, 1989). Among vervet monkeys in Kenya, a fight between two monkeys in different families sometimes spreads in such a way that the relatives of the two combatants also end up fighting (Cheney & Seyfarth, 1986). It certainly does not require much imagination to find human analogues to these situations.

Territorial Systems

The discussion of attraction and courtship in Chapter 9 described how males of some species establish mating territories within

TABLE 13.1 ◆ Factors Related to Dominance

Factor	Reason
Size and strength	Large, strong animals usually win competitive encounters.
Gender	Males are usually dominant over females, because there is often sexual selection for size and strength in males.
Aggressiveness	Aggressiveness (usually strongest in males because of sexual selection) tends to enhance competitive and reproductive success.
Experience	The experience of winning fosters development of skill and confidence.
Seniority and prior residency	It generally takes time to move up the social hierarchy.
Kinship ties	In certain primates an ability to remember kinship ties facilitates the "passing on" of status to relatives.

which they have free access to females. Territories may also be established that allow individual animals access to other types of resources such as food or shelter. We may define a **territorial system** as a system that enables an individual to become dominant in a particular area. From this definition it is clear that territorial systems and dominance hierarchies are closely related, in that the concept of dominance applies to both systems. Furthermore, once established, both dominance hierarchies and territorial systems function to reduce intraspecies aggression.

The close relationship between social hierarchies and territorial systems is also illustrated by the fact that one system may easily be replaced by the other, depending on environmental conditions. For example, when a food source is patchily distributed, birds known as honeyeaters establish and defend territories. However, when there is a heavy enough concentration of nectar in a small area to feed a large number of birds, the territorial system breaks down and a dominance hierarchy develops (Craig & Douglas, 1986). The attempt to defend a very rich area would require considerable energy, and an animal has little or nothing to gain by excluding other animals in such a situation.

In contrast to a territory, which is typically defended against the intrusion of conspecifics, a **home range** is the entire area in which an animal lives. Thus, a territory is generally smaller than the home range and includes some resources that are valuable to the animal—such as food or shelter, or something else that will attract a sex partner. Obtaining a territory provides major benefits for an animal, in that a territorial animal has access to resources without constant searching and fighting.

A territorial system also benefits a group of animals as a whole. Territoriality functions to create space between animals and, consequently, to reduce the risks of parasitism and cannibalism. Furthermore, territoriality reduces the possibility of animals' depleting renewable food sources. Nonetheless, as we have seen, group benefits do not usually affect the evolution of a system. Therefore, to understand how territoriality may have evolved and can be maintained, we must concentrate on the benefits and costs at an individual level.

Balanced against the benefits of increased access to resources are several costs associated with establishing and defending a territory. A previous owner must often be ousted, and the encounter involves certain risks and outputs of energy. Risks and outputs are also involved in territorial defense—depending, of course, on the size of the territory and the number and strength of competitors. Numerous studies of social behavior indicate that the establishment and maintenance of territories reflect animals' sensitivity to this cost–benefit ratio.

The Sizes of Territories

The size of a territory depends on several factors, including the extent of an animal's resource requirements, the animal's ability to patrol the area, what types of resources need to be protected, the distribution of the resources, and how much energy it takes to protect the territory. To put it simply, the more the protected resources are spread out, and the greater the animal's ability to patrol and protect the area, the larger the territory is likely to become.

Male birds of certain species hold on to the same territory over a period of years. At the other extreme, male birds of lekking species usually retain a territory for only a day or two, just long enough to attempt to mate with females during the short period in which the females are fertile and visit the lek.

Most species of animals, however, establish a territory for a breeding season. Among the smallest territories are the colonial nest sites of gulls and terns, which are established in close proximity to the nest sites of conspecifics. In fact, the size of the "territory" is determined by how far the bird can reach to

peck at another bird while sitting on its nest. Another small-sized territory is established by a male sea lion on the rocky beach of a deserted island; each male's individual territory is so small that his harem of females and their offspring are crowded together (Campagna et al., 1992).

Eagles establish the largest territory, an area that may be several hundred square kilometers. This large size is related to the fact that eagles' prey is widely distributed; also, the eagles are able to identify prey as well as intruding conspecifics from a considerable distance.

In a few cases, a male bird such as a pied flycatcher establishes more than one breeding territory and attempts to attract a female to each location. If he is successful, he can mate with a female in each territory. However, females resist this strategy; the primary female will often attack the female in the secondary territory. Consequently, multiple-territory males tend to have the greatest reproductive success if they establish territories that are distant from one another.

The size of a territory can vary from time to time, depending on the richness and distribution of resources. For example, the area of the territory of nectar-feeding birds in Australia shrinks when the nectar resource becomes more concentrated. This adjustment can be understood in terms of energy expenditure. If a bird can obtain its required calories from a small area, it need not waste energy defending an area larger than is required (Paton & Ford, 1983).

There are, however, situations in which birds face large fluctuations of food supply in the winter. Under these circumstances, the birds consistently defend a territory that supplies more food than is needed, on average, for their daily caloric requirement. Apparently these birds are taking into consideration long-term effects; that is, they are allowing for the fact that there will be some winter days during which they will need all the food their large territory can provide (Houston et al., 1985).

Another factor that affects size of territory is competition. Songbird males establish relatively large territories in the late winter or early spring. But if an intruder is persistent enough, the resident male may back off somewhat, resulting in a territorial division between the two males. In essence, the energy and risk involved in further confrontations are not worth the value of the lost area. Similarly, as more hummingbirds intrude on other hummingbirds' territories, the size of an individual's territory shrinks (Eberhard & Ewald, 1994).

Finally, there are cases in which birds will abandon a territory when the distribution of food changes. For example, African golden-winged sunbirds defend a territory including their food, flowering mint, when the plant is patchily distributed. When the plant is widely distributed, however, they stop defending their territory and forage in a broad home range (Gill & Wolf, 1978). Again, this shift in strategy seems reasonable: When there is no longer a particular area that is special, there is no advantage to defending it.

Gender and Territoriality

Most territoriality is related, directly or indirectly, to mating and rearing the young. Either the territory is used exclusively for mating, as in the case of a lek, or the territory contains resources that are needed for reproduction, such as food or nesting material. If only one gender in a species is territorial, game theory would predict that it must be the gender that is least discriminating in the choice of a mate; because the evolutionarily stable strategy is the one in which the least discriminating partner tries to attract the most discriminating one. It is usually the male that is the least discriminating, so males are most likely to be territorial. Consistent with this game theory interpretation, we have seen that there is a gender-role reversal in territoriality in polyandrous species such as the spotted sandpiper. Polyandrous females are territorial and are also less discriminating in their choice of partners than are the males.

Females may also establish territories related to rearing the young. For example, female poplar aphids (insects that feed on poplar leaves) fight intensely to gain access to a leaf on a poplar tree. The winner then attempts to probe the leaf, and the probing results in the formation of a gall that functions to feed her offspring. The high level of intensity of the fights seems to be related to the fact that a leaf with a single gall will yield many more offspring than a leaf on which there is also the gall of another aphid (Whitham, 1986).

In a few cases, both the male and the female of the species establish a territory related to feeding. Male and female aquatic insects known as water striders, for example, fight with each other over an area on the water surface that is likely to have a large abundance of prey. The insects that establish rich territories are the most successful in foraging; attain the greatest body mass; and, in the case of females, exhibit the greatest fecundity the following spring (Blanckenhorn, 1991).

The Vigor of Territorial Defense

As the poplar aphid illustrates, an animal will fight vigorously for a territory containing a valuable resource; the more valuable the resource, the more intense the territorial dispute. This principle has been experimentally demonstrated in hummingbirds. When the richness of nectar was manipulated by the experimenter, it was found that hummingbirds fought most vigorously for a resource that they had previously found to be rich than for one that they experienced as poor in nectar quality (Ewald, 1985). Also, the probability of intrusion is greater when the territory contains a rich resource; as the nectar yield improves, more hummingbirds intrude on the territory (Marchesseault & Ewald, 1991).

Once an animal has established a territory, it will generally fight more energetically to defend it—especially in the center, or core area—than the intruding animal will fight to expel the resident. This differential in fighting energy may be related, to a certain extent, to familiarity with the area; but it also makes sense in terms of game theory. The territorial strategy of fighting when in one's own territory but leaving when threatened in another animal's territory becomes evolutionarily stable in a population when matched up against other strategies. A strategy of fight-no-matter-what is unstable, because it will have less fitness payoff than the territorial strategy. That is, the fight-no-matter-what strategist will, on average, lose half the fights and sustain injury or, at the very least, considerable loss of time and energy. A leave-always strategy will never result in territorial acquisition, so it will also be inferior to the territorial strat-egy and, consequently, unstable (Maynard Smith, 1982).

Territories tend to remain stable over relatively long periods of time. This stability is reflected by the fact that once adjacent territories are established, there tend to be fewer hostile exchanges between residents. White-cheeked honeyeater males, for instance, are much less likely to attack nearby resident male birds than to take on strange males that come close to their nests (Armstrong, 1991).

Many territorial bird residents recognize the calls of neighbors. With mynah birds, the experimental broadcast of recordings of calls of strangers evokes more aggression than recordings of calls of neighbors. Over time, there is another effect that reduces aggressiveness between neighbors: The calls of neighbors within a region become more similar (Bertram, 1970). As I mentioned in Chapter 3, this trend toward similarity produces dialects, or geographic variations, in certain bird calls.

PEACEMAKING

We have just seen how dominance hierarchies and territorial systems serve to limit the expression of aggression. However, aggressive encounters may still exact significant tolls, especially in animals such as ground-dwelling primates, which fight for many reasons besides resource acquisition.

Despite their strong tendency to aggress in a destructive manner, recent evidence indicates that chimpanzees and bonobos often engage in highly effective peacemaking gestures following the expression of aggression. Much of the discussion that follows is based on work by Frans DeWaal (1989) and his associates, who analyzed peacemaking through extensive observations of chimpanzees in the colony at the Arnhem Zoo in the Netherlands and of bonobos in the colony at the San Diego Zoo in California.

We must remember that observations of behaviors that occur in seminatural conditions are not always representative of behaviors in the wild. However, the similarity of DeWaal's observations to the somewhat limited ones of scientists who have investigated free-ranging chimpanzees and bonobos indicates that certain generalizations to free-ranging animals seem justified. And the great advantage of observations made in a seminatural state is that data may be amassed continuously, a condition that is particularly important for an analysis of peacemaking behavior.

Reconciliation

In the Dutch colony of chimpanzees, a male named Nikkie was observed slapping a female named Hennie on her back during an aggressive display. Fifteen minutes later, Nikkie slowly approached a group that included Hennie and another female named Mama. Hennie then reached out to Nikkie, offering him the back of her hand. Nikkie responded by kissing her hand, and this gesture was followed by a mouth-to-mouth kiss. After Nikkie left, Hennie walked over to Mama with a grin—which, in chimpanzees, seems to indicate nervousness. Mama responded by placing a hand on Hennie's shoulder and gently patting her, and the signs of nervousness disappeared.

This anecdote captures several elements typical of chimpanzee peacemaking. More than 40 percent of aggressive encounters in the colony involved reconciliations within a half hour. The reconciliation is usually delayed for a short time following the aggressive incident and often involves reaching out with a hand and kissing. It is also quite common for an ally of one of the chimpanzees—often an older individual or one with higher status—to exhibit behaviors that resemble consolation, usually in the form of a hug or gentle pat. Before reconciliation takes place, the two chimpanzees that were involved in an aggressive encounter establish eye contact. If one chimpanzee looks away while the other is focusing on its eyes, it is unlikely that reconciliation will take place, at least in the immediate future.

While physical gestures and eye contact are basic to reconciliation in chimpanzees, among baboons vocal gestures are important both for reconciliation and for facilitating other interactions. When a dominant female baboon grunts while approaching other females, she is more likely to have friendly interactions than when she approaches silently. Furthermore, grunts reconcile opponents after an aggressive interchange. Even in the absence of other friendly gestures, grunts have a reconciling influence (Cheney et al., 1995).

Do reconciliations have an effect on future aggression? It seems that they do. Conflicts are significantly less likely to occur between two individual chimpanzees that have reconciled after a conflict than between individuals that have not.

In most circumstances, the dominant and the subordinate chimpanzee in an encounter are equally likely to initiate a reconciliation.

But after severe fights (which are rare), the dominant animal is unlikely to initiate or participate in a reconciliation. Such fights are most likely to occur when there is a power struggle over status, and especially when the position of the alpha male is at stake. The power struggle does not end until one of the males makes submissive gestures to the other.

As we have seen, tension resulting from aggression often spreads throughout a group of chimpanzees. Conversely, when a power struggle has been settled, there is more hugging and grooming in the group in general. In the Dutch chimpanzee colony, at the moment of the apparent resolution of the power struggle between two males named Luit and Yeroen, several of the other chimpanzees went up to the former adversaries and hugged both of them (DeWaal, 1989).

Incompatible Responses and Mediation

Other factors, in addition to reconciliation, also seem to reduce conflicts and aggression in chimpanzees and bonobos. For example, responses that are incompatible with aggression—such as eating or sex—may facilitate peacemaking. When chimpanzees began to eat in the Dutch colony, there was a general reduction of aggression. In the bonobos, individuals were especially likely to have sexual contact after aggressive outbreaks, as illustrated when a young female named Leslie tried to push past a young male named Kako on the branch of a tree. Kako did not move, and tension built up—until Leslie rubbed her

vulva against Kako's shoulder, and the two animals seemed to relax. Such apparent substitutions of sex for aggression were quite common in the San Diego bonobo colony as well as in bonobos studied in the wild (Kano, 1992).

In some cases third parties seem to act as mediators following periods of aggression. When two male bonobos have fought but have not made peace for a period of time, it is not unusual for a female to walk up to one of the males, touch him, and then walk over to the second male with the first one following. The female may then sit down next to the second male, and both she and the first male may groom him. Mediation occurs among chimpanzees, too; and certain individuals, such as the female named Mama, are especially likely to serve as mediators.

TABLE 13.2 ◆ Factors Related to Peacemaking in Chimpanzees and Bonobos

Peacemaking Behaviors	Examples
Reconciliation	Eye contact; kissing; hand on shoulder; hugging
Incompatible responses	Eating; sex
Mediation	Intervention by a third individual that may initiate touching and grooming involving former combatants

◆ HUMAN EVOLUTION

Although there are obvious differences between humans and nonhuman animals in the expression of aggression, ways of limiting aggression, and peacemaking, there are also many important similarities. An analysis of these similarities can provide valuable insight into the roots of human aggression, and may suggest some ways of limiting destructive aggression.

THE EXPRESSION OF AGGRESSION

There is some controversy about the question of where humans stand relative to other animals in the amount of destructive intraspecies aggression expressed. We sometimes accuse ourselves of being the most violent of all animals. However, as E. O. Wilson (1975) states, we observe or are aware of many more human interactions than any other intraspecific interactions. Consequently, we may overestimate the relative violence of humans. Nonetheless, most of us would agree that we need to find new and better ways to reduce our violence—violence that results not only in the needless deaths of humans but in the deaths of countless other animals as well.

As with nonhuman animals, access to resources is closely related to human aggression. Property considerations that result in theft and disputes of various kinds are a major cause of physical violence. Unromantic though it may be, if we include access to mates as a category of resource aquisition, the relationship between resources and aggression is even stronger. In addition, conflicts from gang rivalries to major wars are often precipitated by disputes over territories and the resources they contain.

Among humans as among nonhuman ground-dwelling primates, other factors also contribute to aggression: Factors such as intervention into the affairs of others, fear of the unfamiliar, and the spread of aggression by contagion (in riots, for instance) are well known to humans. Furthermore, some human aggression, such as serial killing, appears to be senseless or aberrant.

Certain technological advances may function to increase human aggressiveness. For example, television, motion pictures, and computer games present violence unrealistically and in large amounts. Numerous studies have demonstrated that exposure to media violence facilitates the expression of aggression in both children and adults, and that this facilitation is especially great among individuals who have exhibited high levels of aggression before viewing the violent material (Liebert et al., 1989). Even aggression in cartoons may contribute to aggression.

Technological advances can also exacerbate the effects of destructive aggression. Modern weaponry may kill people before they have a chance to make submissive gestures and before aggressors have time to develop second thoughts about their actions. In addition to these direct consequences, modern weaponry can enhance aggression in very subtle ways. In a classic experiment, Berkowitz and LePage (1967) found that the mere presence of a gun in the room where subjects were being tested resulted in subjects' setting unusually high levels of shocks to be given (supposedly) to other subjects. Apparently the subjects were cued to be unusually aggressive by the presence of the gun, even though they had been told that the gun was being used in another experiment and simply happened to be present.

DOMINANCE HIERARCHIES AND TERRITORIAL ORGANIZATIONS

As in the case of many nonhuman animals that are highly competitive, human dominance hierarchies function to limit destructive aggression. In U.S. business organizations, for example, there is typically a well-defined social hierarchy. Not only do high-status persons in the organization have power over lower-status persons; they also have symbols of rank such as oriental rugs on the floors of their offices and special perks such as access to private jets. Communication is also different going from higher- to lower-status persons than vice versa. Low-status people have restricted access to high-status ones, but high-status people can communicate with low-status people at almost any time. Failure to follow the hierarchical structure often provokes aggression.

Territoriality is also well represented in human societies. When people are asked to report their feelings in various types of territories, they generally indicate feeling more confident in their own domain than in that of someone else. For example, nursing home residents report the highest level of comfort in nursing homes that have private areas consistent with the formation of territories (Duffy et al., 1986). As is the case with social hierarchies, violations of a territory are often met with aggression.

Why are dominance hierarchies and territorial systems such an integral part of human societies? As among nonhuman animals, the strategies behind the development of these systems are evolutionarily stable. In other words, there are no consistently better long-term strategies for dealing with competition than playing by the simple rules of social hierarchies and territorial organizations.

PEACEMAKING

Fortunately, humans, like other animals, have the ability to make peace after aggressive encounters. Some of the more effective peacemaking techniques utilized by humans are similar to those used by nonhuman primates. For example, physical contacts involving kisses, hugs, or handshakes are common symbols of resolution after conflicts. Although it may be unflattering to humans to look at it this way, verbal expressions such as "excuse me" or "I'm sorry" have effects similar to those of the grunts of baboons. When apologies are used as a social strategy, research indicates that the apologies have strong positive effects on human conflict resolution (Weiner et al., 1987).

Mediators can also help to reduce aggression, not only among chimpanzees but in human disputes. Human mediators can enable the conflicting parties to save face and may reduce the possibility of escalating conflicts. Interestingly, the best mediators among chimpanzees appear to be female. This finding raises some interesting questions; should human disputants turn more often to women as conflict mediators?

The development of therapeutic techniques provides further hope for successful conflict resolution. Cognitive therapies that decrease people's tendency to attribute other people's behavior to hostile intentions have been found to reduce angry responses. For example, a simple exercise that encourages people to identify possible alternative causes for others' anger-producing behavior may produce positive results in a relatively short time (Seligman, 1989).

Another therapeutic strategy that has yielded promising results is to encourage people to engage in positive activities that generate feelings incompatible with aggression—especially before these individuals encounter situations that have triggered destructive conflict in the past. Feelings found to be especially effective in combating aggressive tendencies are empathy and, as we saw in the Chapter 12, humor (Baron & Richardson, 1994).

There is also a trend in government systems that provides some cause for optimism. In recent decades there has been a slow but steady increase in the number of democratic national governments, particularly among economically powerful nations. Democratic governments show less of a tendency to initiate armed conflict than totalitarian governments. In fact, there has never been a war between two democratic nations! This fact may be at least partly explained in terms of the distribution of costs. In a totalitarian nation the leader does not have to pay a high price for an unpopular war; the leader can retain power by coercion. In a democratic nation, however, the leadership must sooner or later answer to the electorate. Consequently, democratic leaders tend to be more conscious of the great humanitarian cost of war.

◆ CHANGING PERSPECTIVES

PAST	PRESENT	FUTURE
Aggression is innate in nonhuman animals. Debate exists as to whether aggression is innate or learned in humans (early twentieth century).	Like other behavior patterns, both human aggression and that of many nonhuman animals develops as a result of an interaction between genetic predispositions and experiential factors. Intraspecies aggression is typically limited by dominance hierarchies and territorial systems. In some primates, reconciliation and mediation function as peacemaking strategies.	How does the interaction between genetic predispositions and experiential factors take place? Can humans learn some methods of reducing destructive aggression by studying competition, aggression, and peacemaking in nonhumans?

SUMMARY

Disputes over limited resources are a primary cause of intraspecies aggression. Ground-dwelling primates, however, fight for a variety of additional reasons.

Whether an animal chooses to fight a rival or to back down depends on the value of the disputed resource, the abundance of the resource, and the status of the animal. Most fights between conspecifics are stylized and do not involve lethal attacks.

Game theory predicts that if a strategy of fighting or not fighting is strongly influenced by genetic factors, a stable polymorphism will be reached between "hawks" and "doves." In many cases animals develop a conditional strategy—to fight only when there is a reasonably good chance of winning—which is also evolutionarily stable.

Although there are exceptions, males are generally more aggressive in competitive situations than females. This relatively great male aggressiveness is related to sexual selection for aggression, especially in polygynous males.

Ground-dwelling primates show high levels of intraspecies aggression, and not just in conflicts over resources. Other motivations for aggression in primates may include revenge, interference in others' affairs, fear of the unfamiliar, group contagion, or apparently senseless aberrant motives.

Dominance hierarchies and territorial systems function to limit the expression of aggression between conspecifics. Dominance hierarchies are formed out of dominance–submission relationships. The animals highest in the hierarchy gain the greatest fitness because of access to resources and lower levels of stress. Among factors related to dominance are size, gender, level of aggressiveness, and (in monkeys) recognition of kinship ties.

Territorial systems, like dominance hierarchies, are built on dominance relationships. A territorial animal establishes dominance in a particular area and then defends the area against intruders. The size of a territory and the vigor with which the animal defends it depend on several factors, including the extent of the animal's resource requirements, the animal's ability to patrol the area, what types of resources need to be protected, the distribution of the resources, and how much energy it takes to protect the territory.

Ground-dwelling primates such as chimpanzees and bonobos have developed highly effective peacemaking gestures. In some cases third parties act as mediators in aggressive disputes.

Human aggressive tendencies are rooted in many of the same factors as nonhuman animals' aggression. Human violence is exacerbated by technological advances such as the promulgation of aggressive models in the media and the development of weaponry. Dominance hierarchies and territoriality help avert human violence. Peacemaking is facilitated by reconciliation gestures, the use of mediators, therapeutic techniques, and democratic procedures.

KEY TERMS

CHAPTER 14

REPRESENTATIVE SOCIAL GROUPS

- ◆ *Why does only the queen honeybee reproduce?*
- ◆ *Why do only the infertile females work for the colony?*
- ◆ *How do worker bees communicate?*

14

W̳e have considered several basic aspects of social behavior, including cooperation, altruism, communication, and aggression. However, we have not yet taken a comprehensive view of how animals interact in complex societies. In an attempt to get a better overview of specific animal societies, let's now look in some detail at several representative animal groups.

Because humans are highly social, and because there has been a traditional tendency to conceptualize humans as very different from nonhuman animals, we often fail to appreciate the high degree of complexity in nonhuman social organizations. However, as we saw in Chapters 12 and 13 and will see once again in this chapter, many nonhuman social organizations surpass human societies in terms of the elaborate cooperation among members.

It appears that sociality evolved independently in a large variety of animals. However, many of the principles that have influenced the evolution of social behavior in these diverse groups of animals are similar. We will begin with invertebrates and then consider three classes of vertebrates—fish, birds, and mammals—and finally humans. Whenever possible, we will focus on how ecological demands on the animals and the animals' prior adaptations interact in the evolution of sociality.

INVERTEBRATES

Several different types of invertebrates have evolved social systems that are highly developed in terms of the degree of cooperation and mutual dependency they represent.

Colonial Invertebrates

Colonial invertebrates are invertebrate species in which individuals are physically joined together and/or are divided into distinct **castes**—classes or forms with specialized roles. (By convention, social invertebrates that have caste systems but are *not* physically joined together, such as ants and bees, are not referred to as "colonial" species.) At the highest level of colonial organization, both physical union and a caste system exist. The physical union may be so complete that it is difficult or impossible to tell one individual from another. Within the caste system, there is typically one caste that is reproductive and another caste or castes that perform nonreproductive functions.

Very important preadaptions for social behavior in colonial invertebrates are related to asexual reproduction and structural simplicity. Colonial coelenterates (radially symmetrical invertebrates) such as Portuguese man-of-war and coral consist of aggregations of individuals that are genetic duplicates or clones of one another. Because clones share 100 percent of their genes, giving up reproduction to become a sterile individual is beneficial if this sacrifice promotes the reproduction of a sister. The asexual reproduction in these colonial coelenterates allows for extremely rapid rates of reproduction. The structural simplicity of coelenterates is also a preadaptation for a colonial existence. It is easier for small, simple animals than for large, intricate ones to evolve structural linkage with one another. These preadaptations enable colonial coelenterates to develop cohesiveness, cooperation, and altruism to a greater degree than any other group of animals.

FIGURE 14.1 ◆ The Portuguese man-of-war, a colonial invertebrate.

The Portuguese Man-of-War

The Portuguese man-of-war resembles a jellyfish. However, this giant coelenterate is made up of individual asexually reproduced animals called zooids that are specialized for different functions; some feed, others reproduce, and still others make up the float. The zooids of the Portuguese man-of-war are so well integrated that the colony functions as a superorganism. A major advantage of this social system is that the colony may grow relatively large—man-of-war tentacles may reach a length of several yards—and can survive successfully in the open ocean (Phillips, 1973; see Figure 14.1).

Coral

Colonial organization is dramatically illustrated by corals, many of which build a calcareous base that supports an extensive colony. There are two types of zooids in these animals: Some are specialized for reproduction and the creation of water currents, while others eat, digest, and distribute food to the rest of the colony. One of the important advantages of this type of colony is that the calcareous skeletons anchor the colony and guard it against sedimentation. The skeletons also provide protection against predators (Coates & Oliver, 1973).

Reefs built by coral not only benefit the coral animals themselves but are basic to an extensive community that includes a great variety of marine organisms. For example, the area around a single isolated tropical reef may contain many different fish species as well as numerous invertebrates. By extrapolation, one can imagine the effect of the Great Barrier Reef off the eastern coast of Australia on oceanic life in that area. This reef—which includes a large number of separate reefs—covers a distance of more than 2,000 kilometers, or about 1,200 miles.

Communal Spiders

Although most species of spiders are solitary, some species of *Metepeira* and other small web-building spiders live in communities that include as many as a thousand individuals. The communal species cooperate in building a web and share in capturing and feeding on prey. This communal behavior offers several advantages: Individuals crowded into web chambers inside the web are protected from predators and extremes of temperature; the individuals in a communal web invest less energy searching for a mate and protecting a territory than solitary individuals; and there is less variability in food availability than when individuals forage on their own.

A major disadvantage of communal living, however, is that competition over prey items and intolerance of other group members may lead to disruptive aggression. The competition is most intense when prey is scarce. Consequently, spiders are much more likely to be colonial in habitats where there is an abundance of prey. Most probably, an abundance of prey was an important preadaptation for the evolution of communal living in spiders.

Eusocial Insects

The **eusocial** insects include termites, ants, some species of wasps, and some species of bees. *Eusocial* means "truly social," and eusociality is characterized by three sets of behaviors: cooperation in the care of the young, support of fertile individuals by nonfertile nest mates, and the presence of two or more generations of individuals cooperating and living together. These behaviors constitute the most complex type of social behavior found among invertebrates.

All of the eusocial insects except termites are members of the order Hymenoptera, which is characterized by haplodiploidy (refer to Chapter 2). Haplodiploidy is a strong preadaptation for social behavior, because there are important fitness benefits associated with cooperation, especially cooperation in reproduction. Since daughters share 75 percent of their genes, on average, there is a relatively great inclusive fitness benefit for a haplodiploid insect female to assist with the reproductive output of a sister, even if it involves giving up her own reproduction (Trivers & Hare, 1976).

Ants

In some respects ants are the dominant form of insect on the planet. They are found on all land masses except the polar regions and are probably the most numerous of all insects. It has been estimated that one colony of driver ants in Africa may contain as many as 22 million workers. One factor in the relative success of ants seems to be related to their ability to nest in soil and exploit energy-rich microhabitats. Another factor is ants' ability to generate a large variety of behaviors within a colony even though there is no single leader that directs or coordinates the activities (Gordon, 1995). (We will consider an extremely important coordinating mechanism that is sensitive to changing environmental conditions when we discuss pheromones in Chapter 17.)

There are three castes of ants: queens, males, and infertile females that function as workers. In ants such as the army ant, the worker caste is further divided into three types with specialized roles: Large workers or soldiers are the defenders of the colony, intermediate-sized workers function as food gatherers, and small workers serve as attendants of the queen and her offspring.

There is also a division of labor among workers in the ant *Leptothorax unifasciatus.* By painstakingly marking individual workers and observing their behavior, researchers found that each worker tended to perform nest duties in a specific area of the nest (Sendova-Franks & Franks, 1995).

All ant workers are wingless. However, the queen and the males grow wings just before the nuptial flight. After the flight, the males die, but the queen pulls off her wings and typically returns to the nest.

Communication regarding food is very efficient in many species of ants. Workers lay down a chemical trail after locating a food source; when other workers follow the trail and locate the food, they reinforce the chemical pathway as they return to the nest. As a result, rich food sources are eventually indicated by strongly marked trails, while depleted sources are abandoned as the chemical trail fades. In some cases the chemical cues are three-dimensional. For example, fire ants lay their chemical trail by releasing a rapidly evaporating substance from a gland located near the tip of their extended stinger, creating a "vapor tunnel" as they move along the ground (Wilson, 1963).

Honeybees

Bees, like ants, are haplodiploid; not all bees are social, however. This fact suggests that haplodiploidy may be a preadaptation for sociality under appropriate ecological conditions, but not under other conditions.

Among bees, honeybees have the most complex social system. A honeybee queen performs no function other than a reproductive one. Honeybee drones (males), like those of all eusocial hymenoptera, are produced only at certain times during the year, and their sole function is to attempt to mate with a queen. The sterile female workers are by far the most numerous of the three castes; they perform all of the nest or hive maintenance functions.

Although the workers occasionally lay sterile eggs, their eggs are generally eaten by other workers. Such egg consumption reflects a subtle fitness-related strategy on the part of the workers. Each worker is related to a greater extent to the queen than to other workers, so destroying workers' eggs supports the queen's reproduction and provides relatively high levels of indirect fitness (Visscher & Dukas, 1995).

In contrast to ants, honeybee workers have specific duties that are age-dependent. For the first 3 weeks of their lives, they clean, feed larvae, construct the comb, and guard the hive. Then, at about 3 weeks of age, they begin to forage, a task that occupies the remaining 3 weeks of their lives (Lindauer, 1961). Much of the activity inside a honeybees' nest is directed toward caring for the larvae. The type of care given to the female larvae has a significant effect on their future development. Female larvae that are fed a normal diet develop into infertile workers; but the same larvae, if fed a protein-rich diet known as **royal jelly,** will develop into fertile queens.

The presence or absence of a pheromone produced by the queen determines the type of diet the workers feed the larvae. When the queen is alive and in good health, the queen pheromone is spread throughout the hive by trophallaxis (workers' exchanging food with each other) and physical contact. Under these conditions, the workers feed the larvae a normal diet (see Free, 1987). But when the queen dies or becomes ill and does not produce sufficient amounts of the queen pheromone, the workers are induced to feed some of the larvae royal jelly. These developing queens then remain in special cells until they are mature. If one new queen matures and emerges before any others, she kills the rest of the pretenders before they can escape from their cells. However, if two new potential queens emerge from their cells at about the same time, they fight to the death; the winner then becomes the reigning monarch. New queens may also be produced when the population of the hive becomes very large. In this case, however, the old queen leaves the hive with a large retinue before the new queens emerge.

Much of the success of honeybees in the temperate regions is related, as we have seen, to the workers' ability to translate directional information presented on a vertical surface (the honeycomb) into information about the location of a food source. Furthermore, unlike most pollen-gathering insects, honeybees have mechanisms that enable the entire colony to survive cold winters. The bees are able to warm their hive by generating and conserving heat from the metabolism of a large number of individuals. As many as 20,000 bees cluster tightly together, preventing the temperature in the hive from approaching the freezing point, even when the outdoor temperature reaches minus 28°C. Bees on the inside of the cluster generate most of the heat by moving restlessly, while bees on the outside serve primarily as an insulating cover. Because the whole colony survives the winter, the bees get a jump on their insect competitors in gathering nectar and pollen in the early spring.

Honeybees are also well adapted to survive the heat of the summer. Workers provide air-conditioning by carrying water into the nest, hanging droplets over the brood cells, and then fanning their wings. These behaviors distribute cool, moist air throughout the nest.

FISH

Social behavior occurs in all major classes of vertebrates and is fairly well developed in bony fishes. We have already seen several examples of territoriality and dominance hierarchies in fishes. Other forms of social behavior in fish include schooling behavior and cooperation in reproduction.

Schooling

Fish that are not territorial often form a school. A school is marked by **collective behavior**—moving in unison with an approximately equal space between individuals. In contrast to many other types of social groups, schools do not have a consistent leader; any individual may stimulate a change in the group's movement. Individuals in a school have an especially sensitive warning system to alert them to danger, because even a slight movement as the result of predator identification will be immediately communicated to other group members. A similar advantage occurs in regard to the identification of a food source.

Individuals in a school of fish are approximately the same size and are mutually attracted to each other. The advantage of joining a school that contains similar-sized fish is that no one individual stands out as different. Fish different in size are more likely to be noticed and taken by a predator (see Ranta et al., 1995).

Most of the time, each fish has a precise orientation to other members of the school, a condition known as polarization. For example, the school starts, stops, and turns in unison. At other times, especially when it is feeding, the school is depolarized in the sense that the individuals have a somewhat random orientation to each other.

The development of this attraction of fish to one another and the tendency to polarize take place gradually as the fish mature. For example, laboratory studies of the common silverside indicate that newly hatched fry dart off after coming close to each other. Older fry swim close to one another for a second or two,

but only if they happen to meet head to tail. But as the fry grow even older, they swim together for longer and longer periods of time, and more than two fish join in parallel swimming. Finally, as adults, the fish engage in parallel swimming and synchronous movement over long periods of time (Shaw, 1958).

I have mentioned how schooling facilitates feeding and defense against predators; another advantage of schooling may be related to hydrodynamic efficiency, particularly during migrations. Scientists have pointed out that the fish in a school are spaced in such a manner that individuals could get a boost from the water currents created by the fish in front of them. Although later studies raise doubt as to how much hydrodynamic advantage schools supply, there is evidence that migrating fish in schools increase the accuracy of their homing, perhaps by sharing information concerning migratory routes (Pitcher & Parrish, 1993). At any rate, migrating fish often do school and probably gain more than one advantage from this form of social behavior.

Schools break up at night, which suggests that visual cues are important in the spacing of the fish. Apparently the fish utilize an optomotor reaction; that is, they "stop" the movement of a stimulus on the retina of the eye by swimming at the same speed as the stimulus. The dark lateral stripes on the sides of many schooling fishes make it easy for each individual to fixate on the side of a neighbor and coordinate the responses necessary for polarized movement (Shaw, 1962).

Sensitivity to changes in water pressure created by the swimming movements of other fish also seems to be involved in schooling. This sensitivity allows the fish to adjust to quick changes in the velocity and heading of the school. Only when fish are both blinded and deprived of their lateral line organ (which functions to mediate sensitivity to changes in water pressure) are they completely unable to school (Partridge & Pitcher, 1980).

Cooperation in Reproduction

Cooperation in reproduction is another form of social behavior. Juveniles of several species of territorial cichlid fish stay in the sheltered nest area and help adults protect the nest. These juveniles seem to have a better chance of taking over a nest area when adults die than of winning a nest territory by aggression (Myles, 1988).

Some fish nest in colonies. For example, breeding male bluegill sunfish build individual nests in the sand on the bottom of a lake; but the nests are very close to one another, enabling the adult males to swim together to chase bullheads away from the nests that contain the bluegills' eggs.

In contrast, pumpkinseed sunfish, which are very closely related to bluegills, do not nest communally; individual pumpkinseed males have nests separated from one another. Why this difference in sociality? Pumpkinseed sunfish have strong mouthparts, which are related to the type of food they eat. These fish are able to defend their nests individually against predatory catfish. In contrast, bluegills feed on softer food and have weaker mouthparts. Because of the weakness of their mouthparts, the bluegills are not able to defend individually against catfish and so have developed a colonial nesting system that facilitates group cooperation (Gross & MacMillan, 1981). In essence, the type of food the bluegills eat—and

the corresponding evolution of soft mouthparts—preadapts these fish for the development of a social defense system.

BIRDS

Birds engage in several kinds of complex social interaction, including cooperation in reproduction, flocking, and cooperation in hunting.

Cooperation in Reproduction

Like bluegill sunfish, some species of birds are colonial nesters; for example, the nests of certain species of swallows are very close together on cliffs. Social nesting birds are more effective in identifying and mobbing predators than solitary nesters. On the negative side of the ledger, however, the density of parasites is greater in communal nests than in isolated nests, and the parasites have a debilitating effect on the nestlings.

The evolution of social nesting in swallows may be related to the tendency of individual birds to nest in sites occupied by others in the past. This tendency to be "traditional" is found in several other groups of animals as well, suggesting that strategies for choosing nest sites that prove to be successful are passed on from one generation to another (Shields et al., 1988).

Another type of cooperative social behavior related to reproduction is for some individual birds to help others rear their young. Florida scrub jays sometimes function as helpers in the nests of other birds, whether re-

FIGURE 14.2 ◆ **Three adult Florida scrub jays.** The two parents and a yearling bird work together to care for the young.

lated or not (see Figure 14.2). The nests of acorn woodpeckers may also include nonrelatives that function as helpers. The woodpecker helpers are found only in territories that include a large cache of acorns, and the reward for these helpers may be a cache of acorns that are left when the residents die or are killed.

Flocking

Many species of birds experience benefits from moving in flocks. Not only is an unpredictable food source easier to locate by a group than by individuals, but the group is often able to utilize resources more efficiently. For example, groups of gulls can fish more ef-

fectively than individuals. Similarly, seed-eating birds feeding on the ground may benefit from being in a group. Comparisons with computer simulations indicate that a flock of seed-eating birds, which pursues a straight course across a field, utilizes the resource with a higher level of efficiency than do birds that feed in isolation (Cody, 1971).

A flock also produces defensive benefits. When one member of a flock of birds suddenly takes off, possibly as the result of spotting a predator, other birds follow suit.

Like a school of fish, a flock of birds in flight often exhibits collective behavior. Not only do the birds move together with approximately equal spacing, but they flap their wings in synchrony. Through this synchrony the flock can easily communicate information about migratory routes and can also gain some aerodynamic advantage by flying in formation.

Cooperation in Hunting

In some circumstances, predatory birds cooperate in the hunting of prey. For example, a juvenile and an adult golden eagle were observed attacking a fox in team fashion. The juvenile dive-bombed the fox from behind, making loud cries that attracted the fox's attention. As the fox turned to jump at the juvenile, the adult eagle dove at the fox and knocked it down. Finally, after repeated attacks and fierce struggles, the two eagles killed the fox and shared in the eating of the carcass.

Pairs of eagles may also cooperate in attacking monkeys in treetops. One eagle functions as a decoy, while a second attacks the distracted monkey. Examples of cooperative hunting, though rare, suggest that avian group cooperation tends to develop in situations where individual hunting strategies are unsuccessful or less than half as successful as group ventures (Ellis et al., 1993).

MAMMALS

At the species level, sociality among mammals is most common in the large species, probably because it is the larger mammals that forage in open areas. These open-area foragers are more vulnerable to predation than nocturnal or burrowing mammals and can benefit from the possibility of group defenses.

Not all large mammals become social, however. Among animals that are extremely sexually dimorphic, such as orangutans, the two genders have different dietary requirements and different methods of foraging. Consequently, it is unlikely that they could successfully forage together.

When sociality does evolve in mammals, a key factor is milk. Because mammalian young are dependent on their mother's milk during their early development, the nursing relationship may become highly interactive and form the basis for extended bonding. Consequently, it is relatively easy for the bonding that occurs during nursing to continue beyond weaning.

Sociality has evolved independently in various different types of mammals. Therefore, we will look separately at several representative groups of mammals.

Rodents

Sociality is rare in rodents but well developed in prarie dogs and naked mole-rats.

Prairie Dogs

Black-tail prairie dogs, which inhabit open areas of the Black Hills of South Dakota, live in prairie dog towns that may contain as many as 1,000 individuals. Towns are subdivided by physical factors—such as ridges or streams—into wards. Each ward, in turn, is divided into basic social units called coteries. A coterie is made up of several adults and their offspring; the size of the group varies, but usually numbers less than 25. Members of a coterie share

◆ UNUSUAL ADAPTATIONS

Eusociality in Naked Mole-Rats

Eusociality was once believed to be restricted to insects. In 1981, however, J. U. M. Jarvis announced the discovery of a social system paralleling that of eusocial insects in a little-known rodent known as the naked mole-rat. These burrowing rodents live in a network of underground tunnels with a central "nest." Each colony of mole-rats has one relatively large breeding female (a queen) and several breeding males (kings). There are also overlapping generations of offspring that do not reproduce. Smaller individuals function as workers (Jarvis, 1981). Since this initial discovery, other species of eusocial mole-rats have been identified; some of these species appear also to have a few individuals specialized as soldiers (Lovegrove & Wissel, 1988).

Interest quickly developed concerning how such an unusual system might have evolved in mammals. Ecological factors seem to be relevant. The mole-rats live in a semiarid environment in East Africa and feed on underground bulbs and tubers. Because the probability of finding these foods in a nearby location under these arid conditions is very low, the usual rodent pattern of dispersal to avoid inbreeding and overcrowding would not be effective. It would be more advantageous to remain in the same locale, inbreed, and (for the nonreproductive caste) gain fitness by indirect selection. Thus, arid conditions and limited distribution of food seem to be strong factors in the evolution of eusociality in mole-rats (Lovegrove & Wissel, 1988).

Although naked mole-rats engage in a high degree of cooperation, research indicates that they do compete for food in certain cases and, as a result of this competition, form social hierarchies (Schieffelin & Sherman, 1995). Thus, the eusocial system of these animals differs significantly from that of eusocial insects, which do not form social hierarchies.

---

burrows, recognize each other as individuals, and spend much time grooming one another and feeding together. Each coterie has its own system of tunnels, and the adults defend a small area at the entrance.

If a prairie dog sights a predator, it gives an alarm call, and this call quickly spreads from burrow to burrow. Individual prairie dogs respond to these alarm calls by retreating to their burrows. Different alarm calls are given for different types of predators. Research indicates that prairie dogs are able to encode surprisingly specific types of information in their calls. Gunnison's prairie dogs, in the southwestern United States, differentiate among humans that vary in size, shape, and color of clothes (Slobodchikoff et al., 1991). Apparently these prairie dogs have become exceptionally sensitive to humans—who have been hunting them for at least 150 years.

Ungulates

Large ungulates that live in open areas are the most highly social. In some species, such as wildebeests and elephants, the adults are large enough to protect themselves; however, a group of adults is necessary to defend the young against predation. Thus, as in many other groups of animals, threat of predation is a driving force in the evolution of sociality among ungulates.

Wildebeests

The blue wildebeest is the most common antelope on the African plains. When grazing, the wildebeest females live in herds with the young, while adult males live in bachelor herds. The males establish territories during the mating season, but these territories function only for courtship and mating.

As we shall see in Chapter 19, wildebeests engage in extensive migrations across the plains of Africa. When the population is on the move, there is no expression of territorial behavior. In fact, a tendency for individual animals to travel close together in single file is basic to the success of their migrations. The wildebeests also leave a very strong scent along the trail so that individuals who become separated from the group can easily find the group again (Estes, 1974).

African Elephants

African elephant social groups are strongly matriarchal. As in the case of the prairie dog, there is a hierarchy of social units. The smallest unit is known as the **family** and consists of 10 to 20 females and their young offspring. The oldest female, known as the matriarch, is usually the leader of the family group. Because elephants continue to grow throughout their lives, the oldest female is also the largest.

In contrast to wildebeest groups, which are relatively temporary, elephant family groups are extremely stable and are likely to include both daughters and granddaughters of the matriarch. The matriarch leads the other members of the family group and takes the forward position when danger threatens.

The second level of social organization in the hierarchy is the **kinship group.** Kinship groups consist of family groups that remain fairly close to one another and include relatives that split off when the family group becomes too large.

When migrating, elephants generally form still another level of social organization known as a **clan,** which may contain as many as 250 elephants. However, the clan is not well organized above the level of the kinship group.

Adolescent male elephants are driven from the family group and thereafter live alone or in loose bands with other males. Even when they are in groups, the males are much less social than females (Douglas-Hamilton, 1973).

African elephants communicate graded levels of aggressiveness and defensive behavior with their head, trunk, and ears (Brown, 1975). Growls, trumpeting, shrieks, and whistles also function in communication. These sounds, the meanings of which are dependent on intensity and context, function to maintain contact among members of the family unit and to express various types of intraspecific aggressiveness. There is also some chemical communication between elephants. Picking up olfactory cues from the ground with the tips of their trunks, individuals that become separated from the family unit are able to follow trails as much as 2 hours old (Douglas-Hamilton, 1973).

For many years elephant populations in Africa have been in decline, largely because of killing by humans. The ivory from the tusks is valuable and until recently was easy to sell. In recent years, however, there has been a crackdown on poaching and an attempt to disrupt the ivory market. Much of the improved outlook for elephant survival is related to a worldwide interest in these animals and their behavior, promoted by television specials and popular books describing the elephants' social system. Thus, research findings on elephant social relationships have had a significant impact on elephant conservation.

Carnivores

In contrast to ungulates, whose sociality is generally related to defensive functions, carnivores benefit from living in social groups because groups may be more efficient hunters than individual animals. As I have mentioned before, grouped carnivores such as lions and wolves may be able to take large prey that are inaccessible to solitary hunters. The grouped hunters are also able to protect their kills from scavengers more effectively than individuals.

Lions

Lions are the most social species of the cat family, living in prides of approximately 15 individuals; a pride consists of two or three adult males and several adult females with their offspring. Female lions show a high degree of cooperation in their hunting behavior. They also cooperate in the rearing of the young, sometimes nursing one another's cubs and taking turns caring for a group of cubs while other females are hunting.

In contrast to the arrangement in many social groups, among lions it is the females that defend the pride's territory. Experiments with recordings of intruders coupled with the presentation of stuffed lion models indicate that the females are sensitive to the number of intruders, approaching the loudspeaker most rapidly when there is a favorable ratio of residents to apparent intruders (Grinnell et al., 1995). Some females, described as "laggards," are slow to join the attack and participate only when they seem to be needed (Heinsohn & Packer, 1995).

The females of the pride lead the group from place to place and do most of the hunting. When a kill has been made, however, the males usually eat first, followed by the females and the young. Nonetheless, some females may join together and force a male to back off from the kill. The males expend most of their energy protecting the group from other lions, especially males that try to take over the pride (Schaller, 1972). Consequently, the males' primary contribution to the survival of the pride is protection.

Wolves

Wolves are among the most efficient social hunters. Hunting in packs, wolves are able to subdue animals larger than themselves. There are two behavioral traits that have preadapted animals of the dog family, such as wolves, to develop pack behavior. First, they hunt in open areas and pursue their prey, a strategy conducive to the development of cooperation. Second, they form a special type of pair bond in which the male brings food to both the young and the mother (Wilson, 1975).

Packs of wolves usually contain 5 to 15 members. A new pack is formed when a pack becomes too large and a mated pair leave and produce a litter of their own. As the puppies grow, two dominance hierarchies are established, one for the males and the other for the females. The father is the alpha male and the mother, the most dominant female. The alpha male is the leader of the pack during hunting pursuits and is the center of attention for the other wolves at most times. On some occasions the whole pack gathers around the alpha male, nuzzling him and making submissive gestures (Mech, 1970).

The dominant female mates with the alpha male and suppresses sexual activity in the other females of the pack. Even though the other females ovulate, they will not breed. As a result of this suppression, the dominant male and female are monogamous and are the only wolves in the pack to reproduce. The fact that only one pair in the pack reproduces is apparently important in the mobility of the pack. If many females were breeding, the pack's mobility would be limited, and the group would not be able to cover the huge home range they need to pursue large prey.

Territories tend to be temporary, because wolves move such great distances within their home range. Their olfactory marks, left by urine, fade within a day or two if not reinforced, and territories are relinquished as the wolves leave the area. Consequently, the home ranges of two packs of wolves may overlap without the groups' coming into contact with each other.

The evidence is strong that domestic dogs evolved from wolves. For anyone who has ever had a dog as a pet, some of the behaviors just described may seem familiar. Essentially, if a dog has been raised from a puppy by its owner, many of its actions toward the owner resemble the responses wolves direct toward the alpha male.

Cetaceans

Large, predatory cetaceans (whales and dolphins) are extremely difficult to observe in the ocean, because they typically avoid humans. Sperm whales, for example, may dive to depths of several hundred meters when approached. However, it has been possible for scientists to observe two smaller species of cetaceans, killer whales and bottle-nosed dolphins, for long enough periods of time to assess certain characteristics of their social behavior.

Killer Whales

Killer whales have been seen using a variety of cooperative feeding strategies. By coordinating their swimming, a group of seven killer whales in the Antarctic created waves that washed a crabeater seal off an ice floe. Near Vancouver Island, British Columbia, a pod of killer whales surrounded a group of sea lions, and different members of the pod took turns attacking the prey. Similar observations were made off the coast of Argentina, and from this sighting it was clear that the killer whales not only cooperated in their hunting but shared food after the killing (see Hoelzel, 1991).

Bottle-Nosed Dolphins

We have more information about bottle-nosed dolphins than about other species of dolphins, because bottle-nosed dolphins are easier than others to observe in the wild. Extended, detailed observations of bottle-nosed dolphins have been possible as the result of an unusual situation that developed in Western Australia. A large number of dolphins became exceptionally tame in a bay near a campground where the dolphins were fed by tourists. Since 1984, more than 300 individuals have been identified and the social relationships of many of the males studied. (It is possible to identify individual dolphins on the basis of scar patterns and the general shape of the dorsal fin.) The dolphins are easy to observe over extended periods of time from small boats, and in many cases the dolphins come up to humans and eat from their hands (Connor et al., 1992).

The Western Australian observations indicate a highly unusual type of social behavior among dolphins. Males in small groups "herd" females or attempt to control their movements. The males form groups of two or three and try to force females to join their group. Since females do not come into estrus very often, it may be to a male's fitness benefit to be in association with a female and thereby increase the probability that he can copulate with her at the appropriate time. There are even situations where two small groups of males will form a temporary alliance against a third group and attempt to steal their females. Some of the acrobatic behaviors that are often seen in captive dolphin shows—synchronized leaping, somersaulting, and belly flopping—are, in the natural state, apparent attempts to intimidate the female. If a female is not intimidated and tries to escape, males will chase after her, slam into her with their bodies, or bite (Connor et al., 1992).

Like fish, cetaceans often travel in schools, not only showing collective behavior in their movements through the water, but also surfacing to breathe in synchrony. Most cetacean schools are mixed, containing males, females, and the young. The adults typically surround the young, affording some protection from predators. Observations of dolphins in the open ocean and studies of dolphins in captivity indicate that as stress (such as the approach of a predator) increases, the school becomes more tightly packed. This reduction of the distance between group members probably facilitates the protection of weaker adults or young dolphins (Maier, 1968).

The schools of cetaceans vary greatly in size. In one case, people in a plane spotted a school of Black Sea dolphins that was estimated to contain 100,000 individuals. This large a group, however, appears to be exceptional and restricted to the breeding areas of fish on which the dolphins feed. When food is scarce, cetaceans typically break up into smaller groups (Slipjer, 1962).

As in the case of elephants, interest in cetacean behavior has grown in recent years. It is to be hoped that this interest, too, can be translated into increased efforts directed toward conservation.

Primates

Because the prime mover in the evolution of primate social behavior is the threat of predation, the most highly social primates are ones that spend at least some time on the ground. Primates that live entirely in the trees would not benefit as much from group defenses as ground-dwelling ones. Furthermore, arboreal primates cannot communicate as well visually as ground-dwelling ones because of the limits placed on visual cues by arboreal vegetation. Let's consider two representative ground-dwelling primates, the hamadryas baboon (a monkey) and the chimpanzee (an ape).

Hamadryas Baboons

Hamadryas baboons live in the semiarid region around the Red Sea and spend almost all of their waking hours on the ground. The adult males have large canine teeth and a mane of wavy gray hair, and are twice the size of adult females. As would be expected in view of this sexual dimorphism, hamadryas baboons are polygynous; they live in basic social units that consist of one male and two to five females with their offspring.

The social structure of hamadryas baboons is what has been described as a "feminist's nightmare" (DeWaal, 1989). The male controls the females' behavior with various forms of aggression, ranging from a hostile stare to a slap or a bite on the neck. Females are punished for such things as straying too far from the male, associating with strangers, or fighting with one another. Fights between females are most likely to break out over access to the male, especially over attempts to groom him.

When hamadryas baboons move from one area to another, they form a larger social group known as a band. The movement away from one area may be stimulated by a male who departs with his social unit. However, the whole band does not move until older males in the band begin to move out. Thus, there is a hierarchy of males, and the most dominant males control decisions about troop movement. Although there are numerous threats and bluffs in the interaction between males, there are very few fights. An encounter between two males usually ends when the subdominant male makes a submissive gesture—turning his head to expose his neck (Kummer, 1968, 1971).

Because harem masters have several females in their harem, there are always numerous males without female consorts. These bachelor males typically form a band of their own. One of the few times that the male band is integrated into the baboon society as a whole is near the end of the day, when several bands, both mixed and all male, come together to form a larger group near a huge rock on which the baboons sleep.

Chimpanzees

Chimpanzees, also highly social primates, are especially interesting because they are the closest living relatives of humans. For many years little was known about the behavior of chimpanzees in the wild, because it was very difficult for human observers to get close enough to watch the chimpanzees in their heavily forested habitats. However, Jane Goodall developed a technique in which she spent days or even weeks waiting quietly, barely moving, in the forest. Eventually the chimpanzees habituated to her and went on with their lives in what appeared to be a normal manner. Thereafter, the chimpanzees almost seemed to accept her as a member of the group (Goodall, 1965).

Observations by Goodall and her associates, as well as by other groups of scientists, indicate that chimpanzees usually live in groups that include several males and females along with their offspring. However, chimpanzee societies are more casual and flexible than those of other nonhuman ground-dwelling primates. Furthermore, chimpanzee groups frequently change in size and makeup. Much of this changeability is related to the fact that individual females move from one group to another and back again. In other primate groups, females typically stay with one group and the males leave.

Juvenile chimpanzees spend a great deal of time in play behavior, typically in same-gender groups. As we saw in Chapter 3, play appears to be important in the development of adult behavior patterns. There are some basic gender differences in the play of juvenile chimpanzees. The play of male juveniles consists to a great extent of rough-and-tumble be-havior; the play of females is less physical, and female juveniles spend more time observing newborn chimpanzees.

Although chimpanzees usually forage on fruit and other vegetable material, they occasionally hunt prey, especially juvenile baboons or colobus monkeys. When hunting, male chimpanzees often cooperate in the capture of the prey. For example, one adult male may recruit other male helpers by means of a series of silent stares and tense body postures. Several males may then chase or fight off adult male baboons that may be attempting to protect a young baboon. While hunting colobus monkeys, chimpanzees sometimes form hunting parties of 10 or more males (Teleki, 1973; Stanford, 1995).

In contrast to vegetable food, which is never passed from one adult to another, the meat from a hunt is almost always shared among chimpanzees. Sharing is often preceded by begging responses; for example, the would-be recipient may hold out the palm of a hand and make soft whimpering noises (Teleki, 1973). Recent research indicates that males may use meat as a resource with which to barter for sex with females or as a means to form a political alliance (Stanford, 1995).

The chimpanzees have a social hierarchy based, to a certain extent, on coalitions. One individual will serve as an ally and support another during confrontations. An effective coalition may be able to bring about the overthrow of the most dominant male. In a chimpanzee colony at a Dutch zoo, for example, a male named Yeroen had been the alpha male for 3 years. However, a coalition between two males called Luit and Nikkie was able to overthrow Yeroen, and Luit became the dominant male. Sitting at the top of the hierarchy, however, places a male in a vulnerable position. The overthrown leader, Yeroen, formed a new coalition with Nikkie and overthrew Luit a year later. Nikkie then dominated but continued to depend on Yeroen for support. In many cases, the rise or fall of a leader is also influenced by support from females (DeWaal, 1987).

There seem to be some basic gender differences in social relationships among chimpanzees. Males form alliances much more frequently than females. As a corollary to this tendency, males are more likely than females to form associations that are transactional.

Consequently, as the political winds shift, male associations or friendships tend to break up.

In contrast, female friendships tend to be based on kinship and what might be called personal preference. For example, at the Dutch zoo a bond between two female chimpanzees named Mama and Gorilla lasted for more than 20 years and transcended many political changes that disrupted male associations. As we have seen, females are also more likely than males to function as mediators in political disputes between males (DeWaal, 1987).

◆ HUMAN EVOLUTION

Several aspects of chimpanzee society bear a clear resemblance to human societies, especially the frequent formation of political coalitions, the differentiation of male and female social roles, and the strong need for social interaction. By analyzing some of the similarities between these aspects of chimpanzee and human societies we can gain some insight into the probable evolution of human social behavior and certain problems that exist in highly technological societies.

THE FORMATION OF POLITICAL COALITIONS

Frans DeWaal (1987) makes the point that the political coalitions of chimpanzees, based on a tit-for-tat strategy of reciprocity, are similar to political coalitions in many human societies. This similarity suggests a relatively early primate evolution of complex tit-for-tat strategies. That is, it seems probable that the ability to form complex political coalitions evolved in the ancestors of humans long before the evolution of language. With the development of language, it was possible to make the coalitions even more complex.

Political coalitions in humans can serve a positive function in overthrowing autocratic, single-interest political groups. However, political coalitions, like single-interest groups, may also discriminate against minorities and other groups that have relatively little power. Thus, like many mechanisms with long evolutionary histories, political coalitions can have either positive or negative social influence. In democratic systems of government, it is important that all viewpoints be considered. Therefore, an effective democratic system requires good communication as well as some sort of protection against secret alliances that may be highly discriminatory against people with little political clout.

GENDER DIFFERENCES

Social scientists assumed for many years that basic differences between men and women were the result of cultural mores and were relatively free from biological and evolutionary influences. But the fact that chimpanzee juveniles show some of the same gender differences as human children—differences that cannot reasonably be explained by cultural traditions—suggests that some gender differences may have an evolutionary history that precedes the establishment of human culture.

As we have seen, juvenile chimpanzees play together in same-sex groups; the play of the males involves a rough-and-tumble type of interaction; and female play has a more social and parental orientation. Comparable gender differences in the play of boys and girls have been found in analyses of interactions on school playgrounds (Youngs, 1985). These observations suggest that the play of juveniles may be preadaptations for the somewhat different roles males and females fill as adults, both in chimpanzee society and in many human societies.

A similar conclusion is suggested by the finding that there are gender differences in the nature of chimpanzee and human political coalitions and friendships. As we have seen, the associations of male chimpanzees are often focused on some instrumental activity such as hunting baboons or cooperating in political alliances. Friendships in female chimpanzees, however, are usually based on kinship or nonpolitical preferences. And studies of verbal interactions among human friends show clear analogies with these chimpanzee patterns. Men spend a good deal of time talking to their male friends about instrumental activities such as job-related issues or sports. In contrast, women frequently talk together about feelings and relationships.

Also, relative to men, women tend to be more perceptive of other people's emotions. For example, women, on average, are more accurate in identifying the emotions expressed in videotaped interviews than are men (Hall, 1987).

Although there is an apparent basis for some gender differences in our early evolutionary history, economic and cultural factors probably account for much of the bias and sexism that developed after we became *Homo sapiens.* The dawn of agriculture was a major factor in promoting this bias and sexism, because the domestication of animals and the possibility of owning land and animals opened the way for an accumulation of wealth and power. Because women were restricted by childbearing, ownership and power tended to be male-dominated. And with power and wealth came discrimination against women and other groups that had little or no power.

In many of the societies that came into being following the development of agriculture, a viewpoint developed that women were simply property. Although this viewpoint has changed in Western societies in recent years, there are still many examples of discrimination against women.

THE NEED FOR SOCIAL INTERACTION

After a lifetime of chimpanzee research, Jane Goodall remarked that if we see chimpanzees only as isolated individuals, we will completely fail to understand them. A comparable statement could certainly be made about humans. And because chimpanzees and humans both evolved as ground-dwelling primates highly dependent on their social group, the chimpanzee–human analogy makes sense.

Some humans tend to be loners, but these individuals rarely thrive or find much personal satisfaction. For example, in an extensive research project spanning 30 years, McAdams and Vaillant (1980) found that individuals who had a high need for personal intimacy were significantly more successful in their work and had fewer social and psychological problems than individuals who had a moderate or low need for intimacy.

Unfortunately, as I have mentioned before, technological advances have tended to isolate people in many modern societies. This isolation has produced a reduced tendency to behave cooperatively and an increased tendency toward destructive aggression. In addition, many individuals who

FIGURE 14.3 ◆ **Depression affects many individuals.** In fact, there has been an increase in the rate of depression among Americans in recent years, much of it related to technological advances that increase psychological isolation.

are psychologically isolated develop depression and anhedonia, or a failure to enjoy anything in life (Wright, 1994; see Figure 14.3).

Because of our evolutionary history as social primates, the human need for others is very deep-seated. Despite the seductions of electronic interaction via the Internet, it is doubtful that anything will replace the satisfactions gained from warm relationships between real human beings.

◆ CHANGING PERSPECTIVES

PAST	PRESENT	FUTURE
Social behavior haphazardly evolved in some types of animals but not in others (early twentieth century).	Certain principles related to the danger of predation and the distribution of resources apply to the evolution of social behavior in many diverse groups of animals. Social evolution is highly sensitive to cost–benefit ratios associated with group living.	How much insight into the evolution of human social needs can we gain by looking at the evolution of nonhuman social behavior? What is the impact of group living on evolution?

SUMMARY

Social evolution is sensitive to the cost–benefit ratios associated with living in groups. Ecological factors such as the danger of predation and the distribution of resources have a strong influence on the development of society.

Social dependency, expressed in terms of the physical union of individuals and a division into specialized castes, reaches its greatest height in colonial invertebrates such as coral. Though not as socially interdependent as coral, some small spiders live in large groups and share in capturing and feeding on prey.

Eusocial (truly social) insects such as ants and honeybees cooperate in the care of young, have an infertile caste that supports fertile nest mates, and live in integrated groups including two or more generations. The high level of co-operation in these eusocial insects enables them to live successfully in a wide variety of habitats.

Social behavior known as collective behavior is seen in many types of fish and birds and facilitates communication regarding such activities as feeding, avoidance of predation, and migration. Cooperation in reproduction also occurs in certain fish and bird species; nest helpers and communal nesting are examples of such cooperation.

In mammals, well-developed social systems generally occur in large animals that forage on the ground in open areas. A significant exception is the naked mole-rat. These rodents are one of the few eusocial mammals.

Among the most social mammals are prairie dogs and elephants, both of which live in a hierarchy of social units. Wolves and lions have high levels of social organization and exhibit intragroup cooperation in their hunting. Killer whales and bottle-nosed dolphins also cooperate with other members of the group in hunting, and male dolphins may form coalitions to "herd" females.

In primates, baboons and chimpanzees live in highly developed social units. A baboon group is polygynous, but chimpanzees live in multimale groups. Male chimpanzees often form coalitions to overthrow a dominant male, while female friendships are usually based on kinship and personal preference.

An analysis of some similarities between chimpanzee and human societies provides insight into important human social behaviors. We have looked at the formation of human political coalitions, gender differences in social behavior, and the need for social interaction from an evolutionary perspective.

KEY TERMS

caste, p. 322
clan, p. 334
collective behavior, p. 327
colonial invertebrates, p. 322

eusocial, p. 324
family, p. 332
kinship group, p. 333
royal jelly, p. 326

CHAPTER 15

SOCIAL RELATIONSHIPS BETWEEN DIFFERENT SPECIES

◆ *Why are these ants carrying vegetation to their nest?*

◆ *How does the fungus that grows on the vegetation benefit from the ants' behavior?*

*S*ome relationships between animals of different species may be considered "social" in the sense that the relationships persist over a relatively long period of time. In recent years animal behaviorists have become especially interested in these ongoing relationships, because they can have a strong effect on the evolution of behavior.

    We will begin by discussing **parasitism**—relationships that benefit one animal and harm another. Then we will consider two types of symbiotic relationships: **commensalism,** or relationships that benefit one animal and have little or no effect on the other, and mutualism, in which both individuals benefit. We will conclude by examining parasitic and mutualistic relationships in which humans are directly involved.

15

PARASITISM

Parasites have a strong effect on the evolution of their hosts, and vice versa. Because the parasite injures the host species, a selection process develops that tends to counter the injurious effect. For example, the host species may develop a tendency to avoid environmental areas with large concentrations of the parasites. The parasite is then selected to counter the defenses of the host, possibly by developing superior ways of locating the host. In other words, there is an evolutionary arms race between hosts and parasites that is comparable to that between predators and prey. As we shall see at several points in this chapter, this arms race produces a relatively rapid rate of evolution in both hosts and parasites (Hamilton et al., 1990).

Conventional Parasitism

In the most familiar type of parasitism, which we will call **conventional parasitism,** the parasite feeds on some of the host's tissue—and, in some cases, reproduces inside the host, where the young are protected and fed. Conventional parasitic relationships vary widely. Some parasites, such as mites and ticks, live on the outside of the bodies of hosts. Other parasites, including tapeworms, roundworms, and numerous protozoans, live inside the

body of their hosts. Certain parasites, such as blood-sucking arthropods and leeches, are temporary visitors; once they have obtained a meal they leave. In contrast, parasitic protozoans and tapeworms spend their entire lives inside their hosts.

Despite this variability in the type of relationship, certain principles apply to parasitic relationships in general. Parasites are typically smaller and reproduce at a faster rate than their hosts. In addition, parasites typically refrain from killing or severely injuring their hosts. Such restraint enables the parasite to accrue fitness benefits over an extended period of time.

In the parasite–host arms race, the more the host adapts to the parasite, the more the parasite is selected to counteradapt. However, the adaptations of parasite and host are liable to move in somewhat different directions. If we look at species in a general way, adaptations require metabolic resources and consequently are limited in degree. In other words, animals may not evolve in all directions at once. Therefore, adaptational investment must be either general (going toward moderate effectiveness in various different circumstances) or specific (moving toward a high degree of effectiveness in restricted circumstances). Because a host usually carries several types of parasites, the host is not able to invest all of its adaptational resources in fighting just one type of parasite. Consequently, hosts tend to evolve general adaptations. These adaptations are usually related to minimizing costs rather than to eliminating parasites completely.

In contrast, parasites typically benefit by becoming specialized for one type of host. It is generally more advantageous for a parasite to be very sure of success with one type of host than to be moderately sure of success with a variety of types (Dawkins & Krebs, 1979). Thus, it is not surprising that most parasites are specialized for parasitizing only one species or a few closely related species.

Intermediate Hosts

Some parasites live entirely off one host, but others have different hosts during different stages of development. The hosts that serve the parasite in its early stages of development are known as **intermediate hosts.** As we will see, the role of intermediate hosts in parasitism is particularly important, because the evolution of a parasite in relation to a specific host species may take one of two directions, each with particular advantages.

In competition between individuals of the parasitic species, the more virulent individual parasites reproduce most rapidly. Consequently, these virulent individuals have a selective advantage—up to a point. That point is when the host is killed and the parasites, lacking a food source, die also. In contrast, more benign parasites have a long-term advantage. Although they reproduce relatively slowly, the benign parasites do not eliminate their food source.

Parasites with intermediate hosts typically interact with a **vector**—an animal that transports them from one host to another. For example, a mosquito is a vector for the malaria parasite. The vector is not harmed but performs a critical function for the parasite.

When a parasite has an intermediate host and a vector, the parasite can afford to be virulent and kill its host; the vector will transport it to another host. In contrast, parasites without intermediate hosts and vectors are dependent on their one and only host and consequently tend to evolve in the benign direction (Ewald, 1987).

This analysis has important implications for our understanding of many human diseases. As many as 50 percent of the infectious

TABLE 15.1 ◆ Types of Parasites

Type	Example	Effect on Host	Benefit for Parasite	Intermediate Host?
Virulent	Malaria parasite	Severe debilitation and/or death	Short-term; rapid reproduction	Usual
Benign	Cold virus	Mild to moderate debilitation but normal recovery	Long-term; host is not killed, so food supply continues	Unusual

diseases that have an intermediate host are classified as severe. In comparison, only 10 percent of non-vector-borne diseases fall into the severe category (Ewald, 1987).

Altering a Host's Physiology and Behavior

In some cases a parasite alters its host's behavior or behavior potential, but the changes do not benefit the parasite. Rather, the changes seem to be a side effect of poor health in the host induced by the parasite. For example, a protozoan parasite reduces the spatial ability of laboratory mice (Kavaliers et al., 1995; Thompson & Kavaliers, 1994).

In other cases, however, a parasite may alter the physiology and behavior of its host in such a way that the parasite obtains some benefit. For example, a mouse that is infected with the malarial parasite is more lethargic and less capable of fighting off the mosquitoes that function as vectors. The mosquitoes engorge themselves with the blood of a mouse host and then transport the malarial parasite from one host to another. Consequently, the parasite gains simply by reducing the energy level of the mouse and making it vulnerable to the vector (Moore & Gotelli, 1990).

A parasite may also induce a more specific behavioral change that provides fitness benefits. For example, a lance fluke (a type of flatworm) increases the probability that its next host will consume its intermediate host—an ant—by inducing behavioral changes in the ant. The parasite selectively consumes the ant's nervous system; as a result of the neural deficit, the ant bites onto a blade of grass and stays attached to it. In this exposed position, the ant is likely to be eaten by the fluke's next host—a sheep (Moore & Gotelli, 1990).

Still another parasite strategy is to alter an intermediate host's physiology in such a way that the host becomes more attractive to a predator. For example, a parasitic worm *Leucochloridium paradoxum* produces changes in the eyestalks of a snail, its intermediate host. The eyestalks enlarge and take on bright colors that attract predatory birds. After feeding on a snail's eyestalk, the bird becomes the worm's next host (Lewis, 1977).

Hosts' Defenses against Parasites

Even though parasites are highly adapted to finding and taking advantage of hosts, the hosts are far from helpless. Some animals live solitary lives and thereby reduce the possibility of parasite transfer. Starlings fight parasites more actively, introducing pungent herbs into their nests that impede the growth of lice and parasitic bacteria.

A rather surprising adaptation to parasitism, **adaptive suicide,** has been identified in a few animals. When infested by parasites, a small insect known as a pea aphid may give itself up to a predator and thereby prevent the parasites from infesting other members of the group, which are closely related. When the parasitized pea aphid is approached by a predatory ladybird beetle, the aphid moves in such a way that it maximizes its chances of being preyed upon by the beetle. This apparent suicide does not occur under all circumstances, but only when the chances of the aphid surviving long enough to reproduce are extremely poor (McAllister et al., 1990).

Adaptive suicide has also been identified in bumblebee workers that have been attacked by a type of parasitoid fly. The parasitized workers tend to remain outside of the nest longer than nonparasitized workers and may

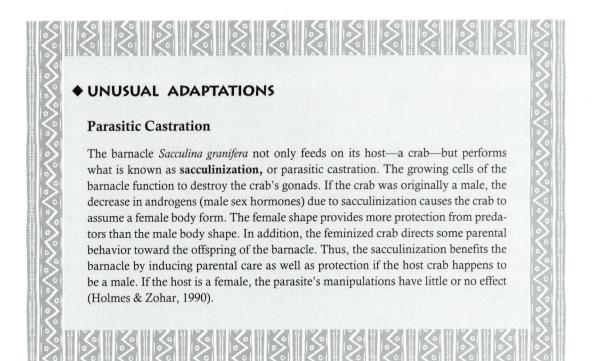

◆ UNUSUAL ADAPTATIONS

Parasitic Castration

The barnacle *Sacculina granifera* not only feeds on its host—a crab—but performs what is known as **sacculinization,** or parasitic castration. The growing cells of the barnacle function to destroy the crab's gonads. If the crab was originally a male, the decrease in androgens (male sex hormones) due to sacculinization causes the crab to assume a female body form. The female shape provides more protection from predators than the male body shape. In addition, the feminized crab directs some parental behavior toward the offspring of the barnacle. Thus, the sacculinization benefits the barnacle by inducing parental care as well as protection if the host crab happens to be a male. If the host is a female, the parasite's manipulations have little or no effect (Holmes & Zohar, 1990).

abandon the nest altogether. By staying away from the nest, the workers prevent the parasites from spreading. However, the workers cannot feed on the colony's stored food and die relatively early. Incidentally, because the parasites may be more likely to survive outside of the bees' nest, the parasites may also benefit from the workers' tendency to stay away from the nest. Thus, the bees and the parasites may both benefit from the workers' altered behavior (Poulin, 1992).

Parasitoidism

We have seen in earlier chapters that certain insects are parasitoid; that is, they deposit their eggs inside another animal such as a caterpillar, and when the eggs hatch, the larvae then feed on the body of the host. Parasitoid insects are extremely selective in that they lay their eggs inside (parasitize) a specific type of host.

Female parasitoid wasps typically identify their host on the basis of chemical cues. In addition, they are sensitive to a chemical cue left by another wasp that has already parasitized the host. This cue is inhibitory and prevents the mother from investing in a host that would prove to be suboptimal; it also protects the investment of the original wasp. Thus, this chemical communication provides a benefit both for the original wasp and for the wasp that refrains from oviposition on this host.

A parasitoid wasp is also sensitive to the relative quality of the potential host. This sensitivity is especially important because, as described in Chapter 8, female parasitoid wasps are able to determine the sex of their offspring. When the host is perceived as large and young—a high-value host—the female wasp lays more eggs that develop into females. Lower-value hosts are the recipients of eggs that generally develop into males. This differential treatment of offspring is apparently related to the fact that female offspring that are well fed develop into large females. Large females have high fecundity and thus provide relatively great fitness benefits for the mother. Males benefit less from growing large and therefore do not provide special fitness benefits for the mother, so the mother produces more males when resources are relatively poor (Brault, 1991).

Parasitoid wasps might be liable to inbreeding and its resulting negative effects, because brothers and sisters develop on the same host. By the time most wasps have reached sexual maturity, however, they have left the area of the host. Furthermore, research on the parasitoid wasp *Bracon hebetor* has uncovered another mechanism that reduces inbreeding. Females become sensitive to environmental cues such as odor associated with their host and avoid mating with their brothers, which give off these cues (Ode et al., 1995).

Kleptoparasitism

Some animals that live a parasitic existence do not inflict structural damage on their hosts but steal resources from other animals—a tendency known as **kleptoparasitism.** We have already seen an example of kleptoparasitism in bowerbirds, which steal ornaments from conspecifics' bowers. Here, we will focus on kleptoparasitism that involves stealing food other animals have recently obtained and, in some cases, stored.

Stealing Prey

The oceanic frigate (or man-of-war) bird is well known for its tendency to pirate from smaller birds that have just captured fish. The frigate bird's dependence on kleptoparasitism is related to the fact that the bird has weak legs, small feet, and nonwaterproof plumage. Consequently, the bird has great difficulty taking off once it has landed on water. The frigate bird spends much of its time soaring; when it sees a smaller bird catch a fish, it swoops down and forces the hunter to regurgitate or drop its fish. The pirate then catches the booty in midair. Nonetheless, the frigate bird is not completely dependent on kleptoparasitism, because it can take fish out of the water with its talons or capture flying fish in the air (see Welty & Baptista, 1988).

A California hawk called the northern harrier is a part-time kleptoparasite but is also vulnerable to kleptoparasitism by other, larger birds. Sensitive to its vulnerability, the harrier chases large hunting birds from its territory but allows smaller hunting birds to remain. The smaller hunters pose no threat and can easily be kleptoparasitized by the harrier (Temeles, 1990).

Kleptoparasitism is not restricted to stealing from other species. Some birds steal prey from conspecifics, especially when the conspecific has captured a large prey animal. The curlew, a wading bird of the Northern Hemisphere, directs its attacks primarily at conspecifics that are lower in dominance. These attacks clearly have a lower energy cost and a higher probability of success than would attacks against more-dominant birds (Ens et al., 1990).

Web-building spiders are particularly vulnerable to kleptoparasitism, because prey caught in their web is exposed for a period of time. Also, the spider's injection of poison predigests portions of the prey, reducing handling costs for a potential pirate. Some insects have actually become specialized for stealing from webs. For example, the legs of certain wasps are constructed in such a way that the wasps can easily walk on the sticky strands of a spiderweb (Barnard, 1990).

Other types of spiders may also steal from spiderwebs. Experiments involving the spider *Argyrodes ululans,* which steals prey from a species of social spider, suggest that the kleptoparasite takes several variables into account as it adjusts its pirating behavior: its own level of hunger, the number of social spiders present to defend the prey, and the size of the prey. Apparently the spider is capable of complex information processing related to its kleptoparasitism (Cangialosi, 1991).

Stealing Hoarded Food

Certain animals raid the larders or cache sites of other animals. A hoard raider such as a grizzly bear may rely on its superior size and strength to invade the territory of a red squirrel and search for a cache of nuts. However, some raiders use more devious strategies. Small cache robbers remain at a distance while a bird such as a jay caches seeds; the thief will then approach the area and search after the jay has left (Vander Wall & Smith, 1987).

A small African bird known as the honeyguide and the ratel, or honey badger, have developed a highly unusual type of relationship that facilitates the stealing of honey. When the bird finds a bees' nest, it flies off and apparently searches for a honey badger. Once it locates a badger, the bird vocalizes vigorously and seems to lead or guide the badger to the bees' nest. The badger tears the nest open with its claws and feeds on the honey and some of the bees' larvae. The honeyguide then takes advantage of the situation and feeds on the wax of the comb as well as eating some of the remaining larvae.

In some remote parts of Africa where tribespeople still collect honey from wild bees, the honeyguides also lead humans to bees' nests in a manner similar to that observed with badgers. Apparently the honeyguides have extended their tendency to include humans—who also open up the bees' nest and thus perform a service for the honeyguides.

Social Parasitism

In **social parasitism** a parasite rears its young at the expense of a host. Thus, in contrast to conventional parasitism and kleptoparasitism, social parasitism exploits not food but the parental tendencies and the time and effort of the host.

Obligate Brood Parasitism

Brood parasitism, the most common type of social parasitism, involves the placement of the parasite's eggs in the nest of the host during a specific time frame in which the host is induced to care for the parasite's offspring.

Brood parasitism occurs in some insects (Tallamy & Horton, 1990) but is most familiar in birds, especially in cuckoos and cowbirds.

Cuckoos are **obligate** brood parasites; that is, they completely depend on other birds to raise their young. The several species of cuckoos that are found in Europe and India show numerous adaptations related to their brood parasitism. In certain species the male approaches the nest of a potential host and induces the resident bird to fly up and give chase. The female cuckoo then enters the temporarily abandoned nest and lays an egg. Cuckoos mimic the eggs of the species they parasitize, increasing the likelihood that the cuckoo's egg will be accepted. Because the cuckoo embryo develops faster than the embryos of the host species, the cuckoo young typically hatches first.

In one species, the young cuckoo places its back against the hosts' eggs and rolls the eggs out of the nest, one at a time. The host parents then feed the cuckoo fledgling as if it were their own. Even in species where the hosts' young are not killed, the developing cuckoo is larger and gives more intense begging cues than the hosts' fledglings, so the parasite is fed first and given the lion's share of the food (Wyllie, 1981).

North American cowbirds are the New World equivalent of Old World cuckoos. Most of the cowbird species are obligate; and, as in the case of cuckoos, cowbird embryos develop faster than those of their hosts. Some potential hosts of cowbirds have evolved defenses against these parasites. For example, yellow warblers often bury cowbird eggs, especially when they are laid in the nest before the warbler's eggs are. Nonetheless, the warbler often accepts cowbird eggs if they are laid

after the warbler starts to incubate (Sealy, 1995).

When we consider brood parasitic relationships in general, the brood parasites tend to have the upper hand in the evolutionary arms race. A likely explanation for this asymmetry is related to the evolutionary pressure on the parasites and their hosts. The cost of failure is much greater for the parasite: If the young brood parasites are not accepted, the genes associated with the strategy will not be passed on. However, a host can fail to recognize a parasite and still be successful in rearing some young of its own (Dawkins & Krebs, 1979).

Facultative Brood Parasitism

Some brood parasites are **facultative;** that is, they sometimes incubate their own eggs but at other times lay their eggs in other birds' nests. Often, facultative parasites lay their eggs in nests of conspecifics.

Facultative parasitism is fairly common, especially in birds that exhibit biparental care. Certain birds employ a conditional parasitic strategy that is adjusted to environmental conditions. For example, when environmental conditions are poor to moderate, a female redhead duck lays her eggs either in another duck's nest or in her own nest. When environmental conditions are favorable, however, she increases her reproductive chances by both laying some eggs in another duck's nest and incubating some eggs on her own (Sorenson, 1991).

As in the case of obligate parasites, facultative parasites must overcome the host's defenses against parasitism. Female barnacle geese intensely attack other female geese that approach their nests. However, a parasite barnacle goose is sometimes able to lay her eggs in the vicinity of a host's nest. The host goose may then retrieve the parasite's eggs as if they were her own (Forslund & Larsson, 1995).

The Evolution of Brood Parasitism

Evolutionary theory suggests that the primitive condition for birds was probably nonparasitic. Then, under conditions in which birds may have experienced destruction of their nests, some birds would have gained fitness benefits by laying their eggs in another bird's nest. Since it is more difficult for a host to discriminate conspecific eggs from her own than to discriminate the eggs of a different species, conspecifics are generally vulnerable to brood parasitism.

Once a bird species evolved a tendency became parasitic, there was a selective advantage to deceiving the host more effectively. At the highest level of adaptation, an obligate parasite became completely dependent on one particular species of host. This species of host would have been the one that the parasite was consistently able to deceive or that was unable to adjust effectively to the threat of brood parasitism (Hamilton & Orians, 1965).

The results of a simple experiment lend support to at least one aspect of this theory. Researchers injected European starlings with a substance that made their eggs fluoresce under ultraviolet light. The researchers then destroyed the nests of these birds and, after a short period of time, looked for fluorescent eggs in the nests of other starlings. The injected starlings' eggs did appear in the nests of other birds, suggesting that facultative parasitism is a response readily available to birds not normally identified as brood parasites (Stouffer & Power, 1991).

Slave Making

Slave making, another form of social parasitism, is found exclusively in certain species of ants. Slave-making workers raid the colony of another species of ant and carry the pupal cocoons of their hosts to their (the slave makers') own nest. In some cases, ants of the raiding species kill resistors by piercing them with saberlike mandibles. In other cases, the slave makers utilize a type of chemical warfare: The raiding ants spray chemical substances that throw the defenders into an agitated state, eliminating the hosts' ability to defend their nest (Regnier & Wilson, 1971).

After the workers of the host species emerge from the pupal state, they carry out the housekeeping activities, including caring for their captors' own eggs and feeding the adults that made them slaves. During this time they respond to their captors in the same way that they would to their own species. In the case of the Amazon ant *Polyergus rufescens,* the slave makers are completely dependent upon their slaves, unable to carry out the housekeeping tasks themselves. Because the slaves are workers and do not reproduce, the slave makers must periodically raid nests to replenish their supply of slaves (Hölldobler & Wilson, 1990).

What might be considered the ultimate form of social parasitism is found in the ant genus *Teleutomyrmex.* The relatively small *Teleutomyrmex* queens enter the nest of a host species without facing resistance, because the parasitic queens are able to mimic the chemical code that identifies the host species. The parasitic queens then spend much of their time riding on the backs of the larger host queens, where they are fed by workers of the host species. The parasitic queens are completely dependent upon the host species, showing considerable degeneration of most organ systems except the reproductive system. Finally,

the parasitic species performs a type of castration; the host species is then able to produce only sterile workers (Wilson, 1975).

Why did slave making evolve in ants but rarely, if at all, in other social insects? The major reason seems to have to do with the tendency of ants to return to the nest of their own species after nuptial flights. In an evolutionary sense, it is a small step for an ant to enter the nest of another species instead of that of its

TABLE 15.2 ◆ Varieties of Parasitism

Variety	Definition	Benefit to Parasite	Examples
Conventional parasitism	Parasite feeds on host.	Parasites gain nutritional and sometimes reproductive advantages.	Most animals serve as hosts for conventional parasites, which include a wide range of organisms, from viruses to worms to insects, etc.
Parasitoid relationships	Parasite lays eggs inside host.	Offspring of parasites are protected by host and feed on host.	Only certain insect species, such as parasitoid wasps, are parasitoid.
Kleptoparasitism	Parasite steals from host.	Parasite gets free meal.	Kleptoparasitism, especially facultative kleptoparasitism, occurs in a variety of animals; frigate birds and honey badgers are examples.
Social parasitism	Parasite lays eggs in host's nest; parasite enslaves host species.	Parental investment is minimized because host provides for young; "slaves" may provide other services as well.	Brood parasitism occurs in several bird species, such as cuckoos, and in a few insect species; slave making occurs in a few ant species.

own. In contrast, bees and termites would be unlikely to become slave makers, because queen bees and queen termites found new colonies after their nuptial flight. It would be an unrealistically large step for these insects to enter another insect's nest (Wilson, 1971).

COMMENSALISM

Commensalism, in which one animal benefits and the other is unaffected, has been studied less thoroughly than parasitism or mutualism. Nevertheless, there are many well-established examples of commensalism in the animal world. Fish known as remoras use their suckers to attach themselves to sharks. As the sharks feed, the much smaller remoras gather some of the food scraps. The remoras gain free transportation and meals but apparently have little effect on the shark's fitness. A similar type of commensalism exists between barnacles and humpback whales. The barnacles that encrust the body of a humpback gain free transportation to food sources but have little influence on the whale.

In some cases one species of animal gains protection from its general association with another species. For example, a sea worm known as the innkeeper provides shelter for a variety of marine animals. The worm bores a tunnel on the ocean's bottom in shallow coastal waters and then feeds by filtering out small organisms that become trapped in a slime net. The innkeeper's commensal animals include such diverse species as goby fish, scale worms, and pea crabs; the commensals gain protection by living in the worm's burrow and/or eat some of the leftovers.

In the Antarctic, a more intimate type of commensalism is found between an amphipod crustacean and a poisonous shelled mollusk. The amphipod gains protection by capturing and then carrying the mollusk on its back. This unique type of association clearly benefits the crustacean but does not seem to significantly affect the mollusk (McClintock & Janssen, 1990) (see Figure 15.1).

One type of interspecies social system frequently evolves into another type, and commensal relationships can turn into parasitic ones. For example, an excessive number of barnacles may reduce a humpback whale's buoyancy, hampering the whale's ability to swim. Similarly, an extraordinarily large number of "guests" in the innkeeper worm's "inn" can significantly reduce the worm's food supply.

Commensalism may also evolve out of other interspecies relationships. For example, a notoriously parasitic protozoan and a type of salamander known as a newt live in apparent harmony in the Shenandoah Mountains of West Virginia. Researchers found the concentration of parasites in the blood of some newts to be so great that the newts should have shown signs of severe debilitation. However, these newts appeared healthy, had normal reproduction, and lived as long as nonparasitized newts.

Why has this parasite evolved so far in the benign direction in regard to this population of newts? Apparently the evolution of the parasite is related to the life cycles of both the parasite and the newt. The intermediate vector for the parasite is a leech found only in ponds. The newt does not return to a pond (to breed) until it is 6 years old. Consequently, even mildly virulent parasites would be likely to

FIGURE 15.1 ◆ **A tiny crustacean gains protection by carrying a poisonous mollusk on its back.** (The magnification of the figures is increased about 50 times.)

shorten the newt's life and bring on their own demise. Thus, there would be a very strong selection pressure for parasites benign to this population of newts to evolve (Mock & Gill, 1984).

MUTUALISM

Mutually beneficial relationships, or mutualism, have played a very important role in the evolution of the complexity of living things. There is strong evidence that organelles (specialized cellular parts) such as mitochondria found in eukaryotes (refer to Chapter 8) are actually the remains of simple, prokaryotic organisms. Presumably the simple organisms were involved in a mutualistic relationship with larger organisms hundreds of millions of years ago and then became permanently incorporated into the cells of the larger, eukaryotic organisms (Ehrman, 1983; Margulis, 1970).

Mutualistic relationships are common in present-day organisms of all types. In some cases the relationship is obligate, in that one species cannot survive without its partner or **symbiont.** In other cases the mutualism is facultative—the two species are mutualistic but are able to survive independent of each other. Facultative mutualism is the most common type, probably because this type of mutualism represents a typical evolutionary starting point of most mutualistic relationships. In some relationships, the symbionts then evolve greater and greater dependency upon one another, to the point that the relationship becomes obligate.

Mutualism between Animals and Plants

Countless plants are exploited by animals, but food plants sometimes have a mutualistic relationship with the animals that eat them. The animals feed on some part of the plant and, in return, transport a plant's seeds or pollen. Seeds of fruit may be carried some distance: After the fruit is eaten, the seeds pass unaltered through the animal's digestive tract. Meanwhile, the animal travels a certain distance. When the animal defecates, it deposits the seeds on the ground along with some fertilizer.

Animals may transport seeds by other means as well. For example, some seeds have barbs or hooks that temporarily fasten to the fur of mammals, facilitating dispersal. One of the most effective long-distance dispersal methods involves a plant dropping seeds onto muddy ground. The mud may then adhere to the feet of migrating birds, and the seeds may be carried thousands of kilometers. If an animal feeds on the plant whose seeds it carries, the relationship is mutual. However, if the animal simply picks up seeds by passing by the plant, the relationship is commensal.

Some of the most complex mutualistic relationships between plants and animals occur between flowering plants and nectar feeders such as bees. The bees feed on the flowers' nectar and pollen and transfer pollen, which collects on the bees' bodies, from one flower to another. This fertilizes the flowers and thus enables the plants to reproduce. But the plants benefit only if the bees consistently fly from one plant to another plant of the same species. This need for **species fidelity**—the movement of pollinators to flowers of the same species—has resulted in certain plant adaptations. For example, plants of the same species grow in patches and bloom at the same time.

There are certain species of orchids in Central America, however, that are widely distributed. This wide distribution is apparently facilitated by the orchid's ability to attract the males of a specific bee species with its fragrance. The male bees, in turn, visit only these specific plants, because the males require a particular orchid product to manufacture the chemical compound that attracts females. In other words, by holding the key to mate attraction for the male bees, the orchids ensure that the bees will develop a tendency to visit the same species of plant, even if the bees must travel a great distance (Dressler, 1968).

Generally, one species of plant flowers at a different time than does another species that tends to be pollinated by the same animal. This blooming schedule reduces competition among plants to attract pollinators.

Hummingbirds, which are found only in the Western Hemisphere, are among the most highly specialized nectar feeders. In contrast to other birds, hummingbirds are specially adapted to extract nectar, thanks to their long

◆ UNUSUAL ADAPTATIONS

Mutualism between Ants and Plants

One of the most unusual examples of plant–animal mutualism is found in the relationship between certain ants and an acacia tree in the tropics. The swollen thorns of the tree provide a shelter for the ants, and the structures at the tips of the leaves give the ants a consistent food supply. The ants, in turn, protect the acacia tree by stinging and biting any other animal that attempts to feed on the tree. The ants also clear away flammable debris from the base of the tree, creating a natural firebreak.

Another unusual type of mutualism involving ants is seen in tropical leaf-cutting ants *(Atta)* and fungi. Worker ants grow an underground garden of fungi, which serves as the ants' food. The fungi, too, benefit—because the ant workers provide pieces of vegetation that nourish the fungi, remove competing species of fungi, and provide anal secretions that function as a fertilizer. Once inside the nest, the workers chew around the edges of leaf fragments they have brought back. Patches of fungi removed from stored leaves are then placed on the new leaves, where they take root and multiply. Using this method, the workers provide a continuous supply of fungus for the ant colony. The leaf-cutter ant workers differ considerably in size and strength. The larger workers cut through relatively dense leaves, while the smaller workers prepare smaller segments of less dense leaves. As a result, the colony can make use of a variety of types of leaves (Wetterer, 1991).

beaks, tubelike tongues, ability to hover in flight, and small size. And as a hummingbird inserts its bill into a flower, its head picks up pollen; subsequently the bird transfers the pollen to other flowers it visits.

A high probability of species fidelity in some hummingbirds is strongly affected by the coevolution of specific structures in the birds and in the flowers pollinated by the birds. For example, the swordtail hummingbird of South America has a bill that is twice as long as the bill of any other hummingbird. The bill is just long enough to fit into the corolla tube of a certain climbing passionflower. Similarly, the Central American sicklebill hummingbird's beak is shaped in such a way that it precisely fits the sickle-shaped corolla tube of certain heliconias.

Mutualism between Animals and Microorganisms

Several examples of obligate mutualism between animals and microorganisms exist, in which microorganisms facilitate the digestion of the animal's food. The digestion of ungulates such as cattle is facilitated by bacteria and protozoans that dwell in the rumen (recall the discussion in Chapter 6). Many primates also benefit from "friendly" bacteria that aid digestion and, in some cases, help fight parasites.

Termites harbor protozoans in their intestines, and the protozoans' enzymes are able to digest the cellulose in wood. The relationship between termites and their protozoans is obligate: The termites cannot use wood as a food source without the protozoans, and the protozoans are unable to survive outside of the termites' intestines. The protozoans are passed from one individual termite to another as the result of trophallaxis—the continual exchange of liquid among colony members. This exchange further enables the termites to pass the protozoans from one generation to another. As in the ants and social bees discussed in Chapter 14, the trophallaxis also functions to provide food for those castes that are unable to feed on their own and enables the termites to exchange chemicals that operate as communication signals.

Because the termite's ability to utilize cellulose is unique among insects, this use of protozoans has enabled termites to penetrate habitats where competition is greatly reduced—even, in many cases, habitats in which no other insects can survive. In addition, the termite's complex social system enables it to alter its environment significantly.

For example, the mounds of certain African termites include a system of air-conditioning that enables the colonies to survive in extremely inhospitable areas.

Mutualism between Animal Species

We have already seen some examples of mutualism between animals of different species in previous discussions. Mullerian mimicry, discussed in conjunction with defense in Chapter 7, consists of a relationship where both the model and the mimic are harmful or distasteful; consequently, both both species benefit from the other species' defensive adaptation. In the cooperation between honeyguides and badgers, both species gain access to food after the honeyguide leads the badger to a beehive.

Certain animals of different species benefit from each other's defenses against predators. For example, African dwarf mongooses often travel with large terrestrial birds called hornbills. When the hornbills fly off in alarm, the mongooses quickly search for cover.

Ungulates in mixed herds on the African plains are often sensitive to nervous reactions of different species—reactions that may signal danger. Similarly, birds are often sensitive to other species' alarm calls. While the courtship songs of birds are quite specific to particular species, alarm calls tend to be very similar across species.

Alarm calls may even be identified across classes of animals. In East Africa, vervet monkeys and starlings show a mutualism in regard to alarm calls. Both the monkeys and the starlings give a different type of call for an airborne predator than for a terrestrial predator. The monkeys and starlings are able to identify and interpret each other's two types of calls and to take appropriate evasive action (see Cheney & Seyfarth, 1990).

In some cases, mutualism provides food for one animal and relief from parasites for the other. For example, oxtail birds that ride on rhinos' backs feed on blood-sucking ticks and flies. Similarly, certain small fishes known as **cleaners,** which live around coral reefs, feed on parasites in a large fish's mouth (see Figure 15.2). The smaller fish gain food and protection, while the large fish is relieved of parasites. These cleaners are typically stationed in a particular area and are brightly colored, which facilitates their identification. Large

fishes sometimes wait in line for the services of a cleaner. Not only are the large fish relieved of parasites, but the cleaning of infected tissue resulting from previous wounds promotes the healing process. Some aspects of cleaners' behavior, however, are parasitic. Cleaners may bite off pieces of fin and other healthy tissue and may even eat some of the larger fish's eggs. As we have seen in many earlier chapters, behaviors do not always fit neatly into single categories.

In conclusion, mutualism varies greatly not only in the forms it takes but in the degree that symbionts depend on one another. In some cases the mutualism is obligate and the symbionts cannot survive without each other. At the other extreme, certain types of facultative mutualism may be difficult to differentiate

FIGURE 15.2 ◆ **A cleaner fish entering the mouth of a large fish.** The cleaner feeds on parasites living off the large fish, so both fish reap benefits from the association.

from neutralism—in which different species live together without significantly affecting one another. Similarly, mutualistic relationships differ in their degree of symmetry. In some cases the symbionts may benefit equally, but in others one symbiont may obtain a larger percentage of the benefits. Finally, some mutation may include elements of parasitism.

◆ HUMAN EVOLUTION

We, like other animals, live in a variety of social relationships with organisms of other species. Both parasitism and mutualism are important for humans; and in technological societies, the basic nature of these relationships has been significantly altered through human manipulation.

PARASITISM

A principle derived from an analysis of the evolutionary arms race concerns the ability of a host to survive an attack by parasites. If a population of hosts has been isolated from certain parasites for many generations, the reintroduction of the parasites is likely to prove lethal to a large percentage of these hosts. The parasites will have evolved new methods of attack, but the isolated population will not have evolved countermeasures.

This principle helps explain a tragic occurrence in world history. Various parasites (disease organisms) introduced to the New World by the Spanish and other Europeans following the discoveries of Columbus killed approximately 75 percent of the native population. Most of the parasites were not lethal or even seriously deleterious to the Europeans; but the indigenous peoples in Central and South America, having been isolated from Europeans for thousands of years, were not adapted to the parasites.

Another principle related to the evolutionary arms race is that organisms not harmful to one species may be strongly deleterious to closely related species that have not had the opportunity to adapt. The AIDS virus, or a very close variant, was associated with green monkeys in central Africa without deleterious effects (Norman, 1986). When the virus was somehow transferred to humans, however, it had a lethal effect. Given time, humans would probably evolve defenses against the AIDS virus by natural selection. However, the cost in lives lost would be huge, and most scientists believe that an aggressive attack on the virus by drugs, education, and other means is a preferable alternative.

Humans have been able to fight a large number of other infectious disease organisms with drugs. If we inhibit the spread of a disease by means of a drug, however, we may put ourself at risk. The parasitic organism will continue to evolve resisistance to the drug, and unless we continue to develop new drugs, the parasite will eventually get the upper hand. We have already seen the development of resistance to antibiotic drugs in many types of bacterial parasites.

Another potential problem: If we—as individuals or as groups—ever find ourselves in a situation where effective drugs are unavailable, we are at extraordinarily high risk. Over time, parasites evolve; but if we have depended on drugs, we have not evolved effective defenses. While few people would suggest that we in industrialized societies completely wean ourselves from the use of drugs to fight disease, it is important to develop new ways of combating illness. Strengthening people's immune systems—by encouraging increased consumption of antioxidants and promoting more effective ways of coping with stress—hold great promise. Perhaps the best news is that strengthening the immune system has no negative effects.

MUTUALISM

Humans have many mutualistic relationships with other organisms. With the advent of agriculture, the relationship between humans and the plants they cultivated became particularly complex.

An analysis of the probable roots of agriculture suggests that agriculture evolved by a series of small steps. At first, early humans may have spared a tree that bore especially large fruit, while cutting down other trees for firewood. This fruitful tree would then reproduce and produce other trees that tended to resemble it in the production of fruit.

Similarly, humans probably picked strains of wild wheat that had the least brittle fibers because this type of wheat was relatively easy to harvest. If they took the wheat back to their base camp, the seeds would be dropped nearby; and after a few generations, there would be a new strain of wheat growing near the base camp. As the process repeated itself, domesticated wheat would become more prevalent without anyone making a conscious decision to plant a crop (Rindos, 1984).

The domestication of dogs probably started accidentally as well. As some wolves with a low fear of humans began to hang around campsites and eat scraps, these animals may have been petted and accepted by members of the human group. Wolves that have persisting juvenile characteristics such as shorter muzzles, smaller size, and a tendency to beg for food are more acceptable to humans than larger, fiercer animals and would be more

likely to benefit from the association with humans. Because wolves have a tendency to develop a subservience to a pack leader, these animals would find it easy to adjust to being dominated by a human "owner." Ultimately, wolf-dogs and humans both benefited: The wolf-dogs received protection and food, while the humans received help in tracking, hunting, and herding other domestic animals. Over time a selection of qualities occurred that humans found particularly appealing.

The benefits that domestic animals such as cattle receive may be less obvious, in view of the fact that cattle are usually eaten by their domesticators. However, domestic animals have a relatively high rate of reproduction and are protected for the earlier parts of their lives. Consequently, cattle and other domestic animals do gain fitness benefits from the association with humans, and the relationship may qualify as mutualism (see Allman, 1994).

Even if pets and domestic animals do benefit in a biological fitness sense, these animals have often been mistreated. We have a serious moral responsibility to minimize suffering and provide as comfortable an environment as possible for animals that live with us and/or serve us. As discussed in Chapter 1, there are now legal sanctions against blatant mistreatment of laboratory animals at most universities and research laboratories. Furthermore, zoos in many parts of the world are making an attempt to keep animals in habitats that resemble those found in nature. Even so, there is still room for improvement.

◆ CHANGING PERSPECTIVES

PAST	PRESENT	FUTURE
Animals statically remain in distinct categories of interspecies relationships such as parasitism, commensalism, and mutualism (early twentieth century).	Interspecies relationships are continuously evolving. For example, parasitic relationships may evolve into mutualistic ones and vice versa.	What are the consequences, from an evolutionary viewpoint, of fighting parasites with drugs?

SUMMARY

Hosts and parasites are in an evolutionary arms race and consequently evolve at a relatively fast rate. Conventional parasites feed off of their hosts. Parasites with intermediate hosts—and vectors that transport them from one host to another—are most likely to evolve virulent strategies. Parasitoid insects lay eggs inside a host, and the insects' offspring feed on the host.

Some parasites maximize gains by altering a host's physiology or behavior. Hosts may actively fight parasitism by avoiding close physical contact with conspecifics that may be parasitized, by introducing antiparasitic plants and animals into their nests, or by commiting adaptive suicide.

Kleptoparasites steal resources—especially prey and hoarded food—from other animals. Social parasites—including brood parasites and slave makers—rear their young at the expense of their hosts. Brood parasites place their eggs in the nest of a host and rely on the host to rear the young. Slave makers—certain species of ants—typically raid the nest of a host species of ant and carry off the host's pupal cocoons.

Commensalism is a relationship between different species in which one species benefits and the other is relatively unaffected. From an evolutionary standpoint, commensalistic relationships are frequently in a state of flux. Parasitic relationships may evolve into commensalistic ones, and commensalistic ones may evolve into mutualistic ones.

Mutualistic relationships (relationships in which both organisms benefit) may be either obligate or facultative. Plant–animal mutualism is complex and highly evolved, especially mutualism between flowering plants and animals that function as pollinators. Mutualism between animals and microorganisms facilitates digestion for the former and provides food for the latter. Two species of animals may develop mutualism when one species feeds on the other's parasites or when both species gain defensive benefits from the association.

Parasitic organisms have played major roles in human history. A risk of combating disease organisms with drugs is that humans may fail to develop immune defenses as fast as parasites evolve new modes of attack. Mutualism between humans and plants and animals takes complex forms, particularly since the development of agriculture.

KEY TERMS

adaptive suicide, p. 348
brood parasitism, p. 351
cleaners, p. 360
commensalism, p. 345

conventional parasitism, p. 346
facultative, p. 352
intermediate hosts, p. 347
kleptoparasitism, p. 350

CHAPTER **16**

THE NEURAL CONTROL OF BEHAVIOR

◆ *What areas in the brain mediate aggression?*

◆ *Are there different types of aggression?*

16

*P*revious chapters have focused on the functional aspects of various behaviors and how they may have evolved. In this and the following two chapters, we will consider the biological mechanisms that mediate and coordinate many of these behaviors. Research into these mechanisms in recent years has provided exciting answers to proximate questions of behavior—and has stimulated new questions about the evolution of neural and biochemical control of behavior. Furthermore, some of the findings have been applied to practical problems related to the health and welfare of both humans and nonhuman animals.

Every multicellular animal, in order to function as a unit, must coordinate the activities of its different systems. In response to this need, two general classes of controls have evolved: chemical controls, which feature the relatively slow transportation of specialized chemical messages; and neural controls, which involve rapid conduction of electrical signals from one part of the animal to another. Because chemical substances are involved in the transmission of neural impulses and neural impulses may stimulate the release of chemical substances, these two control systems overlap considerably. However, for purposes of exposition, I will treat neural and chemical controls separately in this chapter and Chapter 17.

In this chapter, we will begin by discussing methods of investigating neural systems. Then we will look at neural transmission and at nervous systems in general. Next, we will focus on the neural control of many of the behavioral systems discussed in previous chapters. Finally, we will consider the evolution of the human brain and the neural control of behavior in humans.

METHODS OF INVESTIGATION

The Greek physician Hippocrates was one of the first people to clearly identify the nervous system as the hub of cognition and behavior. Hippocrates noted that injury to the human brain resulted in deficits such as impaired speech and movement. Some 700 years later, the Roman physician Galen performed what could be called the first experiment in neurophysiology; he experimentally destroyed specific parts of the brains of laboratory animals and produced changes in the animals' behavior. Then, in the nineteenth century, two German physicians, Gustav Fritsch and Edward Hitzig, developed a different technique to investigate the relationship between brain and behavior: Using human volunteers as subjects, they applied minute electric shocks to what has come to be known as the motor area of the cerebral cortex and evoked specific muscle movements on the opposite side of the body.

The two general types of experimental approaches just mentioned—creating experimental **lesions** (damage to neural tissue) and artificially stimulating the brain—are still used today, but with considerable refinement. For example, researchers can now create experimental lesions in very specific neural areas of the brains of laboratory animals. In some cases experimenters pass electrical current through a steel wire, and this current initiates chemical reactions that destroy cells in the region of the tip of the wire. In other cases high-frequency alternating current is used to produce the lesions; the passage of the current through neural tissue produces heat, which in turn destroys nearby cells. In still another technique, experimenters use neurotoxins, or nerve poisons, to destroy parts of neural cells so as to determine which parts of the neuron have specific effects on behavior.

Brain stimulation techniques have also become highly refined. Researchers can now stimulate tiny individual nerve cells with microelectrodes. They can also permanently implant tiny electrodes in an animal's brain and then, after the animal recovers from surgery, stimulate the animal by remote control in a free-ranging environment. Brain stimulation may also be applied chemically, with advantages comparable to those associated with the use of neurotoxins; that is, only cell bodies in an area are stimulated, so researchers can assume that changes in behavior are due to the chemical excitation of cell bodies and not to other causes.

The development of the microcomputer has fostered the use of imaging techniques that can also provide information on brain–behavior relationships. For example, the positron emission tomography or PET scan is sensitive to the metabolic activity of various areas of the brain and thus can provide information about how active these areas of the brain are in different situations. The experimental animal—or human patient—is injected with a mildly radioactive form of glucose, which is absorbed by brain cells in proportion to the cells' level of activity. The information from the PET scan is then computer enhanced and printed out in color, enabling physicians or researchers to easily compare activity in various parts of the brain.

Other injection techniques make it possible to identify neurons that are susceptible to stimulation by specific chemicals, especially steroid hormones. For example, scientists may inject an animal with a radioactive hormone. They can later locate the neurons that have taken up the substance, thereby discovering which neurons have receptors sensitive to the particular hormone.

NEURAL TRANSMISSION

A **neuron,** or nerve cell, is a cell specialized for the transmission of information from one area of the body to another. All multicellular animals except sponges exhibit neural transmission of information. Although nonneural cells conduct excitation to a certain extent, there are several advantages to neural transmission over the type of nonneural transmission found in sponges. In the first place, neural conduction is rapid. A neural impulse may travel more than 200 miles per hour (100 meters per second). Furthermore, neural conduction occurs without decrement; that is, the message arriving at the far end of a neuron is as robust as the stimulation at the near end of the neuron. The fact that neural conduction is both rapid and nondecremental enables large, fast-moving animals to coordinate activities in distant parts of their bodies and to respond quickly to stimulation.

Neurons communicate with other neurons, forming a neural pathway that may include many individual neurons. Because the pathway may be highly variable, the excitation may end up at any of numerous locations. Consequently, there is the possibility of great diversity in behaviors, especially in animals with large numbers of neurons.

Excitation may persist for some time after a stimulus is removed. This persistence of excitation enables the animal to make responses that are delayed or may be influenced by other types of stimulation as well.

Although most neurons are stimulated by other neurons or by stimuli coming from sensory receptors, certain neurons generate excitation independent of external stimulation. Thus, a neuron or group of neurons may contain a code programmed by genes. This genetic programming makes it possible for certain behaviors to occur spontaneously, independent of external stimulation.

The Structure of Neurons and Supporting Cells

In vertebrates, most neurons are found in the brain and spinal cord, which make up the central nervous system (CNS). Neurons in the peripheral nervous system (PNS) conduct information to and from the CNS and communicate with sense organs, muscles, and glands on the peripheral, or distal, parts of the body.

Neurons differ greatly in size and shape. Most neurons have the same basic four parts, however. The **cell body** houses the nucleus and is the center for life processes in the neuron. **Dendrites** carry information toward the cell body, while **axons** carry information away from the cell body. At the end of the branched axon are **terminal buttons,** rounded swellings located close to other neurons' dendrites. The tiny gap between the terminal buttons and the dendrites of adjacent neurons is called the synapse.

In addition to neurons, the nervous system contains supporting cells, the most important of which are **glial cells.** Some glial cells provide physical support and clean up debris in the brain. Other glial cells produce a **myelin sheath** that encloses axons. Myelin, a whitish fatty material, functions to insulate the axon and enables it to transmit information with maximum speed (see Figure 16.1).

Conduction within the Neuron

The process of neural conduction within a single neuron is similar in virtually all nervous systems. When a neuron is in a resting state, the inside of the cell has a slightly negative electrical charge relative to the outside. This negative charge, called the **resting potential,** occurs because there are a relatively large number of negative ions inside the cell. The resting potential is maintained by the action of a mechanism that pumps positive ions back outside when they leak into the cell through

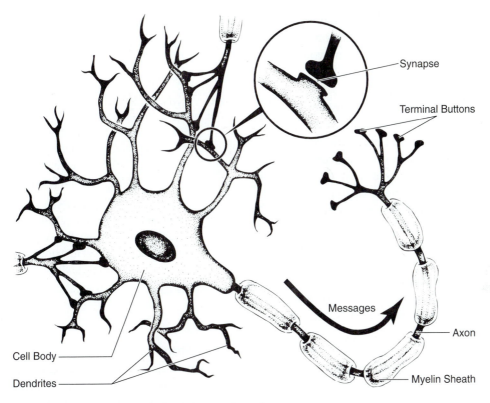

Synapse

Terminal Buttons

Messages

Axon

Myelin Sheath

Cell Body

Dendrites

FIGURE 16.1 ◆ A schematic representation of a neuron.

the semipermeable membrane that separates the inside from the outside of the cell.

When the neuron is stimulated beyond a certain threshold, the permeability of the membrane suddenly changes and positive ions rush in, eliminating the resting potential. In fact the rush is so great that, for a very short time, the interior of the cell becomes positively charged. Then the pump mechanism works again, bringing the negative ions back in and restoring the resting potential. The swings back and forth in electrical charge are known as the **action potential,** or firing, of the neuron. Once the action potential is generated in one part of the neuron, the potential moves down the neuron until it reaches the axon terminal buttons.

An unmyelinated axon conducts information in a manner analogous to a line of dominos falling against other dominos and thereby conducting the excitation to the domino at the end of the line. However, the excitation in myelinated neurons jumps along the axon, enabling the neural message to travel much more quickly.

Myelinated axons are necessarily thicker than unmyelinated ones. Furthermore, for all neurons, the greater the diameter of the axon, the faster the neuron conducts excitation. Therefore, there is a trade-off. More room is needed in a particular element of the nervous system if information is to travel rapidly than if it travels slowly.

The action potential travels in one direction—from the area of stimulation on the dendrites or cell body to the terminal buttons at the end of the axon branches of the neuron. Usually the area of stimulation is at a dendritic branch or at the membrane surrounding the cell body. When a neuron fires, or generates an action potential, it fires full force—a principle known as the **all-or-none law.** After a neuron fires, there is an interval during which it cannot fire again—the refractory period. This occurs because it takes time to restore the resting potential after an action potential has been generated.

If all neurons either fire or fail to fire, how does an individual neuron code for the intensity of stimulation? The answer is provided by the **rate law:** Strong stimulation induces rapid firing of a neuron, while weaker stimulation induces slower firing. In addition, strong stimulation typically results in the firing of a relatively large number of neurons in the general area of excitation.

In conclusion, the observation that all neurons generate action potentials in much the same way suggests that the basic "plan" of neural transmission evolved early in the evolution of animals, probably billions of years ago. Then modifications in the degree of specialization of neurons evolved. Such factors as the presence or absence of myelinization, the size of the neurons, and the degree of dendritic and axonal branching evolved in conjunction with more specific demands of an animal's environment and the nature of the behavioral system. For example, giant myeli-

TABLE 16.1 ◆   General Principles Related to Neural Firing

Principle	Definition	Result
All-or-none law	Nerves either fire or do not fire.	Perceived intensity is not related to strength of individual neural firing.
Rate law	Strong stimulation induces rapid firing.	Perceived intensity is related to speed of individual neural firing.

nated nerve fibers have evolved in certain fishes that benefit greatly from making quick evasive movements in order to escape from predators. In contrast, fibers that convey messages related to digestion are unmyelinated. There is less advantage to rapid communication of information related to digestion.

Synaptic Transmission

Once the action potential reaches the terminal buttons, structures within the buttons called **synaptic vesicles** are stimulated. The vesicles then approach the cell membrane, where they open and deposit chemicals into the synapse. These chemicals influence the reactions of **postsynaptic neurons**—neurons across the synapse from the neuron that just fired. The critical chemicals that send the message across the synapse are neurotransmitters, or transmitter substances.

The Effects of Neurotransmitters

Neurotransmitters have either excitatory or inhibitory effects. When excitatory, the effect is to stimulate a decrease in the resting potential of the postsynaptic neuron. If this decrease is sufficient, the postsynaptic neuron fires, or generates an action potential. When the effect is inhibitory, the neurotransmitter inhibits firing or makes the postsynaptic neuron more difficult to fire.

After the neurotransmitter substance crosses the synapse, it is often taken back by the neuron that released it, a process known as **reuptake.** In other cases, the substance is deactivated by enzymes found in the synapse.

In actuality, a very large number of axon buttons from many neurons converge at receptor sites on the dendrites of a postsynaptic neuron. Consequently, many neurons have input into the "decision" concerning the firing of the postsynaptic neuron. The "decision" concerning whether or not excitation should continue across a synapse is complex; neurotransmitters from many neurons are involved, some inhibitory and others excitatory. The timing of the arrival of action potentials and transmitter substances is also important. In addition, the threshold for the generation of action potentials shifts, depending on factors taking place in other parts of the body. This complexity is related to the great potential for complex and variable behavior, especially in animals with large numbers of highly branched neurons packed closely together.

Neurotransmitters Associated with Emotional Responses

Although we cannot know if nonhuman animals experience emotions comparable to those of humans, animals such as birds and mammals exhibit behavioral responses that are very similar to signs of emotion in humans. For example, rats show responses that closely resemble human responses to pain, pleasure, sexual arousal, and aggression. And the neurotransmitters that mediate these responses are similar in humans, rats, and other nonhuman animals. Therefore, if we are careful not to make unwarranted assumptions about what nonhumans feel—or don't feel— we can use the term **emotional responses** when discussing certain nonhuman animals.

Some of the most important neurotransmitters associated with arousal and emotional responses are **monoamines,** a family of chemical substances that are produced by neurons in several parts of the brain. These substances tend to modulate activity in widespread parts of the brain. For example, **dopamine** is a monoamine that has both excitatory and inhibitory functions, depending upon the nature of the postsynaptic receptor. A closely related substance, **norepinephrine** (also called noradrenalin), has excitatory effects and plays a role in responses that involve strong emotional arousal, such as sex and aggression. A third monoamine, **serotonin,** produces inhibitory postsynaptic potentials and generally has inhibitory effects on behavior. Thus, serotonin is sometimes involved in responses associated with lower levels of arousal and may have effects opposite to those of norepinephrine.

Endorphins

Another class of chemical substances, **endorphins,** function somewhat like neurotransmitters. Endorphins stimulate special receptor sites throughout the brain and function to reduce pain sensations (Fields & Basbaum,

TABLE 16.2 ◆ Monoamines Functioning as Neurotransmitters

Substance	Effect
Dopamine	Both excitatory and inhibitory effects.
Norepinephrine	Excitatory effects associated with emotional arousal.
Serotonin	Inhibitory effects.

1984). It is because of the effects of endorphins, as I mentioned when describing the reactions of an animal wounded by a predator (Chapter 7), that an animal (or person) is able to delay responding to injuries until it is in a relatively safe position.

Some endorphins also produce a positive or pleasurable sensation. The enhancement of positive sensations is particularly important in the facilitation of activities such as running, which are often basic to the survival of mammals. Similarly, during events such as parturition (childbirth), endorphins facilitate fitness by turning a painful event into a positive one.

Although the types of activities and functions associated with neurotransmitters and endorphins differ from one species of animal to another, the neurotransmitters themselves are virtually identical for a large variety of animals. Thus, a neurotransmitter extracted from an insect may be used to stimulate the nerves of a mammal. Apparently the chemical structures of neurotransmitters and endorphins evolved at a very early point and have not changed over billions of years (Krieger, 1983).

THE STRUCTURE AND EVOLUTION OF NERVOUS SYSTEMS

Although all animals' neurons are basically very similar in their structure and function, there are large differences in the way neurons are organized in the nervous systems of different species. Furthermore, there is great variability in the total number of neurons in a given animal, ranging from a few thousand in certain worms to more than 100 billion in humans. These organizational and numerical variations are related to differences in the behaviors of diverse species of animals.

Consistent with the emphasis on the behavior of vertebrates in previous chapters, I will devote most of my attention in this section to the nervous systems of vertebrates. One of the best ways to gain a general understanding of nervous systems is to look at their probable evolution, and I will consider evolution at several points in the discussion.

The vertebrate nervous system is highly bilaterally symmetrical; also, as mentioned earlier, neural impulses travel in only one direction. These two factors, bilateral symmetry and one-way communication, enable vertebrates to exert a hierarchy of control. Thus, a central processing area receives information and sends directives to lower centers. The neural areas in the brain and spinal cord are specialized for most of the processing of information. In contrast, long axons that run from the spinal cord to the brain—or from one level of the brain or spinal cord to another—transmit information between neural levels.

Fossil evidence indicates that ancestral jawless fishes gave rise to the modern classes of fishes. Fishes then gave rise to amphibians. Later, reptiles evolved from ancestral amphibians. Finally, birds and mammals evolved from reptiles. Consequently, we may develop hypotheses about vertebrate evolution by looking at representatives of the various classes of vertebrates.

The Basic Five Brain Lobes of Vertebrates

All vertebrates have the same basic five brain lobes: the myelencephalon and metencephalon (hindbrain), the mesencephalon (midbrain), and the diencephalon and telencephalon (forebrain). The evolutionary trend was to elaborate on the development of these basic lobes, particularly the **diencephalon** and **telencephalon,** which are the most anterior (farthest forward) lobes of the vertebrate brain. Thus, in an ancestral-type fish such as the lamprey, the diencephalon, telencephalon, and midbrain are all about the same size. In a reptile such as a turtle, however, the diencephalon and telencephalon are considerably larger than the midbrain.

The diencephalon of mammals is particularly well developed and is differentiated. As we shall see, areas of the diencephalon, particularly the **hypothalamus,** are important in several behavioral systems.

The mammalian telencephalon is developed to an even greater extent than the diencephalon. The cerebral hemispheres—the two symmetrical halves of the telencephalon—are surrounded by an outer covering, or cortex. There are, generally speaking, two types of cortical areas. The paleocortex consists of a single layer of cells surrounding the cerebral hemispheres and is differentiated into structures that make up part of the **limbic system.** As we shall see, the most important structures in the limbic system are the **amygdala** (associated with aggression) and the **hippocampus** (associated with visual/spatial memory). Because the hypothalamus is intimately involved with structures derived from the paleocortex, the hypothalamus is also considered part of the limbic system.

The Neocortex and Cerebral Hemispheres

The most apparent evolutionary development in mammals is the appearance of a six-layered cortex—the neocortex. This brain structure is rather poorly developed in ancestral-like mammals such as the opossum. At the other extreme, the cortex is large and well developed in ground-dwelling primates. In the chimpanzee the cortex is deeply fissured and makes up more the one half of the total volume of the brain (see Figure 16.2).

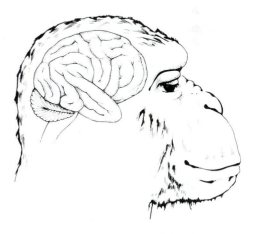

FIGURE 16.2 ◆ The brain of a chimpanzee.
Note the relatively large, convoluted cerebral cortex.

Several motor and sensory functions are associated with the cortex covering the cerebral hemispheres. A strong evolutionary trend in the evolution of the mammalian brain was for recently evolved structures to take over some of the functions that were performed by more primitive structures in ancestral vertebrates. For example, the primary visual center in the brain of fishes is located in the midbrain. However, the primary visual area in the brain of mammals is in the neocortex of the posterior part of the cerebral hemispheres; only certain primitive visual reflexes are regulated by the mammalian midbrain. The division of labor in a mammalian sensory system allows for much more complex information processing than that seen in ancestral vertebrates.

Another trend in the evolution of the mammalian cortex was the development of large **association areas**—areas of the cortex that do not have any specific sensory or motor function. These areas are small or nonexistent in ancestral-like mammals but make up a large percentage of the chimpanzee's cortex. The association areas seem to function as integration centers; they appear to enable the chimpanzee to engage in information processing more complex than that in ancestral mammals.

Hemispheric Symmetry and Asymmetry

Earlier in this section I described the vertebrate nervous system as highly bilaterally symmetrical. But although there is a large amount of right–left symmetry, a certain amount of asymmetry in brain functions has evolved in the cerebral hemispheres of certain vertebrates. Until recently only humans were believed to have significant right brain–left brain asymmetry—associated largely with the neural representation of language and the type of motor coordination associated with tool use. However, in rats, the right hemisphere is more involved in affective (emotional) responses than the left hemisphere. In chimpanzees, there is right hemisphere dominance in processing information about shapes of objects (see Hellige, 1993). There is also a certain amount of asymmetry in birds. For example, the areas of the brain associated with birdsong generally show cerebral asymmetry (see Bradshaw & Rogers, 1993).

Why has there been an evolution for a basic symmetrical pattern interrupted, in some cases, by asymmetry? Let us begin by considering the first part of the question. Because freely moving animals must be equally sensitive to stimulation impinging upon their right and left sides, sensory organs evolved a symmetrical placement, enabling the animals to be equally alert to both sides. Similarly, limbs evolved symmetrical placement so that animals could move efficiently in a straight line. Those parts of the brain that controlled sensory and motor functions obviously would be most efficient if symmetrically placed.

There is no particular advantage, however, to symmetrical placement of neural areas that process certain types of information, especially complex information. In fact, redundancy may be reduced and more efficient use made of limited space if information is processed in different hemispheres. However, this asymmetry of information processing can work effectively only if information can be transferred from one hemisphere to the other (Corballis, 1991).

Basic to hemispheric asymmetry in mammals, therefore, was the evolution of the **corpus callosum**—a structure that transfers neural excitation from one hemisphere to the other. Ancestral species of mammals such as opossums lack a corpus callosum and show little or no asymmetry. In contrast, more recently evolved species, especially old-world monkeys and apes, have a well-developed corpus callosum and a relatively large amount of cerebral asymmetry.

Neural Specializations

The previous discussion may have given the impression that the evolution of the brain has followed a straight line, with recently evolved species of primates clearly at the highest point. But such a linear view of evolution, as Hodos and Campbell (1969) pointed out in a classic paper, would not be accurate. Comparable to what we have seen when we considered the evolution of behavior throughout this book, the evolution of neural structures resembles a bush much more than a ladder. There are specializations within neural areas that have taken place at many points on the evolutionary "bush." For instance, a high degree of specialization has developed in memory areas in the male vole's hippocampus, even though this rodent has a small brain in comparison with that of most primates. Similarly (as we shall see in Chapter 18), bats have highly specialized neural areas for processing the auditory cues associated with echolocation.

Nonetheless, Hodos and Campbell suggest it is useful to compare certain recently evolved animals with the living descendants of animals whose early forebears were the apparent ancestors of those more recently evolved animals. For example, the **encephalization,** or general brain development, of tree shrews, which are similar to the most primitive primates, may be compared to that of old-world monkeys and apes. This comparison may be made on the basis of an encephalization quotient, or **EQ**—the ratio of brain weight to overall body weight (Jerison, 1991). The EQ for the average mammal is given as 1.00, so EQs greater and smaller than 1.00 give a rough comparative estimate of encephalization. By using a ratio we take into account the fact that large animals have large brains and large brain cells—but not necessarily more or better-developed brain cells than smaller animals.

When the three types of primates are compared, the ancestral-like tree shrews have the lowest EQs, while recently evolved apes have the highest. Jerison (1991) argues that with a high EQ, neurons are available in excess of those required for routine bodily functions. These excess neurons may then be invested in complex information processing. Supporting Jerison's argument is the finding, discussed in Chapter 5, that apes do quite well on tests of complex information processing and cognition.

Other factors that have little or nothing to do with complex learning ability are also related to EQ, however. For example, animals that store fat increase their body weight much more than their brain weight—altering their EQ downwards—but probably do not drop in complex learning ability. Similarly, animals that have evolved from much larger ancestors have a large EQ partly because the body evolves a smaller size much more rapidly than the brain. Thus, there is no evidence that dolphins or domestic cats, which have higher EQs than whales or large felines, are superior in complex information processing. In conclusion, EQ is a fairly good predictor of general brain development, but other factors must also be taken into consideration.

THE NEURAL CONTROL OF BEHAVIORAL SYSTEMS

Now that we have looked at how neurons work and how the nervous system is put together, we can obtain a better understanding of the neural control of many of the behaviors we have considered in previous chapters. We will begin by looking at the reward circuits that are basic to the expression of many behaviors. Then we will look at some examples of research on neural factors in learning and memory, feeding behavior, reproductive behavior, and aggression.

Reward Circuits

A basic assumption about the control of behavior is that animals are motivated to engage in behaviors that produce pleasurable sensations and to avoid behaviors that result in unpleasant or painful sensations. The theory is that animals have evolved a tendency to "enjoy" engaging in behaviors that ultimately result in fitness and to "dislike" engaging in fitness-reducing behaviors.

There is considerable support for this assumption. Research with rats and other mammals indicates that there are special neural circuits that mediate "pleasure" and "pain." A classic laboratory study by Olds and Milner (1954) indicated that rats would press a bar over and over again to obtain mild electrical stimulation of the hypothalamus. In contrast, when electrodes were placed in other brain locations, rats would press bars to terminate the stimulation.

Later studies indicated that there is a system of neural fibers called the **mesotelencephalic dopamine system** that connects areas of the midbrain with several areas in the telencephalon. As in the case of hypothalamic stimulation, rats in an experimental setting will press a bar a large number of times to obtain stimulation of this system, and levels of dopamine in the area rise after this stimulation (see Phillips et al., 1992).

Some behaviors may be experienced as pleasurable because engaging in the behaviors leads to a release of endorphins, which then stimulate neural reward or "pleasure" circuits. Rats in an experimental setting will press a bar to inject endorphinlike substances into their system (Goeders et al., 1984). This finding helps to explain why endorphins produce their positive effects.

Under natural conditions, the performance of fitness-related activities probably evolved a tendency to stimulate the mesotelencephalic system—and perhaps other pleasure-related systems. Consequently, the fitness of an animal was enhanced by the operation of the reward system. Of course, a behavior could not invariably induce stimulation of the reward system, because such behaviors as eating and sex would then occur all of the time. As we shall see, there has been an evolutionary tendency to link certain behaviors with rewarding stimulation, but only under appropriate circumstances.

Most scientists agree that some human behaviors cannot be explained by a motivation to induce pleasure and/or avoid pain (see Kagan, 1996). However, the pleasure-seeking, pain-avoidance paradigm does seem to explain some human behavior and much of nonhuman animal behavior.

Learning and Memory

For more than 2,000 years, people have correctly assumed that learning and memory took place somewhere in the brain. Only in the last 30 years, however, have we developed reasonable hypotheses concerning the physiological basis of these processes. As in the case of reward circuits, learning and memory are important to a variety of behavioral systems.

Learning

When we considered habituation as a type of learning in Chapter 4, we saw that the sea slug's simple nervous system includes very large neurons that are relatively accessible to experimental investigation. Consequently, researchers were able to identify what happened to sea slugs' neurons when there was a habituation of the gill response. Kandel and Schwartz (1982) observed that when stimulation leads to habituation, there is less neurotransmitter substance released from presynaptic neurons. This reduction leads to a cessation of the gill response. In other words, the learned response involved changes that took place at the synaptic level.

These and other types of changes at the level of the synapse, which occur in a wide variety of animals, help to explain why certain types of repeated stimulation ultimately lead to changes in the pattern of neural firing in an area of the brain. As Donald Hebb (1949) hypothesized even before these mechanisms were clearly understood, changes in the pattern of neural firing provide the basis for learning.

In some cases these changes at the synaptic level remain for a long time. Consequently, experiences may build on each other, and an animal may show incremental changes in performance. In conclusion, the synaptic change model of learning seems to apply to many different types of learning and to virtually all animals investigated (Roitblat & von Fersten, 1992).

Memory

Karl Lashley (1929) performed a series of experiments with rats showing that destruction of even large areas of the rat's brain does not eliminate memories for well-learned responses. Later research indicated that, although destruction of brain tissue may result in short-term memory loss, the old memories are durable. For example, monkeys with damage to the limbic system failed to remember solutions to problems they learned after the trauma. However, they retained old memories (Mishkin & Appenzeller, 1987). This relatively great durability of long-term memories is adaptive, because what an animal learns early in life is especially important for survival and reproductive success.

Another adaptation of memory systems is related to types of experience: Negative experiences are retained in a more durable manner than positive experiences. For example, rats in the laboratory that are stressed by a foot shock retain the memory for a much longer time

TABLE 16.3 ◆ Memory for Negative and Positive Experiences

	Retention	Ultimate Explanation
Negative Experience	Relatively long	Relatively great evolutionary pressure for the development of mechanisms for negative memory.
Positive Experience	Relatively short	Relatively little evolutionary pressure for the development of mechanisms for positive memory.

than rats experiencing positive events. Remembering negative experiences better than positive ones is related to the life/dinner principle discussed in Chapter 6. That is, forgetting a bad experience could result in death—but forgetting a good experience probably costs the loss of something equivalent to a good dinner. Therefore, there is greater evolutionary pressure for the development of mechanisms related to retention of negative experiences, especially strongly negative ones.

Specialized Memory Areas

Certain neural areas are specialized for specific types of learning and memory (see Squire, 1987). For example, part of a rabbit's cerebellum (a structure in the hindbrain) is associated with the rabbit's ability to retain a conditioned eye-blink response to a tone followed by a puff of air (McCormick & Thomp-

son, 1984). In monkeys, the superior temporal lobe (part of the forebrain) is involved in the retention of an auditory task—but not of a visual task (Colombo et al., 1990).

One of the most widely researched memory areas is the hippocampus of the limbic system, an area associated with visuospatial memories. Lesions in the hippocampus disrupt a rat's performance in a radial maze; however, when spatial information is well learned, hippocampal lesions do not disrupt spatial memory (Poucet et al., 1991). As suggested earlier, long-term memories are stored in a way that makes them highly durable.

Because the hippocampus is specialized for the mediation of spatial memories, it is not surprising that animals with good spatial memories have a relatively large hippocampus. Thus, male meadow voles have a larger hippocampus than females of the same species (Sherry et al., 1992). As we saw in Chapter 5, male meadow voles have better spatial learning ability and spatial memory than females. Apparently there has been a sexual selection for the development of spatial learning and memory in meadow voles.

Is the hippocampus an all-purpose spatial memory storage area, or is it specialized to store specific types of spatial memories? A study with two closely related species of tits, marsh tits and blue tits, suggests that the hippocampus is specialized for certain types of memory storage. The marsh tit is a bird that caches seeds, while the blue tit does not. The study showed that the two species were approximately equal in their ability to learn a location where they had eaten a peanut. However, the marsh tit was vastly superior to the blue tit in its ability to remember the location of cached food (Healy & Krebs, 1992).

In conclusion, there seems to be a domain specificity in memory storage that is comparable to the domain specificity of learning discussed in Chapter 4. In other words, there has presumably been a natural selection process associated with relatively specific types of learning and memory. Those types of learning and memory that have been selected, of course, are those that have a relatively high fitness payoff.

Feeding Behavior

An important center for the neural control of feeding in mammals is the ventromedial area of the hypothalamus (VMH). Experimental lesioning of the VMH of rats results in extreme obesity (see Figure 16.3). However, the relationship between the VMH and hunger is not as simple as it might appear. For example, rats with experimental lesions of the VMH eat more than normal rats, but only if the food is very tasty; if available food is somewhat untasty, the VMH-lesioned rats eat less than normal rats (Powley, 1977). If the VMH does not influence food intake by regulating hunger directly, what is its role? At least part of the answer is related to fat storage. Rats with VMH lesions convert more food to stored fat than do normal rats (Duggan & Booth, 1986).

Other neural areas—including the lateral hypothalamus (LH) and bundles of nerve fibers passing through the hypothalamus—are also involved in control of feeding. These fibers use dopamine as a neurotransmitter, so it is not surprising that dopamine levels in the areas are related to feeding (see Stricker, 1983).

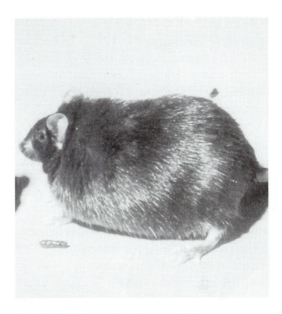

FIGURE 16.3 ◆ An obese rat. The rat was given free access to food following lesioning of the VMH.

A negative feedback mechanism operates between cells throughout the body and the neural centers in the brain controlling hunger. That is, as the level of supply of nutrients from the previous meal drops, a hunger signal is sent to the neural centers. In an attempt to explain this mechanism, J. Mayer (1955) proposed the **glucostatic hypothesis:** the theory that the signal for hunger is a drop in blood glucose.

There is considerable support for the glucostatic hypothesis. When animals are given free access to food, a drop in blood glucose typically precedes eating. Nonetheless, sensitivity to glucose levels does not completely explain hunger. There are comparable mechanisms sensitive to levels of fatty acids and possibly to levels of amino acids (components of proteins) (Ritter et al., 1992). In keeping with the long evolutionary history of feeding, it seems that a variety of mechanisms have become involved in the neural control of feeding behaviors.

Reproductive Behavior

Sexual and parental behaviors, like many of the other behaviors I have discussed, have multiple representations in the brains of mammals. This multiple representation is probably related to the fact that reproductive behaviors have become highly complex in the more recently evolved mammals as compared to ancestral vertebrates. The more complex information-processing systems have tended to evolve neural representation in the more recently evolved areas of the brain.

Experimental lesions of the ventromedial area of the hypothalamus of female rats lead to a loss of sexual responsiveness; this finding suggests that the VMH is basic to female sexual behavior. In fact, females with these lesions will actually attack amorous males. Consistent with these findings, stimulation of the VMH increases the incidence of sexual behaviors (Pfaff & Sakuma, 1979; Richmond & Clemens, 1988).

In addition to the VMH, another neural area, known as the periaqueductal gray matter of the midbrain (PAG), is involved in female sexual behavior. Lesions in the PAG stop female rats from assuming a receptive posture in preparation for copulation, whereas electrical stimulation of the PAG evokes this normal sexual response (Sakuma & Pfaff, 1979). Apparently the VMH and the PAG communi-

cate with each other, both neurally and hormonally, to jointly mediate female sexual behavior (Harlan et al., 1982).

In males, one of the major areas associated with sexual behavior is the medial preoptic area (MPA), an area in the diencephalon anterior to the hypothalamus. Thus, stimulation of this area in male rats elicits mounting and intromission, while destruction of the MPA eliminates these behaviors (Sachs & Meisel, 1988).

The limbic system is also involved in male sexual behavior. Early researchers working with male cats made general experimental lesions in the cats' limbic systems; they found that the cats attempted copulation with a variety of inappropriate sex objects, including the experimenters (Green et al., 1957). Later researchers, working with rats, identified the critical limbic structure as the medial amygdala. Specific lesions in this area disrupted male sexual behavior (De Jonge et al., 1992).

Interestingly, the neural areas associated with female parental behavior are similar—and in some cases identical—to those involved in the sexual behavior of males. Thus, the experimental destruction of the MPA, the same area that causes loss of sexual behavior in males, results in the loss of parental behavior in female rats. Females with these brain lesions ignore their pups but continue to show normal sexual behavior (Numan, 1974).

Another neural similarity between male sexual behavior and female parental behavior is seen in the limbic system. Lesions in the limbic system result in a disorganization of parental responses. For example, a mother rat with experimental lesions picks up a pup, walks around in an aimless fashion, drops the pup outside the nest, and generally appears

TABLE 16.4 ◆ Neural Centers Involved in Reproduction

Type of Reproductive Behavior	Neural Center
Female sexual behavior	VMH, PAG
Male sexual behavior	MPA, limbic system
Parental behavior	MPA, limbic system

confused (Slotnick, 1967). It seems that the MPA and parts of the limbic system have evolved an interaction effect. This interaction effect, however, is expressed in the neural control of different behaviors—sexual behavior in the male and parental behavior in the female.

Aggression

As you will recall from Chapters 7 and 13, there are two general types of aggression. Offensive aggression functions to establish territories or to defeat other animals competing for resources. In contrast, defensive aggression protects an animal against predation and attacks from conspecifics.

In male rats, a midbrain structure known as the ventral tegmental area (VTA) seems to be involved in offensive aggression. Lesions of the VTA disrupt the aggression (Adams, 1986).

Another neural structure, the corticomedial amygdala of the limbic system, influences offensive aggression in a subtle way. Under normal circumstances rats will make submissive gestures after they have been defeated by

another rat. However, rats with lesions in this part of the limbic system fight just as vigorously after defeat as they do the first time they met their opponent (Bolhuis et al., 1984). Apparently the limbic system lesions interrupt the development of the normal fear reaction that prevents animals from persisting in encounters they are likely to lose.

The neurotransmitters norepinephrine and serotonin are both involved in offensive aggression, but they appear to have opposite effects. Animal research has shown that high levels of norepinephrine are associated with increased aggression, whereas high levels of serotonin are correlated with reduced aggression (Siegel & Pott, 1988). An understanding of these neurotransmitter effects has considerable practical significance for efforts to deal with destructive aggression in humans.

Defensive aggression is related to somewhat different neural areas than is offensive aggression. In research with cats, stimulation of either the PAG of the midbrain or the me-

TABLE 16.5 ◆ Neural Influences on Aggression

Type of Aggression	Function	Neural Centers and Neurotransmitters
Offensive aggression	Resource acquisition	VTA, corticomedial amygdala of limbic system, norepinephrine, serotonin
Defensive aggression	Defense against predators and conspecifics	PAG, medial hypothalamus

dial hypothalamus produces such defensive behaviors as hissing and growling (Clemente & Chase, 1973; Shaikh & Siegel, 1989).

In conclusion, not only are offensive and defensive aggression behaviorally and functionally distinct; each of these types of aggres-sion is regulated by different neural areas and neurotransmitters. Thus, although it is common to speak of aggression as if it were a single system, it is very important to make a distinction between the types of aggression.

◆ HUMAN EVOLUTION

Research into the neural basis of human behavior has generated great inter-est in recent years, not only for theoretical reasons but because the findings have many practical applications. We will begin by comparing the human brain with that of other mammals, particularly other primates. Then we will look at some examples of research on neural bases of human behavioral systems.

THE HUMAN BRAIN

Some of the evolutionary trends discussed earlier in conjunction with pri-mates are particularly pronounced in the evolution of the human brain. For example, the large association areas seen in the telencephalon of apes are even larger in humans. Humans also have a more extensive cerebral cortex than apes. The human cortical areas that show the greatest increase in size compared to those of apes are the areas functionally related to the sensory and motor control of the hands and to the production and perception of speech. In contrast to what was once believed, areas of the brain strongly associated with speech—such as the region known as Broca's area—are not unique to humans; Broca's area is simply more highly developed in humans than in other primates.

The well-developed association areas and cerebral cortex contribute to a human EQ that is exceptionally high—higher than that of any other ani-mal (Jerison, 1991). These relatively large areas in the human brain are as-sociated with fine coordination of the hands, language development, and complex learning processes and cognitive ability.

Cerebral asymmetry, too, is exceptionally great in humans, particularly in regard to speech and other advanced cognitive abilities. For example, speech areas and analytic centers tend to be concentrated on the left side of the cerebral cortex, while most neural control of spatial perception and emotional evaluations tends to originate on the right side. There is a great deal of overlap between functions, however; so the distinction between "right brain" and "left brain" is not as clear-cut as is popularly believed. Furthermore, there is constant interaction between the cerebral hemispheres via the extremely well-developed corpus collosum (Hellige, 1993).

Generally speaking, the difference between humans and nonhuman animals in regard to cerebral asymmetry is more quantitative than qualitative. We probably evolved an exceptionally high degree of asymmetry because we needed as much cerebral area as possible to mediate our rapidly evolving speech and advanced cognitive ability (Bradshaw & Rogers, 1993).

THE NEURAL CONTROL OF HUMAN BEHAVIORAL SYSTEMS

Findings from recent studies of the neural bases of behavioral systems have tremendous practical significance in many areas. Here, we will look at examples related to the understanding and treatment of two disorders—clinical depression and disordered eating patterns.

Clinical Depression

Our ancestors may have reaped some benefit from a period of emotional depression. Individuals who expressed depressed feelings over experiences such as the loss of a loved one probably evoked positive responses from other group members, and the bonds among group members may have been strengthened as a result. Furthermore, a period of depressed activity may have been spent in contemplation and a reevaluation of strategies. For example, if a friend was killed, the bereaved individual may have spent useful time figuring out what went wrong and what could be done differently in the future (see Allman, 1994).

However, major or clinical depression—defined as a long period of debilitating depression—is antithetical to fitness. Yet clinical depression is common in several technologically advanced societies. For example, clinical depression is the most common psychiatric disorder in the United States. More than 21 percent of American women and 12 percent of American men suffer from a period of major depression at some point in their lives (Kessler et al., 1994). Approximately 15 percent of people with major depressive episodes commit suicide (Kaplan & Sadock, 1991).

How can this obviously nonadaptive phenomenon be explained by evolutionary theory? As we shall see when we discuss stress in Chapter 17, technologically advanced societies tend to produce long-term stress for which we are not well adapted. Continued stress and depressed mental states are associated with changes in brain chemistry. For example, severely depressed individuals have abnormal levels of the crucial neurotransmitters norepinephrine, dopamine, and serotonin (Goodwin & Jamison, 1990).

Antidepressant drugs are often able to help relieve depression by reestablishing normal levels of these neurotransmitters. This normalizing effect occurs when the antidepressant alters the reuptake of the neurotransmitter, changes the pattern of breakdown of the transmitter substance, or produces a shift in the quantity of neurochemicals that interact with the neurotransmitter. But there are large individual differences in responses to antidepressant drugs and in the period of time needed before any change is felt. Some of these differences can be explained by the resistance of the human body to changing neurotransmitter levels and by the complexity of the interactions between neurochemicals. At present the most effective treatment for major depression involves administering of different drugs in varying dosages while maintaining a vigilant evaluation of results. Generally speaking, psychotherapy in conjunction with drug treatment has been found to produce the most satisfactory results (Weiss, 1995).

Disordered Eating Patterns

People in technologically advanced societies are, as noted in Chapter 6, apt to choose poor diets. This tendency, in combination with other factors, has resulted in a near epidemic of eating disorders. One of the most common eating disorders, failure to inhibit caloric consumption, results in obesity— defined as having a body weight exceeding the healthy range by 20 percent or more. Obesity is nonadaptive because it shortens life and diminishes the quality of life; it heightens risk of diabetes, heart disease, breast and colon cancers, bone and joint problems, gall-bladder disorders, and other ills. But the number of people classified as obese in the United States is increasing rapidly. In 1980 the obesity rate was 1 in 4 people, but the figure surpassed 1 in 3 in 1991 and is continuing to increase (Kuczmarski et al., 1994).

Stress is one contributing factor in obesity. Most normal-weight people respond to stress by eating less. Overweight people, however, generally respond to stress by increasing their caloric intake (Herman & Polivy, 1984).

Obese people are also highly sensitive to external cues related to hunger, such as the sight or smell of desirable food. Even when they have just eaten and moved away from the table or begun other activities, obese people find it more difficult to resist eating again when food is present than do normal-weight people (Rodin, 1984).

 Still another factor is a heightened sensitivity to endorphins related to pleasure. Obese people seem to prolong eating once they begin because they have a continued pleasurable reaction to the taste of food. That is, their pleasurable reaction to food is slow to satiate compared to that of nonobese people (Reid, 1990). In essence, much of the research on obesity suggests that the problem is often one of ineffective neural satiety mechanisms.

◆ CHANGING PERSPECTIVES

PAST	PRESENT	FUTURE
The nervous system of nonhuman animals is quite different from that of humans (nineteenth century, pre-Darwin).	Although the brain of the human contains more neurons than that of any other animal, the general organization of the human nervous system is very similar to that of other mammals, especially other primates.	How and why did the human brain evolve to a relatively large size and complexity in a relatively short period of time?

SUMMARY

Researchers investigate the nervous system in two general ways: by destroying part of the system or by stimulating part of the system and then observing changes in behavior. It is also possible to investigate brain–behavior relationships by producing computer images of changes that take place in the brain during a behavior and/or by tracing radioactive hormones in the brain.

The nervous system mediates responses in animals by rapidly conducting electrical signals from one part of the animal to another. Conduction within a neuron involves movement of an action potential down a neuron to the terminal buttons at the end of an axon branch.

At the synapse, neurotransmitters either facilitate or inhibit the generation of an action potential in the postsynaptic neuron. Endorphins function somewhat like neurotransmitters and can reduce pain or induce pleasure.

The evolution of the vertebrate nervous system features increasing growth and differentiation of the brain, particularly in the diencephalon and telencephalon. In primates, the evolution of a high degree of complexity in the cerebral cortex, cortical association areas, and hemispheric asymmetry is of special significance. A general but fairly meaningful measure of brain complexity is EQ, or encephalization quotient.

Reward circuits in the brains of mammals may provide positive feedback for behaviors related to fitness. These circuits include the mesotelencephalic dopamine system, which is sensitive to stimulation by endorphins.

Learning of a wide variety of responses takes place at the synaptic level. Memories are stored in several different areas of the brain. Long-term memories and negative memories are generally more durable than short-term memories or memories of positive events.

Feeding is regulated by the VMH and other neural areas. These areas are sensitive to blood glucose levels and, to a certain extent, to levels of fatty acids and amino acids.

Reproductive behaviors are regulated by an interaction between neural centers, especially ones in the midbrain and the limbic system. However, the specific areas involved are somewhat different for male sexual behavior, female sexual behavior, and parental behavior.

Aggression is also regulated by an interaction between neural centers in the midbrain and the limbic system. Offensive and defensive aggression are controlled by somewhat different neural centers. Norepinephrine and serotonin are among the most important neurotransmitters related to aggression.

Differences between the human brain and that of other primates are more quantitative than qualitative. We have considered the application of some neural research to human problems such as clinical depression and disordered eating patterns.

KEY TERMS

CHAPTER 17

THE CHEMICAL CONTROL OF BEHAVIOR

◆ *Why are ants the most successful animals on Earth?*

◆ *How do ants communicate?*

In this chapter we will explore two chemical systems whose effects we have already encountered in the course of several discussions. We will begin with pheromones, the chemical substances that communicate information between conspecifics. Then we will focus on hormones, the chemical messengers within an individual animal's body. Finally, we will turn to the effects of these chemical systems in humans. As we shall see, pheromones and hormones communicate vast amounts of information in many species.

17

PHEROMONES

Pheromones were discovered relatively recently. Starting in the 1930s, Adolph Butenandt, a German chemist and Nobel laureate, began trying to identify the sex attractant in female silkworm moths (*Bombyx mori*). The task for Butenandt and his associates proved to be extraordinarily difficult, because the pheromone that acted as a sex attractant—and that later came to be known as bombykol—is present only in extremely small quantities. Thus, it took almost 20 years and the extraction of bombykol from more than 500,000 female moths before researchers could identify the chemical structure of bombykol and confirm the effects of this specific chemical substance. Thanks to advances in molecular biology, the identification of pheromones is now much easier, and a great variety of pheromones have been classified in the last 25 years. Well over a thousand different pheromones have now been identified.

Different species' communication pheromones may be passed from one animal to another in several ways. In many mammals, volatile pheromones contained in urine or other body secretions are released after the secretion has been deposited on or rubbed against some object in the environment. Fish and other aquatic animals, however, may simply release pheromones into the water.

Some animals transmit pheromones by direct contact with conspecifics. For example, eusocial insects often exchange pheromones by feeding other colony members in the technique known as **trophallaxis.** Similarly, a male queen butterfly transmits his pheromone to the female by dusting her antennae with powdery, pheromone-laden particles from the bristles of his antennae.

During the breeding season, male black-tailed deer and certain other mammals take some of the female's urine into their mouths, raise their heads, curl their upper lips, and breath deeply. These behaviors enable the male to be directly sensitive to the presence or absence of a pheromone in the female's urine.

Another method of pheromone transfer is seen in domestic pigs. The salivary gland of the mature male secretes a pheromone that is passed on to the female via his breath. The scent of the boar's breath, which resembles the smell of urine, is apparently highly attractive to a receptive sow. Most estrous females respond to an artificial aerosol preparation of the pheromone by showing lordosis (mating posture) and a willingness to mate. Pork breeders are able to take advantage of the sow's response to this aerosol treatment: The breeders use the aerosol to identify sows in estrus, then artificially inseminate these sows (see Agosta, 1992).

Pheromones are especially important in reproduction and in other aspects of social interaction. We will now look at reproductive pheromones, then consider the role of pheromones in social behavior.

Reproductive Behavior

There are two general types of reproductive pheromones. **Signal pheromones** (also referred to as sexual pheromones) have an immediate effect, communicating such things as attraction, sexual readiness, and fitness. In contrast, **primer pheromones** have a delayed and relatively long-lasting effect, stimulating physiological changes related to reproduction.

Signal Reproductive Pheromones in Insects

As you may recall from Chapter 9, male silkworm moths may be attracted by the pheromone bombykol from a distance of several kilometers. The pheromone is particularly effective when carried downwind on consistent nocturnal breezes. The pheromone emitted by a queen honeybee on her nuptial flight does not carry as far as that of a female silkworm moth; but even so, the bee's pheromone attracts a very large number of males. There is great competition among males for a chance to mate with the queen—despite the fact that the successful male loses his intromittent organ and his life in the process.

The female of the corn earworm shows a remarkable adaptation related to the timing of mating. Responding to a chemical in the corn silk, she releases her reproductive pheromone just as the corn ripens. Then the female can time her mating and egg laying to coincide with the ripening of the corn, which serves as food for the larvae (Raina et al., 1992).

Research on insect pheromones has resulted in some practical applications. Traditionally, insect infestations have been treated with insecticides—chemicals that kill specific insect pests. Insecticides have severe drawbacks, however. They often kill beneficial insects, and they can have a negative effect on the environment by tainting the food of harmless animals such as birds that naturally feed on the insects. Furthermore, insect pests ultimately evolve an immunity to an insecticide, so it is necessary to use increasing amounts of toxins or keep developing new toxins.

Sexual attractant pheromones have a general advantage over insecticides as a tool for insect control. Over a few generations, animals may evolve an immunity to insecticides—but they cannot evolve an immunity to sexual pheromones. (If an individual did have an immunity, it would be unsuccessful in mating and could not pass on the immunity to its offspring.) Thus, the same pheromone can be used repeatedly over a long period of time. Farmers can bait large numbers of traps with a pheromone, capturing or killing at least one gender of the pest. The reduction of one gender in the local population will, of course, lead to a population crash in the next generation. Another method is to spread the pheromone evenly throughout a crop area. Then, when an insect attempts to find a mate, the insect cannot appropriately zero in on the natural source of the pheromone (see Agosta, 1992).

Signal Reproductive Pheromones in Mammals

We have already seen examples of signal pheromones that act as sex attractants in male deer and pigs. In black-tailed deer, not only does the female's urine contain a signal pheromone; both sexes have glands on their foreheads that secrete a pheromone that attracts the opposite sex. They deposit their pheromones by rubbing their hind legs over their foreheads and later touching dry twigs with their legs (Müller-Schwartze, 1971).

Although we usually conceptualize one *individual* as chemically attracting another, chemical attraction may also take place between gametes. Many examples of sperm and eggs attracting each other occur in the ocean. In addition, there is research evidence indicating that human eggs attract sperm with the aid of a pheromone. During in vitro fertilization, sperm swim fairly directly toward the egg. Researchers have also discovered receptors in sperm tissue that are similar to odor-detecting protein molecules in the olfactory system (see Agosta, 1992).

Another type of pheromone, a **maternal pheromone,** also affects the interaction between mother mammals and their offspring. Using the kind of apparatus shown in Figure 17.1, researchers have learned that when rat pups are about 14 days old, the mother rat produces a pheromone that attracts the pups and keeps the young in the area of the mother. When the young are weaned at about 27 days of age, the pheromonal output stops, contributing to the dispersal of the young (Leon & Moltz, 1971; Moltz & Leidahl, 1977).

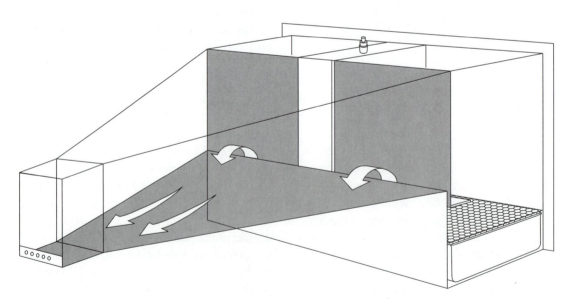

FIGURE 17.1 ◆ **Apparatus used in maternal pheromone study.** The young are placed in the small chamber at the left. Then they must choose one of the two compartments on the right, one of which contains olfactory cues left by the mother. (The white arrows indicate air currents.)

Primer Reproductive Pheromones in Mice

In contrast to signal pheromones, primer pheromones influence reproductive behavior by altering reproductive physiology. Pheromones in the urine of mice have several primer effects. A male mouse's urine accelerates sexual maturity in immature females and also induces estrus in mature females. This priming of sexual readiness in females is known as the **Vandenbergh effect** (Vandenbergh et al., 1975). As a consequence of the Vandenbergh effect, females come into estrus shortly after the arrival of a male; so the effect provides fitness advantages for both the male and the female.

If the female mouse is already pregnant and the male is unfamiliar to her, however, the effect of the pheromone in the male's urine is very different. A new resident male's urine induces the **Bruce effect**—abortion or resorption of the embryos (Bruce, 1960). The termination of the female mouse's pregnancy facilitates the male's fitness, in that he has an opportunity to inseminate the female earlier than if she had carried the fetuses to term. Although it is less obvious, the termination could also be advantageous to the female. A new male is likely to kill the offspring after they are born, so the death of the fetuses allows the female to start a new pregnancy that is likely to result in viable offspring.

The odor of a male mouse's urine also produces the **Whitten effect:** synchronization of estrous cycles in a group of females. Female mice that are introduced to a male—or simply to the odor of the pheromone in his urine—quickly adjust their estrous cycles so that they come into estrus simultaneously (Whitten, 1959). As a result of this synchronization, many of the females give birth at about the same time. Because mice typically nurse their offspring communally, this synchronization facilitates the survival of the young. If a mother dies or is killed, other lactating females in the group are able to nurse and protect the young. In addition, because females in the group are typically close relatives, the foster mothers benefit as the result of indirect fitness.

TABLE 17.1 ◆ Effects of Primer Reproductive Pheromones in the Urine of Mice

Name of Effect	Specific Effect	Benefits
Vandenburgh effect	Pheromone in male urine primes sexual readiness in females.	Females hasten puberty and come into estrus shortly after male arrives.
Bruce effect	Pheromone in urine of new resident male induces abortion.	Females become ready for new pregnancies.
Whitten effect	Pheromone in male urine produces synchrony in females' estrous cycles.	The group may cooperate in nursing and/or protecting the young.

Social Behavior

Pheromones have a number of social functions in addition to reproductive ones. Insects and mammals both have good chemical sensitivity and engage in complex social interactions, so it is not surprising that these two classes of animals utilize social pheromones to a great extent.

Social Pheromones in Insects

Insect pheromones are involved in a wide variety of social behaviors. For instance, they help insects aggregate, communicate alarm, recognize colony members, establish a trail, and determine the condition of a queen. Let's look at a few representative examples of these functions.

Many insects leave an **alarm pheromone**—a substance secreted in response to dangerous conditions that stimulates conspecifics to leave the area. In some cases, too, alarm pheromones stimulate colony members to respond aggressively rather than leave. For example, bees have a pheromone in their venom that induces other bees to congregate in the area and sting intruders. Thus, if a person is stung by one bee, it is likely that other bees in the vicinity will attempt to sting also (see Free, 1961).

One of the most important pheromones in eusocial insects is the **recognition pheromone**—a substance that is exclusive to the individual colony. Workers at the entrance of a nest will attack an insect that does not give off this pheromone. Thus, if a colony member is experimentally rubbed with the body of a foreign insect, workers will attack the tainted member as if it were an intruder. Conversely,

a foreigner rubbed with the body of a conspecific will be admitted without attack.

A specialized type of recognition pheromone known as a **funeral pheromone** signals the death of an insect colony member. When a colony member dies, the decaying body gives off a pheromone that causes workers to transport the body out of the nest. If a live ant is experimentally rubbed with a dead one, the live ant will be carried out like a corpse and placed on a refuse pile. Impelled to return to the nest, the tainted ant will then be carried out again and again until the chemical marker eventually dissipates (Wilson, 1963).

Another specialized recognition pheromone induces workers to cannibalize aberrant nest members. Occasionally, as the result of some physiological error in sexual development, a fertilized egg develops into a male. (As we saw in Chapter 14, fertilized eggs of eusocial insects normally develop into females.) Worker bees consume these aberrant males shortly after they hatch, saving the colony the expense of supporting colony members that are reproductively useless and perform no nest duties. When experimenters rub normal males against an aberrant male, the normal males are also consumed; therefore, we can assume the cannibalism is due to a pheromone (see Free, 1987).

As described in Chapter 14, ants locate food and carry it back to the nest. In many species, critical communication about the location and quality of food sources takes place via pheromones. Worker ants lay down a chemical residue that functions as an **odor trail** after they locate a food source. Once the source is depleted, the chemical trail fades. One ant species, the fire ant, produces three-dimensional trails or "vapor tunnels" by releasing a rapidly evaporating pheromone (Wilson, 1963). These "tunnels" help other members of the colony find the food.

Finally, eusocial insects broadcast a **queen pheromone** that indicates the condition of the queen. If the queen is alive and in good health, she produces the pheromone; its dissemination reinforces the status quo of the colony. For example, the attendants of the queen honeybee pick up the queen's pheromone by trophallaxis and physical contact; they then spread the pheromone throughout the hive as they have contact with their nest mates. As long as the queen pheromone is present in the hive, the workers feed the larvae a normal diet. When the queen dies or becomes ill, however, she does not produce a sufficient quantity of queen pheromone. Workers respond to the lack of queen pheromone by feeding some of the larvae royal jelly, and then these individuals develop into potential

queens. Then, as Chapter 14 described, the workers arrange encounters between potential queens; and within a short time, the old queen is replaced (Free, 1987).

Social Pheromones in Mammals

Pheromones are important in social behavior of many mammals, particularly in territorial marking, aggression, and social recognition. Because dogs and humans have been living together for more than 8,000 years, the raising of a male dog's leg to urinate on a tree may have been one of the first expressions of pheromonal communication consistently observed by humans.

A pheromone in the urine of dogs and several other mammals functions to mark a tree or other object as a boundary of a territory. However, animal behaviorists have observed that the effectiveness of the pheromone

TABLE 17.2 ◆ Social Pheromones in Insects

Type	Specific Effect	Benefits
Alarm pheromone	Stimulates colony members to leave area or become aggressive.	Coordinates escape or defense.
Recognition pheromone	Stimulates colony members to behave positively toward healthy colony members.	Enables colony members to exclude intruders, dead individuals, and/or unhealthy individuals.
Odor trail	Stimulates workers to follow trail.	Enables workers to locate quality food sources.
Queen pheromone	Promulgates information on condition of queen.	Enables workers to facilitate replacement of ill or dead queen.

fades within a day or two, and the marker must be reinforced if the territory is to be maintained. In the case of wolf packs, which move great distances within their home ranges, the fact that the territorial pheromones fade out with time enables packs to have overlapping ranges (Mech, 1970).

Mice also communicate via pheromones contained in the urine. A male mouse will consistently attack another male. However, castrated males do not elicit male aggression; apparently the testes produce a pheromone that elicits the aggressive response. As we shall see in Chapter 20 when we consider population regulation, a high concentration of the pheromone is associated with crowding, and this stimulates an unusually large amount of aggression. The aggression then functions as a population control mechanism.

Many mammals, like eusocial insects, recognize members of their social group on the basis of pheromones. In addition, dogs and mice are very accurate in individual recognition based on pheromones and other chemical cues. In mice, differences in odor can be traced to very slight variations in a protein that affects the odors of urine and other secretions. Consequently, the potential for individual variation is vast; this fact helps to account for the well-developed olfactory discrimination of many mammals (see Agosta, 1992).

In conclusion, social pheromones affect behavior in a wide variety of animals, especially social insects and mammals. In social insects the pheromones exert their influence in a relatively stereotypical manner: A pheromone from any individual of the same caste in the colony will have the same effect. In contrast, mammals typically learn to differentiate the pheromones of different individuals, al-lowing members of the group to respond differentially to the smells of individual group members.

The Benefits and Costs of Pheromonal Communication

Pheromonal communication provides numerous benefits, particularly for eusocial insects. The potential for complex communication in these insects is great because they produce so many chemical substances that can act as pheromones. For example, more than 50 potential pheromones have been identified in the glands of certain ants. There is probably not a specific effect associated with each chemical substance; but the number of possible messages is very large, because a blend of substances may produce a unique message. In other words, substances A and B together produce a different effect than either A or B alone. Furthermore, the same pheromone may have different effects, depending on the specific context (Agosta, 1992; Wilson, 1975).

Nonetheless, there can be disadvantages to some types of pheromonal communication if pheromones are perceptible to animals other than conspecifics. For example, if a pheromone related to attractiveness leads to attempts at mating with individuals of other species, there is a waste of reproductive potential at the very least. It is also possible that one of the individuals could be injured or killed.

Another possible disadvantage is that an individual from a different species may be attracted by a pheromone and prey on its sender. In response to this possibility, there has been a natural selection for pheromones that are highly specific to a given species, particularly in regard to attraction.

The possibility of communicating with individuals from other species is less of a problem in regard to alarm pheromones than in regard to reproductive pheromones. In fact, if two species develop a sensitivity to each others' alarm substances, this mutual sensitivity can be the basis for mutualism. We saw in Chapter 12 how a mutual sensitivity to alarm calls can benefit two or more species. Thus, it is not surprising that alarm pheromone molecules are generally smaller and less complex—and therefore less species-specific—than molecules of reproductive pheromones. In addition, these smaller molecules are less biologically expensive to produce and travel more rapidly in the air (Wilson, 1975).

Recently, however, researchers have identified a parasitoid fly (*Apocephalus paraponerae*) that exploits an ant alarm pheromone to parasitize several ant species. These flies have evolved a sensitivity to the pheromone and utilize it to zero in on their ant hosts (Feener et al., 1996). As I have pointed out before, the fact that animals are constantly coevolving means that no solution is perfect or invulnerable in a world filled with opportunists.

HORMONES

The notion that various substances in the body promote normal functioning goes back to ancient times. In the fifth century B.C., the Greek physician Hippocrates suggested that good health resulted from the proper balance of four fluids. It was not until the 1840s, however, that the first successful experiment related to hormones was performed: A. A. Berthold castrated roosters, observed changes in their behavior, and then returned a testis to the animal's body. Berthold found that the rooster subsequently returned to normal sexual behavior, and he concluded that the testes normally release something into the blood that functions to maintain sexual behavior.

In the early part of the twentieth century, researchers began systematically experimenting with extracts from endocrine glands and the term *hormone* was first introduced. Berthold's general method of removing an animal's endocrine gland, observing behavioral changes, and then observing changes after a hormone produced by the gland is restored remains a popular experimental procedure to this day. It is now possible to identify local effects of hormones by implanting a hormone in a discrete area of the animal's body, especially in parts of the brain. Researchers can then observe the specific effects on both behavior and neural activity and can draw inferences about the role of the hormone in question (see Turner & Bagnara, 1976).

As discussed in Chapter 2 in connection with the development of gender differences, researchers may also observe the results of natural differences in effective hormone levels. These differences may be associated with such factors as rat fetuses' positions in the uterus or congenital insensitivities to certain hormones.

Most hormones, especially those of vertebrates, are secreted directly into the blood by endocrine glands (see Figure 17.2). Once in the bloodstream, hormones travel throughout the animal's body, often exerting their influence in distant areas. As with the two types of pheromonal effects, hormones have two general types of effects. **Organizational effects** stimulate relatively permanent structural changes in neural organization. These changes generally occur early in life during a sensitive period of development. In contrast,

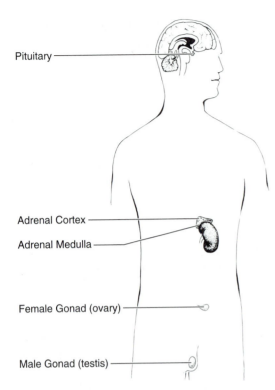

FIGURE 17.2 ◆ **The locations of several important endocrine glands in a human.**

Pituitary

Adrenal Cortex

Adrenal Medulla

Female Gonad (ovary)

Male Gonad (testis)

activational effects are transient and last only while the hormone is present in large amounts. Activational effects of hormones bring into play neural patterns that are already present.

Reproductive Behavior

We will now look at the organizational and activational effects of sex hormones on reproductive behavior. Two closely related steroid hormones produced by the gonads—**testos-**

terone and **estradiol**—have critical effects on reproductive behavior. The closeness of the relationship between these sex hormones can be seen in their biochemical structure as well as in their synthesis (see Figure 17.3). Estradiol is in fact synthesized from testosterone, with the aid of a special enzyme. Many cells in the brain contain this enzyme, and testosterone may enter a cell, undergo synthesis into estradiol, then produce its effect as a synthesized molecule of estradiol (Bonsall et al., 1992).

High levels of testosterone are basic to several aspects of male sexuality. Also, as Chapter 2 explained, a low level or lack of testosterone is basic to the development of female sexuality.

Testosterone is the most influential member of a class of hormones called androgens. Unfortunately, the term *androgen,* which is derived from the Greek word for "man," is somewhat misleading, because androgens may affect the behavior of females as well as males. In a comparable way, estradiol is the most potent of the estrogens, a category of hormones whose name is derived from the Greek word for "woman." Once again, the term *estrogen* is misleading, because estrogens can affect the behavior of both males and females.

Various classes of vertebrates produce testosterone and estradiol, and the biochemical composition of each is very similar across classes. Consistent with this similarity, the same testosterone that influences the development of a mating tendency in a male frog stimulates the growth of a mane in male lions. Although the specific "tasks" of the sex hormones have changed, little or no evolutionary change in the structure of these hormones has taken place over millions of years.

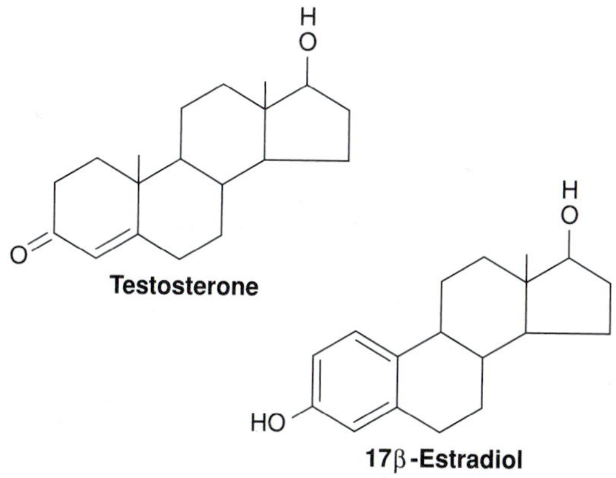

FIGURE 17.3 ◆ **The chemical structures of testosterone and estrogen.** Note the extreme similarity in the structures.

Organizational Effects of Hormones on Reproductive Behavior

In Chapter 2 we saw that rat fetuses exposed to differential amounts of testosterone under natural conditions develop differing degrees of masculinization. There is also evidence from castration studies that testosterone has an organizing effect on reproduction-related neural centers early in young animals' development. For example, males with normal amounts of testosterone develop a preoptic area (in the brain) that is twice as large as the same area in rats castrated immediately after birth (Jacobson, 1978). The preoptic area is involved, as we have seen, in the sexual behavior in males.

Because testosterone is associated with a masculinization effect in the development of both sex organs and nerves related to male sexual behavior, it is not surprising that a significant relationship between testosterone and sexual behavior exists. Thus, if a male is ex-perimentally castrated at birth, it will show a lowered tendency to exhibit male sexual ability as an adult, even if it is given injections of testosterone at this time. The castrated male will also show an increased tendency to exhibit female behavior, an example of the feminization effect. In keeping with these findings, female rats given shots of testosterone at birth show fewer female-type behaviors and more male-type behaviors as adults than rats reared normally (Svare, 1988).

The principles of masculinization and feminization—related to the presence or absence of testosterone during a sensitive period of development—apply to hormones' organizational effects on several structures and behaviors related to mating. However, the sensitive periods are different for the development of sex organs, specific neural development, and the development of sexual behavior potential.

Activational Effects— Male Sexual Behavior

Testosterone stimulates growth of secondary sex characteristics such as the colorful plumage of many male birds, the antlers of stag deer, and the manes of male lions. The output of testosterone is regulated by an anterior pituitary hormone known as follicle-stimulating hormone, or **FSH.** In most species of birds, and in deer, FSH production is sensitive to diurnal cycles (the length of the day). Consequently, FSH production is seasonal, and the males develop their secondary sex characteristics during the mating season.

In many other mammals, however, the production of FSH and testosterone is relatively constant. Consequently, animals such as male lions retain their secondary sex characteristics throughout the year. This constancy is possible because of a negative feedback circuit between certain parts of the brain and the testes. When FSH levels are high, the testes are stimulated to secrete testosterone. Then, when receptors in the hypothalamus detect a high level of testosterone in the blood, a chemical message is sent to the anterior pituitary that reduces FSH secretion. The low FSH levels result in a drop in testosterone secretion. After the testosterone level drops, inhibition of the FSH secretion ceases, and the testosterone level rises again. This feedback circuit enables most male mammals to retain their secondary sex characteristics throughout the year.

In addition, male mammals retain their sexual interest throughout the year, because testosterone is generally directly linked to male sexual drive. There are important exceptions to this rule, however. Castration of primates with prior sexual experience does not usually eliminate sexual interest. It seems that primates' sexuality is less dependent on testosterone and more dependent on experience than the sexuality of most other mammals (Daly & Wilson, 1983).

After ejaculation, males typically enter a **refractory period;** that is, a period during which they are unresponsive to sexual stimulation. What is the proximal mechanism for this temporary loss of sexual interest? Two hormones produced by the pituitary gland, **oxytocin** and **prolactin,** are secreted in large amounts during ejaculation. These hormones seem to induce quiescence and loss of sexual interest following ejaculation (Oaknin et al., 1989).

Activational Effects— Female Sexual Behavior

In mammals such as the rat, female receptivity to mating is regulated by two hormones: estradiol and **progesterone,** a steroid hormone secreted by the corpus luteum of the ovaries. Studies involving the experimental blocking of these hormones indicate that estradiol "primes" the female. Then, if she receives stimulation from progesterone within 18 to 24 hours, she develops receptivity (Takahashi, 1990).

The priming by estradiol followed by progesterone has additional effects. Female animals are not simply passive recipients of male sexual advances but, in many cases, exhibit proceptivity, or the tendency to encourage sexual contact with males. Thus, the female rat wiggles her ears, crouches, and moves her tail to one side—behaviors that greatly excite the male.

Estradiol and progesterone also enhance a female's attractiveness to males by stimulating physical changes. For example, the urine of female dogs and cats in estrus attracts males, sometimes from a great distance. The female chimpanzee in estrus develops a pink, swollen area in her genital region that induces sexual advances from males.

The hormone FSH stimulates output of estradiol in females, much as FSH triggers testosterone output in males. At the beginning of the female's estrus or menstrual cycle, FSH levels are low. As FSH levels build up during the early part of the cycle, estradiol is secreted. Estradiol, in turn, stimulates the release of another anterior pituitary hormone, LH (luteinizing hormone). LH induces ovulation; it also stimulates development of the corpus luteum and the production of progesterone. Finally, when estradiol and progesterone levels reach a high point, they are antagonistic to the production of FSH and LH, and the female returns to the beginning stage of the cycle. In other words, the interaction between two hormones produced by the ovaries (estradiol and progesterone) and two hormones produced by the anterior pituitary (FSH and LH) regulate the rhythmic recurrence of the female reproductive cycle.

As mentioned in Chapter 9, certain primates such as bonobo chimpanzee females are sexually receptive throughout much of their menstrual cycle. Apparently the bonobos do *not* depend heavily on estradiol to support their receptivity (see Kano, 1992). At least part of this continuous receptivity throughout the menstrual cycle is related to a relationship between testosterone and sexual receptivity. Testosterone, which is secreted in small amounts by the adrenal glands of females, is correlated with sexual interest (Everitt et al., 1972). Because testosterone is secreted throughout the menstrual cycle, this hormone functions to stabilize sexual interest in certain primates.

Activational Effects— Parental Behavior

Following mating, hormones continue to facilitate reproduction by influencing parental care. Large quantities of progesterone and prolactin work in conjunction with each other to mediate such varied types of parental responses as incubation behavior in domestic hens and nursing behavior in mammals (see Johnson, 1986).

In addition to progesterone and prolactin, oxytocin is involved in the nursing behavior of mammals. Oxytocin stimulates the letting down of milk into the area of the nipples, a response that is necessary before the young can obtain the milk. When the young first begin to nurse, their stimulation of the mother's nipples induces the release of oxytocin and the subsequent letting down of milk. Then, as the young continue to nurse, their stimulation keeps oxytocin levels high, and this high level of oxytocin stimulates the production of more prolactin as well as the letting down of milk. Finally, the high levels of prolactin result in continued milk production. This positive feedback circuit enables the mother to produce oxytocin and prolactin only for the duration of the nursing relationship (Lehrman, 1961).

As long as the mother is nursing her offspring, she does not come into estrus, because high levels of prolactin inhibit the output of estradiol. Thus, prolactin not only facilitates parental behavior but prevents the mother from engaging in sexual activities and becoming pregnant. As noted in Chapter 11, the spacing of offspring may be an important reproductive strategy.

In conclusion, there is often an interaction between behavior and hormonal output. Not only do hormones affect behavior, but behavior may affect hormonal output.

The Interaction between Hormones and Neurons in Reproduction

The finding that testosterone stimulation early in life results in growth of the preoptic area in males' brains is one example of how hor-

TABLE 17.3 ◆ Organizational and Activational Effects of Hormones

Effect	Length of Effect	Period of Sensitivity	Examples
Activational	Transient	Whenever hormones are present in large amounts	Testosterone is associated with sex drive in adult males.
Organizational	Permanent	During and early, sensitive period of development	Testosterone induces masculinization of genitals in males.

mones interact with neurons in the control of reproductive behavior. Another example is the development of testosterone-sensitive receptors on individual neurons. Early stimulation by testosterone increases the number of these receptors on neurons in the preoptic area (Roselli et al., 1989). Thus, the masculinization effects of hormones can occur as the result of both an increase in the number of neurons and an increase in the individual neurons' sensitivity.

In the case of feminization, there is evidence that early testosterone stimulation results in a reduction in the number of estrogen receptors on brain neurons (Rainbow et al., 1984). Under normal circumstances males develop relatively few estrogen receptors and, consequently, are less likely to develop female-type behaviors than are females.

Social Behavior

No only does testosterone directly facilitate reproduction in males; this hormone makes an important indirect contribution to a male's fitness by increasing aggressiveness toward con-

specific males. This aggressiveness facilitates success in encounters with competing males and in some cases enables males to acquire a mating territory. And the influence of testosterone on aggressiveness is both activational and organizational.

Activational Effects of Hormones on Aggression

In a large variety of animals, testosterone has an activational effect on aggression. Experimental studies support this conclusion, in that shots of testosterone generally raise levels of male–male aggressiveness, while castration lowers them. This facilitation of aggression seems to result from a combination of factors. First, testosterone may lower the threshold for attack, causing the animal to respond aggressively in a relatively wide variety of situations. Second, testosterone may enhance attention to stimuli related to attack. For example, the period of sustained attention to an opponent preceding attack seems to be lengthened by testosterone. Third, increased muscular development and size, which is stimulated by testosterone, may indirectly increase the ten-

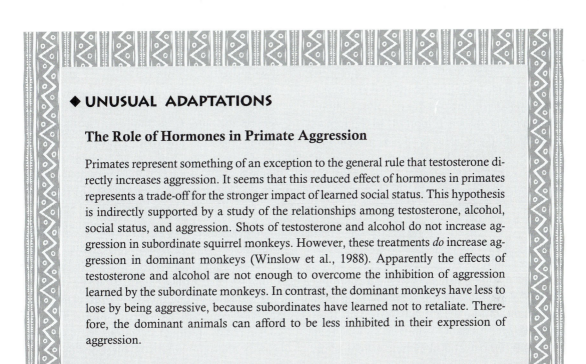

◆ UNUSUAL ADAPTATIONS

The Role of Hormones in Primate Aggression

Primates represent something of an exception to the general rule that testosterone directly increases aggression. It seems that this reduced effect of hormones in primates represents a trade-off for the stronger impact of learned social status. This hypothesis is indirectly supported by a study of the relationships among testosterone, alcohol, social status, and aggression. Shots of testosterone and alcohol do not increase aggression in subordinate squirrel monkeys. However, these treatments *do* increase aggression in dominant monkeys (Winslow et al., 1988). Apparently the effects of testosterone and alcohol are not enough to overcome the inhibition of aggression learned by the subordinate monkeys. In contrast, the dominant monkeys have less to lose by being aggressive, because subordinates have learned not to retaliate. Therefore, the dominant animals can afford to be less inhibited in their expression of aggression.

dency to aggress. Greater strength and size heighten the probability of winning; and, as we have seen, winning can be reinforcing and can foster the tendency to provoke encounters. Finally, the testosterone-induced development of secondary sex characteristics may promote the tendency of conspecific males to respond aggressively to combative signals (Archer, 1988).

The multiple effects of testosterone on aggression are illustrated by male songbirds. Males with high levels of testosterone develop bright coloration, which tends to provoke attack from conspecific males. In addition, the testosterone promotes a high level of activity called **migratory restlessness.** Migratory restlessness is associated with a tendency to fly in

a certain direction; but migratory restlessness also increases the tendency of males to behave aggressively. Finally, testosterone stimulates males to sing their territorial and courtship songs. Like bright coloration, the singing tends to provoke conspecific males to attack.

Although the relationship between aggression and testosterone is typically associated with males, females in a few species also illustrate the relationship. The enlarged clitoris or pseudopenis of the female spotted hyena (see Chapter 12) apparently evolved because of a natural selection process favoring high levels of aggressiveness promoted by testosterone. Hyenas need aggressiveness to fight for food, and the pseudopenis develops in female fetuses as the result of large amounts of testosterone secreted by the mother during her pregnancy. A similar relationship between female aggressiveness and high levels of testosterone is found in the spotted sandpiper, the polyandrous bird we discussed in Chapter 10. Aggressiveness is important to the female spotted sandpiper because she must fight with other females to establish a territory to attract a male partner (Oring, 1985). In a few instances, then, female animals benefit from heightened levels of aggressiveness. In these cases, a tendency to utilize the testosterone produced by the female's adrenal glands apparently evolved.

It seems that estradiol has an effect opposite to that of testosterone; estradiol reduces aggression. If female animals have had their ovaries experimentally removed so that they have little or no estradiol in their system, shots of testosterone induce aggressiveness toward other females. In contrast, shots of estradiol diminish aggression (Van de Poll et al., 1988).

Organizational Effects of Hormones on Aggression

As we have seen, the reduced *activational* effects of hormones in certain primates relate to sexual behavior as well as to aggression. With the evolution of the relatively large, well-developed primate brain, the central place of learning has tended to overshadow dependence on hormonal mechanisms. Nonetheless, the *organizational* effects of hormones are basic to primate behavior as well as to the behavior of nonprimates.

Testosterone administered to female rhesus monkeys late in fetal development results in an increase in rough-and-tumble play after birth. It seems that the prenatal effects of testosterone—which is normally secreted for a short time during the fetal development of males—organizes brain development in such a way that aggression is facilitated, much the way testosterone organizes brain development related to sexual behavior. However, the timing of the sexual and aggressive organizational effects is different. Testosterone treatment early in fetal development causes hypersexual behavior, while later treatments of testosterone (shortly before birth) result in increased aggressiveness (Goy et al., 1988).

In songbirds it is often estradiol rather than testosterone that has organizing effects on singing and aggression. Thus, female songbirds, which normally have low levels of estradiol early in life, do not sing even if they are injected with testosterone as adults. Only if the females receive injections of estradiol shortly after hatching plus injections of testosterone when they reach maturity will they sing like males (Pohl-Apel & Sossinka, 1984). Studies with zebra finches indicate how the early estradiol has its effect. Normally, estradiol stimulates the development of neural areas related to song development only in males. However, experimental implantation of estradiol also stimulates growth of these neural areas in females. Then, in adulthood, the females can be stimulated to sing malelike songs (DeVoogd, 1991).

In conclusion, we have seen that certain hormones have both organizational and activational effects on reproduction and social processes. We should keep in mind, however, that there is not always a clear line of distinction between organizational and activational effects. For example, activational effects are sometimes delayed, taking several days or even weeks before they can be observed. The delay may be caused by the time necessary for a hormone to metabolize or break down, or it may result from the complex interactions among hormones. At any rate, dichotomies are seldom absolute—as we have discovered several times throughout this book.

Stress

The subject of stress arose in Chapter 7 when we considered defense against predation. We will now look at the hormonal responses to stressful events—responses that help explain why long-term stress can be deleterious to an animal's health.

Stress Reaction in Adults

Animals exhibit the same type of general physiological reaction to predators or to threatening conspecifics, whether the threatened animals are preparing to fight, flee, or freeze. The hormones epinephrine and norepinephrine, secreted by the adrenal medulla, function to mobilize the body's resources and provide extra energy. (As you will remember from Chapter 16, epinephrine and norepinephrine also serve as neurotransmitters.) Under continued threat of predation or other types of stress, a condition that experimenters can simulate in the laboratory by delivering periodic electric shocks, animals exhibit what has been called the **general adaptation syndrome** (Selye, 1976).

The general adaptation syndrome consists of three stages. The first stage, known as the alarm stage, involves the responses just discussed—secretion of adrenal hormones that function to provide immediate extra energy. The second stage, called the resistance stage, features the secretion of **corticosteroid hor-mones** by the adrenal medulla; these keep the body's temperature, blood pressure, and respiration high, thereby providing resources over a longer period of time.

If the stress reaction continues for too long a time, however, the animal enters the third stage—exhaustion. Essentially, the animal has been living on borrowed resources. When the resources are depleted, the animal's resistance to disease in general is lowered, and it is likely to develop stress-related diseases such as ulcers. In some cases the prolonged stress may be lethal.

In essence, the evolved mechanisms for dealing with stress are helpful up to a point; but when stress becomes too intense and/or prolonged, the results are deleterious. Researchers are now beginning to understand some of the specifics of the relationship between stress and health. In one study, for example, rats stressed in the laboratory showed increased output of **glucocorticoids.** These hormones are important in carbohydrate and protein metabolism; but the exceptionally high concentration of glucocorticoids functioned to decrease the number of **natural killer cells**—cells in the immune system that destroy cells infected by viruses (Keller et al., 1983). Consequently, the rats became susceptible to opportunistic diseases.

Other laboratory experiments have suggested that animals learn to be helpless in situations where their attempts to escape or control events have failed. This **learned helplessness** then generalizes to different situations—even to situations where adaptive responses are readily available. For example, researchers have strapped dogs in a harness and given them repeated shocks in a laboratory setting. Later, when placed in a situation in which they could escape shock by simply jumping over a hurdle, the dogs cowered and made no attempt to escape the shock (Seligman & Maier, 1967).

Prenatal Responses to the Mother's Stress

In a classic experiment, Richard Thompson (1957) shocked pregnant rats and found that not only the mothers but their unborn young were affected by the stress. The young of these stressed mothers showed reduced rates of activity after birth.

Later studies with laboratory animals indicated that the effects of prenatal stress may last into adulthood, especially in males. When the male offspring of prenatally stressed mothers become adult, the males have a smaller-than-usual penis and are less likely to show normal male sexual behavior than are offspring of nonstressed mothers (Ward & Weisz, 1980). Consistent with this finding,

male offspring of stressed mothers are less aggressive than normally reared offspring (Kinsley & Svare, 1986).

These effects on the adult offspring seem to result from the mothers' large output of corticosteroids. These hormones have their effect by reducing the production of testosterone in the male fetuses. This reduced testosterone production is, in turn, linked to inhibition of the masculinization process necessary for both sexual and aggressive behavior in the male.

Finally, there is evidence that prenatal responses to maternal stress make animals more susceptible to later stress. Thus, rats whose mothers have been stressed react abnormally strongly to stress as adults (Takahashi et al., 1992). It seems that the inability of animals to adapt to long-term stress or to adjust to the deleterious effects of long-term stress on their mothers can create serious problems.

◆ HUMAN EVOLUTION

The same classes of chemical factors that influence the behavior of nonhuman animals also affect humans. An increased understanding of these factors has resulted in some significant breakthroughs in the treatment of certain human problems, particularly in regard to our reactions to long-term stress.

PHEROMONES

Generally speaking, humans and primates in general are less dependent on pheromonal communication than are many eusocial insects and rodents. As we have seen, ants and mice communicate a very large amount of social information on the basis of pheromones. In contrast, primates rely to a great extent on auditory and visual communication.

Nonetheless, humans are more sensitive to pheromones than we believed in the past. For many years scientists assumed that an olfactory organ that is sensitive to pheromones in most mammals—the vomeronasal organ—was vestigial and nonoperative in humans. But research evidence has now revealed that humans have somewhat active vomeronasal organs and are sensitive to certain pheromones (Garcia-Velasco & Mondragon, 1991). In one study, for example, people were able to tell on the basis of olfactory cues whether a T-shirt had previously been worn by a man or by a woman (Russell, 1976).

As in nonhuman animals, human pheromones have a primer effect. For example, women who do not live or work around males—and males' normal body odors—often experience disturbances in their menstrual cycles and a failure to ovulate. In contrast, women who work with or spend a large amount of time in the company of men have relatively short menstrual cycles. Furthermore, women who live together tend to synchronize their menstrual cycles, an effect that is similar to the Whitten effect in mice (McClintock, 1971).

The benefit of synchronizing menstrual cycles in humans is not clear. It is possible, however, that this synchronization resulted in an increased probability that females within a group of our hominid ancestors would become pregnant and deliver young at the same time. With infants of approximately the same age, the possibility of sharing nursing responsibilities was increased, and mothers in the group could babysit one another's infants.

It appears that these effects in humans are due to pheromones. Support for this conclusion comes from an experiment involving the systematic presentation of odor cues from underarm perspiration. A woman who served as a donor placed cotton pads under each arm for a period of 24 hours. A group of women functioning as recipients then rubbed the pads on their upper lips, just below their noses, three times a week. The recipients showed a significant tendency to synchronize their menstrual cycles with the cycle of the donor (Russell et al., 1978).

Why did scientists fail for so long to identify the significant roles of pheromones and other chemical stimuli in human behavior? Part of the reason is that since Victorian times many people have tended to deemphasize olfactory cues by covering them up with artificial fragrances and by refraining from discussing natural odors with the same openness afforded visual and auditory cues (see Schaal & Porter, 1991). Consequently, Western technological societies have tended to overlook some potentially important factors in human behavior.

HORMONES

Hormones are associated with the same general types of behavior patterns in all vertebrates. However, there are significant differences between the activational effects of hormones in humans and in other vertebrates, particularly in regard to sexual behavior and stress.

Sexual Behavior

Female sexual desire (proceptivity and receptivity) is generally facilitated by estradiol; but in primates such as the bonobo, female sexual desire is more closely regulated by testosterone than by estradiol. A similar relationship between testosterone and sexual desire is seen in human females. For example, women with low levels of estradiol resulting from menopause or ovariotomy (removal of the ovaries) do not lose sexual interest (Persky et al., 1978).

Why was there a shift to testosterone-controlled sexual desire in female bonobos and humans? Because testosterone is secreted in relatively constant amounts during the cycle, this shift enables females of these primate species to engage in coitus throughout the menstrual cycle and to associate sexual interaction with functions other than reproduction. This association between sex and nonreproductive functions, seen in bonobos and in chimpanzees, is even more pronounced in humans.

Stress

In humans as in nonhuman animals, physiological responses to long-term stress can have strongly negative effects. Why has there not been an evolutionary trend to counter these negative effects? One of the reasons is that most animals do not remain stressed for long periods of time under natural conditions. Either the imminent threat of predation passes, or the animal is eaten. Similarly, animals adjust to social pressures or leave the group; and social animals are seldom or never forced into social isolation.

However, humans in technologically advanced societies often remain under some type of stress for long periods of time—noisy environments, crowded or menacing conditions, and job situations that are highly demanding and in which they feel they have little control. There are also breakdowns in close relationships as the divorce rate rises and people move more often from one community to another. In sum, humans in technological societies often face types of stress for which we are poorly adapted; and we do not always utilize effectively the coping mechanisms we do possess. For example, our ancestors' lifestyle provided two very effective means of stress reduction—exercise and close communion with other group members (see De Angelis, 1995).

Research on stress in humans supports the findings I have outlined in conjunction with nonhumans. Prolonged stress compromises the immune system and makes us more vulnerable to opportunistic diseases. For example, college students are more likely to develop respiratory diseases at exam time than during the rest of the semester. This increase in susceptibility is related to a significant drop in immunoglobulins that are part of the body's primary defense against respiratory infections (Jemmott & Magloire, 1988).

The findings of the "executive" rat study are particularly applicable to humans. In a classic study, human subjects were exposed to an unpleasant noise. One group of subjects had the opportunity to turn off the noise when they felt too much stress, although they typically decided not to exert this option. However, these subjects showed fewer negative reactions to the stress than subjects who did not have the opportunity to exert control. The minimally stressed subjects also made fewer errors on a subsequent proofreading task than did those who had had no control options (Glass et al., 1969). Apparently even the possibility of exerting control mitigated the effects of the stress.

Following the lead of this and other similar studies, more recent research indicates that if people are hopeful and believe they have some kind of control over events that may be stressful, they experience fewer negative effects of stress (Zimmerman, 1990). The combined effects of positive attitudes, general physical health, and regular exercise are a powerful deterrent to a variety of diseases (Roth et al., 1989).

Fortunately, there is evidence that coping skills involving these principles can be taught to children in a relatively short period of time. Sixth-grade children were given an 8-hour stress management program that emphasized coping skills. Both self-reports and reports of teachers indicated that the program significantly reduced children's stress levels (DeWolfe & Saunders, 1995). Despite increasing stress in our society, the possibility of developing widely utilized stress management programs such as this is cause for some optimism.

◆ CHANGING PERSPECTIVES

PAST	PRESENT	FUTURE
Chemical systems are quite independent of neural and sensory systems (early nineteenth century).	There is a complex interaction among chemical, neural, and sensory systems.	How did pheromonal, hormonal, neural, and sensory systems affect one another's evolutions?

SUMMARY

Pheromones are chemical messengers passed from one conspecific to another. Signal pheromones have an immediate effect on behavior. In eusocial insects, the pheromones may influence sexual attraction, communicate alarm, facilitate recognition of colony members, establish a trail, or communicate regarding the condition of the queen. In mammals, signal pheromones may affect reproduction by acting as a sex attractant, as an attractant between eggs and sperm, or as a maternal attractant. Signal pheromones are also important in mammals' social behavior, functioning as territorial markers, increasing male–male aggressiveness, and facilitating social recognition.

Primer pheromones influence an animal's physiological condition and consequently have a delayed effect on behavior. In rodents, primer pheromones may accelerate the sexual maturity of females, promote abortion and resorption of embryos, or synchronize estrous cycles.

Hormones are chemical messengers typically carried in the blood from one part of an animal's body to another. Immediate, activational effects of hormones such as testosterone influence the development of secondary sex characteristics, sex drive, and the onset of parental behavior. An interaction of several hormones controls the development of sexual and parental behaviors. Testosterone also has an influence on the social behavior of males, contributing to intraspecies aggressiveness, especially against other males.

Hormones also have organizational effects, stimulating structural changes that are relatively permanent. Testosterone has an organizational effect on reproduction, as illustrated by the masculinizing effect of testosterone on the prenatal development of sex organs and neurons related to sexual behavior. Testosterone and estradiol are also related to social behavior, as demonstrated by their effects on aggression in mammals and singing in birds.

Hormones are also secreted in response to stress, sometimes causing serious problems. Long-term stress can compromise the immune system, especially if animals have no control over the cause of the stress. In addition to its effects on adults, stress can negatively influence mammals when it occurs prenatally.

An understanding of the evolution of the chemical control of behavior helps to explain certain previously ill-understood aspects of human behavior. Examples include the roles of pheromones as primers and of hormones in regulating human sexual behavior and stress reactions.

KEY TERMS

activational effects, p. 400
alarm pheromone, p. 396
Bruce effect, p. 395
corticosteroid hormones, p. 407
estradiol, p. 400
FSH, p. 401
funeral pheromone, p. 396
general adaptation syndrome, p. 407
glucocorticoids, p. 407
learned helplessness, p. 407
maternal pheromone, p. 394
migratory restlessness, p. 405
natural killer cells, p. 407
odor trail, p. 396

organizational effects, p. 399
oxytocin, p. 402
primer pheromone, p. 393
progesterone, p. 402
prolactin, p. 402
queen pheromone, p. 397
recognition pheromone, p. 396
refractory period, p. 402
signal pheromone, p. 393
testosterone, p. 400
trophallaxis, p. 392
Vandenbergh effect, p. 395
Whitten effect, p. 395

SENSORY SYSTEMS AND BIOLOGICAL CLOCKS

◆ *How do bats avoid flying into obstacles in the dark?*

◆ *Can bats identify one another in the dark?*

In this third chapter on biological mechanisms, we will consider sensory systems and biological clocks. Because some animals have mechanisms quite different from those of humans, it is only recently that we have come to appreciate the great diversity of ways in which nonhuman animals gather information about the world.

The division between the systems we discussed in Chapters 16 and 17 and those we will consider here is necessarily arbitrary, in that neural and chemical processes interact

18

with sensory systems. Furthermore, biological clocks influence neural functioning and hormonal secretions—and vice versa. However, following the pattern set in previous chapters, this chapter will discuss sensory systems and biological clocks separately.

We will begin by surveying sensory systems in general and how they evolved. Then we will take a comparative look at each of the major sensory systems, and we'll consider examples of how sensory information affects behavior. Next, we will examine biological clocks—timing mechanisms that have a direct effect on behavior as well as on many structural adaptations related to behavior. Finally, we will consider human sensory systems and biological clocks.

SENSORY SYSTEMS

Most sensory systems have three components. The first component, a receptor, is sensitive to a particular type of energy (or chemical compound) and transduces, or changes, this energy into electrical nerve impulses. The sensory receptors are highly selective, responding only to certain types of energy and, generally, to a very narrow band of that energy. For example, vertebrate eyes respond to electromagnetic energy with wavelengths of approximately 440 to and 700 nm and are oblivious to longer or shorter wavelengths. (One nm—nanometer—is a billionth of a meter.)

In certain cases, stimulation of a receptor results in a series of enzyme-catalyzed biochemical or mechanical steps that serve to amplify the signal. This series of steps enables some highly specialized senses to respond to minute amounts of stimulation. For example, the middle ear bones of birds and mammals greatly amplify the sound signal, enabling many of these animals to be extremely sensitive to airborne vibrations.

The second component of sensory systems is a conductor that transmits coded information to higher neural levels, such as the sensory areas in the central nervous system of vertebrates. In vertebrates the conductors are usually long axons that carry the neural message from the sense organ to the neural center.

Some of the coding of sensory information takes place spatially; that is, the interpretation of the neural message is dependent on the area of the brain involved. For example, animals that are experimentally stimulated in the visual area generally respond as if they perceived a visual message, and animals stimulated in the auditory area react as if this excitation resulted from an auditory stimulus.

Coding also takes place at a temporal level; that is, the coding is dependent on time sequences. For example, neural firing at a slow rate generally indicates that the stimulus is weak, while a rapid rate of firing is associated with strong stimulation.

The third component of sensory systems is the neural center. The neural center receives sensory information, integrates this information with that coming from other parts of the nervous system, and communicates with effector systems—different areas of the brain involved in the mediation of responses and the storage of memories. In very complex sensory systems, such as the visual systems of birds and mammals, there are several neural centers, each with different specializations.

Typically, sensory systems do not respond with the same level of intensity at all times. **Sensory adaptation,** or showing less response after a period of continuous stimula-

tion, may occur in any or all of the three components of the sensory system. This adaptation process enables an animal to pay less attention to constant stimulation and, consequently, to be more sensitive to changes in the amount or type of stimulation impinging upon it. Sensitivity to change is generally adaptive, because change is likely to signal a significant event.

The Evolution of Sensory Systems

The ancestral single-celled organisms that lived hundreds of millions of years ago did not, by definition, have sensory systems. A system implies multiple cells cooperating in a highly integrated manner. To survive, however, those early organisms must have been sensitive to certain aspects of the environment. This sensitivity became elaborated as multicellular animals evolved and as individual cells became specialized and worked in concert with other cells. Let's turn now to some important factors in the evolution of sensory systems.

Ecological Factors

An animal's habitat has a particularly strong influence on the evolution of sensory systems. For example, air is a poor conductor of electricity; accordingly, it not surprising that sensitivity to shifts in electrical potential has evolved only in aquatic animals. Similarly, animals such as bats that are active only at night or certain fish that live in dark and murky water where vision is ineffective have been selected for active sensory systems such as echolocation and electrolocation.

TABLE 18.1 ◆ The Components of Sensory Systems

Component	Function
Receptor	Detection and amplification of signal
Conductor	Coding and transmission of information to higher neural levels
Neural center(s)	Integration of information and communication with other neural areas

The type of food eaten also has a strong effect on the evolution of sensory systems. Animals that eat foods such as decaying vegetation or rotting meat, which give off strong odors, have evolved a sensitivity to chemical cues. In contrast, birds that feed on seeds, which do not have a strong odor, have tended to evolve a sensitivity to visual cues. Furthermore, as we shall see, the type of food eaten has influenced the evolution of color vision.

Another factor that shapes the evolution of sensory systems is danger of predation. Thus, lizards have evolved an acute sensitivity to smells associated with predatory snakes; moths have evolved an auditory system that is sensitive to predatory bats' calls; and European toads have evolved "feature detectors" that are maximally sensitive to predatory storks and cranes.

The evolution of sensory systems is also related to how rapidly an animal must make a decision. A frog does not have time to evaluate carefully the qualities of a fly that passes overhead. Consequently, there has been a natural selection for a quick-response food-detection sensory system in frogs. A cow, in contrast, has more time to make a decision about the acceptability of food. This animal has evolved a sensitivity to characteristics of grass that are indicative of quality.

Prior Adaptations

As we saw in our discussion of learning in Chapter 4, a prior adaptation or basic foundation is necessary before a system can evolve. In regard to sensory systems, a species must be preadapted to evolve certain types of sensitivities and behavior tendencies. For example, certain fish were preadapted—because they possessed special organs that are sensitive to waterborne vibrations—to evolve electroreceptors. Then a few fish that were sensitive to electrical fields produced by other fish became sensitive to their own electrical fields. Similarly, the bat was preadapted to develop a sophisticated system of echolocation (use of sound waves to locate objects) because, like most mammals, it had a well-developed auditory system.

Because sensitivities to stimulation evolve according to principles of natural selection, a sensory system does not always analyze information in a manner that is predictable or appears logical. A human engineer starting from scratch would undoubtedly design a type of eye or ear very different from what we find in the natural world, and in some cases the engineer's design would be more efficient. However, natural selection works with different tools and under different constraints than a human engineer. The fact that natural selection has produced such a variety of sensory systems adapted to such vastly different conditions—and featuring, in many cases, tremendous sensitivity to minute amounts of stimulation—never ceases to fascinate animal behaviorists.

Now that we have a general overview of sensory systems, let us look at some of the most important sensory systems in more detail.

Chemoreception

We will begin by discussing chemoreception—a specialized sensitivity to molecules of particular chemical compounds. Chemoreception is probably one of the first sensory systems to evolve (see Doty, 1995). The primary chemical sensory systems include olfaction (smell), which is specialized for detection of substances at a distance; and gustation (taste), which functions to identify substances on contact.

Olfaction

In land animals, a stimulus must be in a gaseous form before it can be detected by the olfactory system, or sense of smell. Although we do not know exactly how an animal classifies odors, a major factor appears to be the shape of a molecule; there is a moderate correlation between the shape of a molecule and the odor quality. However, odor quality is also affected by molecular properties such as electrical charge and chemical reactivity (see Cain, 1988).

Chemical substances or pheromones are basic to intraspecies communication; and among the most highly specialized pheromone receptors are those of the male silkworm moth, which include feathery antennae containing multiple chemoreceptors. These receptors are so sensitive that males are neurophysiologically excited by as little as a trillionth of a microgram of the female attraction pheromone. This extraordinary sensitivity enables the male to sense the presence of a female several kilometers away. The male then locates the female by flying upwind and adjusting to the relative concentration of the pheromone as detected by the two antennae; that is, he turns to the left if the left antenna receives more stimulation and to the right if stimulation is greatest on the right antenna (Schneider, 1974).

An important factor in the evolution of the extreme specialization of the male silkworm moth's chemoreception seems to be the flightlessness of the female. Because she is un-

able to move any great distance, males have become selected for identifying females from greater and greater distances. Females, in turn, have become selected for producing more and more potent attractants.

For many animals olfaction is important in the detection of food. Snakes, which facilitate the detection of odor by tongue flicking, are highly sensitive to the odor of their prey. Because the snake's tongue is forked, it can sample two points of a chemical gradient at the same time. Consequently, a snake can accurately follow the chemical trail left by its potential prey.

Rattlesnakes and other poisonous snakes in the family Elapidae first strike their prey, then release it and follow the its chemical trail. By releasing the prey and waiting to eat it until after the venom has had its deadly effect, the snake avoids having to swallow a struggling victim.

Conversely, the prey of snakes often use olfactory cues to identify the presence of their predators. For example, if the odor of a predatory snake is left in the cage of a laboratory lizard, the lizard shows long periods of immobility, hesitant movements, and an increased rate of tongue flicking. All of these responses indicate a state of preparation for the possibility of predatory attack.

Dogs have especially well-developed olfactory systems. In addition to locating prey from a distance, dogs can detect the odor trails of a prey animal. In some cases dogs are able to follow trails laid up to 4 days earlier. This remarkable olfactory ability is related to the dog's unusually large number of auditory receptors (approximately 1 billion) and to the fact that a large portion of the canine forebrain is devoted to processing olfactory information (see Moulton, 1977).

Gustation

In contrast to olfactory stimuli, which cannot be classified into a small number of categories, gustatory stimuli are easily classified into four primary taste qualities—sweet, sour, salty, and bitter. Most vertebrates are sensitive to all four taste qualities.

As the section on feeding behavior in Chapter 6 explained, animals typically have preferences for taste qualities associated with needed nutriments. Moreover, animals tend to avoid those taste qualities that indicate spoilage or poison. For example, rats avoid sour tastes (associated with high levels of bacterial activity in spoiled food) and bitter tastes (often linked with poisonous plant alkaloids). In addition, some feeding generalists develop nutritional wisdom—the preference for certain tastes following a deprivation of the nutrients associated with those tastes.

In many cases olfaction and gustation work together in the location and evaluation of a food source. The interaction of smell and taste in a mammal is easily illustrated if one blocks the sense of olfaction and observes the partial loss of taste discrimination. Most of us have noticed that food is less tasty when we have the nasal blockage associated with a common cold.

Thermoreception

Thermoreception, or sensitivity to temperature, is closely related to chemoreception, in that thermoreceptor function is based on temperature-induced changes in the speed of certain chemical reactions. Thermoreceptors are sensitive to specific temperatures as well as to changes in temperature, enabling many animals to select environments that are optimal or to make a quick escape from a deteriorating environment. In addition to a sensitivity to ambient temperature, a few animals possess extreme sensitivity to the temperature of distant objects. For example, mosquitoes are able to locate people on the basis of their body heat. Incidentally, mosquitoes are especially attracted to individuals with a high body temperature (Herter, 1962).

Rattlesnakes (Elapidae) and their cousins (Crotalidae) have highly specialized heat receptors that allow them to locate their prey at a distance. These pit organs, which are located between each eye and nostril, can detect a warm object such as a mouse in complete darkness. By moving its head back and forth, the snake can identify the boundaries of the object, select prey of an appropriate size, and strike at the center of the prey with great accuracy (Newman & Hartline, 1982).

Mechanoreception

Mechanoreception includes a variety of sensory systems that are sensitive to some form of mechanical stimulation. Essentially, mechanical stimulation results in a deformation or change in a specialized sensory cell membrane, which is then transduced into a neural response.

Touch Receptors

Land animals are typically sensitive to direct touch and, in some cases, to the movement of air caused by approaching danger. In many animals the touch receptors are sensory hairs that are displaced by tactual stimulation. For example, cockroaches have multiple wind-sensitive hairs located on two appendages, called cerci, projecting from the posterior end of their bodies. When a predator such as a cat creates a small gust of wind as it moves a paw to strike at the roach, the mechanoreceptors alert the roach and it runs for cover. These receptors are finely tuned; they do not respond to all gusts of wind, only to those in the intensity range of the wind generated by a predatory strike.

Mammals often have sensory hairs that are displaced by tactual stimulation. Social mammals may communicate arousal and positive emotional states via touch.

Web-building spiders have mechanoreceptors that are sensitive to vibrations conducted by the web. As the spider sits in its retreat with one leg in contact with a strand of the web, it can detect tremors in the web resulting from the struggles of a victim. (The web is constructed in such a way that movement in any part of the web will be conducted to the area of the spider's retreat.) Strong vibrations, which indicate a large and formidable prey, induce the spider to approach the prey rapidly, throw silk over the victim, and then apply a paralyzing bite. Less intense vibrations evoke a more leisurely approach; the relatively small victim may even be ignored for a time. Fortunately for the males of the species, which are typically smaller than the females, females can usually identify the web movements caused by approaching conspecific males and thus refrain from attacking the males (see Witt & Rovner, 1982).

Lateral Line Organs

Several varieties of fish—and a few amphibians—have mechanoreceptors known as **lateral line organs,** which are sensitive to water-borne vibrations. The lateral line organs, located in a canal that runs down the sides of the fish, signal the position of other animals in the water. These receptors also indicate the presence of obstacles, because the water movements created by the swimming of the fish are reflected by obstacles. Some fish have lateral line receptors on their heads and are highly sensitive to cues from surface waves created by insects trapped at the water surface. Like the mechanoreceptors of cockroaches, the lateral line receptors of fish that feed on insects are finely tuned, enabling the fish to discriminate prey from other causes of surface waves such as raindrops (see Popper & Platt, 1983).

Kinesthetic Receptors

Kinesthetic receptors, or proprioceptors, are mechanoreceptors located in the joints, muscles, and tendons that indicate the relative positions of body parts, particularly the appendages. When compared to other types of mechanoreceptors, some proprioceptors show very slow rates of sensory adaptation, thereby allowing the animal to remain aware of the position of a limb over an extended period of time.

Studies of kinesthetic receptors in rhesus monkeys suggest that there are several types of receptors: Some indicate whether a muscle is flexed or extended and also the velocity of movement; others are sensitive to the degree of flexion or extension; and still others respond to static position rather than to movement. In addition, some neurons indicate flexion in combinations of joints (see Costanzo & Gardiner, 1981). This complex organization of feedback is especially important for monkeys and apes, which utilize fine motor coordination in swinging from one branch to another in the trees and also in grasping objects such as fruit hanging from a tree. In addition, kinesthetic feedback is basic to the development of complex skills such as termite fishing in the chimpanzee.

Auditory Receptors

Because sound waves create pressure waves that stimulate receptors mechanically, auditory receptors are considered a type of mechanoreceptor. In certain insects, receptors known as **sensory hairs** are tuned to vibrations of specific frequencies, much like the strings on a piano. When a sound of a particular frequency occurs, the sensory hair is deflected back and forth, and this mechanical energy is transduced into neural impulses.

Auditory systems in animals may be so finely tuned that only one type of sound is audible. For example, a moth's auditory system is unresponsive to most environmental sounds but is capable of obtaining highly specific information on the approach of bats by analyzing the bats' ultrasonic echolocating calls. Laboratory studies indicate that a critical cue for the moth is the intensity of the bat's call. Systematic manipulation of the intensity of sounds emitted from a loudspeaker indicates that when the sound reaches a critical intensity normally associated with a bat's physical closeness, the moth will dive toward the ground in a twisting, unpredictable manner.

Even before the bat approaches close enough to evoke the diving response, the moth is able to obtain information about the location of the bat—whether it is above or below, to the right or to the left. The moth's auditory system gleans this information by comparing the intensity of sound received by the two receptors on the opposite sides of the moth's body. The moth is then able to move in a direction away from the approaching bat (Roeder, 1970). Although fossil evidence suggests that insects such as the ancestors of crickets evolved hearing before the arrival of bats, moths seem to have evolved hearing strictly as an adaptation to bat predation (Hoy, 1992).

As mentioned earlier, the vibrations of the tympanic membrane (eardrum) of birds and mammals are amplified by one or more inner ear bones, giving birds and mammals an especially acute sense of hearing. Birds and mammals use sound for a variety of functions, including intraspecific communication, predator identification, and, in many cases, foraging (see Klump et al., 1995).

Many of these functions are possible because of the ability to localize sound. This ability exists in all birds and mammals, but in the night-hunting barn owl the ability is extraordinarily well developed. The barn owl can locate rodents in complete darkness, using only the sounds made by movements of the prey. Like many animals, the owl obtains information on the horizontal direction of the sound source by analyzing the tiny difference between the times the sound arrives at each of its ears as well as the sound's relative loudness in each ear. For example, if the sound comes from straight ahead, it arrives at both ears at the same time and is equally loud; if it comes from an area slightly to the left, the sound arrives at the left ear slightly before it arrives at the right ear and is also slightly louder to the left ear. The barn owl is unique, however, in that one ear is located higher on the head than the other. This differential placement enables the owl to determine vertical as well as horizontal direction, because the ear that is lower on the head receives the sound stimulation

◆ UNUSUAL ADAPTATIONS

Echolocation

Some animals not only respond to sounds from the environment, but produce sounds themselves and gain information by analyzing the pattern of echoes from nearby objects. This ability, known as **echolocation,** is particularly well developed in bats that catch insects in flight.

The fact that bats use their auditory sense to avoid obstacles was known at least as early as the eighteenth century. However, it was not until much later that Griffin and Galambos (1941) discovered *how* bats use their auditory ability to avoid obstacles. They found that little brown bats (*Myotis lucifugus*) were able to find their way among a series of fine wires spaced about a foot apart, but only if their mouth and ears were unobstructed. Clearly, the bats were responding to some sound that they emitted from their mouths. Later, with more sophisticated electronic equipment, Griffin found that the bats emitted extremely intense high-pitched sounds—sounds too high for the human auditory system to detect. The bats then analyzed the echoes reflected from objects. Of special significance was the finding that the bats could also locate food with these sonar systems (Griffin, 1958).

With even more sophisticated equipment, researchers found that many of bats' sound pulses are very short in duration and repeated rapidly, enabling the bat to process large amounts of information in a short time. Bats such as the Mexican free-tail bat (*Tadarida brasiliensis*) emit two types of echolocation calls. **Constant frequency calls** remain at the same pitch; they provide detailed information about the target's rate of movement and whether it is moving toward or away from the bat. In contrast, **frequency modulated calls,** which start at a particular pitch and then sweep downward about an octave, provide maximal information about the shape, size, and texture of the target. The bat uses a constant frequency call as it is searching for prey; then, once it detects a target, it switches to a signal that is increasingly frequency modulated. The frequency modulated signal enables the bat to identify its target and make a decision on whether or not to attack.

Another line of research indicates that the adaptive specialization of the bat's calls is matched by specializations in the bat's auditory system. Typically, vertebrate auditory receptors become temporarily insensitive after the animal makes a sound as intense as that of the bat. The bat, however, is able to contract a muscle in the middle ear that dampens the vibrations of middle ear bones for the duration of a cry. The

(continued)

muscle relaxes approximately 5 milliseconds after the cry, enabling the auditory system to be receptive to the relatively soft echo that follows.

The reception of the echo is further facilitated in the auditory center of the bat's brain, where specialized nerve cells are located. These "echo-detection cells" are highly sensitive to echoes, because they respond maximally to the second of two sounds that occur in rapid succession (Pollak et al., 1977). Finally, there are cells in the bat's brain that track the general movement of the prey. These cells continue to respond only if there is a continuing decrease in the interval between the bat's cry and the echo, a situation that would result only if the bat was getting closer and closer to its prey.

To sum up, the bat's ability to echolocate is highly evolved in several respects: The bat emits calls specialized to produce echoes that are relatively easy to analyze; the auditory system is specialized to detect echoes; and the nervous system is highly specialized to process information provided by the sonar system. Over millions of years the sound-emitting, sound-receiving, and sound-analyzing systems have interacted with one another to drive the evolution of one of the most complex information-processing systems in the animal world (see Popper & Fay, 1995).

Whales and dolphins also echolocate, although in some respects their ability is less sophisticated than that of bats. Dolphin echolocation is especially useful in deep or murky water, both for the avoidance of obstacles and for locating food. Experiments with blindfolded captive dolphins indicate that the animals are able to locate a dead fish within seconds (see Au, 1993).

Under most circumstances, the bottle-nosed dolphin is able to integrate information obtained by echolocation with information supplied by visual cues. In fact, one dolphin was able to recognize visually objects she had only previously "heard" by echolocation—and vice versa. The dolphin's sonar provides images of the world that are apparently comparable in some respects to images provided by the eyes (Pack & Herman, 1995).

In contrast, one species of dolphin—the river dolphin of India—relies almost entirely on echolocation. It feeds in murky water near the bottom, and its vestigial eyes are incapable of forming an image.

In addition to providing sensory information, there is evidence that dolphins' echolocation signals help these animals hunt fish. Strong echolocation signals may stun prey fish or at least cause disorientation in a school of fish (see Richardson et al., 1995).

first if the sound source is located below the owl. When the owl is perched above the plane of its prey, it can then utilize both horizontal and vertical directional information to pinpoint the prey's location (Konishi, 1985).

Equilibratory Systems

The equilibratory system is a mechanoreceptor system that is anatomically associated with the auditory system of many animals. Equilibratory receptors are sensitive to the position of the body in relation to gravity; in some cases these receptors also provide information about acceleration and deceleration. Virtually all animals that locomote possess an equilibratory system. Compared to other sensory systems linked to stimuli that change position periodically—such as light, odor, and sound—equilibratory systems depend on gravity, a cue that is stable in both magnitude and direction. Consequently, the equilibratory

systems have not evolved complex neural centers associated with information processing like those involved in echolocation.

The equilibratory systems of animals vary, but all have two basic elements in common: a mass that is affected by forces such as gravity and inertia, and hair cells or other cells that are affected by the movement of the mass. Generally speaking, animals that move rapidly require a more sophisticated equilibratory system than slow-moving animals, and this differential need is reflected in the relatively complex systems of flying insects, cephalopods (such as the squid and octopus), and vertebrates (see Budelmann, 1988).

Electroreception

Electroreceptors are found only in aquatic vertebrates, a finding consistent with the fact that water is a good conductor of electricity while

TABLE 18.2 ◆ Mechanoreceptors

Type	Definition	Function
Touch receptors	Cells especially sensitive to a displacement of the cell membrane; sensory hairs on specialized organs.	Predator detection; tactile communication
Lateral line organs	Organs on side or head of animal that are sensitive to waterborne vibration.	Identification of obstacles and other animals
Kinesthetic receptors	Receptors in joints, etc., that indicate relative positions of body parts.	Fine motor coordination
Auditory receptors	Sensory hairs or tympanic organ sensitive to sound.	Detection of other animals; communication; echolocation
Equilibratory receptors	Gravity-sensitive organs often associated with auditory system.	Indication of body's position or acceleration/deceleration

◆ UNUSUAL ADAPTATIONS

Electrolocation

Two groups of fishes that live in extremely murky water—one group in Africa (Moryriformes) and the other in South America (Gymnoformes)—produce a weak electrical field around their bodies and are sensitive to distortions of this field produced by another animal or an obstacle (see Figure 18.1). The fish detects the distortions with the aid of electroreceptors located along the length of its body. Thus, this **electrolocation** is analogous to echolocation, in that both systems involve an output of energy as well as a highly adapted sensory system. Furthermore, the systems are used for analogous functions—detection of prey and avoidance of obstacles. In addition to identifying prey and obstacles, some species utilize their electrolocation system in courtship. For example, an African electric fish, *Pollomyrus isidori,* is able to recognize an opposite-sex conspecific on the basis of electrical output (Crawford, 1991). In *Eigenmannia,* a courting male is able to induce spawning (the laying of eggs) by producing a special pattern of electrostimulation (Heiligenberg, 1993).

Like bats, electrolocating fish have specialized areas of the brain that are adapted for their active sensory system. These adaptations enable the fish to distinguish the size of objects that distort their electrical field as well as to differentiate edible from nonedible objects.

The neural areas also show adaptations that function to prevent one fish from interfering with another's electrolocation system. For example, *Eigenmannia* has a "jamming avoidance reflex" that enables an individual fish to adjust its electrical discharge rate in such a way that the rate is distinct from that of a neighbor. Consequently, each individual fish has its own private electrolocation "channel" and avoids any interference (see Moller, 1995).

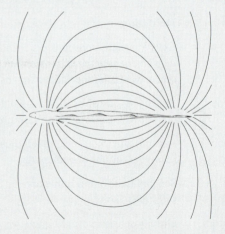

FIGURE 18.1 ◆ The electrical field generated by a weakly electric fish, *Gymnarchus.* The fish is sensitive to an interruption of this field caused by another animal or an obstacle.

air behaves as an insulator. Because electroreceptors appear in the most primitive living fishes, it appears that these sense organs have an ancient origin (Zakon, 1988).

Electroreception is usually associated with detection of prey. For example, the little skate (*Raja erinacea*) is sensitive to weak electrical fields produced by the muscle tissue in the body of its prey. This sensitivity enables skates to locate prey animals in muddy water or even victims buried in the sand on the bottom (Bullock & Heiligenberg, 1986). The skate's electroreceptors are specialized lateral line organs distributed in clusters on the pectoral fins and the head region.

The Australian platypus is the only mammal with electroreception. The receptors are located in its ducklike bill. During the night the platypus probes its bill in the mud and stones of a stream bottom and stirs up the aquatic invertebrates that are its prey. The platypus is then able to use electroreception to zero in on the prey animals as they attempt to swim away.

Magnetoreception

Some animals are sensitive to magnetic energy and, as we shall see in detail in Chapter 19, navigate by using cues from the earth's magnetic field. There appear to be several types of magnetic receptors. For example, sharks, rays, and skates may be able to use their electroreceptors to sense the earth's magnetic field (see Kalmijn, 1988).

In contrast, the homing pigeon has a magnetic material located in the retina that is sensitive to the earth's magnetic field and can use the magnetic field in navigation. The pigeon's retina responds to light differently if the magnetic field is altered, so it seems that in this

bird there is an integration of information provided by light and information about the earth's magnetic field. Further evidence for the role of the visual system in magnetoreception comes from the finding that pigeons are incapable of homing after being transported to an unfamiliar release site in total darkness (see Wiltschko & Wiltschko, 1995).

Studies of pigeons also indicate that information about the direction of gravity from the equilibratory system is integrated with visual and magnetosensory information at several centers in the brain, especially in the pineal gland (Semm et al., 1984). Thus, as in the case of many sensory systems, there seems to be a complex integration of sensory information, especially in birds and mammals.

Photoreception

Photoreceptors are specialized for the detection of electromagnetic energy in the range of 300 to 10,000 nm in wavelength. Within this range, some animals are sensitive to wavelengths that are invisible to others. For example, humans perceive electromagnetic energy around 560 nm in wavelength as red light, but nocturnal mammals do not respond to this energy range. Consequently, we can observe nocturnal mammals under red light in a zoo or laboratory setting, but the animals react as if they were in total darkness. Conversely, bees are sensitive to ultraviolet light that is invisible to humans. As a result, bees can discriminate between two flower colors that we perceive as exactly the same color.

The basic nature and complexity of photoreception or visual systems vary even more than the ranges of sensitivity. At one extreme, the one-celled organism *Euglena* has a simple photosensitive area known as an **eye spot** proximal to a ridge. The ridge casts a microscopic shadow, which enables the eye spot to provide the organism with general information about the angle of light so that the organism can orient toward the sun. This orientation is very important, because *Euglena,* like green plants, produces its own food by photosynthesis. (*Euglena* can also absorb nutrients from the water when sunlight is not available. This dual method of feeding supports *Euglena's* survival under a variety of environmental conditions—as illustrated by the large numbers of these animals found in the green scum on the surface of freshwater ponds.)

In contrast to the extremely simple photoreception of *Euglena,* the visual systems of many animals are highly complex. The most complex visual systems are found in rapidly moving animals such as insects, cephalopod mollusks such as the octopus, and vertebrates.

The visual system of adult insects includes **compound eyes,** organs made up of individual visual units called **ommatidia.** Each ommatidium is a tube with its own lens that focuses light on an individual photoreceptor cell, and its own nerve fiber to convey visual information to the insect's brain (see Figure 18.2). The compound eye forms an image consisting of a mosaic of dots that vary in brightness. The larger the number of ommatidia, the greater the concentration of dots and the finer the image. Thus, the dragonfly, which has as many as 20,000 ommatidia in each eye, is able to form a fairly good visual image and identify the small flying insects that serve as its prey. The compound eye is especially sensitive to movement, which also facilitates the dragonfly's detection of its prey (see Elzinga, 1997).

Cephalopod mollusks such as the octopus also have well-developed visual systems that enable them to identify small, fast-moving prey. Their eyes resemble a camera, with a lens at the anterior end that focuses an image

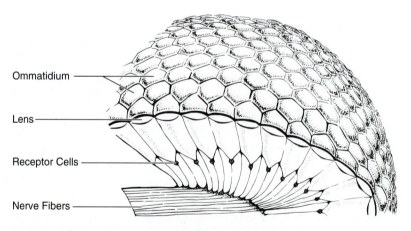

Ommatidium

Lens

Receptor Cells

Nerve Fibers

FIGURE 18.2 ◆ **The compound eye of an insect.** Each ommatidium has its own lens, receptor cell, and nerve fiber that carries messages to the insect's brain.

of an object on a layer of photosensitive cells in the retina. The lens can be moved back and forth, enabling the octopus to focus on either distant or close objects.

The optic system of a vertebrate, like that of the octopus, has a lens that focuses the image on photosensitive cells in the retina. In contrast to the octopus, however, the vertebrate lens focuses objects at varying distances not by moving but by changing shape. Furthermore, the retinas of most vertebrates have many more photosensitive cells than those of the octopus; in some birds and mammals, there are 100 million photoreceptors. The

heavy concentration of photosensitive cells, many of which have direct neural connections, enables these animals to form very fine visual images and gives these animals outstanding **visual acuity**—an ability to distinguish objects in clear focus.

Feature Detectors

In some cases animals learn to discriminate among objects on the basis of the retinal image. However, there are many examples of visual discrimination that require no learning. These discriminations are facilitated by **feature detectors**—neurons in certain parts of the brain that respond selectively to particular aspects of visual input. For example, the frog *Rana pipiens* has feature detectors (sometimes called "bug detectors") that consist of nerve cells maximally sensitive to any small, erratically moving object passing through the visual field at about the rate of a flying insect. Such stimulation immediately evokes head turning, general orientation, and a strike by the frog. Obviously these feature detectors are basic to the frog's feeding response.

European toads also have feature detectors. However, the toad's detectors are maximally sensitive to cues provided by a long, thin object moving slowly across the visual field. This is the type of stimulation provided by worms—the primary prey of toads. Thus, frogs and toads have evolved feature detectors that are sensitive to the type of food they consume. The toads also have feature detectors that identify potential predators. These specialized cells in the thalamus respond strongly to objects moving at a certain speed and casting a perpendicular image on the retina. These cues are likely to be associated with two of the toads' major predators: herons and storks.

TABLE 18.3 ◆ Photoreception Systems

Type	Example	Sensitivity
Eye spot	Euglena (protozoan)	Sensitive to location of light source.
Compound eye	Adult insects	Sensitive to movement; multiple ommatidia can form fairly good image.
Cephalopod eye	Octopuses and their relatives	Moving lens; produces good image and visual acuity.
Vertebrate eye	Vertebrates	Adjustable lens shape combined with multiple photoreceptors; provides outstanding visual acuity.

When the toad receives the appropriate neural messages in the thalamus, it crouches inconspicuously (Ewert, 1980).

Groups of neurons in the temporal lobe of the rhesus monkey's brain also seem to function as feature detectors. Experimental tests indicate that these neurons respond more to drawings of monkey faces than to any other type of drawing (see Fridlund, 1994). Such hypersensitivity to faces clearly has advantages for social interaction and the development of social strategies—advantages that, as we saw in Chapter 12, are basic to the fitness of social primates.

Color Vision

Animals such as honeybees, certain fish, birds, and most primates have color vision; that is, they can discriminate among objects on the basis of the dominant wavelength reflected from each object. The mechanisms mediating color vision are different for each group of animals, however. For example, the eye of the pigeon has different-colored oil droplets that filter out certain wavelengths; consequently, it is the oil droplets that mediate color discrimination. In contrast, the eyes of apes, old-world monkeys, and humans lack oil droplets but have cone cells (color-sensitive retinal cells) with three different types of pigments, each maximally sensitive to different wavelengths. Specifically, red-sensitive cones absorb wavelengths around 560 nm, green-sensitive cones are maximally sensitive to wavelengths of 530 nm, and blue-sensitive cones absorb wavelengths around 420 nm. The differentiation of cones into three types accounts for human color sensitivity.

Why did some animals evolve excellent color vision while others evolved only limited sensitivity or no color sensitivity at all? A major factor seems to be diet and time of feeding. Animals that feed on brightly colored objects in bright illumination experience considerable fitness benefits from color vision. For example, bees that forage on the nectar of flowers and monkeys that forage for ripe fruit are able to make fine discriminations among flowers and fruits. The plants that bear flowers and fruit also benefit from attracting foragers; therefore, there has been a complementary evolutionary trend in plants toward bright coloration in flowers and fruits.

Whereas cones are specialized for vision in bright illumination, rods (rod cells in the retina) are maximally sensitive to dim light. Thus, nocturnal animals have predominantly rod vision, while diurnal animals (animals active in daytime) have mostly cones, especially in the **fovea**—the area of the retina that receives the most direct aspect of the visual image. Because rods are incapable of mediating color vision, nocturnal animals are color-blind. Conversely, many diurnal animals have color vision but relatively poor night vision.

Sensitivity to Polarized Light

As light waves from the sun travel through the earth's atmosphere, they become **polarized;** that is, they vibrate in a single plane. The eyes of some animals, especially the complex eyes of insects, are highly sensitive to polarized light. The water bug *Notonecta* uses its sensitivity to polarized light to locate water; because light waves reflected off water are very strongly polarized, the bug is able to distinguish the sky above a pond from sky above the land.

Honeybees use the polarization of light too; they can identify the position of the sun even when it is obscured by clouds, as long as there is a patch of blue sky. The bees are able to do this because the plane of polarization detectable in the open sky indicates the position of the sun.

Birds such as the pigeon are also able to detect the plane of polarization of the sun's light. Polarization of the sun's rays is particularly great at sunset—and many birds start their migration at sunset, because they can get the most accurate "compass reading" at this time (Helbig, 1991).

BIOLOGICAL CLOCKS

As noted in Chapter 6, no two species of animals can occupy precisely the same ecological niche at the same time. But if different species are active at different times of the day—or at different times of the year—they may occupy the same location. Consequently, the ability of animals to time their patterns of activity enables two competing species to live in the same place. The timing of patterns of activity also enables animals to search for food at times when it is most likely to be available, to become active when predators are least likely to find them, and to coordinate the quest for mates between the two sexes.

What mechanism controls when an animal is active or what time schedule it follows? For many years we assumed that external cues drove animals' biological rhythms. For example, it seemed logical that certain animals slept when it became dark and awoke when light intensity increased. However, if animals of many different species—and plants as well— are placed in experimental conditions where no external cues are available, they still show a rhythm or cycling of behavior and physiological processes. The mechanism behind this

cycling is now known as a **biological clock,** or internal timing device that governs biological rhythms.

We will first consider different kinds of biological rhythms and the ways in which they are tuned to significant external events in animals' lives. Then we will look at external cues that set or **entrain** biological clocks. Finally, we will discuss the physiological mechanisms that mediate biological clocks.

Biological Rhythms

Many different types of animals show **circadian rhythms**—patterns of activity that approximate the length of a day. For example, fruit flies (*Dacus tryoni*) always mate at about the same time in the evening; they continue to show this cyclical pattern of mating even when external cues indicating the time of day are not available (Tychsen & Fletcher, 1971). This pattern enables the flies to mate under cover of darkness, when the danger of predation is reduced.

Another common cycle in the animal world is a **circannual rhythm,** a cycle lasting approximately one year. A circannual pattern makes it possible for an animal to engage in a behavior during the appropriate season. For example, the golden-mantled ground squirrel (*Citellus lateralis*) enters into hibernation at approximately the same time every year, during the late fall. Like the fruit flies, the ground squirrel maintains its rhythm when kept in a laboratory, isolated from external factors that could indicate the season. For example, ground squirrels kept in rooms with constant temperature and unchanging light–dark cycles showed a consistent hibernation schedule over a 4-year period (Pengelley & Asmundson, 1970).

Animals that must coordinate their activities with the ocean tides in order to survive often show cycles that correspond with the position of the moon—a cycle that is appropriate, in that the gravitational pull of the moon influences the tides. Thus, an oyster opens its shell every 12.4 hours, an interval that corresponds to the timing of high tide. By opening their shells at high tide and closing them at low tide, the oysters can feed when they are bathed in water and protect themselves when they are in shallow water or on the shore and vulnerable to predation and desiccation (drying out). Again, this cycling is independent from external cues: If oysters are taken inland, where there are no cues from the ocean's movement, the oysters continue to show the same temporal pattern of shell opening and closing (Brown et al., 1970).

Another example of a lunar-related rhythm, but a rhythm of greater length, is seen in the palolo worm of the South Pacific. During a period when palolo worms remain sheltered in their rock or coral crevices beneath the surface of the ocean, the male and female adult worms start to develop sexual segments, or **epitokes,** at the posterior end of their bodies (see Figure 18.3). On a night in October or November at the beginning of the last lunar quarter, the mature epitokes break away from the worms and swim to the surface of the ocean. At the surface the epitokes perform a nuptial dance, swimming in circles and releasing their gametes in the presence of opposite-sex epitokes. The Samoan people have become aware of the time of epitoke swarming, and Samoans celebrate annual feasts after catching the tasty epitokes in nets cast from small boats.

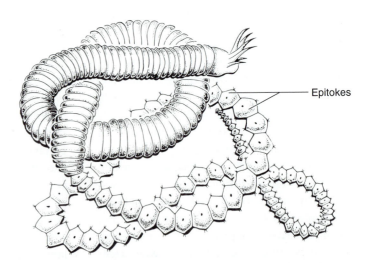

Epitokes

FIGURE 18.3 ◆ A palolo worm with a long chain of epitokes. At a predictable time of the year, regulated by the worm's biological clock, the epitokes break off and swim to the surface of the ocean, where they perform a nuptial dance.

Perhaps the longest cycle regulated by a biological clock mechanism is that of the 17-year cicada. As described in the discussion of the dilution effect in Chapter 7, these insects live for 17 years as larvae and then emerge as adults in great numbers in the spring of the final year. It seems that the clocks of animals have become specialized for a great variety of time intervals, intervals that are consistent with external events significant in their lives.

Why do so many animals show biologically regulated rhythms as opposed to relying on external or environmental cues for regulation of behaviors? In the first place, environmental cues are not always reliable indicators of significant events. If oysters adjusted the opening and closing of their shells to the presence or absence of water, they would sometimes make inappropriate responses. For example, a shoreline oyster would be likely to open its shell during or after a heavy rain and, in the process, expose itself to predation from birds. Similarly, if birds began their northern migration as soon as the temperature reached a certain point, they could be induced to migrate during an unseasonable warm spell and find themselves in dangerously cold weather later on.

Another advantage of biological clocks is that behavior patterns can be regulated in such a way that animals can anticipate a significant environmental change. For example, palolo worms may time the development of epitokes so that the mature epitokes emerge and swarm at the appropriate time. Furthermore, because both the male and the female worm have comparable biological clocks, it is possible to coordinate the swarming activity and fertilization.

Finally, biological clocks enable animals to learn time relationships. As explained in Chapter 4, temporal learning has important fitness benefits and is well developed in several animals.

The Role of External Cues

Although external cues do not control rhythmic activity, these cues play critical roles. Primarily, external cues function to entrain the biological clock. For example, when oysters are taken to a location with different tidal rhythms, they adjust their shell openings and closings to correspond to the new rhythms. Consequently, oysters can be successfully transplanted from the Atlantic to the Pacific Ocean. Similarly, the rhythm of activity levels of rats can be entrained to artificial light–dark cycles. Actually, the cycles of rats in constant illumination show a cycle a little longer than 24 hours; but if the schedule is entrained every day by the light coming on, the cycles function on a 24-hour schedule.

An external cue that functions to entrain cycles is known as a **zeitgeber**—literally translated, a time giver. Light is one of the most important zeitgebers, especially for birds. Light penetrates a bird's skull and reaches the pineal gland in the center of the brain. Consequently, even blind birds are able to maintain their normal biological rhythms (Somers & Klein, 1984).

In mammals, however, the optic system is necessary for entrainment by light. A structure in the hypothalamus known as the suprachiasmatic nucleus (SCN) receives neural fibers from the retina that provide information about light intensity. Thus, in contrast to the situation with birds, the experimental destruction of the tract connecting the retina with the

SCN of rats disrupts the biological clock relating general activity to the light–dark cycle (Sadun et al., 1984).

Physiological Mechanisms

Even single-celled organisms show biological rhythms, so it is clear that a clock mechanism may be located in an individual cell. Laboratory experiments not only support this hypothesis of an intracellular clock mechanism but suggest that the mechanism is located in the cytoplasm (the part of the cell outside of the nucleus) rather than in the nucleus. Thus, a clock continues to function even when a cell nucleus is experimentally removed (Woolum, 1991).

What is the nature of this clock mechanism? Some studies suggest that protein synthesis is the basic process. For example, a substance that inhibits protein synthesis in the cytoplasm disrupts the clock (Sargent et al., 1976). It is possible that the rate of synthesis

provides the "tick" of the clock. However, there is also evidence that other types of reactions in the cell may be involved as well (see Nakashima, 1986).

Most animals have several biological clocks. Thus, it is possible for multiple clocks to combine in various patterns and produce a clock with a relatively long time period (Dowse et al., 1987). In many cases there appears to be a **master clock** or clocks that regulate and synchronize the other clocks in the body. This central control coordinates cycles and different rhythmic processes so that they occur at appropriate times.

An experimental study of hamsters indicates that the master clock is located in the suprachiasmatic nucleus (SCN). Experimenters removed the SCN from a group of hamsters that showed a normal 24-hour cycle of activity. They then transplanted into these animals neural tissue from the SCNs of hamsters that showed abnormal activity cycles of less than 24 hours. The animals receiving the transplants took on the abnormal activity cycles of the donor hamsters (Ralph et al., 1990).

◆ HUMAN EVOLUTION

The sensory systems and biological clocks of humans, like those of nonhuman animals, reflect adaptations related to humans' evolutionary history. A greater understanding of the evolutionary basis of these systems has resulted in several practical applications, especially in regard to people's sleeping patterns. We will begin by looking at sensory systems and then consider biological clocks.

SENSORY SYSTEMS

Generally speaking, the sensory systems of all animals, including humans, are similar at the level of the individual receptor cell; but there are considerable variations in the number of receptor cells. For example, all vertebrates have comparable photoreceptors (rods and/or cones). However, vertebrates with eyes specialized for acuity have many more individual receptors concentrated in the fovea than do animals with less specialization. The concentration of cones in the fovea of eagles, which can spot a rabbit from a distance of more than a mile, greatly surpasses the concentration of cones in the fovea of humans and other mammals (Reymond, 1985).

In a comparable way, individual chemical receptor cells are similar for animals as diverse as moths, flies, and humans. However, the number of cells as well as the chemical properties of molecules that stimulate the cells are quite different in these animals.

The greatest degree of specialization takes place at the neural level, in the brain. What often separates humans from nonhuman animals in regard to sensory systems is the degree to which humans can integrate sensory information and use this information to build sophisticated cognitive strategies. Much of the relatively large human brain is involved in processing complex sensory information. Let's look more closely at two of the most highly specialized human senses, vision and hearing.

Photoreception

In keeping with our ancestry as diurnal primates, we have visual acuity and color vision superior to that of nonprimate mammals. Our ancestors clearly experienced strong fitness benefits from recognizing the shape and bright colors of food such as ripe fruit during daylight.

In humans as in other primates, the two eyes are set in the front of the head, enabling the visual fields of the two eyes to overlap. Primates also have a restricted fovea, which is stimulated when we look directly at an object. These adaptations provide for good visual acuity and depth perception, factors obviously important in reaching for fruit and leaping from branch to branch. In contrast, ungulates and rodents have eyes on the sides of their heads and a wide fovea, enabling them to develop a wide angle of vision but relatively poor acuity and depth perception. For these and other animals that are particularly vulnerable to predation, the wide angle of vision facilitates predator detection.

Although humans are diurnal, we have large numbers of rods peripheral to the fovea. Consequently, our night vision is more sensitive than that of animals such as eagles that have an all-cone retina, but inferior to that of animals such as cats that have predominantly rod retinas. Cats also have a reflective substance in the eye that facilitates the detection of small amounts of light.

Like other primates, humans have feature detectors that are specialized for identifying faces of conspecifics (Heit et al., 1988). These feature detectors consist of highly specialized single neurons in the cerebral cortex. Our perception of the face as a whole depends on a pattern of scanning that covers the critical areas of the face, particularly the eyes and the mouth. The acquisition of speech comprehension and production seems to be related to this scanning pattern (see Fridlund, 1994). Feature detectors are clearly very important in the development of complex social strategies. Not only do these perceptual systems facilitate facial recognition and sensitivity to facial expression, but they contribute to the development of language.

Audition

The human auditory system is adapted for a wide range of auditory sensitivity but has less sensitivity to sound frequencies at the extremes of the possible range. For example, we cannot hear the very high frequency sounds emitted by mice and bats or the low-frequency sounds made by elephants and whales. This difference between various species is related to the fact that a small cochlea (bony part of the inner ear) such as that of mice and bats is maximally sensitive to high-pitched sounds, while the large cochleas of elephants and whales are maximally sensitive to low-frequency sounds. Essentially, our auditory system is most sensitive to sounds with frequencies in the range of the human voice. Auditory sensitivity and vocal production must have influenced each other during our evolutionary history.

Humans have a well-developed ability to localize sounds. One of the most important cues for this sound localization is the relative time of arrival of a sound at each of the two ears. Because sounds arrive first at the ear nearest the sound source, we have a good indication of the direction of the source. Interestingly, sound localization is most highly developed in mammals that also have a narrow visual fovea. This accurate sound localization is important for the coordination of vision and sound in the identification of objects in the environment, because we can accurately direct our gaze at a sound source (Fay, 1994).

We also have an outstanding ability to detect changes in the intensity of sound, better than that of any other animal tested (Long, 1994). This sensitivity may be an adaptation for detecting emotional expression in the vocal communication of other humans. This ability would have fitness value in terms of our ability to form a theory of mind (recall Chapter 5) related to other people's emotions.

Still another outstanding auditory ability is humans' perception of complex sounds, an ability associated with the perception of speech. Recent evidence suggests that other primates also share this ability (see Stebbins and Moody, 1994). Consistent with the ability to perceive complex sounds, gorillas and other primates communicate in fairly complex ways with grunts (Seyfarth et al., 1994). Apparently the evolutionary beginnings of human speech perception and production took place in our primate ancestors. This conclusion is further supported by the observation that shortly before human infants begin to make syllabic babbling sounds, they use grunts for communication (McCune et al., 1996). The roots of human language in the grunts and other sounds produced by our ancestors argues against a long-held notion that spoken language had its origin entirely with the species *Homo sapiens.*

BIOLOGICAL CLOCKS

Biological clocks serve many of the same functions in humans as in nonhumans—facilitating the regulation of sleep cycles, general activity patterns, and autonomic activities such as changes in body temperature and energy levels. However, humans living in highly technological societies often get out of synchrony with natural rhythms, because we must frequently change our activity patterns to match externally dictated schedules. Asynchrony is particularly great when we change from one work shift to another or travel long distances in a short period of time.

Studies of changes in working hours indicate that when people move from one shift to another, they experience increased irritability and difficulty sleeping—especially when they move to a schedule requiring a significantly earlier starting time. Because the natural human circadian rhythm is a little longer than 24 hours (approximately 25 hours), research indicates it is easier to shift to a later schedule than to an earlier one. Furthermore, it is easier to adjust to an anticipated shift by staying up an hour later each night than by trying to arise an hour earlier each day (Czeisler et al., 1982).

Similarly, because the natural rhythm is approximately 25 hours, people usually have fewer problems with jet lag going west and adjusting to the sun setting at a later time than they do going east and adjusting to the sun setting earlier.

There are definite individual differences in the timing of circadian rhythms. For example, individuals known as "morning persons" show relatively high body temperatures and higher energy levels early in the morning, and lower temperatures and less energy in the evening. In "night persons" the pattern is reversed. The reason for differences in the peaks and valleys is not clear, but it clearly maximizes an individual's efficiency if he or she can arrange a schedule of activity compatible with these peaks and valleys (Melton & Bartanowicz, 1983).

◆ CHANGING PERSPECTIVES

PAST	PRESENT	FUTURE
Sensory systems, like all other animal systems, are immutable and thus the same as they were when animal species were first created. Animal rhythms are inexplicable (nineteenth century, pre-Darwin).	Sensory systems, like all other animal systems, evolved according to the principles of natural selection. Animal rhythms are typically regulated by biological clocks.	How are sensory experiences organized and stored in the nervous system? Are there as yet unidentified influences of biological clocks on behavior and cognition?

SUMMARY

Sensory systems have three components: Receptors change energy received from the environment into nerve impulses; conductors transmit coded information to higher neural centers; and neural centers integrate information and communicate with effector systems. Sensory adaptation takes place in all three systems.

The evolution of sensory systems is influenced by a combination of ecological factors and prior adaptations. In many cases the evolution of one sensory system in an animal has significant effects on the evolution of other systems.

Chemoreception includes olfaction (generally associated with identification of a variety of relevant stimuli from a distance) and gustation (associated with the acceptance or rejection of food). A complex integration of olfactory and gustatory information takes place in feeding behavior.

Thermoreception—sensitivity to specific temperatures as well as to changes in temperature—is related to habitat selection in many animals. In addition, a few animals can locate prey with specialized thermoreceptors.

Mechanoreception systems include lateral line organs, kinesthetic receptors, auditory receptors, and equilibratory systems. Auditory systems are especially well developed in birds and mammals and include an ability to localize sounds. Some animals, especially bats, have an extremely sophisticated echolocation system that enables them to capture prey and avoid obstacles.

Electroreception is found in a few aquatic vertebrates and is usually associated with the detection of prey. Two groups of fishes produce a weak electric field used in electrolocation; in some cases, too, a fish can recognize the opposite sex on the basis of electrical output.

Magnetoreception—sensitivity to magnetic energy—is found in a wide diversity of animals and is often related to navigation. There seem to be several different types of magnetoreceptors.

Photoreception is common in the animal world and is a highly developed sense in many animals, especially cephalopods, birds, and mammals. Specializations in photoreception include mechanisms that mediate feature detection, color vision, and sensitivity to polarized light.

Biological clocks function as internal timing devices that are finely tuned to significant external events in an animal's life. Biological rhythms such as circadian and circannual rhythms enable animals to avoid dependency on certain environmental cues that might be unreliable, to anticipate significant environmental changes, and to form the basis for learning time relationships.

External cues or zeitgebers function to entrain biological clocks. Basic processes within an individual cell—such as protein synthesis—seem to provide the "tick" of the clock. In many animals a master clock regulates and synchronizes other clocks in the body. Internal communication about rhythms may be either hormonal or neural.

Human sensory systems exhibit special adaptations associated with social communication. For example, we are extremely sensitive to changes in facial expression and to changes in the intensity and complexity of sound. Human biological clocks are apparent in several cyclical activities, especially sleep patterns.

KEY TERMS

biological clock, p. 431
circadian rhythm, p. 431
circannual rhythm, p. 431
compound eye, p. 428
constant frequency calls, p. 423
echolocation, p. 423
electrolocation, p. 426
entrain, p. 431
epitokes, p. 432
eye spot, p. 427
feature detectors, p. 429

fovea, p. 430
frequency modulated calls, p. 423
lateral line organs, p. 421
master clock, p. 434
ommatidia, p. 428
polarized, p. 430
sensory adaptation, p. 417
sensory hairs, p. 422
visual acuity, p. 429
zeitgeber, p. 433

CHAPTER 19

MIGRATION AND NAVIGATION

- ◆ *Why do some animals migrate thousands of miles each year?*
- ◆ *How do migrating animals find their way?*

*T*he ability to move about is basic to the survival of animals. Even sessile animals (animals that remain in one place as adults) generally locomote in their larval stages. In this chapter and in Chapter 20, we will focus particularly on the relatively long-range movements of animals, the function of these movements, and the types of cues that regulate them.

19

*This chapter will start with **migration**—the round-trip movements of animals from one habitat to another and back again. Then we will discuss the navigational abilities that enable animals to find their way from one habitat to another as well as to move about within a single habitat with a high degree of efficiency. We'll conclude with a look at migrations and navigation among humans.*

MIGRATION

A large variety of animals migrate during some period of their lives. Some animals migrate only a few yards; others migrate halfway around the world. The most extensive migrators are flying or swimming animals. Flying has an advantage in that it is rapid, and under certain circumstances birds can utilize favorable winds to reduce energy expenditure. Swimming is slower than flight but is energy efficient, particularly for larger animals.

In contrast, animals that locomote across land run into such discontinuities as mountains, rivers, and deserts as well as human-made barriers. Consequently, long-range terrestrial migrations are rare. When they do occur, they tend to be made by large animals that inhabit areas relatively free of physical barriers (Waterman, 1989).

Benefits and Costs of Migration

The evolution of migration, like the evolution of many other behaviors considered in previous chapters, has been strongly influenced by the balance between benefits and costs. One of the most important benefits is the possibility of utilizing food from two or more distinct habitats. For example, wildebeest migrations in Africa enable these antelope to feed on vegetation in the parts of Africa receiving seasonal rainfall.

Migratory animals may also benefit from dividing their time between areas that are optimal for adult feeding and areas that are best suited for the rearing of young. For example, several species of whale feed in cold Arctic waters, where food is plentiful, and then travel thousands of miles to tropical waters to reproduce. The young can survive only in the warm tropical water.

Feeding in one area and breeding in another may have other advantages, particularly for birds that migrate between extreme northern and semitropical or temperate habitats. Young birds may be exposed to more predators and parasites in the semitropical or temperate climate than in the northern habitat, so there is an advantage to breeding and rearing the young, vulnerable offspring in the cold habitat with fewer predators and rare or nonexistent parasites. Furthermore, the young may benefit from the long hours of daylight during summers in extreme northern climates.

In addition to the advantages related to feeding and breeding, a bird's temporary absence from a particular area may make it difficult for a population of predators to build up to high levels in that area. Unless the predators have an alternative food source, their population will be limited by the temporary absence of the birds.

Migrations may also provide a subtle advantage in that the movements involved in migration may expose an animal to new, potentially useful environments. An animal may then use the information gained to make optimal habitat choices. For example, some codfish began to move into new spawning grounds off the western coast of Greenland after a general increase in water temperatures in the early 1900s. These fish had apparently discovered the new habitat as the result of explorations that accompanied their migratory behavior (see Baker, 1981).

On the cost side of the ledger, migrations may demand a large expenditure of energy—and, as we shall see, some animals do not feed

along their migratory routes. Some animals are also at risk of attack by predators during migration. Several types of predators are familiar with the wildebeests' route and wait along the way, including crocodiles that inhabit rivers crossed during the migration. Also, the rivers the wildebeests cross are often swollen by heavy rains, and there is a danger that the high water may sweep individuals downstream and result in drownings.

Comparable weather-related hazards face birds crossing large bodies of water. Unpredictable storms and adverse wind conditions take the lives of many migrating birds. Under certain weather conditions, high buildings and city lights can cause migrating birds to become disoriented and crash fatally into window panes (see Alerstam, 1990). Research by animal behaviorists has, however, provided information on how buildings can be designed or modified to minimize these occurrences.

TABLE 19.1 ◆ Benefits and Costs of Migration

Benefits	Costs
Use of food from different habitats	Large expenditure of energy
Use of feeding and breeding habits that are different	Attack by predators along the way
Temporary absence, which prevents buildup of predator populations	Exposure to adverse weather conditions during migration
Exposure to new, potentially useful environments	

Methods of Investigation

Scientists have long sought to study and understand animal migrations. Researchers may observe movements of large groups of birds and mammals from some distance, especially with the aid of small aircraft. Radar helps researchers follow the movements of airborne animals and is particularly effective at night, when visual sightings are difficult or impossible. In contrast, sonar is a useful tool for tracing underwater migrations, particularly those of large schools of fish.

However, these techniques provide little or no information on the migration of individual animals. An increasingly common technique for tracing individual animal movements is **telemetry:** Researchers attach radio-wave transmitters to individual animals and can then trace the source of the waves as the animals move about. Recent technological advances have resulted in the development of smaller and less intrusive transmitters—transmitters so small that their size is determined only by the size of the battery. Scientists can now identify not only the location of an animal but its pattern of movement and physiological status. Furthermore, by using satellites, scientists can trace the animals' activities from a relatively great distance (see Berthold, 1993).

Data about migratory movements may also be collected indirectly. For example, researchers may number and tag an individual animal with instructions asking anyone finding the animal to report its location. Similarly, researchers may tag large numbers of animals at one end of their migratory range and then, at what may be presumed to be the other end, check individuals to see if they belonged to the original tagged population. Using this technique, researchers can also estimate how long it took the animals to complete the migration.

Another indirect technique is to identify the stomach contents of the migrating animals. If the food discovered grows only in one area, it may be concluded that the animals were recently in that area.

Preparation for Migration

Many species of animals that migrate great distances, especially certain species of birds and whales, must make adjustments before the journey begins. Migrating whales go for many months without eating, so they feed extensively and build up large stores of fat before leaving their feeding grounds. Birds typically eat at some points along the migratory route, but they also store fat and build up their flight muscles before they begin their migration.

Birds that are preparing to migrate also exhibit unusually high levels of fluttering, a behavior known as migratory restlessness. This restlessness is particularly noticeable in birds caged outdoors during their normal spring and fall migratory periods. Interestingly, the migratory restlessness lasts for a period of time matching the normal duration of the bird's migration. Furthermore, the movements are in the direction of the bird's normal migration. This appropriately timed and spatially oriented migratory restlessness appears in individual birds that have never migrated before, suggesting that it is relatively independent of experience (see Berthold, 1993).

Are birds motivated to migrate for a fixed period of time? Scientists investigated this question by placing birds at various points along their migratory route and seeing how long they continued to travel. When European starlings were experimentally released south of their normal starting points in the fall, they flew beyond the normal end point of their migration. This finding supported the hypothesis of a predetermined, fixed period of time for the migratory flight. Nonetheless, the starlings did not stop their flight at the end of the fixed time period if they were over inhospitable terrain. Instead, they continued to fly until they were over suitable terrain (Perdeck, 1964). It seems that birds have a strong tendency to fly for a minimal amount of time and then to start searching for an appropriate stopping point.

Patterns of Migration

The investigative methods discussed above have revealed a great diversity of migratory patterns. Some migrations are daily and occur in a vertical direction. For example, small crustaceans that make up part of the zooplankton (minute animal life in the sea) move to the ocean surface shortly after dawn, descend into deep water during the day, then rise again during the late afternoon. These movements allow the animals to feed on phytoplankton (minute plant life) near the surface at times when light intensity is reduced and the crustaceans are difficult for predators to locate. Because zooplankton do not rely on visual cues to locate phytoplankton, the reduced illumination does not present an obstacle to their feeding.

The most common type of migration is seasonal. Spiny lobsters spend the spring and summer in shallow inshore water, then migrate to deep water offshore in the fall and winter. During the migration they walk along the bottom in a more or less straight line, each lobster touching the one in front of it. The movement enables the lobsters to feed in food-rich shallow areas but to reproduce in deeper water where they run less risk of predation. Furthermore, because the deep water is cooler, metabolism is slowed down, so energy can be conserved during the times the lobsters are not feeding (see Baker, 1981).

Pacific salmon migrate only once in their lives, moving from the river tributaries in which they hatch to the open ocean and then returning at the end of their lives to the same tributaries to reproduce. Why did the fish evolve the tendency to return to the exact tributary from which they started? It seems that each population of salmon is adapted to the specific conditions of its microhabitat. When the young fish are experimentally introduced into tributaries other than the ones in which they hatched, there is an unusually high rate of mortality (Quinn & Dittman, 1990). (We will consider how the salmon find their natal tributary when we discuss navigation later in the chapter.)

There are also considerable variations in the distances animals migrate. The vertical migrations of the crustacean zooplankton cover only a few meters. Red-bellied newts also migrate a relatively short distance. These salamanders breed in streams in the redwood belt of northern California, then move high up the forested mountain slopes to feed and, later, to hibernate. In the spring the newts return again to the breeding area, typically choosing the same 50-meter stretch of water in which they spawned the year before. Newt migration is constrained because amphibians cannot travel too far from a source of water during their lifetimes; unlike other animals that are terrestrial, amphibians are unable to drink water and must absorb liquids through their skin (see Stebbins & Cohen, 1995).

In contrast to these short-distance migrators, the Arctic tern flies from the Arctic to the Antarctic and back again, a round-trip of 40,000 kilometers. This around-the-world travel occupies a large portion of the bird's adult life. Equally impressive, in some respects, are the nonstop flights of birds over hostile environments. For example, the bristle-thighed curlew must fly 10,000 kilometers over the Pacific Ocean to reach its winter home in Polynesia.

The Migration of Birds

Birds are the ultimate migrators. Almost half of all bird species are migratory, a much higher percentage than is seen in any other class of animals. Furthermore, as we've seen, some birds migrate great distances and spend a large percentage of their lives in migratory movement. Generally, the most efficient migrators are medium-sized birds such as the curlew and tern. Large birds such as geese are unable to add much reserve fat, because the added weight would make it impossible for the birds to get airborne. At the other extreme, small birds are limited by a slower speed of flight and their susceptibility to adverse wind conditions.

Because many species of birds produce altricial young that require large quantities of food, the advantages of extreme northern and southern latitudes during the summertime are particularly important. The long daylight hours for food gathering, the reduced competition, and the relative lack of parasites compensate for the rigors of extended travel.

In North America the most common migratory movements of birds are from a northern summer home and breeding area to a southern winter area. Prominent geographic features such as mountain ranges, great rivers, lakes, and coastlines tend to run north–south, so these features may function as landmarks and facilitate navigation during part of a bird's migration. In fact, North America's four major migratory routes, sometimes called **flyways,** run along such prominent features as the West Coast, the Rocky Mountains, the Missouri–Mississippi Rivers, and the Great Lakes.

Many songbirds and shorebirds travel from North America to Central and South America by flying out to sea from the Atlantic states and passing over the area around Bermuda en route to South America. Typically, they wait for favorable winds to take them toward Bermuda; then, when they pass over the Sargasso Sea, they change altitude and pick up the north-east early trade winds, which push them toward South America. Other birds, particularly birds of prey that are not well suited for flying over water, follow an overland route through Central America.

Although some birds go without feeding during their migration, especially if they are land birds flying over the ocean, others feed extensively along the way. In certain cases this means taking a different route north during the spring than south during the fall. For example, the golden plover makes a loop between northern Canada and southern South America, evidently taking advantage of the late-summer berries in New England and Labrador.

A large number of birds that breed in Europe and Asia winter in Africa. However, two major barriers prevent a direct north–south migration route for many of these birds: the Mediterranean Sea and the Sahara Desert. Birds tend to cross the Mediterranean at one of its narrowest points, the Straits of Gibraltar or the Bosporus, and travel along the eastern and western boundaries of the Sahara. Large birds such as storks and eagles use these narrow crossings of the Mediterranean and, at certain times of the year, fill the sky in great numbers. Other, more efficient migrators such as warblers fly across Italy and use Sicily and Malta as stepping stones to Africa. However, relatively few birds cross the Mediterranean at its widest point or fly across the Sahara.

Some species of European birds make migrations much longer than necessary to reach Africa. Instead of heading directly south, flycatchers that breed in the area around Moscow fly west to the coast of Portugal before beginning their southward flight. The establishment of this circuitous route seems to have been related to the retreat of the ice during the last ice age. As the weather in northern Europe became warmer and more hospitable, birds from what is now Portugal began to move into the north and east. Because the birds had become familiar with the Portugal-to-Russia route and were successful using this route, there was no evolutionary pressure on them to explore possible alternative routes over unfamiliar terrain (Baker, 1981).

Individual Differences in Bird Migration

The discussion so far may have given the impression that all birds within a species behave in the same way; that is, that individuals are either consistently migratory or consistently nonmigratory. However, some individuals are opportunistic, shifting their migratory strategy depending on environmental conditions. For example, an individual of a migratory species may not migrate in certain years, especially when there is a mild winter, reduced competition, or an abundance of food. Individuals may also alter the timing of their migration to wait out unfavorable weather conditions. Because birds are extremely sensitive to barometric pressure, they are able to predict weather changes with a high degree of accuracy (see Alerstam, 1990).

Sometimes an individual bird's migratory pattern is related to its place in the dominance hierarchy. For example, subordinate birds often migrate farther than dominant ones, allowing the subordinate individuals to avoid territorial competition that they would probably lose. Similarly, younger, lower-ranking birds may migrate earlier than older ones. This seems to allow the younger birds to establish territories early and thus to hold their own against older, more dominant individuals (Cristol et al., 1990).

The Evolution of Bird Migration

Fossil evidence suggests that many birds migrating between tropical and temperate or arctic zones lived originally in the tropics. They probably began to migrate north in the spring as population pressures or the threat of predation increased. However, they would have found it necessary to move back to the warmer climate for the winter.

There is also evidence, however, that some birds that had established themselves as year-round northern residents started to migrate south when the winters grew colder or northern population pressures built up. For example, periods of glaciation in the Pleistocene would have forced such birds to fly south during the winter (Sauer, 1963).

It is also likely that some patterns of bird migration were related to continental drift. As the continents slowly drifted apart over millions of years, birds would have continued to move from one area to another, even though this migration became progressively longer with each passing century (Wolfson, 1948).

Considering the great variety of migratory patterns in birds, it seems reasonable that there have been several evolutionary trends related to migration. Furthermore, some birds' migratory patterns may have been the result of a combination of trends.

Land Mammals

Land mammals show less migratory behavior than birds, often relying on hoarding and hibernation to adjust to fluctuations in food supply. Mammals' migratory patterns are greatly influenced by climate, which, of course, directly affects the availability of food. For example, chimpanzees in the highlands of Tanzania migrate about 10 kilometers and thus feed in different areas during the wet and dry seasons. Kangaroos in Australia migrate following a rain, moving from areas near permanent water to outland areas. Because rainfall is unreliable in Australia, the kangaroos' migratory pattern is less predictable than that of chimpanzees.

Ungulates in Africa are the most extensive migrators among land mammals, sometimes covering more than 1,500 kilometers in each direction. Unlike the many migrants that follow a to-and-fro pattern, wildebeests travel in an elliptical pattern, taking advantage of areas where food is available during the dry season. The details of the pattern vary from year to year, depending largely on rainfall. In some cases herds of wildebeests may move toward storm clouds even if the clouds are more than 80 kilometers distant.

Ungulates that live in alpine regions also undertake seasonal migrations. For example, moose of the Canadian Rockies spend the summer in high coniferous forests near a stream or lake. In the autumn, as the snows arrive, the moose move down into the valleys. They spend the winter in the lowlands; then, when warm weather comes in the spring, they begin their uphill trek to the summer range. The movement is highly dependent on specific weather conditions. Thus, at any time of year, adverse weather drives the moose to lower levels of elevation.

Caribou in arctic regions show a similar migration, but in this case the animals move from the tundra in the north to forested areas farther south. Caribou travel in huge herds—which may include 100,000 individuals—and may travel more than 1,000 kilometers in each direction. On the spring trip north, pregnant females lead the migration, followed by males and immature caribou in lines that are sometimes more than 200 kilometers long. The major purpose of the northward leg of the journey is apparently to arrive at a location relatively free from wolves at the time that the females give birth (Bergerud et al., 1990; see Figure 19.1).

Flying Mammals

Bats, the only flying mammals, have the same potential as birds to migrate seasonally and exploit food resources from two or more sepa-

FIGURE 19.1 ◆ **Migrating caribou moving through Alaska.**

rate habitats. However, most bats that live in temperate zones do not show the avian pattern of migrating to warmer climates during the winter. Instead, bats migrate to caves, where they hibernate for the winter. Another difference between bats and birds is that bat females, independent of the males, seasonally move to caves where they bear their young. The young are left in huge crèches (aggregations of young) and nursed by their mothers, who return periodically to the cave to care for their offspring.

Some bats' journeys between winter caves and summer areas are fairly extensive. For example, the bat *Myotis sodalis* hibernates in caves in Kentucky and flies to summer quarters more than 500 kilometers away in Ohio, Indiana, and Michigan. Perhaps more remarkable is the finding that individual bats are able to return to the same spot on the wall of a cave several hundred meters deep and teeming with thousands of other bats.

Aquatic Mammals

Whales are the most extensive migrators among mammals; in some cases whales travel a distance of 18,000 kilometers between polar and tropical waters. These extensive migrations are related to the fact that newborn whales cannot tolerate cold water. Also, whales have an advantage over land mammals, in that whales are able to sleep part of the time while continuing on their journey.

Both male and female baleen whales spend the summer months feeding in the cold water of the Arctic or the Antarctic, where the concentration of food is 10 times greater than it is in warm waters. The whales then spend the winter months in tropical or subtropical waters, where mating takes place and the young from previous matings are born.

The migratory route of gray whales (large baleen whales) is easier to identify than that of other whales, because grays travel close to the shore and can easily be observed. They start their journey in the Bering Sea off Alaska and travel to a specific lagoon in Baja California, Mexico (see Figure 19.2). During the journey they periodically straighten their bodies vertically and stick their heads out of the water, apparently orienting to the coastline.

Northern fur seals migrate north in spring and give birth to their young, conceived the previous year, when they arrive at their island breeding grounds in the North Pacific. The

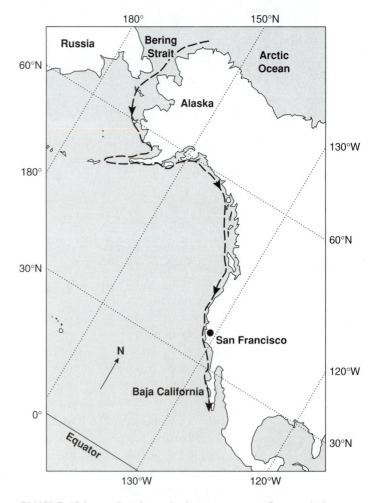

FIGURE 19.2 ◆ Southward migratory route of gray whales.

◆ UNUSUAL ADAPTATIONS

The Long-Distance Migration of Monarch Butterflies

Most insects do not migrate far from the place where they hatch. However, monarch butterflies (*Danaus plexippus*) make a remarkable long-distance migration—remarkable especially when the extent of their journey is considered in relation to their body size. After hatching, some monarchs of the eastern United States and Canada migrate more than 1,600 kilometers to mountain fir forests near Mexico City, where they mate and spend the winter. During the winter, they show greatly reduced activity and aggregate, several layers deep, on the trunks of certain trees (see Figure 19.3). Then, in the spring, they fly back to their summer location; lay their eggs; and, shortly thereafter, die. Thus, it is the offspring, none of which have any migratory experience, that make the trip south the next fall (see Waterman, 1989).

FIGURE 19.3 ◆ Monarch butterflies overwintering after a long migratory journey.

(continued)

These butterflies generally fly during the day and rest in trees and shrubs at night. One of the reasons that such extensive migrations are possible is that insects have a highly efficient system of gas exchange. That is, the vigorous motions of flying pump air directly through microscopic tubelets to the muscles, where oxygen is delivered and carbon dioxide removed. The gases do not enter into solution in the blood as they do in vertebrates and most other migrating animals.

The monarchs benefit from traveling such a great distance to a wintering site because they require a very specific type of environment, found almost exclusively in the fir forests of Mexico. This habitat is consistently cool but does not drop below freezing, allowing the butterflies to conserve their energy resources but not freeze (Calvert & Brower, 1986).

How did these butterflies evolve a tendency to lay their eggs such a great distance from where they spent the winter? Historically, it seems that milkweed, which serves as an exclusive food source for the larvae, became less and less available near the wintering area. Over the millennia, generations of monarchs apparently adjusted the length of their migration to meet the demands of an increasingly great travel distance (Urquart, 1987).

males arrive first and fight with each other to establish territories. Then, several weeks later, the females arrive. After the breeding season the males migrate southward, but they stay within 800 kilometers of the breeding site. The females, however, migrate as much as 1,400 kilometers farther south.

In contrast to fur seals, which give birth to their young on land, female walruses give birth on ice floes. Consequently, the migratory movements of walruses depend on the movement of the ice pack. In the winter walruses are generally found in open water passages produced by the action of wind and currents on the ice. In the spring the females give birth to young on ice floes; and throughout much of the spring and summer, groups of adults and young spend time drifting about on the floes. Thus, much of the movement of the walruses is passive, depending on winds and current.

NAVIGATION

Migrating animals must be able to navigate through unfamiliar environments and locate a destination that, in some cases, may be quite a small area. Nonmigratory animals, too, must be able to navigate in order to move about in their home area. In fact, one of the animals most widely studied in regard to navigation, the pigeon, is nonmigratory: The pigeon has a remarkable ability to find its way back to its home site—an ability known as **homing**—when displaced into areas it has never visited before.

The remarkable ability of animals to navigate during extensive migrations—in some cases, over trackless terrain or water—has been a source of fascination to animal watchers for thousands of years. Although some mysteries remain, animal researchers in recent decades have provided many answers to the age-old questions about animal navigation. We will begin our discussion with a brief overview of some of the methods used by these researchers. Then we will consider the most commonly used navigational techniques.

Methods of Investigation

In order to navigate, animals need both a "compass" and a "map," or representation of an area. Scientists investigate the cues involved in compass orientation and map representation by subjecting animals to a variety of treatments and then observing their behavior. For example, researchers may eliminate or disrupt a sensory system that is presumably important in navigation. In a classic study, Charles Walcott (1972) strapped magnets to the heads of pigeons, confusing their magnetic sense. This treatment disrupted the navigation of pigeons under some circumstances, suggesting that the magnetic sense was a significant factor in the birds' navigation.

Another method is to test an animal's ability to navigate after being moved to a different location. Wehner and Srinivasan (1981) displaced desert ants when the ants had traveled a certain distance from their nest and

were beginning to return to their nest. The ants then traveled a distance and in a direction that would have been appropriate had they not been displaced. Thus, the researchers concluded that the ants did not rely on landmarks to find their nest but utilized some other mechanism that gave them a sense of direction and distance.

In some experiments researchers expose animals to artificial conditions, such as a planetarium in which the apparent pattern of stars may be manipulated. E. G. F. Sauer (1971) placed warblers in a planetarium and reversed the normal pattern of stars. The warblers tended to orient in the direction opposite to that of their normal migration, suggesting that some birds are able to use the pattern of stars as a compass.

It is also possible to look at the correlation between natural disruptions (such as magnetic storms) and disruptions in navigation. For example, Frei (1982) found that during magnetic storms, pigeons tend to head off in a direction different from that appropriate for returning to their loft.

Dead Reckoning

One complex but effective method of navigation is **dead reckoning.** Dead reckoning involves estimating direction and distance to a goal, obtaining measures of the distance and direction traveled at several points along the journey, calculating present position at each point, and then making appropriate adjustments in the direction headed. This method is particularly useful when an animal is traveling over or in open water devoid of landmarks.

Once an animal obtains its initial orientation, it is usually able to stay on course—to continue in the same direction—for a period of time. Even if the animal veers from its set course to avoid an obstacle, it is able to adjust in such a way that it returns to the correct course without using external cues. This ability is facilitated by an **internal inertia system,** a system that indicates the degree of a turn and allows the animal to reorient with considerable precision (see Waterman, 1989).

The effectiveness of a dead reckoning system depends on many factors, including the effectiveness of the internal inertial system, the ability of flying or swimming animals to compensate for wind or current, the distance the animals must travel using the dead reckoning system exclusively, and the accuracy of the initial reading of direction.

The desert ant has a remarkable ability to use a type of dead reckoning system. The ant makes a tortuous journey of up to 100 meters away from its nest in search of food. Then, after finding food, it heads directly for the nest and travels to within a few meters of the nest. At this point the ant begins searching movements that shortly bring it to the opening of the nest. Apparently the ant "calculates" the direction it must head as well as the distance that must be traveled on the basis of angles of turns and the time spent moving in each direction (Wehner & Srinivasan, 1981). And this "computing" is accomplished by an animal with a brain the size of a grain of sand!

The Use of Celestial Cues

Another remarkable ability in many animals is the use of celestial cues in navigation. This navigational method is impressive particularly because the relative positions of celestial objects are constantly changing.

The Sun

A large variety of animals use the sun as a compass and compensate for its movement across the sky during the day. An experiment with pigeons illustrates one way in which the sun-compass reaction has been investigated. Researchers placed the birds, for a period of several weeks, in a closed room with artificial lighting. They exposed the birds to shifting light and dark periods out of phase with those in the real world—a technique known as "clock shifting." For example, instead of normal light associated with the sunrise at 6:00 A.M., the artificial lights came on at midnight. When taken from the room and placed in sunlight, the pigeons oriented improperly toward their home loft, flying at an angle to the sun that was off by 6 hours (Walcott, 1972).

Many species of birds rely on the sun as a compass during their migration. As we saw earlier, studies of migratory restlessness indicate that North American birds caged outdoors consistently orient in the direction of their normal migration; that is, they flutter in a northerly direction in the spring and in a southerly direction in the fall. If the birds are placed indoors in artificial light, however, they flutter in various directions without any specific orientation.

Garden warblers (a European species) are of special interest to researchers, because they normally fly southwest toward the Straits of Gibraltar for 2 months and then turn and fly southeast for 2 months toward central and southern Africa. Thus, the question arises, will these birds change their direction of migratory restlessness if they are caged during their normal period of migration?

The answer is yes. Caged garden warblers mimic the orientation of the migrating birds, fluttering in a southwesterly direction for the first 2 months, then in a southeasterly direction for the next 2 (see Waterman, 1989). It seems that there is a biological clock mechanism that signals the birds to orient in the new direction after a certain period.

Compensation for the Movement of the Sun

A special problem exists for the honeybee and other animals that use the sun as a compass. The rate of change in the sun's **azimuth,** or amount of horizontal displacement, is different depending on the time of day, the season, and the latitude. Consequently, if the bee "assumed" that the amount of change was the same in every hour or every season or every latitude, it would make significant errors in its navigation. But, as I have described before, the honeybee is able to compensate for differences in the rate of azimuth change in navigating its return to the hive.

To investigate how bees do this, James Gould (1980) captured bees and held them prisoner for 2 hours—from 11:00 A.M. until 1:00 P.M. He then released the bees and measured their angle of flight. Gould's hypothesis was that the bees would "calculate" their angle of flight on the basis of information they received just before their incarceration. If this hypothesis was correct, the bees should be slightly inaccurate in their orientation, because the sun moves across the sky faster during the period between 11:00 and 1:00 than it does just before 11:00. The bees' predicted inaccuracy was very close to that actually observed, so the hypothesis was confirmed. How did the bees deal with this inaccuracy? They were able to adjust their navigational error after they were set free and could again observe the sun's movement. Apparently bees take periodic readings of the rate of movement of the sun when they are able to see the sun. They then base their estimates of the sun's movement on these readings. Furthermore, they can readjust if they cannot see the sun for a period of time.

Polarized Light

Chapter 18 discussed certain animals' sensitivity to the pattern of polarization of sunlight. Because the pattern of polarization shifts in a predictable way as the sun moves across the sky, these animals receive information about the position of the sun if they can see a patch of blue sky. Thus, honeybees are able to use the sun as a compass even on partly cloudy days (Wehner, 1987).

There is another advantage to a sensitivity to the pattern of polarization. Natural light is strongly polarized at sunset, and there is a band of maximal polarization that runs north to south as the sun sets in the west. Thus, the many birds that begin their migratory movements at sunset may use the pattern of polarized light at sunset to set their direction of flight. Experiments involving the experimental manipulation of the pattern of polarization strongly suggest that the birds do in fact utilize cues from polarized light in their orientation (Helbig, 1991).

The Pattern of Stars

Warblers migrate at night, when cues from the sun are not available, and use the pattern of stars to navigate. Since the 1960s, researchers have learned that many other species of birds also navigate by the stars.

How do the birds utilize information extracted from the pattern of stars in the night sky? Stephan Emlen (1975) conducted experiments with indigo buntings that helped to answer this question. By selectively shifting certain patterns of stars, Emlen found that the birds do not respond to the total pattern of stars but to patterns within 35 degrees of the **celestial pole**—the center of rotation of the night sky. Also, different individual birds apparently learn to respond to different constellations or combinations of constellations. The blocking of one constellation might disrupt one bird, but not another.

As we saw in Chapter 3 when we discussed the development of behavior, birds apparently learn to identify the celestial pole in relation to nearby constellations when they are very young and then use this information as migrating adults. Because the celestial pole is consistently in the northern part of the sky, the birds are able to use it as a compass.

In conclusion, it seems that some nocturnal migrators get a fix on the direction they must travel at sunset and then get additional directional information from the pattern of the stars. Nocturnal migration presents many advantages; winds are more consistent at night than they are in the day, and there is also a reduced threat from predators after dark. Unfortunately, however, artificial lights from structures such as lighthouses and tall buildings may interfere with navigation, especially when weather conditions make it difficult for migrating birds to pick up natural navigational cues (Alerstam, 1990).

The Moon

Because the moon is visible on only half of the days of the year, very few animals have evolved a tendency to use it as a compass.

However, the beach hopper *Talitrus saltitor* is an exception. This small crustacean, which moves approximately 100 meters up and down the beach in a 24-hour period, uses the sun as a compass during the day and, when it is available, the moon at night. A simple experiment using mirrors demonstrated the role of the moon as a compass; when the experimenters altered the apparent position of the moon with a mirror, the beach hopper predictably changed its orientation (Papi & Pardi, 1959).

The Use of the Earth's Magnetic Field

When it was first suggested, many years ago, that animals responded to magnetic fields, the idea was met with great skepticism. However, as you will recall from Chapter 18, magnetoreceptors have been identified in several animals. Furthermore, Walcott's (1972) classic experiment in which pigeons' magnetic sense was disrupted demonstrated the effects of magnetism on bird orientation. However, Walcott found that the disrupting effect occurred only on cloudy days. The magnetically disoriented birds oriented correctly when released on sunny days. Apparently pigeons utilize the more reliable cues from the sun's position whenever possible and rely on their sensitivity to the earth's magnetic field as a backup system.

Marine animals are also sensitive to magnetic cues. Laboratory studies with hatchling loggerhead turtles (*Caretta caretta*) indicate that when the surrounding magnetic field is experimentally reversed, the turtles reverse their direction of orientation (Lohmann, 1991).

Whales may also use magnetic fields in their orientation. The ocean floor has bands of

TABLE 19.2 ◆ Celestial and Magnetic Cues Utilized in Navigation

Cues	Special Adaptations	Examples
Sun	Compensation for movement of the sun across the sky	Birds and honeybees
Polarized light	Sensitivity to the pattern of polarization	Birds and honeybees
Pattern of stars	In young warblers, ability to learn constellations close to the celestial pole	Warblers
Moon	Unknown	Beach hoppers
Earth's magnetic field	Sensitivity to magnetism	Birds, loggerhead turtles, whales

solidified lava that form a sort of magnetic highway, and it is possible that whales use magnetic cues from this highway during their migration. Indirect evidence supporting this conclusion comes from an analysis of whale strandings. In many cases, these strandings occur in areas with magnetic anomalies that could confuse the whales (Klinowska, 1986).

The Use of Landmarks

Using information from a compass alone, animals would be unable to pinpoint their home from any significant distance. Even the most accurate navigator would be likely to miss its home site by several kilometers. Once an animal arrives in the general vicinity of its home, however, it can find its way by orienting to familiar landmarks. An animal may also use visual, auditory, and olfactory landmarks as "maps" to set its course for migration, to gain information about its position en route, and to recognize the appropriate general area at the end of the journey.

Visual Landmarks

The role of visual landmarks in bird navigation is suggested by evidence such as the finding that bird migrations often follow prominent geographical features, especially landmarks that are readily discernible from the air. Furthermore, pigeons allowed to become familiar with the area around their loft return home more quickly than birds that have not familiarized themselves with the area. As a matter of fact, when young birds of migratory species first leave their nest, they spend a large amount of time randomly flying around the area, presumably learning landmarks. Migratory species spend considerably more time in this activity—especially in flying at a distance from the nest—than do nonmigratory species.

In birds that migrate in flocks, such as geese, younger adult birds seem to rely on older birds that have migrated for years to identify landmarks along the migratory route. First-time migrators that are not in the company of experienced older birds are less efficient at finding their destination. Presumably, the V formation in which geese fly allows changes in the flight pattern of individual birds, which may reflect some knowledge of the migratory route, to be communicated easily to the other birds.

Visual landmarks do not seem to be very important in the migrations of aquatic animals. Light does not penetrate the water to the degree that aquatic animals can see the bottom, except in very shallow water. However, the gray whale is an exception; as we have seen, this whale occasionally sticks its head out of the water in what seems to be an attempt to orient itself relative to the shoreline.

Acoustic Landmarks

Although we do not usually think of sounds as being reliable landmarks, some sounds—such as distant surf pounding against the shore or wind murmuring in forested areas—can be very effective beacons, especially when visual cues are limited. Some birds have evolved a sensitivity to very low-frequency sounds associated with surf and winds and are able to detect shorelines and forests at a distance of several hundred kilometers (see Alerstam, 1990).

Sounds also facilitate the navigation of bats, but in this case, it is echoes from the echolocation system that provide the cues. Experimental research indicates that deafened bats have great difficulty in homing. Nonetheless, it seems likely that bats rely to some extent on a combination of cues in their navigation. Enough light is present in postsunset glow and from the stars to allow for some visual cues to provide information in addition to that provided by the acoustic cues.

The evidence for linking echolocation and navigation in dolphins is more indirect. However, because dolphins follow underwater escarpments while making echolocating sounds, it seems likely that they, like bats, make use of the echoes for navigation to some extent (see Waterman, 1989).

Homing Guided by Chemical Cues

Several types of animals use chemical cues in their navigation. These animals are able to discriminate among different levels of concentration of a particular chemical substance. Thus, by moving in the direction of greatest concentration, the animals are able to home in on the source of the substance.

Homing in Salmon

A classic series of experiments by Hasler and Larson (1956) indicated that young salmon learn distinctive chemical cues associated with water from particular tributaries and use these cues in their well-developed homing response as adults. Experimenters plugged the nasal sacs of salmon and found that without the use of olfactory cues, the fish were unable to find the tributary in which they hatched. Apparently the salmon fry (juvenile fish) had learned the chemical properties of the water in their natal area. (The specific chemical properties of a stream are stable over a period of years, reflecting such factors as the type of vegetation in the area.) Other research suggests that there is a short sensitive period during which the salmon fry are able to learn to discriminate tributaries on the basis of subtle chemical cues in the water. At the end of this sensitive period—at the time when the salmon begin their migration out to the ocean—the fish lose this discriminatory ability. The salmon's brief period of sensitivity, then, enables this fish to develop certain preferences and behavior tendencies that will be retained over a long period of time and that are resistant to interference by later learning.

How the salmon on their return migration are able to find their way to the choice point where they can sense odors from the natal area remained a mystery for many years. However, research indicates that the salmon are also able to recognize the odors of other streams they pass on their way back up the river. Consequently, once the salmon are swimming upstream, they can make correct choices at the forks of various streams and tributaries.

Homing in Green Sea Turtles

A population of green sea turtles migrates from the coastal waters of South America to Ascension Island, a distance of more than 2,000 kilometers. The turtles have to navigate extremely accurately, because Ascension Island is only 8 kilometers wide. How do they do it? The most plausible explanation is that, as young turtles, they are carried away from Ascension Island by the equatorial current that takes them to South America. Then, on the return trip as adults several years later, the turtles follow the countercurrent that flows beneath the surface in the opposite direction (Baker, 1978).

The remarkable ability of the green sea turtles to find Ascension Island may also be explained on the basis of sensitivity to chemical cues similar to that shown by salmon. The turtles must surface to breathe, so they periodically pass through the equatorial current on their way to the surface and may be able to recognize the chemical cues in that current. (Like rivers, ocean currents have a distinct chemical signature.) The turtles could then follow the chemical trail and home in on the island (Baker, 1981; Carr, 1965).

It appears that the turtles learn cues associated with the Ascension Island breeding area when they first hatch; then, when they are older, they learn cues related to the South American feeding grounds. DNA analyses of populations in both locations indicate that the turtles show extreme fidelity to both the breeding site and the feeding area (Limpus et al., 1991).

Why do these turtles migrate such a great distance when there are suitable nesting sites that are closer to South America? It may be that the migratory pattern was established millions of years ago, when South America and Ascension Island were closer together (The same geological forces that caused South America and Africa to drift apart were at play in this situation.) Because the turtles could continue to find the island by following currents—even if the distance became progressively greater—the tendency to migrate in this pattern survived (Carr & Coleman, 1974).

Homing in Pigeons

We have already seen that pigeons rather clearly home by using cues from the earth's magnetic field and the sun. Do pigeons also use olfactory cues? Studies of the role of olfaction in navigation have produced considerable controversy. On the one hand, when researchers make pigeons insensitive to smell by experimentally disrupting their olfactory system, the birds often have problems homing (Wallraff, 1983). On the other hand, it is not clear how the olfactory cues are used by the birds. Furthermore, some experimenters have suggested that the experimental birds fail to home because, lacking a sense of smell, they have lost their motivation to fly (see Wiltshko

& Wiltshko, 1995). To make matters even more confusing, pigeons tested in Italy are generally impaired by disruption of the olfactory system, while pigeons tested in Germany are not.

Nevertheless, studies that do not involve experimental disruption of the olfactory system indicate that many pigeons do indeed use olfactory information in their navigation. The differences between Italian and German birds seem to be related to such factors as the type of loft in which the pigeons are raised and the types of cues that are present during the pigeons' development (Benvenutti et al., 1990). However, the olfactory information is not in itself sufficient for homing. As in the case of other species of animals, pigeons apparently need to integrate olfactory information with other types of information in order to home.

◆ HUMAN EVOLUTION

The migrations of humans, like those of several species of nonhuman animals, may be quite extensive under certain circumstances. We will first look briefly at some human migrations, especially those that took place before the use of navigational aids, and then consider aspects of human navigational ability.

MIGRATIONS

The hominid ancestors of humans probably migrated from one part of Africa to another in response to food availability. Once *Homo sapiens* evolved, some migrations became more extensive. There is evidence of migrations covering thousands of kilometers, including voyages across vast expanses of open ocean. For example, artifacts indicate that during the twelfth to fourteenth centuries, Tahitians made round-trips between Tahiti and Hawaii, a total distance of more than 6,000 kilometers (3,700 miles).

A few years ago a Micronesian sailor supported the hypothesis that such trips did indeed take place. He sailed, unaided by navigational instruments, from Tahiti to Hawaii in a replica of a traditional sailing vessel. Fortunately for today's scientists, there are still Micronesian and Polynesian navigators living on the islands who can explain the traditional navigational techniques. Interestingly, these techniques are very similar to those apparently used by the Persians, the Chinese, and even the Phoenecians more than 3,000 years ago (Waterman, 1989).

NAVIGATION

Without navigational aids, humans are insensitive to some of the important cues utilized by certain nonhuman animals. We cannot orient in relation to cues from the earth's magnetic field, as some birds can; we are unable to use cues from the polarized light of the sun when the sun is not visible, as honeybees can. Humans also rely to a much greater extent on the cultural learning of navigational techniques than do nonhumans. In many cases nonhuman animals are able to navigate without previous experience; and even when experience is involved, animals' reliance on "teaching" by conspecifics is limited. For example, experienced older birds may facilitate the navigation of younger birds by acting as models, but even without this help, inexperienced birds may find their destination eventually.

In contrast, human navigators depend greatly on learning and techniques passed on from one generation to another. For example, the art of traditional navigation practiced by Pacific Islanders requires a long period of training in an awareness of every possible natural cue used in navigation, including types of waves, clouds, fish, and birds. The teachers sometimes employ pebbles, sticks, and shells to construct charts on the ground as teaching aids for their students during land training. Once at sea, however, these island navigators use no chart, ruler, or protractor. Dead reckoning and celestial navigation are their key tools for setting the course and estimating time of travel between landmarks. Much of the trip between Hawaii and Tahiti is out of sight of any land, so the use of landmarks is limited to short periods of time at the beginning and the end of the journey. Nonetheless, the types of waves and the number and types of fish and birds present give some indication of proximity to land and ocean currents (Waterman, 1989).

It seems that humans were not strongly selected to develop techniques for accurate navigation over large expanses of ocean water, because extensive migrations over water are relatively rare. Because we have the potential for high levels of cultural learning, however, certain Pacific Islanders have been able to build a tradition of remarkable navigational ability over many generations. And interestingly, the cues utilized by these Pacific island navigators are very similar to many of the cues used by nonhuman animals.

◆ CHANGING PERSPECTIVES

PAST	PRESENT	FUTURE
Migratory strategies are inflexible; the navigational methods of migrating animals are mysterious (early twentieth century).	Many migration strategies are flexible and sensitive to ecological factors, including population dynamics. Most animals use several types of cues in their navigation.	Are there still unidentified cues used in navigation? How do they function?

SUMMARY

Migration can enable animals to exploit food in two or more different habitats, remain in consistently favorable environments, avoid predators and parasites, produce young under optimal conditions, and gain information about possible future habitats. On the other hand, costs of migration include considerable energy expenditure, vulnerability to attack, and susceptibility to adverse weather conditions.

Scientists investigate migration in animals with the aid of devices and techniques such as radar, sonar, telemetry, and the tagging of individual animals. Scientists study navigational ability by eliminating or disrupting certain sensory systems in animals or by placing animals in artificial conditions and then observing their behavior.

Monarch butterflies, salmon, and whales are among the animals that exhibit long-distance migrations. Some land mammals also migrate, often in search of food. However, birds are the champion migrators, both in terms of distances traveled and in terms of the number of species that migrate. Migrating species typically prepare for their journeys by building up flight muscles and storing fat; if prevented from migrating, birds show migratory restlessness. Although migratory patterns can be identified in a species as a whole, there may be individual differences in the tendency to migrate.

Animals use many different navigational cues in their migrations and to facilitate efficient movement within their habitat. Dead reckoning is a method of determining position on the basis of both distance and direction traveled. Many animals use celestial cues as a compass and can compensate for the apparent movement of the sun, the stars, and in rare cases the moon across the sky during a given period of time.

Some animals can use the sun as a compass even when it is not visible, orienting to the pattern of polarized light. Nocturnally migrating birds use the constellations of the night sky, relying on the fixed position of the celestial pole. A few animals are also sensitive to the earth's magnetic field, using the magnetic sense as a backup navigational system.

Many animals use visual or acoustic landmarks to provide "maps." A few animals, including salmon, green sea turtles, and pigeons, are able to use chemical cues as a guide for homing.

Human migrations and navigational ability can be quite extensive under some circumstances. However, navigation without the use of a compass is strongly dependent on learning and the accumulation of knowledge over several generations.

KEY TERMS

azimuth, p. 455
celestial pole, p. 456
dead reckoning, p. 453
flyways, p. 446

homing, p. 453
internal inertia system, p. 454
migration, p. 442
telemetry, p. 444

CHAPTER 20

EMIGRATION, HABITAT SELECTION, AND POPULATION REGULATION

- ◆ *Why do lemmings move in such large numbers?*

- ◆ *Do some lemmings kill themselves on their marches?*

In Chapter 19 we looked at animal movement in terms of migration and navigation. In this chapter we will consider three other processes related to animal movement: emigration, habitat selection, and population regulation. Although these processes are somewhat distinct, they are interrelated in important ways. Factors related to emigration influence where animals travel; habitat selection is concerned with when animals

20

stop emigrating and settle down; and the population density depends, to a certain extent, on emigration patterns and habitat selection.

We will begin by considering patterns of emigration and the various functions these movement patterns serve. Then we will discuss how animals choose their habitat and the complex interaction that may take place between genetic and environmental factors in habitat selection. Next, we will analyze the large number of ways in which the population of animals is regulated. Finally, we will consider aspects of human emigration and habitat selection.

EMIGRATION

Emigration is movement out of a particular area without a return to that area. Emigration may promote optimal breeding conditions, because young animals tend to disperse and avoid breeding with extremely close relatives. Emigration may also reduce competition with conspecifics, some of whom are likely to be close relatives. Finally, emigration may constitute escape from a deteriorating environment or crowded conditions.

Optimal Outbreeding Related to Natal Dispersal

Some animals exhibit **natal philopatry;** that is, they remain in the area of their birth or hatching and share a territory or home range with parents and siblings. Natal philopatry enables animals to remain within familiar territories where they are relatively safe and well adapted.

In contrast, the offspring of many species exhibit **natal dispersal**—movement from the natal area to a new area where their reproduction takes place. A significant advantage of natal dispersal is that the possibility of inbreeding is reduced. As we saw in Chapter 2 when we discussed genetics, inbreeding is generally disadvantageous for both the parents and the offspring.

In some cases of natal dispersal, the parents chase the offspring out of the area just before they reach reproductive age. In monogamous species of birds, for example, daughters in particular are forced out of the nest area. This sex bias is probably related to the fact that daughters may parasitize the parents by laying eggs in their nest. In polygynous species, both sexes of offspring present a threat; the daughter may be a nest parasite, and the son may "steal" copulations with the mother. Therefore, unsurprisingly, there is no sex bias in the way the young are treated in polygynous bird species (Liberg & von Schantz, 1985).

Although the parents are often the initiators, the offspring initiate dispersal in some species. For example, screech owl young have an intrinsically timed "dispersal restlessness" similar to the migratory restlessness discussed in Chapter 19. When raised in isolation, the young owls have an activity level that increases up until the time when they would normally disperse, remains high for the period corresponding to their normal departure, and then drops at about the time they would normally settle down (Ritchison et al., 1992).

Greater Dispersal in One Gender Than in the Other

In most cases of natal dispersal, one gender of offspring disperses and the other gender either stays or remains relatively close to the natal area. This system of dispersal makes it unlikely that brothers and sisters will mate. In most songbird species only the female disperses; or, if both genders disperse, the female travels the greater distance. This gender difference seems to be related to the relative costs of dispersal. Because most male songbirds are monogamous and establish a territory, a male bird derives an advantage from staying close to the natal area where he already knows the location of resources and predators. For females, who are not usually involved in establishment or defense of territories, the cost of emigration is not as great (Greenwood, 1980).

The opposite pattern prevails among mammals. In contrast to most birds, the fe-

male mammal usually provides for her young on her own; and there are relatively great advantages to remaining in the general area, where she is familiar with resources and predators. Thus, the cost of emigration is less for male mammals than it is for females, and the male typically emigrates farther than the female. For example, male Belding's ground squirrels emigrate when they reach maturity, while the females remain in the natal area (Holecamp & Sherman, 1989). When lions reach maturity, it is also the male that leaves while the female stays. Young males may depart on their own, or they may be chased out, if a coalition of males takes over from their father (Pusey & Packer, 1987).

In both ground squirrels and lions, the degree of dispersal is such that it promotes breeding with cousins or females of intermediate genetic relationship. This is an optimal degree of outbreeding and results, as we saw in Chapter 2, in higher levels of fitness than either inbreeding or extreme outbreeding.

Primate males that live in social groups, such as vervet monkeys, usually do not leave an area but join a separate troop. This redistribution of males has a function similar to that of male dispersal; that is, because animals that live in different troops do not usually mate, the possibility of incest is reduced. Male vervet monkeys may change groups again when they get older. The pattern of males shifting from group to group is such that the likelihood of mating between individuals that are intermediately related is greater than the likelihood of two completely unrelated individuals' mating.

As suggested earlier, there is another possible advantage of male dispersal in mammals. If the males did not disperse, they would be competing with male relatives for re-

◆ UNUSUAL ADAPTATIONS

Dispersal in Blind Mole-Rats

So far, we have considered the dispersal of animals that either fly or walk to a new area. But how do animals that live underground disperse? Research on blind mole-rats provides some answers and also uncovers an unusual method of communication.

The blind mole-rat, in contrast to the naked mole-rat introduced in Chapter 14, is a highly solitary animal that lives in its own tunnel system and never leaves the system unless it is forced out. After birth, the blind mole-rats live with their mothers. As they get older, however, they dig their own tunnels as extensions of the maternal tunnel. Then, when they are about 12 weeks old, they seal off their tunnels and begin the solitary existence typical of adults. Nonetheless, they are able to communicate with other mole-rats by the use of seismic signals: The rats strike their heads on the ceilings of their tunnels, producing vibrations that carry long distances through the soil (Rado et al., 1991). The rats seem to use these signals to regulate their spacing in the environment and also for sexual communication.

sources. This type of competition would lower indirect fitness (Hamilton & May, 1977). A study of the population density of white-footed mice (*Peromyscus leucopus*) over a period of a year offers indirect support for this competition hypothesis. When few receptive females were available, older male mice displaced younger males at a relatively high rate—a finding that suggests that competition over the females was an important factor in dispersal (Korytko & Vessey, 1991).

Escape from a Deteriorating Environment

Unstable environments periodically deteriorate, so even a slim chance of finding a superior environment makes emigration or disper-

TABLE 20.1 ◆ Natal Dispersal

Type of Animal	Greatest Dispersal	Reason
Birds	Female offspring	Dispersal less costly for females
Mammals	Male offspring	Dispersal less costly for males

sal advantageous. An adaptation for small, light animals is to make themselves vulnerable to wind conditions and allow the wind to transport them or their potential offspring to new areas. For example, organisms known as slime-mold amoebas are free-living most of their lives; but when their food source dwindles, they aggregate and form a colony. As the number of aggregating organisms becomes relatively large, the amoebas join together in a sausage-shaped slug. Then the cells differentiate; some form a cylindrical stalk, while others move to the top of the stalk and form a small sphere enclosing reproductive spores. The spores are eventually released and carried by the wind to a new area, where the next generation of amoebas will live (Bonner, 1963; see Figure 20.1).

Some species of spiders that live in periodically deteriorating habitats also use the wind to emigrate, utilizing a method known as ballooning. The spider climbs to the top of vegetation or some projecting object, orients its abdomen into the air, and extrudes long strands of silk. When the wind is in an acceptable direction and the wind speed is less than 10 kph (7 mph), the spider releases its hold on the substrate and takes off with the wind. The length and direction of the trip is very much dependent upon the wind and is not always favorable in terms of the spider's fitness; under certain conditions, ballooning spiders have been carried hundreds or even thousands of miles and have landed on ships far out at sea.

Escape from an Overpopulated Environment

While spiders leave a deteriorating environment, the function of lemming emigration is primarily to escape from overcrowded conditions. For some poorly understood reason, the population of lemmings explodes every 3 or 4 years. Naturalists once thought that these small rodents, which live in mountainous areas of Norway, Sweden, and Finland, committed suicide to relieve the overpopulation—because every few years great numbers of lemmings run down mountainsides and throw themselves or push one another into large bodies of water. However, this putative suicide was very hard to explain, because it would clearly be selected against at the individual level.

An explanation that is compatible with modern evolutionary theory is that many lemmings are unable to establish territories in the usual summer feeding grounds because of the high population pressure. Consequently, these animals continue down the mountain en

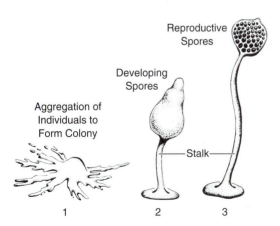

Reproductive Spores

Developing Spores

Aggregation of Individuals to Form Colony

Stalk

1   2   3

FIGURE 20.1 ◆ **Adjustment of the slime-mold amoeba to deteriorating conditions.** (1) The individual organisms aggregate. (2) Some cells differentiate into stalk cells and form a stalk, while others form a sphere. (3) Some cells form reproductive spores that are dispersed by the wind.

masse and keep moving, in a more or less straight line, across lakes and rivers. Actually, lemmings are reasonably good swimmers, and a relatively small percentage of them drown. The survival chances of lemmings that undergo a long emigration—including lake crossings and exposure to numerous predators—may not be great; but the probable fitness benefits are greater for them than for lemmings that do not emigrate and are unable to establish a territory or reproduce (see Stenseth & Ims, 1993).

Escape from a Temporarily Suboptimal Environment

A basic difference between migration and emigration is that in migration, individuals return to their place of departure. In contrast, emigrating individuals make only a one-way journey. But desert locusts (*Schistocerca gregaria*) are classified somewhere between migrants and emigrants, because second- or third-generation descendants often return to the place of departure.

At one time scientists believed there were two species of desert locusts—one species that emigrated, was highly social, and ate voraciously, and another species that did not emigrate, was solitary, and ate relatively small amounts. However, we now know that there is only one species and that the locust population can regulate when individuals develop into the social, emigratory type. A dense population of locusts produces a particularly heavy concentration of a pheromone produced by males. This pheromone stimulates females to mature rapidly and produce an unusually large number of eggs. When these

young mature, they develop into the emigrant type, which feed voraciously and form large swarms. Thus, when conditions are favorable for the locusts, as reflected by the dense population of individuals that starts the process, the emigratory type is produced.

A large concentration of voracious locusts quickly outstrips the local food supply. However, because the emigratory locusts keep moving, they are exposed to fresh food supplies. One locust swarm in East Africa was estimated to be more than 30 meters (100 feet) deep and more than a kilometer across. The swarm took 9 hours to pass a particular point and devastated virtually all vegetation in its path (see Figure 20.2). During their long emigration, desert locusts move toward storm clouds or rain so as to devour vegetation in temporarily fertile areas along the way (see Farb et al., 1962; Johnson, 1969).

In contrast to ballooning spiders, desert locusts are not at the complete mercy of the wind. The locusts shift their pattern of flight, depending on the wind direction. When the wind is against them, they fly close to the ground, where the wind velocity is reduced. When flying with the wind, however, some of the locusts fly high above the ground, moving faster than the lower ones—which often drop to the ground to feed. The high-flying ones eventually arrive at the front of the swarm, after which they fly downwards and move back toward the center of the swarm. Thus, the pattern of some individuals' movement is something resembling the track of a tank, functioning to keep the locusts in a tight swarm.

When conditions are favorable, mating and oviposition take place. Later, after the eggs are laid and the adults grow old, the

FIGURE 20.2 ◆ An emigrating swarm of desert locusts in Ethiopia.

swarm gradually dies out. However, when the eggs hatch and develop into young adults, new swarms arise and continue on the next leg of the journey. Thus, second- or third-generation individuals often end up in the same area from which the movement began.

HABITAT SELECTION

After an animal emigrates, it must find a place to settle down. In some species, such as the ballooning spiders, external forces determine where animals settle. In other cases there may be **competitive exclusion**—one species of animal may be driven out of a preferred site by competition with a highly similar species. For example, competition is strong between the coho and chinook salmon in many streams and rivers that run into the Pacific Ocean. In pool-like habitats, the coho dominate the chinook and force them into less desirable areas (Taylor, 1991). As the result of competitive exclusion, animals end up living in a **realized niche;** that is, a niche that is more restricted than it would be if there were no competition.

Individuals may also force conspecifics into less desirable habitats. Because competition for nesting sites is intense among kittiwakes, many of these birds end up nesting in relatively poor locations where reproductive success is limited (Porter, 1990).

TABLE 20.2 ◆ Functions of Emigration

Function	Mechanism	Examples
Promotion of optimal outbreeding	Natal dispersal	Many species of birds and animals
Escape from deteriorating environment	Adaptations for dispersal via wind	Slime-mold amoebas; certain spiders
Escape from overpopulated conditions	Mass emigrations	Lemmings
Escape from temporarily suboptimal conditions	Departure and return generations later	Desert locusts

Nonetheless, many animals select a habitat independent of competition, sometimes taking several variables into account. As we shall see, the factors involved in habitat selection vary from relatively simple mechanisms to complex information-processing systems.

Basic Orienting Mechanisms

Some animals orient with the aid of mechanisms that more or less automatically direct them toward favorable environments and away from unfavorable ones. There are two types of basic orienting mechanisms: taxes (the singular is taxis) and kineses (the singular is kinesis).

A **taxis** is a movement directly toward or away from a stimulus. A movement toward a stimulus is known as a positive taxis. If animals have receptors on both sides of the body, they move in the direction associated with maximum stimulation. For example, certain aquatic arthropods that benefit from finding water exhibit a positive taxis toward humidity. Thus, the response leads the animal to the favorable aquatic environment.

In contrast, a movement away from a stimulus is known as a negative taxis. Planarians can be damaged by light, so this simple response enables the animal to avoid a dangerous habitat.

Migrating salmon also exhibit tactic responses. In this case, the animal's response is to the movement of water against the body, a response called a rheotaxis. Positive rheotaxis induces a tendency to swim against the current. This response is predominant when the salmon swims upstream during its migration as an adult.

Kineses are also movements in response to stimuli, but a **kinesis** is a response to the intensity of stimulation. This type of response *indirectly* leads an animal into a favorable environment or away from an unfavorable one. There are two general types of kineses. **Or-**

thokinesis is a change in the speed of movement dependent on intensity of stimulation. An animal moves faster in an unfavorable environment and slows down or stops in a favorable one. As a result, the animal is likely to end up eventually in a favorable environment. For example, the larvae of brook trout (*Lampetra planeri*) end up buried in the mud at the bottom of a stream as the result of an orthokinetic response to light. The larvae have a light-sensitive area near the tip of the tail. As a larva digs in the mud at the bottom, the light receptor becomes covered and the animal stops moving (Jones, 1955).

Klinokinesis is a change in the rate of turning related to intensity. Turning rate increases as the animal enters an unfavorable area. Although a change in turning rate in itself is not likely to benefit an animal, the occurrence of klinokinesis in combination with orthokinesis can have a favorable effect. For example, an animal may continue to turn until it is headed in a favorable direction and then stop moving as it enters a favorable area. Consequently, these kinetic responses often occur in conjunction with each other (Budenberg, 1991).

Statistical analyses of the movements of animals that exhibit taxes and kineses indicate that the animals are usually employing several of these basic orienting mechanisms in combination (Benhamou & Bovet, 1992). Furthermore, the types of responses are liable to change as the physiological condition of the animal changes. For example, a tick that is food-deprived shows a negative geotaxis (a movement away from the ground) and moves to the top of a blade of grass, where it is more likely to encounter a host. After eating, however, the tick exhibits a positive geotaxis and moves down to the ground, where it is less likely to encounter predators (Fraenkel & Gunn, 1961). It appears, then, that although taxes and kineses are simple mechanisms, they provide for a fairly large range of adaptive responses.

TABLE 20.3 ◆ Taxis and Kineses

Mechanism	Definition	Effect
Taxis	Movement directly toward (positive taxis) or away from (negative taxis) a stimulus	Taxis directly places animal in favorable environment.
Orthokinesis	Increased rate of movement in unfavorable environment	In combination with klinokinesis, orthokinesis indirectly places animal in favorable conditions.
Klinokinesis	Increased rate of turning in unfavorable environment	In combination with orthokinesis, klinokinesis indirectly places animal in favorable conditions.

Complex Methods
of Habitat Selection

Despite their many advantages, taxes and kineses have clear limitations: They cannot provide the types of information that allow animals to make complex habitat choices. And complex choices are required of many animals, especially animals that must travel a certain distance to find an appropriate habitat. We will now look at the more complex processes that enable animals such as honeybees, lizards, birds, and mammals to find specific types of habitat.

Communication and "Group Decision"
in Honeybee Nest Site Choice

A colony of honeybees must locate a site that is some distance from their original site. Because half of the bees remain at the old nest, the emigrating bees must move far enough so that there is not too much competition for nectar in the immediate area. The emigrating bees form a swarm and find a temporary refuge hanging in a solid mass from the limb of a tree, the workers surrounding the queen. During the next few days, workers fly out in search of potential nest sites. When a suitable site is found, a worker returns and performs a dance much like the waggle dance that communicates the location of a food source (Chapter 12). The dance communicates the quality, distance, and direction of the potential nest site.

At first there may be several workers indicating different site choices. Soon, however, workers that have been recruited to an appealing nest site will also dance in support of this site; when the "votes" on a given location reach a critical point, the entire swarm will fly to this site. Thus, the system of communication allows for a type of group consensus. The main factors honeybees consider in choosing a nest site are the volume of the cavity, the degree of insulation (at least for bees living in temperate zones), and the distance between the new site and the nest from which the bees emigrated (Lindauer, 1961; Seeley, 1977).

Social Factors in a
Lizard's Habitat Choice

We once believed that the presence of territorial conspecifics would discourage animals from settling in an area because of the pressure of competition (Kluyver & Tinbergen, 1953). In fact, however, field observations indicate that emigrants in search of a site prefer to settle next to established territorial residents. Further evidence of this "social" decision making comes from a controlled field study of lizards. These animals show a preference for settling in areas near conspecifics until the point when the habitat becomes saturated (Stamps, 1991). As we saw in Chapter 7 when we considered defensive strategies, there are significant advantages to living in large groups.

The Role of Photoperiod
in Birds' Habitat Choice

Many animals, especially birds, assess the quality of an environment on the basis of visual cues. The use of visual cues is illustrated by the finding that birds are able to choose a habitat based on information contained in a photograph. Moreover, the particular photographic scene that is most appealing depends on the season. For example, birds in a laboratory experiment preferred a scene from the winter habitat in the winter, and they were most likely to choose one from the summer habitat in the summer (Roberts & Weigl, 1984).

We might think that this differential choice would reflect the birds' sensitivity to temperature. However, an experimental presentation of slides of various habitats to dark-eyed juncos indicated that the birds' choice depends on photoperiod, or length of daylight versus darkness. When presented with a color slide of both their summer and winter habitats, the juncos spent the most time in front of the image of their winter habitat after they had been kept in the laboratory with 9 hours of light and 15 hours of darkness (the winter photoperiod). Conversely, they spent the most time in front of the summer habitat slide after they had been kept under the summer photoperiod of 15 hours of light and 9 hours of darkness (Roberts & Weigl, 1984).

The Role of Experience in Habitat Selection of Birds and Mammals

Laboratory studies indicate that the experience of birds alters their preferred habitat. Chipping sparrows, which normally prefer pine branches, were reared in a room with oak branches and compared to a control group of sparrows reared without any vegetation. When tested 2 months later, the group with the special oak-branch experience spent about equal amounts of time on oak and pine branches, while the control group showed a definite preference for pine (Klopfer, 1963). Apparently the sparrow's basic preference for pine, which is influenced by hereditary factors, can be modified by early experience—though not entirely eliminated.

The resilience of the basic preference is further illustrated by a subsequent experiment with the chipping sparrows raised with oak boughs. After the testing at the end of the first phase of the experiment, these birds were placed in an aviary in a pine forest for 8 months. The birds then preferred the pine branches when given a choice between pine and oak, indicating that the basic preference had returned (Klopfer, 1963).

Experiments with laboratory mice indicate a similar interaction between inherited preferences and early experience. Mice were raised on one of two types of materials: cedar shavings or a commercial cellulose material. When tested, they preferred the bedding on which they had been raised. However, later tests showed a "drift" toward a preference for the cedar bedding (Anderson, 1973). It may be concluded that, for at least some mammals and birds, habitat preferences may be modified by experiential factors. However, genetically influenced tendencies are not replaced and may return under certain circumstances.

POPULATION REGULATION

In some instances, animals that emigrate to a new area are so successful that there is a rapid increase in density, a depletion of environmental resources—and, ultimately, a danger that the resources will be depleted to the extent that there is a population crash. Because this danger exists, different species have evolved different mechanisms for population regulation. We will now look at the various methods of population regulation and at how they evolved at an individual level.

Some population pressure is alleviated by dispersal and other types of emigration. In addition, a population is regulated by **abiotic** conditions, or conditions imposed by nonliving aspects of the environment. Some abiotic factors such as floods, fires, volcanic eruptions, or rapid climatic changes are catastrophic and out of animals' control. These catastrophic events are called **density independent,** because they are not influenced by how many animals are present in a particular area. Animals that are *r* selected are then the first ones to colonize an area after a catastrophe (MacArthur & Wilson, 1967; Pianka, 1970). (As discussed in Chapter 8, *r* selection means that animals are capable of reproducing rapidly when the population is below carrying capacity.)

More predictable population regulation factors are **biotic,** or related to living things. Many of these biotic factors are **density dependent**—influenced by the number of animals in a particular area. Density-dependent factors place effective limits on population growth when density reaches high levels. There are two general types of regulation related to biotic factors: regulation imposed by different species, and regulation imposed by conspecifics.

Regulation Imposed by Different Species

The fact that density-dependent factors such as food, predators, parasites, and competitors control population growth is not surprising. However, as we shall see, the relationship between these ecological factors and population density is far from simple.

Abundance of Prey Animals and Other Food Sources

The abundance of prey animals sets an upper limit on the population density of predators. We saw in Chapter 7 how a population of predators fluctuates in synchrony with the prey population. Similarly, the abundance of food is related to population density in nonpredators. For example, artificially placing food in a particular area increases the density of shrews (*Sorex*) up to a certain point; then the population stabilizes (Holling, 1959).

Similar results were obtained by John Calhoun (1962, 1973) in a classic series of laboratory studies on population regulation in mice and rats. He provided a room with a plethora of food, water, and resting sites and then observed the rodents' behavior and population growth. The populations consistently showed an S-shaped growth curve and then reached a point of stability. Within a finite space, apparently, many animals limit their population growth long before they are likely to overrun the food supply. (We'll return to Calhoun's studies shortly.)

Predation

Predators, of course, limit the population density of prey animals. Thus, when nest boxes that provide shelter from predators are provided for pied flycatchers, these birds significantly increase their population (von Haartman, 1953). Similar population increases occur with the artificial introduction of shelters for marine animals. Sunken ships provide refuges and lead to rapid increases in populations of several species of fishes and marine invertebrates. In some cases conservationists have actually sunk old ships in order to increase fish populations and create new opportunities for fishing (MacArthur & Connell, 1966).

A more direct way of looking at the effect of predators on a population of prey animals is to compare populations of animals with and without the presence of predators. In the Bahamas, lizards that prey on orb-weaving spiders live on certain islands but not on other islands that have similar habitats. The population of orb-weaving spiders is several times greater on the lizardless islands than on the islands with spider-eating lizards (Schoener & Toft, 1983).

Nonetheless, the removal of a predator does not always result in a long-term increase in the population of prey animals—as illustrated by a classic observation. In 1911 a group of 25 reindeer was introduced to a 21-square-mile island off the coast of Alaska where there were no reindeer predators. By 1938 the reindeer population had risen to more than 2,000. Then, in the 1940s, the effects of overgrazing resulted in a population crash—and by 1950 there were only 8 reindeer on the island (Krebs, 1972). If predation is a primary factor that keeps a population of prey animals from reaching the limits set by food availability, then a sudden disappearance of the predator can have a strongly negative long-term effect on the population of prey animals.

The disappearance of a predator can disrupt the natural balance in other ways as well. Paine (1966) removed starfish that normally prey on a variety of marine animals from a test area of the intertidal seacoast of the Olympia peninsula in Washington State. The starfish were allowed to remain in a comparable area (the control site). In the test area, the population of one species of mussel that was nor-

mally preyed upon by the starfish increased. However, the total number of marine invertebrate species was reduced to 8, while the number in the control site remained at 15. Apparently the removal of the predator allowed the mussel to dominate the area and drive out competing species. In contrast, when the predator was present, it prevented domination of available space by one species.

The Natural Balance between Predators and Prey

The results of predator removal are very difficult to predict, because there is a delicate and complex natural balance between predators and prey. Under natural conditions, it is unusual for a predator to appear suddenly in a habitat. Predatory patterns typically evolve slowly, and in response to these changes, the prey animals evolve defenses. Thus, predators are much less likely to drive animals to extinction under natural conditions than when a predator is introduced by humans. Human intervention can be especially disastrous in an island environment, where it is impossible for most animals to find an effective refuge or to disperse far enough to escape an area of heavy predation. A very sad example is found in the Hawaiian Islands, where a large percentage of the original population of bird species has been brought to extinction by the introduction of human pets and domestic animals.

Often, the relationship between predator and prey populations oscillates as a result of an interaction effect. As the prey population expands, predators have more food and increase in number. However, the predation pressure reduces the prey population; and as the prey population drops, many predators fail to find enough food to survive, so their population also drops.

The average point around which the oscillation occurs depends on the efficiency of the predator. If the predator is inefficient, it cannot exploit the prey until the prey population becomes very dense, so the average prey density is relatively great. In contrast, an efficient predator can exploit the prey even at low levels of density, so the population of prey animals remains relatively low on the average. If the predators become too efficient, the prey population can be driven to extinction. The possibility of extinction is especially great if the predators have an alternative food source to exploit when the prey population drops to a very low point.

Except in cases involving extremely efficient predators and/or predators with alternative food sources, however, the average population balance between predators and prey tends to remain fairly stable over time. Nonetheless, the predator–prey balance may be altered by other limiting factors that affect the populations differentially, such as an increase in parasitism or climatic changes. Therefore, the population balance is never assured.

Parasitism

In a manner somewhat similar to predators, parasites may act as population regulators by reducing the fitness of their hosts. As you may remember from Chapter 15, some parasites castrate their hosts. Other parasites may decrease their hosts' fitness by reducing their hosts' ability to escape from predators. For example, malarial parasites diminish the running stamina of lizards. The malarial parasite also detracts from the lizard's fitness by forcing a reduction of clutch size (number of eggs

laid) in females (Schall, 1982). We have also seen how a parasite may lessen its host's fitness by inducing risk proneness and by altering a host's behavior so that it is more likely to become prey for another animal.

Thus, although parasites do not usually kill their hosts, especially adult hosts, they can have a stabilizing effect on the population of their hosts. Because parasites are more likely to be transmitted from one host to another under crowded conditions, the parasites can limit the population growth of their hosts in much the same way that predators can limit the population growth of prey animals.

Interspecific Competition

An animal from a different species that is in competition for the same resource or resources can also function as a population regulator. A classic experimental study of two species of barnacles found in the same general shoreline habitat illustrates the effect of interspecific competition. Joseph Connell (1961) removed one of the species from rock surfaces on the coast of Scotland. The other species quickly occupied the vacated spaces. It turns out that under normal conditions, the species that Connell removed grows rapidly and uses its strong shell to pry individuals of the other species off the rocks. However, the physically weaker species is able to remain in the area because this barnacle is able to survive in dryer parts of the intertidal zone. Consequently, the stronger species limits the population of the weaker species but does not drive it to extinction.

Mobile animals may also limit the population of a related species. For example, two species of voles (mouselike rodents) are found in the Rocky Mountains. One species is specialized for living in relatively dry habitats, while the other thrives in wetter areas. When one species was experimentally trapped and removed from its preferred habitat, some individuals from the other species moved into the vacated area. It seems that under normal circumstances, the aggression of the species in the habitat for which it is maximally adapted keeps the related species out and, consequently, serves as a population regulator.

Unfortunately, humans sometimes introduce an alien species into an area where the species thrives at the expense of native animals. I have already mentioned an example of such a catastrophe—the loss of many bird species after the arrival of humans and their domestic animals in the Hawaiian Islands. A more recent example was the introduction of zebra mussels into the Great Lakes. Apparently a foreign ship brought over this native of the Caspian Sea in 1986 and introduced the mussel into its new habitat as the ship flushed out ballast water. The zebra mussel has already threatened the survival of many native species of mussels and clams. Furthermore, because it clogs industrial and municipal water intake pipes, controlling the zebra mussel will have cost more than a billion dollars by the year 2000. Humans have learned a hard lesson from artificially altering natural environments. We have driven a large number of plants and animals to extinction by changing natural habitats to suit our immediate needs. Clearly, an understanding of ecology and government policies that control potential threats to ecological balance are strongly needed. The research of ecologists and animal behaviorists can contribute significantly to public awareness and can support the efforts of those who are pressing for wise environmental policies.

Regulation Imposed by Conspecifics

The Calhoun experiments with mice and rats suggested that there was some sort of population regulation—independent of food, predation, parasitism, and interspecific competition—that limited the rodent populations in the experimental setting. Calhoun's observations suggested that the limiting factor was what he called "social pathology." When the rat population became extremely crowded, some males became indiscriminant in their choice of sex partners, approaching both females and other males. Other males were inactive sexually and failed to enter into the dominance hierarchy. Females also behaved abnormally, failing to build nests and in some cases refusing to mate at all. In the high-density mouse population, large numbers of mice would withdraw and form a pile of inactive individuals. Furthermore, females that bore young often abandoned them.

What causes this social pathology? Subsequent research has suggested that there are several proximate causes, including pheromones, hormones, and increased levels of aggression and stress. There also seem to be genetic factors that influence the development of this social pathology.

Pheromones

Part of the social pathology and population-limiting effect of extreme population density may have been due to pheromones. We saw in Chapter 17 that a pheromone in the urine of a strange male will cause abortion to take place in a female. Under crowded conditions there is a strong concentration of this pheromone. Furthermore, the urine of females contains a socially significant pheromone: High concentrations of this pheromone delay sexual maturation in other females (Novotny et al., 1986).

Aggression and Stress

When mice are given tranquilizers that reduce the expression of aggression and the experience of stress in general, the mouse population increases to near the carrying capacity of the environment (Vessey, 1967). An apparent explanation for this finding is that the stress associated with fighting and crowding over a relatively long period of time produces increases in adrenocortical hormones. High levels of adrenocortical hormones compromise an animal's immune system, and the animal becomes open to a variety of opportunistic diseases. It seems likely, then, that stress acts together with pheromones to limit population growth in some animals.

Another indication that aggression is a limiting factor in population growth comes from a study in which test mice were exposed to 2 minutes per day of fights with a mouse trained to fight. Because the test mouse invariably lost, the stress was presumably quite great. This short period of exposure to aggression was enough to evoke stress reactions and decreased resistance to parasitism (Patterson & Vessey, 1973).

Nonetheless, the population-controlling relationship among crowding, stress, and aggression does not hold for all animals. Chimpanzees in the Dutch zoo colony discussed in Chapter 14, when kept in tight winter quarters, showed little or no increase in aggression over that observed in the more spacious summer quarters. However, there were significant increases in the amount of grooming behavior and the number of appeasement gestures. Apparently potential hostilities in chimpanzees are minimized by these social interactions (DeWaal, 1989).

Siblicide

There is another way in which aggression may limit a population: In the phenomenon known as **siblicide,** one sibling may kill another sibling.

In great egrets, where siblicide is common, the parents do nothing to intervene (Mock, 1984). Size difference between the siblings is great, because the eggs are laid—and hatch—1 or 2 days apart. (In most other birds, the separation between laying times fails to make a difference, because embryonic development does not begin until the entire clutch is laid.) Such differences in size and strength increase the possibility of siblicide, especially because the great egret young have a high level of aggressiveness. The failure of these birds to develop a mechanism to produce synchrony in development of the embryos, and the parents' failure to stop lethal aggression, suggest that siblicide may have a fitness benefit for the parents. In times of food shortage—which are relatively frequent for owls and great egrets—siblicide may be a more efficient method of dealing with limited resources than the slow starvation of one or more of the offspring (Mock & Ploger, 1987).

Siblicide has also been identified in a mammal that normally produces twins—the spotted hyena. In this case, however, the lethal aggression does not seem to be proximally related to food shortage. The extremely intense fighting between hyena siblings is due, to a large extent, to masculinization associated with the high levels of testosterone in the mother. (We have already seen the effects of the testosterone in the development of the pseudopenis of the female.) Because siblicide is more common in same-sex siblings, it appears that the ultimate function of the behavior is the reduction of intrasex competition (Frank et al., 1991).

Territoriality

As Chapter 13 explained, territoriality and dominance hierarchies function to reduce intraspecies aggression in certain animals, particularly in social birds and mammals. Consequently, when territorial rights are violated because of high population density, more aggression is expressed.

Territoriality may also have a limiting effect on reproduction in crowded populations. For example, territorial defense of a resource can force some animals into marginal areas where they are unable to reproduce or where their reproductive potential is greatly reduced. In contrast, when population density is low, a high percentage of individuals are able to establish territories of good quality. The effect of a reduction in population density is illustrated by a study of great tits in a wooded area of England. Each season the birds occupy all of the optimal areas for breeding in the woods; surplus birds live in hedgerows, where reproductive success is lower. When birds are experimentally removed from the wooded area, they are replaced within hours by birds from the hedgerows (Krebs, 1971).

In some cases the size of an animal's territory is related to the food supply. For example, red squirrels establish larger territories when the food supply is limited. This expansion of the size of an individual territory allows the squirrel to obtain adequate food during hard times. But the expansion of each squirrel's territory during periods of food shortage tends to reduce the total number of territories available. Consequently, territoriality may have the function of limiting population growth most severely during times of food shortage (Smith, 1968).

Dominance Hierarchies

Dominance hierarchies may also place limits on reproduction. In animals as diverse as paper wasps and wolves, the dominant female suppresses reproduction in other females. In times when food is plentiful, more wasp females will become foundresses, starting their own nests. Similarly, in good times, young wolves will be more likely to leave the pack and start a pack of their own.

Dominance hierarchies may limit population growth even when dominant females do not suppress breeding in other females. In a flock of chickens, dominant animals have first choice of feeding opportunities. If there is a shortage of food, only the chickens highest in the social hierarchy are able to obtain enough to eat, and low-status birds are unlikely to survive. Consequently, low-status birds in a social hierarchy are somewhat like surplus birds in a territorial species—when conditions are poor, the low-status individuals are expendable.

Genetic Factors

Clearly, conditions are very different for animals living under crowded conditions than for uncrowded ones. Thus, it is possible that dif-

TABLE 20.4 ◆ Population Regulation Imposed by Conspecifics

Factor	Effect	Examples
Pheromones	High levels of pheromones (associated with dense population) disrupt reproduction.	Mice and other rodents
Aggression and stress	The stress of crowding and aggressive encounters compromise the immune system and lead to a higher death rate.	Mice and other rodents
Siblicide	One sibling kills another sibling.	Great egrets and owls
Territoriality and dominance hierarchies	Territorial behavior and dominance hierarchies can trigger aggression and limit reproduction in overcrowded conditions.	Many animals, including birds and mammals

ferent genotypes (genetic makeups) will be more successful at high population levels than at low ones. If this were true, there would be selection for two distinct types of individuals: specialists for crowded conditions and specialists for uncrowded ones. Support for this hypothesis comes from a study of voles, which normally have 3- to 4-year population cycles. During these rodents' cyclical population downturns, the population continues to decline even under conditions that appear to be favorable. An explanation for this decline is that the dense-population specialists are highly aggressive, intolerant, and poor breeders; although these animals are survivors under crowded conditions, they cannot take advantage of opportunities provided under less-dense population pressure. It is not until the population level has been low for a few years that the low-density specialists, which

are fast breeders and less aggressive, can establish themselves in the population. At this point the population begins to expand again (Chitty, 1960).

It also seems logical that differences in aggressiveness related to genetic factors would be associated with population density. When population density is high, there is more likelihood of interaction with nonkin than when density is low. Since nonkin interactions tend to be more aggressive, this could explain some of the heightened aggressiveness in high-density populations (Charnov & Finerty, 1980).

The Evolution of Self-Regulatory Systems

The original explanation for the evolution of regulation of population by conspecifics was related to a "for the good of the group" concept. Researchers assumed that groups of animals that regulated their population would be most likely to survive and pass on their genes (Wynne-Edwards, 1962). However, as we have seen in several different contexts, group selection processes are open to question. Group selection for population regulation seems unlikely, because individuals would maximize their own fitness by reproducing rapidly and would exert a strong, rapid selection effect *against* population regulation. In other words, selfishly reproducing animals would pass their genes on and destroy the regulation effect.

A more reasonable hypothesis is consistent with animals' operating in their own self-interest. This hypothesis suggests that individuals that showed restraint in their own reproduction during times of overcrowding and saved their reproductive efforts for periods when the young would be more likely to survive would be following a sound individual strategy. Furthermore, individuals that interfered with others' reproduction by means such as expressing disruptive aggression or limiting access to needed resources would enhance the chances of survival of their own offspring by reducing overpopulation (Chitty, 1960).

It seems, then, that population-limiting mechanisms such as territoriality and dominance hierarchies evolved primarily as a means of facilitating individual fitness. The population-limiting effect benefited the population as a whole, but this limitation effect does not seem to have been a prime mover in the evolution of the systems.

◆ HUMAN EVOLUTION

Several of the topics covered in this chapter are basic to an understanding of human evolution and shed light on the human condition in some unexpected ways. We will begin by considering the emigration of early *Homo sapiens* out of Africa and then look at the function of biophilia in human habitat selection.

EMIGRATION

For many years anthropologists generally believed that ancient ancestors of humans known as *Homo erectus* emigrated out of Africa more than a million years ago. Thus, they assumed that separate pockets of these hominids gave rise to the different races of humans. Recent evidence suggests, however, that all humans descended from a band of *Homo erectus* that lived in Africa. Presumably, the bands of *Homo erectus* that had migrated to various parts of the world at the early time died out.

According to the modern "out of Africa" theory, all modern humans descended from the same band relatively recently—about 200,000 years ago. A major source of support for this theory comes from the finding that all people living today share mitochondrial DNA that is very similar. As opposed to the types of DNA discussed in Chapter 2, mitochondrial DNA is passed on via the mother and does not enter into recombination with DNA from the father. Consequently, this DNA does not change from generation to generation except as the result of slow mutations.

Taking into account the average rate of mutation, it took 200,000 years or less to produce the diversity in mitochondrial DNA that we see in present-day humans. This finding suggests that all humans have a recent common ancestor, much more recent than previously believed. Specifically, the older theory indicated that human racial differences might have dated back more than a million years, at least 5 times as far back as the "out of Africa" theory indicates.

The hypothesis that humans have a relatively recent common ancestor has strong social ramifications. For example, it is possible for a white person to be just as closely related, from a genetic standpoint, to an African or an Asian as to another white person (see Brown, 1991). Thus, the "out of Africa" theory implies that human racial differences are not as fundamental or as ancient as many people had previously supposed.

From a genetic standpoint, skin pigmentation is a particularly misleading attribute to include in any definition of race. Human skin color, like the color of the hair or scales of many nonhuman animals, may change in just a few generations—or even within an individual's lifetime—as a simple adaptation to environmental conditions. Differences in skin color are certainly not an indication of deep-seated genetic differences.

If race is not a significant concept from a biological standpoint, why have humans traditionally paid so much attention to racial differences? Lawrence Hirschfeld (1996) argues that the concept of race emerged as the result of evolutionary forces associated with life in small, tightly knit groups. In primordial hominid groups there would have been a natural selection for accuracy in identifying individuals who were not members of the group and might pose a threat. In other words, a basic tendency to separate people into "us" and "them" categories evolved early in our hominid ancestory.

What can be done to reduce the destructive inherited tendency toward racism? Hirschfeld believes that it is difficult and unproductive to ignore ethnic and racial differences but that we can appreciate that these differences are superficial. Furthermore, it is possible to celebrate the many advantages of diversity. We can attempt to understand the origins of cultural differences, and we can teach our children the dangers and the falseness of racial and ethnic stereotypes.

HABITAT SELECTION

There is considerable support for Wilson's (1984) biophilia hypothesis—the hypothesis, identified in Chapter 1, that people "love living things." Extending the literal meaning of biophilia, Wilson hypothesized that our ancestors were naturally selected to be attracted to environments where existing animal and plant life was conducive to the fitness of hominids. This extended definition of biophilia also includes certain nonliving environmental factors such as clear water and a balance between sunshine and rainfall.

If we think about our own attitudes toward our physical habitats, we encounter many examples of biophilia. Healthy-looking trees provide shade and fruit. Flowers are a sign that fruit will be produced. The presence of songbirds is associated with an abundance of seeds and other edible substances. Grassy areas, clear running water, and grazing animals suggest not only potential food sources but a generally healthy environment. Hills provide an opportunity to survey the landscape. In essence, our ancestors were inclined to select biophilic habitats, and this tendency was passed on to us (Orians & Heerwagen, 1992).

A traditional belief is that people prefer the habitat most closely resembling the one in which they were raised, no matter what its nature. However, experimental tests using pictures of various environments indicate that virtually all Western people prefer the kind of environment described in the last paragraph, including people raised in crowded city environments (see Kellert & Wilson, 1993).

Even paintings and architectural designs that simulate a biophilic environment or are in harmony with a natural environment are perceived as attractive. People prefer large expanses of walls to be painted with soft colors that are similar to water, the sky, or grassy areas. In contrast, smaller architectural or decorative elements may include bright colors such as the bright reds, pinks, or purples associated with flowers. As in the case of flowers, these bright colors tend to occur in relatively small patches in most human-made habitats (Kellert & Wilson, 1993). Thus, in addition to our habitat selection, many of our aesthetic preferences seem to have been influenced by the natural selection of our ancestors living on the open savanna lands of Africa. Significantly, the findings of these studies of biophilia are consistent with our concern over the natural evironment.

◆ CHANGING PERSPECTIVES

PAST	PRESENT	FUTURE
Emigration patterns and habitat selection are inflexible and often nonadaptive. Population regulation mechanisms evolve at the group level (early twentieth century).	Emigration patterns and habitat selection are flexible and generally adaptive. Population regulation mechanisms evolve at the individual level.	How have humans affected nonhuman emigration patterns, habitats, and populations? What can we do to promote environmental conservation and live in harmony with the natural world? Can we control human population growth and still live in harmony with our moral values?

SUMMARY

Emigration—movement out of a particular area without a return to that area—may prove advantageous if the environment is deteriorating or is overcrowded. Certain spiders and the desert locust have developed special adaptations for dispersing from a deteriorating environment. The emigrations of lemmings, which show cyclic population explosions, are associated with escape from overcrowded conditions.

Natal dispersal—the emigration of young animals from the natal area—promotes optimal outbreeding. In birds, the females typically disperse to a greater degree than the males; but in mammals, the males show relatively greater dispersion. These gender differences are related to different optimal cost–benefit ratios for the two genders.

After emigrating, many animals actively select the habitat in which they settle down. The simplest orienting and habitat selection mechanisms are taxes (movements directed toward or away from a stimulus) and kineses (movements that respond to intensity of stimulation and indirectly lead an animal into a favorable environment).

Honeybees and vertebrates—especially birds and mammals—take numerous variables into account when selecting a habitat. Experimental research indicates that a complex interaction between genetic factors and early experience influences habitat selection in birds and mammals.

A variety of factors serve to regulate the population of animals. Some population regulation mechanisms are unpredictable and density independent; that is, they are not influenced by the density of the population. However, many mechanisms are density dependent and are regulated by such ecological factors as food availability, predation, and parasitism. In some cases, density-dependent regulatory factors imposed by different species function to maintain a fairly stable population density.

Many animals have also evolved density-dependent mechanisms of population regulation induced by conspecifics. In some cases crowding produces social pathology. The proximate causes of this social pathology include high levels of pheromones, hormones, and aggressiveness. These mechanisms affect both the mortality of individuals and their reproductive success.

Territoriality and dominance hierarchies may also function to limit population growth. Although the mechanisms function to benefit the species as a whole, they clearly evolved at the individual level of selection.

Studies of probable human emigration patterns and habitat preferences have several social implications. For example, the "out of Africa" hypothesis implies that all humans have a relatively recent common ancestor and sheds light on presumed racial differences. The biophilia hypothesis supports concerns over environmental preservation.

KEY TERMS

abiotic, p. 476
biotic, p. 476
competitive exclusion, p. 471
density dependent, p. 476
density independent, p. 476
emigration, p. 466
kinesis, p. 472

klinokinesis, p. 473
natal dispersal, p. 466
natal philopatry, p. 466
orthokinesis, pp. 472–473
realized niche, p. 471
siblicide, p. 480
taxis, p. 472

EPILOGUE

THE RELATIONSHIP BETWEEN HUMAN AND NONHUMAN ANIMALS

At several points in this book I have alluded to our tradition of anthropocentrism—our tendency to view ourselves as more important than, and superior to, other animals. This superiority complex has a long history in the Western world; it is seen in the Old Testament and in the philosophical doctrines of Plato and Aristotle and continues with the writings of early Christians. By feeling more important than nonhuman animals, we have elevated our egos and protected ourselves from feeling guilty if we mistreated other animals.

In many respects the results of anthropocentrism are similar to those of ethnocentrism. In its extreme forms, ethnocentrism produces prejudice and genocide while anthropocentrism is associated with wanton destruction of nonhuman animals and their environment.

Ironically, the decimation of "their" environment is the decimation of "our" environment, because it is impossible to separate one from the other. As a familiar example, the cutting down of uninhabited rain forests in Brazil reduces the oxygen content of the air throughout the world and can ultimately affect the health of humans everywhere. Furthermore, destruction or even partial destruction of a rain forest brings about the extinction of many animals and plants, some of which have never been identified. Many of us feel that humans do not have the moral right to drive species to extinction.

We can question another aspect of anthropocentrism as well—the assumption that there is a huge essential difference between humans and nonhumans. As this book has emphasized in every chapter, there is strong evidence that humans, like nonhumans, have evolved by natural selection and that certain basic components of our behavior are influenced by fitness-related strategies. Furthermore, some of the traditional definitions of humans as being the only animals to make and use tools and to have cultural traditions no longer stand up. Distinctions between humans and nonhumans in regard to toolmaking and culture now appear to be only a matter of degree.

There is also evidence that some nonhuman animals exhibit cognitions such as the formation of search images, numerical competence, self-concept, intentionality, insight, and concept formation. Perhaps most compelling is the evidence that certain nonhumans are capable of learning the rudiments of language. Although there is still controversy concerning the interpretation of many studies of animal cognition, there is little doubt that the more we understand nonhuman animals, the smaller the gulf between "us" and "them" appears to be.

Historically, our technology has contributed to our destructive anthropocentrism. It is now possible to cut down vast expanses of rain forest cheaply. Furthermore, one oil spill from a supertanker can pollute the ocean for thousands of square miles.

Nonetheless, technology can also provide solutions. We have the technology to identify environmental problems and to promote the survival of endangered species. Furthermore, our sophisticated educational and communication networks can effectively promote environmentalism and a concern for all life. In the last analysis, verdant forests, brightly colored flowers, and melodically singing birds not only lift our spirits, but are basic to our thriving and ultimately to our survival.

APPENDIX

CLASSIFICATION OF ANIMALS

Aristotle was the first known person to propose a systematic classification system for animals. His system was based on the animal's habitat—land, sea, or air—and the next significant improvement in classification did not occur for more than 2,000 years. Then, in the eighteenth century, a Swedish scientist named Karl von Linné—or, in Latin, Carolus Linnaeus—developed a system based on the animal's physical structure. With minor changes, Linneaus' system is still used today. To facilitate communication throughout the scientific world, Linnaeus used Latin names. (He even used the Latin version of his own name.) Linnaeus classified all animals into six major categories. Arranged from higher (broader) to lower (more specific) levels of classification,

these categories are: phylum, class, order, family, genus, and species (see Table A.1). In referring to a specific animal, Linnaeus used the animal's genus and species name and placed them in italics; for example a house cat was (and still is) denoted as *Felis domesticus.*

One of the great advantages of Linnaeus' system of classification is that it is consistent with the theory of evolution. (Linnaeus did not realize this, of course, because he lived a hundred years before Darwin.) Animals that are in the same category at a low level of classification are more closely related, from an evolutionary standpoint, than animals that appear in a common category at a higher level of classification. For example, a dog and a fox, which are both canids (members of the family

TABLE A.1 ◆ The Classification of the Domestic Cat

Phylum	Class	Order	Family	Genus	Species
Chordata	Mammalia	Carnivora	Felidae	*Felis*	*domesticus*

Canidae) are more closely related than dogs and cats, which belong to different families. Nonetheless, dogs and cats are both carnivores (order Carnivora) and thus are more closely related than dogs are to dolphins (order Cetacea). Linnaeus' system of classification embraced all living things known at the time, both animals and plants. Here, I will survey some of the important subgroupings of two important animal categories; invertebrates and vertebrates.

INVERTEBRATES

Ninety-five percent of the species of animals are classified as invertebrates—animals without backbones. They are a tremendously varied lot, and there is some controversy about how to classify them. Some biologists prefer to place one-celled animals in a separate kingdom known as the protists. However, this book follows the traditional classification and includes one-celled animals, or protozoans, as a subgroup of invertebrates.

Protozoans exhibit many types of symmetry as well as great variation in size and complexity of structure and behavior. Because protozoans have only one cell, this cell must, by itself, carry on all of the varied life processes.

The coelenterates, such as jellyfish, hydroids, coral, and sea anemones, are radially symmetrical animals; that is, their bodies consist of a central axis with parts radiating out in a symmetrical pattern. Radial symmetry is well suited for sessile (nonmoving) animals or for animals that move slowly, because this arrangement of body parts enables the individual to respond equally well to predators or prey that approach from any direction.

In contrast to coelenterates, flatworms are bilaterally symmetrical: The two halves are similar. There is some centralization of control in a primitive brain located at the anterior end of the body.

Annelids are round worms that have a somewhat more centralized nervous system. This centralization is reflected in the gathering of nerve axons into cords and the clustering of nerve cell bodies into ganglia (masses of nerve tissue).

Mollusks include a variety of soft-bodied animals, many of which excrete a shell. The bivalves (oysters and clams) and gastropods (certain shells, snails, and slugs) are sessile or slow-moving. In contrast, cephalopods such as octopuses and squid are extremely quick in their movements, propelling themselves with a type of jet propulsion.

Arachnida is a class of the phylum Arthropoda—animals with jointed legs and a hard exoskeleton (exterior skeleton). Arachnids, which include scorpions and spiders, are eight-legged and, for the most part, terrestrial. Fossil evidence suggests that the ancestors of modern arachnids were aquatic forms that became adapted to living on land.

Crustaceans are a large class of arthropods and, like all arthropods, have an exoskeleton or cuticle that covers their entire body. Included in this class are lobsters, crabs, shrimps, barnacles, and amphipods (such as beach fleas); the vast majority of crustaceans are adapted to an aquatic environment.

Insects make up the largest class of arthropods; in fact, the insect class contains more species than all other groups of animals combined. Insects are found in every habitat except the deeper recesses of the sea. One of the major factors related to their success is the ability of most insects to fly, which facilitates their avoidance of predators and enables them quickly to move into and colonize new environments.

VERTEBRATES

The vertebrates—animals with backbones—include five major classes. Of these, the fishes are the most numerous and diverse. More than 20,000 species of fishes have been identified, and they inhabit virtually every aquatic environment, including the open ocean, the depths of the ocean, freshwater lakes, mountain streams, and desert springs. Fishes are divided into three groups: jawless fishes (lampreys and hagfishes); cartilaginous fishes (sharks, skates, and rays); and bony fishes, most of which are teleosts. Teleosts were the last fishes to evolve and include the vast majority of living fish.

Amphibians include frogs, toads, and salamanders. There are approximately 2,600 species of amphibians; most of them are frogs. The word *amphibian* has two meanings. In popular usage, it means living both on land and in the water. However, the more accurate definition of amphibian, "having two lives," refers to the fact that the larval and adult stages of amphibians are often very different. When amphibians are on land, their body water evaporates even when the relative humidity is 100 percent; so amphibians are never completely free from a dependency on free water.

Reptiles, which include more than 6,000 distinct species, are the ancestral vertebrates completely adapted to terrestrial life. Reptilian skin does not have to be kept moist like that of amphibians. The eggs of reptiles—and also the amnion, or sac, that surrounds the de-veloping embryo—are adapted to form a protective barrier and prevent dehydration. The primary groups of reptiles are turtles, crocodilians, lizards, snakes, and the extinct dinosaurs.

Birds, which evolved from reptiles, are a remarkably successful class of vertebrates, numbering about 8,500 species and colonizing virtually all habitats except the deep ocean. There are 27 orders of birds, but the majority of species are passerines, or perching birds. Of the perching birds, most are songbirds. Birds' success, like that of insects, is related to flight: By flying, birds can avoid predators and can cover great distances in search of food. In addition, flight gives birds access to habitats such as cliffs, from which other comparably sized animals are excluded.

Birds are differentiated from all of the other animals discussed so far in that they are "warm-blooded" animals, or endotherms. Endotherms maintain a high, constant body temperature independent of the environmental temperature. In contrast, invertebrates and the more primitive classes of vertebrates are "cold-blooded" animals, or ectotherms. Ectotherms are primarily dependent on the environment to supply heat for their bodies.

Mammals, like birds, evolved from reptiles; and mammals are also endotherms. Mammals are distinguished from the other classes of vertebrates by possessing hair and producing milk to feed their young. There are approximately 4,000 species of mammals, varying in size from shrews less than 5 centimeters (2 inches) long to whales more than 100 meters (110 feet) in length. Mammals are divided into three general groups: the rare, egg-laying monotremes, such as the platypus; the pouched marsupials, such as kangaroos and opossums; and placental mammals, which are the most recently evolved and by far the most familiar and numerous.

Of the placental mammals, primates are of particular interest because of the complexity of their behavior, the size of their brain, and the fact that humans are primates. Non-human primates consist of four main groups: prosimians (lemurs and tamarins); new-world monkeys (such as howlers and squirrel monkeys); old-world monkeys (including rhesus monkeys and baboons); and apes (gibbons, orangutans, gorillas, and chimpanzees). Humans are classified in a family by themselves (Hominidae).

GLOSSARY

abiotic Nonliving and unrelated to living things.

abstract concepts Concepts that depend on an even greater degree of abstraction than object concepts.

action potential The swinging back and forth in the electrical charge of a nerve cell that constitutes the firing of the cell.

activational effects Transient hormonal effects that occur only when a hormone is present in large amounts; activate existing neural patterns.

adaptation An inherited trait or behavioral disposition that provides fitness advantages in some way.

adaptive radiation A group of animals' rapid evolution in several different directions after they enter a hospitable area.

adaptive suicide Among certain insects, a pattern of behavior in which one member of the group may give itself to a parasite to prevent it from infesting other members of the group.

aggressive mimicry A predatory mechanism through which a predator develops a resemblance to an inanimate object or another animal to help ambush its prey.

alarm pheromone An insect pheromone secreted in response to dangerous conditions that stimulates conspecifics in the area.

allele An alternate form of a gene.

alloparental care An animal's caring for offspring that are not its own.

all-or-none law A principle stating that when a neuron fires, or generates an action potential, it does so full force.

altricial species Species in which the young are relatively undeveloped at hatching.

altruism Selfless and helpful behavior.

altruistic sperm Sperm from the same male that may cooperate with one another instead of competing.

amplexus The mating embrace of frogs, in which the male grasps the female's legs and holds her until she releases her eggs.

amygdala A structure in the limbic system that influences aggression.

ancestral Showing no development of significant evolutionary trends; contrasts with *specialized*.

antiaphrodisiac A substance that reduces the attractiveness of a female to males who might try to mate with her after one male has already inseminated her.

aposematic coloration   Bright coloration that serves to warn predators; found only in toxic species.

area-restricted search hypothesis   A theory suggesting that an animal uses a decreased speed of locomotion and/or sharp turns when foraging a favorable feeding area; this allows the animal to remain in the area as long as it is rich in food.

association areas   Areas of the mammalian cerebral cortex that function as information integration centers.

association hypothesis   A theory suggesting that the gender that is present when the eggs or young first appear will most likely be parental.

assortative mating   The matching of mating partners according to a significant trait, such as size.

axon   A neural structure that carries information away from the cell body of the neuron.

azimuth   The amount of horizontal displacement of the sun; changes according to the time of day, season, and latitude.

Bateman's principle   A principle stating that because of gender differences in the ability to attract mates, there is more variability in the reproductive success of males than of females.

Batesian mimicry   The resemblance of some harmless animals to animals that can defend themselves or are toxic.

behavioral ecology   The study of the relationship between ecology and behavioral patterns.

big bang strategy   A reproductive strategy in which the animal reproduces only after waiting an extremely long time and then in one large reproductive bout.

binary fission   A type of asexual reproduction in which, after the chromosomes are duplicated, the animal simply splits into two more or less equal parts.

biological clock   The internal timing device that governs biological rhythms in many animals and plants.

biophilia   An interest in animals and other parts of the natural environment that is deeply rooted in evolutionary principles.

biotic   Being related to living things.

biparental care   Care of the young provided by both the mother and father.

blocking   A phenomenon that occurs when a conditioned stimulus is presented in combination with a second stimulus; under these circumstances, it is unlikely that an animal will learn to respond to the second stimulus when presented alone.

bright bird hypothesis   The theory that bright coloration may serve as an honest signal of fitness in bird species that are subject to parasitism.

brood parasitism   The placement of the parasite's eggs in the nest of the host during a specific time frame, in which the host is induced to care for the parasite's offspring.

Bruce effect   The abortion or resorption of mouse embryos induced by a pheromone in an alien male's urine.

caste   In colonial invertebrates, a specialized class or form with particular functions.

celestial pole   The center of rotation of the night sky.

cell body   The structure that houses the nucleus and is the center for life processes in the neuron.

central-place foraging   Taking food to an area from which there are several escape routes.

certainty of parenthood hypothesis   A theory stating that the greater the certainty that an animal is the true biological parent, the greater the probability that it will provide parental care.

chunk   To organize information into a small number of manageable categories so as to facilitate memory.

circadian rhythm   A cyclical pattern of activity that lasts approximately one day.

circannual rhythm   A cyclical pattern of activity that lasts approximately one year.

clan   The largest group in the hierarchy of elephant social units; generally forms for migration but is not well organized.

classical conditioning   The passive development of a response to a previously neutral stimulus.

cleaners   Small fish that live around coral reefs and feed on parasites in the mouths of larger fish.

Clever Hans phenomenon   The phenomenon of a human cueing a nonhuman animal to give a putatively intelligent response.

coevolution hypothesis   The theory that animals are most likely to benefit from genetic variability when they are significantly affected by another group of animals, such as predators.

cognitive map   A mental representation, or schema, of the spatial environment that an animal uses to plan movements that are difficult for predators to predict.

collective behavior   Behavior that occurs simultaneously in a group of animals.

colonial invertebrates   Invertebrate species in which the individuals are physically joined or divided into distinct castes that have specialized roles.

color resemblance   A form of camouflage in which an animal's color matches that of its background.

commensalism   A type of symbiotic relationship that benefits one animal but has little or no effect on the other.

comparative psychologists   Social scientists who focus on the study and comparison of behavior in different species.

competitive exclusion   A form of habitat selection in which one species of animal is driven out of a preferred site by competition with a highly similar species.

compound eye   An insect's eye; made up of numerous visual units.

concept formation The formation of a category or extraction of a general principle.

concordance rate The degree of similarity between identical twins.

conditional strategies Alternative strategies that animals adopt under certain conditions.

conditioned stimulus (CS) A neutral stimulus that, after being paired with an unconditioned stimulus (UCS), evokes a conditioned response.

confusion effect A phenomenon of group defense that results primarily from the difficulty a predator has visually fixating on and pursuing a single individual amidst a group.

conjugation A sexual process found in certain one-celled organisms in which two organisms come together and exchange their small nuclei while retaining their large nuclei; as a result, both individual organisms are modified genetically, but there is no increase in the number of organisms.

conspecifics Other members of the same species.

constant frequency calls Echolocation calls that remain the same pitch and provide detailed information about a target's rate of movement and whether it's moving away from or toward the bat.

contextual effect A phenomenon in which the context in which a communication signal is given affects the message.

continuous reinforcement The reinforcement that follows a given behavior 100 percent of the time.

conventional parasitism Parasitism in which the parasite feeds on some of the host's tissue and in some cases reproduces inside the host, where the young are protected and fed.

convergence An evolutionary pattern that occurs when animals that are very different fill similar niches and consequently become more similar.

copulation The direct placement of sperm into a female receptacle.

corpus callosum A structure that transfers neural excitation from one hemisphere of the brain to the other.

corticosteroid hormones Hormones that keep the body's temperature, blood pressure, and respiration high, thereby providing resources during times of stress.

countershading A type of camouflage effected through reducing differences in reflectance on an animal's body; darker markings on top of the animal create the illusion of flatness, which allows the animal to blend in with the background.

créche A "nursery" or gathering of offspring of many parents.

cuckold To put a male animal in the position of investing in the rearing of another male's offspring.

dead reckoning A method of navigation that involves estimating direction and distance to a goal.

death feigning Behavior in which immobility is used as protection against predation.

defeminization Inhibition of the development of female traits due to the presence of testosterone.

defensive aggression Fighting against a predator.

delayed matching-to-sample paradigm A research technique in which experimenters present an animal with a stimulus and then, after a period of time, test to determine if the animal can recognize the stimulus.

dendrite A neural structure that carries information toward the cell body of the neuron.

density dependent The condition of being influenced by the number of animals in a particular area.

density independent The condition of not being influenced by the number of animals in a particular area.

developmental homeostasis The tendency for organisms to buffer themselves against extreme conditions that might occur under natural circumstances.

dialects Birdsongs that vary from one geographic region to another.

diencephalon A brain lobe that is well developed in highly evolved animals, particularly mammals.

dilution effect The phenomenon in which individual animals in a large group gain defensive benefits because predators can take only a small percentage of the total group.

dioecism The condition in which an animal is either a male (producing sperm) or a female (producing eggs).

diploid Containing the full complement of chromosomes.

direct fitness Success in passing on copies of one's genes by parenting offspring that survive and reproduce.

discrete signal A communication signal that is either present or absent; it does not vary along a continuum.

displays Signals or behavior patterns that are specialized to convey information.

disruptive coloration Irregular patches of contrasting colors; when one or more patches match the color of the background, part of the animal fades from view and the rest is seen as an irregular, nonanimal-shaped object.

divergence The tendency for animals of different species that may start out being similar to become more distinct over many generations, as they live in very different niches.

domain-specific learning Learning that reflects an evolved sensitivity to certain stimuli, whereby animals are more likely to learn certain types of relationships than others.

dominance In genetics, the relationship between alleles, in which one is expressed while another (recessive) is inhibited; also describes genetically determined traits.

dopamine A type of monoamine that has both excitatory and inhibitory functions, depending upon the nature of the postsynaptic receptor.

double imprinting A condition in which an animal becomes imprinted to two different species.

dove strategy A strategy that favors backing off rather than fighting.

DNA Deoxyribonucleic acid; the molecular "blueprint," or record of precise instructions, for heredity found in the nucleus of each cell.

echolocation The process of producing sounds and analyzing the patterns of their echoes; gives animals such as bats information about nearby objects.

ecological plasticity The ability of feeding generalists to adapt to changing food supplies and a variety of habitats.

electrolocation A type of electroreception in which a fish detects distortions of its electrical field with the aid of receptors located along the length of its body; aids in detecting prey and avoiding obstacles.

emigration Movement out of a particular area without returning to it.

emotional responses Behavioral responses exhibited by animals that are very similar to signs of emotion in humans.

encephalization General brain development.

endorphins Chemical substances that stimulate special receptor sites throughout the brain and function to reduce sensations of pain.

entrain To set in motion; for instance, as with a biological clock.

epigenesis The complex interaction between genetic and environmental factors.

epiphenominal The quality of being derivative or incidental; for instance, the idea that consciousness may simply accompany problem solving, not have a causal link in the process.

epitokes Sexual segments at the posterior ends of male and female adult palolo worms' bodies.

EQ Encephalization quotient; the ratio of brain weight to overall body weight.

estradiol A steroid hormone (one of the estrogens) produced in the gonads; has critical effects on female reproductive behavior.

ethology The study of animal behavior in natural or seminatural settings.

eukaryote An organism that has a distinct cell nucleus.

eusocial Being characterized by cooperation in care of the young, support of fertile individuals by nonfertile nest mates, and the presence of two or more generations of individuals cooperating and living together.

evolutionarily stable strategy A strategy that is so effective that it will not likely be replaced by an alternative strategy.

evolutionary arms race Competition between prey and predator groups of organisms, in which each group responds by adjusting to the other, such that neither wins.

evolutionary psychologists Social scientists interested in the evolution of human behavior.

expectancy Anticipatory behavior that may facilitate memory.

exploitation phase The phase of feeding in which foraging animals spend most of their time in the richest patch.

external fertilization Fertilization that takes place as the eggs are deposited or shortly thereafter.

eye spot A photosensitive area on a one-celled organism.

eye spots Markings on the hind wings of some species of butterflies and moths that function to frighten predators.

facultative Occurring at some times but not others; for instance, brood parasites sometimes incubate their own eggs but other times lay their eggs in the nests of other birds.

family In African elephants, the smallest unit of the social hierarchy; consists of 10 to 20 females and their young.

feature detectors Neurons in the brain that respond selectively to certain aspects of visual input—namely, aspects that correspond to relevant features in the animal's environment.

fecundity The condition of being fruitful in producing offspring; relates to the number of eggs the female produces.

female defense polygyny A type of polygyny in which a male defends a harem of females against other males.

filial imprinting Development of a tendency for young birds to follow their mother.

fitness The degree of likelihood that an animal will survive and successfully reproduce relative to other animals.

flyways The major routes of bird migration; there are four in North America.

fovea The area of the retina that receives the most direct visual stimulus.

freezing A temporary immobility used as a defense against predation; involves tenseness that can be converted into sudden action.

frequency modulated calls Echolocation calls that start at a particular pitch and then sweep down an octave; provide maximum information about the shape, size, and texture of the bat's target.

FSH Follicle-stimulating hormone; an anterior pituitary hormone that regulates the output of testosterone.

full song The normal, complex song of a songbird species.

funeral pheromone An insect pheromone that signals the death of a colony member.

gametes Eggs and sperm; cells that contain half the full number of chromosomes.

game theory A strategy that considers competitors' behaviors.

gene flow The introduction of genes from potentially interbreeding individuals of different populations.

gene pool The aggregate of types of genes that are found in a given population of animals.

general adaptation syndrome A three-stage physiological response mediated by hormones; helps animals deal with short-term stress.

generalists Animals that eat a wide variety of foods.

genes The basic "blueprints" for development and inheritance.

genetic drift Changes in the frequency of alleles that occur in a population solely by chance.

genital lock An adaptation in certain mammals in which the male sex organ becomes locked inside that of the female for a period of time; functions to keep the penis inserted long enough for all the semen to enter the vagina.

genotype The genetic makeup of an individual.

glial cell The most important kind of supporting cell in the nervous system.

glucocorticoids Hormones involved in carbohydrate and protein metabolism, among other functions.

glucostatic hypothesis The theory that the signal for hunger is a drop in the blood glucose level.

graded signal A communication signal that is variable in intensity and duration and thus conveys information about the level of the sender's motivation.

gravid female A female carrying eggs.

habituation An animal's developing tendency to react less vigorously to a stimulus that has been consistently present but has little or no effect on it.

haplodiploidy A phenomenon among certain insects in which males develop from infertile (haploid) eggs while females develop from fertile (diploid) eggs.

haploid Containing half of an organism's original number of chromosomes.

hawk strategy A strategy that favors fighting rather than backing off.

hemipenes Two intromittent organs, one on each side of the body; remain flush against the body when the male is relaxed but protrude when the male is sexually aroused.

hermaphroditic Being characterized by the production of both sperm and eggs by the same individual.

heterozygous Being affected by two or more alleles that differ (as in heterozygous traits).

hippocampus A structure in the limbic system that is associated with visual/spatial memory.

home range The entire area in which an animal lives.

homing An animal's ability to find its way back to its home site.

hominids Various species classified within the family of humans; all but one are now extinct.

homozygous Being affected by identical alleles (as in homozygous traits).

hormones Chemical substances that alter the activities of tissues and organs, including those of the nervous and reproductive systems.

hypothalamus A structure in the diencephalon that is important in regulating many responses.

imprinting The rapid development of a strong, stable preference for a particular type of stimulus that is present for a short, sensitive period of development.

inbreeding depression Reduced fitness associated with the breeding of close relatives.

inclusive fitness The sum of direct and indirect fitness.

incubation The transfer of heat from a heat source (usually a parent's body) to the eggs.

indirect fitness Fitness associated with the successful reproduction of close relatives who are not direct descendants.

individual level of selection hypothesis A theory of natural selection at the individual level; argues that there must be a selective advantage for individual animals if evolution is to occur.

induced ovulators Females that ovulate only when they are mated; almost always become pregnant following copulation.

injury feigning A strategy in which a parent acts as if it is injured so as to lead predators away from the nest site.

intention movements Movements that normally precede a behavior pattern; may develop into communication signals.

intermediate hosts The hosts that serve a parasite in its early stages of development.

internal fertilization Fertilization that occurs while the eggs remain in the female's reproductive tract.

internal inertia system A system that indicates the degree of a turn and allows an animal to reorient with considerable precision.

intrinsic reinforcement Reinforcement directly associated with an activity.

kamikaze sperm Sperm that compete aggressively with sperm from other males' copulations.

kinesis Movement by an animal in response to the intensity of stimulation.

kin selection *See* theory of kin selection.

kinship group The second level in the hierarchy of elephant social organization; includes several family groups.

kleptoparasitism Parasitic animals' stealing of resources from their hosts.

klinokinesis An intensity-related change in the rate of turning in an animal's movement.

larder hoarding Placement of all hoarded food in one or several closely placed sites.

lateral line organs Sensory receptors along the sides of fish that are sensitive to waterborne vibrations.

learned helplessness The generalized response of acting helpless that is learned through repeated experiences in situations where attempts to escape or control events have failed.

learning A relatively persistent change in behavior resulting from experience.

lek polygyny A polygynous mating system centered in a particular assembly area that serves as a setting for male display and mating.

lesions In brain research, damage to neural tissue.

life/dinner principle A principle stating that the risk for the predator is much less than the risk for the prey; that is, if the prey wins (escapes), the predator loses only its dinner, but if the predator wins, the prey loses its life.

limbic system A group of brain structures that is activated by motivated behavior and arousal.

linear dominance hierarchy A social structure in which one animal is dominant over all others, a second is dominant over all others but the first, and so on.

lottery hypothesis A theory suggesting that in a variable environment, there is a better chance for at least some offspring to survive if they are different from one another than if they are extremely similar.

many-eyes hypothesis A theory suggesting that as the size of a group increases, there are more eyes (or ears or noses) on the lookout for predators, making predator detection more rapid.

marginal value theorem A theory predicting that an animal will leave a food patch at the point when the net calorie intake drops to the level that approximates the average level for the habitat as a whole.

masculinization The effect of testosterone on the development of structures and behaviors related to mating.

master clock The biological clock that regulates and synchronizes the other clocks in an organism's body.

matching of attractiveness A phenomenon in which the individuals that make up a couple are approximately equal in level of attractiveness.

maternal pheromone A pheromone that affects the interaction between mother mammals and their offspring.

mating systems Systems that determine how many sexual partners an animal has and how long the partners stay together.

medley A mixture of two or more communication signals presented together; produces an effect that is different from that of either signal alone.

meiosis A process in sexual reproduction that brings about variability in genetic makeup; results in the production of cells that contain half the original number of chromosomes and enter into the process of fertilization.

memorability The likelihood that a sender's communication display will be remembered by the receiver.

mesotelencephalic dopamine system A system of neural fibers that connects areas of the midbrain with several areas in the telencephalon and is involved with the process of reward.

metacommunication Communication about the meaning of communication.

migration The round-trip movements of animals from one habitat to another.

migratory restlessness A high level of migratory activity; usually related to an animal's tendency to move to new regions.

mitosis The process of asexual cell replication.

mixed evolutionarily stable strategy An animal's tendency to employ more than one strategy, such that its competition will be unable to anticipate strategies as easily.

mobbing A group defensive behavior in which adult birds leave their nests and cooperatively attack or dive at a predator.

monoamines   A family of neurotransmitters that are produced by neurons in several parts of the brain.

monogamous   Being characterized by a pattern in which one male mates more or less exclusively with one female.

mouthbreeders   A type of fish in which a parent (usually but not always the male) carries the eggs in its mouth until they hatch.

Mullerian mimicry   Mimicry in which both the model and the mimic are harmful.

mutations   Random errors in genetic coding and replication that continually introduce new genes and alleles into the population.

mutualism   Cooperation or coordination (as in the quest for food) that directly benefits two or more animals.

myelin sheath   A sheath of fatty, whitish material (produced by glial cells) that wraps around the axon of a nerve cell.

natal dispersal   The movement of animals from the area of their birth to a new area where their reproduction takes place.

natal philopatry   The tendency for animals to remain in the area of their birth and share a territory or home range with parents and siblings.

natural killer cells   Cells in the immune system that destroy cells infected by viruses.

natural selection   *See* theory of natural selection.

neophilia   An attraction to novel objects.

neophobia   An avoidance or fear of strange or unfamiliar objects.

neuron   Nerve cell; a cell specialized for the transmission of information from one area of the body to another.

neurotransmitters   Chemical communicators that regulate the transmission of neural impulses and consequently are intimately involved with the functioning of the nervous system.

niche   An animal's specific habitat and role within it.

niche rule   A principle stating that no two species can exist in the same locale and utilize the same resources at the same time.

nonconditional strategies   Male courtship strategies, whether primary or alternative, that are strongly influenced by genetic factors.

norepinephrine   A neurotransmitter involved in responses characterized by strong emotional arousal, such as sex and aggression.

nutritional wisdom   The tendency to choose a well-balanced diet when different types of foods are available.

obligate   Being completely dependent on a system; for instance, as when one bird depends on another to raise its young.

object concepts   Concepts that apply to groups of objects belonging together or being functionally classified together.

object permanence   The concept that an object still exists even when it is no longer visible.

odor trail   A pheromone pathway created by worker ants to lead from a food source to the nest.

ommatidia   Visual units that make up the compound eyes of insects.

operant conditioning   A type of learning in which an animal actively operates on its environment to produce favorable consequences.

optimality theory   A theory stating that a natural selection process for efficiency exists for virtually all animal behaviors.

optimal outbreeders   Animals that mate with partners that are somewhat similar to themselves and thus avoid both inbreeding and outbreeding depression.

organizational effects   Hormonal effects that stimulate relatively permanent changes in neural organization during sensitive periods of development.

orthokinesis   A change in an animal's speed of movement that is dependent on the intensity of stimulation.

os penis   A bone that supports the male penis.

outbreeding depression   Suboptimal outcomes in the offspring of parents with highly diverse genetic backgrounds; caused by too much breeding with dissimilar animals.

oviparous   Being characterized by the production of eggs that hatch after being extruded from the mother's body.

oxytocin   A posterior pituitary hormone related to reproduction.

pair bond   The tendency for two animals to stay together.

parasitism   A long-term relationship that benefits one animal and harms another.

parental investment   *See* theory of parental investment.

parthenogenesis   The development of unfertilized eggs.

partial reinforcement   Reinforcement that follows a behavior less than 100 percent of the time.

Pavlovian conditioning   Another term for *classical conditioning; see* classical conditioning.

personal space   An area surrounding an animal that it protects against intrusion.

phenotype   An observable characteristic.

pheromones   Chemical substances that influence the behavior of other individuals in the same species.

play   An activity that imitates elements of goal-directed behavior but does not lead to an immediate goal.

pleiotropy   The influence of one gene on the development of several different structures or traits.

polarized   Vibrating in a single plane; for instance, light waves after they travel through the earth's atmosphere.

polyandry   A mating system in which the female has several partners while the male has one (or at least fewer partners than the female); the opposite of *polygyny.*

polygeny   The influence of several different genes on the expression of a trait or behavior.

polygynandry A mating system in which animals live in groups and both males and females mate with a variety of partners within their group.

polygynous Being characterized by a mating system in which a few males mate with many females while other males do not mate at all.

polygyny threshold The point at which it benefits a female to shift from a monogamous to a polygynous relationship.

postsynaptic neuron The neuron across the synapse from the neuron that just fired.

precocial species Species in which the young are well developed at hatching.

predator inspection A group defensive strategy in which a few potential prey animals move close to a potential predator to assess its motives.

predictive value The consistency with which a conditioned stimulus precedes the unconditioned stimulus.

Premack's principle A rule stating that any activity may be reinforced (rewarded) by a preferred activity.

primacy effect A phenomenon in which several male animals copulate with a female within a short period of time; usually the first male's sperm inseminates the eggs.

primer pheromone A pheromone that has a delayed and relatively long-lasting effect, stimulating physiological changes related to reproduction.

prior adaptation An adaptation that serves as a foundation for the development of new adaptations.

progesterone A female steroid hormone secreted by the corpus luteum of the ovaries.

prokaryotes Primitive bacteria that do not have a clearly differentiated cell nucleus.

prolactin A posterior pituitary hormone related to reproduction.

proximate questions Questions concerned with the immediate causes of behavior.

pseudocopulation False copulation in spiders; occurs when a male intromits his organ into the female without having filled it with sperm.

pseudopenis A greatly enlarged clitoris.

queen pheromone A pheromone in eusocial insects that indicates the condition of the queen.

rate law A principle stating that strong stimulation induces rapid firing of a neuron while weaker stimulation induces slower firing.

realized niche A niche that is more restricted than it would be if there were no competition.

recency effect A phenomenon in which the sperm of the last male to mate with a female fertilizes the largest share of her eggs.

recessive Being masked by another dominant allele or trait.

reciprocal altruism The return of selfless and helpful behavior; often performed when the cost of helping is small and the benefits of being helped in return are relatively large.

recognition pheromone An insect pheromone that is exclusive to the individual insect colony.

recombinant DNA DNA spliced together from two separate organisms.

refractory period A period following ejaculation during which males are unresponsive to sexual stimulation.

reinforcement The presentation or removal of a stimulus that functions to increase the probability of a behavior.

repair hypothesis A theory suggesting that there is a selective advantage to sexual processes because the recombination of genetic material that takes place during meiosis provides for repair of possible damage to the DNA.

resource defense polygyny A type of polygyny in which males gain sexual access to multiple females by establishing a territory that includes some type of resource needed by females.

resting potential The slightly negative electrical charge inside the nerve cell when it is in a resting state.

reuptake In neural firing, the process by which a neurotransmitter is taken up by the neuron that released it.

ribosomes Specialized structures within the cell that function as the "workshop" that constructs proteins.

ritualization The process by which behaviors become more stereotyped as they take on functions as communication signals.

round dance A honeybee dance performed by returning foragers when the food source is less than 25 meters away.

royal jelly A special protein-rich food that when fed to honeybee larvae causes them to develop into fertile queens.

RNA Ribonucleic acid; a type of RNA known as *transfer RNA* carries or transfers critical information from the DNA to another part of the cell, where a protein is constructed.

rumen A chamber in the digestive system of ungulates that facilitates the breakdown of cellulose found in leaves and grasses.

runaway selection hypothesis A theory describing an exaggerated sexual selection process that results from females' preferences for extreme characteristics in males.

sacculinization Parasitic castration, in which the growing cells of the parasite function to destroy the gonads of its host.

sampling phase The phase of feeding during which animals randomly search through various food patches.

satellite A silent male frog that remains near a singing male and attempts to intercept females approaching the singer.

scatter hoarding The practice of widely distributing caches of food; practiced by most food-hoarding birds.

scramble competition polygyny A type of polygyny in which males scramble around in an attempt to mate as many times as possible in a short period of time.

search image A cognitive representation of the stimulus an animal is seeking.

selfish herd hypothesis   A theory suggesting that since prey animals tend to move toward the middle of the group, they also tend to form tight groups when threatened with predation.

self-matching   Comparing a quality of another individual (such as a scent) with the same quality in oneself.

sensory adaptation   The diminution of sensory response after a period of continuous stimulation.

sensory hairs   Hairs that are deflected by mechanical stimulation; the mechanical energy of the hairs' motion is then transduced into neural impulses.

serial position effect   The tendency to remember information at the beginning and end of a series more effectively than that in the middle.

serotonin   A monoamine that produces inhibitory postsynaptic potentials and generally has inhibitory effects on behavior.

sexual cannibalism   A phenomenon in which the female eats the male after mating; seen in praying mantises and certain spiders.

sexual dimorphism   A difference between genders in morphology or behavior.

sexual imprinting   Development of a tendency to show sexual responses to a type of animal or object present during a sensitive period.

sexual pheromone   A type of reproductive pheromone that communicates such qualities as attractiveness, sexual readiness, and fitness.

sexual selection   A type of natural selection that acts differentially on the two genders.

shaping   Reinforcing a response that is close to a desired response and then incrementally requiring higher degrees of accuracy or desirability before presenting additional reinforcement.

siblicide   The killing of one sibling by another.

signal pheromone   A pheromone that has an immediate effect.

sign tracking   The development of a food-related response to a conditioned stimulus in the absence of any reinforcement.

simultaneous hermaphroditism   A form of reproduction in which a single animal produces male and female gametes at roughly the same time.

slave making   A form of social parasitism in which ants carry off other ants' pupae and make them their slaves.

sneaker   A male fish that slips into a larger male's territory and attempts to fertilize the eggs of a spawning female.

social–cognitive theory   Albert Bandura's theory combining social learning and cognition to explain certain aspects of human behavior.

social grooming   Reciprocal grooming that has a calming effect and reinforces social bonds between group members.

social learning   The transfer of skills developed or information obtained by one animal (the model) to another (the observer).

social parasitism   A type of parasitism in which one animal rears its young at the expense of another.

sociobiology The study of social behavior in animals with an emphasis on evolved biological mechanisms.

spatial learning The acquisition of information about spatial relationships in the environment.

specialized Being highly evolved in regard to a particular adaptive mechanism or behavior.

species fidelity The movement of pollinators from one plant to another of the same species.

spermatophore A packet of sperm deposited by the male on the ground or the bottom of a body of water, which the female picks up later.

spillover hypothesis A theory suggesting that if an area is associated with frequent successful copulations, other males will tend to go there in the future.

stable polymorphism The stable relationship that develops between animals that fight and those that back off (such as hawks and doves).

stimulus enhancement A type of social learning in which a model emphasizes the location or object to which an observer should orient.

stotting Repeated leaping about 20 inches off the ground by gazelles; signals predators that their efforts will be fruitless.

strategy A rule of thumb that has resulted in generally favorable outcomes throughout an animal's evolutionary history.

subsong A simple song that is a precursor to the full song of a given songbird.

successive hermaphroditism A change from one sex to the other at some point in an animal's life.

symbiont A partner in a symbiotic, mutualistic relationship.

synaptic vesicle A structure within the neuron's terminal buttons that contains a neurotransmitter.

synchronization in hatching The simultaneous hatching of embryos, which facilitates their being reared as a group.

taste aversion learning Development of an avoidance of certain foods whose taste has become associated with illness.

taxis Movement directly toward or away from a stimulus.

telemetry A technique for tracing individual animal movements; researchers attach a radio-wave transmitter to an animal and then trace the source of the waves as the animal moves about.

telencephalon The most anterior brain lobe; particularly well developed in mammals.

temporal learning The ability to learn time intervals; similar to operant conditioning.

terminal buttons Round swellings at the ends of the axons of a neuron; located close to other neurons' dendrites.

termite fishing A process in which a chimpanzee inserts a probe (such as a twig) into a termite nest, withdraws the probe, and then eats the termites clinging to it.

territorial system A system that enables an individual to become dominant in a particular area.

testosterone   A steroid hormone (one of the androgens) produced in the gonads; has critical effects on male behavior, particularly reproductive behavior.

theory of kin selection   A theory suggesting that animals are naturally selected to help relatives because this helping behavior has indirect fitness value.

theory of mind   An ability to infer states of knowledge, intentions, and feelings in another animal, particularly cognitions different from one's own.

theory of natural selection   A theory suggesting that only animals well equipped to survive and reproduce will pass on their inherited traits; the backbone of Charles Darwin's explanation for evolution.

theory of parental investment   An optimality theory applied to the development of reproductive strategies; namely, reproduction at a given point uses up time and energy and reduces the probability of successful reproduction in the future, yet waiting too long risks the possibility of dying before having reproduced.

tit-for-tat strategy   A strategy that involves cooperating on the first move but then matching the other individual's moves on succeeding occasions.

town   A community of as many as 1,000 prairie dogs.

trace theory of memory   A theory suggesting that memory consists of a neutral trace that fades over time.

trophallaxis   The exchange of food and fluid between social insects.

tutor   An individual animal that functions as a model or teacher in the development of a behavior pattern.

ultimate questions   Questions related to distant, often evolutionarily based causes.

unconditioned stimulus (UCS)   A stimulus that normally evokes a response and is paired with a conditioned stimulus (CS) during operant conditioning.

ungulates   Hoofed animals.

vaginal plug   Viscous material left in the vagina of a female mouse after the male has copulated, which functions as a barrier to further copulation.

Vandenbergh effect   A phenomenon characterized by the priming of sexual readiness in females by a male pheromone.

vector   An animal that transports parasites from one host to another.

vestigial structure   A structure that was useful at an earlier time in the evolutionary history of a species but has no present function.

visual acuity   The ability to distinguish objects in clear focus.

viviparous   Being characterized by live birth of the young.

vocal mimicry   The ability of certain birds to copy sounds in the environment in addition to those produced by their conspecifics.

waggle dance   A honeybee dance that indicates the distance and direction of a food source if it is more than 25 meters away.

war of attrition   A battle between animals in which the winner is the one that stays the longest at the point of encounter, rather than the one that fights the most vigorously.

Whitten effect   A phenomenon characterized by the synchronization of estrous cycles in female mice; produced by a male signal pheromone.

zeitgeber   An external cue that entrains biological cycles; literally, a time giver.

zooids   Asexually reproduced individuals in a compound organism; may be specialized for different functions.

REFERENCES

Acharya, L. (1995). Sex-biased predation on moths by insectivorous bats. *Animal Behaviour, 49,* 1461–1468.

Adamo, S. A., & Hoy, R. R. (1995). Agonistic behaviour in male and female field crickets, *Gryllus bimaculatus,* and how behavioural context influences its expression. *Animal Behaviour, 49,* 1491–1501.

Adams, D. B. (1983). Hormone-brain interactions and their influence on agonistic behavior. In B. B. Svare (Ed.), *Hormones and aggressive behavior.* New York: Plenum Press.

Adams, D. B. (1986). Ventromedial tegmental lesions abolish offense without disturbing predation or defense. *Physiology and Behavior, 38,* 165–168.

Ader, R., & Cohen, N. (1984). Behavior and the immune system. In W. D. Gentry (Ed.), *Handbook of behavioral medicine.* New York: Guilford Press.

Agosta, W. C. (1992). *Chemical communication: The language of pheromones.* New York: Freeman.

Agren, G. (1990). Sperm competition, pregnancy initiation and litter size: Influence of the amount of copulatory behaviour in Mongolian gerbils, *Meriones unguiculatus. Animal Behaviour, 40,* 417–427.

Alatalo, R.V., & Helle, P. (1990). Alarm calling by individual willow tits, *Parus montanus. Animal Behaviour, 40,* 437–442.

Alatalo, R. V., Lundberg, A., & Ståhlbrandt, R. (1984). Female mate choice in the pied flycatcher *Ficedula hypoleuca. Behavioral Ecology and Sociobiology, 14,* 253–262.

Albrecht, D. J., & Oring, L. W. (1995). Song in chipping sparrows, *Spizella passerina:* Structure and function. *Animal Behaviour, 50,* 1233–1241.

Alcock, J. (1972). The evolution of the use of tools by feeding animals. *Evolution, 26,* 464–473.

Alcock, J. (1987). The effects of experimental manipulation of resources on the behavior of two calopterygid damselflies that exhibit resource-defense polygyny. *Canadian Journal of Zoology, 65,* 2475–2482.

Alerstam, T. (1990). *Bird migration.* Cambridge, England: Cambridge University Press.

Allman, W. F. (1994). *The Stone Age present.* New York: Simon & Schuster.

Alsop, B., & Honig, W. K. (1991). Sequential stimuli and relative numerosity discriminations in pigeons. *Journal of Experimental Psychology, 17*(4), 386–395.

Altmann, J. (1990). Primate males go where the females are. *Animal Behaviour, 39,* 193–194.

Anderson, L. T. (1973). An analysis of habitat preference in mice as a function of prior experience. *Behaviour, 47,* 302–339.

Anderson, O. R. (1988). *Comparative protozoology: Ecology, physiology, life history.* Berlin, Germany: Springer-Verlag.

Andersson, M. (1982). Female choice selects for extreme tail length in a widowbird. *Nature, 299,* 818–820.

Andersson, M. (1994). *Sexual selection.* Princeton, NJ: Princeton University Press.

Andrade, M. C. B. (1996). Sexual selection for male sacrifice in the Australian redback spider. *Science, 271,* 70–71.

Antolin, M. F. (1992). Sex ratio variation in a parasitic wasp. II. Diallel cross. *Evolution, 46,* 1511–1524.

Archer, J. (1988). *The behavioural biology of aggression.* New York: Cambridge University Press.

Arkes, H. R., Herren, L. T., & Isen, A. M. (1988). The role of the potential loss in the influence of affect on risk-taking behavior. *Organizational Behavior and Human Decision Processes, 42,* 181–193.

Armstrong, D. P. (1991). Aggressiveness of breeding territorial honeyeaters corresponds to seasonal changes in nectar availability. *Behaviour Ecology and Sociobiology, 29,* 103–111.

Ash, M., & Roberts, W. A. (1992) Central-place foraging by rats on the radial maze: The effects of patch size, food distribution, and travel time. *Animal Learning & Behavior, 20,* 127–134.

Association for the Study of Animal Behaviour. (1996). Guidelines for the treatment of animals in behavioural research and teaching. *Animal Behaviour, 51,* 241–246.

Au, W. W. L. (1993). *The sonar of dolphins.* New York: Springer-Verlag.

Austad, S. N., & Sunquist, M. E. (1986). Sex-ratio manipulation in the common opossum. *Nature, 324,* 58–60.

Axelrod, R. (1984). *The evolution of cooperation.* New York: Basic Books.

Axelrod, R., & Hamilton, W. D. (1981). The evolution of cooperation. *Science, 211,* 1390–1396.

Azar, B. (1996). Sound patterns: Learning language keys. *The APA Monitor, 20.*

Azar, B. (1997). Nature, nurture: Not mutually exclusive. *The APA Monitor, 28*(5), 1, 28.

Baerends, G. P., & Baerends-van Roon, J. M. (1950). An introduction to the study of the ethology of the cichlid fishes. *Behaviour Supplement, 1,* 1–243.

Baerends-van Roon, J., & Baerends, G. P. (1979). The morphogenesis of the behavior of the domestic cat, with a special emphasis on the development of prey-catching. *Proceedings of the Royal Netherlands Academy of Sciences, 72.*

Baird, T. A., Ryer, C. H., & Olla, B. L. (1991). Social enhancement of foraging ephemeral food source in juvenile walleye pollock, *Theragra chalcogramma. Environmental Biology Fish, 31,* 307–311.

Baker, R. (1996). *Sperm wars: The science of sex.* New York: Basic Books.

Baker, R. R. (1978). *The evolutionary ecology of animal migration.* London, England: Hodder & Stoughton.

Baker, R. R. (1981). *Human navigation and the sixth sense.* New York: Simon & Schuster.

Baker, R. R., & Bellis, M. A. (1993). Human sperm competition: Ejaculate manipulation by females and a function for the female orgasm. *Animal Behaviour, 46,* 887–909.

Balda, R. P. (1980). Recovery of cached seeds by a captive *Nucifraga caryocatactes. Zeitschrift für Tierpsychologie, 52,* 331–346.

Baldi, R., Campagna, C., Pedraza, S., & Burney, J. (1996). Social effects of space availability on the breeding behaviour of elephant seals in Patagonia. *Animal Behaviour, 51,* 717–724.

Baldwin, J. D. (1986). Behavior in infancy: Exploration and play. In G. Mitchell & J. Erwin (Eds.), *Comparative primate biology; Vol. 2A. Behaviour, conservation, and ecology.* New York: Liss.

Balkema, G. W., Mangini, N. J., & Pinto, L. H. (1983). Discrete visual defects in pearl mutant mice. *Science, 219,* 1085–1087.

Balshine-Earn, S. (1995). The costs of parental care in Galilee St. Peter's fish, *Sarotherodon galilaeus. Animal Behaviour, 50,* 1–7.

Bandura, A. (1986). *Social foundations of thought and action: A social cognitive theory.* Englewood Cliffs, NJ: Prentice-Hall.

Barash, D. P. (1977). Sociobiology of rape in mallards *(Anus platyrhynchos):* Responses of the mated male. *Science, 197,* 788–789.

Barnard, C. J. (1990). Parasitic relationships. In C. J. Barnard & J. M. Behnke (Eds.), *Parasitism and host behavior.* London, England: Taylor & Francis.

Baron, R. A., & Richardson, D. R. (1994). *Human aggression* (2nd ed.). New York: Plenum Press.

Basic Behavioral Science Task Force of the National Advisory Mental Health Council. (1996). Basic behavioral science research for mental health: Thought and communication. *American Psychologist, 51*(3), 181–189.

Basolo, A. L. (1991). Male swords and female preferences. *Science, 253,* 1426–1427.

Bateman, A. J. (1948). Intra-sexual selection in *Drosophila. Heredity, 2,* 349–368.

Bateson, M., & Kacelnik, A. (1995). Accuracy of memory for amount in the foraging starling, *Sturnus vulgaris. Animal Behaviour, 50,* 431–443.

Bateson, P. P. G. (1982). Preference for cousins in Japanese quail. *Nature, 295,* 236–237.

Beach, F. A. (1950). The snark was a boojum. *American Psychologist, 5,* 115–124.

Beach, F. A. (Ed.). (1965). *Sex and behavior.* New York: Wiley.

Bean, N. J. (1982). Modulation of agonistic behavior by the dual olfactory system in male mice. *Physiology and Behavior, 29,* 433–437.

Beck, B. B. (1980). *Animal tool behaviour: The use and manufacture of tools by animals.* New York: Garland STPM.

Beecher, M. D., & Beecher, I. M. (1979). Sociobiology of bank swallows: Reproductive strategy of the male. *Science, 205,* 1282–1285.

Begley, S. (1996). Holes in those genes—Not even DNA can live up to all the hyped claims. *Newsweek,* 57.

Bellis, M. A., & Baker, R. R. (1990). Do females promote sperm competition? Data for humans. *Animal Behaviour, 40,* 997–998.

Belsky, J., Steinberg, L., & Draper, P. (1991). Childhood experience, interpersonal development, and reproductive strategy: An evolutionary theory of socialization. *Child Development, 62,* 647–670.

Benhamou, S., & Bovet, P. (1992). Distinguishing between elementary orientation mechanisms by means of path analysis. *Animal Behaviour, 43,* 371–377.

Benvenutti, S., Fiaschi, V., Gabliardo, A., & Luschi, P. (1990). Pigeon homing: A comparison between groups raised under different conditions. *Behavior Ecology & Sociobiology, 27,* 93–98.

Bergerud, A. T., Ferguson, R., & Butler, H. E. (1990). Spring migration and dispersion of woodland caribou at calving. *Animal Behaviour, 39,* 360–368.

Berglund, A. (1993). Risky sex: Male pipe fishes mate at random in the presence of a predator. *Animal Behaviour, 46,* 169–175.

Berkowitz, L., & LePage, A. (1967). Weapons as aggression-eliciting stimuli. *Journal of Personality and Social Psychology, 11,* 202–207.

Bernstein, H., Byerly, H. C., Hopf, F. A., & Michod, R. E. (1984). Origins of sex. *Journal of Theoretical Biology, 110,* 323–351.

Bernstein, H., Byerly, H. C., Hopf, F. A., & Michod, R. E. (1985). Genetic damage, mutation, and the evolution of sex. *Science, 229,* 1277–1281.

Berthold, P. (1993). *Bird migration: A general survey.* New York: Oxford University Press.

Bertram, B. C. R. (1970). The vocal behavior of the Indian hill mynah, *Gracula religiosa. Animal Behavior Monographs, 3*(2), 79–192.

Bertram, B. C. R. (1978). Kin selection in lions and evolution. In P. P. G. Bateson & R. A. Hinde (Eds.), *Growing points in ethology.* New York: Cambridge University Press.

Birch, H. G. (1945). The relation of previous experience to insightful problem solving. *Journal of Comparative Physiology, 38,* 295–317.

Birgersson, B., Ekvall, K., & Temrin, H. (1991). Allosuckling in fallow deer, *Dama dama. Animal Behaviour, 42,* 326–327.

Birkhead, T. R., & Moller, A. P. (1992). *Sperm competition in birds: Evolutionary causes and consequences.* London, England: Academic Press.

Blanckenhorn, W. U. (1991). Fitness consequences of food-based territoriality in water striders, *Gerris remigis. Animal Behaviour, 42,* 147–149.

Blest, A. D. (1957). The function of eye-spot patterns in the *Lepidoptera. Behaviour, 11,* 209–256.

Blough, D. S. (1959). Delayed matching in the pigeon. *Journal of the Experimental Analysis of Behavior, 2,* 151–160.

Blough, P. M. (1991). Attentional priming and visual search in pigeons. *Journal of Experimental Psychology: Animal Behavioral Processes, 15,* 358–365.

Boccia, M. L. (1986). Grooming site preferences as a form of tactile communication and their role in the social relations of rhesus monkeys. In D. M. Taub & F. A. King (Eds.), *Current perspectives in primate social dynamics.* New York: Van Nostrand Reinhold.

Boesch, C. (1991). Teaching among wild chimpanzees. *Animal Behaviour, 41,* 530–532.

Boesch, C. (1996). The question of culture. *Nature, 379,* 207–208.

Böhner, J. (1990). Early acquisition of song in the zebra finch, *Taeniopygia guttata. Animal Behaviour, 39,* 369–374.

Bolhuis, J. J., Fitzgerald, R. E., Dijk, D. J., & Koolhaas, J. M. (1984). The corticomedial amygdala and learning in an agonistic situation in the rat. *Physiology and Behaviour, 32,* 575–579.

Bolles, R. C. (1973). The comparative psychology of learning: The selection association principle and some problems with "general" laws of learning. In G. Bermant (Ed.), *Perspectives in animal behavior.* Glenview, IL: Scott, Foresman.

Bolles, R. C., & Fanselow, M. S. (1980). A perceptual-defensive-recuperative model of fear and pain. *Behavioral and Brain Science, 3,* 291–323.

Bolles, R. C., & Moot, S. A. (1973). The rat's anticipation of two meals a day. *Journal of Comparative and Physiological Psychology, 83,* 510–514.

Bonner, J. T. (1963). How slime molds communicate. *Science in America, 209*(2), 84–93.

Bonsall, R. W., Clancy, A. N., & Michael, R. P. (1992). Effects of the nonsteroidal aromatase inhibitor, Fadrozole, on sexual behavior in male rats. *Hormones and Behavior, 26,* 240–254.

Borgia, G. (1985). Bower destruction and sexual competition in the satin bowerbird *(Ptilonorhnchus violaceus). Behavioral Ecology and Sociobiology, 18,* 91–100.

Borgia, G. (1995). Why do bowerbirds build bowers? *American Scientist, 83*(11), 542–547.

Bossert, W. H., & Wilson, E. O. (1963). The analysis of olfactory communication among animals. *Journal of Theoretical Biology, 5,* 443–469.

Bouchard, T. J., Jr., Lykken, D. T., McGue, M., Segal, N. L., & Tellegen. A. (1990). Sources of human psychological differences: The Minnesota study of twins reared apart. *Science, 250,* 223–228.

Bourlière, F. (1954). *The natural history of mammals* (H. M. Parshley, Trans.). New York: Knopf.

Bouton, M. E., & Bolles, R. C. (1979). Contextual control of the extinction of conditioned fear. *Learning Motivation, 10,* 445–466.

Boysen, S. T., & Berntson, G. G. (1995). Indicating acts during counting by a chimpanzee *(Pan troglodytes). Journal of Comparative Psychology, 109,* 47–51.

Bradbury, J. W. (1982). The evolution of leks. In R. D. Alexander & D. W. Tinkle (Eds.), *Natural selection and social behavior.* New York: Chiron.

Bradbury, J. W., & Gibson, R. M. (1983). Leks and mate choice. In P. Bateson (Ed.), *Mate choice.* Cambridge, England: Cambridge University Press.

Bradshaw, J., & Rogers, L. J. (1993). *The evolution of lateral asymmetries, language, tool use, and intellect.* San Diego: Academic Press.

Bradshaw, J. W. S. (1992). *The behaviour of the domestic cat.* Wallingford: C.A.B. International.

Braitenberg, V. (1986). *Vehicles.* Cambridge: MIT Press.

Brault, S. (1991). Host choice and offspring sex allocation in a solitary parasitic wasp. *Behavioral Ecology and Sociobiology, 29,* 353–360.

Breland, K., & Breland, M. (1961). The misbehavior of organisms. *American Psychologist, 16,* 661–664.

Brodie, E. D., III. (1993). Differential avoidance of coral snake banded patterns by free-ranging avian predators in Costa Rica. *Evolution, 47,* 227–235.

Brodie , E. D., III, & Moore, A. J. (1995). Experimental studies of coral snake mimicry: Do snakes mimic millipedes? *Animal Behaviour, 49,* 534–536.

Bronson, F. H., & Marsteller, F. A. (1985). Effect of short-term food deprivation on reproduction in female mice. *Biological Reproduction, 33,* 660–667.

Bronson, F. H., & Rissman, E. F. (1986). The biology of puberty. *Biological Review, 61,* 157–195.

Brouette-Lahlou, I., Vernet-Maury, E. & Chanel, J. (1991). Is rat-dam licking behavior regulated by pups' preputial gland secretion? *Animal Learning & Behaviour, 19* (2), 177–184.

Brower, L. P. (1985). Foraging dynamics of bird predators on overwintering monarch butterflies in Mexico. *Evolution, 39,* 852–868.

Brower, L. P., & Calvert, W. H. (1984). Chemical defence in butterflies. In R. I. Vane-Wright & P. R. Ackery (Eds.), *The biology of butterflies.* London, England: Academic Press.

Brower, L. P., Ryerson, W. N., Coppinger, J. L., & Glazier, S. C. (1968). Ecological chemistry and the palatability spectrum. *Science, 161,* 1349–1351.

Brown, D. (1991). *Human universals.* New York: McGraw-Hill.

Brown, F. A., Jr., Hastings, J. W., & Palmer, J. D. (1970). *The biological clock: Two views.* New York: Academic Press.

Brown, J. L. (1975). *The evolution of behavior.* New York: Norton.

Brown, P. L., & Jenkins, H. M. (1968). Auto-shaping of the pigeon's key peck. *Journal of Experimental Analysis of Behavior, 11,* 1–8.

Bruce, H. M. (1960). A block to pregnancy in the mouse caused by proximity of strange males. *Journal of Reproduction and Fertility, 1,* 96–103.

Budenberg, W. J. (1991). Redefinition of klinokinesis is not appropriate. *Animal Behaviour, 42,* 156–158.

Bull, J. J. (1983). *Evolution of sex determining mechanisms.* California: Benjamin/Cummings.

Bullock, T. H., & Heiligenberg, W. (Eds.). (1986). *Electroreception.* New York: Wiley.

Burger, J., Gochfeld, M., & Murray, B. G. (1992). Risk discrimination of eye contact and directness of approach in Black Iguanas *(Ctenosaura similis). Journal of Comparative Psychology, 106,* 97–101.

Burke, T., Davies, N. B., Bruford, M. W., & Hatchwell, B. J. (1989). Parental care and mating behaviour of polyandrous dunnocks *Prunella modularis* related to paternity by DNA fingerprinting. *Nature, 338,* 249–251.

Burkhardt, D., & de la Motte, I. (1983). How stalk-eyed flies view stalk-eyed flies: Observations and measurements of the eyes of *Cyrtodiopsis whitei (Diopsidae, Diptera). Journal of Comparative Physiology, 151,* 407–421.

Burley, N. (1981). Mate choice by multiple criteria in a monogamous species. *American Naturalists, 117,* 515–528.

Burley, N. (1982). Facultative sex-ration manipulation. *American Naturalists, 120,* 81–107.

Burley, N., Krantzberg, G., & Radman, P. (1982) Influence of colour-banding on the conspecific preferences of zebra finches. *Animal Behaviour, 30,* 444–455.

Burton, R. (1985). *Bird behavior.* New York: Knopf.

Busnel, M. C., Granier-Deferre, C., & Lecanuet, J. P. (1992). Fetal audition. *Annals of the New York Academy of Sciences, 662,* 118–134.

Buss, D. M. (1989). Sex differences in human mate preferences: Evolutionary hypotheses tested in 37 cultures. *Behavioral and Brain Sciences, 12,* 1–49.

Buss, D. M. (1991). Evolutionary personality psychology. *Annual Review of Psychology, 42,* 459–491.

Buss, D. M. (1993). Strategic individual differences: The role of personality in creating and solving adaptive problems. In J. Hettema & I. J. Deary (Eds.), *Foundations of personality.* Dordrecht, The Netherlands: Kluwer Academic.

Buss, D. M., Larsen, R., Westen, D., & Semmelroth, J. (1992). Sex differences in jealousy: Evolution, psysiology, and psychology. *Psychological Science, 3,* 251–255.

Buss, D. M., & Schmitt, D. P. (1993). Sexual strategies theory: A contextual evolutionary analysis of human mating. *Psychological Review, 100,* 204–232.

Butler, R. A. (1954). Incentive conditions which inflence visual exploration motivation. *Journal of Experimental Psychology, 48,* 19–23.

Byers, J. A., Moodie, J. D., & Hall, N. (1994). Pronghorn females choose vigorous mates. *Animal Behaviour, 47,* 33–43.

Cain, W. S. (1988). Olfaction. In R. A. Arkinson, R. J. Hernstein, G. Lindzey, & R. D. Luce (Eds.), *Stevens' handbook of experimental psychology* (Vol. 1). New York: Wiley.

Calhoun, J. B. (1962). Population density and social pathology. *Science in America, 206,* 139–148.

Calhoun, J. B. (1973). Death squared: The explosive growth and demise of a mouse population. *Processes of the Royal Society of Medicine, 66,* 80–88.

Calvert, W. H., & Brower, L. P. (1986). The location of monarch butterfly *(Danaus plexippus L.)* overwintering colonies in Mexico in relation to topography and climate. *Journal of the Lepidopterists Society, 40,* 164–187.

Calvin, W. H. (1991). *The ascent of mind: Ice age climates and the evolution of intelligence.* New York: Bantam Books.

Campagna, C., Bisioli, C., Quintana, F., Perez, F. & Vila, A. (1992). Group breeding in sea lions: Pups survive better in colonies. *Animal Behaviour, 43,* 541–548.

Cangialosi, K. R. (1991). Attack strategies of a spider kleptoparasite: Effects of prey availability and host colony size. *Animal Behaviour, 41,* 639–647.

Caraco, T. (1980). On foraging time allocation in a stochastic environment. *Ecology, 61,* 19–128.

Caraco, T., Blanckenhorn, W. U., Gregory, G. M., Newman, J. A., Recer, G. M., & Zwicker, S. M. (1990). Risk-sensitivity: Ambient temperature affects foraging choice. *Animal Behaviour, 39,* 338–345.

Caraco, T., Matindale, S., & Whittham, T. S. (1980). An empirical demonstration of risk-sensitive foraging preferences. *Animal Behaviour, 28,* 820–830.

Carey, M., & Nolan, V., Jr. (1979). Population dynamics of indigo buntings and the evolution of avian polygyny. *Evolution, 33,* 1180–1192.

Caro, T. M. (1986). The functions of stotting: A review of the hypotheses. *Animal Behaviour, 34,* 649–662.

Caro, T. M. (1987). Indirect costs of play: Cheetah cubs reduce maternal hunting success. *Animal Behaviour, 35,* 295–297.

Caro, T. M. (1995). Short-term costs and correlates of play in cheetahs. *Animal Behaviour, 49,* 333–345.

Caro, T. M., FitzGibbon, C. D., & Holt, M. E. (1989). Physiological costs of behavioural strategies for male cheetahs. *Animal Behaviour, 38,* 309–317.

Carr, A. (1965). The navigation of the green turtle. *Scientific American, 212,* 79–86.

Carr, A., & Coleman, P. J. (1974). Seafloor spreading theory and the odyssey of the green turtle from Brazil to Ascension Island, Central Atlantic. *Nature, 249,* 128–130.

Carranza, J., Alvarez, F., & Redondo, T. (1990). Territoriality as a mating strategy in red deer. *Animal Behaviour, 40,* 79–88.

Carranza, J., Garcia-Muñoz, A. J., & De Dios Vargas, J. (1995). Experimental shifting from harem defence to territoriality in rutting red deer. *Animal Behaviour, 49,* 551–554.

Chapman, C., & Chapman, L. J. (1990) Spider monkey alarm calls: Honest advertisment or warning kin? *Animal Behaviour, 39,* 197–198.

Charnov, E. L. (1976). Optimal foraging: The marginal value theorem. *Theoretical Population Biology, 9,* 129–136.

Charnov, E., & Finerty, J. (1980). Vole population cycles: A case for kin-selection? *Oecologia, 45,* 1–2.

Cheney D. L., & Seyfarth, R. M. (1977). Behaviour of adult and immature male baboons during inter-group encounters. *Nature, 269,* 404–406.

Cheney, D. L., & Seyfarth, R. M. (1990). *How monkeys see the world: Inside the mind of another species.* Chicago: University of Chicago Press.

Cheney, D. L., & Seyfarth, R. M. (1991). Truth and deception in animal communication. In C. A. Ristau (Ed.), *Cognitive ethology: The minds of other animals.* Hillsdale, NJ: Erlbaum.

Cheney, D. L., Seyfarth, R. M., & Silk, J. B. (1995). The role of grunts in reconciling opponents and facilitating interactions among adult female baboons. *Animal Behaviour, 50,* 249–257.

Cheney, D. L., Seyfarth, R. M., & Smuts, B. (1986). Social relationships and social cognition in non-human primates. *Science, 234,* 1361–1366.

Chitty, D. (1960). Population processes in the vole and their relevance to general theory. *Canadian Journal of Zoology, 38,* 99–113.

Chloe, J. C. (1994). Sexual selection and mating system in *Zorotypus gurneyi Choe (Insecta: Zoraptera). Behavioral Ecology and Sociobiology, 34,* 87–93.

Chloe, J. C. (1995). Courtship feeding and repeated mating in *Zorotypus barberi (Insecta: Zoraptera). Animal Behaviour, 49,* 1511–1520.

Cigliano, J. A. (1995). Assessment of the mating history of female pygmy octopuses and a possible sperm competition mechanism. *Animal Behaviour, 49,* 849–851.

Clark, M. M., & Galef, B. G., Jr. (1989). Measuring rates of sexual development in female Mongolian gerbils. *Developmental Psychobiology, 22,* 173–182.

Clark, M. M., Tucker, L., & Galef, B. G., Jr. (1992). Stud males and dud males: Intra-uterine position effects on the reproductive success of male gerbils. *Animal Behaviour, 43,* 215–221.

Clark, N. E., & Reis, H. T. (1988). Interpersonal processes in close relationships. *Annual Review of Psychology, 39,* 609–672.

Clarke, A. M., & Clarke, A. D. B. (Eds.). (1976). *Early experience: Myth and evidence.* New York: Free Press.

Cleland, G. G., & Davey, G. C. L. (1983). Autoshaping in the rat: The effects of localizable visual and auditory signals for food. *Journal of Experimental Analysis of Behavior, 40,* 47–56.

Clemente, C. D., & Chase, M. H. (1973). Neurological substrates of aggressive behavior. *Annual Review of Physiology, 35,* 329–356.

Clutton-Brock, T. H. (1984). Reproductive effort and terminal investment in iteroparous animals. *American Naturalists, 123,* 212–229.

Clutton-Brock, T. H., Albon, S. D., Gibson, R. M., & Guinness, F. E. (1979). The logical stag: Adaptive aspects of fighting in red deer. *Animal Behaviour, 27,* 211–225.

Cody, M. L. (1971). Finch flocks in the Mohave Desert. *Theoretical Population Biology, 2,* 142–158.

Colombo, M., D'Amato, M. R., Rodman, H. R., & Gross, C. G. (1990). Auditory association cortex lesions impair auditory short-term memory in monkeys. *Science, 247,* 336–338.

Connell, J. H. (1961). The influence of interspecific competition and other factors on the distribution of the barnacle *Chthamalus stellatus. Ecology, 42,* 710–723.

Connor, R. C. (1995). Impala allogrooming and the parcelling model of reciprocity. *Animal Behaviour, 49,* 528–530.

Connor, R. C., Smolker, R. A., & Richards, A. F. (1992). Two level of alliance formation among male bottlenose dolphins. *Processes of the National Academy Science, 89,* 987–990.

Cooney, R., & Cockburn, A. (1995). Territorial defense is the major function of female song in the superb fairy-wren, *Malurus cyaneus. Animal Behaviour, 49,* 1635–1647.

Cooper, W. E., Jr., & Vitt, L. J. (1985). Bluetails and autotomy: Enhancement of predation avoidance in juvenile skinks. *Zeitschrift für Tierpsychologie, 70,* 265–276.

Corballis, M. C. (1991). *The lopsided ape: Evolution of the generative mind.* Oxford, England: Oxford University Press.

Cosmides, L., & Tooby, J. (1995). From evolution to adaptations to behavior: Toward an integrated evolutionary psychology. In *Biological perspectives on motivated activities.* Norwood, NJ: Ablex.

Costanzo, R. M., & Gardiner, E. B. (1981). Multiple-joint neurons in somatosensory cortex of awake monkeys. *Brain Research, 24,* 321–333.

Cote, I. M., & Hunt, W. (1993). Female redlip blennies prefer older males. *Animal Behaviour, 46,* 203–205.

Cotman, C., & Nieto-Sampedro, M. (1982). Brain function, synapse renewal, and plasticity. *Annual Review of Psychology, 33,* 371–402.

Cott, H. B. (1957). *Adaptive coloration in animals.* London, England: Methuen.

Craig, J. L., & Douglas, E. (1986). Resource distribution, aggressive asymmetries and variable access to resources in the nectar feeding bellbird. *Behavioral Ecology and Sociobiology, 18,* 231–240.

Crawford, J. D. (1991). Sex recognition by electric cues in a sound-producing Mormyrid fish, *Pollimyrus isidori. Brain, Behavior and Evolution, 38,* 20–38.

Crelin, E. S. (1987). *The human vocal tract: Anatomy, function, development, and evolution.* New York: Vantage Press.

Cresswell, W. (1994). Flocking is an effective anti-predation strategy in redshanks, *Tringa totanus. Animal Behaviour, 47,* 433–443.

Crews, D. (1989). Unisexual organisms as model systems for research in the behavioral neurosciences. In R. M. Dawley & J. P. Bogart (Eds.), *Evolution and ecology of unisexual vertebrates.* Albany: New York State Museum.

Crews, D. (1994). Animal sexuality. *Scientific American, 270,* 108–114.

Cristol, D. A. (1992). Food deprivation influences dominance status in dark-eyed juncos, *Junco hyemalis. Animal Behaviour, 43,* 117–124.

Cristol, D. A., Nolan, V., & Ketterson, E. D. (1990). Effect of prior residence on dominance status of dark-eyed juncos, *Junco hyemalis. Animal Behaviour, 40,* 580–586.

Crook, J. H. (1964). The evolution of social organization and visual communication in the weaver birds *(Ploceinae). Behaviour, 10,* 1–178.

Curio, E. (1978). The adaptive significance of avian mobbing. I. Teleonomic hypotheses and predictions. *Zeitschrift für Tierpsychologie, 48,* 175–183.

Czeisler, C. A., Moore-Ede, M. C., & Coleman, R. M. (1982). Rotating shift work schedules that disrupt sleep are improved by applying Circadian principles. *Science, 217,* 460–462.

Daly, M., & Wilson, M. (1983). *Sex, evolution and behavior* (2nd ed.). Boston: Willard Grant.

Daly, M., & Wilson, M. (1987). Evolutionary psychology and family violence. In C. Crawford, M. Smith, & D. Krebs (Eds.), *Sociobiology and psychology.* Hillsdale, NJ: Erlbaum.

Darby, C. L., & Riopelle, A. J. (1959). Observational learning in the rhesus monkey. *Journal of Comparative and Physiological Psychology, 52,* 94–98.

Darwin, C. (1859). *On the origin of species.* London, England: Murray.

Darwin, C. (1871). *The descent of man and selection in relation to sex.* London, England: Murray.

Davey, G. (1989). *Ecological learning theory.* London, England: Routledge.

Davies, N. B. (1983). Polyandry, cloaca-pecking and sperm competition in dunnocks. *Nature, 302,* 334–336.

Davies, N. B. (1992). *Dunnock behaviour and social evolution.* Oxford, England: Oxford University Press.

Davies, N. B., Hartley, I. R., Hatchwell, B. J., Desrochers, A., Skeer, J., & Nebel, D. (1995). The polygynandrous mating system of the alpine accentor, *Prunella collaris*. I. Ecological causes and reproductive conflicts. *Animal Behaviour, 49,* 769–788.

Dawkins, R. (1977). *The selfish gene.* New York: Oxford University Press.

Dawkins, R. (1980). Good strategy or evolutionarily stable strategy? In G. W. Barlow & J. Silverberg (Eds.), *Sociobiology: Beyond nature/nurture?* Boulder, CO: Westview.

Dawkins, R., & Krebs, J. R. (1979). Arms races between and within species. *Processes of the Royal Society of London, 205,* 489–511.

De Angelis, T. (1995). The state of relationships: A special focus. *The APA Monitor, 26,* 1, 46.

de Fanis, E., & Jones, G. (1995). The role of odour in the discrimination of conspecifics by pipistrelle bats. *Animal Behaviour, 49,* 835–839.

De Fries, J. C., Hegmann, J. P., & Halcomb, R. A. (1974). Response to 20 generations of selection for open-field activity in mice. *Behavioral Biology, 11,* 481–495.

De Jonge, F. H., Oldenburger, W. P., Louwerse, A. L., & Van de Poll, N. E. (1992). Changes in male copulatory behavior after sexual exciting stimuli: Effects of medial amygdala lesions. *Physiology and Behavior, 52,* 327–332.

Delius, J. D., & Nowak, B. (1982). Visual symmetry recognition by pigeons. *Psychology Research, 44,* 199–212.

De Nault, L. K., & McFarlane, D. A. (1995). Reciprocal altruism between male vampire bats, *Desmodus rotundus. Animal Behaviour, 49,* 855–856.

Denny, M. R. (1980). Introduction and overview. In M. R. Denny (Ed.), *Comparative psychology: An evolutionary analysis of animal behavior.* New York: Wiley.

DeVoogd, T. J. (1991). Endocrine modulation of the development and adult function of the avian song system. *Psychoneuroendocrinology, 16,* 41–66.

DeVore, I. (1963). Mother-infant relations in free-ranging baboons. In H. L. Rheingold (Ed.), *Maternal behavior in mammals.* New York: Wiley.

DeWaal, F. B. (1987). Tension regulation and nonreproductive functions of sex in captive bonobos *(Pan paniscus). National Geographic Research, 3,* 318–335.

DeWaal, F. B. (1989). *Peacemaking among primates.* Cambridge: Harvard University Press.

DeWaal, F. B. (1991). Complementary methods and convergent evidence in the study of primate social cognition. *Behaviour, 118,* 297–320.

DeWolfe, A. S., & Saunders, A. M. (1995). Stress reduction in sixth-grade students. *The Journal of Experimental Education, 63,* 315–329.

Dewsbury, D. A. (1972). Patterns of copulatory behavior in male mammals. *Quarterly Review of Biology, 47,* 1–33.

Dewsbury, D. A. (1990). Deer mice as a case study in the operation of natural selection via differential reproductive success. In D.A. Dewsbury (Ed.), *Contemporary issues in comparative psychology.* Sunderland, MA: Sinauer Associates.

Dewsbury, D. A. (1995). Americans in Europe: The role of travel in the spread of European ethology after World War II. *Animal Behaviour, 49,* 1649–1663.

Dewsbury, D. A., Bauer, S. M., Pierce, J. D., & Shapiro, L. E., et al. (1992). Ejaculate disruption in two species of voles (Microtus): On the PEI matching law. *Journal of Comparative Psychology, 106,* 383–387.

Dial, B. E., & Fitzpatrick, L. C. (1983). Lizard tail autotomy: Function and energetics of postautotomy tail movement in *Scincella lateralis. Science, 219,* 391–393.

Diamond, J. (1996). Why women change. *Discover, 17,* 130–137.

Dilger, W. C. (1962). The behavior of love-birds. *Scientific American, 206,* 88–98.

Dixon, A. K., & Mackintosh, J. H. (1971). Effects of female urine upon the social behaviour of adult male mice. *Animal Behaviour, 19,* 138–140.

Domjan, M., & Burkhard, B. (1986). *The principles of learning and behavior* (2nd ed.). Monterey, CA: Brooks/Cole.

Domjan, M., & Purdy, J. E. (1995). Animal research in psychology: More than meets the eye of the general psychology student. *American Psychologist, 50,* 496–503.

Doty, R. L. (Ed). (1995). *Handbook of olfaction and gustation.* New York: Marcel Dekker.

Douglas-Hamilton, I. (1973). On the ecology and behaviour of the Lake Manyara elephants. *East African Wildlife Journal, 11,* 401–403.

Dowse, H. B., Hall, J. C., & Ringo, J. M. (1987). Circadian and ultradian rhythms in period mutants of *Drosophila melangaster. Behavioral Generation, 17,* 19–35.

Dressler, R. L. (1968). Pollination by euglossine bees. *Evolution, 22,* 202–210.

Drickamer, L. C., & Vessey, S. H. (1973). Group changing in male free-ranging rhesus monkeys. *Primates, 14,* 359–368.

Duffy, M., Bailey, S., Beck, B., & Barker, D. G. (1986). Preferences in nursing home design: A comparison of residents, administrators, and designers. *Environment and Behavior, 18,* 246–257.

Dugatkin, L. A. (1992). Sexual selection and imitation: Females copy the mate choice of others. *The American Naturalist, 139*(6), 1384–1389.

Dugatkin, L. A., & Alfieri, M. (1991). Guppies and the tit-for-tat strategy: Preference based on past interaction. *Behavioral Ecology and Sociobiology, 28,* 243–246.

Dugatkin, L. A., & Godin, J. J. (1993). Female mate copying in the guppy *(Poecilia reticulata):* Age-dependent effects. *Behavioral Ecology, 4,* 289–292.

Duggan, J. P., & Booth, D. A. (1986). Obesity, overeating, and rapid gastric emptying in rats with ventromedial hypothalamic lesions. *Science, 231,* 609–611.

Dunbar, R. I. M. (1988). *Primate social systems.* Ithaca, NY: Comstock.

Dunbar, R. I. M. (1995). The mating system of callitrichid primates: I. Conditions for the coevolution of pair bonding and twinning. *Animal Behaviour, 50,* 1057–1070.

Dutton, D. G., & Aron, A. P. (1974). Some evidence for heightened sexual attraction under conditions of high anxiety. *Journal of Personality and Social Psychology, 30,* 510–517.

Dyer, F. C., Berry, N. A., & Richard, A. S. (1993). Honey bee spatial memory: Use of route-based memories after displacement. *Animal Behaviour, 45,* 1028–1030.

Eberhard, J. R., & Ewald, P. W. (1994). Food availability, intrusion pressure and territory size: And experimental study of Anna's hummingbirds *(Calypte anna). Behavioral Ecology and Sociobiology, 34,* 11–18.

Eberhard, W. G. (1985). *Sexual selection and animal genitalia.* Cambridge: Harvard University Press.

Edminster, F. C. (1947). *The ruffed grouse.* New York: Macmillan.

Edwards, C. A., & Honig, W. K. (1987). Memorization and "feature selection" in the acquisition of natural concepts in pigeons. *Learning and Motivation, 18,* 235–260.

Eens, M., Pinxten, R., & Kempenaers, B. (1995). Do female tree swallows guard their mates by copulating frequently? A comment on Whittingham et al. *Animal Behaviour, 50,* 273–276.

Ehrman, L. (1983). Endosymbiosis. In D. Futuyma & M. Slatkin (Eds.), *Coevolution.* Sunderland, MA: Sinauer Associates.

Eibl-Eibesfeld, I. (1970). *Ethology: The biology of behavior.* New York: Holt, Rinehart and Winston.

Eibl-Eibesfeld, I., & Sielmann, H. (1962). *Beobachtungen am Spechtfinken Cactospiza pallida (Sclater und Salvin). Journal of Ornithology, 103,* 92–101.

Eisner, T. E. (1966). Beetle spray discourages predators. *Natural History, 75,* 42–47.

Elgar, M. A., & Crespi, B. J. (Eds.). (1992). *Cannibalism, ecology and evolution among diverse taxa.* Oxford, England: Oxford Science.

Elgar, M.A. (1986). House sparrows establish foraging flocks by giving chirrup calls if the resource is divisible. *Animal Behaviour, 34,* 169–174.

Elliott, A. J. (1981). *Child language.* Cambridge, England: Cambridge University Press.

Ellis, D. H., Bednarz, J. C., Smith, D. G., & Flemming, S. P. (1993). Social foraging classes in raptorial birds. *BioScience, 1,* 14–20.

Elzinga, R. J. (1977). *Fundamentals of entomology* (4th ed.). Englewood Cliffs, NJ: Prentice-Hall.

Emlen, S. T. (1975). Migration: Orientation and navigation. In D. S. Farner & J. R. King (Eds.), *Avian biology.* New York: Academic Press.

Endler, J. A. (1986). *Natural selection in the wild.* Princeton, NJ: Princeton University Press.

Enquist, M., & Leimar, O. (1990). The evolution of fatal fighting. *Animal Behaviour, 39,* 1–9.

Ens, B. J., Esselink, P., & Zwarts, L. (1990). Kleptoparasitism as a problem of prey choice: A study on mudflat-feeding curlew, *Numenius arquata. Animal Behaviour, 39,* 219–230.

Esch, H. (1967). The evolution of bee language. *Scientific American, 216,* 96–104.

Evans, R. M. (1990a). Embryonic fine tuning of pipped egg temperture in the American white pelican. *Animal Behaviour, 40,* 963–968.

Evans, R. M. (1990b). Vocal regulation of temperature by avian embryos: A laboratory study with pipped eggs of the American white pelican. *Animal Behaviour, 40,* 969–979.

Everitt, B. J., Herbert, J., & Hames, J. D. (1972). Sexual receptivity of bilaterally adrenalectomised female rhesus monkeys. *Physiology and Behavior,* 406–415.

Ewald, P. W. (1985). Influence of asymmetries in resource quality and age on aggression and dominance in black-chinned hummingbirds. *Animal Behaviour, 33,* 705–719.

Ewald, P. W. (1987). Transmission modes and evolution of the parasitism-mutualism continuum. *Annals of the New York Academy of Science, 503,* 295–306.

Ewert, J. P. (1980). *Neuro-ethology.* New York: Springer-Verlag.

Ewing, L. S. (1967). Fighting and death from stress in a cockroach. *Science, 155,* 1035–1036.

Faaberg, G. (1988). *Ornithology: An ecological approach.* Englewood Cliffs, NJ: Prentice-Hall.

Fagen, R. M., & George, T. K. (1977). Play behaviour and exercise in young ponies *(Equus caballus). Behavioral Ecology and Sociobiology, 2,* 267–269.

Fanselow, J. S., & Lester, L. S. (1988). A functional behavioristic approach to aversively motivated behavior: Predatory imminence as a determinant of the topography of defensive behavior. In R. C. Bolles & M. D. Beecher (Eds.), *Evolution and learning.* Hillsdale, NJ: Erlbaum.

Fanselow, J. S., & Sigmundi, R. A. (1982). The enhancement and reduction of defensive fighting by naloxone pretreatment. *Physiological Psychology, 10,* 313–316.

Farb, P., & the Editors of Time-Life Books. (1962). *The insects.* New York: Time.

Fay, R. R. (1994). Comparative auditory research. In R. R. Fay & A. N. Popper (Eds.), *Comparative hearing: Mammals.* New York: Springer-Verlag.

Feener, Jr., D. H., Jacobs, L. F., & Schmidt, J. O. (1996). Specialized parasitoid attracted to a pheromone of ants. *Animal Behaviour, 51,* 61–66.

Fields, H. L., & Basbaum, A. (1984). Endogenous pain control mechanisms. In P. D. Wall & R. Melzack (Eds.), *Textbook of pain.* Edinburgh, Scotland: Churchill Livingstone.

Fiorito, G., & Scotto, P. (1992). Observational learning in *octopus vulgaris. Science, 256,* 545–547.

Fisher, R. A. (1930). *The genetical theory of natural selection.* Oxford, England: Clarendon.

FitzGerald, G. J. (1993). The reproductive behavior of the stickleback. *Scientific American, 4*(4), 80–85.

Fitzgibbon, C. D. (1990). Why do hunting cheetahs prefer male gazelles? *Animal Behaviour, 40,* 839–845.

Fitzgibbon, C. D. (1994). The costs and benefits of predator inspection behaviour in Thomson's gazelles. *Behaviorial Ecology and Sociobiology, 34,* 139–148.

Flinn, M. V. (1988). Step-parent/step-offspring interactions in a Caribbean village. *Ethology and Sociobiology, 9,* 335–369.

Foltz, D. W., & Schwagmeyer, P. L. (1989). Sperm competition in the thirteen-lined ground squirrel: Differential fertilization success under field conditions. *American Naturalist, 133,* 257–265.

Fontaine, R. P. (1994). Play as physical flexibility training in five ceboid primates. *Journal of Comparative Psychology, 108*(3), 203–212.

Ford, C. S., & Beach, F. A. (1951). *Patterns of sexual behavior.* New York: Harper & Row.

Formanowicz, D. R., Jr., Brodie, E. D., Jr., & Bradley, P. J. (1990) Behavioural compensation for tail loss in the ground skink. *Animal Behaviour, 40,* 783–784.

Forslund, P., & Larsson, K. (1995). Intraspecific nest parasitism in the barnacle goose: Behavioural tactics of parasites and hosts. *Animal Behaviour, 50,* 509–517.

Fraenkel, G. S., & Gunn, D. L. (1961). *The orientation of animals—Kineses, taxes and compass reactions.* New York: Dover.

Frank, L. G., Glickman, S. E., & Licht, P. (1991). Fatal sibling aggression, precocial development, and androgens in neonatal spotted hyenas. *Science, 252,* 702–704.

Free, J. B. (1961). The stimuli releasing the stinging response of honey bees. *Animal Behaviour, 9,* 193–197.

Free, J. B. (1987). *Pheromones of social bees.* Ithaca, NY: Comstock.

Frei, U. (1982). Homing pigeons' behaviour in the irregular magnetic field of Western Switzerland. In F. Papi & H. G. Wallraff (Eds.), *Avian navigation.* Berlin, Germany: Springer-Verlag.

Fridlund, A. J. (1994). *Human facial expression: An evolutionary view.* San Diego: Academic Press.

Friedman, M. I., & Bruno, J. P. (1976). Exchange of water during lactation. *Science, 191,* 409–410.

Frith, H. J. (1957). Experiments on the control of temperature in the mound of the Mallee-Fowl, *Leipoa ocellata* Gould *(Megapodiidae). Commonwealth Scientific and Industrial Research Organization, Wildlife Research, 2,* 101–110.

Gabor, C. R., & Jaeger, R. G. (1995). Resource quality affects the agonistic behaviour of territorial salamanders. *Animal Behaviour, 49,* 71–79.

Gagnon, S., & Dore, F. Y. (1992). Search behavior in various breeds of adult dogs *(Canis familiaris):* Object permanence and olfactory cues. *Journal of Comparative Psychology, 106*(1), 58–68.

Galef, B. G., Jr. (1990). An adaptationist perspective on social learning, social feeding, and social foraging in norway rats. In D. A. Dewsbury (Ed.), *Contemporary issues in comparative psychology.* Sunderland, MA: Sinauer Associates.

Galef, B. G., Jr., & Whiskin, E. E. (1992). Social trasmission of information about multiflavored foods. *Animal Learning and Behavior, 20,* 56–62.

Galef, B. G., Jr., & Whiskin, E. E. (1995). Learning socially to eat more of one food than of another. *Journal of Comparative Psychology, 109*(1), 99–101.

Galef, B. G., Jr., & Wigmore, S. W. (1983). Transfer of information concerning distant foods: A laboratory investigation of the "information-centre" hypothesis. *Animal Behavior, 31,* 748–758.

Galef, B. G., Jr., & Wright, T. J. (1995). Groups of naive rats learn to select nutritionally adequate foods faster than do isolated naive rats. *Animal Behaviour, 49,* 403–409.

Gallistel, C. R. (1990). *The organization of learning.* Cambridge: Bradford Books/MIT Press.

Gallup, G. G., Jr. (1970). Chimpanzees: Self-recognition. *Science, 167,* 86–87.

Gallup, G. G., Jr. (1982). Self-awareness and the emergence of mind in primates. *American Journal of Primatology, 2,* 237–248.

Garcia, J., Hawkins, W. G., & Rusiniak, K. W. (1974). Behavioral regulation of the milieu interne in man and rats. *Science, 185,* 824–831.

Garcia, J., & Koelling, R. A. (1967). Relation of cue to consequence in avoidance learning. *Psychological Science, 4,* 123–124.

Garcia-Velasco, J., & Mondragon, M. (1991). The incidence of the vomeronasal organ in 1,000 human subjects and its possible clinical significance. *Journal of Steroid Biochemistry and Molecular Biology, 39,* 561–563.

Gardner, R. A., & Gardner, B. T. (1969). Teaching sign language to a chimpanzee. *Science, 165,* 664–672.

Garland, T. (1988). Genetic basis of activity metabolism. I. Inheritance of speed, stamina, and antipredator displays in the garter snake *Thamnophis sirtalis. Evolution, 42,* 335–350.

Gaulin, S. J. C., & FitzGerald, R. W. (1986). Sex differences in spatial ability: An evolutionary hypothesis and test. *American Naturalist, 127,* 74–88.

Geary, D. C. (1995). Reflections of evolution and culture in children's cognition: Implications for mathematical development and instruction. *American Psychologist, 50,* 24–37.

Gibbon, J. (1991). Origins of scalar timing. *Animal Learning and Behavior, 22,* 3–38.

Gibbons, J. A., & Lillywhite, H. B. (1981). Ecological segregation, color matching, and speciation in lizards of the *Amphibolurus decresii* species complex *(Lacertilia: Agamidae). Ecology, 62,* 1573–1584.

Gibbs, H. L., Weatherhead, P. J., Boag, P. T., White, B. N., Tabak, L. M., & Hoysak, D. J. (1990). Realized reproductive success of polygynous red-winged blackbirds revealed by DNA markers. *Science, 250,* 1394–1397.

Gilbert, L. E. (1976). Postmating female odor in *Heliconius* butterflies: A male-contributed anti-aphrodisiac? *Science, 93,* 419–420.

Gill, F. B., & Wolf, L. L. (1978). Comparative foraging efficiencies of some montane sunbirds in Kenya. *Condor, 80,* 391–400.

Gisiner, R., & Schusterman, R. J. (1991). California sea lion pups play an active role in reunions with their mothers. *Animal Behaviour, 41,* 364–366.

Gisiner, R., & Schusterman, R. J. (1992). Sequence, syntax, and semantics: Responses of a language-trained sea lion *(Zalophus californianus)* to novel sign combinations. *Journal of Comparative Psychology, 106*(1), 78–91.

Gittleman, J. L., & Harvey, P. H. (1980). Why are distasteful prey not cryptic? *Nature, 286,* 149–150.

Glass, D. C., Singer, J. E. & Friedman, L. N. (1969). Psychic cost of adaptation to an environmental stressor. *Journal of Personality and Social Psychology, 12,* 200–210.

Godin, J. J., & Briggs, S. E. (1996). Female mate choice under predation risk in the guppy. *Animal Behaviour, 51,* 117–130.

Goeders, N. E., Lane, J. D., & Smith, J. E. (1984). Self-administration of methionine enkephalin into the nucleus accumbens. *Pharmacology, Biochemistry, and Behavior, 20,* 451–455.

Goldfoot, D. A., Westerborg-van Loon, H., Groeneveld, W., & Koos Slob, A. (1980). Behavioral and physiological evidence of sexual climax in the female stump-tailed macaque *(Macacca arctoides). Science, 208,* 1477–1478.

Goodall, J. (1963). My life among wild chimpanzees. *National Geographical Magazine, 124,* 272–308.

Goodall, J. (1965). Chimpanzees of the Gombe Stream Reserve. In I. DeVore (Ed.), *Primate behavior.* New York: Holt, Rinehart and Winston.

Goodall, J. (1986). *The chimpanzees of Gombe: Patterns of behaviour.* Cambridge: Harvard University Press.

Goodwin, F. K., & Jamison, K. R. (1990). *Manic-depressive illness.* New York: Oxford University Press.

Gordon, D. M. (1995). The development of organization in an ant colony. *American Scientist, 83.*

Gosling, L. M., & Petrie, M. (1990). Lekking in topi: A consequence of satellite behaviour by small males at hotspots. *Animal Behaviour, 40,* 272–287.

Gotmark, F., Winkler, D. W., & Anderson, M. (1986). Flock-feeding on fish schools increases individual success in gulls. *Nature, 319,* 589–591.

Gottlieb, G. (1965). Components of recognition in ducklings. *Natural History, 74*(2), 12–19.

Gottlieb, G. (1971). *Development of species identification in birds.* Chicago: University of Chicago Press.

Gottlieb, G. (1978). Development of species identification in ducklings. IV. Change in species-specific perception caused by auditory deprivation. *Journal of Comparative and Physiological Psychology, 92,* 375–387.

Gould, J. L. (1980). The case for magnetic field sensitivity in birds and bees. *American Scientist, 68,* 256–267.

Gould, J. L. (1986). The locale map of honey bees: Do insects have cognitive maps? *Science, 232,* 861–863.

Gould, S. J. (1965). *The panda's thumb.* New York: Norton.

Gould, S. J. (1984). Only his wings remained. *Natural History, 93,* 10–18.

Goy, R. W., Bercovitch, F. B., & McBrair, M. C. (1988). Behavioral masculinization is independent of genital masculinization in prenatally androgenized female rhesus macaques. *Hormones and Behavior, 22,* 552–571.

Grammer, K., & Thornhill, R. (1994). Human *(Homo sapiens)* facial attractiveness and sexual selection: The role of symmetry and averageness. *Journal of Comparative Psychology, 108*(3), 233–242.

Green, J. D., Clemente, C., & DeGroot, J. (1957). Rhinencephalic lesions and behavior in cats. *Journal of Comparative Neurology, 108,* 505–545.

Greenberg, R. (1989). Neophobia, aversion to open space, and ecological plasticity in song and swamp sparrows. *Canadian Journal of Zoology, 67,* 1194–1199.

Greenberg, R. (1990). Feeding neophobia and ecological plasticity: A test of the hypothesis with captive sparrows. *Animal Behaviour, 39,* 375–379.

Greenwood, P. J. (1980). Mating systems, philopatry, and dispersal in birds and mammals. *Animal Behaviour, 28,* 1140–1162.

Griffin, D. R. (1958). *Listening in the dark.* New Haven, CT: Yale.

Griffin, D. R. (1981). *The question of animal awareness.* New York: Rockefeller University Press.

Griffin, D. R. (1992). *Animal minds.* Chicago: University of Chicago Press.

Griffin, D. R., & Galambos, R. (1941). The sensory basis of obstacle avoidance by flying bats. *Journal of Experimental Zoology, 86,* 481–506.

Grinnell, J., Packer, C., & Pusey, A. E. (1995). Cooperation in male lions: Kinship, reciprocity or mutualism? *Animal Behaviour, 49,* 95–105.

Gross, M. R. (1982). Sneakers, satellites, and parentals: Polymorphic mating strategies in North American sunfishes. *Zeitschrift für Tierpsychologie, 60,* 1–26.

Gross, M. R., & Charnov, Y. (1980). Alternative life histories in bluegill sunfish. *Proceedings of the National Academy of Sciences, 77,* 6937–6940.

Gross, M. R., & MacMillan, A. M. (1981). Predation and the evolution of colonial nesting in bluegill sunfish *(Lepomis macrochirus). Behavioral Ecology and Sociobiology, 8,* 163–174.

Guhl, A. M. (1956) The social order of chickens. *Science in America, 194*(2), 42–46.

Guilford, T., & Dawkins, M. S. (1991). Receiver psychology and the evolution of animal signals. *Animal Behaviour, 42,* 1–14.

Gunter, G., & McCaughan, D. (1959). Catalepsy in two common marine animals. *Science, 130,* 1194–1195.

Gustavson, C. R., Garcia, J., Hawkins, W. G., & Resniak, K. W. (1974). Coyote predation control by aversive conditioning. *Science, 184,* 581–583.

Gwynne, D. T. (1984). Courtship feeding increases female reproductive success in bushcrickets. *Nature, 307,* 361–363.

Gyger, M., & Marler, P. (1988). Food calling in the domestic fowl, *Gallus gallus:* The role of external referents and deception. *Animal Behaviour, 36,* 358–365.

Hall, J. A. (1987). On explaining gender differences: The case of nonverbal communication. In P. Shaver & C. Hendrick (Eds.), *Review of Personality and Social Psychology, 7,* 177–200.

Hall, K., & Schaller, G. (1964). Tool-using behavior of the California sea otter. *Journal Mammal, 45,* 287–298.

Halliday, T. (1982). *Sexual strategy.* Chicago: University of Chicago Press.

Halonen, J., & Denny, M. R. (1980). Defense against predation. In M. R. Denny (Ed.), *Comparative psychology: An evolutionary analysis of animal behavior.* New York: Wiley.

Hamilton, J. B., & Mestler, G. E. (1969). Mortality and survival: Comparison of eunuchs with intact men and women in a mentally retarded population. *Journal of Gerontology, 24,* 395–411.

Hamilton, W. D. (1964). The evolution of social behavior. *Journal of Theoretical Biology, 7,* 1–52.

Hamilton, W. D. (1971). Geometry for the selfish herd. *Journal of Theoretical Biology, 31,* 295–311.

Hamilton, W. D. (1972). Altruism and related phenomena, mainly in social insects. *Annual Review of Ecology and Systematics, 3,* 193–232.

Hamilton, W. D., Axelrod, R., & Tanese, R. (1990). Sexual reproduction as an adaptation to resist parasites: A review. *Proceedings of the National Academy of Sciences, 87,* 3566–3573.

Hamilton, W. D., Henderson, P. A., & Moran, N. A. (1981). Fluctuation of environment and coevolved antagonist polymorphism as factors in the maintenance sex. In R. D. Alexander & D. W. Tinkle (Eds.), *Natural selection and social behaviour.* New York: Chiron Press.

Hamilton, W. D., & May, R. M. (1977). Dispersal in stable habitats. *Nature, 269,* 578–581.

Hamilton, W. D., & Orians, G. H. (1965). Evolution of brood parasitism in altricial birds. *Condor, 67,* 361–382.

Hamilton, W. D., & Zuk, M. (1982). Heritable true fitness and bright birds: A role for parasites? *Science, 218,* 984–987.

Hannon, S. J., & Eason, P. (1995). Colour bands, combs and coverable badges in willow ptarmigan. *Animal Behaviour, 49,* 53–62.

Harcourt, R. (1991). Survivorship costs of play in the South American fur seal. *Animal Behaviour, 42,* 509–511.

Harlan, R. E., Shivers, B. D., Kow, L. M., & Pfaff, D. W. (1982). Intrahypothalamic colchicine infusions disrupt lordotic responsiveness in estrogen-treated female rats. *Brain Research, 238,* 153–167.

Harlow, H. F. (1960). Primary affectional patterns in primates. *American Journal of Orthopsychiatry, 30,* 676–684.

Harlow, H. F., & Harlow, M. K. (1962). Social deprivation in monkeys. *Scientific American, 207,* 136–146.

Harlow, H. F., & Zimmerman, R. R. (1958). The development of affectional responses in infant monkeys. *Proceedings of the American Philosophical Society, 102,* 501–509.

Hasler, A. D., & Larson, J. A. (1956). The homing salmon. *Science in America, 193*(2), 72–77.

Hatfield, E., & Walster, G. W. (1981). *A new look at love.* Reading, MA: Addison-Wesley.

Hausfater, G. (1975). Dominance and reproduction in baboons *(Papio cynocephalus):* A quantitative analysis. *Contributions in Primatology, 7,* 1–150.

Haverkamp, L. J., & Oppenheim, R. W. (1986). Behavioral development in the absence of neural activity: Effects of chronic immobilization on amphibian embryos. *Journal Neuroscience, 6,* 1332–1337.

Hayes, K. J., & Hayes, C. (1952). Imitation in a home raised chimpanzee. *Journal of Comparative and Physiological Psychology, 45,* 451–459.

Hazlett, B. (1996). Assessments during shell exchanges by the hermit crab *Clibanarius vittatus:* The complete negotiator. *Animal Behaviour, 51,* 567–573.

Hazlett, B. A. (1992). The effect of past experience on the size of shells selected by hermit crabs. *Animal Behaviour, 44,* 203–205.

Healy, S. D., & Krebs, J. R. (1992). Comparing spatial memory in two species of tit: Recalling a single positive location. *Animal Learning and Behavior, 20,* 121–126.

Heath, A. C., & Martin, N. G. (1993). Genetic models for the natural history of smoking: Evidence for a genetic influence on smoking persistence. *Addictive Behaviors, 18,* 19–34.

Hebb, D. O. (1949). *The organization of behaviour.* New York: Wiley Interscience.

Hedrick, A. V., & Dill, L. M. (1993). Mate choice by female crickets is influenced by predation risk. *Animal Behaviour, 46,* 193–196.

Heiligenberg, W. (1993). Electrosensation. In D. H. Evans (Ed.), *The physiology of fishes.* New York: Wiley.

Heinberg, L. J., & Thompson, J. K. (1992). Social comparison: Gender, target importance ratings, and relation to body image disturbance. *Journal of Social Behavior and Personality, 7,* 335–344.

Heinrich, B. (1995). Neophilia and exploration in juvenile common ravens, *Corvus corax. Animal Behaviour, 50,* 695–704.

Heinrich, B., & Bartholomew, G. A. (1979). The ecology of the African dung beetle. *Scientific American, 241,* 146–156.

Heinrich, B., & Collins, S. L. (1983). Caterpillar leaf damage, and the game of hide-and-seek with birds. *Ecology, 64,* 592–604.

Heinrich, B., & Marzluff, J. M. (1991). Do common raven yell because they want to attract others? *Behavior Ecology and Sociobiology, 28,* 13–21.

Heit, G., Smith, M. E., & Halgren, E. (1988). Neural encoding of individual words and faces by the human hippocampus and amygdala. *Nature, 333,* 773–775.

Helbig, A. J. (1991). Inheritance of migratory direction in a bird species: A cross-breeding experiment with SE and SW migrating blackcaps *(Sylvia atricapilla). Behavioral Ecology and Sociobiology, 28,* 9–12.

Hellige, J. B. (1993). *Hemispheric asymmetry: What's right and what's left?* Cambridge: Harvard University Press.

Herman, D., & Polivy, J. (1984). A boundary model for the regulation of eating. In A. J. Stunkard & E. Stellar (Eds.), *Eating and its disorders.* New York: Raven.

Herman, L. M. (1987). Receptive competencies of language-trained animals. In J. S. Rosenblatt, C. Beer, M. C. Busnel, & P. J. B. Slater (Eds.), *Advances in the study of behavior* (Vol. 17). San Diego: Academic Press.

Hernstein, R. J. (1985). Riddles of natural categorization. *Philosophical Transactions of the Royal Society of London, B308,* 129–144.

Herter, K. (1962). *Der temperatursinn der tiere.* Wittenbery, Germany: Ziensen Verlag.

Hess, E. H. (1956). Natural preferences of chicks and ducklings for objects of different colors. *Psychological Report, 2,* 477–483.

Hess, E. H., (1973). *Imprinting: Early experience and the developmental psychobiology of attachment.* New York: Behavioral Science.

Heyes, C. M. (1994). Reflections on self-recognition in primates. *Animal Behaviour, 47,* 909–919.

Higgins, L. E., & Buskirk, R. E. (1992). A trap-building predator exhibits different tactics for different aspects of foraging behavior. *Animal Behaviour, 44,* 485–499.

Hildemann, W. H. (1959). A cichlid fish, *Symphysodon discus,* with unique nurture habits. *American National, 43,* 27–34.

Hill, K., & Hurtado, A. M. (1989). Hunter-gatherers of the new world. *American Scientist, 77,* 437–443.

Hirschfeld, L. A. *Race in the making: Cognition, culture and the child's construction of human kinds.* Cambridge: MIT Press.

Hirsh, S. M., & Bolles, R. C. (1980). On the ability of prey to recognize predators. *Zeitschrift für Tierpsycholiogie, 54,* 71–84.

Hitchcock, C. L., & Sherry, D. F. (1990). Long-term memory for cache sites in the black-capped chickadee. *Animal Behaviour, 40,* 701–712.

Hodos, W., & Campbell, C. B. G. (1969). Scale naturae: Why there is no theory in comparative psychology. *Psychological Review, 76,* 337–350.

Hoelzel, A. R. (1991). Killer whale predation on marine mammals at Punta Norte, Argentina: Food sharing, provisioning and foraging strategy. *Behavioral Ecology and Sociobiology, 29,* 197–204.

Hoglund, J., Alatalo, R. V., Gibson, R. M., & Lundberg, A. (1995). Mate-choice copying in black grouse. *Animal Behaviour, 49,* 1627–1633.

Holecamp, K. E., & Sherman, P. W. (1989). Why male ground squirrels disperse. *American Scientist, 77,* 232–239.

Hölldobler, B., & Wilson, E. O. (1990). *The ants.* Cambridge: Belknap Press/Harvard University Press.

Holling, C. S. (1959). The components of predation as revealed by a study of small mammal predation of the European pine sawfly. *Canadian Entomology, 91,* 293–320.

Hollis, K. L. (1982). Pavlovian conditioning of signal-centred action patterns and autonomic behavior: A biological analysis of function. *Advances in the Study of Behavior, 12,* 1–64.

Hollis, K. L. (1990). The role of Pavlovian conditioning in territorial aggression and reproduction. In D.A. Dewsbury (Ed.), *Contemporary issues in comparative psychology.* Sunderland, MA: Sinauer Associates.

Hollis, K. L., Dumas, M. J., Singh, P., & Fackelman, P. (1995). Pavlovian conditioning of aggressive behavior in blue gourami fish *(Trichogaster trichopterus):* Winners become winners and losers stay losers. *Journal of Comparative Psychology, 109*(2), 123–133.

Holmes, J. C., & Zohar, S. (1990). Pathology and host behavior. In C. J. Barnard & J. M. Behnke (Eds.), *Parasitism and host behaviour.* London, England: Taylor & Francis.

Holmes, W. G. (1984). Predation risk and foraging behavior of the hoary marmot in Alaska. *Behavioral Ecology and Sociobiology, 15,* 293–302.

Holmes, W. G. (1991). Predator risk affects foraging behaviour of pikas: Observational and experimental evidence. *Animal Behaviour, 42,* 111–119.

Holmes, W. G., & Sherman, P. W. (1982). The ontogeny of kin recognition in two species of ground squirrels. *American Zoologist, 22,* 491–517.

Holmes, W. G., & Sherman, P. W. (1983). Kin recognition in animals. *American Scientist, 71,* 46–55.

Hoogland, J. L. (1995). *The black-tailed prairie dog: Social life of a burrowing mammal.* Chicago: University of Chicago Press.

Houk, J., & Geibel, J. (1974). Observation of underwater tool use by the sea otter, *Enhydra lutris Linnaeus. California Fish & Game, 60,* 207–208.

Houston, A. I., McCleery, R. H., & Davies, N. B. (1985). Territory size, prey renewal, and feeding rates: Interpretation of observations on the pied wagtail *(Motacilla alba)* by stimulation. *Journal of Animal Ecology, 54,* 227–239.

Hoy, R. R. (1992). The evolution of hearing in insects as an adaptation to predation from bats. In D. B. Webster, R. R. Fay, & A. N. Popper (Eds.), *The evolutionary biology of hearing.* New York: Springer-Verlag.

Hrdy, S. B. (1977). Infanticide as a primate reproductive strategy. *American Scientist, 65,* 40–49.

Hrdy, S. B. (1988). The primate origins of human sexuality. In R. Belling & G. Stevens, *The evolution of sex.* San Francisco: Harper & Row.

Hubel, D. H., & Wiesel, T. N. (1979). Brain mechanisms of vision. *Science in America, 241,* 150–162.

Hudson, P. J., & Newborn, D. (1990). Brood defence in a precocial species: Variations in the distraction displays of red grouse, *Lagopus Lagopus scoticus. Animal Behaviour, 40,* 254–261.

Hunt, G. (1996). Manufacture and use of hook-tools by New Caledonian crows. *Nature, 379,* 249–251.

Huntingford, F. A., Lazarus, J., Barrie, B. D., & Webb, S. (1994). A dynamic analysis of cooperative predator inspection in sticklebacks. *Animal Behaviour, 47,* 413–423.

Hurly, T. A. (1992). Energetic reserves of marsh tits *(Parus palustris):* Food and fat storage in response to variable food supply. *Behavioral Ecology, 3,* 181–188.

Huxley, J. S. (1923). Courtship activities in the red-throated diver *(Colymbus stellatus Pontopp.);* Together with a discussion of the evolution of courtship in birds. *Journal of the Linnean Society of London, Zoology, 35,* 253–292.

Immelmann, K. (1972). The influence of early experience upon the development of social behavior in estrildine finches. In *Proceedings of the 15th International Ornithology Congress.* The Hague, the Netherlands.

Immelmann, K. (1985). The natural history of bird learning. In P. Marler & H. S. Terrace (Eds.), *The biology of learning.* New York: Springer-Verlag.

Itani, J. (1958). On the acquisition and propagation of a new food habit in the troop of Japanese monkeys at Takasakiyama. *Primates, 1,* 131–148.

Jackson, F. R., Bargiello, T. A., Yun, S.-H., & Young, M. W. (1986). Product of per locus in Drosophila shares homology with proteoglycans. *Nature, 320,* 185–188.

Jacobs, K. M., Mark, G. P., & Scott, T. R. (1988). Taste responses in the nucleus tractus solitarius of sodium-deprived rats. *Journal of Physiology, 406,* 393–410.

Jacobson, M. (1978). Developmental neurobiology. In G. Gottlieb (Ed.), *Studies of the development of behavior and the nervous system, II. Aspects of neurogenesis.* New York: Academic Press.

Jacobson, M. (1978). *Developmental neurobiology.* New York: Plenum Press.

Jaeger, R. G., Schwarz, J., & Wise, S. E. (1995). Territorial male salamanders have foraging tactics attractive to gravid females. *Animal Behaviour, 49,* 633–639.

Janes, S. (1976). The apparent use of rocks by a raven in nest defense. *Condor, 78,* 409.

Jarman, M. V. (1974). The social organisation of antelope in re ecology. *Behaviour, 58,* 215–267.

Jarvis, J. U. M. (1981). Eusociality in a mammal: Cooperative breeding in naked mole-rat colonies. *Science, 212,* 571–573.

Jemmott, J. B., III, & Magloire, K. (1988). Academic stress, social support, and secretory immunoglobulin. *Journal of Personality and Social Psychology, 55,* 803–810.

Jensen, D. (1966). The hagfish. *Science in America, 214,* 82–90.

Jerison, H. J. (1991). *Brain size and the evolution of mind.* New York: American Museum of Natural History.

Johnsgard, P. A. (1967). Dawn rendezvous on the lek. *Natural History, 76*(3), 16–21.

Johnson, C. G. (1969). *Migration and dispersal of insects by flight.* London, England: Methuen.

Johnson, J. H. (1986). *Life events as stressors in childhood and adolescence.* Beverly Hills, CA: Sage.

Johnston, R. E. (1993). Chemical signals and reproductive behavior. In J. G. Vandenbergh (Ed.), *Pheromones and reproduction in mammals.* New York: Academic Press.

Johnston, R. E. O., & Robinson, T. A. (1993). Cross-species discrimination of individual odors by hamsters *(Muridae: Mesocricetus auratus, Phodopulus campbelli). Ethology, 94,* 317–325.

Johnston, T. D. (1981). Selective costs and benefits in the evolutioin of learning. In J. S. Rosenblatt, R. A. Hinde, C. Beer, & M. C. Busnel (Eds.), *Advances in the study of behavior.* New York: Academic Press.

Jones, D., & Hill, K. (1993). Criteria of facial attractiveness in five populations. *Human Nature, 4,* 271–296.

Jones, F. R. H. (1955). Photo-kinesis in the ammocoete larva of the brook lamprey. *Journal of Experimental Biology, 32,* 492–503.

Kagan, J. (1996). Three pleasing ideas. *American Psychologist, 51,* 901–908.

Kalin, N. H. (1993). The neurobiology of fear. *Scientific American, 268,* 94–101.

Kallander, H. (1978). Hoarding in the rook *Corvus frugilegus. Answer Supplement, 3,* 124–128.

Kalmijn, A. J. (1988). Detection of weak electric fields. In J. Atema, R. R. Fay, A. N. Popper, & W. N. Tavolga (Eds.), *Sensory biology of aquatic animals.* New York: Springer-Verlag.

Kamin, L. J. (1968). Atttention-like processes in classical conditioning. In M. R. Jones (Ed.), *Miami symposium on the prediction of behavior: Aversive stimulation.* Miami: University of Miami Press.

Kandel, E. R. (1979). Small systems of neurons. *Scientific American, 241,* 66–76.

Kandel, E. R., & Schwartz, J. H. (1982). Molecular biology of learning: Modulation of transmitter release. *Science, 218,* 433–443.

Kano, T. (1992). *The last ape.* Palo Alto, CA: Stanford University Press.

Kaplan, H. I., & Sadock, B. J. (1991). *Synopsis of psychiatry: Behavioral sciences and clinical psychiatry* (6th ed.). Baltimore: Williams & Wilkins.

Katano, O. (1990). Dynamic relationships between the dominance of male dark chub, *Zacco temmincki,* and their acquisition of females. *Animal Behaviour, 40,* 1018–1034.

Kavaliers, M., Colwell, D. D., & Galea, L. A. M. (1995). Parasitic infection impairs spatial learning in mice. *Animal Behaviour, 50,* 223–229.

Kawai, M. (1965). Newly acquired precultural behavior of the natural troop of Japanese monkeys on Koshima Island. *Primates, 6,* 1–30.

Keane, B. (1990). The effect of relatedness on reproductive success and mate choice in the white-footed mouse, *Peromyscus leucopus. Animal Behaviour, 39,* 264–273.

Keller, S. E., Weiss, J. M., Schleifer, S. J., Miller, N. E., & Stein, M. (1983). Stress-induced suppression of immunity in adrenalectomized rats. *Science, 221,* 1301–1304.

Kellert, S. R., & Wilson, E. O. (Eds). (1993). *The biophilia hypothesis.* Washington, DC: Island Press.

Kempenaers, B. (1995). Polygyny in the blue tit: Intra- and inter-sexual conflicts. *Animal Behaviour, 49,* 1047–1064.

Kendler, K. S., Heath, A. C., Neale, M. C., Kessler, R. C., & Eaves, L. J. (1992). A population-based twin study of alcoholism in women. *Journal of the American Medical Association, 268,* 1877–1882.

Kessel, E. L. (1955). Mating activities of balloon flies. *Systematic Zoology, 4,* 97–104.

Kessler, R. C., McGonagle, K. A., Zhao, S., Nelson, C. B., Hughes, M., Eshelman, S., Wittchen, H., & Kendler, K. S. (1994). Lifetime and 12 month prevalence of DSM-III-R psychiatric disorders in the United States: Results from a national comorbidity survey. *Archives of General Psychiatry, 51,* 8–20.

King, A. P., & West, M. J. (1990). Variation in species-typical behavior: A contemporary issue for comparative psychology. In D. A. Dewsbury (Ed.), *Contemporary issues in comparative psychology.* Sunderland, MA: Sinauer Associates.

Kinsley, C., & Svare, B. (1986). Prenatal stress reduces intermale aggression in mice. *Physiology and Behavior, 36,* 783–785.

Kirkpatrick, M. (1982). Sexual selection and the evolution of female choice. *Evolution, 36,* 1–12.

Klinowska, M. (1986). Diurnal rhythms in Cetacea—A review. *Report of the International Whaling Commission (Spec. Issue), 8,* 75–88.

Klopfer, P. H. (1963). Behavioral aspects of habitat selection: The role of early experience. *Wilson Bullentin, 75,* 15–22.

Klump, G. M., Dooling, R. J., Fay, R. R., & Stebbins, W. C. (1995). *Methods in comparative psychoacoustics.* Basel: Birkhauser Verlag.

Kluyver, H. N., & Tinbergen, L. (1953). Territory and the regulation of density in titmice. *Arch. Neerl. Zoology, 10,* 265–287.

Koeniger, G. (1990). The role of the mating sign in honey bees, *Apis mellifera:* Does it hinder or promote multiple mating? *Animal Behaviour, 39,* 444–449.

Komers, P. (1996). Obligate monogamy without paternal care in Kerk's dikdik. *Animal Behaviour, 51,* 131–140.

Konishi, M. (1965). The role of auditory feedback in the control of vocalization in the white-crowned sparrow. *Zeitschrift für Tierpsychology, 22,* 770–783.

Konishi, M. (1985). Birdsong: From behavior to neuron. *Annual Review Neuroscience, 8,* 125–170.

Koopman, P., Gubbay, J., Vivian, N., Goodfellow, P. N., & Lovell-Badge, R. (1991). Male development of chromosomally female mice transgenic for Sry. *Nature, 351,* 117–121.

Korytko, A. I., & Vessey, S. H. (1991). Agonistic and spacing behaviour in white-footed mice, *Peromyscus leucopus. Animal Behaviour, 42,* 913–919.

Kraak, S. B. M., & van Den Berghe, E. P. (1992). Do female fish assess paternal quality by means of test eggs? *Animal Behaviour, 43,* 865–867.

Kramer, S. N. (1963). *The Sumerians.* Chicago: University of Chicago Press.

Krebs, C. J. (1972). *Ecology: The experimental analysis of distribution and abundance.* New York: Harper & Row.

Krebs, J. R. (1971). Territory and breeding density in the great tit, *Parus major L. Ecology, 52,* 2–22.

Kruuk, H. (1972). *The spotted hyena.* Chicago: University of Chicago Press.

Kuczmarski, R. J., Flegal, K., Campbell, S. M., & Johnson, C. L. (1994). Increasing prevalence of overweight among U.S. adults. *Journal of the American Medical Association, 272,* 205–211.

Kuhme, W. (1963). Ethology of the African elephant (*Loxodonta africana,* Blumenbach 1797) in captivity. In C. Jarvis and D. Morris (Eds.), *International zoo yearbook* (Vol. 14). London, England: Hutchinson.

Kummer, H. (1968). *Social organization of hamadryas baboons: A field study.* Chicago: University of Chicago Press.

Kummer, H. (1971). *Primate societies: Group techniques of ecological adaptation.* Chicago: Aldine-Atherton.

Lashley, K. S. (1929). *Brain mechanisms and intelligence.* Chicago: University of Chicago Press.

Laviola, G., & Alleva, E. (1995). Sibling effects on the behavior of infant mouse litters *(Mus domesticus). Journal of Comparative Psychology, 109*(1), 68–75.

Lawrence, S. E. (1992). Sexual cannibalism in the praying mantid, *Mantis religiosa:* A field study. *Animal Behaviour, 43,* 569–583.

LeClerc, R., & Reberg, D. (1980). Sign-tracking in aversive conditioning. *Learning and Motivation, 11,* 302–317.

Leffelaar, D., & Robertson, R. J. (1984). Do male tree swallows guard their mates? *Behavioral Ecology and Sociobiology, 16,* 73–80.

Lehrman, D. S. (1961). Hormonal regulation of parental behavior in birds and infrahuman mammals. In W. C. Young (Ed.), *Sex and internal secretions* (3rd ed.). Baltimore: Williams & Wilkins.

Leon, M., & Moltz, H. (1971). Maternal pheromone: Discrimination by preweanling albino rats. *Physiology and Behavior, 7,* 265–267.

Leonard, J. T., & Lukowiak, K. (1991). Sex and the simultaneous hermaphrodite: Testing models of male-female conflict in a sea slug, *Navanax inermis (Opisthobranchia). Animal Behaviour, 41,* 255–266.

Leslie, A. M. (1991). The theory of mind impairment in autism: Evidence for modular mechanisms of development? In A. Whiten (Ed.), *The emergence of mind reading.* Oxford, England: Blackwell.

Lewis, P. D., Jr. (1977). Adaptations for the transmission of species of leucochloridium from molluscan to avian hosts. *Proceedings of the Montana Academy of Sciences, 37,* 70–81.

Liberg, O., & von Schantz, T. (1985). Sex-biased philopatry and disperal in birds and mammals. The Oedipus hypothesis. *American Naturalist, 126,* 129–135.

Liebert, R. N., Sprafkin, J. H., & Davidson, E. S. (1989). *The early window: Effects of television on children and youth* (3rd ed.). New York: Pergamon Press.

Ligon, J. D., & Zwartje, P. W. (1995). Female red junglefowl choose to mate with multiple males. *Animal Behaviour, 49,* 127–135.

Lima, S. L. (1985). Maximizing efficiency and minimizing time exposed to predators: A trade-off in the black-capped chickadee. *Oecologia, 66,* 60–67.

Lima, S. L. (1990). The influence of models on the interpretation of vigilance. In M. Bekoff & D. Jamieson (Eds.), *Interpretation and explanation in the study of animal behavior: Vol. 2. Explanation, evolution and adaptation.* Boulder, CO: Westview Press.

Lima, S. L. (1995). Back to the basics of anti-predatory vigilance: The group-size effect. *Animal Behaviour, 49,* 11–20.

Limpus, C. J., Miller, J. D., Parmenter, C. J., Reimer, D., McLachland, N., & Webb, R. (1991). Migration of green (*Chelonia mydas*) and loggerhead (*Caretta caretta*) turtles to and from eastern Australian Rookeries. *Australian Wildlife Reserves.*

Lindauer, M. (1961). *Communication among social bees.* Cambridge: Harvard University Press.

Liu, X., Lorenz, Yu Q, Hall, J. C., & Rosbash, M. (1988). Spatial and temporal expression of the period gene in Drosophila melanogaster. *Genes and Development, 2,* 228–238.

Lloyd, J. E. (1975). Aggressive mimicry in *Photuris* fireflies: Signal repertoires by *femmes fatales. Science, 197,* 452–453.

Lohmann, K. J. (1991). Magnetic orientation by hatchling loggerhead sea turtles. *Journal of Experimental Biology, 155,* 37–49.

Long, G. R. (1994). Psychoacoustics. In R. R. Fay & A. N. Popper (Eds.), *Comparative hearing: Mammals.* New York: Springer-Verlag.

Lorenz, K. (1942). Die angeborenen Formen mglicer Erfahrung. *Zeitschrift für Tierpscholiogie, 5,* 235–409.

Lorenz, K. Z. (1935). Der Kumpan in der Umweld des Vogels; die Artenosse als auslösende Moment sozialer Verhaltungswiesen. *Journal für Ornithologie, 83,* 137–213, 324–413.

Losas, J., & Irschick, D. (1996). The effect of perch diameter on escape behaviour of *Anolis* lizards: Laboratory predictions and field tests. *Animal Behaviour, 51,* 593–602.

Lovegrove, B. G., & Wissel, C. (1988). Sociality in mole-rats: Metabolic scaling and the role and risk sensitivity. *Oecologia, 74,* 600–606.

Lucas, J. R. (1994). Regulation of cache stores and body mass in Carolina chickadees *(Parus carolinensus). Behavioral Ecology, 5,* 171–181.

Lucas, J. R., Creel, S. R., & Waser, P. M. (1996). How to measure inclusive fitness, revisited. *Animal Behaviour, 51,* 225–228.

MacArthur, R. H. (1958). Population ecology of some warblers in coniferous forests. *Ecology, 39,* 599–619.

MacArthur, R. H., & Connell, J. H. (1966). *The biology of populations.* New York: Wiley.

MacArthur, R. H., & Pianka, E. R. (1966). On optimal use of a patchy environment. *American Naturalist, 100,* 603–609.

MacArthur, R. H., & Wilson, E. O. (1967). *Theory of island biogeography.* Princeton, NJ: Princeton University Press.

Macuda, T., & Roberts, W. A. (1995). Further evidence for hierarchical chunking in rat spatial memory. *Journal of Experimental Psychology: Animal Behavior Processes, 21,* 20–32.

Madsen, T., Shine, R., Loman, J., & Hakansson, T. (1992). Why do female adders copulate so frequently? *Nature, 355,* 395–396.

Magurran, A. E., & Pitcher, T. J. (1987). Provenance, shoal size and the sociobiology of predator-evasion behaviour in minnow shoals. *Procession Royal Society of London, Ser. B., 229,* 439–465.

Maier, N. R. F., & Schneirla, T. C. (1935). *Principles of animal psychology.* New York: McGraw-Hill.

Maier, R. A. (1963a). Maternal behavior in the domestic hen: The role of pretest restriction of movement. *Journal of Comparative & Physiological Psychology, 56,* 350–356.

Maier, R. A. (1963b). Maternal behavior in the domestic hen: The role of physical contact. *Journal of Comparative & Physiological Psychology, 56,* 357–361.

Maier, R. A. (1964). The role of the dominance-submission ritual in social recognition of hens. *Animal Behaviour, 12,* 59.

Maier, R. A. (1968). The effects of stress upon social distance in dolphins. *Perceptual & Motor Skills, 27,* 862.

Maier, R. A., Jr. (1983). *The relationship between perceived attractiveness and facial features of premature and full-term infants.* Doctoral dissertation, Loyola University, Chicago.

Mann, N. I., & Slater, P. J. B. (1995). Song tutor choice by zebra finches in aviaries. *Animal Behaviour, 49,* 811–820.

Marchesseault, L., & Ewald, P. W. (1991). Effect of territory quality on intrusion rate in non-breeding hummingbirds. *Behavior Ecology and Sociobiology, 28,* 305–308.

Margoliash, D., Staicer, C. A., & Inoue, S. A. (1991). Stereotyped and plastic song in adult indigo buntings, *Passerina cyanea. Animal Behaviour, 42,* 367–388.

Margulis, L. (1970). *Origin of eukaryotic cells.* New Haven, CT: Yale University Press.

Margulis, L., & Sagan, D. (1988). Sex: The cannibalistic legacy of primordial androgynes. In R. Belling & G. Stevens (Eds.), *The evolution of sex.* San Francisco: Harper & Row.

Marks, I. M. (1987). *Fears, phobias, and rituals.* New York: Oxford University Press.

Marler, P. (1970). Birdsong and speech development: Could there be parallels? *American Scientist, 58,* 669–673.

Martin, G. M., & Bellingham, W. P. (1979). Learning of visual food aversions by chicken *(Gallus gallus)* over long delays. *Behavioral Neural Biology, 24,* 58–68.

Martin, P. (1984). The time and energy costs of play behaviour in the cat. *Zeitschrift für Tierpsychologie, 64,* 298–312.

Mason, W. A. (1978). Social experience and primate cognitive development. In G. M. Burghardt & M. Bekoff (Eds.), *The development of behavior: Comparative and evolutionary aspects.* New York: Garland STPM.

Masserman, J. H. (1943). *Behavior and neurosis.* Chicago: University of Chicago Press.

Massey, A. (1988). Sexual interactions in red-spotted newt populations. *Animal Behaviour, 36,* 205–210.

Mathis, A., Chivers, D., & Smith, R. (1996). Cultural transmission of predator recognition in fishes: Intraspecific and interspecific learning. *Animal Behaviour, 51,* 185–201.

Mauck, R. A., & Grubb, T. C., Jr. (1995). Petrel parents shunt all experimentally increased reproductive costs to their offspring. *Animal Behaviour, 49,* 999–1008.

Mayer, J. (1955). Regulation of energy intake and the body weight: The glucostatic theory and the lipostatic hypothesis. *Annals of the New York Academy of Science, 63,* 15–43.

Maynard Smith, J. (1973). The logic of animal conflict. *Nature, 246,* 15–18.

Maynard Smith, J. (1974). The theory of games and the evolution of animal conflict. *Journal of Theoretical Biology, 47,* 209–221.

Maynard Smith, J. (1982). *Evolution and the theory of games.* Cambridge, England: Cambridge University Press.

McAdams, D. P., & Vaillant, G. E. (1982). Intimacy motivation and psychosocial adjustment: A longitudinal study. *Journal of Personality Assessment, 46,* 586–593.

McAllister, M. K., Roitberg, B. D., & Weldon, K. L. (1990). Adaptive suicide in pea aphids: Decisions are cost sensitive. *Animal Behaviour, 40,* 167–175.

McClintock, J. B., & Janssen, J. (1990). Pteropod abduction as a chemical defence in a pelagic antarctic amphipod. *Nature, 346,* 462–464.

McClintock, M. K. (1971). Menstrual synchrony and suppression. *Nature, 229,* 224–245.

McComb, K. E. (1991). Roaring by red deer stags advances date of oestrus in hinds. *Nature, 330,* 648–649.

McCormick, D. A., & Thompson, R. F. (1984). Cerebellum: Essential involvement in the classically conditioned eyelid response. *Science, 223,* 296–299.

McCracken, G. F. (1993). Locational memory and female-pup reunions in Mexican free-tailed bat maternity colonies. *Animal Behaviour, 45,* 811–813.

McCune, L., Roug-Hellichius, L., Vihman, M. M., Bordenave Delery, D., & Gogate, L. (1996). Grunt communication in human infants *(Homo sapiens). Journal of Comparative Psychology, 110,* 27–37.

McDonald, D. B. (1989). Correlates of male mating success in a lekking bird with male-male cooperation. *Animal Behaviour, 37,* 1007–1022.

McNamara, J. M., & Houston, A. I. (1992). Evolutionarily stable levels of vigilance as a function of group size. *Animal Behaviour, 43,* 641–658.

Mech, L. D. (1970). *The wolf: The ecology and behavior of an endangered species.* Garden City, NY: Natural History Press.

Melton, C. E., & Bartanowicz, R. S. (1983). *Biological rhythms and rotating shift work: Some consideration for air traffic controllers and managers.* Springfield, VA: U.S. Department of Commerce.

Menzel, C. R. (1991). Cognitive aspects of foraging in Japanese monkeys. *Animal Behaviour, 41,* 397–402.

Metz, K. J., & Weatherhead, P. J. (1991). Color bands function as secondary sexual traits in male red-winged blackbirds. *Behavioral Ecology and Sociobiology, 28,* 23–27.

Michelsen, A., Andersen, B. B., Storm, J., Kirchner, W. H,. & Lindauer, M. (1992). How honeybees perceive communication dances, studied by means of a mechanical model. *Behavioral Ecology and Sociobiology, 30,* 143–150.

Milinski, M. (1984). Parasites determine a predator's optimal feeding strategy. *Behavioural Ecology and Sociobiology, 15,* 35–38.

Milinski, M. (1992). Predator inspection: Cooperation or "safety in numbers"? *Animal Behaviour, 43,* 679–680.

Milton, K. (1993). Diet and primate evolution. *Scientific American, 269,* 70–77.

Mishkin, M., & Appenzeller, T. (1987). The anatomy of memory. *Scientific American, 256,* 80–89.

Mitani, J. C. (1984). The behavioral regulation of monogamy in gibbons *(Hylobates muelleri). Behavioral Ecology and Sociobiology, 15,* 225–229.

Mock, B. A., & Gill, D. E. (1984). The infrapopulation dynamics of trypanosomes in red-spotted newts. *Parasitology, 88,* 267–282.

Mock, D. W. (1984). Siblicidal aggression and resource monopolization in birds. *Science, 225,* 731–733.

Mock, D. W., & Ploger, B. J. (1987). Parental manipulation of optimal hatch asynchrony in catle egrets: An experimental study. *Animal Behaviour, 35,* 150–160.

Moffatt, C. A., & Hogan, J. A. (1992). Ontogeny of chick responses to maternal food calls in the Burmese Red Junglefowl *(Gallus gallus spadiceus). Journal of Comparative Psychology, 106,* 92–96.

Moffitt, T. E., Caspi, A., Belsky, J., & Silva, P. A. (1992). Childhood experience and the onset of menarche: A test of a sociobiological model. *Child Development, 63,* 47–58.

Moller, A. P. (1990). Effects of a hematophagous mite on the barn swallow *(Hirundo rustica):* A test of the Hamilton and Zuk hypothesis. *Evolution, 44,* 771–784.

Moller, P. (1995). *Electric fishes: History and behaviour.* London, England: Chapman & Hall.

Moltz, H., & Leidahl, L. C. (1977). Bile, prolactin, and the maternal pheromone. *Science, 196,* 81–83.

Moore, J., & Gotelli, N. J. (1990). A phylogenetic perspective on the evolution of altred host behaviours: A critical look at the manipulation hypothesis. In C. J. Barnard & J. M. Behnke (Eds.), *Parasitism and host behaviour.* London, England: Taylor & Francis.

Morris, D. (1957). "Typical intensity" and its relation to the problem of ritualization. *Behaviour, 11,* 1–12.

Morris, D. (1967). *The naked ape.* New York: McGraw-Hill.

Morris, P. H., Reddy, V., & Bunting, R. C. (1995). The survival of the cutest: Who's responsible for the evolution of the teddy bear? *Animal Behaviour, 50,* 1697–1700.

Morton, E. S. (1977). On the occurrence and significance of motivation-structural roles in some bird and animal sounds. *American Nautralist, 111,* 855–869.

Moulton, D. G. (1977). Minimum odorant concentrations detectable by the dog and their implications for olfactory receptor sensitivity. In D. Miller-Schwarze & M. M. Mozell (Eds.), *Chemical signals in vertebrates.* New York: Plenum Press.

Mountjoy, D. J., & Lemon, R. E. (1996). Female choice for complex song in the European starling: A field experiment. *Behavioral Ecology Sociobiology, 38,* 65–71.

Mountjoy, P. T. (1980). An historical approach to comparative psychology. In M. R. Denny (Ed.), *Comparative psychology: An evolutionary analysis of animal behavior.* New York: Wiley.

Moynihan, M. H. (1970). Control, suppression, decay, disappearance and replacement of displays. *Journal of Theoretical Biology, 29,* 85–112.

Müller-Schwarze, D. (1971). Pheromones in black-tailed deer *(Odocoileus hemiounus colombianus). Animal Behaviour, 19,* 141–152.

Mundinger, P. C., (1995). Behaviour-genetic analysis of canary song: Inter-strain differences in sensory learning, and epigenetic rules. *Animal Behaviour, 50,* 1491–1511.

Myers, D. G. (1983). *Social psychology* (5th ed). New York: McGraw-Hill.

Myles, T. G. (1988). Resource inheritance in social evolution from termits to man. In *The ecology of social behavior.* San Diego: Academic Press.

Nakashima, H. (1986). Phase shifting of the circadian conidiation rhythm in *Neurospora crassa* by calmodulin antagonists. *Journal of Biological Rhythms, 1,* 163–169.

Nelson, D. A., Marler, P., & Palleroni, A. (1995). A comparative approach to vocal learning: Intraspecific variation in the learning process. *Animal Behaviour, 50,* 83–97.

Newman, E. A., & Hartline, P. H. (1982). The infrared "vision" of snakes. *Science in America, 246,* 116–124.

Nicholson, N. A. (1982). *Weaning and development of indepedence in olive baboons.* Doctoral dissertation, Harvard University, Cambridge, MA.

Nilsson, J. A., & Smith, H. G. (1994). Energetic bottle-necks during breeding and reproductive costs of being too early. *Journal of Animal Ecology, 63,* 200–208.

Noirot, E. (1972). Ultrasounds and maternal behavior in small mammals. *Developmental Psychobiology, 5,* 371–387.

Norman, C. (1986). Politics and science clash on African AIDS. *Science, 230,* 1140–1141.

Norris, K. (1993). Seasonal variation in the reproductive success of blue tits: An experimental study. *Journal of Animal Ecology, 62,* 287–294.

Nottebohm, F. (1987). Plasticity in adult avian central nervous system: Possible relations between hormones, learning, and brain repair. In F. Plum (Ed.), *Higher functions of the nervous system, Sec. 1, Vol. 5: Handbook of physiology.* Washington, DC: American Physiology Society.

Nottebohm, F. (1991). Reassessing the mechanisms and origins of vocal learning in birds. *Trends in Neuroscience, 14,* 206–210.

Novotny, M., Jemiolo, B., Harvey, S., Wiesler, D., & Marchlewska-Koj, A. (1986). Adrenal-mediated endogenous metabolites inhibit puberty in female mice. *Science, 231,* 722–725.

Nowak, R. (1991). Senses involved in discrimination of merino ewes at close contact and from a distance by their newborn lambs. *Animal Behaviour, 42,* 357–366.

Nowak, R., Poindron, P., & Putu, I. G. (1989). Development of mother discrimination by single and multiple newborn lambs. *Developmental Psychobiology, 22,* 833–845.

Numan, M. (1974). Medial preoptic area and maternal behavior in the female rat. *Journal of Comparative and Physiological Psychology, 87,* 746–759.

Oaknin, S., Rodriguez del Castillo, A., Guerra, M., Battaner, E., & Mas, M. (1989). Change in forebrain Na,K-ATPase activity and serum hormone levels during sexual behavior in male rats. *Physiology and Behavior, 45,* 407–410.

Ode, P. J., Antolin, M. F., & Strand, M. R. (1995). Brood-mate avoidance in the parasitic wasp *Bracon hebetor* Say. *Animal Behaviour, 49,* 1239–1248.

Oden, D. L., Thompson, R. K. R., & Premack, D. (1988). Spontaneous transfer of matching by infant chimpanzees. *Journal of Experimental Psychology: Animal Behavior Processes, 14,* 140–145.

Olds, J., & Milner, P. (1954). Positive reinforcement produced by electrical stimulation of septal area and other regions of rat brain. *Journal of Comparative and Physiological Psychology, 47,* 419–427.

Olton, D. S., & Samuelson, R. J. (1976). Remembrance of places passed: Spatial memory in rats. *Journal of Experimental Psychology: Animal Behavioral Processes, 2,* 97–116.

Orians, G. H., & Heerwagen, J. H. (1992). Evolved responses to landscapes. In J. Barkow, L. Cosmides, & J. Tooby (Eds.), *The adapted mind.* New York: Oxford University Press.

Oring, L. W. (1985). Avian polyandry. *Current Ornithology, 3,* 309–351.

Overmann, S. R. (1980). Feeding behaviors. In M. R. Denny (Ed.), *Comparative psychology: An evolutionary analysis of animal behavior.* New York: Wiley.

Owens, D., & Owens, M. (1996). Social dominance and reproductive patterns in brown hyaenas, *Hyaena brunnea,* of the central Kalahari desert. *Animal Behaviour, 51,* 535–551.

Pack, A., & Herman, L. (1995). Sensory integration in the bootlenosed dolphin: Immediate recognition of complex shapes across the senses of echolocation and vision. *Journal of Accoustical Society of America, 98,* 722–733.

Packer, C. (1977). Reciprocal altruism in *Papio anubis. Nature, 265,* 441–443.

Packer, C. (1986). The ecology of felid sociality. In D. J. Rubenstein & R. W. Wrangham (Eds.), *Ecological aspects of social evolution.* Princeton, NJ: Princeton University Press.

Packer, C., Scheel, D., & Pusey, A. E. (1990). Why lions form groups: Food is not enough. *American Nature, 136,* 1–19.

Paine, R. T. (1966). Food web completexity and species diversity. *American Nature, 100,* 65–76.

Papi, F., & Pardi, L. (1959). Nuovi reperti sull' orientamento lunari di Talitrus saltator Montagu *(Crustacea Amphipoda). Z. Vergl. Physiology, 41,* 583–596.

Parker, G. A. (1974). Assessment strategy and the evolution of fighting behaviour. *Journal of Theoretical Biology, 47,* 223–243.

Partridge, B. L., & Pitcher, T. J. (1980). The sensory basis of fish schools: Relative roles of lateral line and vision. *Journal of Comparative Physiology, 135A,* 315–325.

Partridge, L. (1980). Mate choice increases a component of offspring fitness in fruit flies. *Nature, 283,* 290–291.

Paton, D. C., & Ford, H. A. (1983). The influence of plant characteristics and honyeater size on levels of pollination in Australian plants. In C. E. Jones & R. J. Little (Eds.), *Handbook of experimental pollination biology.* New York: Van Nostrand Reinhold.

Patterson, M. A., & Vessey, S. H. (1973). Tapeworm *(Hymenolepis nana)* infection in male albino mice: Effect of fighting among the hosts. *Journal of Mammal, 54,* 784–786.

Pavlov, I. P. (1927). *Conditioned reflexes.* Oxford, England: Oxford University Press.

Payne, K. B., Langbauer, W. R., Jr., & Thomas, E. M. (1986). Infrasonic calls of the Asian elephant *(Elephas maximum). Behavioral Ecology & Sociobiology, 18,* 297–301.

Payne, R. S., & McVay, S. (1971). Songs of humpback whales. *Science, 173,* 585–597.

Pearce, J. M. (1987). *Introduction to animal cognition.* Hillsdale, NJ: Erlbaum.

Pengelley, E. T., & Asmundson, S. J. (1970). The effect of light on the free-running circnnual rhythm of the golden-mantled ground squirrel, *Citellus lateralis. Comparative Biochemical Physiology, 30,* 177–183.

Penna, M., & Solis, R. (1996). Influence of burrow acoustics on sound reception by frogs *Eupsophus (Leptodactylidae). Animal Behaviour, 51,* 255–263.

Pepperberg, I. M. (1992). Proficient performance of a conjunctive, recursive task by an African gray parrott *(Psittacus erithacus). Journal of Comparative Psychology, 106*(3), 295–305.

Perdeck, A. C. (1964). An experiment on the ending of autumn migration in starlings. *Ardea, 52,* 133–139.

Perrill, S. A., Gerhardt, H. C., & Daniel, R. (1978). Sexual paraitism in the green tree frog *(Holy cinerea). Science, 200,* 1179–1180.

Persky, H., Lief, H. L., Strauss, D., Miller, W. R., & O'Brien, C. P. (1978). Plasma testosterone level and sexual behavior of couples. *Archives of Sexual Behavior.*

Petranka, J. W., & Thomas, D. A. G. (1995). Explosive breeding reduces egg and tadpole cannibalism in the wood frog, *Rana sylvatica. Animal Behaviour, 50,* 731–739.

Petrie, M. (1983). Female moorhens compete for small fat males. *Science, 220,* 413–415.

Petrie, M., Halliday, T., & Sanders, C. (1991). Peahens prefer peacocks with elaborate trains. *Animal Behaviour, 41,* 323–331.

Petrinovich, L. (1990). Avian song development: Methodological and conceptual issues. In D. A. Dewsbury (Ed.), *Contemporary issues in comparative psychology.* Sunderland, MA: Sinauer Associates.

Pfaff, D. W., & Sakuma, Y. (1979). Deficit in the lordosis reflex of female rats caused by lesions in the ventromedial nucleus of the hypothalamus. *Journal of Physiology, 288,* 203–210.

Pfennig, D. W., Loeb, M. L. G., & Collins, J. P. (1991). Pathogens as a factor limiting the spread of cannibalism in tiger salamanders. *Oecologia, 88,* 161–166.

Pfennig, D. W., Reeve, H. K., & Sherman, P. W. (1993). Kin recognition and cannibalism in spadefoot toad tadpoles. *Animal Behaviour, 46,* 87–94.

Phelps, M. T., & Roberts, W. A. (1989). Central-place foraging by Rattus Norvegicus on a radial maze. *Journal of Comparative Psychology, 103,* 326–338.

Phillips, A. G., Coury, A., Fiorino, D., LePiane, F. G., Brown, E., & Fibiger, H. D. (1992). *Annals of the New York Academy of Sciences, 654,* 199–206.

Pianka, E. R. (1970). On *r* and *K* selection. *American Nature, 102,* 592–597.

Picker, M. D., Leon, B., & Londt, J. G. H. (1991). The hypertrophied hindwings of Palmipenna aeoleoptera Picker, 1987 *(Neuroptera: Nemopteridae),* reduce attack by robber flies by increasing apparent body size. *Animal Behaviour, 42,* 821–825.

Pitcher, T. J., & Parrish, J. K. (1993). Functions of shoaling behavior in teleosts. In T. J. Pitcher (Ed.), *Behavior of teleost fishes* (2nd ed.). London, England: Chapman & Hall.

Pohl-Apel, G., & Sossinka, R. (1984). Hormonal determination of song capacity in females of the zebra finch: Critical phase of treatment. *Zeitschrift für Tierpsychologie, 64,* 330–336.

Poindron, P., & LeNeidre, P. (1980). Endocrine and sensory regulation of maternal behaviour in the ewe. *Advanced Study of Behavior, 11,* 75–119.

Pollak, G. D., Marsh, D., Bodenhamer R., & Souther A. (1977). Echo-detecting characteristics of neurons in inferior colliculus of unanesthetized bats. *Science, 196,* 675–677.

Popper, A. N., & Fay, R. R. (Eds.). (1995). *Hearing of bats.* Berlin, Germany: Springer-Verlag.

Popper, A. N., & Platt, C. (1983). Sensory surface of the saccule and lagena in the ears of ostariophysan fishes. *Journal of Morphology, 176,* 121.

Porter, J. M. (1990). Patterns of recruitment to the breeding group in the kittiwake *Rissa tridacyla*. *Animal Behaviour, 40,* 350–360.

Poucet, B. (1993). Spatial cognitive maps in animals: New hypotheses on their structure and neural mechanisms. *Psychological Review, 100,* 163–182.

Poucet, B., Herrmann, T., & Buhot, M. C. (1991). Effects of short-lasting inactivations of the ventral hippocampus and medial septum on long-term and short-term acquisition of spatial information in rats. *Behavioural Brain Research, 44,* 53–65.

Poulin, R. (1992). Altered behaviour in parasitized bumblebees: Parasite manipulation or adaptive suicide? *Animal Behaviour, 44,* 174–176.

Poulin, R., & Vickery, W. L. (1996). Parasite-mediated sexual selection: Just how choosey are parasitized females? *Behavioral Ecology and Sociobiology, 38,* 43–49.

Povinelli, D. J. (1993). Reconstructing the evolution of mind. *American Psychologist, 48,* 493–509.

Povinelli, D. J., Nelson, K. E., & Boysen, S. T. (1990). Inferences about guessing and knowing by chimpanzees. *Journal of Comparative Psychology, 104,* 203–210.

Powlesland, R. G. (1980). Food-storing behavior of the South Island robin. *Mauri Ora, 8,* 11–20.

Powley, T. L. (1977). The ventromedial hypothalamic syndrome, satiety, and a cephalic phase hypothesis. *Psychological Review, 84,* 89–126.

Premack, D. (1965). Reinforcement theory. In D. Levine (Ed.), *Nebraska symposium on motivation* (Vol. 13). Lincoln: University of Nebraska Press.

Premack, D. (1971). On the assessment of language competence in the chimpanzee. In A. M. Schrier & F. Stollnitz (Eds.), *Behavior of nonhuman primates* (Vol. 4). New York: Academic Press.

Prescott, C. A., Hewitt, J. K., Truett, K. R., Heath, A. C., Neale, M.C., & Eaves, L. J. (1994). Genetic and environmental influences on lifetime alcohol-related problems in a volunteer sample of older twins. *Journal of Studies on Alcohol, 55,* 184–202.

Profet, M. (1993). Menstruation as a defense against pathogens transmitted by sperm. *Quarterly Review of Biology, 68,* 335–386.

Provine, R. R. (1995). The study of laughter provides a novel approach to the mechanisms and evolution of vocal production, perception and social behavior. *American Scientist, 84.*

Pugesek, B. H. (1981). Increased reproductive effort with age in the California gull *(Larus californicus). Science, 212,* 822–823.

Pusey, A. E., & Packer, C. (1987). The evolution of sex-biased dispersal in lions. *Behaviour, 101,* 275–310.

Quinn, T. P., & Dittman, A. H. (1990). Pacific salmon migrations and homing: Mechanisms and adaptive significance. *Trends in Ecology and Evolution, 5,* 174–177.

Rado, R., Wolleberg, Z., & Terkel, J. (1991). The ontogeny of seismic communication during dispersal in the blind mole rat. *Animal Behaviour, 42,* 15–21.

Rainbow, T. C., Snyder, L., Berck, D. J., & McEwen, B. S. (1984). Correlation of muscarinic receptor induction in the ventromedial hypothalamic nucleus with the activation of feminine sexual behavior by estradiol. *Neuroendocrinology, 39,* 476–480.

Ralls, K., Brugger, K., & Ballou, J. (1979). Inbreeding and juvenile mortality in small populations of ungulates. *Science, 206,* 1101–1103.

Ralph, M. R., Foster, R. G., Davis, F. C., & Menaker, M. (1990). Transplanted suprachiasmatic nucleus determines circadian period. *Science, 247,* 975–978.

Randall, J. A. (1989). Individual footdrumming signatures in banner-tailed kangaroo rats *Dipodomys spectabilis. Animal Behaviour, 38,* 620–630.

Randall, J. A. (1995). Modification of footdrumming signatures by kangaroo rats: Changing territories and gaining new neighbors. *Animal Behaviour, 49,* 1227–1237.

Ranta, E., Peuhkuri, N., Laurila, A., Rita, H., & Metcalfe, N. B. (1995). Producers, scroungers and foraging group structure. *Animal Behaviour, 51,* 171–175.

Reebs, S. G., & Colgan, P. W. (1991). Nocturnal care of eggs and circadian rhythms of fanning activity in two normally diurnal cichlid fishes, *Cichlasoma nigrofasciatum* and *Herotilapia multispinosa. Animal Behaviour, 41,* 303–311.

Regnier, F. E., & Wilson, E. O. (1971). Chemical communication and "propaganda" in slave-maker ants. *Science, 172,* 267–269.

Reichman, O. J. (1979). Subtly suited to a seedy existence. *New Scientist, 81,* 658–660.

Reid, L. D. (1990). Rates of cocaine addiction among newborns. Personal communication, Rensselaer Polytechnic Institute.

Renner, M. (1960). Contribution of the honey bee to the study of time sense and astronomical orietation. *Cold Spring Harbor Symposia on Quantitative Biology, 25,* 361–367.

Rescorla, R. A. (1988). Pavlovian conditioning: It's not what you think it is. *American Psychologist, 43,* 151–160.

Rescorla, R. A., & Wagner, A. R. (1972). A theory of Pavlovian conditioning: Variations in the effectivenesss of reinforcement and nonreinforcement. In A. H. Black & W. F. Prokasy (Eds.), *Classical conditioning II: Current research and theory.* New York: Appleton-Century-Crofts.

Reyer, H. U. (1984). Investment and relatedness: A cost/benefit analysis of breeding and helping in the pied kingfisher. *Animal Behaviour, 32,* 1163–1178.

Reymond, L. (1985). Spatial visual acuity of the eagle *Aquila audax:* A behavioural, optical and anatomical investigation. *Vision Research, 25,* 1477–1491.

Reynolds, J. D. (1987). Mating system and nesting biology of the red-necked phalarope *Phalaropus Iobatus. Ibis, 129,* 225–242.

Richardson, W. J., Greene, C. R., Jr., Malme, C. I., & Thomson, D. H. (1995). *Marine mammals and noise.* San Diego: Academic Press.

Richmond, G., & Clemens, L. (1988). Ventromedial hypothalamic lesions and cholinergic control of female sexual behavior. *Physiology and Behavior, 42,* 179–182.

Richter, C. P. (1943). Total self-regulatory functions in animals and human beings. *Harvey Lecturer, 38,* 63–103.

Rindos, D. (1984). *The origins of agriculture: An evolutionary perspective.* Orlando, FL: Academic Press.

Rintamaki, P. T., Alatalo, R. V., Hoglund, J., & Lundberg, A. (1995). Male territoriality and female choice on black grouse leks. *Animal Behaviour, 49,* 759–767.

Ritchison, G., Belthoff, J. R., & Sparks, E. J. (1992). Dispersal restlessness: Evidence for innate dispersal by juvenile eastern screech-owls? *Animal Behaviour, 43,* 57–65.

Ritter, S., Calingasan, N. Y., Hutton, B., & Dinh, T. T. (1992). Cooperation of vagal and central neural systems in monitoring metabolic events controlling feeding behavior. In S. Ritter, R. C. Ritter, & C.D. Barnes (Eds.), *Neuroanatomy and physiology of abdominal vagal afferents.* Boca Raton, FL: CRC.

Roberts, E. P., Jr., & Weigl, P. D. (1984). Habitat preference in the dark-eyed junco *(Junco Hyemalis):* The role of photoperiod and dominance. *Animal Behaviour, 32,* 709–714.

Roberts, W. A. (1992). Foraging by rats on a radial maze: Learning, memory, and decision rules. In I. Gormezano & E. A. Wasserman (Eds.), *Learning and memory: The behavioral and biological substrates.* Hillsdale, NJ: Erlbaum.

Roberts, W. A., & Grant, D. S. (1976). Studies of short-term memory in the pigeon using the delayed matching to sample procedure. In D. L. Medin, W. A. Roberts, & R. T. Davis (Eds.), *Processes of animal memory.* Hillsdale, NJ: Erlbaum.

Rodd, F. H., & Sokolowski, M. B. (1995). Complex origins of variation in the sexual behaviour of male Trinidadian guppies, *Poecilia reticulata:* Interactions between social environment, heredity, body size and age. *Animal Behaviour, 49,* 1139–1159.

Rodin, J. (1984). A sense of control. *Psychology Today*, 38–45.

Roeder, K. D. (1970). Episodes in insect brains. *American Scientist, 58*, 378–389.

Roitblat, H. L., & von Fersten, H. (1992). Comparative cognition: Representations and processes in learning and memory. *Annual Review Psychology, 43*, 671–710.

Roitblat, H. L., & von Fersten, L. (1992). Representations and processes in learning and memory. *Annual Review Psychology, 43*, 671–710.

Rongstad, O. J., & Tester, J. R. (1971). Behavior and maternal relations of young snowshoe hares. *Journal of Wildlife Management, 35*, 338–346.

Rose, L. M., & Fedigan, L. M. (1995). Vigilance in white-faced capuchins, *Cepus capucinus*, in Costa Rica. *Animal Behaviour, 49*, 63–70.

Roselli, C. E., Handa, R. J., & Resko, J. A. (1989). Quantitative distribution of nuclear androgen receptors in microdissected areas of the rat brain. *Neuroendocrinology, 49*, 449–453.

Rosenzweig, M., Krech, D., Bennett, E. L., & Diamond, M. (1962). Effects of environmental complexity and training on brain chemistry and anatomy: A replication and extension. *Journal of Comparative and Physiological Psychology, 55*, 429–437.

Roth, D. L., Wiebe, D. J., Fillingim, R. G., & Shay, K. A. (1989). Life events, fitness, hardiness, and health: A simultaneous analysis of proposed stress-resistance effects. *Journal of Personality and Social Psycholgy, 57*, 136–142.

Rothstein, S. I., Yokel, D. A., & Fleischer, R. C. (1988). The agonistic and sexual functions of vocalizations of male brown-headed cowbirds, *Molothrus ater. Animal Behaviour, 36*, 73–86.

Rowe, M. P., Coss, R. G., & Owings, D. H. (1986). Rattlesnake rattles and burrowing owl hisses: A case of acoustic Batesian mimicry. *Ethology, 72*, 53–71.

Rumbaugh, D. M., & Gill, T. V. (1976). The mastery of language-type skills by the chimpanzee Pan. *Annals of the New York Academy of Sciences, 280*, 572–578.

Russell, M. J. (1976). Human olfactory communication. *Nature, 260*, 520–522.

Russell, M. J., Switz, G. M., & Thompson, K. (1978). *Olfactory influences in the human menstrual.* Paper presented at the meeting of the American Association for the Advancement of Science, San Francisco.

Russon, A. E., & Galdikas, B. M. F. (1995). Constraints on great apes' imitation: Model and action selectivity in rehabilitant orangutan *(Pongo pygmaeus)* imitation. *Journal of Comparative Psychology, 109*, 5–17.

Rutter, M. L. (1997). Nature-nurture integration: The example of antisocial behavior. *American Psychologist, 52*, 390–398.

Sachs, B. D., & Meisel, R. L. (1988). The physiology of male sexual behavior. In E. Knobil & J. Neill (Eds.), *The physiology of reproduction.* New York: Raven Press.

Sadun, A. A., Schaechter, J. D., & Smith, L. E. H. (1984). A retinohypothalamic pathway in man: Light mediation of circadian rhythms. *Brain Research, 302*, 371–377.

Sakuma, Y., & Pfaff, D. W. (1979). Facilitation of female reproductive behavior from mesencephalic central grey in the rat. *American Journal of Physiology, 237*, R278–R284.

Sandell, M., & Smith, H. G. (1991). Dominance, prior occupancy, and winter residency in the great tit *(Parus major). Behavioral Ecological Sociobiology, 29*, 147–152.

Sargent, R. C. (1981). *Sexual selection and reproductive effort in the three spine sticleback* Gasterosteus aculeatus. Doctoral dissertation, State University of New York, Stonybrook.

Sargent, R. C. (1989). Parental investment decision rules and the Concorde fallacy. *Behavior Ecology and Sociobiology, 17*, 43.

Sargent, R. C., & Gross, M. R. (1985). Parental investment decision rules and the Concorde fallacy. *Behaviour Ecology and Sociobiology, 17*, 43–45.

Sargent, R. C., Gross, M. R., & Vanden Berghe, E. P. (1986). Male mate choice in fishes. *Animal Behaviour, 34*, 545–550.

Sauer, E. G. F. (1963). Migration habits of golden plovers. *Processes of the 13th International Ornithological Congregation, 454–467.*

Sauer, E. G. F. (1971). Celestial rotation and stellar orientation in migrating warblers. *Science, 173,* 459–460.

Savage-Rumbaugh, E. S. (1986). *Ape language: From conditioned response to symbol.* New York: Columbia University Press.

Savage-Rumbaugh, E. S. (1988). A new look at ape language: comprehension of vocal speech and syntax. In D. W. Leger (Ed.), *Nebraska symposium on motivation.* Lincoln: University of Nebraska Press.

Savage-Rumbaugh, E. S., & Lewin, R. (1994). *Kanzi: At the brink of the human mind.* New York: Wiley.

Savory, T. (1965). Courtship behavior of arachnids. *National History, 74,* 52–56.

Schaal, B., & Porter, R. (1991). "Microsmatic humans" revisited: The generation and perception of chemical signals. In P. Slater, J. Rosenblatt, C. Beer, & M. Milinski (Eds.), *Advances in the study of behavior.* San Diego: Academic Press.

Schall, J. J. (1982). Lizard malaria: Parasite-host ecology. In R. B. Huey, E. R. Pianka, & T. W. Schoener (Eds.), *Lizard ecology: Studies of a model organism.* Cambridge: Harvard University Press.

Schaller, G. B. (1972). *The Serengeti lion.* Chicago: University of Chicago Press.

Schenkel, R. (1967). Submission: Its features and function in the wolf and dog. *American Zoologist, 7*(2), 319–329.

Schieffelin, J. S., & Sherman, P. W. (1995) Tugging contests reveal feeding hierarchies in naked mole-rat colonies. *Animal Behaviour, 49,* 537–541

Schlupp, I., Marler, C., & Ryan, M. J. (1994). Benefit to male sailfin mollies of mating with heterospecific females. *Science, 263,* 373–374.

Schneider, D. (1974). The sex-attractant receptor of moths. *Scientific American, 231*(1), 28–35.

Schoener, T. W., & Toft, C. A. (1983). Spider populations: Extraordinarily high densities on islands without top predators. *Science, 219,* 353–355.

Schrier, A. M., & Brady, P. M. (1987). Categorization of natural stimuli by monkeys *(Macaca mulatta):* Effects of stimulus set size and modification of exemplars. *Journal of Experimental Psychology: Animal Behavior Processes, 13,* 136–143.

Schwagmeyer, P. L. (1995). Searching today for tomorrow's mates. *Animal Behaviour, 50,* 759–767.

Schwagmeyer, P. L., & Parker, G. A. (1990). Male mate choice as predicted by sperm competition in thirteen-lined ground squirrels. *Nature, 348,* 62–64.

Scott, D., & Jackson, L. L. (1990). The basis for control of post-mating sexual attractiveness by *Drosophila melanogaster* females. *Animal Behaviour, 40,* 891–900.

Scott, J. P., & Fredericson, E. (1951). The causes of fighting in mice and rats. *Physiological Zoology, 24,* 273–309.

Scott, M. P., & Traniello, J. F. A. (1990). Behavioural and ecological correlates of male and female parental care and reproductive success in burying beetles *(Nicrophorus spp.). Animal Behaviour, 39,* 274–283.

Sealy, S. G. (1995). Burial of cowbird eggs by parasitized yellow warblers: An empirical and experimental study. *Animal Behaviour, 49,* 877–889.

Searcy, W. A., Eriksson, D., & Lundberg, A. (1991). Deceptive behavior in pied flycatchers. *Behavioral Ecology and Sociobiology, 29,* 167–175.

Sebeok, T. (1979). Performing animals. *Psychology Today, 79,* 78–91.

Seligman, M. (1995). *The optimistic child.* Boston: Houghton Mifflin.

Seligman, M. E. P. (1975). *Helplessness: On depression, development and death.* San Francisco: Freeman.

Seligman, M. E. P. (1989). Explanatory style: Predicting depression, achievement, and health. In M. D. Yapko (Ed.), *Brief therapy approaches to treating anxiety and depression.* New York: Brunner/Mazel.

Seligman, M. E. P. (1991). *Learned optimism.* New York: Knopf.

Seligman, M. E. P., & Maier, S. (1967). Failure to escape traumatic shock. *Journal of Experimental Psychology, 74,* 1–9.

Selye, H. (1976). *The stress of life* (2nd ed.) New York: McGraw-Hill.

Semm, P., Nohr, D., Demaine, C., & Wiltschko, W. (1984). Neural basis of the magnetic compass: Interaction of visual, magnetic, and vestibular inputs in the pigeon's brain. *Journal of Physiology, 155,* 283–288.

Sendova-Franks, A. B., & Franks, N. R. (1995). Spatial relationships within nests of the ant *Leptothorax unifasciatus* (Latr.) and their implications for the division of labour. *Animal Behaviour, 50,* 121–136.

Seraganian, P. (Ed.). (1993). *Exercise psychology: The influence of physical exercise on psychological processes.* New York: Wiley.

Seyfarth, R., Cheney, D. L., Harcourt, A. H., & Stewart, K. J. (1994). The acoustic features of gorilla double grunts and their relation to behavior. *American Journal of Primatology, 33,* 31–50.

Shaikh, M. B., & Siegel, A. (1989). Naloxone-induced modulation of feline aggression elicited from midbrain periaqueductal gray. *Pharmacology, Biochemistry, and Behavior, 31,* 791–796.

Shaw, E. (1958). The development of visual attraction among schooling fishes. *Biology Bullentin, 115,* 365.

Shaw, E. (1962). The schooling of fishes. *Scientific American, 206*(6), 128–141.

Sherman, P. W. (1985). Alarm calls of Belding's ground squirrels to aerial predators: Nepotism or self-preservation? *Behavioral Ecology and Sociobiology, 17,* 313–323.

Sherry, D. F. (1982). Food storage, memory and marsh tits. *Animal Behaviour, 30,* 631–633.

Sherry, D. F. (1984). Food storage by black-capped chickadees: Memory for the location and contents of caches. *Animal Behaviour, 32,* 451–464.

Sherry, D. F., Jacobs, L. F., & Gaulin, S. J. C. (1992). Spatial memory and adaptive specialization of the hippocampus. *Trends in Neuroscience, 15,* 298–303.

Sherry, D. F., Krebs, J. R., & Cowie, R. (1981). Memory for the location of stored food in marsh tits. *Animal Behaviour, 29,* 1260–1266.

Shettleworth, S. J., Hampton, R. R., & Westwood, R. P. (1995). Effects of season and photoperiod on food storing by black-capped chickadees, *Parus atricapillus. Animal Behaviour, 49,* 989–998.

Shields, W. R., Crook, J. R., Hebblethwaite, M. L., & Wiles-Ehmann, S. S. (1988). Ideal free coloniality in the swallows. In C. Slobodchikoff (Ed.), *The ecology of social behavior.* San Diego: Academic Press.

Siegel, A., & Pott, C. B. (1988). Neural substrates of aggression and flight in the cat. *Progress in Neurobiology, 31,* 261–283.

Sillén-Tullberg, B. (1985). Higher survival of an aposematic form than of a cryptic form of a distasteful bug. *Oecologia, 67,* 411–415.

Silverman, I., & Eals, M. (1992). Sex differences in spatial abilities: Evolutionary theory and data. In J. Barkow, L. Cosmides, & J. Tooby (Eds.), *The adapted mind.* New York: Oxford University Press.

Simons, R. (1990). Copulation patterns of African marsh harriers: Evaluating the paternity assurance hypothesis. *Animal Behaviour, 40,* 1151–1157.

Simpson, G. G. (1958). The study of evolution: Methods and present status of theory. In A. Roe & G. G. Simpson (Eds.), *Behavior and evolution.* New Haven, CT: Yale University Press.

Simpson, S. J., & White, P. R. (1990). Associative learning and locus feeding: Evidence for a "learned hunger" for protein. *Animal Behaviour, 40,* 506–513.

Singh, D. (1993). Adaptive significance of waist-to-hip ratio and female attractiveness. *Journal of Personality and Social Psychology, 51,* 293–307.

Skinner, B. F. (1953). *Science and human behavior.* New York: Macmillan.

Slagsvold, T., & Lifjeld, J. T. (1990). Influence of male and female quality on clutch size in tits *(Parus spp.). Ecology, 71,* 1258–1266.

Slagsvold, T., & Lifjeld, J. T. (1994). Polygyny in birds: The role of competition between females for male parental care. *American Naturalist, 143,* 59–94.

Slijper, E. J. (1962). *Whales.* New York: Basic Books.

Slobodchikoff, C. N., Kiriazis, J., Fischer, C., & Creef, F. (1991). Semantic information distinguishing individual predators in the alarm calls of Gunnison's prarie dogs. *Animal Behaviour, 42,* 713–719.

Slotnick, D. M. (1967). Disturbances of maternal behavior in the rat following lesions of the cingulate cortex. *Behaviour, 29,* 203–236.

Smith, C. C. (1968). The adaptive nature of social organization in the genus of tree squirrel *Tamiasciurus. Ecological Monographs, 38,* 31–63.

Smith, J. N. M., & Sweatman, H. P. A. (1974). Food searching behaviour of tit mice in patchy environments. *Ecology, 55,* 1216–1232.

Smith, R. L. (1976). Male brooding of the waterbug *Abedus Herberti (Hemiptera: Belostomatidae). Annual Entomology of Social America, 69,* 740–747.

Smith, R. L. (1979). Paternity assurance and altered roles in the mating behavior of a giant water bug *Abedus herberti (Heteroptera: Belostomatidae). Animal Behaviour, 27,* 716–728.

Smuts, B. (1987). What are friends for? *Natural History, 2,* 36–44.

Somers, R. L., & Klein, D. C. (1984). Rhodopsin kinase activity in the mammalian pineal gland and other tissues. *Science, 226,* 182–184.

Sorenson, M. D. (1991). The functional significance of parasitic egg laying and typical nesting in redhead ducks: An analysis of individual behaviour. *Animal Behaviour, 42,* 771–796.

Spear, N. E., Miller, J. S., & Jagielo, J. A. (1990). Animal memory and learning. *Annual Review of Psychology, 41,* 169–211.

Spear, N. E., & Rudy, J. W. (1991). Tests of the ortogeny of learning and memory: Issues, methods & results. In H. N. Shair, G. A. Barr, & M. A. Hofer (Eds.), *Developmental psychobiology.* New York: Oxford University Press.

Squire, L. R. (1987). *Memory and brain.* New York: Oxford University Press.

Staddon, J. E. R. (1983). *Adaptive behavior and learning.* Cambridge, England: Cambridge University Press.

Stamps, J. A. (1991). The effect of conspecifics on habitat selection in territorial species. *Behavioral Ecological Sociobiology, 28,* 29–36.

Stander, P. E. (1992). Cooperative hunting in lions: The role of the individual. *Behavioral Ecology and Sociobiology, 29,* 445–454.

Stanford, C. B. (1995). Chimpanzee hunting behavior and human evolution. *American Scientist, 83.*

Stattin, H., & Magnusson, D. (1990). *Pubertal maturation in female development.* Hillsdale, NJ: Erlbaum.

Stebbins, R. C., & Cohen, N. W. (1995). *A natural history of amphibians.* Princeton, NJ: Princeton University Press.

Stebbins, W. C., & Moody, D. B. (1994). How monkeys hear the world: Auditory perception in nonhuman primates. In R. R. Fay & A. N. Popper (Eds.), *Comparative hearing: Mammals.* New York: Springer-Verlag.

Stenseth, N. C., & Ims, R. A. (1993). *The biology of lemmings.* London, England: Academic Press.

Stephens, M. (1982). Mate takeover and possible infanticide by a female northern jacana *(Jacana spinosa). Animal Behaviour, 30,* 1253–1254.

Stern, J. M. (1989). A revised view of the multisensory control of maternal behaviour in rats: Critical role of tactile inputs. In R. J. Blanchard, D. C. Blanchard, S. Parmigiani, & P. F. Brain (Eds.), *Ethoexperimental approaches to the study of behavior.* The Hague, the Netherlands: Nijhoff.

Stewart, K. J. (1987). Spotted hyaenas: The importance of being dominant. *Trends in Ecology and Evolution, 2,* 88–89.

Storey, A. E., & Joyce, T. L. (1995). Pup contact promotes paternal responsiveness in male meadow voles. *Animal Behaviour, 49,* 1–10.

Stouffer, P. C., & Power, H. W. (1991). Brood parasitism by starlings experimentally forced to desert their nests. *Animal Behaviour, 41,* 537–539.

St. Paul, U. V. (1982). Do geese use path integration for walking home? In F. Papi & H. G. Wallraff (Eds.), *Avian navigation.* New York: Springer-Verlag.

Stricker, E. M. (1983). Brain neurochemistry and the control of food intake. In E. Satinoff & P. Teitelbaum (Eds.), *Handbook of behavioral neurobiology. Vol. 6: Motivation.* New York: Plenum Press.

Suomi, S. J. (1973). Surrogate rehabilitation of monkeys reared in total social isolation. *Journal of Children Pschological Psychiatry, 14,* 71–77.

Suter, R. B. (1990). Courtship and the assessment of virginity by male bowl and doily spiders. *Animal Behavior, 39,* 307–313.

Svare, B. (1988). Genotype modulates the aggression-promoting quality of progesterone in pregnant mice. *Hormones and Behavior, 22,* 90–99.

Svensson, E. (1995). Avian reproductive timing: When should parents be prudent? *Animal Behaviour, 49,* 1569–1575.

Swaddle, J. P. (1996). Reproductive success and symmetry in zebra finches. *Animal Behaviour, 51,* 203–210.

Sweeney, B. W., & Vannote, R. L. (1982). Population synchrony in mayflies: A predator satiation hypothesis. *Evolution, 36,* 810–821.

Symons, D. (1979). *The evolution of human sexuality.* New York: Oxford University Press.

Takahashi, L. K. (1990). Hormonal regulation of sociosexual behavior in female mammals. *Neuroscience and Biobehavioral Reviews, 14,* 403–413.

Takahashi, L. K., Baker, E. W., & Kalin, N. H. (1990). Ontogeny of behavioral and hormonal responses to stress in prenatally stressed male rat pups. *Physiology and Behavior, 47,* 357–364.

Takahashi, L. K., Turner, J. G., & Kalin, N. H. (1992). Prenatal stress alters brain catecholaminergic activity and potentiates stress-induced behavior in adult rats. *Brain Research, 574,* 131–137.

Tallamy, D. W., & Horton, L. A. (1990). Costs and benefits of the egg-dumping alternative in *Gargaphia* lace bugs *(Hemiptera: Tingidae). Animal Behaviour, 39,* 352–359.

Taylor, E. B. (1991). Behavioural interaction and habitat use in juvenile chinook, *Oncorhynchus tshawytscha,* and coho, *O. kisutch,* salmon. *Animal Behaviour, 42,* 729–744.

Teleki, G. (1973). *The predatory behavior of wild chimpanzees.* Lewisburg, PA: Bucknell University Press.

Teleki, G. (1974). Chimpanzee subsistence technology: Materials and skills. *Journal of Human Evolution, 3,* 575–594.

Telford, S. R., & Dangerfield, J. M. (1990). Manipulation of the sex ratio and duration of copulation in the tropical millipede *Alloporus uncinatus:* A test of the copulatory guarding hypothesis. *Animal Behaviour, 40,* 984–985.

Temeles, E. J. (1990). Interspecific territoriality of northern harriers: The role of kleptoparasitism. *Animal Behaviour, 40,* 361–366.

ten Cate, C. (1987). Sexual preferences in zebra finch males raised by two species: II. The internal representation resulting from double imprinting. *Animal Behaviour, 35,* 321–330.

ten Cate, C. (1991). Behaviour-contingent exposure to taped song and zebra finch song learning. *Animal Behaviour, 42,* 857–859.

ten Cate, C., & Slater, P. J. B. (1991). Song learning in zebra finches: How are elements from two tutors integrated? *Animal Behaviour, 42,* 150–152.

Terrace, H. S., Petitto, L. A., Sanders, R. J., & Bever, T. G. (1979). Can an ape create a sentence? *Science, 206,* 891–902.

Terrick, T. D., Mumme, R. L., & Burghardt, G. M. (1995). Aposematic coloration enhances chemosensory recognition of noxious prey in the garter snake *Thamnophis radix. Animal Behaviour, 49,* 857–866.

Thompson, S. N., & Kavaliers, M. (1994). Physiological bases for parasite-induced alterations of host behaviour. *Parasitology Supplement, 109,* 119–138.

Thompson, W. F. (1957). Influence of prenatal maternal anxiety on emotionality in young rats. *Science, 125,* 698–699.

Thornhill, R. (1981). *Panorpa (Mecoptera: Panorpidae)* scorpionflies: Systems for understanding resource-defense polygyny and alternative male reproductive efforts. *Annual Review of Ecology and Systematics, 12,* 355–386.

Thornhill, R., & Alcock, J. (1983). *The evolution of insect mating systems.* Cambridge: Harvard University Press.

Thorpe, W. H. (1961). *Bird song.* Cambridge, England: Cambridge University Press.

Tinbergen, N. (1951). *The study of instinct.* London, England: Oxford University Press.

Tinbergen, N. (1959). Comparative studies of the behavior of gulls *(Laridae):* A progress report. *Behaviour, 15,* 1–70.

Tinbergen, N. (1963). The shell menace. *Natural History, 72,* 28–35.

Tinbergen, N., & Perdeck, A. C. (1950). On the stimulus situation releasing the begging response in the newly hatched herring gull chick *(Larus argentatus* Pont). *Behaviour, 3,* 1–38.

Tinklepaugh, O. L. (1928). An experimental study of representative factors in monkeys. *Jounal of Comparative Psychology, 8,* 197–236.

Tokarz, R. R., & Slowinski, J. B. (1990) Alternation of hemipenis use as a behavioural means of increasing sperm transfer in the lizard *Anolis sagrei. Animal Behaviour, 40,* 374–379.

Tolman, E. C., Ritchie, B. F., & Kalish, D. (1946). *Journal of Experimental Psychology, 36,* 13–24.

Tomback, D. F. (1978). Foraging strategies of Clark's nutcrackers. *Living Bird, 16,* 123–161.

Tomlinson, W. T., & Johnston, T. D. (1991). Hamsters remember spatial information derived from olfactory cues. *Animal Learning & Behavior, 19*(2), 185–190.

Toth, N., & Rumbaugh, S. (1993). Pan the toolmaker: Investigations into the stone tool-making and tool using capabilities of a bonobo *(Pan paniscus). Journal of Archeological Science, 20,* 89.

Townshend, T. J., & Wootton, R. J. (1985). Adjusting parental investment to changing environmental conditions: The effect of food ration on parental behaviour of the convict cichlid, *Cichlasoma nigrofasciatum. Animal Behaviour, 33,* 494–501.

Trivers, R. L. (1971). The evolution of reciprocal altruism. *Quarterly Review of Biology, 46,* 35–57.

Trivers, R. L. (1972). Parental investment and sexual selection. In B. Campbell (Ed.), *Sexual selection and the descent of man.* Chicago: Aldine.

Trivers, R. L. (1974). Parent-offspring conflict. *American Zoologist, 14,* 249–264.

Trivers, R. L. (1985). *Social evolution.* Menlo Park, CA: Benjamin/Cummings.

Trivers, R. L., & Hare, H. (1976). Haplodiploidy and the evolution of the social insects. *Science, 191,* 249–263.

Trivers, R. L., & Willard, D. E. (1973). Natural selection of parental ability to vary the sex ratio of offspring. *Science, 179,* 90–92.

Trumler, E. (1959). Das "Rossigkeitsgesicht" und ähnliches Ausdrucksverhalten bei Einhufern. *Zeitschrift für Tierpsychologie, 16,* 478–488.

Tryon, R. C. (1940). Genetic differences in maze-learning ability in rats. In *39th yearbook national society studies education* (Part I). Bloomington, IL: Public School Publishing.

Turner, C. D., & Bagnara, J. T. (1976). *General endocrinology* (6th ed.). Philadelphia: Saunders.

Turner, G. F., & Robinson, R. L. (1992). Milinski's tit-for-tat hypothesis: Do fish preferentially inspect in pairs? *Animal Behaviour, 43,* 677–678.

Turner, J. R. G. (1986). Drinking crocodile tears: The only use for a butterfly. *Antenna, 10,* 119–120.

Tuttle, M. D., Taft, L. J., & Ryan, M. J. (1982). Evasive behaviour of a frog in response to bat predation. *Animal Behaviour, 30,* 393–397.

Tychsen, P. H., & Fletcher, B. S. (1971). Sudies of the rhythm of mating in the Queensland Fruit fly, *Dacus tryoni. Journal of Insect Physiology, 17,* 2139–2156.

Urquhart, F. A. (1987). *The monarch butterfly: International traveler.* Toronto, Canada: University of Toronto Press.

Van de Poll, N. E., Taminiau, M. S., Endert, E., & Louwerse, A. L. (1988). Gonadal steroid influence upon sexual and aggressive behavior of female rats. *International Journal of Neuroscience, 41,* 271–286.

van Lawick-Goodall, J. (1970). Tool-using in primates and other vertebrates. In D. Lehrman, R. Hinde, & E. Shaw (Eds.), *Advances in the study of behavior* (Vol. 3). New York: Academic Press.

van Lawick-Goodall, J., & Van Lawick, H. (1966). Use of tools by the Egyptian vulture. *Neophron percnopterus. Nature, 212,* 1468–1469.

Vandenbergh, J. G., Witsett, J. M., & Lombardi, J. R. (1975). Partial isolation of a pheromone accelerating puberty in female mice. *Journal of Reproductive Fertility, 43,* 515–523.

Vander Wall, S. B., & Smith, K. G. (1987). Cach-protecting behavior of food-hoarding animals. In A. C. Kamil, J. R. Krebs, & R. H. Pulliam (Eds.), *Foraging behavior.* New York: Plenum Press.

Verner, J. (1964). Evolution of polygamy in the long-billed marsh wren. *Evolution, 18,* 252–261.

Vessey, S. H. (1967). Effects of chlorpromazine on aggression in laboratory populations of wild house mice. *Ecology, 48,* 367–376.

Vierke, J. (1973). Das Wassersprucken der Artn Gattung Colisa (Pisces: Anabantidae). *Bonn. Zool. Beitr. 24,* 62–104.

Vince, M. (1969). Embryonic communication, respiration, and the synchronization of hatching. In R. A. Hinde (Ed.), *Bird vocalizations: Their relations to current problems in biology and psychology.* Cambridge, England: Cambridge University Press.

Vincent, A. C. J. (1995). A role for daily greetings in maintaining seahorse pair bonds. *Animal Behaviour, 49,* 258–260.

Visalberghi, E., & Fragaszy, D. M. (1990). Food-washing behavior in tufted capuchin monkeys, *Cebus apella,* and crabeating macaques, *Macaca fascicularis. Animal Behaviour, 40,* 829–836.

Visalberghi, E., & Fragaszy, D. (1995). The behaviour of capuchin monkeys, *Cebus apella,* with novel food: The role of social context. *Animal Behaviour, 49,* 1089–1095.

Visscher, P. K., & Dukas, R. (1995). Honey bees recognize development of nestmates' ovaries. *Animal Behaviour, 49,* 542–544.

von Frisch, K. (1971). *Bees: Their vision, chemical senses and language.* Ithaca, NY: Cornell University Press.

von Haartman, L. (1953). Was reizt den Trauer fliegenschnäpper *(Muscicapa hypoleuca)* zu füttern? *Die Vogelwarte, 16,* 157–164.

Vos, D. R. (1995). The role of sexual imprinting for sex recognition in zebra finches: A difference between males and females. *Animal Behaviour, 50,* 645–653.

Waage, J. K. (1973). Reproductive behavior and its relation to territoriality in *Calopteryx maculata (Beauvois) (Odonata: Calopterygidae). Behaviour, 47,* 240–256.

Wahlsten, D. (1995). Increasing the raw intelligence of a nation is constrained by ignorance, not its citizens' genes. *The Alberta Journal of Educational Research, 41,* 257–264.

Wahlsten, D., & Gottlieb, G. (in press). The invalid separation of effects of nature and nurture: Lessons from animal experimentation. In R. J. Sternberg & E. L. Grigorenko (Eds.), *Intelligence, heredity and environment.* New York: Cambridge University Press.

Walcott, C. (1972). Bird navigation. *Natural History, 81,* 32–43.

Wallraff, H. G. (1983). Relevance of atmospheric odours and geomagnetic field to pigeon navigation: What is the map basis? *Comparative and Biochemical Physiology, 76A,* 643–663.

Walls, S. C., Mathis, A., Jaeger, R. G., & Gergits, W. F. (1989). Male salamanders with high quality diets have faeces attractive to females. *Animal Behaviour, 38,* 546–548.

Walsh, C., & Cepko, C. L. (1992). Widespread dispersion of neuronal clones across functional regions of the cerebral cortex. *Science, 28,* 434–440.

Wang, Z., & Novak, M. A. (1994). Alloparental care and the influence of father presence on juvenile prairie voles, *Microtus ochrogaster. Animal Behavior, 47,* 281–288.

Ward, I., & Weisz, J. (1980). Maternal stress alters plasma testosterone in fetal mice. *Science, 207,* 328–329.

Washburn, D. A., & Rumbaugh, D. M. (1991). Ordinal judgments of numerical symbols by macaques *(Macaca Mulatta). American Psychological Society, 2*(3), 190–193.

Washburn, S., & Jay, P. (1967). More on tool-use among primates. *Current Anthropoly, 8,* 253–254.

Wasserman, E. A. (1993). Comparative cognition: Beginning the second century of the study of animal intelligence. *Psychological Bulletin, 113,* 211–228.

Wasserman, E. A., Grosch, J., & Nevin, J. A. (1982). Effects of signalled retention intervals on pigeon short-term memory. *Animal Learning and Behavior, 10,* 330–338.

Waterman, T. H. (1989). *Animal navigation.* New York: Freeman.

Watson, P. J., & Thornhill R. (1994). Fluctuating asymmetry and sexual selection. *Tree, 9*(1), 21–25.

Weary, D. M., & Kramer, D. L. (1995). Response of eastern chipmunks to conspecific alarm calls. *Animal Behaviour, 49,* 81–93.

Webster, J. (1995). *Animal welfare: A cool eye towards Eden.* Oxford, England: Blackwell Science.

Wehner, R. (1987). "Matched filters": Neural models of the external world. *Journal of Comparative Physiology A., 161,* 511–531.

Wehner, R., & Srinivasan, M. V. (1981). Searching behavior of desert ants, genus *Cataglyphis (Formicidae,* Hymenoptera). *Journal of Comparative Psychology, 142,* 315–338.

Weiner, B., Amirkhan, J., Folkes, V. S., & Verette, J. A. (1987). An attributional analysis of excuse giving: Studies of a native theory of emotion. *Journal of Personality and Social Psychology, 52,* 316–324.

Weisfeld, G. E. (1993). The adaptive value of humor and laughter. *Ethology and Sociobiology, 14,* 141–169.

Weiss, J. M. (1995). *Stress-induced depression: What we have found and where we are going.* Paper presented at the Wisconsin Symposium on Emotion, Inaugural Meeting, Madison, WI.

Wells, M. J., & Wells, J. (1972). Sexual displays and mating in *Octopus vulgaris* Cuvier and *O. Cyanea* Gray and attempts to alter performance by manipulating the glandular condition of the animals. *Animal Behaviour, 20,* 293–308.

Welty, J. C., & Baptista, L. (1988). *The life of birds.* Fort Worth, TX: Harcourt Brace Jovanovich.

Wenner, A. M. (1971). *The bee language controversy.* Boulder, CO: Educational Programs Improvement.

Wetterer, J. K. (1991). Allometry and the geometry of leaf-cutting in Atta cephalotes. *Behavior Ecology Sociobiology, 29,* 347–35.

Whiten, A., Cusance, D., Gomez, J. C., Teixidor, P., & Bard, K. (1996). Imitative learning of artificial fruit processing in children *(Homo sapiens)* and chimpanzees *(Pan troglodytes). Journal of Comparative Psychology, 110,* 3–14.

Whitham, T. G. (1986). Costs and benefits of territoriality: Behavioral and reproductive release by competing aphids. *Ecology, 67,* 139–147.

Whitten, W. K. (1959). Occurrence of anestrus in mice caged in groups. *Journal of Endocrinology, 18,* 102–107.

Whittingham, L. A., Dunn, P. O., & Robertson, R. J. (1995). Testing the female mate-guarding hypothesis: A reply. *Animal Behaviour, 50,* 277–279.

Wickler, W., & Seibt, U. (1981). Monogamy in Crustacea and man. *Zeitschrift für Tierpsychologie, 57,* 215–234.

Wiklund, C., & Sillén-Tullberg, B. (1985). Why distasteful butterflies have aposematic larvae and adults, but cryptic pupae: Evidence from predation experiments on the monarch and the European swallowtail. *Evolution, 39,* 1155–1158.

Wilcox, R. S. (1988). Surface wave reception in invertebrates and vertebrates. In J. Atema, R. R. Fay, A. N. Popper, & W. N. Tavolga (Eds.), *Sensory biology of aquatic animals.* New York: Springer-Verlag.

Wilczynski, W., Rand, A. S., & Ryan, M. J. (1995). The processing of spectral cues by the call analysis system of the tungara frog, *Physalaemus pustulosus. Animal Behaviour, 49,* 911–929.

Wildhaber, M. L., Green, R. F., & Crowder, L. B. (1994). Bluegills continuously update patch giving-up times based on foraging experience. *Animal Behaviour, 47,* 501–513.

Wilkinson, G. S. (1984). Reciprocal food sharing in the vampire bat. *Nature, 308,* 181–184.

Williams, G. C. (1975). *Sex and evolution.* Princeton, NJ: Princeton University Press.

Williams, R. W., Cavada, C., & Reinoso-Suárez, F. (1993). Rapid evolution of the visual system: A cellular assay of the retina and dorsal lateral geniculate nucleus of the spanish wildcat and the domestic cat. *The Journal of Neuroscience, 13*(1), 208–228.

Wilson, E. O. (1963). Pheromones. *Science in America, 208*(5), 100–114.

Wilson, E. O. (1971). *The insect societies.* Cambridge: Belknap Press.

Wilson, E. O. (1975). *Sociobiology: The new synthesis.* Cambridge: Harvard University Press.

Wilson, E. O. (1975). *Sociobiology: The new synthesis.* Cambridge: Harvard University Press.

Wilson, E. O. (1984). *Biophilia. The human bond with other species.* Cambridge: Harvard University Press.

Wiltschko, R., & Wiltschko, W. (1995). *Magnetic orientation in animals.* New York: Springer-Verlag.

Winslow, J. T., Ellingoe, J., & Miczek, J. A. (1988). Effects of alcohol on aggressive behavior in squirrel monkeys: Influence of testosterone and social context. *Psychopharmacology, 95,* 356–363.

Wisenden, B. D., Lanfranconi-Izawa, T. L., & Keenleyside, M. H. A. (1995). Fin digging and leaf lifting by the convict cichlid, *Cichlasoma nigrofasciatum:* Examples of parental food provisioning. *Animal Behaviour, 49,* 623–631.

Witt, P. N., & Rovner, J. S. (1982). *Spider communication: Mechanisms and ecological significance.* Princeton, NJ: Princeton University Press.

Wolfson, A. (1948). Bird migration and the concept of continental drift. *Science, 108,* 23–30.

Woolbright, L. L., Greene, E. J., & Rapp, G. C. (1990). Density-dependent mate searching strategies of male woodfrogs. *Animal Behaviour, 40,* 135–142.

Woolfenden, G. E., & Fitzpatrick, J. W. (1984). *The Florida scrub jay: Demography of a cooperative-breeding bird.* Princeton, NJ: Princeton University Press

Woolum, J. D. (1991). A re-examination of the role of the nucleus in generating the circadian rhythm in *Acetabularia. Journal of Gioll Rhythms, 6,* 129–136.

Wourms, M. K., & Wasserman, F. E. (1985). Butterfly wing markings are more advantageous during handling than during the initial strike of an avian predator. *Evolution, 39,* 845–851.

Woyciechowski, M., Kabat, L., & Krol, E. (1994). The function of the mating sign in honey bees, *Apis mellifera:* New evidence. *Animal Behaviour, 47,* 733–735.

Wright, A. A., Santiago, H. C., Sands, S. F., Kendrick, D. F., & Cook, R. G. (1985). Memory processing of serial lists by pigeons, monkeys, and people. *Science, 229,* 287–289.

Wright, J., & Cuthill, I. (1990). Manipulation of sex differences in parental care: The effect of brood size. *Animal Behaviour, 40,* 462–471.

Wright, R. (1994). *The moral animal: The new science of evolutionary psychology.* New York: Pantheon.

Wynne-Edwards, V. C. (1962). *Animal dispersion in relation to social behaviour.* Edinburgh, Scotland: Oliver & Boyd.

Ydenberg, R. C., & Dill, L. M. (1986). The economics of fleeing from predators. *Advances in the Study of Behavior, 16,* 229–249.

Yoshikubo, S. (1985). Species discrimination and concept formation by rhesus monkeys *(Macaca mulatta). Primates, 26,* 285–299.

Youngs, B. B. (1985). *Stress in children.* New York: Arbor House.

Zach, R. (1979). Shell dropping: Decision-making and optimal foraging in northwestern crows. *Behaviour. 68,* 106–117.

Zahavi, A. (1975). Mate selection—A selection for a handicap. *Journal of Theoretical Biology, 53,* 205–214.

Zahavi, A. (1987). The theory of signal selection and some of its implications. In V. P. Delfino (Ed.), *International symposium of biological evolution.* Bari: Adriatica Editrice.

Zajonc, R. B. (1985). Emotion and facial efference: A theory reclaimed. *Science, 228,* 15–21.

Zakon, H. (1988). The electroreceptors: Diversity in structure and function. In J. Atema, R. R. Fay, A. N. Popper, & W. N. Tavolga (Eds.), *Sensory biology of aquatic animals.* New York: Springer-Verlag.

Ziegler, T. E., Epple, G., Snowdon, C. T., Porter, T. A., Belcher, A. M., & Kuderling, I. (1993). Detection of the chemical signals of ovulation in the cotton-top tamarin, *Saginus oedipus. Animal Behaviour, 45,* 313–322.

Zimmerman, M. A. (1990). Toward a theory of learned hopefulness: A structural model and analysis of participation and empowerment. *Journal of Research in Personality, 24,* 71–86.

NAME INDEX

SUBJECT INDEX

Photo and Figure Credits

Page xxii/Photo, © Patti Murray/Animals Animals. **Page 4/Figure 1.1,** Pierre Berger/Photo Researchers. **Page 7/Figure 1.2,** North Wind Picture Archives. **Page 24/Photo,** Gregory G. Dimijian/Photo Researchers. **Page 27/Figure 2.1,** From *Biology: Exploring Life* (p. 459), by G. D. Brum & M. McKane, 1989, New York: Wiley. Copyright 1989 by Wiley. Reprinted with permission. **Page 50/Photo,** Tom Vezo/The Wildlife Collection. **Page 56/Figure 3.2,** From *Imprinting: Early Experience and the Developmental Psychobiology of Attachment* (p. 191), by E. H. Hess, 1973, Belmont, CA: Wadsworth. Copyright 1973 by Wadsworth. Reprinted with permission. **Page 65/Figure 3.3,** Tim Davis/Photo Researchers. **Page 72/Photo,** © Miriam Austerman/Animals Animals. **Page 79/Figure 4.1,** Courtesy of the National Library of Medicine. **Page 82/Figure 4.2,** Courtesy of Pfizer, Inc. **Page 85/Figure 4.4,** Tim Davis/Tony Stone Images. **Page 88/Figure 4.5,** From "Honeybee Navigation," by James L. Gould and Fred C. Dyer, 1983, *American Scientist,* 71: 587–597. Reprinted with permission of American Scientist. **Page 98/Photo,** Lawrence Migdale/Photo Researchers. **Page 105/Figure 5.1,** Language Research Center, Georgia State University. **Page 108/Figure 5.2,** William Munoz. **Page 110/Figure 5.3,** From "Remembrance of Places Past: Spatial Memory in Rats," by D. S. Olton and R. J. Samuelson, 1976, *Journal of Experimental Psychology: Animal Behavior Processes, 2,* 97–116. Copyright © 1976 by the American Psychological Association. Reprinted with permission. **Page 122/Photo,** M. Phillip Kahl/Photo Researchers. **Page 128/Figure 6.1,** Donald Patterson/Photo Researchers. **Page 139/Figure 6.3,** Miguel Castro/Photo Researchers. **Page 146/Photo,** Craig K. Lorenz/Photo Researchers. **Page 158/Figure 7.3,** © Miriam Austerman/Animals Animals. **Page 168/Photo,** John Mitchell/Photo Researchers. **Page 189/Figure 8.3,** From "Sex Ratio of White Births in the United States during the Second World War" (p. 289), by B. MacMahon and T. F. Pugh, 1954, *American Journal of Human Genetics, 6,* 284–292. Copyright 1954 by the University of Chicago Press. Reprinted with permission. **Page 194/Photo,** Tom McHugh/Photo Researchers. **Page 206/Figure 9.2,** From *Animal Behavior: An Evolutionary Approach,* 4th ed. (p. 401), by J. Alcock, 1989, Sunderland, MA: Sinauer Associates. Copyright 1989 by Sinauer Associates. Adapted with permission. **Page 220/Photo,** © Rue/Vandermolen/Animals Animals. **Page 225/Figure 10.1,** © Leonard Lee Rue III/Animals Animals. **Page 244/Photo,** Art Wolfe/Tony Stone Images. **Page 264/Figure 11.4,** Toni Angermayer/Photo Researchers. **Page 270/Photo,** Suen-O Lindblad/Photo Researchers. **Page 276/Figure 12.2,** © Krishman/Animals Animals. **Page 281/Figure 12.2,** From *Comparative Animal Behavior* (p. 234), by R. A. Maier and B. M. Maier, 1970, Belmont, CA: Brooks/Cole. Copyright 1970 by Brooks/Cole. Reprinted with permission. **Page 296/Photo,** Ian Cleghorn/Photo Researchers. **Page 300/Figure 13.1,** W. B. Allen, Jr./Photo Researchers. **Page 320/Photo,** © Donald Specker/Animals Animals. **Page 323/Figure 14.1,** Robert C. Hermes/Photo Researchers. **Page 341/Figure 14.3,** Will Hart. **Page 344/Photo,** Bryan Mullennix/Tony Stone Images. **Page 356/Figure 15.1,** John Janssen, Loyola University Biology Department. **Page 366/Photo,** Mary Eleanor Browning/Photo Researchers. **Page 381/Figure 16.3,** NIH/Science Source/Photo Researchers. **Page 390/Photo,** Ross E. Hutchins/Photo Researchers. **Page 394/Figure 17.1,** From "Bile, Prolactin, and the Maternal Pheromone," by H. Moltz & L. C. Leidahl, 1977, *Science, 196,* 81–83. Copyright 1977 by the American Association for the Advancement of Science. Adapted with permission. **Page 414/Photo,** Merlin Tuttle/Photo Researchers. **Page 426/Figure 18.1,** From *Comparative Animal Behavior* (p. 87, part a), by R. A. Maier and B. M. Maier, 1970, Belmont, CA: Brooks/Cole. Copyright 1970 by Brooks/Cole. Reprinted with permission. **Page 440/Photo,** Renee Lynn/Photo Researchers. **Page 449/Figure 19.1,** © Leonard Lee Rue III/Animals Animals. **Page 451/Figure 19.3,** Ron Sanford/Tony Stone Images. **Page 464/Photo,** Tom McHugh/Photo Researchers. **Page 471/Figure 20.2,** Gianni Tortoli/Photo Researchers.